Evans & Smith
The Law of
Landlord and Tenant

Evans and Smith
The Law of
Landlord and Tenant

Fifth edition

P F Smith BCL, MA
Reader in Property Law
University of Reading

Butterworths
London, Edinburgh, Dublin
1997

United Kingdom	Butterworths a Division of Reed Elsevier (UK) Ltd, Halsbury House, 35 Chancery Lane, LONDON WC2A 1EL and 4 Hill Street, EDINBURGH EH2 3JZ
Australia	Butterworths, SYDNEY, MELBOURNE, BRISBANE, ADELAIDE, PERTH, CANBERRA and HOBART
Canada	Butterworths Canada Ltd, TORONTO and VANCOUVER
Ireland	Butterworth (Ireland) Ltd, DUBLIN
Malaysia	Malayan Law Journal Sdn Bhd, KUALA LUMPUR
New Zealand	Butterworths of New Zealand Ltd, WELLINGTON and AUCKLAND
Singapore	Reed Elsevier (Singapore) Pte Ltd, SINGAPORE
South Africa	Butterworths Publishers (Pty) Ltd, DURBAN
USA	Michie, Charlottesville, VIRGINIA

A CIP Catalogue record for this book is available from the British Library.

ISBN 0 406 06563 2

Printed by Redwood Books, Trowbridge, Wiltshire

Preface

The principal aim of this book, now in its fifth edition, is to provide a concise yet reasonably detailed account and analysis of the general law of landlord and tenant, for students, legal practitioners and other professional people. Much of the text of this edition is new, owing to the sheer width and bulk of changes which have taken place in the last four years.

Both equity and the common law have been active in the general law of landlord and tenant. The common law had begun to relax some aspects of the continuing post-assignment liability of an original lessee before legislation arrived. There have been developments in other fields. The courts have been active in relation to consents to assignments, interpretation of repairing covenants, remedies (such as repudiation), surrender, and relief against forfeiture. These and other perhaps less predictable developments – there were cases concerned with the Landlord and Tenant Act 1730 and the Distress for Rent Act 1739 – across the whole field of the common law, meant that many parts of the text of Parts A to C of this book needed to be revised and in some cases re-written.

The period since the appearance of the last edition has seen much legislative change. The principles governing the enforcement of leasehold covenants have been reformed by the Landlord and Tenant (Covenants) Act 1995. Part III of the Housing Act 1996 alters the rules applicable to private sector residential tenancies still further in the direction of deregulation and so away from any vestiges of security for tenants. The 1996 Act also affects other areas of the law, notably service charges abuse and secure tenancies. So far as was known, most of the relevant provisions of this Act were in force at the time of writing this Preface.

The enfranchisement process has been extended to long lessees of flats by the Leasehold Reform, Housing and Urban Development Act 1993. In pursuance of deregulation, the Agricultural Tenancies Act 1995 was passed. It removes security of tenure for new tenancies of agricultural land and allows diversification into non-farming activities. I hope that the quite large tracts of text affected by these substantial changes have been sufficiently re-written to reflect the impact of both this mass of legislation and of the significant number of cases arising across the whole field of the various statutory provisions covered in Parts D to F of this work.

Rules originating in European Union directives, promulgated by subordinate domestic legislation, needed to be discussed, if only *ex abundanti cautela*. The terms and possible applicability of these regulations are discussed in a generally

v

revised chapter 4. Their arrival into our law may be only the first step in other interventions from across the Channel, at least in the field of residential tenancies, which may be conceived of in Brussels as equivalent to consumer contracts.

The treatment of repairing obligations and secure tenancies has been expanded. The treatment of the Rent Act 1977 was reduced, mostly so as to prevent unacceptable increases in the length of the text, but I hope without jettisoning any material of present-day significance.

The permission of the Law Society is gratefully acknowledged for the reproduction of the Law Society Business Leases in the Appendix. I am also grateful to Messrs Sweet & Maxwell and to the author of the precedent concerned for permission to reproduce in the Appendix a typical short residential lease.

I should also wish to acknowledge my indebtedness to my publishers for their kindness and consideration at all times. I am grateful to the staff of the Reading University Law Library for their patience and helpfulness in dealing with my various inquiries. I am also indebted to those readers, especially although not exclusively legal practitioners, who have been kind enough to make comments and criticisms of the text of this work, but any remaining errors or omissions in this book are my sole responsibility.

The law as stated in this book is that as it was believed to be as at the beginning of January 1997, when the text went to press, although in the production stages of the manuscript it was possible to make a certain number of final adjustments and insertions to the text.

P F Smith,
Reading,
March 1997

Contents

PART B RIGHTS AND OBLIGATIONS OF THE PARTIES

Abbreviations and Bibliography

The following *abbreviations* are used in the text (not included are references to standard series of Law Reports published by the Incorporated Council or Butterworths):

CLJ	Cambridge Law Journal
CLP	Current Legal Problems
CLY	Current Law Year Book
Conv(NS)	Conveyancer (New Series)
Conv	Conveyancer
EG	Estates Gazette
EGLR	Estates Gazette Law Reports
HLR	Housing Law Reports
NLJ	New Law Journal
LQR	Law Quarterly Review
LS	Legal Studies
LT	Law Times
MLR	Modern Law Review
PM	Property Management

Bibliography

The following books are referred to by name in the text:

Arden and Hunter	*Manual of Housing Law*, 5th edn, A Arden and C Hunter (1992)
Bernstein and Reynolds	*Handbook of Rent Review*, looseleaf
Bright & Gilbert	*Landlord and Tenant Law*, S Bright and G Gilbert (1995)
Cheshire and Burn	*Modern Law of Real Property*, 15th edn, EH Burn (1994)
Clarke	*Leasehold Enfranchisement*, DN Clarke (1993)
Clarke and Adams	Rent Reviews and Variable Rents, 3rd edn, DN Clarke and JW Adams (1990)
Crabb	*Leases, Covenants and Consents*, L Crabb (1991)

Davey	*Residential Rents*, M Davey (1990)
Evans	*Agricultural Tenancies Act 1995*, D Evans (1995)
Foa	*Foa's General Law of Landlord and Tenant*, 8th edn, H Heathcote-Williams QC (1957)
Hague	*Leasehold Enfranchisement*, 2nd edn (1987) Hague
Halsbury	*Halsbury's Laws of England*, Vol 17
Hanbury and Martin	*Modern Equity*, 14th edn, J Martin (1993)
Martin	*Residential Security*, 2nd edn, J Martin (1995)
Matthews and Millichap	*A Guide to the Leasehold Reform, Housing and Urban Development Act 1993*, P Matthews and D Millichap (1993)
Megarry	*The Rent Acts*, 11th edn, J Stuart Collyer, Sir R Megarry et al, (1988)
Megarry and Wade	*The Law of Real Property*, 5th edn, Sir Robert Megarry and HWR Wade (1984)
McLoughlin	*Commercial Leases and Insolvency*, 2nd edn, P McLoughlin (1996)
Muir Watt	*Agricultural Holdings*, 13th edn, J Muir Watt (1987)
Murdoch	*The Law of Estate Agency and Auctions*, 3rd edn, J Murdoch (1994)
Pawlowski	*Forfeiture of Leases*, M Pawlowski (1993)
Pawlowski and Brown	*Casebook on Landlord and Tenant Law*, M Pawlowski and J Brown (1995)
Plucknett	*A Concise History of the Common Law*, 5th edn, T Plucknett (1956)
Privity of Contract	*Privity of Contract*, by Riley, Rogers, Fogel and Slessenger (1995)
Rodgers	*Agricultural Law*, CP Rodgers (1991)
Ross	*Drafting and Negotiating Commercial Leases* 4th edn, Ross.
Simpson	*History of Land Law*, 2nd edn, AW Simpson (1986)
Smith	*Property Offences*, ATH Smith (1995)
Snell	*Snell's Equity*, 29th edn, PV Baker and P St J Langan (1990)
Sydenham & Mainwaring	*Farm Business Tenancies*, A Sydenham & N Mainwaring (1995)
Thornton	Property Disrepair and Dilapidations (1992)
Treitel	*Frustration and Force Majeure*, G Treitel (1994)
West	*West's Law of Dilapidations*, 10th edn, PF Smith (1995)
Wolstenholme and Cherry	*Wolstenholme and Cherry's Conveyancing Statutes*, 13th edn, JT Farrand (1971)

Table of statutes

References in this Table to *Statutes* are to Halsbury's of England (Fourth Edition) showing the volume and page at which the annotated text of an Act may be found.

List of cases

PART A
CREATION OF TENANCIES

Chapter 1

Introduction

I GENERAL

The law of landlord and tenant deals with the rules of law applicable to leases. Under a lease, an owner of land permits another person, a tenant, to occupy the land exclusively for a period which is determined by agreement, in return for regular payments of rent. One of the advantages of granting a lease from a freeholder's point of view is that he does not forever give up the right to resume possession of his land: at the expiry of the lease, at common law, the freeholder is entitled to resume possession. A person may take a lease for many reasons, as where he has a short-term use for land which he has no wish to own. Freehold and leasehold interests alike are capable of being investments, whose value will be governed, in part, by the length of the term granted by the lease.

The modern law of landlord and tenant is dual in nature. It is founded on principles of common law and equity of considerable antiquity, which continue to evolve and which statute has sometimes modified. These principles are subjected to a series of statutory codes which regulate various aspects of specific types of lease or tenancy. Although these statutes often interfere with or distort common law and equitable principles, knowledge of them is essential, for reasons which will become apparent in the course of this work.

Brief historical perspective[1]

The law governing leaseholds was not part of the law of real property. Logically, therefore, it is unnecessary in relation to landlord and tenant to outline the feudal system of land tenure, because it did not recognise leaseholds as real property, as they were classified as personal property along with chattels and labelled 'chattels real'. In consequence, leaseholds were purely contractual relationships, so that the landlord merely hired his land to the tenant for a limited period, in return for the payment by the tenant of rent. The remedies of a freeholder who was wrongfully dispossessed from land were real or in rem; in contrast, a tenant in occupation was denied any real remedies for the recovery of the land following wrongful eviction by the landlord. Later, the position of tenants was improved. It appears that during the thirteenth century a special writ in trespass was introduced, *de ejectione firmae*, under which a tenant wrongfully ejected from his land could first claim damages and eventually

---

1 For a detailed discussion, see Cheshire & Burn, chs 2 and 3; Simpson, p 68ff.

recovery of the term, against his landlord and the latter's successors in title.[2] With this remedy, a tenant's right to recover his lease or term was protected; but, as a non-freeholder, he never had *seisin* or possession of the land itself, and as has been pointed out,[3] the real actions (the writ of right and the possessory assizes) were never made available to him.

As to the reasons why leaseholds were treated as chattels real, one may have been economic pressure, and in any case a leasehold was regarded as a valuable investment, as where a tenant with no sufficient capital of his own was able to work another's farm land; a lease also provided a means of evasion of the usury laws so that a debtor would lease land to his creditor at a nominal rent, and the creditor would draw the rents and profits from the land.[4]

Certain advantages were apparent from the general classification of leaseholds as personal property: first, that leaseholders were exempted from the burdensome system of feudal incidents. Second, leaseholds, unlike real property, could be freely disposed of by will. Third, though the action for ejectment was originally limited to actions by the tenant against the landlord and his successors in title, it was later expanded to allow actions against any wrongful dispossessor of the tenant, and was so efficacious that freeholders in due course elected for it because of the (by then) more cumbersome and formalised (real) actions available to them: they did this by pleading the fiction that they held a leasehold.[5]

Nonetheless, possession remained with the landlord not the tenant. As time progressed, the law deliberately assimilated many, but not all, of the rules applicable to leases, as chattels real, and real property. It is also an irony that, after the reforms of the 1925 property statutes, all forms of tenure were abolished except one (socage tenure, the standard freehold tenure). Yet that tenure, which results from the granting and acceptance of a lease, has been stated[6] to be fundamental to the relationship of the parties to a lease. So, a tenant who purported to grant a sub-lease for a longer period than the length of his own lease caused his own lease to be assigned by operation of law.[7] The 'sub-tenant' held direct from the landlord for the residue of the former tenant's lease; and the latter became a stranger to the land. Thus, leases, as chattels real, though in origin personal property, have been said to be part property, part contract and so hybrid in nature,[8] although one writer has contended that contractual principles govern the interpretation of leases as a whole.[9]

For the purposes both of their formal classification within the scheme of property legislation and conveyancing matters, notably assignments, leases are

---

2 See Plucknett, p 373ff.
3 Cheshire & Burn, ch 1, p 35.
4 See further Plucknett, pp 571–574.
5 The enactment of the Common Law Procedure Act 1852 rendered the pleading of this fiction unnecessary.
6 *Milmo v Carreras* [1946] KB 306, [1946] 1 All ER 288, CA.
7 See also *Stretch v West Dorset District Council* [1996] EGCS 76.
8 *Linden Gardens Trust Ltd v Lenesta Sludge Disposals Ltd* [1994] 1 AC 85, 108H, [1993] 3 All ER 417, 432, HL.
9 Pawlowski [1995] Conv 379; also the argument of counsel in *Ingram v IRC* [1995] 4 All ER 334, 340–341; the High Court left this open.

assimilated with the rules governing real property. Nevertheless, important contractual principles, which lie outside the confines of real property law, govern the interpretation of the scope of leasehold covenants, and certain general principles of contract law govern other aspects of the landlord and tenant relationship, such as the determination of periodic joint tenancies,[10] the principles under which terms may be implied into leases and tenancies,[11] and the rights and remedies of the parties, such as a landlord's right to rescind a tenancy for fraud or a tenant's more controversial apparent ability to accept a landlord's repudiation by conduct of a short residential tenancy on account of disrepair.[12]

Effects of the 1925 property legislation

The 1925 legislation is a convenient label for a whole series of reforming and consolidating statutes passed in 1925, which resulted in the enactment, in particular, of the Law of Property Act 1925, the Land Registration Act 1925, and the Land Charges Act 1925 (now the Land Charges Act 1972).

A number of important reforms, partly with the overall aim of simplifying conveyancing, were incorporated into Part I of the Law of Property Act 1925. One general reform was that the number of legal estates in land was reduced to two by s 1(1) of the 1925 Act: the fee simple absolute in possession and the term of years absolute.[13] This second expression is statutory shorthand for all types of lease or tenancy with a few exceptions. This definition includes fixed-term leases; and the statutory definition proceeds, deliberately, to include legal short-term periodic tenancies. The 1925 Act differentiates between 'family' leases for life (which are normally rent-free and which take effect in equity behind a trust) and commercial leases for a fixed period which are determinable by notice on the termination of a life (such as that of the lessee) which fall within the statutory definition of 'term of years absolute'.[14]

The Law of Property Act 1925, having reduced the maximum number of legal estates to two, then provides in s 1(3) that: 'all other estates, interests and charges in or over land take effect as equitable interests'. Generally, the status of a lease (whether legal or equitable) makes no difference to the substantive rights of the parties thereunder.[15] As will be seen, however, the formalities of creation of legal and equitable leases differ and equitable leases require protection against third parties by registration.

Equitable substantive rules applicable to legal and equitable leases developed alongside relevant legal rules; equitable remedies, such as an injunction or specific performance, are available to enable a landlord or tenant of a legal or equitable lease to enforce their respective rights, for example, under covenants

10 *Hammersmith and Fulham London Borough Council v Monk* [1992] 1 AC 478, [1992] 1 All ER 1, HL.
11 See eg *Barrett v Lounova (1982) Ltd* [1990] 1 QB 348, CA; also eg *Killick v Roberts* [1991] 4 All ER 289 (rescission of statutory tenancy allowed for fraud); see Bright [1993] Conv 7.
12 See eg *Killick v Roberts* [1991] 4 All ER 289 (rescission for fraud of statutory tenancy); *Hussein v Mehlman* [1992] 2 EGLR 87 (further discussed in ch 9).
13 As defined by Law of Property Act 1925, s 205(1)(xxvii).
14 See further ch 2.
15 *Walsh v Lonsdale* (1882) 21 Ch D 9, CA.

restrictive of the user of the demised premises, which are often preferable to the standard common-law remedy of damages. Some rights in leaseholds are only recognised by equity, such as those of a tenant holding under a void legal lease or certain rights arising out of equitable estoppel.

The classification of leasehold estates in land has not been altered by the fact that there is high authority for the view that the substantive, rather than merely the administrative, rules of law and equity have been 'fused' as a result of the Judicature Acts 1873 and 1875.[16] However, the 1925 property legislation, as will appear, distinguishes between legal and equitable leases and insists on different formalities for the creation, assignment, registration and surrender of each type of lease. One member of the House of Lords has indicated *obiter* that English law now has one single law of property made up of legal and equitable interests.[17] Differences of substance as opposed to form between legal and equitable leases would not ordinarily, if this view prevails, be retained. For example, the benefit and burden of leasehold covenants are capable of running with the land on a formal assignment of an equitable, as well as a legal, lease: this particular development is adopted by new legislation relating to the enforcement of leasehold covenants.[18]

Main terminology

Those new to landlord and tenant find themselves confronted with a series of technical terms, some of which are interchangeable. These terms are used throughout this book and are outlined in what follows.

1   *Lease or demise*   Generally 'lease' is a noun to describe a formal document under which land or premises is 'demised' or 'leased' to a tenant. In the case of informal leases, such as weekly or monthly tenancies, this process is sometimes spoken of as 'letting'. 'Demised premises' is a label for the land with a building or buildings, or land consisting of a building or part of a building or land with a defined boundary, demised by the habendum of a lease.

2   *Landlord or lessor*   These alternative terms describe the estate owner who grants the lease in question. 'Landlord' is a slightly flexible term, as it describes not only a head landlord, but also a mesne landlord where appropriate, as the following diagram shows:

A_____99_____B_____21_____C

---

16   *United Scientific Holdings Ltd v Burnley Borough Council* [1978] AC 904 at 925, HL; but see Baker (1977) 93 LQR 529; Martin [1994] Conv 13.
17   *Tinsley v Milligan* [1994] 1 AC 340 at 371A-B, [1993] 3 All ER 65 at 86, HL (Lord Browne-Wilkinson).
18   Landlord and Tenant (Covenants) Act 1995 (discussed in ch 5).

A lets land to B for 99 years and B, the mesne landlord, who is also A's tenant, later sub-lets the land to C for 21 years.

3 *Tenant or lessee* Obviously these interchangeable words describe the person who accepts a lease. In the diagram above, both B and C are lessees, or, as the case may be, sub-lessees. B's lease may contain a covenant obliging him to notify A of any sub-leases granted by B.

4 *Assignor and assignee* Subject to any expressly imposed restrictions or limitations on the transfer of leases, leases are freely assignable. Likewise the freeholder's interest, his reversion expectant on the lease, is freely assignable. By assignment is meant the outright transfer (by deed) of the leasehold interest, or freehold reversion, as the case may be. The assignor is the person making the assignment and the assignee the person accepting it.

5 *Sub-demises or sub-leases* A sub-lease takes place where a mesne landlord (such as B in the above diagram) lets the demised premises or part to a tenant, who, vis-à-vis the head landlord (A) is a sub-tenant. The sub-tenant's interest depends on the continued existence of the head lease whose destruction by forfeiture terminates, automatically, any sub-leases derived out of it.[19]

Many leasehold estates

Complex chains of assignments and sub-demises may readily build up where the head lease has been granted for a substantial term of years. Several leasehold estates in the same land may therefore exist. The position may be illustrated by the following diagram.

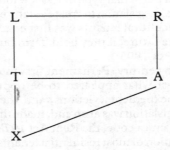

L was head landlord of T, but having assigned his freehold reversion to R, and T having assigned the residue of his lease to A, R occupies L's position as against A. Tenure exists between R and A. T has no tenure with R. X now holds as sub-lessee of A, with tenure between them. R is X's head landlord.

19 See *Viscount Chelsea v Hutchinson* [1994] 2 EGLR 61, CA.

II   SCOPE OF THIS SUBJECT

Main methods of creation of leases

Leases and tenancies arise in a number of different ways which are explored in chapter 2. For present purposes, they may arise in the following two ways, at common law:

1   by express agreement, as where L demises land to T1 for a 21-year fixed term;
2   by implied agreement, as where T2 enters L's land with L's consent, has exclusive possession and pays a weekly rent. T2 is weekly periodic tenant of L even though there may be only an oral agreement between the parties.

In the case of periodic tenants, T2 in the above example has a legal estate in land, derived from his exclusive possession and the payment and acceptance of rent for a periodic term. This is as much a legal estate as that demised to a tenant holding under a 999-year fixed-term lease.

Outline of effect of statutory controls

Parliament has not been content to leave the regulation of the law of landlord and tenant to the common law, even at the price of complexity. For example, there is a long history of legislative control of the exercise of landlords' remedies. The law of distress for unpaid rent has been subject to statutes regulating this self-help remedy for at least 300 years. Statute conferred an automatic right for tenants to obtain relief against forfeiture for non-payment of rent in 1852. Recent legislation is more detailed and specific. The Landlord and Tenant Act 1987 confers remedies, such as the appointment of a manager, against recalcitrant landlords of a particular type of lessee – long residential lessees – of one type of premises – flats. Legislation to create a statutory form of compensation for improvements to agricultural tenants was first enacted in 1875,[20] and these tenants are subject for the future, if they hold 'farm business tenancies', to the Agricultural Tenancies Act 1995.

During the twentieth century, Parliament first intervened so as to protect residential tenants against what appeared to be oppressive and, in wartime conditions, politically inexpedient evictions, and then, once the immediate cause of the protecting legislation was at an end, made the legislation permanent, with the result that it became a code, the Rent Act 1977, for the protection and rent control of the occupation of most residential tenants despite the termination of their tenancies. The 1977 Act cannot apply to most residential tenancies entered into on or after 15 January 1989. These are subjected to Part I of the Housing Act 1988, which creates assured and assured shorthold tenancies. The general balance between the competing parties has been adjusted almost as firmly in the landlord's favour as it had been tilted in the tenant's by the old rent restriction legislation. Thus, an assured shorthold tenant has no right to an automatic renewal of his tenancy once it has ended, and he has to pay whatever the landlord feels able to extract from him, unless the amount is wholly

20   Agricultural Holdings (England) Act 1875.

excessive by comparison to comparable rents in the local vicinity; the rent is to be paid no matter what the state and condition of the property. Although it is commonly supposed that commercial or business tenants are well able to fend for themselves, Parliament has intervened to confer a qualified right to renewal of business tenancies, albeit at a market rent (Landlord and Tenant Act 1954, Part II).

Thus, and in contrast to the common law, Parliament differentiates between three different types of tenancies, depending on whether the premises are residential, business or agricultural. Most of the relevant 'codes' allow the tenant, instead of having to quit the premises when his lease runs out, to remain in occupation against the landlord's wishes unless and until the landlord is able to terminate the tenancy within the relevant statutory rules. As a general principle, the more recent the enactment, the easier such termination is likely to be: thus, an assured tenancy is easier to terminate for non-payment of rent than is a Rent-Act protected or statutory tenancy, and a 'farm business tenancy' is not renewable under statutory rights, as opposed to by agreement in the way a business tenancy may be, even if the parties cannot agree to a renewal.

III COMMONHOLD PROPOSALS

Introduction

Owing to the fact that positive covenants do not run with freehold land, at present there is no reliable method of ensuring that successive owners and occupiers of land which is in multiple occupation, such as a block of flats, observe covenants which involve spending money such as to repair or to pay for repairs. Accordingly, where blocks of flats have been developed, it has been the practice to grant to the occupiers long leases, taking advantage of the rules governing the transmission of positive covenants. However, in recent times, the long leasehold method has given rise to some dissatisfaction on the part of lessees. Some landlords, with the obligation to keep the premises housing the flats concerned in proper repair and condition, have failed to comply with their responsibilities, either by neglecting to undertake any necessary work, or by failing to collect service charges from lessees to pay for the cost of works. There have been complaints of overcharging by unscrupulous landlords, as well as of landlords who buy up freeholds solely for the purpose of enforcing large arrears of service charges in the hope that they will be able to terminate the leases. As the term of a long lease diminishes, it becomes difficult or impossible to secure mortgage finance to purchase the residue of the lease, so rendering certain long leases unassignable.

Parliament has enacted a range of legislation in the field of landlord and tenant which tries, at the price of complexity, to address the problems of overcharging for repairs, neglect of maintenance and other abuses by landlords of long residential lessees, as well as enabling tenants of flats to buy out the freeholder or to extend their individual long leases. This legislation is examined in Part D of this book. However, in the view not least of the Lord Chancellor's office, the time has come for more radical reform. At some time we may see the enactment of commonhold legislation.[1]

The proposals, if implemented in the form proposed in a draft Commonhold Bill, published for consultation in the middle of 1996,[2] would create a 'new kind of freehold ownership with special statutory incidents'.[3] The commonhold idea originated in the report of a working group of the Law Commission.[4] That group referred to some of the perceived problems with long leases and also noted that as there was no standard form of lease, buying and selling leases might also be more complex and expensive than a freehold sale would be.[5]

Outline of commonhold ownership

The basis of commonhold ownership as proposed in 1987 was that it would be a system for freehold ownership 'where the emphasis is on co-operation between owners living within a defined area'.[6] The government Consultation Paper of 1996 argues that, if most European, American and Commonwealth countries have similar schemes to commonhold, it is deficient of English law not to have 'an adequate system for the ownership of freehold flats'.[7] The revised scheme envisaged the application of commonhold both to developments of flats and also to commercial developments where there were multiple units, as with a business park or block of offices.

One of the advantages claimed for commonhold (as against long leases) is that the unit holders in a commonhold development would be able themselves to manage the arrangements for the repair and maintenance of the building, through a commonhold association, without the presence of a superior freehold interest. Rules in what would be intended to be a standard form governing the extent of the association's liabilities and related matters would be made: these would assist efficient management of the development. Time alone will test the correctness of these beliefs.

Possible effects on leases

Commonhold legislation, if ever passed, might have effects on leases granted in a commonhold development and on the leasehold system more generally. If commonhold legislation is enacted in the form canvassed in 1996, it would have two particular limiting effects on leases of commonhold land. Once a commonhold scheme had been established and duly registered, and a

1   The latest proposals are summarised by Aldridge 98 LS Gazette 18 and Williams Estates Gazette Vol 37 (1996) p 128.
2   According to *The Times*, 28 October 1996, the government-funded Leasehold Enfranchisement Advisory Service condemned the draft Bill on the ground of inadequacies in controls on service charges and in respect of dispute resolution between unit holders and the commonhold association.
3   Draft Bill (1996) cl 1(1); but it appears that no legislation to implement the proposals in the form proposed in the Draft Bill will be enacted in the Parliamentary Session which must end in May 1997.
4   Cm 179 (1987).
5   Ibid, para 1.4.
6   Ibid, para 1.10.
7   Consultation Paper (1996) para 1.1.

commonhold association duly constituted, no lease of a commonhold unit could be granted for a term exceeding 25 years. Moreover, any lease in a development which converts into commonhold, as where the freeholder has been bought out by the head long lessees, would be cut down to a 25-year term.[8] These proposed restrictions showed an intention to subordinate leaseholds to commonhold developments as a whole, long leases being perceived as inconsistent with commonhold. In addition, where a commonhold association is wound up, there is under the 1996 proposals a Draconian rule. Any tenancy granted prior to the winding up is deemed to be held from the association, and not from the unit holder who granted the lease. The association would have an overriding power to put the lease to an end and to recover possession of the relevant land if it requires the premises for commonhold redevelopment purposes.[9] The severity of this principle is shown by a further proposed rule that if the tenant had any statutory protection, it would be overridden by operation of law where the conditions precedent of the new rule had been satisfied.

That there might well be wider effects on the law of landlord and tenant as a whole if commonhold eventually comes into being cannot be denied. At the time of writing these remain a matter of speculation. However, commonhold might supercede long leases as a means of developing land in the future to be used for residential flats, depending on the attractiveness of commonholds as opposed to long leaseholds for the holders of units. Some conversions from long leasehold into commonhold by use of voluntary or existing legislative means might be encouraged by the advent of commonhold. Should commonhold be available to commercial developers, some developments of business parks might well proceed under commonhold, if it is cheaper and simpler to operate than the leasehold system, which would remain to be seen. On the other hand, some developers might prefer to continue to use long leases, so as to retain ultimate control over the property, and may find the prohibition on the grant of long leases of commonhold land oppressive and a deterrent to the use of commonhold. Other prospective occupiers of multiple units might prefer the flexibility and finite duration of a business tenancy.

---

8 Draft Bill cll 2 and 13.
9 Draft Bill, cl 37.

Chapter 2

Relationship of landlord and tenant

I NATURE OF THE RELATIONSHIP

The relationship of landlord and tenant arises where one person, who possesses either a freehold or leasehold property interest expressly or impliedly grants to another, by means of a contract, an estate in that property which is less than the freehold interest or for a shorter duration than the leasehold interest of the grantor, as the case may be. The contractual obligations of both the original parties last throughout the term of the lease, where granted by deed, unless the original tenant, on assigning the lease, obtains an express release from the landlord.[1] This, and other aspects of the transmission of the benefits and burdens of leasehold covenants have been modified by recent legislation.[2]

Tenure

The granting of a lease by deed creates tenure between the parties and the results of this are as follows.

1   The respective assignees of each party to the lease will be bound by its terms (under 'privity of estate') if, but only if, the covenant runs with the land. In the case of a tenancy granted on or after 1 January 1996, all covenants in the tenancy are enforceable, by legislation, by and against the landlord and tenant for the time being.
2   Rent is an incident of tenure and so it issues out of the land, not simply out of any buildings on the land: this means that the landlord is entitled to distrain for unpaid rent over the land as a whole.
3   The landlord and tenant are mutually estopped from denying each other's title.

Grant of lease creates estate in tenant

Any express grant of a lease which follows any correct formalities required for the purpose, passes a legal or at least an equitable estate or interest to the tenant. Moreover, it follows from this that:

---

1 See eg *City of London Corpn v Fell* [1994] 1 AC 458, [1993] 4 All ER 968, HL.
2 Landlord and Tenant (Covenants) Act 1995 (ch 5).

1 Throughout the tenant's estate, there must be two concurrent estates in the land, the lease and the landlord's reversion, which may itself be either freehold or leasehold.

2 The duration of the lease must be certain, it must either be a fixed-term lease (sometimes called a 'term certain') of a duration both as regards commencement and termination, which is certain. Or it must be a periodic tenancy, in which case its maximum duration cannot be determined at the commencement of the tenancy, which ends if one party serves a notice to quit on the other.

3 The tenant has the right, in principle, to assign or mortgage his lease, and to create sub-leases out of it, but no tenant may validly sub-let for a longer period of years than he is entitled to under his own lease at the date of the sub-lease. Moreover, leases commonly restrict and sometimes completely remove the ability of the tenant to dispose of his interest.

4 A fixed-term lease expires by effluxion of time; a periodic tenancy is terminated following the expiry of a valid notice to quit. In either event, the tenant's estate in the land determines at common law. It has been held that a statutory tenancy under the Rent Acts, which is a continuation by statute of the common law tenancy, is a mere personal right of occupation, but that an assured periodic tenancy by succession under s 39 of the Housing Act 1988, being a new tenancy, is an estate in land.[3]

Manner relationship arises

The relationship of landlord and tenant may arise in various different ways between the original parties. One has been mentioned: express or implied agreement.

Another way in which the relationship of landlord and tenant may arise is by attornment. Attornment is a useful device for ensuring that tying covenants run with the land in question – as with a mortgage where the borrower attorns himself tenant of the mortgagee.[4]

The relationship of landlord and tenant may continue despite the wish of one of the parties to terminate it. For example, on expiry of a fixed-term or periodic tenancy of a dwelling house protected by the Rent Act 1977, or the Housing Act 1988, automatically a statutory tenancy arises. The landlord has no choice but to accept this state of affairs.[5]

---

3 *Jessamine Investment Co v Schwartz* [1978] QB 264 at 270; [1976] 3 All ER 521 at 526, CA; *Johnson v Felton* [1994] EGCS 135, CA (statutory tenancies); *N & D (London) Ltd v Gadsdon* [1992] 1 EGLR 112 at 116 (assured periodic tenancy by succession). It is not clear whether a continuing business tenancy under s 24(1) of the Landlord and Tenant Act 1954 is an estate: in *City of London Corpn v Fell* supra, the issue was left open.

4 Assuming tying covenants do not contravene EU law: see eg *Inntrepreneur Estates (GL) Ltd v Boyes* [1993] 2 EGLR 112, CA. Law of Property Act 1925, s 151(1)(a) renders an attornment by the lessee unnecessary where the reversion is assigned by deed.

5 Another example of this process is the continuation of business tenancies under Part II of the Landlord and Tenant Act 1954.

II SUBJECT MATTER

All land and interests in land lie in grant[6] and so may be leased. 'Land' is defined by s 205(1)(ix) of the Law of Property Act 1925 as including:

'...land of any tenure, and mines and minerals, whether or not held apart from the surface, buildings or parts of buildings (whether the division is horizontal, vertical or made in any other way) and other corporeal hereditaments; also a ... rent and other incorporeal hereditaments, and an easement, right, privilege, or benefit in, over, or derived from land; but not an undivided share in land...'

Corporeal hereditaments consist of the land itself (including mines and minerals) and permanent structures on the land, such as buildings parts of buildings and fixtures.

Incorporeal hereditaments are rights issuing out of land, and include rights of way, easements generally, sporting rights and other profits à prendre, tolls, commons and estovers and so on: all these may be leased but a deed is required to pass the legal estate.[7]

If a lease of a right of way over land adjoining the tenant's premises is expressly granted, the grantor is not obliged by Part II of the Landlord and Tenant Act 1954 to renew the lease on its expiry, since the tenant is not in occupation for statutory purposes.[8] If the tenant entitled to the lease of a right of way also holds a lease of adjoining premises protected by Part II of the 1954 Act, then the relevant holding for statutory purposes includes the lease of the right of way.[9]

Goods and chattels cannot be let as such. Plant and machinery may be leased by a separate agreement to that leasing the land where they are situated. If chattels and land are let in the same agreement, as with furnished lettings, the rent issues out of the land as a whole and so the whole rent – including any part payable for the use of the furniture – is distrainable.

Easements in a lease

A tenant may obtain the benefit of easements in the lease, by express or implied grant, or express or implied reservation. For present purposes 'easement' means: 'a right attached to a particular piece of land which allows the owner of that land (the dominant owner) either to use the land of another person (the servient owner) in a particular manner ... or to restrict its user by that other person to a particular extent ...'[10] However, one lessee cannot acquire easements prescriptively by common law, lost modern grant or, it seems, statute, against a neighbouring lessee;[11] nor may he prescriptively acquire easements for his sole

---

6 Law of Property Act 1925, s 51(1).
7 Law of Property Act 1925, s 52(1). An equitable lease of an incorporeal hereditament may be validly granted.
8 *Land Reclamation Co Ltd v Basildon District Council* [1979] 2 All ER 993, CA.
9 *Nevill Long & Co (Boards) Ltd v Firmenich & Co* (1983) 47 P & CR 59, CA.
10 Cheshire & Burn, p 518.
11 *Kilgour v Gaddes* [1904] 1 KB 457, CA; *Simmons v Dobson* [1991] 4 All ER 25, CA.

benefit against neighbouring land, whether it is held by his landlord or any other person.[12]

The extent of any particular grant or reservation of an easement in favour of a tenant is a matter of construction,[13] and the question of whether the rights so conferred have been interfered with is a question of fact. Where, for example, the landlords of a block of flats to lessees (A) expressly reserved A a right of vehicular access over a driveway, and then demised the driveway to another lessee (B), it was held that A was entitled to an injunction against B to restrain the building of a car wash, whose erection would substantially interfere with the rights of access, though not render them impossible.[14] In the case of the right to erect signboards, these are generally construed as capable of passing, if at all, as an easement,[15] but the right to erect a signboard may be spelt out of a demise 'with appurtenances'.[16]

The tenant may in the absence of express grant or reservation obtain certain easements by implication under one of four headings.

1 *An easement of necessity* This is limited in principle to a right of access over the landlord's retained land (if any) if at the time of the demise there was no other means of access to the demised premises, however inconvenient: an easement of necessity is limited to the purposes of the lessee at the date of the demise.[17]

2 *Intended easements* Intended easements are readily implied into leases to enable the purposes of the tenant, if known to the landlord, to be effectually carried out, as where a tenant was held entitled to install a ventilation system in the basement kitchen of a restaurant, let as such.[18]

3 *Continuous and apparent quasi-easements* Continuous and apparent quasi-easements are implied under the rule in *Wheeldon v Burrows*[19] but they must be continuous and apparent; necessary for the reasonable enjoyment of the demised premises; and used by the landlord up to the date of the grant of the

---

12 *Gayford v Moffatt* (1868) 4 Ch App 133.
13 In *Civil Service Musical Instrument Association v Whiteman* (1899) 68 LJ Ch 484, a lessee with a right of way over a passage to the demised shop who to the landlord's knowledge spent money on the passage was held not bound to restore the passage to its original condition nor to remove his signboard; also *Coopind UK Ltd v Walton Commercial Group Ltd* [1989] 1 EGLR 241.
14 *Celsteel Ltd v Alton House Holdings Ltd* [1986] 1 All ER 608, [1986] 1 WLR 512, CA; cf *Soames-Forsyth Properties Ltd v Tesco Stores Ltd* 27 February 1991, Unreported.
15 In *Francis v Hayward* (1882) 22 Ch D 177, CA, signboards were construed as part of the demised premises, but this was a very special case.
16 *William Hill (Southern) Ltd v Cabras Ltd* (1986) 54 P & CR 42, CA. Such right may not be construed out of a qualified prohibition against putting up signboards, ibid.
17 *Pinnington v Galland* (1853) 9 Exch 1; *Titchmarsh v Royston Water Co Ltd* (1899) 81 LT 673; *Nickerson v Barraclough* [1980] Ch 325, [1979] 3 All ER 312.
18 *Wong v Beaumont Property Trust Ltd* [1965] 1 QB 173, [1964] 2 All ER 119, CA. The ventilation system, which had to be built against the landlord's back wall, was essential if public health regulations were to be complied with and in this sense 'necessary'.
19 (1879) 12 Ch D 31, CA.

lease, for the benefit of the demised land or premises. It was, for example, held that this rule enabled the equitable lessee of a house to use an unmetalled way over the landlord's land as a means of access to and from the house.[20]

4   *Section 62(1) of the Law of Property Act 1925*   Any lease by deed automatically passes to the tenant a long list of easements, rights and reputed rights, 'at the time of conveyance demised, occupied or enjoyed with, or reputed or known as part or parcel of or appurtenant to the land or any part thereof'. The scope of any easements or rights passed by s 62 is a question of fact.[1] This is supposed to be merely a word-saving provision in relation to leases and other conveyances. In fact where land is demised to a tenant and he under the lease enjoys a precarious right, such as to use a coal-shed on the landlord's land, and the lease is renewed, the right, unless expressly and clearly excluded on renewal,[2] is converted into a full easement.[3] A precarious easement not known to the law will not pass under s 62, such as a right to a supply of hot water and central heating.[4] Subject to that, any right de facto enjoyed with the demised premises at the date of renewal of the lease, such as a way, will pass automatically on renewal under s 62.[5]

III   THE PARTIES

General

Any person[6] not under a legal disability may take or grant a lease. For present purposes, 'disability' means a restriction imposed on a person's capacity to grant or accept a lease. All relevant restrictions are statute-imposed except that in the case of a corporation, its own constitutive instrument may contain further restrictions on the ability to grant or accept leases. In general, therefore, a lease may be granted by any person with capacity to do so on any terms and conditions thought fit. Statute expressly prohibits any discrimination against potential lessees on the grounds of race and sex.[7]

---

20 *Borman v Griffith* [1930] 1 Ch 493.
 1 See *Handel v St Stephens Close Ltd* [1994] 1 EGLR 70 (car-parking).
 2 The grant of a lease 'with appurtenances' is insufficient to exclude s 62: *Hansford v Jago* [1921] 1 Ch 322.
 3 *Wright v Macadam* [1949] 2 KB 744, [1949] 2 All ER 565, CA. This rule applies to a licence to use a right of way or other advantage granted to a tenant let into occupation prior to the granting of a lease: on grant, the right becomes a full easement unless s 62 is excluded: *Goldberg v Edwards* [1950] Ch 247, CA.
 4 *Regis Property Co Ltd v Redman* [1956] 2 QB 612, [1956] 2 All ER 335, CA; nor a right to have one's flank outside wall proofed against the elements: *Phipps v Pears* [1965] 1 QB 76, [1964] 2 All ER 35, CA, nor a right to unlimited grazing: *Anderson v Bostock* [1976] Ch 312, [1976] 1 All ER 560.
 5 *International Tea Stores Co v Hobbs* [1903] 2 Ch 165.
 6 Common law disabilities on the power of a married woman to grant or accept leases were removed by s 1 of the Law Reform (Married Women and Tortfeasors) Act 1935. A contract to grant a lease to an enemy alien is void at common law (but in any case war regulations would strike down such contract).
 7 Race Relations Act 1976, s 21(1); Sex Discrimination Act 1975, s 30(1).

A lease may be void or voidable for other reasons apart from disabilities. In particular, general contractual rules rendering any contract void or voidable apply as much to contracts for a lease as to any contract. Accordingly, a lease made under duress or undue influence is voidable by the other party. So too is a lease procured by fraud or innocent misrepresentation – in this latter case it makes no difference that the lease may have been executed.[8] A lease entered into when one of the parties was in such a state of intoxication as not to know what he was doing, is voidable, provided the other party knew of the fact.[9] A lease made under a genuine mistake of fact as to the identity of the parties or the property is void.[10]

If the grantor purports to grant a lease or sub-lease for a longer term than he himself is entitled to, the 'lease' operates as an out-and-out assignment of the residue of his term.[11] Moreover, two persons may not validly grant a lease of property of which they are owners.[12] A single individual cannot grant a lease to himself, nor a nominee a lease to his principal.[13] Such transactions would be absurd: for example, the notion of a person enforcing covenants in the lease against himself will not bear serious consideration. By reason of s 72(3) of the Law of Property Act 1925, tenants in common of land are enabled validly to lease land, by deed, to themselves in another capacity.

Minors

Minority or infancy is a disability and, accordingly, by s 1(6) of the Law of Property Act 1925, ' a legal estate [in land] ... is not capable of being held by an infant'. The effect of granting a legal lease to a minor has been altered by the Trusts of Land and Appointment of Trustees Act 1996. Until the passing of this Act, the grant of a legal lease to a minor was to cause the creation of a strict settlement owing to s 1(1)(d) of the Settled Land Act 1925. The legal estate in the lease was vested, during the minority of the infant, in trustees of the settlement (1925 Act s 26). However, the 1996 Act was passed with a view to simplifying and modernising the law. It creates a unified system of holding successive or concurrent interests in land. The new system is a trust of land, and from the commencement of the 1996 Act (which was on 1 January 1997) no new settlements may be created or arise (1996 Act, s 2(1)).

The new rules appear to have the following effect. If a legal lease[14] is granted to a minor alone, the legal estate cannot pass to the minor. Instead, the lease operates as a declaration that the demised land is held on trust for the minor.[15]

8 Misrepresentation Act 1967, s 1. See further ch 4.
9 *Gore v Gibson* (1845) 13 M & W 623.
10 The remedy is rectification once the lease has been executed and parol evidence of mutual mistake is admissible even though the lease appears complete in itself: *Craddock Bros v Hunt* [1923] 2 Ch 136, CA. See also ch 4.
11 *Milmo v Carreras* [1946] KB 306, [1946] 1 All ER 288, CA.
12 *Rye v Rye* [1962] AC 496, [1962] 1 All ER 146, HL.
13 *Ingram v IRC* [1995] 4 All ER 334.
14 Sch 1 para 1 of the 1996 Act refers to a 'conveyance' but this expression includes a lease owing to the incorporation by s 23(2) of the 1996 Act of s 205(1)(ii) of the Law of Property Act 1925.
15 Trusts of Land and Appointment of Trustees Act 1996, Sch 1, para 1(1). The same result follows where the purported legal lease is to two or more minors.

Thus, if A grants a legal lease to B, who is a minor, A holds the leasehold estate as trustee for B absolutely. Where a purported grant of the legal lease is to a minor and an adult person jointly, the 1996 Act deems the demised land to be vested in the adult person in trust for the minor and himself.[16] The terms of the lease would determine whether the minor and the adult grantees held beneficially as joint tenants or as tenants in common, in accordance with the general law.

Patients

Where a legal estate in land is vested in a patient (i e by s 1 of the Mental Health Act 1983, a person suffering or appearing to suffer from a mental disorder), either solely or jointly with any other person, s 22 of the Law of Property Act 1925 provides that his receiver (or if none any person authorised in that behalf), must, by order of the judge with jurisdiction under Part VII of the 1983 Act, make or concur in making all dispositions required to convey or create a legal estate in his name and on his behalf. By s 93 of the 1983 Act the judge has all powers to do anything necessary or expedient in relation to the property which the patient would have had, and may in particular, under s 96, make orders or directions for the sale, charging, etc, of any of the patient's property; hence he may grant leases of such property.

Bankrupts

On bankruptcy, the bankrupt's estate, including all freehold and leasehold property[17] vests in a trustee in bankruptcy as soon as the latter's appointment takes effect.[18] When a person is adjudged bankrupt, he loses his power to grant leases: any lease (as a 'disposition') is void except to the extent that it is made with the consent of the court or was subsequently ratified by the court.[19] The statutory prohibition applies from the day of presentation of a petition for a bankruptcy order, and it ends with the vesting of the bankrupt's estate in the trustee in bankruptcy.[20] This is of little solace to the bankrupt since the trustee is invested by statute with the bankrupt's former power to grant leases.[1]

Executors and administrators

On a person's death, all his property, real and personal, vests in the executors of his will immediately on his death, or if none are appointed or he dies intestate, upon his administrators when they are granted letters of administration. Until the distribution of the assets, they have all the powers of trustees for sale and tenant for life.[2] They have powers to grant leases, therefore, though they would

---

16 Sch 1, para 1(2).
17 Insolvency Act 1986, s 283 as amended, so as to exclude from a bankrupt's estate most assured, protected and assured tenancies.
18 Insolvency Act 1986, s 306.
19 Insolvency Act 1986, s 284(1).
20 Insolvency Act 1986, s 284(3).
 1 Insolvency Act 1986, s 314 and Sch 5, Part II, para 12.
 2 Administration of Estates Act 1925, s 39; Law of Property Act 1925, s 33.

not normally do so, except where the property vested in them, for example, during a minority. The concurrence of all personal representatives, if there are two or more, is required on the grant of a lease.[3]

Trustees of land

In the case of land jointly or successively owned or subject to will trusts, the law has been radically reformed by the Trusts of Land and Appointment of Trustees Act 1996.[4] The Act creates a unified system, the trust of land. For the purpose of exercising their functions, trustees of land have, in relation to all the land subject to the trust, the powers of an absolute owner (s 6(1)).[5] The trustees may therefore grant leases of any length to any person, including an adult beneficiary of the trust (s 6(2)). However, the Act allows these powers to be expressly restricted or limited by the relevant will or trust (s 8). In addition, the trustees must, if they grant a lease, observe any relevant rules of statute, of law and of equity (s 6(6)). Thus they would be bound by such rules as the formal requirements of contracts for a lease and the rule of equity which requires them to take reasonable care in their exercise of trust powers.

The exercise of the trustees' leasing powers may also be limited by s 11 of the Act. Any adult trust beneficiary with an interest in possession in the land concerned has a statutory right to be consulted by the trustees, so far as practicable. Indeed, so far as is consistent with the general interest of the trust, the trustees must give effect to their wishes – or to those of a majority of beneficiaries – unless and to the extent that the disposition under which they hold excludes the consultation duty (s 11(2)).

If a person takes a legal lease of unregistered land from trustees of a private trust of land who have failed to consult beneficiaries where required, the lessee, as a 'purchaser', is not concerned to see that the requirement has been complied with (s 16(1)). His title is unaffected by the trustees' breach of duty. This rule does not apply to registered land. If a trust beneficiary is in occupation of registered trust land pursuant to his statutory right of occupation (s 12) his occupation rights would presumably override the registered title to the freehold and could be discovered by prior inspection of the land.

Where land is held in succession, thanks to a conveyance or other instrument such as an operative will, prior to the commencement of the 1996 Act, the powers of leasing are not vested in trustees. Where a strict settlement continues to exist, there is a statutory and specific power to grant legal leases, subject to certain restrictions as to the maximum length of the term. This power is conferred on the tenant for life by the Settled Land Act 1925, and not on the trustees.[6] Although the tenant for life exercises a trusteeship in the exercise of his powers (s 107), he may exercise his powers of leasing, provided he stays

---

3   Administration of Estates Act 1925, s 2(2). See *Harrison v Wing* [1988] 2 EGLR 4, CA.
4   The Act was brought into force on 1 January 1997 (SI 1996/2974) and was passed to implement Law Com No 181; see Pottage (1989) 53 MLR 683 and the summary in Cheshire & Burn, p 211.
5   It is provided by s 6(6) that the trustees must not exercise their powers in contravention of statute, nor of any rule of common law or equity.
6   For some further details see eg Cheshire & Burn, p 187 and also the previous edition of this book, pp 15–16.

within the four corners of the Act, at a time and in conditions of his choosing and in that sense without regard to the interests of any other beneficiaries.[7] In contrast to the position with new style trusts of land, the role of the trustees of a settlement is limited, notably to the receipt of any premium due from the lessee.

In the case of land held on trust for sale created prior to the commencement of the 1996 Act, the trustees for sale have, by s 28 of the Law of Property Act 1925, the leasing powers of a tenant for life. As from the commencement of the 1996 Act, trustees for sale become trustees of land with the new statutory powers and duties of such trustees.[8]

Mortgagors and mortgagees

Leases granted under his common law power by a freeholder, who has created a prior legal mortgage (or legal charge) over his land, without the concurrence of the mortgagee, do not bind the latter, whose legal interest is paramount. Section 99 of the Law of Property Act 1925 confers a statutory power of leasing on a mortgagor in possession without the concurrence of the mortgagee.[9] This may be expressly excluded or curtailed by the mortgage deed (s 99(13),[10] or extended by a written agreement therein contained or collateral thereto (s 99(14)).

Application of power The statutory power enables a mortgagor in possession (s 99(1)) to grant leases or agreements for a lease, which will bind the mortgagor and mortgagee, of the whole or any part of the land in question.

Relevant leases By s 99(3), after 1925 only two kinds of lease are allowed:

(a) agricultural or occupation leases for up to 50 years; and
(b) building leases for up to 999 years.

Formalities Leases under the statutory power must comply with four formalities:

(a) The lease must take effect in possession not later than 12 months after its start date (s 99(5)).
(b) It must reserve the best rent reasonably obtainable in all the circumstances and no premium is allowed (s 99(6)).
(c) The lease must contain a covenant by the lessee for payment of rent (s 99(7)).[11]

---

7 See *Wheelwright* v *Walker* (1883) 23 Ch D 752 (power of sale).
8 1996 Act, ss 1, 4 and 5 and Sch 4 (repealing Law of Property Act 1925, s 28).
9 A mortgagee in possession is empowered by s 99(2) to grant leases binding on all prior incumbrancers and the mortgagor.
10 No such exclusion or curtailment is allowed in the case of mortgages of agricultural land after 1 March 1948, which fall within the Agricultural Holdings Act 1948, nor in the case of mortgages of a new business tenancy under Part II of the Landlord and Tenant Act 1954 (s 36(4)). There is no corresponding statutory prohibition in the case of farm business tenancies, so that s 99 of the 1925 Act may there validly be excluded (Agricultural Tenancies Act 1995, s 31(4)).
11 The lease must contain a condition for re-entry for non-payment of rent within a time of up to 30 days: Law of Property Act 1925, s 99(7).

(d) A counterpart of the lease must be executed by the lessee and delivered to the lessor (s 99(8)) and also, any counterpart of a lease granted by the mortgagor must, within one month of its making, be delivered to the mortgagee or first mortgagee (s 99(11)).[12]

These formalities probably do not apply to oral tenancies;[13] they appear to apply to written agreements for a lease. As with leases by a tenant for life under a settlement, which are not formally valid, if the lack of formality is the sole reason for the invalidity, then the lease may be saved and take effect in equity under s 152(1) of the Law of Property Act 1925.[14] A lease which is not authorised by s 99, or granted by a mortgagor whose statutory power of leasing is excluded or curtailed, binds the lessor and lessee by estoppel but not a prior legal mortgagee who is entitled to assert his legal interest against both parties. The lessee will lack the protection of the Rent Act 1977 as against the mortgagee.[15] Should the mortgagee or his receiver accept rent from the tenant, a new tenancy, binding on the mortgagee, may be created by implication of law,[16] but only if the circumstances warrant this inference, which is not automatic.[17]

Receivers

Receivers appointed by the High Court have no powers of leasing, without the authority of the court. It is not usual for the court to insert, in the order appointing a receiver, a general authority to grant leases: as a rule each individual proposal for a lease must be considered by the court on its merits.[18] If a receiver is appointed by a mortgagee under s 101 of the Law of Property Act 1925, all leasing powers of the mortgagor are thereby vested in the mortgagee (s 99(19)), and are only exercisable by the receiver with his written authority; and the lessee will not obtain a legal estate unless the legal owner is a party to the lease.

The Crown

By virtue of s 1 of the Crown Estate Act 1961, the Crown Estate Commissioners may lease any part of the Crown Estate at the best rent obtainable, for any term not exceeding 100 years. A lease must take effect in possession not later than 12 months after its date, or in reversion after a lease having at that date not more than 21 years to run; and no option or contract may be made for a lease to

---

12 The lessee is not concerned to see that this is complied with: Law of Property Act 1925, s 99(11).
13 *Rhodes v Dalby* [1971] 1 WLR 1325, 1331.
14 The onus is then on the lessee to show that, apart from non-compliance with the statutory power, the lease is otherwise valid: *Davies v Hall* [1954] 2 All ER 330, [1954] 1 WLR 855, CA.
15 *Dudley and District Benefit Building Society v Emerson* [1949] Ch 707, [1949] 2 All ER 252, CA; the same might apply to the protection of the Housing Act 1988. Cf Smith (1977) 41 Conv (NS) 197.
16 *Chatsworth Properties Ltd v Effiom* [1971] 1 All ER 604, [1971] 1 WLR 144, CA.
17 See *Javad v Aqil* [1991] 1 All ER 243, 251-253, CA.
18 Leases will be granted in the name of the estate owner and the best terms must be obtained: *Wynne v Lord Newborough* (1790) 1 Ves 164.

commence more than 10 years from the date of contract, unless the rent under such lease is left to be fixed as at the commencement of the term in such a manner as in their opinion is calculated to ensure the best consideration reasonably obtainable at that date. They may, with the royal assent, under the Sign Manual grant leases, either gratuitously or at such rent as they think fit, of land for development, improvement or general benefit of the Crown, if it is to be used for any of the purposes specified in s 5, or for any public or charitable purposes connected with Crown Estate Land, or tending to the welfare of persons residing or employed on it (s 5).

Government departments authorised to acquire land from time to time for public purposes are generally given power to lease any part of it which is not required for that purpose immediately. Their powers of leasing in such cases are limited strictly to the terms of the enabling Act.[19] Whether they can claim Crown privilege or not, eg whether such a lease is subject to the Rent Act, depends upon whether they can be regarded as acting as agents of the Crown, or merely servants of the Crown; in the latter case they do not enjoy Crown privilege.

Corporations

A corporation is an artificial person, whose legal personality is unchanged. The leasing powers of corporations depend on whether and to what extent they are empowered to grant leases by their constitutive instrument (e g in the case of a company, its memorandum of association). The grant of a lease by a corporation must generally be by deed to pass the legal estate in the land.[20] In the case of a company incorporated under the Companies Acts, the same formalities apply to the granting of legal and equitable leases by it as apply to an individual, in the absence of a contrary intention in the company's memorandum of association.[1] A person who enters possession of corporate land under an unsealed lease may, it seems, still become a tenant from year to year at law.[2] The powers of a statutory corporation will be governed by the statute which creates it.[3]

Local authorities

As to the leasing powers of local authorities, statute confers a general power on them to grant leases,[4] so that, for example, county councils, district councils and London Borough councils generally have power to grant leases of any length. If the consideration is less than the best rent which can reasonably be obtained, a lease cannot be granted except with the consent of the Secretary of State. Excepted from this latter requirement are short tenancies. Local authorities

---

19 As in Civil Aviation Act 1982, s 41.
20 A lease is executed by a company by the affixing of its common seal, but this is not necessary, provided that Companies Act 1985, s 36A is complied with.
1 Companies Act 1985, s 36.
2 *Ecclesiastical Comrs v Merral* (1869) LR 4 Exch 162.
3 See eg Iron and Steel Act 1982, s 14(1); New Towns Act 1981, ss 17, 37 and 64.
4 See Local Government Act 1972, s 123.

are also empowered to grant or assign leases at a premium of land acquired for the purposes of Part II of the Housing Act 1985, subject to the consent of the Secretary of State,[5] which is not required in the case of the grant of a secure tenancy.

Agents

Prospective parties to a lease may authorise an agent to act on their behalf, with regard to negotiating its terms, and also to the granting and accepting of a lease, if they so desire. Authority to negotiate, to sign a binding contract, and even to enter into a lease which does not have to be by deed, requires no formality; but authority to execute a formal lease by deed must itself be given by deed, i e by a power of attorney. An agent should execute a lease in the name of his principal.

An estate agent who is instructed to find a tenant, has no implied authority thereby to sign a contract for a lease, nor let prospective tenants into possession. A bailiff, on the other hand, may have a limited authority to grant leases, eg tenancies from year to year, by virtue of his contract of employment. An agent who exceeds his authority cannot bind his principal, though, of course, his unauthorised acts may be ratified,[6] and such ratification will date back to then. A principal's knowledge will not be imputed to an agent, so that if an agent makes an innocent misrepresentation, an action will not lie against him in consequence, nor against the principal, unless the principal had deliberately kept his agent in ignorance (e g of a serious defect) in order to mislead the purchaser, ie fraudulently.[7] On the other hand, fraudulent mis-statements of an agent will be imputed to the principal. Similarly, where the agent, without the landlord's knowledge or authority, received an illegal premium from a tenant, the landlord was held liable, for the act was within the apparent authority of the agent.[8]

An agent employed to let property is under a duty at common law:[9]

1   to make reasonable enquiries as to the solvency of a prospective tenant if such a duty falls within the scope of his employment;[10]
2   to obtain the best price reasonably obtainable; and
3   until his principal accepts an offer, to disclose to him any other offers made to him.[11]

An agent's right to payment will depend upon any express terms of the agreement between himself and his principal. The contract may stipulate that

5   Housing Act 1985, s 32.
6   See *Worboys v Carter* [1987] 2 EGLR 1, CA.
7   *Armstrong v Strain* [1952] 1 KB 232, [1952] 1 All ER 139, CA.
8   *Navarro v Moregrand Ltd* [1951] WN 335, CA; also *Saleh v Robinson* [1988] 2 EGLR 126, CA.
9   See also duties imposed by Estate Agents Act 1979. By s 2(1)(b): any lease or tenancy granted at an open market rent is seemingly excluded from the Act, whereas the grant of a long lease at a low rent seems to be caught. See Murdoch, ch 6. For criminal liability for certain misdescriptions see Property Misdescriptions Act 1991, ss 1 and 2.
10 *Heys v Tindall* (1861) 1 B & S 296; *Bradshaw v Press* [1983] 2 EGLR 16, CA (on facts estate agent not in breach of duty as nothing in (bogus) reference put him as reasonable agent on further inquiry).
11 *Keppel v Wheeler* [1927] 1 KB 577, CA.

he will be entitled to his fee on the introduction of a willing 'purchaser', for example, or only if a lease is granted. In such a case it is possible that a term will be implied that the principal will not dispose of the property himself or through other means, preventing the agent from receiving any commission.[12] A stipulation for sole letting rights will affect the position between the parties. Any deposit taken by the agent is held by him as agent for the landlord, and therefore, if the agent absconds with the money, the loss falls upon the landlord.[13]

IV TYPES OF LEASES AND TENANCIES

If a lease is to exist as a legal estate, it must fall within the statutory definition of 'term of years absolute'.[14] If the lease falls outside the definition, it may exist in equity.[15] The definition of terms of years absolute is wide.[16] It includes:

1   'A term of years (taking effect either in possession or in reversion whether or not at a rent) . . . subject or not to another legal estate,[17] and either certain or liable to determination by notice, re-entry, operation of law, or by a provision for cesser on redemption or any other event'.[18] This part of the definition therefore includes leases for a fixed term of years, which may last for any length of time (whether for one year or 99 years) provided it is for less than perpetuity.[19] A lease may thus remain a term of years absolute though it expressly enables the landlord to re-enter or forfeit the term for breach of covenant. A 'term of years' such as a fixed-term lease for 10 years is only capable of being a legal estate: to create a legal lease, the parties will have to execute a deed. Special rules apply to the creation of short terms certain.[20]

2   Under the definition clause, 'the expression 'term of years' includes a term for less than a year, or for a year or years and a fraction of a year or from year to year'. All types of periodic tenancies are thereby included, whether they are weekly, monthly, quarterly or yearly. This is deliberate. It is permitted to create a legal periodic tenancy orally or in writing.

---

12 *Luxor (Eastbourne) Ltd v Cooper* [1941] AC 108, [1941] 1 All ER 33, HL.
13 *Goding v Frazer* [1966] 3 All ER 234, [1967] 1 WLR 286.
14 Law of Property Act 1925, s 1(1)(b).
15 Law of Property Act 1925, s 1(3). In this case, if title is unregistered, the lease must be registered as a Class C(iv) land charge on pain of voidness against a purchaser for money or money's worth of the land (Land Charges Act 1972, s 4(5)); for the position where title is registered see ch 4.
16 Law of Property Act 1925, s 205(1)(xxvii).
17 Thus allowing the creation of a sub-lease, a sub-underlease and so on, all derived from a head leasehold estate.
18 The last two expressions are designed (i) to cover a term in a mortgage by demise under which the mortgage term comes to an end on repayment of the mortgage and (ii) to allow for the insertion of an option by one or other party to break the lease on notice.
19 See *Siew Soon Wah v Yong Tong Hong* [1973] AC 836, PC (tenancy described as 'permanent' held grant for longest period landlord had power to demise).
20 As to the formalities applicable to the creation of legal leases, see further ch 4.

3   Certain types of lease are excluded from the statutory definition. A lease determinable on 'the dropping of a life, or the determination of a determinable life interest' cannot be a legal lease. A term of years 'determinable with life or lives or with the cesser of a determinable life interest' is also excluded from being a term of years absolute (and exists behind a trust). A lease created after 31 December 1925 which is 'not expressed to take effect in possession within twenty-one years after the creation thereof where required by this Act to take effect within that period' cannot be a legal lease.[1]

Concurrent leases

A concurrent lease is a term limited to commence before the expiry of an existing lease of the same premises. It operates as an assignment of part of the head landlord's reversion. The concurrent lessee becomes entitled to the rent payable and to enforce the tenant's covenants under the earlier lease.[2] For example, where X held a concurrent lease on a flat occupied by T, it was held that X was 'lessor' for the purpose of recovery from T of a proportion of a service charge.[3] There is no limit on the number of concurrent legal leases which may be granted. Each subsequent term operates as a reversion expectant on the term next preceding it. The subsequent term may be longer than the term next above it or it may be shorter, in which case the legal reversion lasts until expiry of the shorter term. All concurrent leases must be by deed to pass a legal estate.[4]

Reversionary leases

The statutory definition of a 'term of years absolute' includes a term taking effect in reversion, in other words at a future date. There is no requirement that a lease must take effect immediately. Reversionary or future leases are therefore permitted to take effect as from the date of grant. So, by 149(2) of the 1925 Act, it is provided that leases are capable of taking effect from the date fixed for commencement, without actual entry, which latter was, until 1 January 1926, a condition precedent of the tenant's acquiring an estate in the land. By s 149(3) of the 1925 Act, some limits are imposed on the creation of reversionary or future leases:

'A term, at a rent or granted in consideration of a fine, limited ... to take effect more than twenty-one years from the date of the instrument purporting to create it, shall be void, and any contract ... to create such a term shall likewise be void.'

This provision does not affect, in particular, leases taking effect under a settlement. It was new in 1925.[5] A contract to create a lease which, when

---

1   The reason for this is to ensure that a leasehold estate in land is capable of taking effect in possession within a relatively short period of the grant of the term, in the interests of certainty.
2   *Re Moore and Hulm's Contract* [1912] 2 Ch 105.
3   *Adelphi (Estates) Ltd v Christie* (1983) 47 P & CR 650, CA.
4   LPA 1925, s 52.
5   The rule against perpetuities does not preclude the granting of a lease to take effect at a remote future date.

granted, will not infringe s 149(3) is not invalidated by that provision, which only strikes down contracts to create leases which will infringe it when granted.[6] Otherwise a renewal option in any lease for over 21 years in duration would be invalidated by s 149(3).[7] Because legislative policy is to discourage excessive renewals, any contract made after 1925 to renew a lease or sub-lease for over 60 years after the termination of the current lease is void.[8]

LEASES FOR A FIXED TERM

A lease for a fixed term is a lease of pre-defined length, such as for six months, one year, ten years, 99 years or 999 years.[9] The term created by such a lease must be expressed with certainty or by reference to something which can be rendered certain at the commencement of the lease, otherwise it is void for uncertainty: hence, a tenancy alleged to be a term certain for the duration of the Second World War was void as such.[10] A tenancy limited to continue unless ended by a month's notice on either side would likewise be invalid as a term certain.[11] Similarly, a term of uncertain maximum duration, which was to continue until the land was required by the landlord for a road-widening scheme, whereupon the lease was terminable on two months' minimum notice, was held to be void for uncertainty by the House of Lords.[12] In addition, applying that decision, a purported grant of a term certain determinable by an event within the control of both parties is invalid as a purported demise determinable on an uncertain future event: both conditions are repugnant to the nature of a term certain. Should both parties take care to map out in the operative part of the lease the maximum duration of the term, it seemingly is no objection that it may be determinable by one side or the other on the occurrence, within that period, of an uncertain future event: thus a term for five years certain may validly be determinable by the tenant if the war ends prior to the expiry of the lease or by the landlord if he wishes to redevelop the premises.

In order to measure the duration of the estate granted by a lease, a term certain is taken to commence as from the date of its execution,[13] but where a lessee takes possession under a prior agreement for a lease, the High Court has held that the date for measuring liability under covenants and for other purposes such as the date from which the exercise of options runs, is that of the agreement.[14]

6   *Re Strand and Savoy Properties Ltd, D P Development Co Ltd v Cumbrae Properties Ltd* [1960] Ch 582, [1960] 2 All ER 327, (1960) 76 LQR 352; *Weg Motors Ltd v Hales* [1962] Ch 49, [1961] 3 All ER 181, CA.
7   The renewal option in *Re Strand and Savoy Properties Ltd* supra was for one renewal of a 35-year term.
8   LPA 1922, Sch 15, para 7(2).
9   For a recent example see *Re Bennington Road, Aston* (1993) Times, 21 July.
10   *Lace v Chantler* [1944] KB 368, [1944] 1 All ER 305, CA.
11   *Onyx (UK) Ltd v Beard* [1996] EGCS 55.
12   *Prudential Assurance Co Ltd v London Residuary Body* [1992] 2 AC 386, [1992] 3 All ER 504, HL. It was held that there was an implied yearly tenancy, under which both parties had the unfettered power to determine it by six months' notice. See Bridge [1993] CLJ 26; Bright (1993) 13 LS 78; Sparkes (1993) 108 LQR 93; PF Smith [1993] Conv 461.
13   *Bradshaw v Pawley* [1979] 3 All ER 273 at 277–278.
14   *Trane (UK) Ltd v Provident Mutual Life Assurance* [1995] 1 EGLR 33.

The period of letting need not be continuous.[15] A lease may validly prohibit personal occupation by the tenant at specified periods such as weekends. Time share lettings are in principle valid: a person may be granted exclusive possession for one specified week in a specified number of years.[16]

A periodic tenancy, such as from year to year, is saved from invalidity on the ground of uncertainty, according to the House of Lords, only because of the unrestricted power of either party to serve a notice to quit to terminate it at the end of any year. The term continues, however, until determined by notice as if both parties had made a new agreement at the end of each year for the ensuing year.[17]

A lease for a fixed term comes to an end automatically (i e without notice) when the term expires, ie by effluxion of time. In addition, such tenancies may be made terminable *before* the expiration of the term on notice given by one party or the other to terminate the tenancy at given intervals during its currency (i e an option to terminate, or 'break-clause' as it is often called, expressed to be exercisable, for example, at the end of the seventh and the fourteenth years of a 21-year lease).

Leases for life or lives or until marriage

Section 149(6) of the Law of Property Act 1925 provides that a lease or a contract for a lease at a rent or in consideration of a fine 'for life or lives or for any term of years determinable with life or lives or on the marriage of the lessee' is automatically converted into a term of 90 years.[18] Such 90-year terms are determinable, by s 149(6), on either side, 'on the death or marriage (as the case may be) of the original lessee', by at least one month's notice in writing given to determine the tenancy on one of the quarter days applicable to it – or if none, then on one of the usual quarter days. They are legal estates by statutory conversion. Since 'fine' includes a benefit in the nature of a premium (s 205(1)(xxiii) of the 1925 Act), the sale of a house at only one-third of its value in exchange for a licence to occupy for life to the former owners fell within s 149(6), and bound a subsequent legal mortgagee of the premises.[19]

Section 149(6) does not apply to any term taking effect in equity under a settlement or created out of an equitable interest under a settlement for mortgage, indemnity, or other like purposes, even if a rent is reserved. These terms take effect in equity behind a trust under s 1(3) of the 1925 Act.

Section 149(6) applies to any term expressed to be determinable with any life or lives or on the marriage of the lessee,[20] whether the life is that of the landlord, the tenant, or the survivor of the tenant and some other person, no

15 *Smallwood v Sheppards* [1895] 2 QB 627 (occupation for three successive Bank Holidays held agreement for single letting).
16 *Cottage Holiday Associates Ltd v Customs and Excise Comrs* [1983] QB 735. Query whether a time-share period exceeding 21 years would infringe s 149(3) of the 1925 Act.
17 *Prudential Assurance Co Ltd v London Residuary Body*, supra; but see Wilde (1994) 57 MLR 117.
18 A contract for a lease within s 149(6) is deemed to be a contract for a 90-year lease terminable by notice.
19 *Skipton Building Society v Clayton* (1993) 66 P & CR 223, CA; Crabb [1993] Conv 478.
20 Ie automatically on death (or marriage): *Bass Holdings Ltd v Lewis* [1986] 2 EGLR 40, CA.

matter how short the term may be. Moreover s 149(6) applies to any term of years determinable with life, as with a term granted by L to T for 21 years if he (T) so long lives. This will be automatically converted into a 90-year lease determinable at the earliest within one month of T's death.[1] The actual intentions of the parties therefore may count for little.

However, s 149(6) does not apply to a lease or tenancy determinable by notice after the dropping of a life or lives, such as a letting to T for three years with power in the landlord to terminate the tenancy by notice in the event of the death of the tenant during the currency of the term.[2]

Leases with a covenant or option for perpetual renewal

The lease may contain a covenant or option for renewal by the tenant. If the covenant or option is such that the right to renew must be reproduced perpetually in all further leases granted, perpetual renewal is created, with the following consequences.

The grant of a term, sub-term or other leasehold interest which is perpetually renewable takes effect as a term of 2,000 years from the commencement date of the term, or a sub-term of 2,000 years less one day, calculated from the date of commencement of the head term out of which it was derived.[3]

Perpetually renewable leases or sub-leases take effect in substitution for the term originally granted. The rent, covenants and conditions of the substituted term are payable or enforceable during its 2,000-year span. Special provisions apply, of which the following[4] should be mentioned:

1 The lessee or underlessee may, on giving written notice to the landlord at least ten days before the date on which the lease would, but for its conversion, have expired, determine the lease on such expiry date.
2 The lessee or underlessee must register all assignments or devolutions of the converted term with the lessor, his agent or solicitor within six months of the assignment.
3 Each lessee or underlessee, whether the original party or not, is only liable for rent accruing and breaches of covenant taking place while the lease or sub-lease is vested in him.

Since the consequences of perpetual renewal are Draconian – for example the rent originally fixed remains for the whole 2,000-year span of the converted term – the courts are reluctant to hold that perpetual renewal is intended except in the face of unambiguous language. Hence, a covenant to renew at the 'like' rent and all covenants in the lease, did not create perpetual renewal.[5] The question whether a particular form of words confers a right to perpetual renewal is one of construction, and unambiguous language indicating an intention to

---

1 The position if L at the date of the grant holds a leasehold reversion of (say) only 22 years is not solved by s 149(6).
2 *Bass Holdings Ltd v Lewis* supra.
3 LPA 1922, s 145 and Sch 15, paras 1 and 2. Identical provision is made for contracts for perpetual renewal: LPA 1922, Sch 15, para 7(1).
4 LPA 1922, Sch 15, paras 10 and 11.
5 *Iggulden v May* (1804) 9 Ves 325.

include the entitlement to renewal in the terms of the renewed lease will be given effect to and perpetual renewal will be created: as with, for example, a covenant to renew 'on identical terms' as the present lease;[6] or to renew at the same rent and with the like covenants 'including the present covenant for renewal'.[7] The same result followed where the relevant words clearly indicated that the covenant to renew must be included in the terms of any renewed lease on every renewal – with the consequent conversion of a five-year term into a 2,000-year term at the same rent as that originally reserved.[8] A formula for renewal of a 21-year lease as often as every 11 years of the term expired was also held to create perpetual renewal.[9] The court may be able to decide what the parties' true intentions in the light of the surrounding circumstances were, and so it was held that words literally wide enough to confer perpetual renewal must be cut down to take these circumstances into account.[10]

Where a renewal covenant in a seven-year lease provided that a renewed lease must contain a renewal covenant for a further seven-year term on expiry of the renewed term, the tenant was held entitled merely to a double renewal – this on the basis that an obligation for perpetual renewal must be expressly spelt out of the lease.[11]

The safest course is to avoid any danger of perpetual renewal by providing expressly that renewal is to be on the same terms (for example) as the current lease excluding any further renewal covenant or option.

PERIODIC TENANCIES

The initial duration of a periodic tenancy is fixed by express or implied agreement of the parties at the commencement of the tenancy. The periods most commonly found are weekly, monthly, quarterly and yearly tenancies, and whatever period is employed, that is bound to be the minimum duration of the tenancy, but until notice of termination is given, its total duration will not be certain. As the tenancy progresses through one period and another, the tenancy is regarded as one continuous tenancy, but a tenancy from year to year (or for any lesser period) is saved from invalidity on the ground of uncertainty solely by reason of the power of the landlord or the tenant to determine it by notice at the end of any year.

Because of this latter rule, any term which purports to preclude the landlord from serving a notice to quit as long as the tenant pays his rent and performs his covenants, might make it impossible for the landlord ever to serve notice, and is repugnant to the nature of a periodic tenancy.[12] The same result follows if a tenancy provides for service of a notice to quit only by the tenant, thus

6 *Northchurch Estates Ltd v Daniels* [1947] Ch 117, [1946] 2 All ER 524.
7 *Parkus v Greenwood* [1950] Ch 644, [1950] 1 All ER 436, CA.
8 *Re Hopkin's Lease, Caerphilly Concrete Products Ltd v Owen* [1972] 1 All ER 248, [1972] 1 WLR 372, CA.
9 *Wynn v Conway Corpn* [1914] 2 Ch 705, CA.
10 *Plumrose Ltd v Real and Leasehold Estates Investment Society Ltd* [1969] 3 All ER 1441, [1970] 1 WLR 52 (the lease out of which the option derived was itself a once-only renewable lease).
11 *Marjorie Burnett Ltd v Barclay* (1980) 125 Sol Jo 199.
12 *Doe d Warner v Browne* (1807) 8 East 165.

rendering it impossible at any time for the landlord to serve notice to quit.[13] A term which entitles the landlord to serve a notice to quit only if a predetermined but uncertain future event arises, such as an undertaking by the landlord of a weekly tenant not to give notice until the landlord required to pull down the demised buildings, is likewise void for repugnancy.[14] These principles of strict certainty were applied by the House of Lords, overruling earlier Court of Appeal authority, to a tenancy which, in terms, was to continue until certain land might be required by the landlord for the purposes of a road-widening scheme. The landlords' successors in title were able to serve notice on the tenant even though they had no road-widening scheme, the term being construed as a tenancy from year to year, and so determinable on six months' notice by either side.[15] It was said to be of the essence of such a tenancy that both parties should be entitled to give notice to terminate it. The application of the certainty rule to periodic tenancies is seemingly qualified by the fact that it is open to the parties to grant a term from year to year with a fetter on the landlord's power to serve a notice to quit for a number of years determined in advance, thus saving a provision under which the landlord would not serve a notice on the tenant during the first three years of the tenancy.[16]

Yearly tenancies

Yearly tenancies (tenancies from year to year) may be created expressly or impliedly, and may be determined at the end of the first or any subsequent year by service of a valid notice to quit. In the absence of agreement to the contrary, six months' notice is required. Where rent is payable on the quarter days, and the tenant enters in the middle of a quarter, the courts will try to hold that the yearly tenancy commenced and is therefore terminable on a quarter day,[17] eg where on entry, the tenant pays a proportionate part of a quarter's rent, in respect of the period between the actual date of entry and the next quarter day.[18] A tenancy 'for one year, and so on from year to year' creates a fixed-term tenancy for one year, followed by a yearly tenancy; accordingly, it cannot be terminated before the end of the second year.[19]

A tenant holding over after the expiry of a fixed-term lease becomes a tenant at will or on sufferance. If he pays a yearly rent, a tenancy from year to year may arise, on terms not inconsistent with those of the previous lease, if the proper inference from the landlord's acceptance of rent coupled with the other circumstances is that both parties intend to create a tenancy.[20] Thus, if the landlord accepted the rent under a mistake, no implied grant of a yearly tenancy

13   *Centaploy Ltd v Matlodge Ltd* [1974] Ch 1, [1973] 2 All ER 720.
14   *Cheshire Lines Committee v Lewis & Co* (1880) 50 LJQB 121.
15   *Prudential Assurance Co Ltd v London Residuary Body* supra.
16   Such a lease creates a determinable term of three years certain even if the landlord may, eg, serve a notice within that period on a stipulated event. Cf *Breams Property Investment Co v Stroulger* [1948] 2 KB 1, [1948] 1 All ER 758, CA.
17   *Croft v William F Blay Ltd* [1919] 2 Ch 343, at 357, CA.
18   *Doe d Holcomb v Johnson* (1806) 6 Esp 10.
19   *Doe d Chadborn v Green* (1839) 9 Ad & El 658; *Addis v Burrows* [1948] 1 KB 444, [1948] 1 All ER 177, CA.
20   *Vaughan-Armatrading Ltd v Sarsah* (1995) 27 HLR 631, CA.

arises.[1] The question of whether an implied periodic tenancy is created is primarily one of the objective intention of the parties,[2] if stated, or of the proper inferences reasonably to be drawn from their conduct, and is thus one of fact. Hence, all the circumstances, including the payment of rent, which latter is an important factor, are taken into account.[3] It is easier to presume an intention to create an implied yearly tenancy where the tenant lacks any statutory protection, than when he is entitled to it. Yet no implied yearly tenancy arose where the landlord accepted, without more, two isolated payments of rent from an erstwhile service occupier (and licensee), as evidence of the real intentions of the parties is required.[4] Similarly, where a former secure tenant was allowed to hold over, after a suspended possession order had been made, he was held to have done so as the result of the course of the possession proceedings and there was therefore no intention to grant him by implication a new tenancy.[5]

If an acceptance of rent by the landlord is explicable on the ground that the tenant has statutory security of tenure, whether in the residential (or business) sector, as a result of which the landlord may have no choice but to accept the rent, because the tenant is entitled to hold over under the statute concerned, no automatic inference of a periodic implied yearly tenancy is made.[6] The courts take into account the fact that statutory security of tenure modifies the common law rule that a fixed term expires with no automatic implied right of renewal by effluxion of time, and the fact that the parties are taken to be aware of these rights.[7] However, the creation by statute of tenancies which lack security, such as residential assured shorthold tenancies or farm business tenancies, may reduce the occasions in the immediate future in which this particular common law doctrine has to be modified by the courts.

A person who goes into possession under a void lease, or a mere agreement for a lease, is a tenant at will, but when he pays, or agrees to pay, rent in accordance with the intended lease, he becomes a tenant from year to year at law upon the terms of the intended lease in so far as they are not inconsistent with a yearly tenancy. He may have other rights in equity, however, for if he has a specifically enforceable agreement, he is treated as holding from the date of entry on the terms of the lease intended by the parties, as if it had been granted, under the doctrine in *Walsh v Lonsdale*.[8] However, the common law presumption of a new yearly tenancy is relevant where for some reason the remedy of specific performance is unavailable, such as failure by either party to perform a condition precedent.[9]

---

1 *Maconochie Bros Ltd v Brand* [1946] 2 All ER 778; *Sector Properties v Meah* (1973) 229 Estates Gazette 1097, CA.
2 *Sopwith v Stutchbury* (1983) 17 HLR 50, 74, CA.
3 *Javad v Aqil* [1991] 1 All ER 243, CA; *Brent London Borough Council v O'Bryan* [1993] 1 EGLR 59, CA; also *Marcroft Wagons Ltd v Smith* [1951] 2 KB 496, 506, CA.
4 *Thompsons (Funeral Furnishers) Ltd v Phillips* [1945] 2 All ER 49, CA.
5 *Greenwich London Borough Council v Regan* [1996] EGCS 15, CA.
6 *Dealex Properties Ltd v Brooks* [1966] 1 QB 542, [1965] 1 All ER 1080, CA; *Longrigg, Burrough and Trounson v Smith* [1979] 2 EGLR 42, CA.
7 *Cardiothoracic Institute v Shrewdcrest Ltd* [1986] 3 All ER 633, 642.
8 (1882) 21 Ch D 9.
9 *Coatsworth v Johnson* (1885) 55 LJQB 220, CA.

There must be clear evidence of an agreement for a tenancy (or a new tenancy, as the case may be), and payment of rent is not in itself decisive; nor is it even essential, if there is other evidence to support the implication. Conversely, the implication of a yearly tenancy may be rebutted by evidence to the contrary, eg by calculation[10] (though not necessarily payment) of the rent by reference to weekly sums.

Where a tenancy from year to year arises by implication, the tenant holds under such of the terms of the former (or as the case may be, intended) lease as are not inconsistent with those of a yearly tenancy, eg covenants to pay rent in advance,[11] to keep the premises in good tenantable repair,[12] provisos for re-entry by the landlord on non-payment of rent or on breach of other covenants,[13] etc, but no onerous covenants to do repairs which would not normally be done by yearly tenants,[14] to paint every three years,[15] an agreement for two years' notice to quit,[16] nor an option for renewal.[17] A notice to quit given to terminate a yearly tenancy must be expressed to expire at the end of any year of the tenancy. If it arose by reason of the tenant holding over, it is terminable on the anniversary of the termination, and not of the commencement of the original term,[18] unless a contrary intention can be inferred.

Periodic tenancies for less than a year

Periodic tenancies for less than a year may be created expressly, or may arise by implication, in the same way as tenancies from year to year. They include weekly, monthly, three-monthly, quarterly, six-monthly and half-yearly tenancies, and the only reason for treating them separately from yearly tenancies is that they are terminable on one full period's notice at common law, ie in the absence of any express agreement to the contrary, and therefore, unlike tenancies from year to year, they would not normally be terminable at the end of the first period. The period upon which a tenancy is based may be ascertained mainly by reference to the way in which the rent is calculated; thus, where the rent reserved is so much per year, a yearly tenancy will be implied, even though the rent is payable monthly. There is a distinction between a monthly or quarterly rent and monthly or quarterly instalments of a yearly rent;[19] and accordingly, where a tenant for a fixed-term at a weekly rent holds over and continues to pay the same weekly rent, the proper inference is that a weekly tenancy was intended.[20]

---

10 *Adler v Blackman* [1953] 1 QB 146, [1952] 2 All ER 945, CA; cf *Javad v Aqil* [1991] 1 All ER 243, [1991] 1 WLR 1007, CA.
11 *Lee v Smith* (1854) 9 Exch 662.
12 *Richardson v Gifford* (1834) 1 Ad & El 52.
13 *Thomas v Packer* (1857) 1 H & N 669.
14 *Bowes v Croll* (1856) 6 E & B 255.
15 *Pinero v Judson* (1829) 6 Bing 206.
16 *Tooker v Smith* (1857) 1 H & N 732.
17 *Re Leeds and Batley Breweries and Bradbury's Lease, Bradbury v Grimble & Co* [1920] 2 Ch 548.
18 *Croft v William F Blay Ltd* [1919] 2 Ch 343, CA; *Addis v Burrows* [1948] 1 KB 444, [1948] 1 All ER 177, CA.
19 *Ladies' Hosiery and Underwear Ltd v Parker* [1930] 1 Ch 304, CA.
20 *Adler v Blackman* [1953] 1 QB 146, [1952] 2 All ER 945, CA.

The difference between three-monthly and quarterly tenancies and between six-monthly and half-yearly tenancies relates to the date of their commencement, and hence to the dates on which they are terminable and the length of notice required. A tenancy commencing on one of the usual quarter days will normally be construed as a quarterly (or half-yearly tenancy) terminable on one quarter's notice on any quarter day (or on two quarters' notice, as the case may be, on either of the usual half-year days). But where such a tenancy commences in the middle of a quarter, it may be construed as a three-monthly or six-monthly tenancy, terminable on so many calendar months' notice[1] given to expire in the middle of a quarter or half-year, though this may be rebutted by payment of a proportionate part of a quarter's rent (i e from the date of entry to the next quarter day) with the result that the tenancy will be deemed to have commenced on the quarter day next after the tenant's entry.[2]

TENANCIES AT WILL

A tenancy at will arises where a person occupies land or premises with the consent, ie 'at the will', of the owner, under a tenancy of uncertain duration; and because the tenant has no certain estate, a tenancy at will is not within the statutory definition of a 'term of years absolute.' For the same reason, such an interest is terminable at any time simply by a demand for possession, or by implication of law, ie by any act which is inconsistent with the landlord's continuing consent, such as the death of either party, alienation of the landlord's interest with notice to the tenant,[3] or waste committed by the tenant.[4] The tenancy can, in effect, be terminated forthwith, and the tenant must quit immediately; he may in such cases re-enter upon the land within a reasonable time thereafter, to remove his goods or crops. Section 5 of the Protection from Eviction Act 1977 (see chapter 19) is inapplicable to tenancies at will.[5] Though the tenant has no estate, the relationship is one of tenure between the parties, and therefore where a rent has been agreed it is distrainable;[6] otherwise the landlord may bring an action for damages for use and occupation.

An implied tenancy at will arises if a tenant holds over rent-free at the end of his lease, with the implied consent of the landlord, or where a tenant under a lease void at law,[7] or under an agreement for a future lease, enters into possession, rent-free, or where a person is let by the vendor into possession without special stipulations, pending completion of a purchase.[8] There was

---

1 'Month' means calendar month, in any agreement taking effect after 31 December 1925 (Law of Property Act 1925, s 61(a)): thus, a month's notice to quit served on 1 January expires on 1 February.
2 For statutory restrictions as to the length of notices to quit in this type of tenancy see ch 19.
3 Eg by mortgage, *Jarman v Hale* [1899] 1 QB 994.
4 Co Lit 57a; *Countess of Shrewsbury's Case* (1600) 5 Co Rep 13b.
5 *Crane v Morris* [1965] 3 All ER 77, [1965] 1 WLR 1104, CA.
6 *Anderson v Midland Rly Co* (1861) 3 E & E 614.
7 *Dossee v Doe d East India Co* (1859) 1 LT 345, PC; *Meye v Electric Transmission* [1942] Ch 290.
8 *Wheeler v Mercer* [1957] AC 416 at 425, HL. This is thought to be unaffected by the dictum of Lord Templeman in *Street v Mountford* [1985] AC 809 at 820, [1985] 2 All ER 289 at 295, HL, that the vendor-purchaser relationship involved a licence.

held to be an implied tenancy at will where a person took possession during negotiations for a lease, though the occupier paid sums towards the rent, because the rent was not calculable by reference to a year – and no lease was ever entered into.[9] Where tenants held over on various extensions of the last of a series of short-term tenancies mutually intended to take effect outside Part II of the Landlord and Tenant Act 1954, paying rent, pending negotiations (which were abortive) for a new lease, they were held to have done so as tenants at will only.[10] Similarly, where a person took possession of unoccupied premises, in anticipation of an agreement on the terms of a fixed-term lease, paying one quarter's rent in advance, thereafter two further quarter's interim rent, but the parties could not agree on the terms of the proposed lease, which was never granted, the occupier held as implied tenant at will rather than as a quarterly tenant.[11] For the principles which apply where an implied tenant at will pays rent which the landlord accepts, see above.

In the case of expressly created tenancies at will rent may be payable under them and its payment and acceptance will not necessarily convert the tenancy at will into a yearly tenancy.[12] Whether it does do so may depend on whether the tenancy at will is genuine or not, given that expressly (and impliedly) created tenancies at will lie outside the protection of Part II of the Landlord and Tenant Act 1954.[13]

It may be different where there is a non-business arrangement, as where a married couple was informally invited to live in part of a house, for so long as they wished, with the hope that it would be for the rest of their lives, which was held to create a tenancy at will, which was converted into a yearly tenancy on payment of rent.[14] In another case, by contrast, the owner allowed a family informally into occupation of his house and frequently visited them there: it was held that the occupiers were licensees: this is explicable today solely on the basis that there was no intention to create legal relations.[15] Generally, at least in the context of residential premises, if there is exclusive occupation rent-free for an indefinite period, this appears to indicate an implied tenancy at will as opposed to a licence,[16] provided that the landlord can put an end to the arrangement at any time without serving notice on the tenant.[17]

The title of the landlord is extinguished as from the expiry of 12 years uninterrupted rent-free occupation by a tenant at will. The 12 years run from the time when the tenancy at will comes to an end.[18]

9   *British Railways Board v Bodywright Ltd* (1971) 220 Estates Gazette 651.
10 *Cardiothoracic Institute v Shrewdcrest Ltd* [1986] 3 All ER 633, [1986] 1 WLR 368.
11 *Javad v Aqil* [1991] 1 All ER 243, CA. Having failed to obtain a fixed-term lease, there was no ground for the occupier to argue for the implication of a wholly different sort of tenancy.
12 *Manfield & Sons Ltd v Botchin* [1970] 2 QB 612, [1970] 3 All ER 143.
13 *Hagee (London) Ltd v Erikson and Larson* [1976] QB 209 at 216, [1975] 3 All ER 234 at 237, CA (Scarman LJ).
14 *Young v Hargreaves* (1963) 186 Estates Gazette 355, CA.
15 *Heslop v Burns* [1974] 3 All ER 406, [1974] 1 WLR 1241, CA, as explained in *Street v Mountford* [1985] AC 809 at 824, [1985] 2 All ER 289 at 298, HL.
16 *Street v Mountford*, supra.
17 See *Colchester Borough Council v Smith* [1991] 1 All ER 29, 51-52, CA.
18 Limitation Act 1980, s 15(6) and Sch 1, para 5.

TENANCIES ON SUFFRANCE

A tenancy on sufferance is said to arise where a tenant wrongfully holds over on termination of a previous tenancy, eg on the expiry of a fixed-term tenancy, without the landlord's consent, after surrender or on the determination of a tenancy at will. It is not really a tenancy at all, and is distinguishable from a tenancy at will by the lack of consent, express or implied, on the part of the landlord. There can then be no payment of rent, under a tenancy on sufferance, but the landlord can sue to recover mesne profits. By acceptance of rent, however, or other acknowledgement the tenancy may be converted into a tenancy from year to year.

The landlord may sue the tenant for possession without demand, for though he entered lawfully, he becomes, in effect, a trespasser, by wrongfully holding over; and if his occupation continues uninterrupted for 12 years, he will acquire a good title as against his landlord, as a squatter. As against the Crown, however, no tenancy on sufferance can arise, for such a tenancy continues only by the *laches* of the landlord (i e his delay or negligence), and the Crown cannot be guilty of *laches*.

TENANCIES BY ESTOPPEL

Non-denial of landlord's title

The tenant cannot deny the title of his landlord to grant a lease and the landlord cannot deny the tenant's right to occupation under it.[19] This recognition of the binding force of tenancies between the parties and their assigns applies no matter what the form of the lease.[20] The rule lasts for the duration of the lease; even after it expires, the tenant cannot set up a want of title in his landlord as a defence to an action for damages for breach of covenant unless the claim is by a third party.[1] On the other hand, once the lease has determined, a lessee paying rent to an ex-lessor thereafter is only estopped from setting up the ex-lessor's want of title if the lessee knew, or had notice of, the true facts as to the lessor's title.[2]

Effect as against legal mortgagees

Once the intending purchaser of a legal title in land has entered into a binding contract of sale, the land is bound in equity from that moment and the purchaser has a specifically enforceable right to a conveyance of the legal estate. He may only be able to afford the cost of the property if he borrows from a building society, bank or other lending institution, which may undertake,

---

19 *Tadman v Henman* [1893] 2 QB 168; generally, J Martin [1978] Conv (NS) 137.
20 *E H Lewis & Son Ltd v Morelli* [1948] 2 All ER 1021, CA.
1 *Industrial Properties (Barton Hill) Ltd v Associated Electrical Industries Ltd* [1977] QB 580, [1977] 2 All ER 293, CA. See also *Butlins v Hawkin* [1989] EGCS 158 (rights of lessor by estoppel may be assigned – in this case, by written assignments and a conveyance).
2 *National Westminster Bank Ltd v Hart* [1983] QB 773, [1983] 2 All ER 177, CA; *Serjeant v Nash, Field & Co* [1903] 2 KB 304 at 312, CA.

possibly under a binding contract, to advance him funds in return for the creation by the purchaser, once he has obtained the legal title, of a binding mortgage or charge on the land. The purchaser may go into possession prior to completion and grant a tenancy which will bind the parties thereto. The House of Lords has decided that the subsequent acquisition by the purchaser of his legal title, and the execution of a legal charge or mortgage over the land, form part of one simultaneous transaction and that the purchaser never in fact acquires more than an equity of redemption, as the land is, from the start, incumbered with the mortgage.[3] Consequently, it seems that a legal chargee or mortgagee will not be bound by any tenancy granted by the purchaser-landlord prior to the execution of the charge or mortgage, and he may evict the tenant, under title paramount, if the landlord defaults with his mortgage repayments. It seemingly makes no difference, given the wide language used in the House of Lords, whether the mortgagee is under a binding contract, entered into prior to the completion of the purchase, to advance the mortgage money to the purchaser or not. Until this ruling, it had been held that, if the landlord had granted tenancies prior to completion, and thereafter obtained the legal estate, the legal title of the tenants was perfected and bound a legal mortgagee, whose security was created after the landlord obtained the legal estate, even if this process took place on the same day, unless the mortgagee and the landlord, prior to completion, had been under a binding contract to advance the mortgage money on completion.[4]

If a landlord grants a tenancy of land which is previously incumbered with a legal mortgage or charge, and the mortgage deed expressly prohibits the letting of the premises without the consent of the mortgagee, so excluding the landlord's statutory leasing power, the tenancy will not bind the mortgagee, who again has a title paramount: he may evict the tenant if he enforces the security against the landlord.[5] The tenant cannot claim the protection of s 98(1) of the Rent Act 1977, no matter whether his tenancy is contractual or statutory, to prevent this.[6] It seems that the protection of Part I of the Housing Act 1988, which applies to assured tenants, would similarly not apply to a tenant faced with eviction by a prior mortgagee under title paramount. If, however, apparently in any case, the mortgagee is not seeking possession in good faith and reasonably in order to enforce his security, the court may refuse him an order for possession against the tenant in its equity jurisdiction.[7] Should a purchaser-landlord, after completion, create tenancies in any period before the lender registers his charge, the chargee will, apparently, be able to avoid these tenancies.

---

3   *Abbey National Building Society v Cann* [1991] 1 AC 56, Goldberg (1992) 108 LQR 380.

4   *Church of England Building Society v Piskor* [1954] Ch 553, CA; also *Universal Permanent Building Society v Cooke* [1952] Ch 95 and *Grace Rymer Investments Ltd v Waite* [1958] Ch 831, which are inconsistent with the *Cann* decision.

5   *Dudley and District Building Society v Emerson* [1949] Ch 707, [1949] 2 All ER 252, CA.

6   Ibid; *Brittania Building Society v Earl* [1990] 1 EGLR 133, CA. It makes no difference that the mortgagee procures the execution of a new charge after the creation of the tenancy to replace an earlier, prior charge: *Walthamstow Building Society v Davies* (1989) 22 HLR 60, CA.

7   *Quennell v Maltby* [1979] 1 All ER 568, [1979] 1 WLR 318, CA.

However, different principles would seem to apply where an owner of freehold registered land grants a protected tenancy under the Rent Act 1977 and subsequently decides to raise money on the security of the property under a legal mortgage. The tenant's interest has been held to override the registered title under s 70(1)(g) of the Land Registration Act 1925, unless there is an express contrary statement on the property or charges register. Where a legal mortgagee advanced money in these circumstances, and the tenant signed a statement agreeing to postpone his interest to that of the mortgagee, the agreement was ineffective to exclude the effect of s 98(1) of the Rent Act 1977; the tenant's interest overrode the registered title, there being no contrary statement on the register, and the mortgagee could not evict the tenant in reliance on the agreement.[8]

8 *Woolwich Building Society* v *Dickman* (1996) 28 HLR 661, CA.

Chapter 3

Leases and licences

I GENERAL PRINCIPLES

Introduction

A lease, because it confers an estate in land, is much more than a mere personal or contractual agreement for the occupation of a freeholder's land by a tenant. A lease, whether fixed-term or periodic, confers a right in property, enabling the tenant to exclude all third parties including the landlord, from possession, for the duration of the lease, in return for which a rent or periodical payment is reserved out of the land.[1] A contractual licence confers no more than a permission on the occupier to do some act on the owner's land which would otherwise constitute a trespass.[2] If exclusive possession is not conferred by an agreement, it is a licence.

The following are clear examples of licences: an agreement for the hiring of a concert hall for several days,[3] the grant of permission to erect advertisement hoardings,[4] or to run boats on a canal,[5] the grant of 'front of house' rights in a theatre,[6] and the use of refreshment rooms in a theatre.[7] In all these cases, the agreements did not confer exclusive possession on the occupier, at a rent for a term, and were therefore held to be licences. The use of the land by the licensee was for strictly limited purposes. There was no question of attempting to use these genuine licences as devices to avoid tenant statutory protection.

Agreements which are not tenancies

The fundamental difference between a tenant and a licensee is that a tenant, who has exclusive possession, has an estate in land, as opposed to a personal permission to occupy. If, however, the owner of land proves that he never

---

1 *Street v Mountford* [1985] AC 809 at 825, [1985] 2 All ER 289 at 299, HL.
2 *Thomas v Sorrell* (1673) Vaugh 330 at 351, Ex Ch.
3 *Taylor v Caldwell* (1863) 3 B & S 826. Also *Verrall v Great Yarmouth Borough Council* [1981] QB 202, [1980] 1 All ER 839, CA (licence to occupy hall for two specified days held enforceable by specific performance).
4 *Wilson v Tavener* [1901] 1 Ch 578.
5 *Hill v Tupper* (1863) 2 H & C 121.
6 *Clore v Theatrical Properties Ltd* [1936] 3 All ER 483, CA.
7 *Edwardes v Barrington* (1901) 85 LT 650, HL. Also the grant of an exclusive right for 21 years to dump rubbish in excavated parts of a site where quarrying continued: *Hunts Refuse Disposals Ltd v Norfolk Environmental Waste Services Ltd* [1997] 03 EG 139, CA.

intended to accept the occupier as tenant, then the fact that the occupier pays regular sums for his occupation does not make the occupier a tenant.[8] If, moreover, a tenant or owner of a house shares part of the premises with an occupier, the courts appear reluctant to infer the grant of a tenancy.[9] There are circumstances, considered during this chapter, where the nature of the occupation, albeit apparently exclusive, is inconsistent with the grant of a tenancy, such as lodgers and service occupiers.

General rules of construction

If an agreement for the occupation of land confers exclusive possession on the occupier, for periodical money payments and for a determined term or period, the agreement will be a tenancy and not a licence, even if it is labelled as the latter.[10] The substance or reality of the transaction must be ascertained. These principles apply to agreements for the occupation of premises by a single occupier and joint occupiers alike. Agreements for joint occupation of premises must be construed in the light of the surrounding circumstances, any relationship between the prospective occupiers, the nature and extent of the accommodation and the intended and actual mode of occupation.[11]

Statutory background

Tenancies of residential, business and agricultural land are covered by various sets of statutory codes, considered later in this book. These do not, generally, apply to licences, and in the case of business and most residential tenancies, there is no specific legislation precluding landowners or lessees from conferring genuine licences to occupy on another person. For instance, genuine licences of residential accommodation lie outside the full protection of the Rent Act 1977.[12] Genuine licences are incapable of being assured tenancies under the Housing Act 1988, and genuine licences of business premises are outside the protection of Part II of the Landlord and Tenant Act 1954.[13] Some owners of residential or business premises may, instead of granting a tenancy which has little or no security of tenure after it expires,[14] take the more risky course of procuring the signature of an occupier on a document, which has been drawn up in advance, without any negotiation, which asserts in terms that it is a licence, and which uses licence terms throughout, and attempts to avoid conferring exclusive possession on the occupier, with the result that on expiry or termination of the agreement, the occupier will lack statutory security of

8　*Isaac v Hotel de Paris* [1960] 1 All ER 348, [1960] 1 WLR 239, PC.
9　See eg *Monmouth Borough Council v Marlog* [1994] 2 EGLR 68, CA.
10　*Street v Mountford* [1985] AC 809, [1985] 2 All ER 289, HL; *AG Securities v Vaughan* [1990] 1 AC 417, [1988] 3 All ER 1058, HL.
11　*AG Securities Ltd v Vaughan* supra; also *Stribling v Wickham* (1989) 21 HLR 381, [1989] 2 EGLR 35, CA.
12　*Fordree v Barrell* [1931] 2 KB 257, CA.
13　*Shell-Mex and BP Ltd v Manchester Garages Ltd* [1971] 1 All ER 841, [1971] 1 WLR 612, CA; also *Esso Petroleum Co Ltd v Fumegrange Ltd* [1994] 2 EGLR 90, CA.
14　As with assured shorthold tenancies or agreements excluding Part II of the 1954 Act.

tenure. The principles of construction which have evolved in recent years have addressed the problems thrown up by these documents.[15]

These principles do not directly bear on the legitimate and long-established use of contractual licences for genuine purposes, as mentioned at the start of this chapter. In the residential sector, genuine licences to occupy are accepted, without serious question (unless they are shams) where an occupation, though exclusive, is due to family or domestic considerations with no intention to create legal relations,[16] or where as the result of a genuine surrender agreement, the status of the occupier is altered from tenant to licensee in return for rent-free occupation.[17] Similarly, a person occupying a room in an hotel or lodging-house or council single persons' hostel is normally regarded as a lodger and, therefore, as a licensee, not a tenant,[18] in contrast to the position of a doctor, who was held to be a tenant of part of a house, using his premises as a surgery, exclusively, and to whom the benefit of a written agreement – which included the cost of purchase of the goodwill of the practice – had been assigned by the previous occupier.[19] Indeed, even where the parties are related, where an occupation is governed by a written (and so a formal) agreement, the hallmarks of a tenancy may be still held to exist, as where an exclusive occupier of a holiday cottage held a tenancy, despite the owner's retention of a duplicate key.[20] Such cases as these demonstrate that there can be no absolute, but only relative, principles in this area of law.

II CONSTRUCTION OF 'LICENCE' AGREEMENTS

A significant change

In 1985 the House of Lords reached a key decision on the construction of 'licence' agreements, *Street v Mountford*.[1] The case was concerned with an agreement for the occupation of land, by a single occupant, which admittedly conferred exclusive possession but which the owner still contended amounted to a licence in view of the stated intentions of the parties. Under the agreement, a weekly 'licence fee' was payable. Even if land is occupied without payment of periodical sums, there may be a licence or a tenancy depending on the intention of the parties and the surrounding circumstances.[2] However, it is usual to expect the payment of periodical sums where there is a tenancy.

15 It is possible that the Unfair Terms in Consumer Contracts Regulations 1994, SI 1994/3159 apply to this type of licence: the point is considered at the end of this chapter.
16 See eg *Cobb v Lane* [1952] 1 All ER 1199, CA.
17 *Foster v Robinson* [1951] 1 KB 149, [1950] 2 All ER 342, CA.
18 *Appah v Parncliffe Investments Ltd* [1964] 1 All ER 838, [1964] 1 WLR 1064, CA; *Luganda v Service Hotels Ltd* [1969] 2 Ch 209, [1969] 2 All ER 692, CA; *Westminster City Council v Clarke* [1992] 2 AC 288, [1992] 1 All ER 695, HL; Cowan [1992] Conv 285.
19 *Vandersteen v Agius* (1992) 65 P & CR 266, CA; it may be that this agreement was treated as in reality a commercial document.
20 *Ward v Warnke* (1990) 22 HLR 496, CA.
 1 [1985] AC 809, [1985] 2 All ER 289; Anderson (1985) 48 MLR 712; Tromans (1985) CLJ 351; Bridge [1986] Conv 344; Clarke [1986] Conv 39.
 2 Payments to satisfy household bills will not ordinarily amount to periodical payments for this purpose, unless labelled as such by the parties: see *Bostock v Bryant* [1990] 2 EGLR 101, CA.

In *Street v Mountford*, the main facts were as follows. M agreed to occupy a furnished room in S's house at a weekly so-called 'licence fee' of £37. The agreement, a 'personal licence', was non-assignable and avoided any overt suggestion of a tenancy. No services were provided by the owner and no onerous obligations placed on the occupier. At the foot of the agreement, there appeared a statement signed only by the occupier: 'I understand and accept that a licence in the above form does not and is not intended to give me a tenancy protected under the Rent Acts'. The House of Lords construed this agreement as creating a tenancy. The agreement admittedly conferred exclusive possession on the occupier, who paid a rent (or periodical payments) for a periodic term. The actual language in which the agreement was dressed up could not alter its true construction.

The House of Lords held that an agreement which one side claims to amount to a licence and the other asserts is a tenancy must be construed not in accordance merely with its formal language, but with regard to whether the agreement, be it express or implied, formal or informal,[3] confers in fact and in substance, exclusive possession on the occupier, in return for periodical payments, however labelled, for a term, fixed-term or periodic. 'If exclusive possession at a rent for a term does not constitute a tenancy then the distinction between a contractual tenancy and a contractual licence becomes wholly unidentifiable.'[4] These principles of construction apply whether or not the agreement relates to single or joint occupation. No one factor either in the agreement or in the surrounding circumstances, taken into account to assist in the construction of the agreement, is decisive. For example, where a homeless person was granted a written licence to occupy a flat and the only fact militating against the conferral of exclusive possession was that the owner retained a key for various purposes (such as to give access for repairs), the occupier was held to have a tenancy.[5]

The courts were invited by the House of Lords to be astute to detect and frustrate sham devices and artificial transactions whose only object is to disguise the grant of a tenancy and to evade the Rent Acts.[6] They may resort to this power, which entitles them to ignore a paper right of an owner to require the occupier to share with any person nominated by him, or a term denying the occupier the right to occupy the premises at a certain time of day, if the terms are suspect, the result being that, without them, the agreement may well confer exclusive possession and so a tenancy. This power may be mainly aimed at suspect terms in residential 'licences', but it applies equally to business and agricultural premises.

3 For an example of informal agreements see *Smith v Northside Developments Ltd* [1987] 2 EGLR 151, CA.
4 *Street v Mountford* supra, at 825 and 299 (Lord Templeman).
5 *Family Housing Association v Jones* [1990] 1 All ER 385, [1990] 1 WLR 779, CA; also *Aslan v Murphy* [1989] 3 All ER 130, [1990] 1 WLR 766, CA.
6 *Street v Mountford* supra, at 825 and 299; also *AG Securities v Vaughan* [1990] 1 AC 417, 458.

42   *Leases and licences*

Traditional distinction

The House of Lords have restored the traditional distinction between leases and contractual licences. The question of whether a lease or licence has been granted in a given case now depends on the true construction of the agreement in the light of the surrounding circumstances, no matter what the professed intentions of the parties may be. It has been said that in the case of some business tenancies the indicia which may make it apparent that a residential occupier is a tenant may not be present,[7] so recognising judicially that agreements for the occupation of business premises may sometimes contain no obviously suspect terms, unlike in the case of residential premises.[8] The same general approach governs occupation agreements for residential, business and agricultural premises alike, with perhaps a predisposition to treat the latter two classes of agreement with less suspicion than the former. The paramount factor is the presence or absence of exclusive possession. If an agreement in reality creates a tenancy, the fact that it may contain paper denials of exclusive possession or be labelled as a licence will, as seen, count for little.[9]

A number of cases illustrate this approach, notably in relation to occupation agreements conferred on one person. Where a residential occupier had exclusive possession, and paid weekly sums for his occupation, and was not a service occupier, he was held a tenant despite an express denial in his agreement that he had a tenancy.[10] A houseparent who was accepted to have exclusive possession of a house owned by his employer, paying rent, under an informal agreement, was held to be a tenant.[11] So too a person taking possession of a house and paying weekly sums, to put the house into good order and then purchase it from the owner, was held in reality to have exclusive possession and so a tenancy, not a licence.[12]

By contrast, where a person occupied a self-contained bed-sitting room suitable for single occupation, in a supervised homeless men's hostel under an agreement containing a 'mobility clause' enabling the landlord to change his accommodation as it directed, he was in reality a licensee.[13] By further contrast, where a flat was suitable for use by a multiple and shifting population and was so used, with occupiers being entitled to give short notice (a right which was in fact exercised), there being no joint obligation to pay a single rent for the whole premises, there was a genuine licence.[14] That much depends on the facts and circumstances is shown by a further case where a couple was held to have exclusive possession of a three-bedroomed house despite formal terms entitling the owner to enter the premises at any time and accepting that the occupiers

7 See *Dresden Estates Ltd v Collinson* (1987) 55 P & CR 47, CA.
8 See eg *London and Associated Investment Trust plc v Calow* [1986] 2 EGLR 80; Bridge [1987] Conv 137.
9 See eg *Aslan v Murphy* [1989] 3 All ER 130, [1990] 1 WLR 766, CA.
10 *Facchini v Bryson* [1952] 1 TLR 1386, CA.
11 *Royal Philanthropic Society v County* [1985] 2 EGLR 109, CA; PF Smith [1986] Conv 215; also *Postcastle Properties Ltd v Perridge* [1985] 2 EGLR 107, CA.
12 *Bretherton v Paton* [1986] 1 EGLR 172, CA.
13 *Westminster City Council v Clarke* [1992] 2 AC 288, [1992] 1 All ER 695, HL.
14 *Stribling v Wickham* [1989] 2 EGLR 35, CA; also *Mikeover Ltd v Brady* [1989] 3 All ER 618, CA (separate obligations to pay share of rent indicated that two identical agreements were licences).

were licensees.[15] However, an occupier was held to have a genuine licence where neither party intended to confer or accept exclusive possession in all the circumstances: the purpose of the agreement was to enable the licensee to grant short-term, non-secure accommodation in the premises concerned, on behalf of the owning council.[16]

In the context of business premises, an agreement for two years certain, relating to tennis courts, placing the 'licensee' under substantial repairing obligations and conferring in substance exclusive possession on the grantee, not least because it reserved the owner a right to enter and inspect the premises, which was unnecessary if exclusive possession had not been conferred, was held to amount to a tenancy, despite its careful use of 'licence' labelling throughout.[17] Where the occupiers of a petrol filling station agreed not to impede the owner's rights of possession and control, so as to enable the latter's servants to visit the premises when they chose, a genuine licence was created.[18] This decision was applied to three agreements for the exclusive use, subject to the overriding right of the owner to retain possession and control, of garage and shop land and premises: the agreements were construed as one.[19] A person who had been granted a series of 'licences' under the latest of which he used the main part of the land concerned exclusively as gallops, and had been required to accept the inclusion in the agreement of scrubland of no use to him, was held to have a business tenancy. The agreement entitled him to the exclusive right to exercise and train horses, and to a similar right to the unused land, despite its 'licence' terminology.[20]

Exclusive possession but no tenancy

There are some circumstances where, though a grantee of occupation rights over residential property has exclusive possession, there is no tenancy. These circumstances were listed, comprehensively, in *Street v Mountford*.

(i)   *No intention to create legal relations*

If the circumstances and the conduct of the parties show that the occupier is to be granted a personal privilege, with no interest in the land, then he will be a licensee – even if apparently in exclusive possession.[1] However, this category is limited to family arrangements, or acts of friendship or generosity.[2] On these principles, a licence was created where an owner allowed a couple rent-free

---

15 *Duke v Wynne* [1989] 3 All ER 130, [1990] 1 WLR 766, CA.
16 *Camden London Borough Council v Shortlife Community Housing Ltd* (1992) 90 LGR 358; Cowan [1993] Conv 157.
17 *Addiscombe Garden Estates Ltd v Crabbe* [1958] 1 QB 513, [1957] 3 All ER 563, CA.
18 *Shell-Mex and BP Ltd v Manchester Garages Ltd* [1971] 1 All ER 841, [1971] 1 WLR 612, CA.
19 *Esso Petroleum Co Ltd v Fumegrange Ltd* [1994] 2 EGLR 90, CA: the degree of control over the conduct of the business at the service station was expressly taken into account.
20 *University of Reading v Johnson-Houghton* [1985] 2 EGLR 113; Rogers [1986] Conv 275. See also *Bracey v Read* [1963] Ch 88, [1962] 3 All ER 472.
 1 *Errington v Errington and Woods* [1952] 1 KB 290 at 297-298, [1952] 1 All ER 149 at 154-155, CA, applied in *Colchester Borough Council v Smith* [1991] 1 All ER 29, 52-54; also *Westminster City Council v Basson* [1991] 1 EGLR 277, CA.
 2 *Facchini v Bryson* [1952] 1 TLR 1386 at 1389, CA.

occupation as an act of generosity,[3] and also where there was occupation under what was, in substance, despite its tenancy labelling, an informal family arrangement.[4] The exact ambit of the principle is uncertain, although it was held that a person who, under an oral agreement, renovated a dilapidated cottage and then resided there had a tenancy and not a licence;[5] but there have been cases outside family and similar arrangements where licences have been held to exist simply because of the absence of intention, in substance, to enter into legal relations. On this basis the occupier, apparently exclusively, of a room in an old people's home was held a licensee,[6] as was a war-time evacuee living in a house under informal arrangements with the owner.[7] Where parties negotiated for the grant of a lease 'subject to contract' but the negotiations broke down, it was held that the individual concerned was only a licensee as it was the mutual intention of the parties to enter into legal relations only if a lease was completed.[8] Indeed, if an occupier who is offered a tenancy refuses to fulfil conditions precedent, there may be no reason for conferring on him even a licence, and he will then be a trespasser, subject to speedy eviction.[9] Where the tenant died, leaving a daughter in residence, and the landlords only accepted rent from her for a short time while considering their position, it was held, on the special facts arising under residential succession provisions, that the landlords had not intended to contract with the daughter at all, and she was held a licensee.[10]

(ii)   *Exclusive possession exists but is referable to legal relations other than a tenancy*

Exclusive possession is not decisive in all cases, because an occupier with exclusive possession is not necessarily a tenant. The occupier may be a lodger or a service occupier or there may be other special circumstances, as where the occupier is a fee simple owner, a trespasser, a mortgagee in possession, or the object of charity, or where the parties are vendor and purchaser,[11] or where the owner, such as a requisitioning authority,[12] has no power to grant a tenancy.

Service occupation   A person is a service occupier where he is a servant in occupation of the house of his master in order to perform his services: the occupation must be strictly ancillary to the performance of the duties of the servant-occupier, and the servant's occupation in this case is deemed to be that of his master.[13] The test is objective: the fact that a particular employee is not

3   *Heslop v Burns* [1974] 3 All ER 406, [1974] 1 WLR 1241, CA.
4   *Barnes v Barratt* [1970] 2 QB 657, [1970] 2 All ER 483, CA, also *Bostock v Bryant* [1990] 2 EGLR 101, CA.
5   *Nunn v Dalrymple* (1989) 21 HLR 569, CA.
6   *Abbeyfield (Harpenden) Society v Woods* [1968] 1 All ER 352n, [1968] 1 WLR 374, CA.
7   *Booker v Palmer* [1942] 2 All ER 674, CA; also *Davies v Brenner* [1986] CLY 163.
8   *Isaac v Hotel de Paris* [1960] 1 All ER 348, [1960] 1 WLR 239, PC; cf *Chohan v Saggar* [1993] EGCS 194, CA.
9   As in *VG Fraulo & Co Ltd v Papa* [1993] 2 EGLR 99, CA.
10 *Marcroft Wagons Ltd v Smith* [1951] 2 KB 496, [1951] 2 All ER 271, CA.
11 See *Essex Plan Ltd v Broadminster Ltd* [1988] 2 EGLR 73.
12 *Finbow v Air Ministry* [1963] 2 All ER 647, [1963] 1 WLR 697.
13 *Smith v Seghill Overseers* (1875) LR 10 QB 422; also *Redbank Schools Ltd v Abdullahzadeh* (1995) 28 HLR 431, CA.

in a position to better perform the duties required of him or that his occupation is in anticipation of such performance makes no difference; equally, if an employee's occupation is a fringe benefit or inducement to occupy in order to enable him to work better, he is a tenant, not a licensee.[14] In the former case, the possession is that of the master, the servant is a licensee, and no tenancy is created.[15] Examples of service occupation include: a surgeon whose post required residence within the hospital concerned,[16] a soldier required to occupy military quarters,[17] and a chauffeur lodged in part of his master's premises.[18] However, the mere fact that the servant occupies the master's house rent-free as part of his remuneration will not of itself make him a service occupier.[19]

Determining whether exclusive possession exists

The agreement to occupy in *Street v Mountford* was conceded to have conferred exclusive possession on the occupier. It was not therefore necessary for the court to examine the terms and the context of the agreement to conclude that it created a tenancy. In the case of joint residential occupiers, the court may have to decide, in determining whether exclusive possession has been conferred, issues of fact such as whether the occupiers are a cohabiting couple, or are independent persons; whether one person is liable for the whole payments for use and occupation, or each person pays only an agreed share of such sums, or different amounts are payable by different persons.[20] The course of the negotiations leading to the agreement may be relevant.

In construing any agreement, but especially for the occupation of residential premises, the courts detect and frustrate sham devices and artificial transactions which are designed to evade statutory protection conferred on tenants.[1] These principles were evolved against the background of the Rent Acts, which conferred rigid protection in favour of some tenants, so encouraging the grant of suspect occupation agreements; with the greater ease of grant of assured shorthold tenancies, which confer almost no security on tenants, these principles may need to be invoked less often. Nevertheless the courts have in the past resorted to their powers to treat a licence as a tenancy in disguise, as the following examples show.

A term entitling the owner to use a room in common with the occupier and permitting him to allow other persons to use the room together with the latter was held not genuine on the facts, as the room was to be occupied by an unmarried couple jointly.[2] Where a licence agreement provided that the flat concerned could only be occupied between midnight and 10.30am and 12noon

14 *Norris v Checksfield* [1991] 4 All ER 327, [1991] 1 WLR 1241, CA.
15 *Mayhew v Suttle* (1854) 4 E & B 347, Ex Ch.
16 *Dobson v Jones* (1844) 5 Man & G 112.
17 *Fox v Dalby* (1874) LR 10 CP 285.
18 *Thompsons (Funeral Furnishers) Ltd v Phillips* [1945] 2 All ER 49, CA.
19 *Hughes v Chatham Overseers* (1843) 5 Man & G 54; *R v Spurrell* (1865) LR 1 QB 72.
20 See *AG Securities v Vaughan* [1990] 1 AC 417, [1988] 3 All ER 1058, HL; Harpum (1989) CLJ 19; Baker (1989) 105 LQR 165; Hill (1989) 52 MLR 408; PF Smith [1989] Conv 128.
 1 *Street v Mountford* supra; *AG Securities v Vaughan* supra; *Aslan v Murphy* [1989] 3 All ER 130, [1990] 1 WLR 766, CA.
 2 *AG Securities v Vaughan* supra.

and midnight, and allowed the owner to remove furniture from the room as he wished, these arguably sham terms raised the question whether a licence was in fact the real agreement between the parties.[3] By contrast, an agreement for the occupation by a person occupying under a 'licence' under which the landlord could change the accommodation offered was a licence in view of the other circumstances, including the fact that the landlord needed to exercise constant control over the occupiers.[4] The powers exist in relation to agreements to occupy business premises. Thus, a 'management agreement' in the form of a licence, admittedly designed to circumvent a prohibition on the creation of sub-leases in the grantor's own lease, which conferred exclusive possession and control on the occupier of a restaurant, was held to create a sub-tenancy.[5]

Occupation with services provided

In *Street v Mountford*[6] it was held that an occupier of residential accommodation is a lodger, and so a licensee, only if the landlord provides accommodation at a rent and, as part of the contract, be it express or implied, attendance or services which require the landlord or his servants to exercise unrestricted access to and use of the premises. A lodger was entitled to live in the premises but could not call the place his own. The view of Blackburn J[7] was adopted, according to which a lodger might have exclusive use of his room, in that no-one else was there, and he could stow his goods there; but the landlord retained for himself exclusive possession. It now appears that the divide is clear as a matter of law. If no services or attendance are provided by the owner, the occupier holds a tenancy, whether he is described in any agreement as a lodger or licensee or not. Accordingly, a person holding a licence of one room in a four-bedroomed flat, whose charge included a payment for services, was genuinely a licensee and not a tenant. The services – the provision of weekly cleaning and fresh linen – were such as genuinely to require unrestricted access by the landlord, using his own key, without needing the occupier's permission.[8] By contrast, where a doctor's surgery room was occupied exclusively, but was occasionally cleaned by the owner of the house concerned, this one fact did not displace the apparent grant of exclusive possession and so of a tenancy.[9]

Ruling out exclusive possession

It is possible for an owner of land genuinely to reserve rights which are sufficiently extensive to prevent the occupier from having exclusive possession. Whether this is in fact achieved by a particular form of words is a question of their construction in the circumstances. For example, a clause in a 'licence' agreement by which the licensees undertook not to impede in any way the

3 *Crancour v Da Silvaesa* [1986] 1 EGLR 80, CA.
4 *Westminster City Council v Clarke* [1992] 2 AC 288, [1992] 1 All ER 695, HL.
5 *Dellneed Ltd v Chin* [1987] 1 EGLR 75; Bridge [1987] Conv 298.
6 [1985] AC 809, [1985] 2 All ER 289 at 817-818 and 293, HL.
7 In *Allen v Liverpool Overseers* (1874) LR 9 QB 180 at pp 191 - 192.
8 *Huwyler v Ruddy* (1995) 28 HLR 550, CA.
9 *Vandersteen v Agius* (1992) 65 P & CR 266, CA.

officers, servants or agents of the licensor in the exercise of the latter's rights of possession of the premises deprived the licensee of exclusive possession,[10] as did an agreement which entitled the owner to make a contemporaneous use of agricultural land with the occupier, so long as it did not interfere with the reasonable exercise of the latter's rights.[11] Likewise a 'milk sharing agreement' which entitled the owner of agricultural land to alter the area of land and fields to which the agreement applied did not confer exclusive possession on the occupier,[12] any more than did a term in a 'licence' to occupy business premises under which the owner was entitled to require the occupier to transfer his occupation to other premises within the owner's adjoining property.[13] By contrast, more limited rights of entry or access may serve to emphasise the grant of exclusive possession.[14] Thus, where an agreement reserved rights of way over agricultural land in the owner's favour, that did not prevent a tenancy from being granted.[15]

III CONCLUSIONS

Uncertainties in the law

Enough has been said to demonstrate that the construction of agreements which one side alleges to be a tenancy and the other a licence is an uncertain business, and in so many cases the result depends on factual considerations which vary with each case, despite the general rules of construction enunciated by the courts. Though common rules are supposed to apply to all classes of agreement, in reality differences of detail exist. If residential accommodation is scarce, this may enable owners to pressure occupiers into accepting any terms on offer: hence, the requirement that the courts should look out for suspect terms or for whole agreements which are tenancies masquerading as licences. Should the parties succumb to the temptation to use sham terms,[16] the courts will disregard these, once the criterion of a sham has been proved, and must discover the true effect of the agreement, even though prima facie parties are taken to mean what they say.[17] The House of Lords has noted that those who frame residential occupation agreements constantly attempt to circumvent statutory protection offered to tenants on termination of a lease, while still wishing to enjoy an income from the property.[18] This cannot fail to influence the approach of the courts to these agreements, and may go some way to

---

10 *Shell-Mex and BP Ltd v Manchester Garages Ltd* [1971] 1 All ER 841, [1971] 1 WLR 612, CA; also *Esso Petroleum Ltd v Fumegrange Ltd* [1994] 2 EGLR 90, CA.
11 *Bahamas International Trust Co Ltd v Threadgold* [1974] 3 All ER 881, HL.
12 *McCarthy v Bence* [1990] 1 EGLR 1, CA; Rogers [1991] Conv 58.
13 *Dresden Estates Ltd v Collinson* [1987] 1 EGLR 45, CA; Bridge (1987) 50 MLR 655; PF Smith [1987] Conv 220.
14 See *Addiscombe Garden Estates Ltd v Crabbe* [1958] 1 QB 513; [1957] 3 All ER 563, CA (right to enter and inspect condition of premises); also *Dellneed Ltd v Chin* supra.
15 *Lampard v Barker* (1984) 272 Estates Gazette 783, CA.
16 See the analysis of these by Purchas LJ in *Hadjiloucas v Crean* [1987] 3 All ER 1008, 1014.
17 *Aslan v Murphy* [1989] 3 All ER 130, 133, [1990] 1 WLR 766, CA.
18 *AG Securities v Vaughan* [1990] 1 AC 417, 459 (Lord Templeman) and 466 (Lord Oliver).

explaining the limits on the power of owners to contract out of the Rent or Housing Acts, despite judicial differences as to the extent of such limits.[19] At the same time, since it is possible to grant certain residential tenancies (notably assured shorthold tenancies) which have no security after they expire, it may be that, with the passage of time, the practical impact of these principles will diminish as the incentive to grant licences is reduced.

In the business sector, where licences to occupy may still be useful, so as to avoid any need for a joint application to the court for the exclusion of Part II of the Landlord and Tenant Act 1954 of a tenancy, there is less perceived need for a suspicious attitude to agreements which purport to be licences, possibly because of the notion that commercial bargainers may look after their own interests unaided by the courts: but, as was seen, 'sham' agreements or terms in a supposed 'licence' may induce the court to hold an agreement to be a tenancy: the same general principle governs licences to occupy agricultural land.

The sea change in the common law

Nevertheless, in 1985 there was a 'sea change in the law'[20] so that the stated intentions of the parties to a 'licence' agreement are only one of a number of matters to be considered. It may have become almost impossible to grant an occupier of self-contained residential premises a licence to occupy, where the owner requires no unlimited access for the purpose of providing personal services or attendance.[1] Irrespective of the labelling of any agreement for the occupation of land, if it confers exclusive possession of the property on the occupier in return for periodical money payments for a term, fixed or periodic, a tenancy is created unless the relationship between the parties cannot be categorised as landlord and tenant but as within some other category already mentioned. The fact that, in this, the occupier may share a small defined area, such as a reception room, with others, does not necessarily detract from this conclusion.[2]

In the residential sector, where premises are occupied by two or more persons jointly, there is no presumption that they have joint exclusive possession against the owner, and a number of factual matters must be taken into account, on principles already discussed, so as to decide whether a particular agreement is a licence or a joint tenancy. These include: whether the parties hold a single indivisible term or separate agreements; and the manner in which liability for payments for the use and occupation of the premises is apportioned (thus where one person is liable for the whole sum this might imply a joint tenancy whereas if no person is liable except for his portion, or is only liable for a particular share, this could imply a licence).[3] Thus, two separate flat-sharing agreements granted to an unmarried couple, which agreements were interdependent, were held to

---

19 As in eg *AG Securities v Vaughan*, supra.
20 *Family Housing Association v Jones* [1990] 1 All ER 385, 390, CA.
 1 See *Westminster City Council v Clarke* (1991) 23 HLR 506, CA; also *Aslan v Murphy* [1989] 3 All ER 130, [1990] 1 WLR 766, CA.
 2 *London and Associated Investment Trust plc v Calow* [1986] 2 EGLR 80.
 3 See *Stribling v Wickham* and *Mikeover Ltd v Brady* supra.

constitute a single joint tenancy. A right of the owner to introduce other occupiers was treated as a pretence designed to avoid the Rent Act. By contrast, in the same combined appeal, separate agreements for the occupation of a four-bedroomed flat, which were made at different times, in return for separate payments by persons who were not related and who paid different amounts of money, did not confer a joint tenancy of the flat but separate licences to occupy.[4]

The EU dimension

We have up to now discussed only the common-law powers of interpretation of suspect or challenged 'licence' agreements. It is possible that the courts may decide that new European Union regulations[5] apply to some of these agreements. Not all licences would be caught: the person challenging the agreement (the 'consumer') would in any event have to show that the 'supplier' (the licensor) of the 'service' (accommodation with or without meals) was granting the agreement for the purposes of his business. Thus, while local authorities, housing associations and Government departments and agencies might well satisfy the business test, there would be more difficulty with private owners who granted licences. If, however, it could be shown that the granting of a given licence formed part of a pattern of business or trading activities of the owner, then the 'consumer' could well satify the business test, so opening the way to a challenge to the 'licence' itself, as discussed in more detail in chapter 4 of this book. Whether the courts would treat any jurisdiction conferred by these regulations as supplementing or supplanting their common law powers of interpretation might depend on whether the regulations were interpreted as conferring on them, as they appear to, certain additional powers (notably in regard to the good faith assessment required for terms presumed unfair by the regulations).

4 *AG Securities v Vaughan* supra.
5 SI 1994/3159.

Chapter 4

Creation and form of leases

I INTRODUCTION

A formal lease must generally be created by the execution of a deed, preceded by the formation of a binding contract or agreement for a lease. Statutory formalities, discussed in this chapter, govern both these stages.

The first thing to consider is the position of a tenant who takes possession of land or premises under a binding agreement for a lease, but whose landlord has not executed a deed in his favour. The liability of both parties under the terms of such a lease will seemingly be measured from the date of the agreement, and not from the later date of execution of a formal lease.[1]

Equitable leases

Where, therefore, a binding contract for a lease has been entered into, but the lease is defective because it is not by deed, so that the legal estate in the land is not passed to the tenant, but he takes possession and pays rent, the common law may imply that he holds as tenant from year to year, on principles already explained (chapter 2).

Equity goes further and treats the tenant, in these circumstances, as holding a specifically enforceable agreement for a lease, under which he may compel his landlord to grant him a deed, and thanks to which the landlord may compel the tenant to accept a deed. Each party is treated as subject to the obligations[2] of the formal, but not executed, lease, because equity treats that as done which ought to be done. Neither party is entitled to plead the absence of a deed as a ground for refusing to be bound by the terms of the agreement. In the case which is the foundation of these principles,[3] the tenant held under a written lease of a mill for a seven-year term, and so held a lease which was void at law. The tenant took possession, despite not having a lease by deed. He fell into arrear with the rent, and the landlord, on his continuing default, exercised the legal remedy of distress. The tenant's claim that the landlord's use of this remedy was in itself illegal, as being limited to a case of a lease by deed, was dismissed. Although the tenant might have held only a tenancy by implication

---

1 *Trane (UK) Ltd v Provident Mutual Life Assurance* [1995] 1 EGLR 33.
2 It will be appreciated that, strictly, the word 'covenant' is reserved for the obligations undertaken under a lease by deed.
3 *Walsh v Lonsdale* (1882) 21 Ch D 9, CA.

of law from year to year, equity regarded him as entitled to hold in accordance with the terms of his (void) legal lease,[4] and indeed to be as well placed as if he were holding under a formal lease by deed. Both parties were bound by the rights and obligations of the agreement, and so to obtain specific performance and to pay rent, even though no deed had been executed. More recently, it has been held that covenants to repair in an equitable lease were as much enforceable as they would have been in a formal lease by deed.[5]

Equitable leases are not quite identical to legal leases, as is shown by the following considerations. The availability of the remedy of specific performance (considered in more detail below) is dependent on the discretion of the court, with the result that it may be refused, as where the party claiming the remedy has failed to perform his obligations or a condition precedent which has not been waived, as where a tenant took possession of land under an agreement for a lease but failed to cultivate the land properly.[6] In addition, an equitable lease, as a contract for the grant of a lease, must be protected by registration in the register of land charges in the case of unregistered titles,[7] or by means of a notice on the register in the case of registered land.[8] However, registration confers protection on the equitable lessee against all the world.[9]

Two other weaknesses of equitable leases may be mentioned. An equitable lessee cannot plead that he is a *bona fide* purchaser of the land in question, with the result that he may discover that he is bound by restrictive covenants entered into before 1 January 1926, which cannot be registered. Because an equitable lease is not a 'conveyance' within the meaning of section 205(1)(ii) of the Law of Property Act 1925, an equitable lessee does not obtain the benefit of any easements or rights which pass to one who takes a 'conveyance' of land.[10]

As from the commencement of the Landlord and Tenant (Covenants) Act 1995, covenants in tenancies granted on or after 1 January 1996 may be enforced by and against an equitable lessee in possession as much as if he were a legal lessee (s 28(1)), so removing certain technical difficulties and inconsistencies in the previous law arising out of the doctrine of privity of estate. The courts had anticipated this principle by holding that an assignee of an informal tenancy granted prior to 1 January 1996 was bound by an undertaking to pay the landlord £40 towards redecoration of the premises immediately before the expiry of the tenancy, as the fact that the tenancy was not by deed did not, after the Judicature Acts, bar enforcement of such a covenant.[11]

---

4 Owing to the fact that, after the enactment of the Judicature Acts 1873 and 1875, the equity rule prevailed over the common law rule, with which, in this case, it conflicted.

5 *Industrial Properties (Barton Hill) Ltd v Associated Electrical Industries Ltd* [1977] QB 580, [1977] 2 All ER 293, CA.

6 *Coatsworth v Johnson* (1885) 55 LJQB 220, CA; also eg *Shelley v United Artists Corpn* [1990] 1 EGLR 103, CA.

7 Land Charges Act 1972, s 2(4) (Class C(iv)).

8 Land Registration Act 1925, s 48. If the tenant takes possession, his occupation will override the registered freehold or leasehold title thanks to s 70(1)(g) of that Act, unless inquiry is made of the lessee of his rights and he does not disclose them.

9 Law of Property Act 1925, s 199(1).

10 *Borman v Griffith* [1930] 1 Ch 493; but he may claim the benefit of continuous and apparent quasi-easements under the rule in *Wheeldon v Burrows* (1879) 12 Ch D 31, CA.

11 *Boyer v Warbey* [1953] 1 QB 234, [1952] 2 All ER 976, CA.

Statutory guarantees of title

At the contract stage, following a recent reform in the law effective as from 1 July 1995, the parties may agree that the landlord will offer a full or limited statutory guarantee of title, designed to give varying degrees of protection to the lessee against previous incumbrances not reasonably discoverable by the lessee. These guarantees of title also imply a covenant by the lessor, where relevant, that there is, at the date of grant, no subsisting breach of covenant and nothing which would render the lease liable to forfeiture.[12] Special provision is made where the landlord conveys the freehold or executes a long lease under enfranchisement or right to buy legislation.[13]

II   FORMALITIES FOR THE CREATION OF LEGAL LEASES

Legislation imposes formalities for the creation of a lease, in order for it to be a legal 'term of years absolute' within s 1(1) of the Law of Property Act 1925. At common law, a legal lease of corporeal rights could validly be created orally. The policy of these rules is to impose a requirement of a deed as a condition precedent of the valid creation of a legal lease, but to except the creation of short tenancies at a market rent from this requirement, thus allowing the valid oral creation of periodic tenancies.

1   In order validly to create a legal lease, which is a 'conveyance' within the 1925 Act, a deed is required.[14] Otherwise the lease is void at law.

2   No deed is, exceptionally, required to create a valid legal lease where the lease takes effect 'in possession for a term not exceeding three years[15] (whether or not the lessee is given power to extend the term) at the best rent which can be reasonably obtained without taking a fine'.[16] The High Court has ruled that to fall within the present exception a tenancy must confer an immediate right to possession, and not be in any sense a reversionary lease. Hence, a tenancy agreement under which a tenant took possession three weeks after signing an acknowledgement letter of the terms of his tenancy fell outside s 54(2).[17] By contrast, a tenancy within the exception may validly be created orally or in writing: thus, the oral creation of a legal lease for a fixed term not exceeding three years is allowed. To fall within this exception,

---

12   Law of Property (Miscellaneous Provisions) Act 1994, ss 3 and 4, resulting, in amended form, from a Report of the Law Commission (Law Com No 199 (1991)). The full or limited guarantees of title may also apply where a tenant assigns the lease.

13   1994 Act, Sch 1, paras 5 and 12 (limited title guarantee is the most which can be required of a landlord who conveys the freehold or creates a new long lease in favour of a long lessee of a house or flat) and para 9 (full title guarantee is obligatory in case of secure tenant's right to buy).

14   Law of Property Act 1925, s 52(1); a lease is a 'conveyance' within s 205(1)(ii).

15   Computed from the day the lease is made: *Foster v Reeves* [1892] 2 QB 255, CA.

16   Law of Property Act 1925, s 54(2).

17   *Long v Tower Hamlets London Borough Council* [1996] 2 All ER 683; the approach taken is that of *Foa*, p 11 note (p) and is consistent with the fact that LPA 1925, s 149(3) restricts the ability to contract for reversionary leases.

the initial duration of the lease is taken: it must be such that it is granted for a period not exceeding three years, even though it makes no difference that the tenant may have an option to extend the initial term beyond that period. A lease for a term exceeding three years which enables it to be determined within that time must be created by deed.[18] However, provided that the initial duration of a tenancy is not for a period exceeding three years, the fact that, in events which happen, it ultimately may exceed that period will not infringe the exception, which accordingly permits the valid creation at law of periodic tenancies for any period, be it for a week, a month or a year.[19]

3 The legislative exception for the valid creation of oral short leases is limited to terms which take effect in possession, which expression does not require physical possession, as it includes the receipt of rent and profits, or the right to receive them,[20] as from sub-tenants of the lessee. Since the lease must take effect in possession, a reversionary lease is excluded[1] and must be granted by deed to be valid at law, no matter how short the term agreed. The word 'fine' means a premium, ie a capitalised rent. Thus, if any part of a market rent is taken from the tenant as a premium, the lease must be created by deed to be valid at law, notwithstanding the exception.

4 If a lease is created orally, but is required by law to be created by deed, it takes effect as a tenancy at will,[2] unless and until it is converted into a tenancy from year to year by operation of law. However, equity is prepared to give effect to the intentions of the parties in full: a void legal lease may take effect in equity, as explained above. No such lease is valid even in equity from 27 September 1989 unless it is in writing sufficient to comply with s 2 of the Law of Property (Miscellaneous Provisions) Act 1989.[3]

5 An oral lease validly created at law is not quite as good as a lease by deed because it is not a 'conveyance' within the 1925 Act,[4] so that implied easements do not pass on its creation.

6 The legislature makes no exceptions to the formal rules in the case of assignments of a lease or tenancy to correspond to those applicable to the creation thereof. Any legal lease, whether required to be created by deed, or, because it falls within the legislative exception allowing for the valid creation of short leases, created in writing or orally, must be assigned by deed if the assignment is to take effect as a valid legal assignment of the term: otherwise it is void at law.[5] Similarly, no assignment of any legal lease, irrespective of its initial length, is valid in equity unless it is in writing.[6] Hence, where a tenant orally undertook to assign a weekly periodic tenancy to his wife, but

---

18 *Kushner v Law Society* [1952] 1 KB 264, [1952] 1 All ER 404.
19 Cf *Ex p Voisey* (1882) 21 Ch D 442 and cases cited on periodic tenancies in ch 2.
20 Law of Property Act 1925, s 205(1)(xix).
 1 See *Bush Transport Ltd v Nelson* [1987] 1 EGLR 71 at 73, CA.
 2 Law of Property Act 1925, s 54(1).
 3 This is without prejudice to s 54(2) of the Law of Property Act 1925 (1989 Act, s 2(5)), see above.
 4 *Rye v Rye* [1962] AC 496 at 512, HL.
 5 Law of Property Act 1925, s 52(1); *Crago v Julian*, infra. The exception in s 52(1)(d) does not apply to assignments. See Sparkes [1992] Conv 252, 357.
 6 Law of Property Act 1925, s 53(1)(a); *Botting v Martin* (1808) 1 Camp 317; *Crago v Julian*, infra.

never assigned it by deed or in writing, no valid assignment had taken place at law or in equity and the tenancy remained vested in the husband.[7] This principle is not unqualified. It does not apply to the assignment of an informally-created tenancy which takes effect by operation of law[8] nor, apparently, to informal assignments of weekly (or, seemingly, other periodic) statutory tenancies under the Rent Act 1977,[9] and it appears that an assignment of a secure tenancy may be informal owing to the overriding effect of the specific legislation applicable in this case.[10]

III   CONTRACTS ENFORCEABLE UNDER LAW OF PROPERTY ACT 1925, S 40

Section 40 of the Law of Property Act 1925 applies to a contract for the grant of a lease entered into on or before 27 September 1989. Section 40(1) provides that no action may be brought upon any contract for the sale or other disposition of land or any interest in land, unless the agreement upon which such action is brought, or some note or memorandum thereof, is in writing, and signed by the party to be charged or by his agent.

It is a condition precedent to the enforceability by action of such a contract that either the agreement itself, or some sufficient memorandum or note thereof, should be in writing and duly signed by or on behalf of the intending landlord. In the case of a final agreement, the relevant document is the contract finally agreed between the parties. If there is a draft contract which is qualified by the words 'subject to contract' then, even if the terms of it would, but for those words, suffice to establish a binding agreement for a lease within s 40(1), the effect of the expression 'subject to contract' is to deprive the document of any binding force, unless both parties agree to remove the qualification.[11] It makes no difference that negotiations may have reached a very advanced stage.[12]

Although in many cases the parties will seek to rely for the purposes of enforcement on a single written agreement, s 40(1) of the 1925 Act allows an enforceable contract for a lease to be proved if the essential terms of the contract are contained in a duly signed memorandum or note.[13] There is a wide meaning of 'memorandum or note', which need not necessarily be a single document, so as to permit the proof of the essential terms of a binding contract by means

---

7   *Crago v Julian* [1992] 1 All ER 744, [1992] 1 WLR 372, CA.
8   Law of Property Act 1925, s 52(1)(g); *Milmo v Carreras* [1946] KB 306, [1946] 1 All ER 288, CA.
9   *Thomas Pocklington's Gift Trustees v Hill* [1989] 2 EGLR 97 at 100, CA.
10   *Westminster City Council v Peart* (1991) 24 HLR 389, CA (s 91(3)(c) of Housing Act 1985).
11   *Tiverton Estates Ltd v Wearwell Ltd* [1975] Ch 146, [1974] 1 All ER 209, CA; *Salomon v Akiens* [1993] 1 EGLR 101, CA.
12   See eg *Derby & Co Ltd v ITC Pension Trust Ltd* [1977] 2 All ER 890.
13   It suffices for the landlord alone to sign, but then the tenant may repudiate the contract with impunity, although the landlord cannot do so. This anomaly is cured by s 2(3) of the Law of Property (Miscellaneous Provisions) Act 1989, which requires the signature of both parties before the contract is enforceable.

of a series of such documents provided that they referred to each other or were otherwise connected.[14] Once the essential terms have been established, it is then open to a party by oral evidence to prove any further, essential, terms.[15] No special form of memorandum is required.

The terms which are considered essential are few. They include the names of the parties,[16] the address of the property or a description sufficient to identify it,[17] the term and its commencement date,[18] and the rent or any premium or fine.

A party to an oral contract to a lease entered into before 27 September 1989 may be able to prove by oral evidence its exact terms by equity, including terms not connected with the part performance, if he is able to establish a sufficient act of part performance by him of the bargain on the faith of the alleged agreement. Where this is so, he may claim to enforce the contract by specific performance. Sufficient acts of part performance include taking possession and paying rent with the landlord's consent,[19] or, in the case of a landlord, spending substantial sums on alterations to the property under the supervision and at the request of the defendant on the faith of a lease being accepted by him.[20] The party seeking to rely on part performance must show that he acted to his detriment, and that the defendant knew of his acts, which must be consistent with the contract alleged,[1] and that the alleged oral contract was complete and binding and, if in writing, it would have been specifically enforceable.[2]

IV CONTRACTS ENFORCEABLE UNDER THE LAW OF PROPERTY (MISCELLANEOUS PROVISIONS) ACT 1989

Introduction

From 27 September 1989, s 2 of the Law of Property (Miscellaneous Provisions) Act 1989 came into force. It altered the rules governing the enforceability of contracts for the grant of a lease, and repealed the previous legislative rules.[3] Section 2 is of general application, except that it does not apply to a contract to grant an oral lease for a term not exceeding three years.

The policy of this provision has been said to be to prevent disputes as to whether parties had entered into a binding agreement or over what terms they had agreed.[4] Hence the requirement that as a precondition of validity, a

---

14 See *Chapronière v Lambert* [1917] 2 Ch 356, CA.
15 *Beckett v Nurse* [1948] 1 KB 535, [1948] 1 All ER 81, CA.
16 *Coombs v Wilkes* [1891] 3 Ch 77; *Lovesy v Palmer* [1916] 2 Ch 233.
17 *Ogilvie v Foljambe* (1817) 3 Mer 53.
18 *Harvey v Pratt* [1965] 2 All ER 786, [1965] 1 WLR 1025, CA.
19 *Brough v Nettleton* [1921] 2 Ch 25. In *Cohen v Nessdale Ltd* [1981] 3 All ER 118, a payment of ground rent in isolation was held to be sufficient.
20 *Rawlinson v Ames* [1925] Ch 96.
 1 *Steadman v Steadman* [1976] AC 536, [1974] 2 All ER 977, HL.
 2 *Maddison v Alderson* (1883) 8 App Cas 467, HL.
 3 1989 Act, s 2(8) and Sch 2. In *McCausland v Duncan Lawrie Ltd* [1996] 4 All ER 995, CA, the new rules were stated to be intentionally strict and to apply to variations in a contract as well as to its original terms.
 4 *Spiro v Glencrown Properties Ltd* [1991] Ch 537, [1991] 1 All ER 600.

contract for a lease must be in writing and must contain all the agreed terms of the contract, which both parties must sign. However, once a lease has been executed, the 1989 Act ceases to apply to the lease and to any agreement taken as one with the lease, as it only applies to executory contracts. So, a landlord who executed a lease, and who in a separate agreement undertook to pay the lessee for the cost of fitting-out works, could not rely on s 2 of the 1989 Act as a ground for evading his obligation to pay, since the executed lease and the agreement were taken as one.[5]

Statutory requirements

These may be summarised as follows.

1   By s 2(1) of the 1989 Act, 'a contract for the sale or other disposition of an interest in land' (and thus a contract for a lease and for a surrender of a lease)[6] can only be made in writing. It must incorporate all the terms which the parties have expressly agreed in one document, or, where contracts are exchanged, in each.

2   The terms of the contract, or some of them, may be incorporated in a document either by being set out in it in full or by reference to some other document (s 2(2)).

3   The document incorporating the terms, or, where contracts are exchanged, one of the documents incorporating them (but not necessarily the same one) must be signed by or on behalf of each party to the contract (s 2(3)).

The general effects of s 2 on the formalities for a contract for the grant of a lease or other disposition and its relationship with other aspects of formalities may be summarised as follows.

Effects of s 2

1   Where the parties agree on a contract for the grant of a term exceeding three years, or for any disposition of the lease, the contract must, by s 2(1), be in writing or it will be invalid. To be valid, therefore, the contract must contain all the terms agreed, but if a document is referred to in the main contract, its terms will be incorporated into the main contract by reference, thanks to s 2(2) of the 1989 Act. However, where it was claimed that the landlord of business premises had transferred a right, personal to the original tenant, to surrender the lease to his assignee, after an exchange of letters, it was held, applying the strict words of the 1989 Act, that since all the terms of the alleged contract to confer the surrender right or 'put option' had not been fully set out in one document as required by s 2, there was no enforceable contract to confer the surrender right on the assignee.[7] Moreover, it seems

---

5   *Tootal Clothing Ltd v Guinea Properties Management Ltd* [1992] 2 EGLR 80, CA.
6   As to the latter see *Commission for the New Towns v Cooper (Great Britain) Ltd* [1995] Ch 259, [1995] 2 All ER 929, CA.
7   *Commission for the New Towns v Cooper (Great Britain) Ltd* supra, CA; also *Enfield London Borough Council v Arajah* [1995] EGCS 164, CA.

that the omission even of a single term agreed between the parties, no matter how insignificant, from the contract would appear to render the entire contract a nullity.

2   It is essential to the validity of a contract for a lease that both parties should sign it. By 'sign' is evidently meant writing one's hand on the document; so, a prospective lessee must in that sense sign any letter signed by the intending landlord, which sets out the supposedly agreed terms of the lease.[8] The same principle would presumably apply to any letter containing draft variations of an existing tenancy. Section 2(3) of the 1989 Act allows for the signature by a duly authorised agent acting for either party.

3   A contract for an oral lease which is for a term exceeding three years is invalid. Equally, a lease by deed for such a period is valid provided the deed is signed and delivered. An oral contract to grant a lease taking immediate effect in possession for a term not exceeding three years, which complies with s 54(2) of the Law of Property Act 1925, is exempt from the 1989 Act requirement of writing and is valid as an agreement for such a lease. But an oral contract for the eventual grant of a written term not exceeding three years appears to be struck down by s 2 of the 1989 Act, if this provision is literally read.

4   A contract for a lease for a term exceeding three years which does not comply with the requirements of s 2 cannot be saved by equity except where a party might be able to claim rectification of the lease.

5   If a tenant is entitled to claim an enforceable written contract for a lease, but the landlord fails to execute a deed, the tenant may assert that he holds a lease valid in equity, which entitles him to claim specific performance.

6   By contrast, if a contract for a lease is void for non-compliance with s 2 of the 1989 Act but the person takes possession and pays regular money sums to the landlord, the common law would in principle recognise him as a periodic tenant by implication of law.

7   Where the parties or their solicitors each prepare draft contracts, these will, seemingly, not become binding unless and until they contain all the terms the parties have agreed and they have been signed by or on behalf of the parties. The practice of conducting all negotiations for a contract for a lease 'subject to contract' may continue despite the enactment of s 2 of the 1989 Act.[9] At the same time it has been said that the passing of the 1989 Act has reduced the significance of the words 'subject to contract'; in the case in question, an informal exchange of letters setting out the conferral of a 'put option' (or right to surrender) on an assignee by the landlord would, it was said, have been a sufficient note or memorandum to satisfy s 40 of the Law of Property Act 1925. It did not suffice to satisfy s 2 of the 1989 Act, which is much stricter.[10]

8   *Firstpost Homes Ltd v Johnson* [1995] 4 All ER 355, [1995] 1 WLR 1567, CA.
9   As in eg *Enfield London Borough Council v Arajah* [1995] EGCS 164, CA.
10 *Commission for the New Towns v Cooper (Great Britain) Ltd* [1995] Ch 259, [1995] 2 All ER 929, CA.

Damages for breach of contract

The two remedies available for breach of contract or agreement to grant a lease, ie an action to compel specific performance of the contract and, where the contract is evidenced in writing, an action for damages are, generally speaking, alternative remedies, for specific performance is only granted where damages would not give an adequate remedy to the plaintiff. Nevertheless, damages may be awarded on a decree of specific performance, in respect of loss caused by the delay in performance of the contract.[11] Sometimes, the landlord undertakes obligations in a contract for a lease which he fails to fulfil after it has been executed: the execution of the lease is no defence to an action for breach of obligation, as where a landlord undertook to construct certain buildings with good quality materials, but failed to comply with this duty: the tenant could claim damages for breach though he had executed the lease.[12]

The measure of damages for breach of contract arising from a defect in the landlord's title, is generally limited to the losses actually incurred by the tenant,[13] but includes also damages for loss of bargain if the landlord is blameworthy, eg if he fails to take the necessary steps to secure possession.[14] Damages were recoverable where the defendant failed to remove a blot on the title.[15] No damages are generally recoverable for mere delays in completion, as time is presumed not to be of the essence in this case.[16] Expenses occasioned by such delays are recoverable generally, but not if solely due to conveyancing difficulties.[17] In addition, the tenant may sue for the recovery of any deposit or premium paid.

V   ACTION FOR SPECIFIC PERFORMANCE

The equitable remedy of specific performance is an order compelling the execution of a legal lease in proper form by the landlord, or the acceptance of such a lease by the tenant. The remedy is particularly appropriate for the enforcement of leases, since, although its award is discretionary, and so will not be awarded where completion of an agreement for a lease would cause grave hardship to either party,[18] damages are deemed not to be an adequate remedy, since no two pieces of land are taken to be alike.[19] An action for specific

---

11 *Jacques v Millar* (1877) 6 Ch D 153.
12 *Optilon Ltd v Commission for New Towns* [1993] 2 EGLR 89.
13 *Keen v Mear* [1920] 2 Ch 574.
14 *Engell v Fitch* (1868) LR 3 QB 314.
15 *Malhotra v Choudhury* [1980] Ch 52, [1979] 1 All ER 186, CA.
16 Law of Property Act 1925, s 41; *Stickney v Keeble* [1915] AC 386, HL.
17 *Rainieri v Miles* [1981] AC 1050, [1980] 2 All ER 145, HL.
18 *Patel v Ali* [1984] Ch 283; however, in *Amec Properties Ltd v Planning Research and Systems plc* [1992] 1 EGLR 70, CA, specific performance was awarded against an occupying lessee in receivership.
19 The plaintiff is not bound to seek specific performance and may elect for dissolution of the contract and then pursue a claim for damages (see *Johnson v Agnew* [1980] AC 367, [1979] 1 All ER 883, HL).

performance may be brought as soon as the date set for completion has passed,[20] or before then if the defendant has repudiated the contract, so showing no intention to perform it.[1] The detailed principles governing this remedy are beyond the scope of this work,[2] but a certain number of salient points deserve mention.

In the first place, specific performance may only be awarded if there is an agreement for a lease which complies with the formal requirements of statute. If the parties have agreed to grant successive building leases as work progresses, then each agreement may be regarded as severable and specifically enforceable apart from the other agreements,[3] but severance of one single agreement, and specific performance only of part, is not generally possible. The agreement must not be open to reasonable objection in other respects. Some objections go to the conduct of the plaintiff. Thus, it is inequitable to order specific performance of a contract for a lease procured by fraud or misrepresentation by the plaintiff, and the remedy will not lie if the plaintiff has been guilty of unnecessary delay in seeking to enforce the contract, leading the other party to change his position in the meantime.[4] However, if the tenant has already been in possession for many years, paying rent, delay is in itself no bar to this remedy.[5] If a landlord has failed, in breach of contract, to complete certain works which he has undertaken to do before the lease is to commence, such as to complete a new house, this is an absolute bar to his obtaining specific performance.[6] Where a contract for a building lease expressly provided that, if for any reason due to the wilful default of the tenant, the development should remain uncompleted by a specified date, the lease must be treated as completed. One year later, no development having taken place, the prospective landlords treated the agreement as repudiated. The prospective tenant could not invoke the deeming clause. He could not take advantage of his own wrong so as to claim specific performance.[7] However, it now appears that a party may not be in repudiatory breach of his agreement for a lease, and so denied specific performance, where the court takes the view that, as a matter of construction, the principal agreement is unaffected, as where a lessee had undertaken not only to take a lease of commercial premises but also to re-imburse certain moneys due to the prospective lessor from other premises, of which latter undertaking he was in breach.[8]

Other objections relate to the security of the assignee's title, so that specific performance of a contract for a sub-lease which, if executed, would be in breach

20 *Marks v Lilley* [1959] 2 All ER 647, [1959] 1 WLR 749.
 1 See *Hasham v Zenab* [1960] AC 316, PC, where a binding contract for the sale of land was torn up by the defendant just after signing it.
 2 See eg Hanbury & Martin, *Modern Equity*, ch 23; *Snell's Equity*, pp 585ff.
 3 *Wilkinson v Clements* (1872) 8 Ch App 96.
 4 *Laurence v Lexcourt Holdings Ltd* [1978] 2 All ER 810, [1978] 1 WLR 1128.
 5 *Sharp v Milligan* (1856) 22 Beav 606.
 6 *Tildesley v Clarkson* (1862) 30 Beav 419; the same applies where it is a tenant, in possession, who has committed waste or has failed to comply with his obligations under the prospective lease: *Gregory v Wilson* (1852) 9 Hare 683.
 7 *Alghussein Establishment v Eton College* [1988] 1 WLR 587, HL.
 8 *Re Olympia and York Canary Wharf Ltd (No 2)* [1993] BCC 159.

of an absolute covenant in the head lease against sub-letting, will not be awarded.[9] Where the tenant of a lease containing a fully qualified covenant against assignments has contracted to assign it, then he must, where the Standard Conditions of Sale have been incorporated into the contract, as a condition precedent to entitlement to specific performance, apply for the landlord's consent and use his best endeavours to obtain it.[10] Indeed, where the landlord's consent is reasonably refused, or a condition is imposed which, though reasonable, is also one which an assignee might reasonably object to, the assignee cannot be forced by specific performance to take the title offered, and he may rescind the contract and claim damages.[11]

If the landlord has no title at the date of the action, this is a good defence by the tenant to an action for specific performance by the landlord.[12] Where the Standard Conditions of Sale apply, and title is registered, the landlord is obliged to deduce a sufficient title to the head or sub-lease, as the case may be, to enable the tenant to register an absolute title at the Land Registry, which requires him, where necessary, to prove the freehold and head leasehold titles.[13]

VI LEASES BY DEED – FURTHER

General requirements

We have seen that, thanks to legislation, a lease for a term certain exceeding three years must be by deed to pass the legal estate. By s 1(2) of the Law of Property (Miscellaneous Provisions) Act 1989, an instrument cannot be a deed unless it makes it clear on its face that it is intended to be a deed by the person making it or the parties to it.

Formal leases by deed, which are ordinarily typed or printed, are made in two parts: the lease, which is executed by the landlord and delivered to the tenant, and the counterpart, which is executed by the tenant.[14] The counterpart may be sued on by the landlord, and it may be used as evidence to correct a clerical error in the lease itself.[15]

The cost of leases is regulated by the Costs of Leases Act 1958. By s 1, accordingly, unless it is otherwise agreed in writing, a party to a lease is not under an obligation to pay the whole or any part of any other party's solicitor's costs of the lease.[16]

Stamp duty is payable on the formal grant of a lease for a definite term of one year or more or for any indefinite term,[17] and is also charged on the rent and

9 *Warmington v Miller* [1973] QB 877, [1973] 2 All ER 372, CA.
10 Standard Conditions of Sale, 8.3; if these do not apply, see *Day v Singleton* [1899] 2 Ch 320.
11 Law of Property (Miscellaneous Provisions) Act 1989, s 3 permits such a claim.
12 *Jones v Watts* (1890) 43 Ch D 574, CA.
13 Condition 8.2.4.
14 Schedules may be attached to the lease, such as dealing with the details of rent review, fixtures or the condition of the premises; these must be connected to the main part of the deed by express references.
15 *Matthews v Smallwood* [1910] 1 Ch 777.
16 'Costs' are widely defined by s 2 of the 1958 Act, and these include stamp duty.
17 Stamp Act 1892, Sch 1; duty is also charged on any definite term for less than a year, and on any furnished letting where the rent exceeds £500 a year.

any fine or premium. An agreement for a lease for a term of less than 35 years is charged as if it were a formal lease.[18] Duty is chargeable ad valorem and rises significantly with the length of the term.

Requirement of execution of deed

To take effect, a lease must be *executed*. As from 31 July 1990, a deed is validly executed by an individual if, and only if, first, it is signed by him in the presence of a witness who attests the signature, or at his direction and in his presence and in the presence of two witnesses who each attest the signature; and it is delivered by him or a person authorised to do so on his behalf.[19] As from 31 July 1990, it is no longer necessary to seal a deed.[20] Actual delivery is not necessary, for the requirement may be satisfied by any act which shows that intention. A deed is taken, in the absence of contrary proof, to be delivered on the day it bears as its date.[1] A wafer or wax seal may be used for sealing a deed; today, sealing is ordinarily by a printed circle which the landlord signs across.[2] A lease may be delivered as an *escrow*, and so expressed to take effect, not upon delivery, but upon the happening of some event, or the performance of some condition. Where execution precedes the date of the deed, the condition may simply be the completion of the contract, by exchange of lease and counterpart, which must be done in a reasonable time.[3] When the conditions of an escrow are satisfied, rent is payable from the date of conditional delivery.[4] It is a question of fact and of the intention of the landlord whether a lease is intended to operate as an escrow.[5] Only when the condition or conditions of an escrow are performed will a lease delivered as an escrow vest the estate granted.[6] But a deed delivered in escrow is not recallable: it becomes binding once the condition is performed.[7] Even in the case of an unexecuted lease, which is enforceable in equity, covenants therein will bind the tenant immediately after the date the agreement is made.[8]

---

18 Stamp Act 1891, s 75(1), which extends, as from 19 March 1984, to agreements for a lease for over 35 years which form part of tax avoidance schemes.
19 Law of Property (Miscellaneous Provisions) Act 1989, s 1(3).
20 Ibid, s 1(1). Nor is it essential to use any special paper.
1 An undated but signed and sealed lease or underlease will bind both parties if it is proved that it was intended to be binding on delivery: see *Bentray Investments Ltd v Venner Time Switches Ltd* [1985] 1 EGLR 39.
2 *First National Securities Ltd v Jones* [1978] Ch 109, [1978] 2 All ER 221, CA.
3 *Kingston v Ambrian Investment Co Ltd* [1975] 1 All ER 120, [1975] 1 WLR 161, CA; *Glessing v Green* [1975] 2 All ER 696, [1975] 1 WLR 863, CA.
4 *Alan Estates v W G Stores Ltd* [1982] Ch 511, [1981] 3 All ER 481, CA.
5 *D'Silva v Lister House Development Ltd* [1971] Ch 17, [1970] 1 All ER 858.
6 *Beesly v Hallwood Estates Ltd* [1961] Ch 105, [1961] 1 All ER 90, CA; *Alan Estates Ltd v WG Stores*, supra.
7 *Beesly v Hallwood Estates Ltd*, supra. The landlords there could not recall the deed just because they thereafter discovered that the option to renew, the basis of the contract, was void for non-registration, the tenant having complied with the condition.
8 *Carrington Manufacturing Co v Saldin* (1925) 133 LT 432; also *Trane (UK) Ltd v Provident Mutual Life Assurance* [1995] 1 EGLR 33.

VII   CONTENTS OF LEASES

Introduction

The contents of a lease are said to be for the parties to agree upon, subject to certain minimum requirements of the common law, as regarding certainty of the term granted. Statute may have an impact on certain types of covenant, as in the case of assignments or repairs, considered later in this work. There are, strictly speaking, no standard forms, as opposed to precedents, for leases. Parliament last attempted to standardise leases in 1845.[9] Many different types of precedent are available for use for formal and indeed informal leases, if only for the sake of convenience.

Freedom of contract

In the traditional view of the common law, freedom of contract prevails in the negotiation and fixing of leasehold obligations. This view may be realistic in the case of some business leases. The High Court has refused to construe a wide covenant to repair in a long lease in accordance with principles applicable to certain commercial documents in standard form and instead examined all the individual words of the covenant.[10] In the field of rent review, although standard forms are produced by the Law Society and RICS, some parties prefer to use their own, specifically negotiated terms, at the risk of uncertainty of interpretation. In both these instances, some variety in clauses may be inevitable, if only because premises differ in their nature. On the other hand, certain types of covenant, as in the case of quiet enjoyment or limiting assignments or alterations, because they have similar overall aims irrespective of detailed differences in the type of premises, may not necessarily differ greatly as between different types of lease or premises.

Unconsionable bargains

The common law traditionally holds that, while a party to an executed lease may later find its terms onerous or even harsh, the only ground for rescission of such a lease is fraud. It may be that equity is prepared to go further than this. The Privy Council has held that an executed lease may be set aside if it appears that the terms of the lease have been imposed by one party on the other in a morally reprehensible manner so as to affect his conscience.[11] Accordingly, a renewed lease was set aside because the tenant had taken an unconscionable advantage of the age, poverty and ignorance of the landlord, facts known to the tenant at the date of renewal, to secure an advantageous renewal for herself. The Privy Council, however, rejected the notion that an executed lease could be set

---

9   In the Leases Act 1845, which for example gives an 81-word standard covenant to repair; but the Act was largely neglected according to the Law Commission, Law Com No 162 (1987) paras 3.8–3.10. The Royal Commission on Legal Services (1979) Cmnd 7648, Annex 21.1, para 13, supported standardisation, especially with regard to residential premises.

10   *Crédit Suisse v Beegas Nominees Ltd* [1994] 4 All ER 803 at 817.

11   *Boustany* v *Piggott* (1993) 69 P & CR 298; Pawlowski [1995] Conv 454.

aside by equity on the ground that the landlord and tenant had unequal bargaining strength, or that the terms of the lease had been harsh, foolish or even unreasonable. It was the unconscionable use by the tenant of the disabling circumstances of the landlord which raised an equity against the tenant in that case.

However, the High Court has held that the Unfair Contract Terms Act 1977 does not apply to the covenants of a lease, and its exclusion is not confined to the words of demise.[12] Thus, terms in leases escape the statutory tests of fairness.

Possible impact of new European regulations

On 1 July 1995, regulations were promulgated to give effect to a European Union directive.[13] In essence, if these regulations apply to residential leases, then some of these may be subject to a test of unfairness, so opening up a wide and so far uncharted field of challenge for tenants.

At first sight, the regulations seem to have no application to any leases. There is so far no direct authority in point, but the common law regards a lease, because it passes an estate in land, as one consistent whole, which is why neither its operative words of demise nor its terms are not subject to the Unfair Contract Terms Act 1977. Hence, as a matter of first impression, these somewhat clumsily-worded regulations which speak of a 'supplier', and a 'consumer', and of 'goods and services', would seem, having regard to the fact that at common law a lease is not merely personal property, not aptly directed at leases or at their terms, save by adopting a rather strained and articifial interpretation of their language.[14]

Nevertheless, it has been argued that the 1995 regulations do indeed apply to leases, as 'land contracts'.[15] Another writer believes they may apply, if only by analogy with Value Added Tax legislation, which treats leases as a supply of services.[16] Moreover, subordinate legislation passed to give effect to European Union directives must, if reasonably so capable, be construed to conform with those obligations, even though this may involve 'some departure from the strict and literal application of the words'.[17] The question is as to how far one is entitled to go.

It remains our view, for reasons given, that these regulations could only be applied to leases and tenancies, as opposed to residential 'licence' or 'lodging' agreements, around which they may be more easily fitted having regard to the history of the matter, by adopting a strained meaning to their language. Such

---

12 *Electricity Supply Nominees Ltd v IAF Group plc* [1993] 3 All ER 372 (giving a wide construction to the excluding Sch 1 to the Act).
13 Unfair Terms in Consumer Contracts Regulations 1994, SI 1994/3159.
14 The regulations seem much more aptly worded for certain types of licence to occupy, as discussed in ch 3.
15 Bright and Bright (1995) 111 LQR 655. They believe that certain licences to occupy would be caught.
16 JE Adams [1995] Conv 10.
17 *Litster v Forth Dry Dock & Engineering Co Ltd* [1990] 1 AC 546, p 559 (Lord Oliver); also Lord Templeman, ibid, p 558.

straining is not required by the House of Lords, even allowing for the 'greater latitude' of interpretation of which it speaks.[18]

It is, however, necessary to mention what the effect of these regulations might be should the courts decide in future to adopt a wide view and rule these regulations applicable in principle to leases.

1   Only *residential tenancies* would be caught, and only those tenancies granted by such bodies as companies, local authorities, housing associations or Government departments. This is because the 'consumer' (the tenant) must act for purposes outside his business; but the 'supplier' (the landlord) must grant the agreement for the purposes of his trade or business, including the activities of local authorities and the like (reg 2).

2   The *effect* of the regulations is, seemingly, that any term which has not been individually negotiated is regarded as unfair, if contrary to a requirement of good faith,[19] it causes a significant imbalance in the parties' rights and obligations to the detriment of the 'consumer' (reg 4(11)). An unfair term in the prescribed sense is not binding on the 'consumer' (reg 4(4)). We then discover that a term is always regarded as not individually negotiated – raising the prospect of its being unfair – if it is drafted in advance and the 'consumer' cannot influence its substance (reg 3(3)). Therefore, if a residential lessee of the prescribed type is presented with a term which is precedent-based, he may be able to argue that he is not bound by it simply for that reason, provided the 'imbalance' test is satisfied. In addition, however, even if any term is individually negotiated, the regulations may still apply if an overall assessment of the 'contract' indicates that it is a 'pre-formulated standard contract' (reg 3(4)). Apart altogether from these requirements and tests, the landlord must ensure that any written term of the agreement is intelligibly expressed (reg 6).[20]

3   The new rules do not apply to any term which 'defines the main subject-matter of the contract' or which concerns the adequacy of the price or remuneration, as against the goods sold or supplied (reg 3(2)). Assuming, then, that the language of these consumer regulations is extended by the courts to apply to real property such as a lease, the *operative words* of a lease (such as the words of demise as well as, presumably, the reservation of rent clause or clauses defining the demised premises and rights attached to them) are not subject to the 1995 regulations. This major exclusion should limit the impact of these regulations.

4   By contrast, the unfairness test could apply to certain of the terms of the prescribed residential leases. The difficulty is then to decide which precise terms might be subject to that test, no easy task in advance. It is possible that a term which regulates the conduct of the lessee might well be the sort of thing which the regulations aim at, such as user restrictions or limitations

---

18   *Litster v Forth Dry Dock Co Ltd* supra, at p 576 (Lord Oliver).
19   An assessment of good faith is to be made and requires regard to be had to a number of specified matters, such as the strength of the bargaining position of the parties (regs, Sch 2).
20   This particular requirement would appear to apply even to the operative parts of a lease, to which otherwise the regs do not apply.

on the keeping of pets or the erection of aerials and the like; likewise covenants imposing a duty to paint the premises with a particular kind of paint. What is to be the fate of more significant terms such as those relating to rent review or the payment and collection of service charges is not clear; an upward-only rent review clause might be at risk, such as those sometimes suggested for assured shorthold tenancies, as might a penal rent clause; but whether a forfeiture or re-entry clause might be at risk would depend on whether it is treated as part of the operative words of a lease or as a one-sided provision for termination which causes an imbalance between the parties. Clauses which absolutely prohibited the assignment or sub-letting of the premises, while the landlord retained his common law freedom to dispose of the freehold as he saw fit might fall foul of the unfairness test as causing the requisite degree of imbalance.

Specific contents of leases

Returning now to the contents of leases, formal leases must state the names of each party, the duration of the term certain, the premises granted, and the covenants of the lease.[1] While in the case of a tenancy granted on or after 1 January 1996, the liability of a tenant, and any assignee, lasts during the period they hold the lease, in the case of a tenancy granted before that date, the original tenant, and any guarantor of his, is subject to a continuing liability to perform the covenants until the expiry of the lease (see further chapter 5).

1 *Duration of lease* – After the date of the lease, a statement as to its duration (giving a commencement date and a termination date) is obligatory, on pain of voidness, in the case of any lease for a term certain (see chapter 2). The date of commencement may precede the date of execution of the lease, as where the tenant has taken possession under an agreement for a lease.

 A lease stated to commence 'on' a specified date is presumed to commence as at that date.[2] By a curious rule of construction, should a lease commence 'from' a specified date, say 1 January, it is taken not to commence on that day, but on the day following. However, this rule readily yields to any contrary indications which demonstrate that the parties intended the lease to commence on the stated day, as where rent is payable in advance on 1 January, 'from' which date the term is stated to run.[3] The High Court has ruled that a lease expressed to run from 24 June 1984 until 24 December 2003, ie from one specified date to another, ran as from 24 June 1984, so rebutting the presumption just mentioned.[4]

---

1 Specimen leases are set out in the Appendix to this work.
2 *Sidebotham v Holland* [1895] 1 QB 378, CA.
3 *Ladyman v Wirral Estates Ltd* [1968] 2 All ER 197; *Whelton Sinclair v Hyland* [1992] 2 EGLR 158, CA (where the parties were mistaken as to the correct commencement date of a renewed lease so that the application of the presumption would have left the premises undemised for one day).
4 *Meadfield Properties Ltd v Secretary of State for the Environment* [1995] 1 EGLR 39, thus rendering invalid a lessee's notice to terminate to expire on 23 June 1994, and so within ten years of the date of demise.

2   The *premises* demised by the lease will be defined, it is hoped clearly, and
there may be a related statement as to the permitted use of the premises. Any
ambiguities or uncertainties are resolved by the courts. Thus, a lease of
'land', which includes premises, will normally also include the outside of
external walls. Where a long lease demised buildings and premises, it was
held that the roof passed with the demise.[5] The question of the scope of any
particular demise is one of fact.[6] In the case of flats, the demise of a flat is
presumed to include the external walls enclosing it[7] but not the external
walls of other flats in the same building.[8] A demise may also include any void
spaces between the actual and 'false' ceilings of a sub-divided house.[9] It is
presumed that a demise will include everything below ground level in a
vertical line, such as a cellar, in the absence of specific words of exclusion.[10]
In a lease 'with appurtenances', 'appurtenances' includes only such things
as outhouses, yards and gardens.[11] If an upper floor of premises is demised
separately from lower floors, the use of staircases passes (in principle) as an
appurtenance to the upper floor tenant, on the basis of necessity if the
staircase is the sole means of access as at the date of the demise.[12] A right of
way in favour of the demised premises will pass as an 'appurtenance' if
enjoyed at the date of the lease.[13]

 Some leases, especially for a long term, contain exceptions and
reservations.

Exceptions A lease of land prima facie includes everything above and
beneath the surface but the landlord may limit the physical extent of his
grant by expressly excluding from it some part of the land such as a field, a
building, or mines and minerals, or sporting rights.[14]

Reservations These are new rights created in the lease in favour of the
landlord subject to which the tenant will take the property, as with the
landlord reserving himself a right of way over the demised premises, or
reserving a right to build to any height on adjoining land notwithstanding
that the buildings may obstruct any light on the demised premises.[15] Any
reservations must be expressly made in the lease,[16] except in the case of a way
of necessity.[17] Reservations are construed against the landlord.[18] Thus a
wide reservation entitling the landlord to do acts which would otherwise
constitute a nuisance or an interference with easements was construed as

5 *Straudley Investments Ltd v Barpress Ltd* [1987] 1 EGLR 69, CA.
6 *Douglas-Scott v Scorgie* [1984] 1 All ER 1086, [1984] 1 WLR 716, CA.
7 *Sturge v Hackett* [1962] 3 All ER 166, [1962] 1 WLR 1257, CA.
8 *Campden Hill Towers v Gardner* [1977] QB 823, [1977] 1 All ER 739, CA.
9 *Greystone Property Investments Ltd v Margulies* (1983) 47 P & CR 472, CA.
10 *Grigsby v Melville* [1973] 3 All ER 455, [1974] 1 WLR 80, CA.
11 *Trim v Sturminster RDC* [1938] 2 KB 508, [1938] 2 All ER 168, CA.
12 *Altmann v Boatman* (1963) 186 Estates Gazette 109, CA.
13 *Hansford v Jago* [1921] 1 Ch 322.
14 See eg *Mason v Clarke* [1955] AC 778, [1955] 1 All ER 914, HL.
15 *Foster v Lyons* [1927] 1 Ch 219.
16 *Re Webb's Lease* [1951] Ch 808, [1951] 2 All ER 131, CA.
17 *Liddiard v Waldron* [1934] 1 KB 435, CA.
18 *St Edmundsbury and Ipswich Diocesan Board of Finance v Clark (No 2)* [1975] 1 All ER 772,
  [1975] 1 WLR 468, CA; as in *Trailfinders Ltd v Razuki* [1988] 2 EGLR 46.

being subject to an implied limitation that the lessees would not be deprived of all access.[19]

3 *Other parts of lease* Any lease would be expected to reserve a rent payable by the tenant, by an initial formula which indicates the annual amount payable in sterling, and the intervals at which the rent is payable, which may be half-yearly, quarterly, monthly or weekly, and in principle on a given day in the month. Many modern leases make provision for the landlord's privilege of a rent review, under which the rent is to be revised upwards, or even downwards, at fixed intervals agreed in advance, say every five years.

Properly-drawn leases contain express covenants or obligations undertaken by both the landlord and tenant. These deal with every aspect of the relationship of the parties, and are discussed in Part B of this book. Thus the landlord may covenant for quiet enjoyment by the tenant, and undertake to insure the premises. As well as being liable for rent, the tenant may undertake to use the premises in only a specified manner, not to alter them, and to keep them in repair. If the landlord wishes to be able to forfeit (or terminate early) a lease for breaches by the lessee of his covenants, he will have to insert a proviso for re-entry or forfeiture.

The lease may also contain *options* by the tenant to purchase the reversion or to renew, and options by the landlord or tenant to break the lease during the term certain. Some leases provide that it is a *condition* of the lease that the tenant does not become insolvent or bankrupt – so terminating the lease on either event. Leases may contain *schedules*, which, as noted, make detailed provisions for general matters specified in the lease, such as rent review procedures or detailed repairing obligations. There may also be a schedule of fixtures, notably where the premises are let with fixtures or furniture, as well as a schedule of condition, which gives the condition of the premises at the date of the lease so that, if this deteriorates due to the tenant's failure in breach of covenant to repair, the landlord may more easily establish his right to forfeiture or damages.

VIII   REGISTRATION OF LEASES

The title of a leaseholder must be registered under the Land Registration Act 1925 on the first grant of a lease where the title of the leaseholder is a legal estate, and the term granted is for more than 21 years. Registration of the title of a leaseholder is also required where there is an assignment on sale, or the grant of an under-lease out of, a registered lease with or for an unexpired term of more than 21 years (1925 Act s 123(1)). Unless registration of title is applied for within two months of the grant, assignment[20] or under-lease in question, these become void for the purpose of passing the legal estate in the land (s 123(1)).

---

19 *Overcom Properties Ltd v Stockleigh Hall Residents Management* [1989] 1 EGLR 75.
20 Ie a legal assignment; see now *Brown & Root Technology Ltd v Sun Alliance and London Assurance Co* (1996) 141 Sol Jo LB 38, CA (where an unregistered assignment of the legal title meant that the original lessee could exercise a personal option to determine the lease).

Where the term granted, or the unexpired residue of the term assigned or sub-let, is just over 21 years at the date of application for registration, applications may be made for registration within the two-month period allowed even though by the time the lease is registered it will have less than 21 years to run (s 8(1A)).[21]

The registration of any lease or underlease originally created for a term not exceeding 21 years is prohibited (s 22(2)). Leases for a term exceeding 21 years which contain an absolute prohibition on assignments inter vivos are registrable (s 8(2)). Any lease originally granted for a term not exceeding 21 years is incapable of being registered and overrides the registered title (s 70(1)(k)).

Leaseholders may be registered with one of four kinds of title:

(a) *Absolute title* (under s 9 of the 1925 Act) where both the title to the leasehold, the freehold and any intermediate leasehold titles must be approved by the Registrar.

(b) *Good leasehold title* (s 10) which requires approval only of the leasehold title, and therefore the Registrar cannot guarantee that the lease was validly granted.

(c) *Qualified title* (s 12) where the title is subject to a specified defect – otherwise the effect is the same as absolute or good leasehold titles.

(d) *Possessory title* (s 11) in which case no guarantee is given as to the title prior to first registration.

Upgrading of these titles under the 1925 Act is possible. In the case of a good leasehold title the registrar must, on application by the proprietor, convert the title to an absolute title provided he is satisfied as to the title to the freehold and the title to any intermediate leasehold (s 77(1)). In the case of a possessory title the registrar must similarly convert the title to good leasehold if he is satisfied as to the title or if the land has been registered as good leasehold for at least 12 years and he is satisfied that the proprietor is in possession (s 77(2)). The registrar must likewise convert a qualified title to good leasehold if satisfied as to the title (s 77(3)). In all cases just mentioned the registrar may convert titles without any application for conversion having been made. Where an adverse claim is pending, no conversion is possible until the claim is disposed of (s 77(4)).

IX   RECTIFICATION AND RESCISSION

Rectification

The court may, on parol evidence of mutual mistake, order the rectification of an executed lease because it fails properly to carry out the common intention of both parties. The common intention must continue until execution and the

---

21   Otherwise, because of the two-month period for applications, if the term fell to below 21 years by the time of registration, s 8 would, prior to being amended, have precluded registration.
1   See *Brimican Investments Ltd v Blue Circle Heating Ltd* [1995] EGCS 18.

lease once rectified must then represent the true agreement of the parties.[1] An example of such rectification is correcting clerical mistakes or other obvious slips in the preparation of the lease.[2] Rectification may be ordered against an assignee with notice.[3] The court may, in its discretion, order rescission, as opposed to rectification, of a lease for mutual mistake, as where there is a misdescription in the lease. Therefore, where by mistake a first floor was included in a lease, rescission was ordered and the tenant given an option to take a new lease without that floor.[4] If the plaintiff has simply made a bad bargain, forgetting a material matter in negotiations, rectification is out of the question.[5] Rectification of a contract for a lease, and subject to the proof of continuing unconscionability until execution, of an executed lease, is exceptionally possible where only one party is mistaken. There must be additional circumstances which render it unconscionable for the party who wishes to stand by the written terms to rely on them. This requirement is satisfied by proof of fraud or undue influence. More generously, an equity of rectification of a contract for a lease was held to arise where A intends B to misconstrue a document by diverting B from discovering his own mistake by making false and misleading statements. Where, in negotiations with a landlord, a tenant diverted attention from a personal surrender or 'put' option by statements which raised only his interest in exercising a different option in the lease, impliedly representing that the tenant was not interested in exercising the 'put' option, the landlord was held to have been induced to contract on this basis and was entitled to rectification of the contract so that the tenant could not surrender the lease.[6]

Subject to the previous considerations, a person claiming to rectify an executed agreement for unilateral mistake must prove the following, otherwise it would be all too easy to set aside leases on this ground. (1) There was a mistake by the plaintiff in executing the deed, so that the deed does not translate that party's subjective intention at the time of the execution of the deed. (2) There is no mistake by the other party, who intends the result in fact achieved. (3) The other party must be both aware of the plaintiff's mistake, and in not correcting it, his conduct must be unconscionable.[7]

Rescission

In the case of an executed lease, by s 1 of the Misrepresentation Act 1967, the fact that a contract has been performed is no longer a bar to a claim for rescission, but the court has a discretion to award damages in lieu of rescission, and this is without prejudice to any claim that the plaintiff might otherwise have for damages if the representation was negligently made. But for rescission to be

2 *Boots the Chemist Ltd v Street* [1983] 2 EGLR 51.
3 *Equity and Law Life Assurance Society Ltd v Coltness Group Ltd* [1983] 2 EGLR 118.
4 *Paget v Marshall* (1884) 28 Ch D 255.
5 *Harlow Development Corpn v Kingsgate (Clothing Productions) Ltd* (1973) 226 Estates Gazette 1960.
6 *Commission for the New Towns v Cooper (Great Britain) Ltd* [1995] Ch 259, [1995] 2 All ER 929, CA.
7 *Kemp v Neptune Concrete Ltd* [1988] 2 EGLR 87, CA.
8 *Curtin v Greater London Council* (1970) 114 Sol Jo 932, CA.

granted, the court must be satisfied that the parties can be put back into substantially the same position as before.[8] Moreover, there must be evidence of conduct verging on fraud, and this applies where rescission is asked for on the grounds of unilateral mistake, eg where plaintiffs claimed rectification or rescission of a lease in which they had failed to insert a term to protect their own interest.[9]

Rescission for fraud was available after the expiry of a Rent Act contractual tenancy which had been granted on the faith of a fraudulent misstatement by the tenant,[10] it being admitted that, had rescission been ordered while the contractual tenancy was still subsisting, any right to a statutory tenancy would have perished with the contractual tenancy.[11] A party entitled to rescind a lease or a contract to assign a lease has an election and may affirm the lease or contract. For this to apply, the party must have knowledge of his legal rights and of the relevant facts. The sooner he thereafter elects to rescind, the better. If a period elapses between knowledge of the facts and of entitlement to rescind, there can be no effective election to affirm during this period.[12] Once any such period elapses, any right to rescind must be promptly exercised. The commencement of negotiations which are inconsistent with an earlier right to rescind, will deprive the party concerned of that right.[13] If a person takes possession knowing that the consent of the landlord to an assignment of a lease to him has not been obtained, this is not waiver of any right to rescind the contract for a lease.[14]

9   *Truman Aviation Ltd v Bingham* [1970] EGD 296.
10   *Killick v Roberts* [1991] 4 All ER 289, [1991] 1 WLR 1146, CA.
11   *Solle v Butcher* [1950] 1 KB 671, [1949] 2 All ER 1107, CA.
12   *Peyman v Lanjani* [1985] Ch 457, [1984] 3 All ER 703, CA.
13   *Aquis Estates Ltd v Minton* [1975] 3 All ER 1043, [1975] 1 WLR 1452, CA.
14   *Butler v Croft* (1973) 27 P & CR 1 (rescission refused at discretion due to conduct of plaintiff).

PART B
RIGHTS AND OBLIGATIONS OF THE PARTIES

Chapter 5

Covenants generally

I INTRODUCTION

Most fixed-term leases and tenancies contain express covenants entered into by the landlord and the tenant: not many parties are content to allow their relationship to rest solely on implied obligations. The obligations entered into by a landlord and tenant are enforceable not merely between the original parties, but by and against any person who takes an assignment of the landlord's reversion or the lease. The benefit and burden of positive and negative covenants of a lease[1] are annexed to the demised premises and the reversion. The law governing the enforcement of leasehold covenants, which originates from the sixteenth century[2] has been recast and reformed by statute, as from 1 January 1996.[3] Much of this chapter is therefore devoted to a consideration of the way in which leasehold covenants may be enforced after an assignment of the lease or the reversion. It begins, however, with an examination of the way the courts interpret leasehold covenants.

No particular form of words is required to create a covenant and the question is one of construction in each case. Thus, a recent form of lease contains covenants by the tenant under the heading 'tenant's obligations' and states that, for example, the tenant 'is to pay' the rent, and 'is to comply' with certain user obligations.[4] Although as a rule an executed lease cannot be set aside, if the landlord is induced to sign it by a misrepresentation of fact, he may claim rescission,[5] and where a landlord was the victim of a fraudulent misrepresentation by a tenant, she was entitled to rescind a Rent Act protected tenancy once the fraud came to light, thus precluding the creation of a statutory tenancy.[6]

1 In the case of an equitable lease, it is strictly inaccurate to speak of covenants, as there is no deed; but the mutual obligations of the parties are enforceable as if there were a lease by deed.
2 As shown by the citations in *City of London Corpn v Fell* [1994] 1 AC 458, 464B–465C, [1993] 4 All ER 968, 972D–973D, HL.
3 Landlord and Tenant (Covenants) Act 1995.
4 Law Society Business Lease (Whole Premises), cll 1 and 3, cited in Appendix.
5 See *Museprime Properties Ltd v Adhill* [1990] 2 EGLR 196.
6 *Killick v Roberts* [1991] 4 All ER 289; [1991] 1 WLR 1146, CA.

Dependent and independent covenants

Some covenants may contain two limbs, and others, such as for repairs and to pay rent or service charges, are related. Disputes may arise as to whether a party can avoid performing his obligations if the other fails to perform his own. The question has sometimes arisen in relation to covenants to repair, where one party undertakes to repair and the other to pay or contribute to the cost, or where one party agrees to supply materials and the other to carry out repairs.

The courts distinguish between *dependent* and *independent* covenants. The former creates a condition precedent to compliance by the other party with his obligation. The latter covenant requires performance by a party irrespective of whether the other party has performed his part. The question of into which type a given covenant falls is one of construction, and particularly in older cases, some seemingly inconsistent results have been reached.[7] As a general guide, the court is more likely to hold that a covenant is dependent where the parties have, as with landlords' works which may require the payment by lessees of service charges, laid down a detailed procedure for the resolution, before any works are begun, of disputes between the parties as to the proposed method and costs of carrying out the work. Thus, where a landlord undertook, before commencing any major or substantial repairs, to submit to the tenants a copy of the specification and estimates, after which the tenant had time to object, the landlord, who ignored these procedures and undertook works, failed to recover some £36,707 in service charges from the lessees. The consultation procedures were a condition precedent to recovery of the charges, because of the dispute resolution procedure.[8]

The court is entitled to take into account any results flowing from an opposite construction, as where the landlord of an agricultural holding had undertaken to carry out certain repairs by 1 September, the tenant agreeing to pay an increased rent as from the previous March. The two obligations were independent and the tenant could not avoid liability to pay the overdue rent on account of any default by the landlord with his repairing obligations.[9] Likewise, prompt payment by the lessee of a flat of his maintenance obligation was held not to be a condition precedent of his landlord's obligation to provide hot water and central heating, owing to the fact that if it were otherwise, the landlords, who had their remedies, could claim to be freed of all their maintenance obligations if the tenant failed to pay promptly.[10]

Collateral contracts

Although the terms of an executed lease are taken to be a complete record of the agreement of the parties, this is not so if the landlord made a representation, prior to the execution of the contract for a lease, which induced the tenant to

---

7 Compare eg *Tucker v Linger* (1882) 21 Ch D 18, CA and *Westacott v Hahn* [1918] 1 KB 495, CA.
8 *Northways Flats Management Co (Camden) Ltd v Wimpey Pension Trustees Ltd* [1992] 2 EGLR 42, CA; also *CIN Properties Ltd v Barclays Bank plc* [1986] 1 EGLR 59, CA.
9 *Burton v Timmis* [1987] 1 EGLR 1, CA.
10 *Yorkbrook Investments Ltd v Batten* [1985] 2 EGLR 100, CA.

sign the deed or other instrument. If so, the statement will amount to a collateral contract, as where the landlord makes a representation to the tenant as to the state of repair or fitness of the premises; or as where he undertakes, prior to such execution, to put down rabbits,[11] or that the drains of the house are in order,[12] or that there was (contrary to the fact) the benefit of planning permission for the whole building.[13]

A tenant seeking to establish a collateral contract must prove, first, that the statement preceded the grant of the lease; second, that he would have refused to complete unless the representation was true; third, the representation must not contradict the terms of the lease itself.[14] If a covenant in the lease deals with the matter inconsistently with the alleged statement, the lease will prevail unless the landlord has estopped himself from enforcing that covenant, at least for the time being. Accordingly, where a landlord induced most sitting flat tenants to take 99-year leases with full repairing covenants by promising the tenants to pay for initial roofing repairs, the landlord was held unable to recover the cost of these repairs from any of the tenants or their assigns as a result.[15] Fortunately, it appears that a tenant does not have to prove that any collateral contract complies with the formal requirements of s 2 of the Law of Property (Miscellaneous Provisions) Act 1989, since such a contract supplements a lease and does not create an interest in land.[16]

The remedies of a tenant for misrepresentation are rescission – even if the lease has been executed – or damages.[17]

II CONSTRUCTION OF COVENANTS

1   The court must discover the mutual intentions of the parties from the terms of the covenant in question. Questions of construction are resolved in an objective fashion: the question is as to what the parties have in fact said, and not what they meant to say.[18] Thus, if a particular form of words is chosen by the parties, and it has a given consequence as a result of a fair interpretation of those words, they are taken mutually to have intended that result. Subject to what follows, the court declines to distort the primary meaning of words of a covenant.[19] Where appropriate, as has occurred with repairing obligations, the court pays attention to each word of the covenant.[20]

11   *Morgan v Griffith* (1871) LR 6 Exch 70.
12   *De Lassalle v Guildford* [1901] 2 KB 215, CA.
13   *Laurence v Lexcourt Holdings Ltd* [1978] 2 All ER 810, [1978] 1 WLR 1128.
14   *De Lassalle v Guildford*, supra (lease silent about the drains); *Henderson v Arthur* [1907] 1 KB 10, CA.
15   *Brikom Investments Ltd v Carr* [1979] QB 467, [1979] 2 All ER 753, CA (the costs were recoverable under the strict terms of the lease). For a case where deceit was proved see *Gordon v Selico & Co* [1986] 1 EGLR 71, CA.
16   *Lotteryking Ltd v Amec Properties Ltd* [1995] 2 EGLR 13.
17   Misrepresentation Act 1967, ss 1 and 2 allow rescission of an executed lease and damages for a negligent misrepresentation which is not fraudulent.
18   *Schuler v Wickman Tools* [1974] AC 235, 263, HL.
19   See eg *Marks v Warren* [1979] 1 All ER 29.
20   As in *Crédit Suisse v Beegas Nominees Ltd* [1994] 4 All ER 803.

2   The intention of the parties is also construed, especially where a particular
     expression is used which is doubtful or ambiguous, with regard to the factual
     background and other surrounding circumstances known to both parties at
     or before the date of the execution of the lease.[1]

3   When construing certain words in a particular covenant, the courts are
     entitled to have regard, as an aid to construction, to other words in that
     covenant in order to elucidate the meaning of the words in dispute. For
     example, if a general covenant is preceded or followed by a specific covenant
     within the same area, the latter covenant may be used as a guide to the
     interpretation of the former.[2] The court is, if in doubt as to the meaning of
     particular words, also entitled to have regard to any other relevant covenants
     in the lease, and even, where necessary, to the purpose of the demise as a
     whole.[3] Equally, although the surrounding circumstances or 'factual matrix'
     may assist the court, they will be disregarded if they conflict with the actual
     language of the covenant and cannot advance its interpretation.[4]

4   The court is entitled to decide objectively on the underlying purpose of a
     covenant. If the landlord and tenant are business parties, the courts presume
     that such underlying purpose, which in the case of rent review clauses is to
     protect the landlord's rent from erosion by inflation or from being rendered
     unrealistic by rises in property values, will govern the interpretation of the
     covenant as a whole, unless the language used is so clear that the court has
     no alternative but to adopt a construction which goes against that purpose.[5]

5   In the case of a covenant which limits the tenant's common law rights (such
     as a covenant limiting his power to assign or sub-let the demised premises)
     or which requires the tenant to undertake a positive act, any ambiguity in
     the covenant is to be resolved against the landlord.[6] A related rule applies
     where it is argued that a covenant which is not clearly worded arguably limits
     or restricts the easements and other rights otherwise passing with the
     demise: such limits are to be construed *contra proferentem*.[7]

6   If a covenant, literally interpreted, produces a ridiculous result, which it is
     taken that the parties could not have intended, or can only be read in a sense
     argued for by one party by doing violence to its language, the court will have
     regard to the overall purpose of the covenant and then interpret it accordingly,
     if necessary modifying its literal meaning.[8] If it is unavoidably necessary to
     make a clause work in accordance with its overall purpose, the court is
     entitled to imply into a covenant such words as will achieve that purpose,
     rather than literally apply expressions in the covenant which will produce an

1   *Philpot's (Woking) Ltd v Surrey Conveyancers* [1986] 1 EGLR 97, 98; *Larksworth Investments
    Ltd* v *Temple House Ltd* [1996] EGCS 86, CA.
2   See eg *Bristol and West Building Society v Marks and Spencer plc* [1991] 2 EGLR 57.
3   *Wolfe v Hogan* [1949] 2 KB 194, CA; *City and Westminster Properties (1934) Ltd v Mudd* [1959]
    Ch 129, [1958] 2 All ER 733; *Russell v Booker* [1982] 2 EGLR 86, CA.
4   *Montross Associated Investments SA v Moussaieff* [1992] 1 EGLR 55, CA.
5   *Co-operative Wholesale Society Ltd v National Westminster Bank plc* [1995] 1 EGLR 97, CA.
6   *Montross Associated Investments SA v Mousaieff supra.*
7   *St Edmundsbury and Ipswich Diocesan Board of Finance v Clark (No 2)* [1975] 1 All ER 772,
    [1975] 1 WLR 468, CA.
8   See *Wyndham Investments Ltd v Motorway Tyres and Accessories Ltd* [1991] 2 EGLR 114, CA.

absurd result.[9] In any event, unless the clear language of a covenant requires an artificial assumption to be made, it is presumed that no such assumption is required at any time during the term.[10] The court will also strive to interpret a covenant to avoid an unreasonable or improbable result, but if the intention of the parties is clear and unambiguously expressed, the court will enforce it, however capricious the result may appear to be – in the absence of contrary indications in other parts of the lease, since it must be construed as a whole, for the sake of consistency.[11]

7   The construction of any particular covenant should be carried out as a matter of principle, rather than by analogy with other authorities, owing to the fact that (especially in relation to repairing obligations and rent review clauses) there exist many different forms of words. The court will then consider any directly relevant authorities which bear either on the question of construction or on general considerations of interpretation, if these aid the task of construction, or if the words used in the covenant in question are identical to those used in another case. These two processes sometimes become inseparable.[12] The courts have so far declined to interpret covenants in leases of business premises by reference to principles of commercial reality or consistency, despite invitations to do so.[13]

III   ENFORCEABILITY OF COVENANTS GENERALLY

There are two sets of rules which govern the enforcement of covenants in a lease. This is because covenants in a lease granted before a recent statutory reform are governed by a mixture of common law and statutory rules. Tenancies granted as from the commencement of the Landlord and Tenant (Covenants) Act 1995, which came into force on 1 January 1996,[14] are governed by this new code. Because these two systems are likely to co-exist for many years, it is necessary to discuss both sets of rules. It may assist if a brief review of the principles of both rules is given.

The old rules are based on the notion that liability to perform leasehold covenants is governed by two principles. As between the original landlord and the original tenant, the parties are said to be in *privity of contract*. All covenants in the lease are enforceable against both parties. If the tenant voluntarily assigns the lease[15] then the assignee, not having originally entered into the lease, is not in privity of contract with the landlord. He holds by *privity of estate*, however,

---

9 *Jollybird Ltd v Fairzone Ltd* [1990] 2 EGLR 55, CA.
10 See eg *Lynnthorpe Enterprises Ltd v Sidney Smith (Chelsea) Ltd* [1990] 2 EGLR 131, CA.
11 *London and Manchester Assurance Co Ltd v GA Dunn & Co* [1983] 1 EGLR 111, CA; *Glofield Properties Ltd v Morley (No 2)* [1989] 2 EGLR 118, CA.
12 As in eg *Prudential Property Services Co Ltd v Capital Land Holdings Ltd* [1993] 1 EGLR 128.
13 See eg *Equity and Law Life Assurance Society plc v Bodfield Ltd* [1987] 1 EGLR 124, 125, CA; *Crédit Suisse v Beegas Nominees Ltd* [1994] 4 All ER 803, 817–818.
14 Landlord and Tenant (Covenants) Act 1995 Commencement Order, SI 1995/2963.
15 As opposed to making an assignment by operation of law, notably in bankruptcy and insolvency.

as having a leasehold tenure with the landlord. Consequently, any covenant which runs with the land, as with standard tenants' covenants, such as to pay rent or service charges, or to undertake repairs, or to use the premises only as permitted by the lease, is enforceable against an assignee by the landlord. Likewise, an assignee may enforce the burden of landlords' covenants which run with the land against the landlord, whether he is the original landlord or a person to whom the reversion has been assigned, on the basis of privity of estate (the direct relationship of landlord and tenant) between them. Once the current assignee in possession has re-assigned the lease, he loses privity of estate with the then landlord automatically. The new assignee is subjected to the burden and subject to the benefit of the tenants' and landlords' covenants of the lease. The erstwhile assignee is freed at common law from the burdens and cannot claim any benefits under the leasehold covenants, as from the assignment date.

By contrast, an original tenant, because he personally covenanted to observe the covenants of the lease until its contractual expiry date, is subjected by the common law, in the absence of release by the landlord, to a continuing liability to observe the burden of tenants' covenants until that date, despite his having assigned the lease and lost the estate in the land.[16] During times of economic stability, the continuing subjection of an original lessee to the burden of having to pay rent or service charges owed by any assignee for the time being, or to pay the landlord damages on account of dilapidations caused by an assignee, might not have seemed oppressive, perhaps because the solvency of assignees was more secure. In times such as the present, of economic uncertainty, landlords have been able to press home claims against original lessees, as well as against any person guaranteeing the performance of the original lessee, where they could not recover rent and service charges from an insolvent or bankrupt assignee.

The Law Commission examined the law.[17] It considered that 'a landlord or tenant of property should not continue to enjoy rights nor be under any obligation arising from a lease once he has parted with all interest in the property'. It also believed that a lease should be regarded as a single bargain for letting the property. A successor should fully take the place of his precedessor, whether as landlord or tenant, and the distinction between covenants which ran with the land, or which touched and concerned it, and those which did not, should be abolished.

After five years had elapsed, the government promised to reform the law, but it was prompted to act only during the middle of 1995, once a Private Member's Bill, which had cross-party support, showed signs of being enacted so as to implement the Law Commission proposals. So as to try to balance the competing interests of landlords and tenants, the government added a large number of new clauses to what is now the Landlord and Tenant (Covenants) Act 1995. This legislation implements the principal recommendation of the Law Commission, so abrogating the continuing liability of an original tenant for any breaches of covenant committed by his assignee or any other assignee, but not, as envisaged by the Commission,[18] in relation to an assignment of a tenancy

16 See Nicholls LJ in *City of London Corpn v Fell* [1993] QB 589, 603, approved [1994] 1 AC 458, 465; [1993] 4 All ER 968, 973E, HL, as being 'an impeccable judgment'.
17 Law Com No 174, *Privity of Contract and Estate* (1988), esp paras 4.1 and 4.46.
18 *Report*, para 4.60.

in existence when the 1995 Act came into force as from 1 January 1996. Moreover, although the 1995 Act takes the opportunity not only, as envisaged by the Commission, to do away, in relation to 'new tenancies', with the ancient doctrine of covenants touching and concerning land, replacing it with a new concept of landlord and tenant covenants, it has also, it is hoped beneficially, re-cast the general rules as to enforcement of leasehold covenants, so that, for example, the doctrines of privity of contract and of estate have been done away with. Thus, a mortgagee in possession of a landlord's reversion is as much entitled to enforce 'tenant covenants' as would have been the landlord himself (s 15(1)(b) of the 1995 Act).

The 1995 Act, as will appear, contains a number of checks and balances so as to render the abrogation of the 'privity of contract' liability of a tenant more palatable to commercial landlords, who were said to regard the new rule with unease, as affecting the stability of their investments. Consequently, as indeed envisaged by the Law Commission,[19] the 1995 Act allows a landlord to require as a condition of any voluntary assignment that the tenant guarantees the performance of his immediate assignee's obligations (s 16). The rules which govern the question of when it may be reasonable for a landlord to impose a condition of an assignment that the tenant enters into such a guarantee have been revised so that the parties to a commercial lease may agree, at the time of its grant, that such a condition may reasonably be imposed, and such a condition will not now be at risk of being held unreasonable by the courts, merely because it has been agreed in advance (s 22). At the same time, the tenant's guarantee is limited to the period his immediate assignee holds the lease. It does not normally extend to any period after the assignee has re-assigned the lease. Moreover, if the immediate assignee defaults, and the tenant has to pay the landlord money on that account, he may insist on being granted a reversionary or 'overriding' lease of the premises, so that he is able to enforce performance against the assignee – or terminate his lease and re-let the premises or occupy them himself.

It is now time to examine the rules governing the enforcement of leasehold covenants which apply to any tenancy granted before the coming into force of the Act and which may continue after that date.

IV ENFORCEMENT OF COVENANTS IN RELATION TO LEASES OR TENANCIES GRANTED BEFORE 1 JANUARY 1996

1 LIABILITY OF ORIGINAL LESSEE AND LESSOR

General principles

An original tenant is liable to perform all the covenants in a lease granted before the 1995 Act commenced, whether these are capable of running with the land because they touch and concern it, or are purely personal obligations to the landlord. If the original lessee expressly assigns the lease, he remains personally

---

19 *Report*, paras 4.11–4.15.

liable at common law[20] for the performance of any covenant which touches and concerns the land, such as, notably, to pay rent, or service charges reserved as rent or for repairs.

This liability of an original lessee to pay for the results of the failure of his or any later assignee is strict. It seems to be based on the idea that the landlord must have at least one person to whom he may ultimately look for performance of the leasehold covenants, especially that to pay rent, throughout the common law term of the lease. It is for this reason, perhaps, that an original lessee could not plead as a complete defence to liability that the assignee had surrendered part of the premises to the landlord.[1] An original tenant may face a claim for assignees' rent arrears not only from the original landlord, but from an assignee of the reversion.[2]

The severity of the so-called privity principle – seeing that the tenant has no control over the performance of his obligations by any assignee in possession[3] – has been recently limited in two ways. First, the personal liability of an original lessee to observe leasehold covenants despite his having assigned the lease, runs only until the expiry of the contractual term agreed for the lease. It therefore does not extend to any continuation term under Part II of the Landlord and Tenant Act 1954.[4] This principle yields to contrary language in the lease, as where the tenant remains liable during the lease and any extension of it by statute or otherwise.[5] Second, it was held that a lessee who had covenanted to pay an annual rent of £12,000 throughout the term of his lease was not liable to pay the full claim of £38,462 of rent arrears, where it appeared that the lessor and an assignee of the lease had varied the original rent reservation so as to require the payment of an annual rent of £35,000. The deed of variation affected the estate in the land and not the personal liability of the original lessee.[6] However, it was accepted that if the original lessee undertook to pay any reviewed rent, he would be liable to pay such a rent even if the review had taken place between the assignee and the landlord, despite his having no chance to influence the result.[7]

The common law is consistent: an original landlord is under a similar continuing liability to observe any landlords' real covenants in the lease.[8] It has been suggested that the original landlord may be liable, under a real covenant,

20 Unless the landlord releases him at the time of the assignment or later.
1   *Baynton v Morgan* (1888) 22 QBD 74, CA; nor that a voluntary arrangement has been made in respect of the tenant's assignee: *March Estates plc v Gunmark Ltd* [1996] 32 EG 75.
2   *Arlesford Trading Co Ltd v Servansingh* [1971] 3 All ER 113, [1971] 1 WLR 1080, CA.
3   This fact is no defence to liability: *Thames Manufacturing Co Ltd v Perrotts (Nicol & Peyton) Ltd* (1984) 50 P & CR 1; hence the overriding lease provisions of the 1995 Act.
4   *City of London Corpn v Fell* [1994] 1 AC 458, [1993] 4 All ER 468, HL.
5   Even so, a tenant was not liable for interim rent as opposed to the lesser contractual rent, as the lease concerned did not expressly render him liable to pay the former sum: *City of London Corpn v Fell*, supra.
6   *Friends' Provident Life Office v British Railways Board* [1995] 2 EGLR 55, CA; see Harrison [1995] 49 EG 117; also *Metropolitan Properties Co (Regis) Ltd v Bartholomew* [1996] 1 EGLR 82, CA (where a subsequent variation in a lessee's obligations did not affect an earlier liability of a surety).
7   See eg *Selous Street Properties Ltd v Oronel Fabrics Ltd* [1984] 1 EGLR 50 as explained in the *Friends' Provident* case.
8   *Stuart v Joy* [1904] 1 KB 362, CA.

direct to an assignee who became tenant after the assignment of the reversion.[9]

So as to try to cover himself against his continuing liability under the privity of contract rule, the original lessee may, on assigning the lease, take an *express indemnity covenant* from the assignee – and the assignee in turn may act similarly on re-assigning.[10] Where a chain of indemnity covenants has thus been set up, and an original lessee is made to pay rent or other sums by the landlord, because the assignee in possession has defaulted, he in turn may claim an indemnity (the whole sums paid) from the assignee in possession, or, at his option, the person, if different, to whom he originally assigned the lease. The original lessee's right of recovery is quasi-contractual in nature: he is recovering moneys paid under compulsion to the landlord.[11]

Statutory mitigations of the principles The Landlord and Tenant (Covenants) Act 1995 has introduced three mitigations of the full impact of the privity of contract rule as it applies to 'old-style' tenancies granted prior to 1 January 1996. These mitigations also apply to any 'new tenancy' (ie one granted after the 1995 Act commences), as where an assigning 'new tenant' has entered into an 'authorised guarantee agreement' in relation to his immediate assignee. No doubt the main beneficiary of the rules will be an original tenant where the assignee in possession has defaulted; where an intermediate assignee has expressly covenanted to observe covenants until the expiry of the lease, and has re-assigned, he could also invoke these rules. The rules cannot be contracted out of in the lease or tenancy and any 'agreement relating to a tenancy' – such as a term in the tenancy or collateral to it or a variation agreement – which has effect to 'exclude, modify or otherwise frustrate' these provisions is void (s 25(1)).

The first mitigation relates to the *time for recovery* of 'fixed charges' and is seemingly designed to prevent the landlord[12] from inflicting stale claims for such matters as rent, service charges or pre-determined sums payable on account of dilapidations[13] owed by the current assignee in possession, on the tenant who assigned him the lease. The essential rule is that the tenant is not liable to pay 'any amount in respect of any fixed charge payable under the covenant unless, within the period of six months beginning with the date on which the charge becomes due'[14] the landlord serves on this former tenant a

---

9 *Celsteel Ltd v Alton House Holdings Ltd (No 2)* [1987] 2 All ER 240 at 244, CA.
10 Covenants of indemnity are implied by Law of Property Act 1925, s 77(1)(C) & (D) (unregistered land) and Land Registration Act 1925, s 24(1)(b) & (2), but, with the enactment of the Landlord and Tenant (Covenants) Act 1995, Sch 2, these provisions cease to have effect in relation to tenancies granted after the commencement of the 1995 Act (s 30(3)).
11 *Moule v Garrett* (1870–72) LR 7 ExCh 101; *Re Healing Research Trustee Co Ltd* [1992] 2 All ER 481. An intermediate assignee may claim against any person to whom he assigned, if he was not responsible for the breach.
12 Including any person entitled to enforce payment of the 'fixed charge' such as a management company (s 17(6)).
13 'Fixed charges' are defined in s 17(6) so as to embrace all three types of sum.
14 A fixed charge due as at the commencement of the Act is treated, in principle, for notice purposes as due at that date, so that the six month period for claiming it runs as from then (s 17(5)).

statutory notice (s 17(2)). The notice must inform the tenant that the charge is now due and that the landlord intends to recover from him the amount specified in the notice and interest on a specified basis – if the latter is not specified, it cannot be recovered. The amount stated in the notice is, by s 17(4), generally the limit of any claim the landlord may make for fixed charges against the former tenant or any guarantor of his (to whom the benefit of this rule extends by s 17(3), entitling him to a separate notice).

The second mitigation of the privity of contract rule or where a guarantee agreement is invoked relates to post-assignment variations as from the commencement of the 1995 Act, of tenancies which might increase the liability of the former tenant. Thus the demised premises might be changed, or their permitted user altered, or the amount of unit or shop floor space allotted to the current tenant might be varied by mutual agreement which becomes part of the lease. Any increased rent recoverable to the extent that it is referable to these types of variation cannot be recovered from the 'former tenant' (s 18(2)).[15] The scope of this relieving provision is narrow. Because it only applies to a variation which, at the time it was made, the landlord could have absolutely refused to allow (s 18(4)(a)), rent review procedures are seemingly excluded from it.[16] Thus, a tenant who is under a continuing liability to pay rent until a tenancy granted before the commencement of the 1995 Act expires will still be subject to the risk of having to pay a rent inflated by an upwards review entered into between the landlord and an assignee, subject only to the notice requirements of s 17.

The third mitigation is that if a tenant or any guarantor of his obligations is subject to the privity of contract rule, he may, if he pays all the moneys owed by any assignee as the result of a default notice under s 17 of the 1995 Act, either may require the landlord by a 12 month notice[17] to grant him an overriding lease under s 19. If two persons have been served with a default notice, it seems that an overriding lease would be awarded to the first applicant (s 19(7)). The landlord must comply with the request unless the relevant tenancy has been determined. With an overriding lease,[18] the erstwhile tenant becomes the immediate landlord of the defaulting assignee for the term of his lease plus, in principle, three days (s 19(2)). He is then, it is presumed, able to enforce his remedies against that person, including forfeiture of the lease and the re-possessing of the premises or granting a new lease to any other person.[19] These

15 The benefit of this rule extends to a guarantor of the performance of the former tenant's obligations (s 18(3)).

16 As pointed out (*Privity of Contract*, p 53), because of s 18(5) of the 1995 Act, if an assignee carries out improvements within the Landlord and Tenant Act 1927 procedure, and an increase in rent resulted, a former tenant could not use s 18 to avoid paying that increase on the default of such assignee.

17 Given at the date of the payment or within 12 months of it (s 19(5)) but there is no prescribed form of notice.

18 Which binds any landlord's mortgagee, including chargee (s 20(7)), automatically (s 20(4)).

19 It has been said (*Privity of Contract*, p 46) that if a landlord accepts rent arrears from a former tenant following a s 17 notice, that could waive (by conduct) a right to forfeit the occupation lease; if this is correct, and it is difficult to see how the landlord's waiver could bind the former tenant, then once the latter obtained an overriding lease, he would find that one of its purposes was frustrated.

rules also apply to a tenant who holds a 'new tenancy' governed by the full benefit of the 1995 Act, if he has entered into an authorised guarantee agreement with the landlord as a condition of the assignment, and whose assignee has defaulted, leaving the former tenant with a liability to the landlord. An overriding lease must state which of the new or pre-1995 Act set of rules apply to it (s 20(1)). If an overriding lease is not within the reformed rules, the former tenant who holds it remains subject to the privity of contract rule *vis-à-vis* the head landlord, so placing him at a substantial potential disadvantage in the future if he cannot rid himself of the lease.

Insolvency of assignee

Where, following the bankruptcy or insolvency of an assignee, the lease is disclaimed by the assignee's trustee in bankruptcy or liquidator, an original lessee remains, at common law, liable under the privity of contract rule, and so for unpaid rent to the landlord. Any guarantor of the original tenant is also liable. The disclaimer does not affect the right of the landlord, if a lease was granted before 1 January 1996, to have recourse to either party.[20] The original lessee may be as exposed in insolvency matters as elsewhere, since the assignee may alter his leasehold estate by entering into an arrangement with his creditors: the terms of the arrangement will bind the original lessee automatically, mitigated only by questions of construction as to the sums covered and the operative date of the arrangement.[1] In order to try to recoup his losses, the lessee is entitled to seek the restoration of a dissolved assignee company to the register of companies, so as to be able to claim an indemnity from him for moneys paid to the landlord.[2] A lessee or guarantor rendered liable in these circumstances could also seek to obtain an overriding lease under s 19 of the 1995 Act.

Position of guarantors

If some person guarantees or stands surety for the performance of the original tenant's obligation, his liability, although secondary to that of the tenant, is co-extensive with the latter's liability. Indeed, the benefit, or right of a landlord to enforce, a covenant of guarantee passes automatically on any assignment by deed of the reversion.[3] Moreover, if a guarantor is released, this has no effect on the primary liability of the original tenant.[4] However, to avoid grave injustice, where a landlord received some £50,348 on account of rent due from a guarantor, whom he then released, he had to give credit for these sums against his claim for rent arrears from the original lessee.[5] The obligations of the original lessee and his guarantors were regarded by the court as a single set of duties, seeing that a guarantor's obligation to pay touched and concerned the land as

20 *Hindcastle Ltd v Barbara Attenborough Associates Ltd* [1997] AC 70, [1996] 1 All ER 737, HL.
1 *Burford Midland Properties Ltd v Marley Extensions Ltd* [1995] 2 EGLR 15.
2 *Allied Dunbar Assurance plc v Fowle* [1994] 1 EGLR 122.
3 *Kumar v Dunning* [1989] QB 193, [1987] 2 All ER 801, CA.
4 *Allied London Investments v Hambro Life Assurance* (1985) 50 P & CR 207, CA.
5 *Milverton Group Ltd v Warner World Ltd* [1995] 2 EGLR 28, CA.

much as did a lessee's. In this way, the common law rule has been equated to that enacted by the Landlord and Tenant (Covenants) Act 1995.

If, however, the terms of a lease are substantially varied so as to prejudice the guarantor, and his consent to the variation has not been sought,[6] the guarantor is released automatically at common law.[7] It is possible to avoid this result by clear language in the lease, but a statement in a surety covenant that any neglect or forbearance by the landlords in enforcing performance of a covenant against the lessee did not release the surety did not suffice to avoid an automatic release of the tenant's sureties, where the lease had been varied so as to allow the use of part of the premises as an off-licence.[8]

2   LIABILITY OF ASSIGNEES

We now discuss the common law principles on which leasehold covenants are enforceable by and against assignees of the reversion and of the lease. These apply to tenancies granted prior to the commencement of the Landlord and Tenant (Covenants) Act 1995.

(1) There must be *privity of estate* between the parties. In the present context, therefore, the parties must hold, directly, as landlord and tenant.[9] The assignee in possession is liable to perform and may enforce leasehold covenants, but once he parts with possession after a re-assignment, his liability to perform covenants ceases.

This doctrine has the effect that a person who does not directly hold a lease from a landlord might, but for statutory or equitable relaxations, be unable to enforce covenants against the landlord. However, owing to statute, a sub-tenant may claim the right to enforce a positive or negative covenant in the head lease against the head landlord, despite the lack of privity of estate between them.[10] Equity allows a head landlord to enforce directly the burden of a restrictive covenant contained in the head lease against a sub-lessee who has notice of it either by the covenant appearing in his sub-lease or owing to registration.

(2) The covenant must be a real covenant: it must *touch and concern* the land. If this is not so, the covenant is a personal covenant and cannot be enforced by or against assignees, though it is enforceable between the original parties.

Covenants touching and concerning land

The requirement that, to be enforceable by or against an assignee of the lease or the reversion a covenant must touch and concern the demised land, or, to use

---

6 See generally HW Wilkinson (1995) 146 NLJ 1141.
7 See eg *West Horndon Industrial Park Ltd v Phoenix Timber Group plc* [1995] 1 EGLR 77.
8 *Howard de Walden Estates Ltd v Pasta Place Ltd* [1995] 1 EGLR 79.
9 Therefore there must have been a legal assignment of the term; but equity has since *Boyer v Warbey* [1953] 1 QB 234, [1953] 1 All ER 269, CA, allowed the benefit (though apparently not the burden) of a lessee's covenant to pass on assignment of an equitable lease.
10 Law of Property Act 1925 s 78(1), which does not apply to tenancies granted after the commencement of the 1995 Act (Landlord and Tenant (Covenants) Act 1995 s 30(4)).

the language of statute, must have reference to the subject matter of the lease, is of ancient origin. The policy of this rule, which had become technical, is to limit the covenants which may be enforced against third parties, the right to enforce being itself a property interest. Covenants in a lease which directly affect the relationship of the parties as landlord and tenant, without regard to the personal identity of the particular parties concerned at any time, may be said to touch and concern the land, and so to run with it through successive assignments of the lease or the reversion. Thus, tenants' covenants to pay rent, insurance premiums, or service charges, as well as to repair, not to assign without consent,[11] not to make structural alterations and limiting the user of the premises will run with the land.

The House of Lords evolved four tests to be applied. A covenant will run with the land if: (1) it is beneficial to the owner of the land for the time being; (2) it affects the nature, quality, user or value of the landlord's land; (3) it is not in terms personal; and (4) the fact that a covenant is to pay a sum of money does not prevent it touching and concerning the land if (1) to (3) apply and the covenant is concerned with something to be done on, or in relation to the land.[12]

All implied covenants touch and concern land.[13] Conditions for re-entry for breaches of covenant which themselves touch and concern the land also do so.[14] Apart from these cases, there have been many examples of covenants which could have fallen into real covenants or personal covenants, and a few of these on either side may be given. A landlord's covenant for quiet enjoyment,[15] not to determine a quarterly tenancy during its first three years,[16] and to supply a housekeeper to clean flats[17] all touch and concern the demised land, as being of real value to any lessee. By contrast, a landlord's covenant to buy chattels, as opposed to fixtures at the end of the lease,[18] or to pay the tenant £500 unless the lease is renewed,[19] or to allow the tenant to display an advertising sign on other premises[20] were all classified as personal: one related to personal property, the other two did not have any direct bearing on the actual premises demised. More controversially, as showing the technical nature of the rule, it had been held that a landlord's covenant to return a deposit to the tenant at the end of the lease was personal and did not bind an assignee of the reversion,[1] whereas by contrast, a tenant's covenant to pay £40 towards redecoration on quitting ran with the land and bound his successor in title.[2]

---

11 As to which see *Goldstein v Sanders* [1915] 1 Ch 549.
12 *P & A Swift Investments v Combined English Stores Group plc* [1989] AC 632, [1988] 2 All ER 885, HL.
13 *Wedd v Porter* [1916] 2 KB 91, CA.
14 See *Horsey Estate Ltd v Steiger* [1899] 2 QB 79, CA.
15 *Campbell v Lewis* (1820) 3 B & Ald 392.
16 *Breams Property Investment Co Ltd v Stroulger* [1948] 2 KB 1, [1948] 1 All ER 758, CA.
17 *Barnes v City of London Real Property Co* [1918] 2 Ch 18.
18 *Gorton v Gregory* (1862) 3 B & S 90.
19 *Re Hunter's Lease* [1942] Ch 124, [1942] 1 All ER 27.
20 *Re No 1 Albemarle Street W1* [1959] Ch 531, [1959] 1 All ER 250.
 1 *Hua Chiao Commercial Bank v Chiaphua Industries Ltd* [1987] AC 99, [1987] 1 All ER 1110, PC; and equally curiously, a tenant's option to purchase is purely personal: *Woodall v Clifton* [1905] 2 Ch 257, as opposed to a landlord's covenant to renew, which is not: *Weg Motors Ltd v Hales* [1962] Ch 49, [1961] 3 All ER 181, CA.
 2 *Boyer v Warbey* [1953] 1 QB 234, [1953] 1 All ER 269, CA.

A covenant by a surety of the tenant to accept a new lease from the landlord if the tenant became insolvent and his lease was disclaimed ran with the leasehold estate,[3] as of obvious value to any lessor, as did, for similar reasons, a covenant tying the lessees to petrol supplies of the lessor,[4] and a covenant from a third party to guarantee the performance of the tenant's obligations,[5] but not, for example, a tenant's covenant to repair chattels (not fixtures).[6]

Enforcement by and against assignees of lease

An assignee of the lease may sue (take the benefit) or be sued (be subject to the burden) of covenants in the lease which touch and concern the land, but, an assignee is liable only for breaches of covenant committed whilst there is privity of estate between himself and the landlord.[7]

In contrast to the original lessee, therefore, an assignee of the lease is not liable to the landlord for the time being[8] for breaches committed before the assignment, unless they are continuing breaches, as with a neglect to repair.[9] Nevertheless, it appears that if an original lessee has broken his covenant to repair, and assigns to a first assignee, who re-assigns to a second person, and the breach continued throughout, the second assignee (and ultimately the original lessee) are solely liable unless there is an express contrary stipulation when the lease was re-assigned.[10]

An assignee of the lease is similarly not liable for any breaches of covenant committed by a person to whom he re-assigns the lease. This rule may be contracted out of by an express agreement, as where on taking an assignment the assignee covenants direct with the landlord to observe all the covenants in the lease and to pay the rent: in this case the assignee's liability for breaches of covenant commences with the date of the assignment and continues from then until the expiry of the term, co-extensively with the liability of the original tenant.[11] This process of direct covenanting with the landlord (sometimes imposed as a condition of the assignments) may take place each time the lease is re-assigned.

Enforcement by and against assignees of reversion

Where the original landlord assigns by deed the reversion of a lease or tenancy granted before the 1995 Act commences,[12] statute provides for the enforcement

3   *Coronation Street Industrial Properties Ltd v Ingall Industries plc* [1989] 1 All ER 979, [1989] 1 WLR 304, HL.
4   *Caerns Motor Services Ltd v Texaco Ltd* [1995] 1 All ER 247, [1994] 1 WLR 1249 – even though successors in title were not mentioned.
5   *Kumar v Dunning* [1989] QB 193, [1987] 2 All ER 801, CA.
6   *Williams v Earle* (1868) LR 3 QB 739; nor a covenant to pay rates in respect of other land: *Gower v Postmaster General* (1887) 57 LT 527.
7   *Wharfland Ltd v South London Co-operative Building Co Ltd* [1995] 2 EGLR 21.
8   As against his potential liability to indemnify the original lessee or a previous assignee under covenants of indemnity.
9   *Granada Theatres Ltd v Freehold Investment (Leytonstone) Ltd* [1959] Ch 592, [1959] 2 All ER 176.
10 *Middlegate Properties Ltd v Bilbao* (1972) 24 P & CR 329.
11 *Lyons & Co v Knowles* [1943] 1 KB 366, [1943] 1 All ER 477, CA; also *Estates Gazette Ltd v Benjamin Restaurants Ltd* [1995] 1 All ER 129, [1994] 1 WLR 1528, CA.
12 It makes no difference whether the lease itself is by deed, or informal (see *Lotteryking Ltd v Amec Properties Ltd* [1995] 2 EGLR 13) or even, it seems, oral (Law of Property Act 1925, s 154).

by and against the assignee of the freehold (or superior leasehold) reversion of the benefit and burden of the real covenants of the tenant and his assignee.[13]

Benefit of covenants   Section 141(1) of the 1925 Act (passing the benefit of landlords' covenants) provides that rent reserved by a lease, and the benefit of every covenant therein, having reference to the subject matter thereof,[14] 'shall be annexed and incident to and shall go with the reversionary estate in the land, immediately expectant on the term granted by the lease, notwithstanding severance of that reversionary estate . . .'

A legal assignee of the reversion (ie a transferee out and out of the whole of the landlord's interest) obtains by s 141(1) of the 1925 Act the right to enforce against the tenant in possession all the real covenants in the lease, to the exclusion of the original landlord. If, therefore, at the assignment date, there are outstanding and unclaimed rent arrears or damages for breaches of covenant, such as to repair, the assignee has the right to enforce these against the tenant, in addition to any further arrears or damages which may accrue during the post-assignment period.[15]

Burden of covenants   Section 142(1) of the 1925 Act (transmitting the burden of real covenants) is, in its first part, cast in similar language to s 141(1), but it further provides that the lessor's obligations 'may be taken advantage of and enforced by the person in whom the term is from time to time vested ...'

In contrast to s 141, s 142(1) of the 1925 Act does not in terms annex to the leasehold estate the right to take advantage of landlords' breaches of real covenant. It has therefore been held that an original landlord's liability for pre-assignment breaches to the tenant remains, and so a tenant of a flat, who had himself re-assigned his lease, recovered damages for breaches of a landlords' covenant to repair, from a former landlord, calculated down to the date of assignment of the reversion.[16] Equally, an assignee of the reversion who is sued for breaches of covenant to repair which continue into the post-assignment period cannot avoid liability unless he is able to show that the breach is spent.[17] The concept of a person who has assigned his whole interest continuing to be burdened by its covenants is not conducive of certainty and the Landlord and Tenant (Covenants) Act 1995 provides for a procedure for releasing original and subsequently assigning landlords in these circumstances, but only where the tenancy was granted after the commencement of the 1995 Act.

Sections 141 and 142 apply 'notwithstanding severance of that reversionary estate' (ie where a part or parts of the reversion fall into separate hands), and apportionment of the benefits and burdens is provided by s 140. A tenant who

---

13 Neither LPA, s 141 or s 142 apply to tenancies granted after the 1995 Act comes into force, unless the tenancy was granted under, in particular, a pre-commencement agreement (Landlord and Tenant (Covenants) Act 1995, s 30(4)).

14 This is the statutory expression corresponding to the common law term 'touching and concerning', and has the same narrowing object – see above.

15 *Re King* [1963] Ch 459, [1963] 1 All ER 781, CA; *A and D London and County Ltd v Wilfred Sportsman Ltd* [1971] Ch 764, [1970] 2 All ER 600, CA.

16 *City and Metropolitan Properties Ltd v Greycroft Ltd* [1987] 3 All ER 839, [1987] 1 WLR 1085.

17 See *Duncliffe v Caerfelin Properties Ltd* [1989] 2 EGLR 38.

is served with a notice to quit in relation to a part of his land (after the reversion of that part has been severed) is given the option under s 140(2) to quit the whole of the land if he so wishes, by serving a counter-notice within one month upon the reversioner in relation to the rest of the land.

Duty to notify tenants of dwellings of assignments

By s 3(1) of the Landlord and Tenant Act 1985, if the interest of the landlord of a tenancy[18] of premises consisting of or including a dwelling is assigned, the new landlord must give written notice of the assignment and of his name and address to the tenant not later than the next day on which rent is payable under the tenancy, unless that date is within two months of the assignment. In that case the period is the end of the period of two months. Failure without reasonable excuse to comply with this requirement is a criminal offence (s 3(3)).

If the above duty is broken, the old landlord remains liable, jointly and severally with the new landlord, to the tenant for any breaches of covenant until written notification is given to the tenant by the new landlord of the assignment and of the new landlord's name and address.[19]

V   ENFORCEMENT OF COVENANTS IN RELATION TO LEASES OR TENANCIES GRANTED AS FROM 1 JANUARY 1996

1   Introductory principles

The Landlord and Tenant (Covenants) Act 1995 has reformed the law relating to the enforcement of covenants in 'new' tenancies, an expression which generally means tenancies granted as from the commencement of the Act, subject to transitional rules (see s 1(6)). It will therefore be appreciated that a new tenancy granted by court order under Part II of the Landlord and Tenant Act 1954, made as from 1 January 1996, will be subject to the removal of the privity of contract liability of the tenant. The provisions of the 1995 Act cannot generally be contracted out of (s 25) although it is provided that nothing in the Act prevents a landlord or tenant from releasing the other from a liability under the tenancy (s 26(1)).

The Law Commission had recommended that the reforms in the law it advocated should take effect as from the first assignment of any lease or tenancy.[20] However, the government considered that, unless the new rules did not apply to tenancies in existence at the commencement of the Act, commercial landlords would not have supported the whole reform 'package' which the 1995 Act represents. Hence, the 1995 Act has the checks and balances referred to

---

18   By s 3(4), 'tenancy' includes a statutory tenancy. However, the duty to notify does not apply to tenancies to which Part II of the Landlord and Tenant Act 1954 applies (s 32(1)).

19   Landlord and Tenant Act 1985, s 3(3A) and (3B), which continue to apply to any tenancy granted as from the commencement of the 1995 Act: Landlord and Tenant (Covenants) Act 1995, s 26(2).

20   *Report*, para 4.59. For a review of these recommendations and of the 1995 Act, see Davey (1996) 59 MLR 1; also Bridge (1996) CLJ 313; Walter [1996] Conv 432.

earlier in this chapter. In particular, the amendments by s 22 to s 19(1) of the Landlord and Tenant Act 1927 (discussed further in chapter 7 of this book) have the general result of enabling the landlord of a commercial tenant to require, as a condition of an assignment of his tenancy, that he enters into an agreement with the landlord, which guarantees the performance of his obligations by the person to whom the tenant has assigned the lease. A refusal of consent to an assignment subject to a guarantee condition of this kind would not be unreasonable merely because the condition had been agreed or envisaged in advance by the parties at the date of grant of the lease.

Nonetheless, the refusal of Parliament to extend the benefit of the abrogation of the 'privity of contract' rule to tenancies granted before the 1995 Act but continuing after then may lame, and partly delay, the effectiveness of the reform and will in any case create two classes of tenancy, subject to different sets of general enforcement rules, a reformed and an unreformed set (subject to the three mitigations already mentioned). Thus, although the long-term result may be to simplify the law, the short-term consequence of these reforms may well be to render it still more complex.

The 1995 Act supersedes the terminology and some of the principles of the common law, in the interests of promoting simplicity. Hence, by s 2(1), it applies to a 'landlord covenant' or a 'tenant covenant' of a 'tenancy':[1]

(a) 'whether or not the covenant has reference to the subject-matter of the tenancy'; and
(b) 'whether or not the covenant is express, implied or imposed by law'.

It will be seen that paragraph (a) supercedes the requirement that, to be enforceable as against assignees of the lease or the reversion, the covenant must touch and concern the land, because personal and real covenants of a tenancy are alike capable of being enforced. To that extent, s 2(1)(a) of the 1995 Act implements the view of the Law Commission. It said that all the terms of a lease should be regarded as a single bargain for letting the property. When the interest of one of the parties changes hands, the successor, they believed, should take his predecessor's place as landlord or tenant, without distinguishing between different categories of covenant.[2] Thus, the aim of simplification of the law is followed by s 2(1), as well as the related aim of certainty: the Law Commission considered that parties to a tenancy should know the extent of their obligations with certainty.[3]

2 NEW RULES AS TO THE TRANSMISSION OF LEASEHOLD COVENANTS

Introduction

The new rules which govern the transmission of leasehold covenants, have, it is hoped, simplified, the relevant principles. As already noted, the rules apply

---

1 'Tenancy' is widely defined so as to mean 'any lease or other tenancy' and includes both a sub-lease and an agreement for a lease but not a mortgage term (s 28(1)).
2 Law Com No 174 (1988), para 4.1.
3 *Report*, supra, para 4.46.

to legal and equitable leases without differentiation, as well as to sub-leases (s 28(1) of the 1995 Act). Thus, any technical difficulties which might have stood in the way of enforcing the benefit and burden of leasehold covenants by and against informal lessees have been removed. The 1995 Act abolishes the privity of contract liability of an original tenant so that, once he has voluntarily assigned a tenancy, he ceases to be bound by its covenants (s 5). He also loses any right to enforce future performance of the covenants of the tenancy against the landlord. After he has assigned the reversion, the landlord is not automatically freed from the burden of his covenants, but may seek a release from them following a special notice procedure.

With the abolition of the doctrine of privity of estate, other technical difficulties cease to apply. As a result of s 15(1) of the 1995 Act, both the freehold reversioner and the immediate landlord entitled to the rents and profits under the tenancy, if different, as well as a mortgagee[4] in possession of the reversion of the premises, may enforce the covenants of the tenant for the time being. Likewise, where any 'tenant covenant' is enforceable against the reversioner, it is expressly provided (s 15(2)) that it may be enforced against any immediate landlord entitled to the rents and profits of the premises and a mortgagee of the reversion.[5]

A new code

1   *Policy of rules*   The governing provision, s 3 of the 1995 Act, is seemingly designed to ensure that the recommendations of the Law Commission are properly integrated into the law of covenants.[6] Section 3 re-states and, it was claimed, clarifies for new tenancies the old rules for the transmission of the benefit and burden of leasehold covenants in a simple statutory code.[7] As already observed, the Law Commission had recommended that, in particular, the ancient distinction between personal covenants, which could not be enforced against any successor in title to the lease or reversion, and covenants touching and concerning land, which were capable of enforcement against third party assignees despite the lack of privity of contract between them, should disappear. The covenants in a 'new tenancy' (one granted as from 1 January 1996) will form the whole bargain between the parties for the time being to that tenancy, unless subsequently varied, binding on the current holders of the lease and reversion and mutually enforceable by them, however the obligations might previously have been classified. However, owing to s 3(6)(a), covenants which are expressed to be personal to a party will not be enforceable under the

---

4   Including chargee (but not, seemingly, a mortgagee) by deposit of documents, which category has seemingly been abolished by the Law of Property (Miscellaneous Provisions) Act 1989, s 2: *United Bank of Kuwait v Sahib* [1996] 3 All ER 215, CA.

5   Similar rules apply to a tenant's mortgagee, both as respects the ability to enforce and be bound by the tenant covenants of the tenancy (s 15(3) & (4)).

6   HL Committee on Landlord and Tenant (Covenants) Bill, 21 June 1995, col 355, (Lord Chancellor).

7   The aim of simplification is taken to the length of making sure that the technical distinction between things in esse and in posse has been finally laid to rest (1995 Act, s 3(7)), as well as by the prospective repeal of ss 78 and 79 of the Law of Property Act 1925.

1995 Act against any other person – so that it will still be possible for landlords to grant personal licences to tenants to use premises in a way not allowed by the lease.

2 *Annexation of benefit and burden* By s 3(1) of the 1995 Act:

'the benefit and burden of all landlord and tenant covenants of a tenancy:
(a) shall be annexed and incident to the whole, and to each and every part, of the premises demised by the tenancy and of the reversion in them, and
(b) shall in accordance with this section pass on an assignment of the whole or any part of those premises or of the reversion in them.'

There is no differentiation in this provision between positive and negative covenants, and so a single set of enforcement rules applies to both. It is indeed provided in connection with restrictive covenants which are contained in a tenancy or which the landlord has entered into that, as well as being capable of enforcement against an assignee, such covenants shall 'be capable of being enforced against any other person who is the owner of occupier of any demised premises to which the covenant relates, even though there is no express provision in the tenancy to that effect' (s 3(5)). Therefore, where a sub-lessee occupies land which is subject to a restrictive covenant, he is bound by this provision to observe it, if enforceable, under the 1995 Act, even if his or a head tenancy is silent as to the covenant.

It will be seen also that s 3(1) draws no distinction between covenants which touch and concern the land and those which do not, so obviating the need to differentiate between purely personal covenants and those which affected the parties in their capacity as landlord and tenant. Nor does s 3 as a whole draw any distinction between rent and other covenants of a lease which might be enforceable by a landlord,[8] in contrast to the opening words of s 141(1) of the Law of Property Act 1925.[9] The 1995 Act, following the aim of promoting simplicity in this part of the law, makes no terminological distinction between the general rules governing the enforcement of landlord or tenant covenants. These are now in a single statutory code, in contrast to the previous rules, which are contained in statute for landlord and the common law for tenants.

The reference of s 3(1)(a) to 'shall be annexed and incident to the whole, and to each and every part...' is seemingly akin to the words of s 141(1) of the 1925 Act 'shall be annexed and incident to...' and the aim seems the same: to ensure that, on an assignment of the reversion or the tenancy, the full benefit and burden of the tenant covenants passes to the assignee, to the exclusion of the assignor. The words of s 3(1)(b) of the 1995 Act 'shall in accordance with this section pass on an assignment...' emphasise that the transmission of the benefit and burden of leasehold covenants is automatic, without the need for any special or additional words in the instrument by which the assignment is carried out.

---

8 Specific provision is made for the statutory transmission on assignment of the whole or any part of the reversion of the benefit of a landlord's right of re-entry in s 4.
9 Which is disapplied to new tenancies (s 30(4)).

3   *Assignment by Tenant*   It is provided by s 3(2) that

'where the assignment[10] is made by the tenant under the tenancy, then as from the assignment the assignee:
(a) becomes bound by the tenant covenants of the tenancy except to the extent that:
(i)   immediately before the assignment they do not bind the assignor, or
(ii) they fell to be complied with in relation to any demised premises not comprised in the assignment.'

A tenant covenant would not bind the assignor immediately before the assignment if it has been released or waived by the landlord, unless the release or waiver has been expressed to be personal to the tenant (as envisaged by s 3(4)) – there is thus a presumption that any waiver or release will not be personal.

By way of mirror provision, by s 3(2)(b), as from the assignment, the assignee 'becomes entitled to the benefit of the landlord covenants of the tenancy' subject to the same qualification as in s 3(2)(a)(ii) above. The same rules as to the taking of the benefit of landlord covenants and the subjection to the burden of tenant covenants applies where the landlord assigns the reversion to an assignee (s 3(3)). However, if a covenant requires registration so as to render it enforceable against any third party assignee, the transmission rules of the 1995 Act do not obviate the need for such registration (s 3(6)) whether under the Land Registration Act 1925 or the Land Charges Act 1972, depending on whether the title to the burdened land is registered or unregistered.

3   ABROGATION OF THE PRIVITY OF CONTRACT LIABILITY

Introduction

The Law Commission's examination of the law in 1988 caused them to make a central recommendation. This was that 'when a tenant assigns the whole of the property demised by a lease ... his responsibility to comply with the covenants in the lease after the assignment should cease'. He should also cease to derive any benefit from the landlord covenants of the tenancy.[11] The Commission based their conclusion, in part, on considerations of equity in the general sense. 'It is intrinsically unfair that anyone should bear burdens under a contract in respect of which they derive no benefit and over which they have no control'.[12] In the earlier part of this chapter, reference was made to some of the apparently harsh results which the invocation of the privity of contract liability had recently produced.

Section 5 of the Landlord and Tenant (Covenants) Act 1995, which abrogates the privity of contract rule, so that the original tenant and any person to whom he assigns the lease are liable, in principle, to perform tenant

10 An assignment of a tenancy is subject to the common law rules governing formal validity.
11 Law Com No 174 *Privity of Contract and Estate* (1988), para 4.9.
12 *Report*, para 3.1.

covenants only during the period they hold the tenancy, provided it was granted as from 1 January 1996, must be seen against certain matters within the legislative reforms taken as a whole.

(a) The landlord may be able to obtain from an assigning tenant a guarantee agreement within s 16, that his immediate assignee will perform the covenants of the tenancy. A difficulty may arise should the landlord insist that a surety or guarantor of the original tenant guarantees his performance of an authorised guarantee agreement. Such a requirement might perhaps contravene the contracting out provision (s 25) of the 1995 Act. Equally, it is arguable that such an agreement is not a covenant, and that, applying s 24(2), any release of a tenant's guarantor is only co-extensive with that of the tenant himself, so that nothing in the 1995 Act precludes the landlord from acting in this way against a guarantor.[13]

(b) In connection with consents, the landlord of a commercial tenant (but not of a residential tenant) may make use of s 19(1A) of the Landlord and Tenant Act 1927[14] so that, if the parties to the tenancy, at the time of the grant, or at the date of the assignment, so agree, consent may be given subject to a condition that the assigning tenant enters into an authorised guarantee agreement under the 1995 Act. Whereas at common law, an attempt in advance to lay down what conditions were to be deemed reasonable might have been risky, as the courts preserved the power to declare any condition unreasonably imposed, it is now intended by these amendments to avoid this particular ground for challenging guarantee conditions.

(c) If part only of the demised premises is assigned, the liability of the former tenant of part may continue over the whole, where it is not possible to attribute a covenant to the part assigned.

(d) The abrogation of the privity of contract liability of a tenant applies only where the assignment was voluntary as opposed to by operation of law. Assignments in bankruptcy or insolvency or which are in breach of covenant are excluded assignments (s 11(1)). The essential rule in these cases is that the assignor tenant continues to be liable for post-assignment breaches of covenant. Only if at a subsequent stage the tenancy is voluntarily re-assigned does this continuing liability of the tenant come to an end (s 11(2) and (3)).

(e) The effect of s 5 of the 1995 Act is that not only an original tenant, but also, provided a purposive and not a literal interpretation is applied to the words of s 5(1) (see further below) any subsequent assignee voluntarily re-assigning the tenancy will be automatically free from the burden of tenant covenants. Neither will he after assignment be any longer able to claim the benefit of landlord covenants. In the case of assignees who re-assign, the 1995 Act is consistent with the previous common law and may operate more strictly. This is because an assignee may have to undertake to guarantee the

---

13 The opposing arguments are set out by Potter & Collins, Estates Gazette, 11 May 1996, p 118 and JE Adams, ibid, 10 August 1996, p 68.
14 Inserted by 1995 Act, s 22.

performance of the obligations of the person to whom he re-assigns, owing to the operation of a condition as pre-arranged in the circumstances laid down by s 19(1A) of the 1927 Act.

Tenants' statutory release

1   *General rule*   It is provided that where a tenant[15] voluntarily assigns the premises demised to him under a tenancy, then:

(a) if he assigns the whole of the premises demised to him under a tenancy, he is released, as from the assignment, by the 1995 Act, from the tenant covenants of the tenancy (s 5(2)(a)); and

(b) he ceases, as from the assignment, to be entitled to the benefit of the landlord covenants of the tenancy (s 5(2)(b)).

In this way, the privity of contract rule is rendered inapplicable, although the original tenant, or any of his assignees who re-assigns the tenancy,[16] cannot use his automatic statutory release as a defence to an action for any breaches of covenant occurring before the release (s 24(1)). The Act takes effect automatically, and as from the assignment date the assignee is solely liable to perform leasehold covenants. In addition, where an assigning tenant is released, then to the same extent any other person, such as a surety or guarantor of his, is automatically released as from the date of the tenant's release (s 24(2)).

Owing to this reform, the need for any implied indemnity covenants from an assignee was removed and the relevant provisions of the Law of Property Act 1925 do not apply to a tenancy entered into on as from the commencement of the 1995 Act.[17] There are elaborate provisions designed to prevent landlords inserting provisions in the tenancy to circumvent the effect of the statutory release from performance of tenant covenants (s 25) – such as by disguised or overt forfeiture or termination or surrender-back clauses. The right of the parties to tenancies granted at any date expressly to release a landlord or tenant from the covenants of the tenancy is preserved (s 26(1)). Special provision was thought necessary where a management company, with no legal estate vested in it in the premises, enters into 'landlord covenants' such as to keep in repair and maintain the premises, and the tenant assigns the lease. By s 12 of the 1995 Act, the benefit of the landlord covenants passes to the assignee tenant, and so does the burden of tenant covenants such as to pay rent and service charges.

2   *Assignment of part of premises*   Where, however, part only of the premises is assigned, the releases mentioned earlier operate only to the extent that the covenant in question falls to be complied with in relation to that part of the

15   Who need not necessarily be a tenant of the whole premises, as where he holds a sub-lease of part (s 5(4)).

16   An argument that an assignee of the original tenant who re-assigns a new lease cannot claim the benefit of an automatic release under s 5(1) because of the statutory reference to premises 'demised to him' is dismissed by Fogel, Estates Gazette 10 August 1996, p 64, as manifestly absurd; but the material words of s 5(1) could be literally interpreted as confined to the original lessee and an assignee has no premises assigned, but only vested in him.

17   Landlord and Tenant (Covenants) Act 1995, ss 14 and 30(2).

demised premises (s 5(3)). Thus, subject to what follows, certain covenants may be attributed to part only of the premises, as with a lease of a shop and rooms above, and the tenant assigns the shop and retains the living accommodation, and the lease has separate user covenants for the shop and the living accommodation.[18] In such a case, the tenant would be released by s 5 from future observance of the user covenants in relation to the shop, which the landlord would have to enforce against the assignee, but not in relation to the living accommodation.

Some covenants cannot be attributed to any part of the premises, since they relate to the whole premises – such as covenants to pay rent, to decorate or to insure, or to give the tenant facilities separate from the demised premises. Where this is so, after the assignment, both the assigning tenant and his assignee are liable jointly and severally to the landlord for the performance of these covenants (1995 Act s 13(1)). However, the tenant and assignee may agree to an apportionment of liability. This agreement may exonerate one party, presumably the assignor-tenant, from all liability under the covenant specified in the agreement (s 9(1) and (3)).[19] The parties may apply for the apportionment agreement to be binding on, for example, a landlord of the whole premises, following a prescribed form notice procedure (ss 10 and 27(1)).

Landlords' statutory release mechanism

1 *Principles of the reform* The landlord may seek a release from the burden of his covenants as at the date when he assigns the reversion in the whole premises; but if he does not, he remains liable, in contrast to an assigning tenant, for performance of the 'landlord covenants' of the tenancy, and entitled to the benefit of the tenant covenants, until the end of the lease. He is however entitled to seek a release under s 7 of the 1995 Act either at the date he assigns the reversion or at any subsequent re-assignment of it by a successor in title.

The Law Commission did not regard landlords as in quite the same position to former tenants. They firstly used empirical arguments. There was 'less need for radical change' since 'in most leases, the landlord undertakes far fewer obligations then the tenant and landlords may not be troubled by the prospect of continuing liability'.[20] They also resorted to the dangers of abuse: 'the landlord's liability would not be limited', they said, 'until the date of the next assignment'. This was necessary 'to avoid landlords arranging to escape liability by the stratagem of assigning first to a nominee who very shortly afterwards assigns the property again'.[1] The Commission pointed out that this escape route was not open, by contrast, to a tenant who had to obtain the consent of the landlord to each assignment. However, the Commission accepted that, because the notice procedure proposed by them and adopted in the 1995 Act is voluntary, some landlords would continue to be liable to observe landlord covenants and others would not, and that where liability continued,

---

18 Example of the Law Commission (*Report*, supra, para 4.32).
19 A similar principle applies where a landlord assigns the reversion in part only of the premises (s 9(2)).
20 *Report*, para 4.16.
1 *Report*, para 4.23.

it would be a full and not a guaranteeing liability. This latter principle was justified on the ground that a tenant cannot control the way the reversion is assigned, in contrast to landlords, who are able to do so by disposition covenants.[2]

2 *Statutory notice procedure* The procedure by which an assigning landlord may seek a release from the landlord covenants of the tenancy follows the recommendations of the Law Commission. By s 6 of the 1995 Act, a landlord who assigns the reversion of premises[3] of which he is the landlord under the tenancy is given the right to seek a release by notice from the landlord covenants of the tenancy. Any eventual release does not affect the liability of any person jointly and severally liable with the landlord (s 13(2)).

Thus, if the landlord has assigned the reversion in the whole of the premises of which he is landlord, the notice releases him from all of the landlord covenants. He ceases to be entitled to the benefit of any tenant covenants, as from the assignment date (s 6(2)). Where the landlord assigns the reversion of part only of the premises, he may apply to be similarly released from the landlord covenants of the tenancy 'to the extent that they fall to be complied with in relation to that part of the premises' (s 6(3)(a)). As envisaged by the Law Commission, a landlord who does not at any time utilise the release procedure remains jointly and severally liable to the tenant for the observance of landlord covenants with his successor in title (s 13(1)), unless he is able to procure a release under s 7 of the Act.

3 *Contents of notice* Since the notice is regarded as an important document, it must be in a prescribed form (s 27(1)), as envisaged by the Law Commission.[4] The notice must therefore give full information to the tenant, on whom it is served, notably that he must be informed that any objections to the proposed release must be made by written notice served within four weeks of the service of the main notice (s 27(2)). Section 8 of the 1995 Act, which governs landlords' release notices, requires that the notice must be served before the assignment or within four weeks beginning with the date of the assignment (s 8(1)). So, the tenant is informed of the assignment and the notice requests a release of the covenants. If no objection is made, s 8(2) releases a covenant to the extent mentioned in the notice. Any release relates back to the date of the assignment (s 8(3)).[5] The tenant has the absolute right to serve a written notice (which does not have to be in a prescribed form) on the landlord objecting to the release. It must be served within four weeks of the date of service of the landlord's notice (s 8(2)(a)). Despite having served such a counter-notice, the tenant may by a

2 *Report,* para 4.25. This type of argument was accepted during the passage of the Bill: *Hansard* HC (Lords' Amendments)Vol 263 col 1240. Hence also the joint and several liability of different landlords as provided for by s 13 of the 1995 Act.
3 Irrespective of whether the landlord is landlord of the whole premises or part only (s 6(4)).
4 *Report,* para 4.18. The form is in Landlord and Tenant (Covenants) Act 1995 (Notices) Regulations 1995, SI 1995/2964, Form No 3.
5 Thus where a former landlord applies for a release, as where L assigned to R and R wishes to re-assign, L cannot escape liability for breaches of landlord covenants down to the date of any re-assignment.

further notice consent to the release.[6] The landlord may, after receiving a tenant's notice of objection, apply to the county court and it may declare that it is reasonable for the landlord to be released (s 8(2)(b)).[7]

4   AUTHORISED GUARANTEE AGREEMENTS BY ASSIGNING TENANTS

It has already been observed that the abrogation of the privity of contract liability of an original tenant is not absolute, owing to the power of landlords to require the tenant to enter into a guarantee of the performance of the person to whom the lease has been assigned. In such a case, the original (or any later assigning tenant) remains secondarily liable to perform tenant covenants until the lease has been re-assigned.

1   *Policy of the guarantee principle*   The Law Commission recognised that there might, especially in the commercial field, be cases where the landlord was anxious to have the assurance of a continuing guarantee from his tenant and where it was objectively reasonable for him to do so.[8] Such a guarantee should be capable of being required only where the lease required the consent of the landlord to any assignment – so that where the lease had been granted for a long period at a low rent and at a premium, and the tenant was free to assign without restriction, no guarantee could be required from him. The Commission therefore recommended that 'a landlord whose consent has to be obtained should be able to impose a condition that the assignor guarantees the assignee's performance of the lease covenants'.[9] The continuing liability would last until the next assignment, whereupon it would come to an end. The assigning tenant had some control over the identity and attributes of his immediate assignee, but not over those of any subsequent assignee, and this realistic limit to the guarantee principle may make its adoption, with some modifications,[10] by the 1995 Act more palatable to tenants while conferring some compensation to landlords for the abrogation of the privity of contract rule itself. However, it should be borne in mind, having regard to s 16, that if the immediate assignee is released from his obligations, so is the tenant-guarantor, as he would be by a material change in the obligations of the lease which was made without his consent.[11]

2   *Authorised guarantee agreements*   Where on an assignment, the original or any subsequent tenant by assignment is released by the 1995 Act from a tenant

---

6   His consent notice must in terms state that any objection notice has been withdrawn; if not, presumably, the objection notice stands (s 8(2)(c)).

7   No guidance appears either in the Act or in the Law Commission's report, supra, as to what criteria are to be used in deciding on such reasonabless and so the issue seems to be entirely discretionary.

8   *Report*, para 4.10.

9   *Report* para 4.11.

10   Notably the enactment of s 19(1A) of the Landlord and Tenant Act 1927 by s 22 of the 1995 Act, as explained below and in ch 7.

11   *Report*, para 4.11: 'this should avoid a former tenant finding himself responsible for obligations much more onerous than those he originally assumed'.

covenant, the tenant may validly enter into an 'authorised guarantee agreement' with respect to the performance of that covenant by the assignee (1995 Act, s 16(1)). Under such an agreement the tenant must guarantee the performance of the relevant covenant to any extent by the assignee (s 16(2)(a)). Thus, a guarantee might extend only to the rent payable or it might extend to all the tenant covenants. Three conditions must be satisfied before an agreement amounts to an authorised guarantee agreement (s 16(3)):

(a) by virtue of a covenant against assignment, the assignment cannot be effected without the consent of the immediate landlord ('the landlord under the tenancy') or some other person;[12]
(b) any consent is given subject to a lawfully imposed condition that the tenant is to enter into an agreement guaranteeing the performance of the covenant by the assignee; and
(c) the agreement is entered into by the tenant under that condition.

The condition referred to in paragraph (b) may include a condition which has been agreed in advance, at the time the lease was granted, under which, if the lease is assigned by the tenant, the landlord, as a condition of the assignment, may require the assigning tenant to enter into an authorised guarantee agreement.[13] Whether a condition of this sort is reasonable may be judged in accordance with the general law as discussed in chapter 7. It may be that some landlords wish to impose an automatic requirement, in new business leases, that the assignor-tenant enters into a guarantee agreement, tempered by an undertaking that, if the assignee satisfies financial criteria, such a requirement would be released.[14] Whether such a practice would undermine the fundamental principle of the 1995 Act, which is to do away with the post-assignment liability of lessees, is open to question.

There are certain safeguards within the 1995 Act for assigning tenants, at the price of additional complexity in the law. A guarantee agreement cannot validly require the tenant to guarantee in any way the performance of the covenant concerned by any person other than the immediate assignee (s 16(4)(a)). It cannot impose on the tenant 'any liability, restriction or other requirement (of whatever nature)' in relation to any time after the assignee is released from the covenant under the Act on re-assignment or otherwise (s 16(4)(b)). This is not to prevent the landlord from obtaining a further guarantee agreement from such assignee on the re-assignment of the lease.

On the other hand, it is provided that a guarantee agreement may impose liabilities on the tenant as sole or principal debtor in respect of the assignee's obligations (s 16(5)(a)) but his obligations must be no more onerous than if he were liable as sole or principal debtor (s 16(5)(b)), so, arguably, precluding a landlord from claiming an additional rent, agreed or determined with an

---

12 Whether the prohibition on assignment is absolute or qualified.
13 Thanks to s 19(1A) of the Landlord and Tenant Act 1927, inserted by s 22 of the 1995 Act, such a condition will not, ipso facto, be unreasonable merely because it is envisaged by the parties' agreement as reasonable.
14 See Fogel, Estates Gazette 10 August 1996, p 64; cf Acheson, Estates Gazette 18 January 1997, p 132.

assignee, as after a rent review, from the assignor-tenant in default. He may be required by the agreement, as where an assignee goes bankrupt or becomes insolvent and there is a disclaimer of the lease, to enter into a new tenancy of the premises whose term expires no later than the term of the tenancy assigned, with tenant covenants no more onerous than those of the tenancy (s 16(5)(c)). The object of this latter provision seems to be to protect the landlord against a tenant who has assigned to a weak assignee and visiting the consequences on the landlord. In order further to protect landlords in bankruptcy or insolvency cases and where an assignment is made in breach of covenant, it is provided that on the occasion of the first voluntary assignment after the involuntary assignment, when the former tenant will be released, he may at that stage be required by the landlord to guarantee the performance of the current assignee of his covenants (s 16(6)(a)).[15]

Since a tenant who assigns the lease and guarantees the performance of his immediate assignee is vulnerable to re-imburse sums not paid to the landlord by the assignee or to pay him damages on account of the latter's breach of covenant, he is entitled, if his liability materialises, to demand an overriding lease from the landlord (s 19) as discussed earlier. In addition, he is entitled to a six-month warning notice of intention to recover fixed charges and to the other safeguards already discussed.

15   This applies even though the assignor may have entered into a guarantee agreement with the landlord.

Chapter 6

Implied covenants

I AMBIT OF IMPLIED COVENANTS

In this chapter, we examine implied covenants (except those respecting repairs) and notably, two covenants which have long been implied by the common law in order to make a lease work. These are a covenant for quiet enjoyment and against derogation from grant. Without these covenants, the tenant would have no protection against his possession and enjoyment being terminated or seriously interfered with by the landlord. They are narrow in scope. If a tenant wishes to obtain additional protection, notably in relation to privacy or amenities, he must obtain an express covenant in the lease. Before discussing the scope of these and other implied covenants, it is convenient to examine the general basis on which covenants may be implied into leases.

The courts are prepared to imply covenants into a lease which contains no express provisions in relation to a matter only if business efficacy requires this. In the present context, the test involves asking whether the lease would be unworkable without the implication of the term contended for. Hence, where leases of flats would have been useless without implied covenants granting access to the flats via stairs, such rights were implied into leases which did not expressly confer them.[1] A covenant may also be implied so as to correlate to an obligation imposed by an express term in the lease: for example, where the tenant undertook to pay charges in respect of a particular service (provision of a housekeeper), it was held that the landlord would be under an implied obligation to provide the service,[2] or, where the tenant was under an express obligation to repair the interior of a house, the landlord was held to be under a correlative implied obligation to repair the exterior.[3]

However, the courts decline to imply covenants into a lease merely in order to fill gaps left by the parties, or even to remedy defects in a lease.[4] Since statute, as in the case of long leases of residential flats, provides a remedy (the appointment of a manager) in support of the landlord's repairing obligations, this was itself held a ground for refusing to imply a term that, if a landlords'

---

1 *Liverpool City Council v Irwin* [1977] AC 239, [1976] 2 All ER 39, HL.
2 *Barnes v City of London Real Property Co* [1918] 2 Ch 18.
3 *Barrett v Lounova (1982) Ltd* [1990] 1 QB 348, [1989] 3 All ER 351, CA; and cf also *Edmonton Corpn v WM Knowles & Son Ltd* (1961) 60 LGR 124.
4 There is, however, power in the county court to vary the service charges provisions of long leases of flats (Landlord and Tenant Act 1987, Part IV, discussed in ch 20).

managing company defaulted, the landlord had an option to remedy the matter.[5] The fact that it might reduce a tenant's costs to imply a term into a lease is not, of itself, sufficient to satisfy the test of business efficacy, so that no term was implied into a lease that the landlord would arrange insurance of the premises at the lowest possible cost to the tenant.[6]

If a lease contains an express covenant in any form which covers the same subject-matter as that sought to be dealt with by an implied covenant, the express covenant will rule out any implied covenant in the same matter.[7] Thus an express covenant for quiet enjoyment rules out the (often wider) implied covenant for quiet enjoyment.

A IMPLIED COVENANTS BY THE LANDLORD

II QUIET ENJOYMENT

Scope of covenant

An implied covenant by the landlord for quiet enjoyment arises from the relationship of landlord and tenant, however created, whether by deed, in writing, or by parol.[8] It entitles the tenant to be put into possession.[9] The landlord covenants that he has title at the commencement of the tenancy. The covenant extends to unlawful acts of the landlord and to lawful acts of other persons claiming under the landlord by way of entry, eviction, or interruption of the tenant's peaceful enjoyment of the land during the tenancy. It protects the tenant from acts which cause *physical* interference, whether those acts are done on the premises or not and from any conduct of the landlord or his agent interfering with the tenant's freedom of action in exercising his rights as tenant.[10] It affords him no remedy in respect of acoustic or visual interference. Hence, noise from machinery in the same building as an hotel has been held not to be a breach of the covenant,[11] but where noise, dust and dirt from building operations on adjacent premises were so intolerable as to render the tenant's premises uninhabitable, it may be otherwise.[12]

The covenant is narrow in scope. It protects ordinary reasonable use of the premises by the tenant, and not the latter's privacy or amenities. It cannot be implied that, where a landlord grants a lease, he undertakes restrictive obligations as to his use of neighbouring or adjoining land which he may retain: the lessee

---

5 *Hafton Properties Ltd v Camp* [1994] 1 EGLR 67.
6 *Havenridge Ltd v Boston Dyers Ltd* [1994] 2 EGLR 73, CA.
7 *Duke of Westminster v Guild* [1985] QB 688, [1984] 3 All ER 144, CA; *Hafton Properties Ltd v Camp*, supra.
8 *Kenny v Preen* [1963] 1 QB 499, [1962] 3 All ER 814, CA.
9 *Miller v Emcer Products Ltd* [1956] Ch 304, [1956] 1 All ER 237.
10 *McCall v Abeless* [1976] 1 All ER 727 at 730-731, CA; *Kenny v Preen* [1962] 3 All ER 814 at 820, CA.
11 *Kelly v Battershell* [1949] 2 All ER 830, CA.
12 *Matania v National Provincial Bank Ltd* [1936] 2 All ER 633, CA; also *Mira v Alymer Square Investments Ltd* [1990] 1 EGLR 45, CA.

may, if he can, obtain an express covenant to give him any further protection he seeks.[13] Where, therefore, the landlord erected an iron external staircase which passed the tenant's bedroom window, destroying her privacy, she had no claim under the covenant.[14] On the other hand, where the entrance to the tenant's shop was barred by scaffolding erected by the landlord, damages were recovered for loss of custom.[15] There had been a direct physical interference which had damaged the tenant's trade.

Harassment of a tenant may constitute a breach of the present covenant, as where the landlord sent his tenant threatening letters and otherwise intimidated her by banging on the door and shouting abuse.[16] Landlords who cut off gas and electricity supplies,[17] or who entered the premises and removed the doors and windows[18] had both broken this covenant. Their conduct had rendered it impossible for the tenant to enjoy the possession of the premises granted them and so it was not necessary for the tenant to prove that the landlord had in fact offered violence to the tenant. This type of conduct might now give rise to liability under statute (Housing Act 1988, s 27). Exemplary damages apart, the statutory method of computation of damages may be more generous to tenants than the common law. To that extent, the statutory scheme to deter harassment may in time supercede that of the common law.

Narrowness of obligation

The minimal nature of the protection offered by an implied covenant for quiet enjoyment is illustrated by the following points.

1   The covenant extends only to the acts of the landlord and those claiming under him. It does not extend to disturbance by title paramount, as where a sub-tenant finds that he is subject to a restrictive covenant in the head lease.[19] Therefore where an injunction was granted to flat tenants, to restrain another tenant, under a later lease, from building a carwash which would contravene a right of way granted by the present freeholder's predecessor in title to the flat tenants, it was held that the covenant for quiet enjoyment did not cover rights or interests granted by a predecessor in title of the current landlord.[20]

2   The implied covenant terminates with the landlord's interest, so that where a tenant with eight and half years to run under his own lease, mistakenly granted a sub-lease for ten and a half years, the sub-tenant had no remedy when evicted by the superior landlord at the end of the eight and a half years.[1] On the other hand, the covenant includes an obligation to put the

---

13   *Browne* v *Flower* [1911] 1 Ch 219, 226–227; also *Romulus Trading* v *Comet Properties* [1996] 48 EG 157.
14   *Browne* v *Flower* supra.
15   *Owen* v *Gadd* [1956] 2 QB 99, [1956] 2 All ER 28, CA.
16   *Kenny* v *Preen* [1963] 1 QB 499, [1962] 3 All ER 814, CA.
17   *Perera* v *Vandiyar* [1953] 1 All ER 1109, [1953] 1 WLR 672, CA.
18   *Lavender* v *Betts* [1942] 2 All ER 72.
19   *Jones* v *Lavington* [1903] 1 KB 253, CA.
20   *Celsteel Ltd* v *Alton House Holdings Ltd (No 2)* [1987] 2 All ER 240, [1987] 1 WLR 291, CA (express covenant).
1   *Baynes & Co* v *Lloyd & Sons* [1895] 1 QB 820.

tenant into possession so that if the previous tenant wrongfully holds over, the new tenant may sue the landlord.[2]

3 While an implied covenant for quiet enjoyment covers all unlawful acts of the landlord on the premises, acts done pursuant to rights under the lease itself cannot constitute a breach of covenant, such as re-entry for breach of covenant or condition or entry to inspect the condition of the premises under a right expressly or statutorily conferred. On the other hand if the landlord lets adjoining premises, such as a flat above, for a purpose, and it is in such a state that no matter how it is used, it will interfere with the reasonable enjoyment of the tenant's adjoining premises below, the landlord will be in breach of covenant.[3]

4 The covenant extends to acts of the landlord (or a person claiming under him) on adjoining, or adjacent land or premises which cause some physical interference with the ordinary enjoyment of the tenant, unless some special purpose of the tenant, which is interfered with, is known to the landlord: if at the date of the demise it is, he will also be liable. Hence, a landlord was liable for interference with a tenant's access to the demised premises.[4] By contrast, where a landlord used a cellar, retained by him, in connection with his trade, and damaged special paper stored by the tenant in his tenanted warehouse above, the tenant had no cause of action as the landlord could not be assumed to have known, when the lease was granted, of the tenant's special purposes.[5]

5 An implied covenant for quiet enjoyment extends to lawful acts of other tenants of the same landlord (ie acts which they may undertake under their own leases) – as with mining operations by a tenant causing the land under another lessee's house to subside.[6] The acts of these tenants must be 'lawful' in the sense explained and the landlord is not liable if the offending tenant exceeds any limits imposed by his lease. So, where the defendants let farms to A, B and C, and A suffered damage from the flooding of drains on B and C's land, the landlords were held liable only for C's proper use of defective drains, but not for B's excessive ('unlawful') use of drains which were in good order.[7]

Damages

The measure of damages for breach is the loss to the tenant resulting from it.[8] This includes removal expenses, damages for inconvenience and shock where appropriate, and legal costs.[9] If all that the tenant is able to prove is trespass, he cannot recover for loss of profits under a separate head.[10] A lessee of a flat who

2 *Miller v Emcer Products Ltd* [1956] Ch 304, [1956] 1 All ER 237, CA.
3 *Sampson v Hodson-Pressinger* [1981] 3 All ER 710, CA.
4 *Hilton v James Smith & Sons (Norwood) Ltd* [1979] 2 EGLR 44, CA.
5 *Robinson v Kilvert* (1889) 41 Ch D 88, CA.
6 *Markham v Paget* [1908] 1 Ch 697.
7 *Sanderson v Berwick-upon-Tweed Corpn* (1884) 13 QBD 547, CA.
8 *Sutton v Baillie* (1891) 65 LT 528.
9 *Grosvenor Hotel Co v Hamilton* [1894] 2 QB 836, CA; *Giles v Adley* [1987] CLY 2121.
10 *Lawson v Hartley-Brown* (1995) 71 P & CR 242, CA (where on account of trespass one and a half years' rent was awarded for loss of trade).

could not let it due to substantial interference caused by the landlord in the course of work to other parts of the premises, was able to recover loss of estimated rental income.[11]

If the landlord commits a tort, such as trespass or nuisance, then an additional separate claim may be framed by the tenant in tort.[12] If the conduct of the landlord has been particularly outrageous, exemplary damages may be awarded: these need bear no relation to the tenant's losses. An example is where the landlord deliberately ignores the tenant's legal rights as by illegally evicting him.[13] It is not necessary for the tenant to plead trespass in his statement of claim as a condition precedent to an award of exemplary damages.[14] Nor is it necessary to show that the landlord made a profit or aimed at one.[15]

III   NON-DEROGATION FROM GRANT

Nature of obligation

The landlord is subject to an implied covenant not to derogate from his grant. This particular covenant is implied into leases (in the absence of an express obligation in relation to the matter) in the interests of fair dealing. If a landlord grants a lease with one hand, he cannot take away the means of enjoying it with the other. He must not frustrate a purpose contemplated by both parties at the date the lease was granted.[16] The connection between this covenant and the implied covenant for quiet enjoyment is at once apparent.

The nature of the covenant is best shown by examples. The landlord is bound not to interfere with any easements which he has granted, such as a right to use the airspace of adjoining land of his for advertising purposes,[17] even if the land to which the complaint relates had been acquired after the grant of the lease. Nor may he interfere with profits à prendre.[18] Non-derogation from grant applies where the landlord retains adjacent land, and gives the tenant remedies in respect of activities on the part of the landlord or any persons claiming under him, which adversely affect the use of the land let. An implied covenant for non-derogation from grant is not excluded by an express covenant for quiet enjoyment,[19] even though the two covenants serve related objects. An express covenant to let for residential purposes only may carry the implication that any letting of part for business purposes is a derogation from grant.[20]

---

11 *Mira v Alymer Square Investments Ltd* [1990] 1 EGLR 45, CA.
12 As in *Guppy's (Bridport) Ltd v Brookling* (1983) 14 HLR 1, CA, where the landlords cut off all water supplies and sanitation as part of their redevelopment of premises.
13 See eg *Drane v Evangelou* [1978] 2 All ER 437, [1978] 1 WLR 455, CA (£1,000 award upheld). Also, *McMillan v Singh* (1984) 17 HLR 120, CA (award of £250 upheld despite tenant being in arrear with rent).
14 *Drane v Evangelou, supra.* Also *Breeze v Eldon & Hyde* [1987] CLY 2120 (Cty Ct).
15 *Amrani v Oniah* [1984] CLY 1974; cf *Daley v Ramdath* (1993) Times, 21 January.
16 *Johnston & Sons Ltd v Holland* [1988] 1 EGLR 264, 267, CA.
17 *Johnston & Sons Ltd v Holland* [1988] 1 EGLR 264, CA.
18 *Peech v Best* [1931] 1 KB 1, CA.
19 *Grosvenor Hotel Co v Hamilton* [1894] 2 QB 836, CA.
20 *Newman v Real Estate Debenture Corpn Ltd* [1940] 1 All ER 131.

Limits of covenant

As with an implied covenant for quiet enjoyment, the protection offered by an implied covenant not to derogate from grant is fairly narrow. The covenant is broken only if the landlord,[1] or a person claiming under him, such as a tenant or assignee of adjoining land, does something which renders the premises less or substantially less fit for the particular purpose or purposes for which they were known to be let. But for this rule, almost unlimited obligations or risks could be imposed on landlords. The covenant was, however, broken where an assignee of the landlord built on adjoining land in such a way as to obstruct the flow of air to the drying sheds in the tenant's timber yard, the premises having been let for that purpose.[2] Similarly, where the plaintiff held a lease of land expressly for the purpose of storing explosives, and the defendant held a lease of adjoining land from the same landlord, with a view to working minerals, and the defendant built too near the plaintiff's magazine, so jeopardising the latter's statutory licence, the plaintiff obtained an injunction to restrain the breach.[3] Other examples of breaches of the implied covenant not to derogate from grant include: the endangering of the stability of the tenant's adjoining premises by vibration from heavy machinery on the landlord's premises,[4] and where the landlord built against an external wall of the tenant's premises, thereby making use of it as a party wall and blocking off the tenant's right to light.[5] In all these cases the degree and nature of the interference with the tenant's enjoyment was substantial and enough to set at naught the known purposes of the tenant.

No action may be brought unless, at the time of granting the lease, the landlord knew the purpose for which the land was to be used, and also, where relevant, knew that any particular user was special or sensitive.[6] Since the test for determining the existence of a breach is whether the premises are rendered less fit or materially less fit for the particular purpose of the lease, if the only complaint is of interference with the tenant's privacy,[7] or that adjoining premises have been let for a competing trade,[8] or that the insurance risks, such as for fire, have been increased by a letting of adjacent premises,[9] there is no implied derogation from grant. In a recent case,[10] the cases just mentioned were reviewed. The established principle that, express covenant apart, it was no breach of a covenant not to derogate from grant for a landlord to have let neighbouring premises for a competing trade to that of the tenants (in that case

1 As opposed to, notably, a local planning authority: see *Molton Builders Ltd* v *City of Westminster London Borough Council* (1975) 30 P & CR 182, CA.
2 *Aldin* v *Latimer Clark, Muirhead & Co* [1894] 2 Ch 437.
3 *Harmer* v *Jumbil (Nigeria) Tin Areas Ltd* [1921] 1 Ch 200, CA.
4 *Grosvenor Hotel Co* v *Hamilton*, supra
5 *Betts Ltd* v *Pickford's Ltd* [1906] 2 Ch 87.
6 *Robinson* v *Kilvert*, supra.
7 *Browne* v *Flower* [1911] 1 Ch 219.
8 *Port* v *Griffith* [1938] 1 All ER 295.
9 *O'Cedar Ltd* v *Slough Trading Co Ltd.* [1927] 2 KB 123. It would obviously have been different if the letting of the adjoining premises had rendered it impossible for the tenants to insure their own premises.
10 *Romulus Trading* v *Comet Properties*, supra; see HW Wilkinson (1997) 147 NLJ 93.

a banking business) was held to be correctly-based; no principle of alleged unfairness required it to be modified. The High Court pointed to the great uncertainty which might follow adopting a more liberal approach; and in any case, if the parties to a lease wish to make express provisions as to competition, they may always insert these in the lease.

B IMPLIED COVENANTS BY THE TENANT

IV RENT

Even if there is no express covenant by the tenant to pay rent, a covenant to pay rent will be implied from the mere contractual relationship of landlord and tenant, or where the parties are in privity of estate, no matter what the nature of the lease or tenancy or its duration. Thus, an obligation to pay rent arrears was held to be an implied term of a weekly tenancy, so that a deceased tenant's personal representative, who was not in possession and did not take any benefit from the tenancy, was liable in respect of two years' rent arrears accruing from the death of the tenant to the service of a notice to quit.[11]

V LIABILITY TO PAY CHARGES IN RESPECT OF THE PROPERTY

It is convenient briefly to mention the principal cases in which the tenant may be liable under one statute or another to pay a rate, tax or charge on the property.

1 From 1 April 1993, tenants of domestic property, if resident on the chargeable day in the relevant dwelling-house, are liable to council tax.[12]
2 In the case of non-domestic property,[13] the tenant is liable, provided he is the rateable occupier, to pay rates.[14] The tenant is generally liable for non-domestic rates (as 'owner', because of his entitlement within the rating legislation, to possession) where the premises are unoccupied.[15]
3 The tenant is also liable, unless the lease expressly stipulates the contrary, to pay water rates and sewerage charges,[16] and to pay drainage rate, whether an owners' or occupiers' rate.[17] If the owner (i e the landlord) is assessed for

---

11 *Youngmin v Heath* [1974] 1 All ER 461, [1974] 1 WLR 135, CA.
12 Local Government Finance Act 1992, s 6.
13 Excluded, most notably, from 'non-domestic property' is agricultural land and buildings (Local Government Finance Act 1988, Sch 5, paras 1 and 2).
14 Local Government Finance Act 1988, s 43.
15 Non-Domestic Rating (Unoccupied Property) Regulations 1989, SI 1989/2261.
16 Water Industry Act 1991, ss 142 and 144.
17 Land Drainage Act 1991, s 49.

drainage rate by an internal drainage board, he has a right to recover from the occupier any amount paid by him which, as between himself and the occupier, the latter is liable to pay.[18]

4   The tenant may be required by the collector of taxes, following a notice procedure, to pay landlords' Schedule A income tax in the event of the latter's default.[19] The tenant is thereafter entitled to deduct the sums paid from subsequent payments of rent: this right cannot be contracted out of in the lease.[20]

VI   DISCLAIMER OF THE LANDLORD'S TITLE

It is an implied condition of every lease, fixed-term or periodic and formal or informal, that the tenant is not expressly or impliedly to deny the landlord's title or prejudice it by any acts which are inconsistent with the existence of a tenancy. Disclaimer of the landlord's title is analogous to repudiation of a contract. The rule is of feudal origin; the courts are not anxious to extend it and so any breach of this condition must be clear and unambiguous.[1] A disclaimer of the whole of the landlord's title is a breach, entitling the landlord to re-enter and forfeit the lease, though it has been held that s 146 of the Law of Property Act 1925 applies, requiring the service of a forfeiture notice on the tenant.[2] There are two ways in which a breach may arise.

(a) *By matter of record* – this is where the landlord's title is denied in proceedings, as where the tenant answers a claim for rent by asserting an adverse title to the whole land, viz, that vested in him[3] or a third party. However, because a general denial of the landlord's allegations was held only to require the landlord to prove his case, it did not constitute a denial of title by matter of record.[4] Likewise, a denial in pleadings that the landlord had any right to let part of premises, coupled with a positive assertion that he had the right to let the rest of the premises, was held not to amount to a disclaimer by matter of record, since a partial disclaimer was insufficient.[5]

(b) *By act in pais* – this is where the tenant by conduct impliedly denies the landlord's title, as where he wrongfully pays rent to a third party, or lets a stranger into possession with the intention of enabling him to set up an adverse title, or purports to dispose of the landlord's, as well as his own, title.[6]

---

18   Likewise, where an occupier is assessed for drainage rate which is payable by the owner, he is entitled to deduct the amount paid from his rent (s 49(3)).
19   Income and Corporation Taxes Act 1988, s 23.
20   Taxes Management Act 1970, s 106(2).
 1   *WG Clark (Properties) Ltd v Dupre Properties Ltd* [1992] Ch 297, [1992] 1 All ER 596.
 2   *WG Clark (Properties) Ltd v Dupre Properties Ltd*, supra; also *British Telecommunications plc v Department of the Environment* (29 October 1996, Unreported).
 3   *Doe d Graves v Wells* (1839) 10 Ad & El 427.
 4   *Warner v Sampson* [1959] 1 QB 297, [1959] 1 All ER 120, CA.
 5   *WG Clark (Properties) Ltd v Dupre Properties Ltd*, supra.
 6   See *Wisbech St Mary Parish Council v Lilley* [1956] 1 All ER 301, [1956] 1 WLR 121, CA.

VII   LANDLORD'S IMPLIED RIGHT TO ENTER

Except for the purpose of distraining for rent arrears,[7] the landlord has generally no implied right to enter the premises, especially to view or repair them during the lease. There are some exceptions to this rule. Where the landlord has expressly covenanted to carry out particular repairs, he has an implied licence to enter and execute that work, where he is in breach of covenant.[8] A similar right is conferred on him in the case of weekly tenancies.[9] Any such implied licence is limited to what is required to enable the breach to be remedied and does not entitle a landlord to enter and execute works which go beyond the work he is under covenant to perform, such as major renewals or improvements in the case of a mere covenant to repair.[10] If the landlord enters without any right to do so, he commits an actionable trespass,[11] unless it is possible to explain his presence by an express or implied licence granted by the tenant on that occasion for the purpose of carrying out the work.[12] If the landlord enters under an implied licence, after suitable notice, to comply with his repairing covenant, and the tenant requires him to leave, he cannot expect to recover damages from the landlord as the latter is not then in breach of his covenant to repair, assuming the remedial work would have sufficed to comply with his covenant.[13]

VIII   USUAL COVENANTS

General rules[14]

Where an agreement for a lease fails to specify the terms which will be inserted in the lease, it is an implied term of the agreement that the lease will contain the usual covenants and provisos.[15] The question of whether a particular covenant is 'usual' is one of fact; but it is proper to take the evidence of conveyancers and others familiar with practice into account.[16] The court will therefore look at the nature of the premises, their situation and locality, the purpose for which they are being let, and the length of the term,[17] and it may, if appropriate, pay due regard to lists of what have been held to be 'usual' covenants in books of precedents.[18] Such lists, particularly if older, must be regarded as capable of

---

7   *Doe d Worcester Trustees v Rowlands* (1841) 9 C & P 734.
8   *Saner v Bilton* (1878) 7 Ch D 815; *Granada Theatres Ltd v Freehold Investment (Leytonstone) Ltd* [1959] Ch 592, [1959] 2 All ER 176, CA.
9   *Mint v Good* [1951] 1 KB 517; also *McAuley v Bristol City Council* [1991] 2 EGLR 64, CA.
10   See *Plough Investments Ltd v Manchester City Council* [1989] 1 EGLR 244.
11   If necessary this will be restrained by an injunction: *Stocker v Planet Building Society* (1879) 27 WR 877, CA; *Regional Properties Ltd v City of London Real Property Co Ltd* (1979) 257 Estates Gazette 64.
12   *McDougall v Easington District Council* [1989] 1 EGLR 93, CA.
13   *Granada Theatres Ltd v Freehold Investment (Leytonstone) Ltd*, supra.
14   See passim Crabb [1992] Conv 18.
15   *Propert v Parker* (1832) 3 My & K 280; *Blakesley v Whieldon* (1841) 1 Hare 176.
16   *Flexman v Corbett* [1930] 1 Ch 672; *Chester v Buckingham Travel Ltd* [1981] 1 All ER 386.
17   See *Chester v Buckingham Travel*, supra.
18   As in *Hampshire v Wickens* (1878) 7 Ch D 555.

extension or reconsideration where needed in the light of prevailing circumstances.[19] The word 'usual' means no more than 'occurring in ordinary use' so that if it is found that in nine out of ten cases a covenant of a particular sort would be in a lease of premises of a given nature and in a given district, the covenant may be 'usual' for the particular premises in question, for that reason.[20] This is simply because the court is determining in an objective manner what is to be the proper form of the agreement for a lease of the type of property in the locality in issue.

Usual covenants

The following have been held to be usual covenants on the facts and circumstances of particular cases: a covenant by the landlord for quiet enjoyment,[1] and the following covenants by the tenant: to pay tenants' rates and taxes, to keep the premises in repair and to deliver them up in repair at the end of the term,[2] not to alter or add to the demised premises without the landlord's consent, not to stop up, darken or obstruct windows or light belonging to the demised premises, not to permit easements to be acquired against the demised premises, not to permit the demised premises to be used for specified purposes, a condition of re-entry for non-payment of rent and a proviso for re-entry for breach of covenants other than to pay rent.[3]

Onerous covenants

Certain covenants are not 'usual' and are onerous or unusual, because they impose obligations which go outside what the law regards as 'usual' covenants. The following have been held to be onerous or unusual covenants: to insure,[4] to repair and rebuild,[5] to pay solicitors' and surveyors' costs,[6] not to assign or sub-let without consent,[7] not to exercise a particular trade (except in the case of a public house),[8] and a proviso for re-entry which extends to the bankruptcy of the lessee.[9] The significance of a covenant being onerous is not merely that it will not be implied into an agreement for a lease: where a lessee contracts to sell his interest, he is under a duty to disclose onerous or unusual covenants to the purchaser.[10]

---

19 *Chester v Buckingham Travel*, supra.
20 *Flexman v Corbett* [1930] 1 Ch 672 at 678-679.
 1 *Hampshire v Wickens*, supra.
 2 Also a covenant by the tenant to permit the landlord, where the latter has covenanted to repair, to enter and view the state of repair of the premises.
 3 See *Chester v Buckingham Travel*, supra.
 4 *Cosser v Collinge* (1832) 3 My & K 283.
 5 *Doe d Dymoke v Withers* (1831) 2 B & Ad 896.
 6 *Allen v Smith* [1924] 2 Ch 308; *Chester v Buckingham Travel*, supra.
 7 *Church v Brown* (1808) 15 Ves 258; *Chester v Buckingham Travel*, supra.
 8 *Propert v Parker*, supra.
 9 *Chester v Buckingham Travel*, supra.
10 *Chester v Buckingham Travel*, supra.

Chapter 7

Express covenants

I INTRODUCTION

Since the covenants implied into a lease are the minimum necessary to maintain the leasehold estate and protect the reversion, it is obvious that a properly drafted lease will contain a number of express covenants. The parties are free, subject to statutory restrictions, to insert covenants in whatever terms they think fit, even though there is a wide range of forms and precedents to assist them in their task.[1] In this and the next two chapters we discuss the interpretation of the main types of covenant ordinarily found in leases.

II RATES, TAXES, ASSESSMENTS AND OTHER OUTGOINGS

The immediate outgoings on the premises, such as rates, taxes, charges and duties, are settled in the first place by statute, as between the authority or utility to whom the payment has to be made, and thereafter between the landlord and tenant by the terms of the lease. There are also occasions where statute requires one party, usually the landlord, to carry out specific types of work on the premises, such as to enable them to comply with fire precautions: again, the terms of the lease may vary the incidence of liability as between the parties. In either case, clear and unambiguous language is required before a covenant is able to vary a liability cast on the other party by statute, as where the tenant expressly undertakes to make the following payments, with value added tax where payable: all periodic rates, taxes and outgoings related to the property, including any imposed after the date of the lease (even if of a novel nature), to be paid promptly to the authority to whom the sums are due.[2] If clear language is not used, the question of liability to pay an outgoing under a covenant seeking to vary the incidence of statutory liability is one of interpretation of the covenant. Some illustrations of this point are now given.

---

1 See eg Law Society Business Lease, reproduced in the Appendix to this book.
2 Law Society Business Lease, supra, cl 2.1, in which case the covenant will be construed literally: see *Stockdale v Ascherberg* [1904] 1 KB 447, CA.

General rules

The form of covenants may vary greatly from the simple 'rates and taxes' to a more comprehensive formula, such as that just mentioned. A tenant's covenant to pay 'rates, taxes and assessments' suffices to render the tenant liable to pay rates and taxes imposed by statute on the landlord, if these are of a recurring nature. The tenant's liability under so limited a covenant for outgoings imposed by legislation after the grant of the lease depends on whether the liability can be brought within a class of outgoing for which the tenant is already liable, having regard to the contemplation of the parties when the lease was granted.[3] The meaning of particular words may be more narrowly construed in a covenant purporting to vary statutory liability so that while a covenant by the tenant to pay 'rates' usually includes the water rate,[4] the same covenant by the landlord will exclude it save in special circumstances, as where the building as a whole is assessed but the lease is only of one floor of the building.[5] A covenant to pay all outgoings, however, will include the water rate.

Where the tenant is liable for 'all assessments' charged on the premises, he remains liable for sums levied during the lease even though no benefit from the payments in fact accrues to him (as where he is out of occupation).[6] Where the burden of outgoings payable by either party increases as the result of a periodic revaluation, if the words of a particular covenant require this, the party will have to bear the increase.[7]

Where the premises have been sub-let, and the sub-lessee has covenanted to perform all the covenants in the head lease, including that to pay rates, taxes or outgoings, the sub-lessee is rendered liable for sums under that covenant in respect of which his sub-lessor is liable even though the sub-lessor is under an identical covenant, and it is not an implied term of liability under the sub-lessee's covenant that the sub-lessor actually pays the sums concerned.[8] Moreover, if a sub-lessor has to pay a particular outgoing, as to a local authority or utility, it is not a condition precedent of the sub-lessee's liability to pay under his covenant that the sub-lessor has in fact paid the sum in question: the same rule applies to a head landlord as against a lessee.[9]

As a matter of construction, the scope of a particular lessee's covenant to pay rates, taxes or outgoings may be qualified by reference to other terms in the lease. For example, a lessee who covenanted to pay 'all rates, taxes, assessments, charges and outgoings' was not liable to pay his landlord the cost of the renewal of the outside drains of the premises at the demand of a local authority, as the landlord had covenanted to repair these items.[10]

---

3 See *Lowther v Clifford* [1927] 1 KB 130, CA; also *Smith v Smith* [1939] 4 All ER 312.
4 *King v Cave-Browne-Cave* [1960] 2 QB 222, [1960] 2 All ER 751.
5 *Bourne and Tant v Salmon and Gluckstein* [1907] 1 Ch 616, CA.
6 *Eastwood v McNab* [1914] 2 KB 361, CA.
7 *Salaman v Holford* [1909] 2 Ch 602 (landlord's covenant to pay rates and taxes 'now payable or hereafter to become payable').
8 *W H Read & Co Ltd v Walter* (1931) 48 TLR 15.
9 *Francis v Squire* [1940] 1 All ER 45.
10 *Howe v Botwood* [1913] 2 KB 387.

A covenant to pay rates and taxes, or outgoings by the lessee, which is silent as to whether the lessee must pay for the cost of capital improvements to the premises raises some difficulty, since not all the authorities are reconcilable. Where a lessor covenanted that he would pay land and other taxes, and the land was improved, he was liable only to the extent of the unimproved value of the premises, the lessee being liable to the extent of the increase in value.[11] If the outgoings which a lessee is liable to pay are increased as a result of improvements, the question of whether he becomes liable to pay increases so caused, is one of construction of the covenant, though the language should be such that it requires the lessee to pay future charges.[12] In some cases it was suggested that the substance and not just the form of the covenant must be taken into account,[13] but it is submitted that these views are inconsistent with subsequent authority and ordinary rules of interpretation of covenants.[14]

Statute often imposes certain obligations on the landlord to carry out work of a particular nature. For example, certain premises cannot be let unless work to ensure safety in the case of fire is carried out,[15] and duties to ensure that particular work is executed are imposed in relation to factory and other premises.[16] In these cases, the lease may apportion the cost of the work as between the parties. Not only are the courts not bound by the terms of the lease in this respect,[17] but under such statutes it is usual to empower the court to apportion the expenses of the work between the parties on the basis of what is just and equitable,[18] due regard being had to the terms of the lease.[19]

Particular words

Rates covers the general rate: as to whether it includes the water rate, see above. Drainage rates are not 'rates'.

'*Taxes*' when used in conjunction with 'rates' is generally taken to refer only to Parliamentary taxes, but when used alone, may be allowed a wider meaning in the context to include other charges levied by local authorities under statutory powers. As to deductibility from rent of landlord's income tax recovered from the tenant, see chapter 6.

'*Assessments*' when used in conjunction with 'rates and taxes' only, has been held not to refer to a sum assessed in respect of work for the permanent benefit of the property, such as paving a street,[20] but its meaning may be widened by

11 *Mansfield v Relf* [1908] 1 KB 71, CA.
12 *Lowther v Clifford* [1927] 1 KB 130; *Villenex Co Ltd v Courtney Hotel Ltd* (1969) 20 P & CR 575.
13 See eg *Wilkinson v Collyer* (1884) 13 QBD 1; also *Valpy v St Leonards Wharf* (1903) 67 JP 402.
14 See *Lowther v Clifford*, supra.
15 See Fire Precautions Act 1971, ss 1 and 3.
16 Eg under Factories Act 1961, Offices, Shops and Railway Premises Act 1963 and Health and Safety at Work etc Act 1974.
17 *Horner v Franklin* [1905] 1 KB 479, CA.
18 See eg Factories Act 1961, s 170; Offices, Shops and Railway Premises Act 1963, s 73(2); Fire Precautions Act 1971, s 28(3).
19 See *Monk v Arnold* [1902] 1 KB 761.
20 *Wilkinson v Collyer* (1884) 13 QBD 1.

the addition of wider terms such as 'duties', 'burdens', 'impositions', or 'outgoings'. *'Duties'* has a much wider meaning than 'assessments', and has been held to include the cost of paving and drainage, and the cost of removing a public nuisance. *'Impositions'* includes the cost of paving and drainage, but not expenses resulting from breach of duty, and otherwise is not distinguishable from 'duty'; and *'burden'* and *'charge'* are synonymous with *'imposition'*. Where impositions, etc, are 'charged upon the property', the tenant will be liable only for charges imposed on the property during the tenancy, but where they are 'charged upon the landlord or upon the tenant', the tenant will be liable for a charge made upon the property before the tenancy, in respect of which the apportionment is made during the tenancy.

Remedies

A landlord's remedy is by exercise of a right of re-entry where one is reserved in the lease, or by action on the covenant, and he may sue in respect of sums which he has not yet paid, if the tenant's liability is expressed to be for sums charged on the landlord or due from him. If, on the other hand, the landlord is liable for any sums already recovered from the tenant, they are deductible by the tenant from the rent next due, unless the right to deduct is precluded by any agreement. If, nevertheless, he deducts the charges, he will, in any action by the landlord, be entitled to counterclaim them. Alternatively, he can pay the rent in full, and sue upon the covenant.

III QUIET ENJOYMENT

An express covenant for quiet enjoyment or for title in any form will displace the implied covenant in qualified form. An express covenant is usually qualified, and will have the same effects as the implied covenant, but will endure throughout the term granted. As long as it is limited to protecting the tenant from lawful eviction or interruption by the landlord or anyone claiming 'by, from or under' him, it will be construed as qualified, and will not protect the tenant from eviction by title paramount, ie by any one with a title superior to that of the landlord. Nor will such a covenant protect the tenant against claims made under a leasehold title granted at an earlier date by predecessors in title to the landlord.[1] Even an unqualified covenant (eg 'by the landlord, or any person claiming under him, or any other person') will thus not protect the tenant against mere claimants of a superior title,[2] for acts of strangers will only be included if they are mentioned expressly, either by name, or as claimants to the landlord's or a superior title. A covenant against acts of a single identifiable person, such as a head lessor, covers lawful and, in contrast to the implied covenant, unlawful (ie unauthorised) acts by the head lessor; but if the head

1 *Celsteel Ltd v Alton Holdings Ltd (No 2)* [1987] 2 All ER 240, [1987] 1 WLR 291, CA.
2 *Young v Raincock* (1849) 7 CB 310.

lessor assigns his superior interest, it is not clear whether the assignee is liable for unlawful acts.[3]

IV INSURANCE

It is advisable for any lease, especially for a substantial period, to provide that the landlord[4] is to take out and pay the premiums of a policy of insurance against risks such as fire damage, and also damage by other risks such as earthquake, subsidence, storm, flood and vehicular and malicious damage. The basis of the cover may be specified, as where it is that normal for the locality of the premises. The landlord may be under an express obligation to re-instate the premises if one of the risks materialises and causes the destruction of the premises, as where they burn down. Equally, the lease concerned may specify that the parties may agree that the premises are not to be re-instated, in which case it may make provision for the sub-division between the parties of any insurance moneys which are payable. Some leases oblige the landlord to produce from time to time at the tenant's request an up-to-date version of the policy. The landlord may also have to notify the tenant of any changes in the policy. It is normal for the tenant to pay the cost of the premiums, which sums are sometimes reserved as rent, so that they may be distrained for if unpaid.

Certain general points have arisen as to the nature and quality of insurance covenants. A covenant to insure is a continuous obligation and is broken if at any time the premises are uninsured, even if no relevant risk in fact materialises.[5] It is established that any covenant of insurance is a covenant of indemnity,[6] so that the expectation is that the insurance moneys will provide full reimbursement to the landlord for the cost of re-instatement, if that is required, based on the value of the property, at current building costs. At the same time, the court refused to imply any term into a lease, on the ground of business efficacy, which required the landlord to show that the premiums were fair and reasonable in amount, as a condition precedent to being able to recover the costs of premiums from his lessee.[7] Some leases allow the landlord to nominate a company of repute with whom insurance could be effected, and where a landlord altered the insurers and the premiums went up, the court refused to imply a term that the insurance would not be substantially more than the tenant might have arranged.[8]

---

3   *Queensway Marketing Ltd v Associated Restaurants Ltd* [1988] 2 EGLR 49, CA (mesne landlord liable to sub-under-lessee where head landlord interrupted latter's business).

4   Should the insurance by carried out by the tenant, his interest in the policy corresponds to that of his leasehold term (*Re King* [1963] Ch 459) which may explain why a lessee who insures should do so in the joint names of the parties.

5   *Penniall v Harborne* (1848) 11 QB 368; unless the damage falls within an exception clause: *Upjohn v Hitchens* [1918] 2 KB 48, CA.

6   *Lonsdale & Thompson Ltd v Black Arrow Group plc* [1993] 3 All ER 648; Haley [1993] Conv 472.

7   *Havenridge Ltd v Boston Dyers Ltd* [1994] 2 EGLR 73, CA.

8   *Berrycroft Management Ltd v Sinclair Gardens Investments (Kensington) Ltd* [1996] EGCS 143, CA.

If the premises are destroyed following an insurable event, the lease may provide for the express re-instatement of the premises by the landlord, using the insurance moneys. This may be important: no obligation to re-instate in these circumstances exists at common law.[9] Indeed, in the case of fire damage, where there is no express or implied[10] obligation to re-instate, the tenant may by an old statute,[11] still in force, require the landlord to spend the insurance moneys on re-instatement. The courts have taken this to mean applying the moneys within a reasonable time of the event, failing which the landlord is in breach of covenant.[12] It may be that the original building which has been destroyed cannot be rebuilt to precisely the same state as before: in such a case, the courts may accept that re-instatement to the modern equivalent of the building will suffice.[13]

There may be circumstances in which re-instatement is impossible, as where the premises have been compulsorily purchased, or where the parties agree that it is not desirable or possible. In such a case, the question of the distribution of the insurance money may depend on the language, if any, of the lease, so that where the lessee covenanted to pay the insurance premiums on a policy effected wholly for his benefit, he was entitled to all the moneys, even though the policy was held for the joint names of the landlord and tenant.[14] Indeed, the lease may provide that if the landlord cannot re-instate (as where he cannot obtain any required planning permissions), the tenant is to be entitled to surrender the lease after due notice.[15] It may be possible to infer a release of an obligation to re-instate by conduct of the parties which is inconsistent with the fulfilment by the landlord of his obligation, as where there was an insufficient sum to pay for re-instatement and the parties were taken to have divided the moneys between them.[16]

Should the premises be destroyed or damaged so that they cannot be used for the time being, some leases enable the tenant to claim a suspension of rent (which would otherwise be due). To cover the landlord against the financial loss so caused, he may wish to insure against loss of such rent. Equally, the lease may provide in terms for a reduction in rent if the premises may only be used to some extent until re-instatement.

V DISPOSITION COVENANTS[17]

Introduction

If a lease or tenancy does not make any express provisions as to assignments or related dispositions, notably sub-lettings, the common law principle is that the

9 *Bullock v Dommitt* (1796) 6 Term Rep 650.
10 As in *Mumford Hotels v Wheler* [1964] Ch 117.
11 Fires Prevention (Metropolis) Act 1774, s 83.
12 *Farimani v Gates* (1984) 271 Estates Gazette 887, CA; and see *Mark Rowlands Ltd v Berni Inns Ltd* [1986] QB 211, [1985] 3 All ER 473, CA.
13 *Reynolds v Phoenix Assurance Co Ltd* [1978] 2 Lloyds Rep 440.
14 *Re King*, supra.
15 As envisaged by *Precedents for the Conveyancer* No 5-58.
16 *Beacon Carpets Ltd v Kirby* [1985] QB 755, [1984] 2 All ER 726, CA.
17 See passim Crabb *Leases: Covenants and Consents*.

tenant is entitled to deal with his lease as he thinks fit, as might be expected with any right in the nature of property. However, restrictions on the tenant's power to dispose of his lease are often found in leases. Short residential leases sometimes completely or *absolutely* prohibit any assignment, sub-letting or parting with the possession of the premises. Leases of business premises might contain an absolute prohibition of this kind, but are more likely to limit the power of the tenant to assign, sub-let or otherwise dispose of the lease. The tenant may be required to apply for the consent of the landlord for the transaction concerned.

Since 1927, Parliament has interfered with this latter type of covenant, so as to require the landlord to refuse consent only on reasonable grounds being shown.[18] A large body of case-law has evolved around the broad concept of reasonableness, whose net effect is to limit the landlord's ability to refuse consent to an assignee whom he might suspect to be less favourable than the lessee, but where he cannot prove his suspicions. The landlord cannot, under this set of principles, limit himself in advance to given grounds or to general matters of property management.

In relation to a lease which is a 'new tenancy' for the purposes of the Landlord and Tenant (Covenants) Act 1995, and which is not a residential lease, s 22 of the 1995 Act inserts new provisions (s 19(1A)–(1E)) into the Landlord and Tenant Act 1927. The details are examined in what follows. The policy of the new provisions is no doubt related to the abrogation of the 'privity of contract' liability of tenants, notably by enabling a landlord to impose a condition on giving consent that the assigning tenant enters into a guarantee of the assignee's performance of his obligations. The general effect of the new sub-sections is to allow the landlord and tenant, either at the date of grant of the lease or subsequently (as on an assignment) to specify the circumstances in which the landlord may withhold his consent to an assignment of the demised premises, or the conditions for the granting of consent. The landlord will not be regarded as witholding consent unreasonably or imposing an unreasonable condition merely because he relies on the pre-arranged circumstances, as where he requires a guarantee agreement from the assigning tenant.

The legislature has thus eased the position of commercial landlords. It had enacted the Landlord and Tenant Act 1988, considered in more detail below, with a view to speeding up the decision of a landlord, to whom a written application for consent has been made. One effect of the 1988 Act, where the general rules of s 19(1) apply, untrammelled by any restrictive terms in the lease, seems to have been to require a rapid decision by landlords, save in cases of real difficulty or complexity, since in default of such a decision they risked an action for breach of statutory duty under s 4 of the 1988 Act. Where a tenancy granted as from the commencement of the 1995 Act sets out an agreement as envisaged by s 19(1A) of the 1927 Act, the effect of the 1988 Act is likely to be less severe on a commercial landlord, as he is now entitled to refuse consent reasonably to any proposed assignment where the previously specified

---

18   Landlord and Tenant Act 1927, s 19(1), considered more fully below.

grounds or conditions apply to it. The relatively small amount of time allowed by the 1988 Act for him to make his decision goes to form and not to substance.

Absolute, qualified and fully qualified covenants

There are three types of prohibitions or restrictions on assignments and related transactions. None of these is banned by legislation. An *absolute* covenant means just that: the tenant cannot carry out the disposition concerned (be it an assignment, sub-letting or other matter specified in the covenant). If the landlord gives the tenant a licence to assign, or sub-let, for example, he cannot later change his mind and claim a forfeiture, but the licence only makes lawful the particular transaction to which it relates.[19] The Law Commission recommended the abolition of absolute covenants, save in the case notably of short residential lettings.[20]

A *qualified disposition covenant* requires the tenant to obtain the prior consent of the landlord to the transaction concerned, but does not expressly require the landlord, as a counterpart, not to withhold his consent unreasonably. Since landlords could, but for legislation, refuse consent on any ground, even a capricious one, so locking the tenant into the lease, in the case of most leases, Parliament has made qualified disposition covenants *fully qualified*, with the result that the landlord cannot refuse his consent unreasonably in such a case, any more than he could if those words expressly appear in the covenant.

Transactions prohibited by the above covenants

The words of a disposition covenant will be read as a whole: thus, although no doubt it may be more prudent and comprehensive expressly to prohibit assignment, sub-letting or parting with the possession of the demised premises or of any part, parts of such a covenant may overlap. Thus, where a tenant had undertaken not to part with possession of certain premises without consent, and assigned them, he was taken to have broken his covenant, as an assignment necessarily involves parting with possession,[1] unless the landlord could not have reasonably withheld consent.[2] It is not clear however whether a covenant against underletting alone precludes an assignment: according to an Irish case, such a covenant indicates the landlord's intention not to have on the premises a person against whom he cannot claim damages and so includes assignments.[3]

Turning to the scope of individual words of covenant, a prohibition on *assignment* without consent or licence[4] is broken by a legal assignment in proper

---

19 Law of Property Act 1925, s 143(1).
20 Law Com No 141, *Covenants Restricting Disposition*, paras 4.17 and 7.7–7.24.
 1 Just as an assignment of the whole premises involves assigning all parts of them and is impliedly caught by a prohibition on assignments of any part of the premises: *Field v Barkworth* [1986] 1 All ER 362, [1986] 1 WLR 137.
 2 *Marks v Warren* [1979] 1 All ER 29.
 3 *Re Doyle* [1899] 1 IR 113; cf *Greenaway v Adams* (1806) 12 Ves 395, and see *Foa* p 276. See also Crabb, loc cit, p 13.
 4 Consents may sometimes be given in the form of a licence, as to the construction of which see eg *Cerium Investments Ltd v Evans* [1991] 1 EGLR 80, CA.

form of the whole residue of the leasehold term.[5] However, such a covenant is not broken by making an agreement to assign a lease, nor by an equitable assignment of the term.[6] An assignment by operation of law (ie involuntarily), as on bankruptcy, is not caught by a covenant against assignment (see further Chapter 11). In the absence of any recent authority, it appears that, since the terms of a will take effect after 1925 only in equity, the mere disposition of a tenancy in a will is not a breach of a covenant against assignment, though it has been argued that the vesting by a deceased tenant's personal representatives of the tenancy in the named beneficiary would constitute a breach, if without the landlord's consent, where required.[7]

Sub-letting   A covenant against sub-letting is broken if the tenant creates a legal sub-tenancy in respect of the whole of the premises (or of part if the covenant is so expressed), and this will include a mortgage by sub-demise.[8] He cannot in any event, without licence, sub-let a part of the premises, and then sub-let the rest.[9]

Parting with possession   Parting with possession only prohibits a transaction by which the lessee entirely excludes himself from legal possession of the premises,[10] whose existence is a question of fact.[11] In the absence of contrary language, this covenant refers to parting with possession only of the whole premises,[12] and is not broken where the tenant creates a mere licence or takes in lodgers or paying guests. The distinction may be difficult to draw. For example, where a lessee formed a company, which took over his business at the premises, and made new agreements for the supply of electricity and water, put up its own signboard and, importantly, paid its own cheque for rent, the latter fact, coupled with the absence of an all-too-easy denial that possession was held by the company, sufficed, taken with the evidence as a whole, to evidence a parting with possession, incurring a forfeiture.[13]

---

5   The grant of a 'sub-lease' for the same or a longer term than the lessee's would amount to an assignment of it: *Milmo v Carreras* [1946] KB 306, [1946] 1 All ER 288, CA.
6   *Doe d Pitt v Hogg* (1824) 4 Dow & Ry 226; also *Gentle v Faulkner* [1900] 2 QB 267. Foa p 274 notes that this survives the administrative fusion of law and equity.
7   Barnsley (1963) 27 Conv (NS) 159. His view is that the personal representatives would be deemed by s 79(1) of the Law of Property Act 1925 to be successors in title, even if the covenant did not in terms apply to them.
8   *Serjeant v Nash, Field and Co* [1903] 2 KB 304, CA; an express prohibition on charging is required, however, to prevent the creation of mortgages by legal charge: *Grand Junction Co Ltd v Bates* [1954] 2 QB 160, [1954] 2 All ER 385.
9   *Chatterton v Terrell* [1923] AC 578; an illegal sub-letting was restrained by mandatory injunction requiring surrender of the sub-term in *Hemingway Securities Ltd v Dunraven Ltd* [1995] 1 EGLR 61.
10 *Stening v Abrahams* [1931] 1 Ch 470.
11 *Chaplin v Smith* [1926] 1 KB 198, CA.
12 *Church v Brown* (1808) 15 Ves 258.
13 *Lam Kee Ying Sdn Bhd v Lam Shes Tong* [1975] AC 247, PC (but relief was granted as consent could not reasonably have been refused).

Statutory framework

As noted above, statute has intervened so as to modify the impact of covenants against assignments or sub-lettings, without the landlord's prior consent. The position is as follows.

1 *Landlord and Tenant Act 1927, s 19(1)(a)* Except in the case of building leases, and also in the case of a lease of an agricultural holding or farm business tenancy (s 19(4)), s 19(1)(a) of the 1927 Act provides that, notwithstanding any express provision to the contrary, a *qualified* disposition covenant in any lease or under-lease (ie a covenant against assignments etc without the landlord's prior consent) is deemed to be subject to a proviso that the landlord's licence or consent is not to be unreasonably withheld. The provisions of s 19(1)(a) are avoided if the lease contains a surrender back clause, under which the need to give consent only comes into play if the landlord decides not to accept a surrender of the lease, which must be offered as a condition precedent to the seeking of consent.[14]

2 *Landlord and Tenant Act 1927, s 19(1)(b)* In the case of a lease granted for more than 40 years and in consideration, wholly or partly, of the erection of buildings, or the substantial improvement, addition or alteration of buildings, both fully qualified and qualified disposition covenants are subject to a proviso that, where the transaction concerned is effected more than seven years before the end of the term, no consent or licence is required from the landlord.[15] This is subject to the condition that notice of the transaction must be given to the landlord within six months after it is effected. The proviso applies notwithstanding any provision to the contrary. In addition, although s 19(1)(b) allows the tenant freedom to assign, etc, within the prescribed limits, it does not prevent the landlord from enforcing a term in the lease which expressly enables the landlord to require, as a condition of the assignment, an acceptable guarantor for the assignee and a direct covenant by the latter to observe the covenants in the lease for the rest of the term.[16] With the abrogation of the privity of contract liability of tenants by the Landlord and Tenant (Covenants) Act 1995, however, s 19(1)(b) was considered inappropriate. It does not apply to a building lease which is a 'new tenancy' – a tenancy granted as from the commencement of the 1995 Act – unless it is a residential lease.[17]

3 In the case of both qualified and fully qualified disposition covenants, s 144 of the Law of Property Act 1925 implies a proviso that no fine or sum of money in the nature of a fine is to be payable for the landlord's consent

---

14 *Adler v Upper Grosvenor Street Investment Ltd* [1957] 1 All ER 229; *Bocardo SA v S and M Hotels Ltd* [1979] 3 All ER 737, CA.
15 There are certain exceptions to s 19(1)(b), notably where the lessor is a Government department or a local or public authority.
16 *Vaux Group plc v Lilley* [1991] 1 EGLR 60.
17 Landlord and Tenant Act 1927, s 19(1D), inserted by Landlord and Tenant (Covenants) Act 1995, s 22. 'Residential lease' means (s 19(1E)) 'a lease by which a building or part of a building is let wholly or mainly as a single private residence'.

unless there is an express provision in the lease to the contrary.[18] This provision does not disentitle the landlord to require payment of a reasonable sum in respect of legal or other expenses in relation to the licence or consent.

4   The abrogation of the privity of contract liability of tenants holding under a 'new tenancy' is subject to the amendments to s 19(1) of the Landlord and Tenant Act 1927 which have been made by s 22 of the Landlord and Tenant (Covenants) Act 1995. These additional changes, in the interests of commercial landlords, were made so as to secure what the government regarded as an essential balancing factor for the loss of the financial security entailed in landlords not being able to bring an action until the expiry of the lease against the original lessee for breaches of covenant, where the latter had voluntarily re-assigned the term. It also appears that the government feared that, but for these changes, landlords might seek to impose absolute prohibitions on assignment.[19] The amendments to the 1927 Act apply only to 'qualifying leases', defined so as to include any tenancy granted on or after 1 January 1996, but also to exclude residential leases granted at any time, but not necessarily farm business tenancies under the Agricultural Tenancies Act 1995. In the case of residential leases, the general principle remains that a landlord who attempts, even with the agreement of his tenant, to pre-specify the grounds on which he may grant or refuse consent to an assignment or as to the conditions to be imposed cannot avoid the risk that the court may hold the pre-set grounds unreasonable for that very reason.[20]

Under s 19(1A) of the 1927 Act, the parties to a 'qualifying lease' may specify by agreement any circumstances in which an immediate (but not, where relevant, a superior) landlord may withhold his licence or consent to an assignment[1] of the whole or any part of the demised premises. The parties may also specify any conditions subject to which any such licence or consent is to be granted. Where either of these rules applies, the landlord is not regarded as unreasonably withholding his licence or consent to any such assignment if he withholds it on the ground, and it is the case,[2] that any such circumstances exist (s 19(1A)(i)). Indeed, if the landlord gives any such licence or consent subject to the pre-specified conditions, he is not regarded as giving it subject to unreasonable conditions (s 19(1A) (ii).[3] An example of the extent of the control which these provisions may give commercial landlords has been given. Some landlords may require that an assignee's

---

18 For the relationship between this provision and s 19(1) of the 1927 Act see Crabb [1993] Conv 215, who contests the view that fines cannot be reasonable. Cf the view of the Law Commission, Law Com No 141, para 3.16, and their recommendation at para 8.16 that no fines should be payable as a condition of consent.

19 HL Report of Landlord and Tenant (Covenants) Bill, *Hansard*, 5 July 1995, col 385.

20 *Creery v Summersell & Flowerdew and Co Ltd* [1949] Ch 751.

 1 Which expression includes a parting with possession or assignment (s 19(1E)(b)) but not, seemingly, a sub-letting.

 2 So, seemingly, requiring a landlord who is challenged to prove the factual truth of his assertions, not applying to this provision the result in *Air India v Balabel* [1993] 2 EGLR 66.

 3 S 1 of the Landlord and Tenant Act 1988 is expressly subject to s 19(1A) of the 1927 Act, emphasising that where the latter applies, the 1988 Act is mainly procedural in effect.

profits or net assets are a specified multiple of the passing rent, on pain of consent being refused for non-compliance with such criteria.[4]

By contrast, if pre-set grounds or conditions do not cover the circumstances of the particular case – as where the dispute between the parties relates to matters other than a tenant's guarantee (or possibly any tenants' guarantor's guarantee) and the matter was not pre-specified – then the general principles governing the assessment of reasonableness of the consent or condition will apply.

On the other hand, if in a new commercial tenancy, the parties agree at the time the lease is granted, that the landlord may impose a condition of the assignment that the tenant is to enter into an authorised guarantee agreement under s 16 of the Landlord and Tenant (Covenants) Act 1995, the tenant cannot claim that, merely because the condition has been envisaged in advance, that it has been unreasonably imposed. Moreover, it appears that a landlord may require an assigning tenant to enter into an authorised guarantee agreement at any time before an application to assign is made, as where no such condition had been pre-specified in the lease when drafted or in any document attached to it (s 19(1B)).

However, a landlord is still not entitled, even in relation to a new commercial tenancy, to pre-specify such matters as an entitlement to refuse consent to an assignment on the ground that a proposed assignee does not have the same financial standing as the current tenant (s 19(1C)) - unless his power to decide this question is required to be exercised reasonably or is subject to determination by an independent person, so leaving the tenant with a right to challenge the landlord's decision.

5   There is a *special procedure where the Landlord and Tenant Act 1988* applies. The landlord is guilty of breach of statutory duty which sounds in damages (s 4) if he refuses his consent in circumstances outside, it is conceived, the limits of any provision specifying the circumstances in which consent will be given or refused (s 1(5)).[5]

The landlord of any tenant, except a secure tenant, is under the special statutory duties in relation to applications for consent to an assignment, under-letting, charging or parting with possession, imposed by the Landlord and Tenant Act 1988. The Act aims to prevent landlords, including mesne and superior landlords, from unduly delaying in dealing with consent applications by tenants, especially where the landlord decides to refuse consent. The 1988 Act imposes the following procedural duties. They are separate from any other obligations of either party. Indeed, the Court of Appeal has rejected an argument that the Act altered, by a side-wind, the previous law governing the question of when it is reasonable for a landlord

---

4   *Current Law Statutes*, notes to s 22 of the 1995 Act.
5   This difficult provision is seemingly directed at a covenant by a landlord that he will not refuse consent to an assignment to a respectable and responsible person, treating his refusal of consent for an assignment to such a person as unreasonable. It is not thought to affect the operation of pre-specified conditions relating to tenant authorised guarantee agreements under s 16 of the Landlord and Tenant (Covenants) Act 1995.

to refuse consent, and also held that since the landlord is not given much time by the Act in which to make up his mind, he is not impliedly required by it to justify the factual basis of each of his assertions.[6]

Where the tenant serves on the landlord or other person who may consent a written application for consent, or licence (s 5(1)) the landlord, by s 1(3), owes the tenant a duty, within a reasonable time:

(a) to give consent, except where it is reasonable not to do so;
(b) to serve on the tenant written notice of his decision

whether or not to give consent.

In view of the short time allowed the landlord in which to make up his mind, he is entitled to decide on the basis of facts available at the time he decides: his conclusion will not be invalidated by subsequent events which might falsify it, such as a later appearing good set of accounts.[7] A landlord's decision notice must specify any conditions attached to consent, or the reasons for withholding it, as the case may be (s 1(3)). The 1988 Act cannot be evaded by imposing an unreasonable condition on a consent: the duty is treated as broken where this is so (s 1(4)).

If a landlord receives a written consent application, where, in addition to his own consent, the consent of a superior landlord (or, say, mortgagee) is required as well, then the recipient is bound to take reasonable steps to secure the receipt, within a reasonable time, of a copy of the application by that person (s 2(1)). The superior landlord then comes under a mirror duty to that of the mesne landlord under s 1, in relation to giving consent within a reasonable time, and so on (s 3).

The landlord must show, if challenged by the tenant, that he gave a consent within a reasonable time. The Act does not lay down any particular period of time as being reasonable; but in ordinary circumstances, with no special difficulty, this period is not likely to exceed a few weeks.[8] Likewise, reversing the common law, the onus is on the landlord or superior landlord to show that any condition is reasonable, where the 1988 Act applies, and if consent is refused, the onus is on the landlord to show that a refusal of consent was reasonable (s 1(6) and 3(5)).

Reasonableness: preliminary matters

The following principles as to 'reasonableness' of a refusal of consent are not applicable where the narrower regime of s 19(1A) of the 1927 Act applies, at least to the extent that the parties to a 'new tenancy' which is not a residential lease have regulated the ground for consents in advance.

Under the general law, unregulated by advance contract, or where such contract does not cover the matter, the only criterion is that of reasonableness. However, if the landlord has undertaken not to refuse consent to an assignment

---

6 *Air India v Balabel* [1993] 2 EGLR 66, CA.
7 See *CIN Properties Ltd v Gill* [1993] 2 EGLR 97.
8 *Midland Bank plc v Chart Enterprises Inc* [1990] 2 EGLR 59 (10 weeks' inadequately explained delay unreasonable on facts); also *Dong Bang (UK) Ltd v Davina Ltd* [1995] 1 EGLR 41.

to a respectable and responsible person, and a proposed assignee satisfies that test, the landlord must consent to the proposed disposition.[9]

The date at which the reasonableness of a refusal of consent is decided on is the date of the landlord's decision – as opposed to that of any subsequent proceedings between the parties.[10] Therefore, facts which might have swayed the landlord either way which appear after his decision cannot be relevant to its reasonableness, which is only fair, having regard to the short time allowed for a decision where the Landlord and Tenant Act 1988 applies.[11] If a landlord, who by the 1988 Act is bound to give reasons, fails to communicate a particular reason for a refusal or condition, which operated on his mind, the question has been raised as to whether he may rely on that reason in later proceedings.[12] While the 1988 Act does not confine the landlord to any stated reasons it could be said to be a breach of statutory duty not to disclose all operative reasons in the decision to the tenant.[13] The fact that consent could not reasonably be withheld does not exclude the tenant's obligation to apply for consent to the landlord.[14] A landlord whose consent is not sought may bring forfeiture proceedings, but relief may be granted if no damage is caused to his reversion, provided he could not reasonably have withheld consent.[15] A tenant has remedies under the 1988 Act (above) for an unreasonable withholding of consent. He may, alternatively, carry out the transaction concerned and risk a forfeiture.[16]

General meaning of 'reasonableness'

The following general principles governing the question of whether a refusal is reasonable may be summarised as follows. Much, however, depends on the facts.

1   A landlord is not entitled to refuse his consent to an assignment on grounds which have nothing to do with the relationship of landlord and tenant in regard to the subject-matter of the particular demise of the premises such as an alleged difficulty in re-letting other premises.[17] Moreover, a landlord is not entitled, it now seems, to impose by means of a condition – such as a requirement on consenting to a sub-letting that a rent deposit be paid into a joint account held in his and the head lessee's name – some benefit giving him additional security beyond that given him by the terms of the lease. Such a condition amounts to an unreasonable collateral advantage with nothing to do with the lessee's performance of his obligations.[18]

9   *Moat v Martin* [1950] 1 KB 175, [1949] 2 All ER 646, CA.
10   *Bromley Park Garden Estates Ltd v Moss* [1982] 2 All ER 890, [1982] 1 WLR 1019, CA.
11   *CIN Properties Ltd v Gill* [1993] 2 EGLR 97.
12   See Crabb [1994] Conv 316.
13   See *Kened Ltd v Connie Investments Ltd* [1997] 04 EG 141, CA. If a reason is not stated, it seems that it could have influenced the mind of the landlord; ibid.
14   *Barrow v Isaacs & Son* [1891] 1 QB 417, CA; also *Wilson v Fynn* [1948] 2 All ER 40.
15   *Scala House and District Property Co Ltd v Forbes* [1974] QB 575, [1973] 3 All ER 308, CA.
16   He may also apply to the county court under s 53 of the Landlord and Tenant Act 1954 for a declaration that consent was unreasonably withheld.
17   *Re Gibbs and Houlder Bros & Co Ltd's Lease, Houlder Bros & Co v Gibbs* [1925] Ch 575, CA.
18   *Straudley Investments Ltd v Mount Eden Land Ltd* [1996] EGCS 153, CA.

2   Similarly, if the landlord refuses his consent to a proposed assignment or sub-letting because of general reasons of good estate management relating to the whole building, not the particular part let to the tenant, his refusal will be unreasonable – as where the landlord had a general policy of refusing consents to assignments of residential tenancies: the refusal of consent to a flat tenant was held unreasonable.[19]

3   It is not necessary for the landlord to prove that the conclusions which led him to refuse consent were justified, if they were conclusions which a reasonable man might reach in the circumstances. For example, it was held reasonable for a landlord to refuse consent where he had grounds for believing that the proposed assignee might well use its position as leaseholder to gain a share in the landlord's redevelopment scheme.[20]

4   It may be reasonable for a landlord to refuse his consent to a proposed assignment on the ground of the purpose for which the assignee intends to use the premises, even though that purpose is not forbidden by the terms of the lease.[1]

5   On the question as to what extent it is permissible in deciding whether a refusal is reasonable, to take into account the consequences to the current tenant of a refusal of consent, the landlord is entitled to consider only his own interests. There may be some exceptional cases where there is such a disproportion between the benefit to the landlord and the detriment to the tenant that a refusal of consent is on that ground unreasonable, and where, therefore, the tenants proved that unless consent to an assignment to a company, which would licence out various parts of the premises for short-life office accommodation, was given, they would be virtually locked into the lease, and where the damage to the landlords' reversion was minimal, it was held that the landlords had unreasonably withheld their consent.[2]

6   A landlord is entitled to refuse consent to an assignment or sub-letting if the assignee or sub-tenant will inevitably use the premises in a manner contrary to the user covenants of the lease.[3] This may be so where the disposition has already taken place to a business tenant who is bound to break the user covenant, as where an assignee intended to dispose of the premises rather than to observe a covenant to carry on a retail trade on the premises.[4] However, a disposition covenant cannot be used as an indirect means of enforcing a user covenant where the landlord is able, after an assignment or sub-letting, to enforce the user covenant, and his right to do so would not be prejudiced by his giving consent: he may be able to reserve his rights to enforce the former covenant when consenting.[5]

19 *Bromley Park Garden Estates Ltd v Moss*, supra.
20 *Pimms v Tallow Chandlers in the City of London* [1964] 2 QB 547, [1964] 2 All ER 145, CA.
 1 *Bates v Donaldson* [1896] 2 QB 241 at 244, CA; *Rossi v Hestdrive Ltd* [1985] 1 EGLR 50.
 2 *International Drilling Fluids Ltd v Louisville Investments (Uxbridge) Ltd* [1986] Ch 513.
 3 *Packaging Centre v Poland Street Estate Ltd* (1961) 178 Estates Gazette 189; *Granada TV Network Ltd v Great Universal Stores Ltd* (1963) 187 Estates Gazette 391.
 4 *FW Woolworth plc v Charlwood Alliance Properties Ltd* [1987] 1 EGLR 53.
 5 *Killick v Second Covent Garden Property Co Ltd* [1973] 2 All ER 337, [1973] 1 WLR 658, CA.

Examples of reasonable and unreasonable withholding of consent

Some examples of *reasonable refusals of consent* may be given: they have in common the fact that the landlord legitimately resisted having an undesirable occupier foisted on him. It was reasonable to refuse consent because of real fears[6] as to the future rent-generating capacity of premises,[7] as well as where the landlord had serious doubts as to the ability of the proposed assignees to pay the rent or to comply with the full repairing obligations of the lease.[8] Similarly, a landlord who gave the original lessee a personal privilege of a right to end the lease reasonably refused consent to a re-assignment to that lessee, the sole purpose of it being to allow the latter to end the lease and with it, all liability for future rent.[9] Where the effect of a proposed disposition would be to give an assignee a right to enfranchise which the current tenant does not have, or to confer a protected sub-tenancy on a sub-tenant, for the first time, it was reasonable for the landlord to refuse his consent as the original basis of the lease would have been altered to his disadvantage.[10] A landlord who had reasonable suspicions as to the manner a proposed assignee would conduct his business had reasonably withheld his consent,[11] as had a lessor whose tenant had been seriously in breach of his covenant to repair, and there was no definite prospect that the assignee would remedy the breaches.[12]

The grounds on which a landlord may reasonably withhold consent have been limited under the general law by two principles: first, that he must confine his reasons to the actual demised premises, and secondly, he cannot plead in aid general matters of good estate management. Therefore, a refusal of consent because it might be hard to re-let premises of the landlord's currently occupied by the proposed assignee was unreasonable,[13] as was a refusal based on the policy of the landlord of recovering vacant possession of flats by means of a surrender where the existing tenants left.[14] These reasons had nothing to do with the merits of the proposed transaction.

A refusal of consent has also been held *unreasonable* for a variety of reasons, as shown by the following examples, which have little in common on the facts but indicate perhaps that the landlord sought to obtain too many advantages from the disposition covenant. A refusal was thus unreasonable where his sole reason was to obtain possession,[15] or where the landlord tried to obtain a result

6   As opposed to imaginary ones: cf *Rayburn v Wolf* (1985) 50 P & CR 463, CA.
7   *Re Town Investments Ltd Underlease* [1954] Ch 301, [1954] 1 All ER 585 (where a sub-lease was proposed at a low rent and a premium).
8   *British Bakeries (Midlands) Ltd v Michael Testler & Co Ltd* [1986] 1 EGLR 64.
9   *Olympia & York Canary Wharf Ltd v Oil Property Investments Ltd* [1994] 2 EGLR 48, CA.
10 *Bickel v Duke of Westminster* [1977] QB 517, [1976] 3 All ER 801, CA; *Leeward Securities Ltd v Lilyheath Properties Ltd* [1984] 2 EGLR 54, CA; also *West Layton Ltd v Ford* [1979] QB 593, [1979] 2 All ER 657, CA.
11 *Rossi v Hestdrive Ltd* [1985] 1 EGLR 50.
12 *Orlando Investments Ltd v Grosvenor Estate Belgravia* [1989] 2 EGLR 74, CA; PF Smith [1989] Conv 371.
13 *Re Gibbs and Houlder Bros' Lease* [1925] Ch 575, CA.
14 *Bromley Park Garden Estates Ltd v Moss*, supra.
15 *Bates v Donaldson*, supra.

not contemplated by the parties at the date of the relevant assignment, as where he refused to agree to an assignment to B until the tenant agreed to execute an earlier licence to assign to A.[16] Likewise, consent was unreasonably withheld where the reason was not bona fide,[17] or where, although the tenant was in breach of covenant, the disrepair was not very serious and the assignee intended to spend a considerable sum on repairs.[18] Where the landlord refused to consent to a proposed sub-letting as the rent level attained was not high enough in his view, the refusal was unreasonable: the rent was within a band of market levels.[19] A refusal of consent for capricious reasons is unreasonable, as where the ground was that a proposed assignee had diplomatic immunity.[20]

VI ALTERATIONS AND IMPROVEMENTS

The landlord may be content to rely on the law of waste to protect his reversion against any damage caused by the tenant making alterations or improvements to the demised premises, but only if substantial damage is proved will he obtain any satisfaction; and he will obtain none if the value of the reversion is enhanced.

It is common to insert express covenants against the making of structural (or indeed any) alterations. These, by exact analogy with disposition covenants, may be absolute, qualified or fully qualified.[1] Some leases may require the tenant to submit drawings and specifications to the landlord before he consents and may enable a written licence to be granted by the landlord for particular work. Where an absolute covenant against the making of structural alterations,[2] or indeed, a similar covenant, is broken, the landlord may, unless he waives the breach, forfeit the lease or claim a mandatory injunction compelling the tenant to re-instate the premises. For example, where a tenant, during certain works, deliberately lowered the height of a parapet wall by some 12 inches, in breach of a covenant not to cut or injure the main walls of the premises, a mandatory injunction was granted compelling her to re-instate the wall to its former height.[3]

---

16 *Roux Restaurants Ltd* v *Jaison Property Development Co Ltd* [1996] EGCS 118, CA.
17 *Lovelock v Margo* [1963] 2 QB 786, [1963] 2 All ER 13, CA; and a refusal based on the possibility of a superior landlord's refusal is unreasonable: *Vienit Ltd v W Williams & Son* [1958] 3 All ER 621, [1958] 1 WLR 1267.
18 *Farr v Ginnings* (1928) 44 TLR 249.
19 *Blockbuster Entertainments Ltd* v *Leakcliff Properties Ltd* [1996] EGCS 151.
20 *Parker v Boggon* [1947] KB 346, [1947] 1 All ER 46; and a refusal based on grounds of race or sex is ipso facto unreasonable: Race Relations Act 1976 s 24; Sex Discrimination Act 1975, s 31.
 1 Sometimes a consent may be conditional, eg on the execution of a licence, as in *Prudential Assurance Co Ltd* v *Mount Eden Land Ltd* [1996] EGCS 179.
 2 As to the construction of which see *Taylor v Vectapike Ltd* [1990] 2 EGLR 12, where the court refused to put any gloss on the clear words used.
 3 *Viscount Chelsea v Muscatt* [1990] 2 EGLR 48, CA.

'Alterations'

An alteration, within the meaning of a covenant against structural alterations, is a change in the form, structure or constitution of a building, such as the conversion of a bedroom into a bathroom, the sub-division of two rooms, the making of two rooms into one, or the insertion of windows into walls, but not just a change in the appearance of the building, unless the covenant expressly so provides. Conversion of a house into flats[4] is a breach of a covenant against alterations, but not the erection of an advertising sign on an external wall unless the covenant extends to appearance.[5] Even a covenant against alterations to the building or the architectural elevation is not broken by changes in appearance which do not affect the fabric.[6]

'Improvements'

A covenant or condition by the tenant not to make an alteration which is an improvement without the landlord's prior licence or consent is converted by s 19(2) of the Landlord and Tenant Act 1927 into a covenant not to carry out the relevant work without the landlord's prior consent, such consent not to be unreasonably withheld. This applies notwithstanding any express provision to the contrary. However, this section does not apply to absolute prohibitions against the making of structural alterations, leaving the landlord free of statutory qualifications in that case. In addition, specific rules govern the making of improvements in the case of certain types of residential tenancies, to the exclusion of those of s 19(2);[7] seemingly, it is thought that the position of both parties should be more tightly regulated than by the general statutory rule. Because specific consent rules apply to agricultural tenants' improvements, s 19(2) is excluded in the case both of a tenancy of an agricultural holding and in the case of a farm business tenancy.[8]

A further limit on the scope of s 19(2) is that it only applies to an alteration which constitutes an improvement.[9] However, useful to tenants is the principle that the question of whether an alteration amounts to an improvement is to be judged from the point of view of the tenant,[10] and not the landlord, whose position is only safeguarded where he takes advantage of certain rights within s 19(2), as mentioned below. Any alteration which would render the tenant's occupation and enjoyment of the demised premises more convenient and comfortable to him appears to constitute an improvement.[11] This beneficial view to tenants may explain why the rules in this branch of the law have

---

4 *Duke of Westminster v Swinton* [1948] 1 KB 524, [1948] 1 All ER 248.
5 *Heard v Stuart* (1907) 24 TLR 104.
6 *Joseph v LCC* (1914) 111 LT 276; also *Bickmore v Dimmer* [1903] 1 Ch 158, CA.
7 Housing Act 1980, ss 81–83. Duties to alter, and to apply for consent, may arise under the Disability Discrimination Act 1995 (s 16). The landlord cannot unreasonably withhold consent: thus, an absolute prohibition on alterations is, where the Act applies, rendered fully qualified.
8 Landlord and Tenant Act 1927, s 19(4), as amended by Agricultural Tenancies Act 1995, Sch, para 6. Mining leases are also outside s 19(2) (s 19(4) of the 1927 Act).
9 *Balls Bros Ltd v Sinclair* [1931] 2 Ch 325.
10 *Lambert v F W Woolworth & Co (No 2)* [1938] Ch 883, [1938] 2 All ER 664, CA.
11 *Woolworth & Co Ltd v Lambert* [1937] Ch 37, [1936] 2 All ER 1523, CA.

remained relatively stable: the present law may induce landlords to prefer to impose absolute prohibitions where possible.

A tenant's proposal to open apertures in the party-wall between the demised premises and adjoining premises, in both of which the tenant traded, was held to constitute an improvement to which the landlord could not reasonably withhold his consent.[12] Likewise, a tenant's proposed alterations which involved enlarging the demised shop premises, by demolishing a wall at the back, so connecting the shop with adjoining land, and then building an enlarged shop over the combined premises, moving the main staircase and staff accommodation to the extended premises, were held to be improvements within s 19(2) of the 1927 Act,[13] as was the conversion of a roof space, demised to the lessee, a first-floor flat tenant, into a dormer window.[14] If the only way the work can be executed will involve a trespass into the landlord's adjoining land, he is entitled to refuse consent on that ground.[15]

Rights of landlord where s 19(2) applies

So as to safeguard the landlord's position, s 19(2) provides that the landlord has the right to require as a condition of any licence or consent to an alteration which amounts to an improvement in the statutory sense:

(i) the payment of a reasonable sum in respect of any damage to or diminution in the value of the premises or any neighbouring premises belonging to the landlord, and

(ii) of any legal or other expenses properly incurred in connection with such licence or consent, and, in the case of an improvement which does not add to the letting value of the holding,

(iii) an undertaking on the part of the tenant to reinstate the premises in the condition in which they were before the improvement was executed, where such a requirement would be reasonable.

If the landlord withholds his consent, the tenant may, as with disposition covenants, apply to the court for a declaration that consent has been unreasonably withheld.[16] If the tenant is advised that consent has unreasonably been withheld, he may, alternatively, simply proceed with the proposed alteration.[17] If consent could reasonably have been withheld, the landlord may bring a forfeiture, subject to the court's discretion to grant relief, which, in the case of a deliberate breach, may well be refused.[18] Or he may claim re-instatement, damages and a declaration.[19]

---

12 *Lilley and Skinner Ltd v Crump* (1929) 73 Sol Jo 366.
13 *Woolworth & Co Ltd v Lambert,* supra.
14 *Davies v Yadegar* [1990] 1 EGLR 71, CA.
15 *Tideway Investment & Property Holdings Ltd v Wellwood* [1952] 1 All ER 1142; *Haines v Florensa* [1990] 1 EGLR 73, CA.
16 See Landlord and Tenant Act 1954, s 53 (generally the county court).
17 *Railway Comr v Avrom Investments Pty Ltd* [1959] 2 All ER 63, [1959] 1 WLR 389, PC.
18 *Duke of Westminster v Swinton* [1948] 1 KB 524, [1948] 1 All ER 248.
19 As in *Mosley v Cooper* [1990] 1 EGLR 124.

Unreasonable and reasonable refusals

In contrast to the position where the Landlord and Tenant Act 1988 applies, the onus of proving that the landlord has unreasonably refused his consent where s 19(2) of the 1927 Act applies[20] is on the tenant. Hence, where a landlord demanded the payment of £7,000 before he consented to structural alterations proposed by the tenant, it was held that the tenant failed, on the facts, to prove that consent was unreasonably withheld.[1] However, if the landlord gives no reason and merely refuses consent, this puts the onus of justifying the refusal on the landlord.[2] If the landlord demands compensation to cover any damage he may suffer, which sum is later determined in proceedings not to be reasonable, and refuses his consent unless that sum is paid, then he will be unable to require any sum, even a reasonable amount, *ex post facto*. If the landlord refuses consent, and so puts it out of his power to require reinstatement as a condition of giving consent, where the value of the reversion is diminished, he cannot later, if his refusal is held unreasonable, require re-instatement. Where therefore a landlord, having originally demanded the payment of £7,000 as a condition of consenting to tenants' improvements, later refused his consent unconditionally, and his refusal was held to be unreasonable, it was held that he could not then claim any money payments or re-instatement.[3] In any event, it may be that a requirement to pay an unreasonable sum in compensation, or the imposition of an unreasonable re-instatement requirement, as a condition of consent in either case, would amount to unreasonable withholding of consent. As to the grounds on which consent may reasonably be refused, there is little authority. It has been said that many reasons, aesthetic, historic or even personal, may be sufficient grounds.[4]

Non-compliance with reasonable re-instatement condition

A tenant who, having given an undertaking to re-instate, fails to carry it out when the time comes, is liable in damages, the measure of which is the reduction in value of the landlord's reversion: if the landlord proves that he intends and is able to carry out the re-instatement himself, and it would be reasonable for him to do so, he may recover the full cost of re-instatement. But, if the landlord suffers no actual damage, he is entitled to nominal damages only.[5]

---

20 Where the special rules governing certain residential tenancies apply, the onus of proof that consent was reasonably withheld is, however, on the landlord (Housing Act 1980 s 82(1)) but he may rely on the matters there set out, eg the extent to which the work might make the house less safe for occupiers.

1 *Woolworth & Co Ltd v Lambert*, supra.

2 *Lambert v F W Woolworth & Co Ltd (No 2)* [1938] Ch 883 at 906, CA (Slesser LJ).

3 Ibid.

4 *Lambert v F W Woolworth & Co Ltd (No 2)* [1938] Ch 883 at 907, CA (Slesser LJ).

5 *James v Hutton and J Cook & Sons Ltd* [1950] 1 KB 9, [1949] 2 All ER 132, CA; *Duke of Westminster v Swinton* [1948] 1 KB 524, [1948] 1 All ER 248.

VII   USER

General principles

At common law, the tenant, in the absence of any contrary covenant, may use the demised premises for any lawful purpose. Even without any covenant restricting the use of the premises, the tenant is prohibited from actively damaging them, by the doctrine of waste. In this section, we examine the way in which user covenants, especially of a negative nature, are construed by the courts and affected by legislation.

Some leases contain restrictions on the user which is allowed in relation to the premises. The scope of any particular user covenant is for the parties to decide on, and the onus of proving that a breach has taken place is on the landlord.[6] It would seem that any user covenants in a sub-lease should be construed independently of those in the head lease.[7] User covenants may specify that only a given type or range of user is permitted, such as use only as a private residence, or user only for certain types of trade or business. Equally, certain types of specified user may be prohibited or restricted, as where a flat was not to be used except as a single residence in one occupation,[8] or where premises could only be used for the business of a named lessee.[9] A positive obligation to use the premises in a particular way may be imposed, at least in theory, but very clear language is required to achieve that result, and a positively-phrased obligation to use premises either for a given trade or for other purposes was insufficient to do so.[10]

Some user covenants are absolute in form, so that the lessee may only change the user of the premises if the landlord is prepared to agree to vary the lease or waive the breach for his benefit. Other user covenants may be either qualified or fully qualified, by analogy with disposition covenants. The Law Commission did not recommend that absolute user covenants should be made fully qualified, owing in part to the danger that this might raise rents, at least in the business sector, where user covenants tended to be more specific, tying the tenant to specific uses within categories.[11]

Qualified covenants

Where the user covenant permits the tenant to alter the use of the premises with the landlord's consent, the landlord is entitled to refuse his consent to a proposed change of user on any grounds, reasonable or not.[12] This means that, if the tenant cannot procure an alteration in the permitted user of the premises, and the user covenant is absolute, he may have to pay any sum demanded by

---

6 *Basildon Development Corpn v Mactro Ltd* [1986] 1 EGLR 137, CA.
7 *Atwal v Courts Garages* [1989] 1 EGLR 63, CA.
8 *Falgor Commercial SA v Alsabahia Inc* [1986] 1 EGLR 41, CA.
9 See eg *Granada TV Network Ltd v Great Universal Stores* (1963) 187 Estates Gazette 391; also *Law Land Co Ltd v Consumers' Association Ltd* [1980] 2 EGLR 109, CA.
10 *Montross Associated Investments SA v Moussaieff* [1990] 2 EGLR 61, CA.
11 *Report*, paras 4.32–4.53.
12 *Guardian Assurance Co Ltd v Gants Hill Holdings Ltd* [1983] 2 EGLR 36.

the landlord for his consent to such change. Legislation does not imply any proviso that the landlord's consent cannot unreasonably be withheld – if this requirement is to exist, it must be expressly mentioned in the covenant itself.[13]

Legislation alleviates the position slightly: it applies both to qualified and fully qualified user covenants, except in the case of leases of agricultural holdings, farm business tenancies and mining leases. By s 19(3) of the Landlord and Tenant Act 1927, if the proposed change of user does not involve any structural alteration of the premises, the covenant is deemed, notwithstanding any express provision to the contrary, to be subject to a proviso that no fine or sum of money in the nature of a fine, whether by way of rent increase or otherwise, is to be payable for any licence or consent of the landlord to that change.[14] The landlord is not precluded from requiring the payment of a reasonable sum in respect of any damage or diminution in the value of the premises or any neighbouring premises belonging to him. He may also require the payment, as part of this sum, of his legal or other expenses. If the tenant disputes the reasonableness of any sum demanded by the landlord as the price of his licence or consent, the court has power to declare that a given sum is reasonable in amount. If this is done, the landlord is bound to consent to the change in user, on being paid that sum. While an offer of consent on payment of money is not a consent, s 19(3) does not prevent a landlord refusing consent, offering to accept a surrender of the lease, and to re-grant a new lease on terms more advantageous to himself.[15]

Fully qualified covenants

The user covenant may provide that the landlord's consent to a change of user is not to be unreasonably withheld. In general, the reasonableness of any refusal of consent is judged in much the same way as in the case of assignments[16] and so, if the refusal seeks to obtain a collateral advantage not contemplated by the lease, it will be unreasonable, as where the landlord sought to exploit the user covenant to attempt to maximise the rents of surrounding premises.[17] The user covenant may, however, provide that consent to a change of user is not to be withheld unreasonably and then restrict this by stating that, if consent is withheld on specified grounds, it will not be treated as having been unreasonably withheld. In such cases, because the second (and excepting) part of the clause cuts down its first part, the excepting part risks being narrowly construed.[18]

If the landlord demands an excessive sum in respect of his consent in relation to a matter set out in s 19(3) of the 1927 Act, the tenant may apply to

---

13 The Law Commission recommended ending the privileged position of qualified user covenants (*Report*, para 6.14–6.16) which would leave a clear line between absolute and fully qualified user covenants, as exists in the case of assignments.
14 If a fine is actually paid before the licence is granted, it is irrecoverable: see *Comber v Fleet Electronics Ltd* [1955] 2 All ER 161, [1955] 1 WLR 566.
15 *Barclays Bank plc v Daejan Investments (Grove Hall) Ltd* [1995] 1 EGLR 68.
16 See *Sood v Barker* [1991] 1 EGLR 87, CA.
17 *Anglia Building Society v Sheffield City Council* [1983] 1 EGLR 57, CA; also *Tollbench Ltd v Plymouth City Council* [1988] 1 EGLR 79, CA.
18 See *Berenyi v Watford Borough Council* [1980] 2 EGLR 38, CA.

the court for a declaration as to what sum is reasonable, on payment of which consent must be granted. If the landlord demands a fine or other sum as the cost of his consent, it may be that s 19(3) permits the tenant to treat the demand as an unreasonable refusal of consent. Where the landlord refuses his consent, or imposes an unreasonable condition, the tenant may apply to the county court for a declaration, in the same way as in the case of assignments.

Modification of restrictive covenants

Statute enables restrictive covenants in residential leases to be modified. Under s 610 of the Housing Act 1985 in particular,[19] the county court may vary the terms of any covenant in a lease of any premises restrictive of user or prohibiting conversions or alterations where it is in effect the case that such works would enable letting, after conversion, into two or more dwelling-houses, where letting as a single tenement is difficult, owing to changes in the character of the neighbourhood, and the appropriate planning permission has been granted for such conversion. The provision applies to a single unit which the lessee wishes to convert by subdivision into two or more units.[20]

Examples of certain types of user covenant

In leases of residential property, tenants commonly covenant to use the premises as a private residence only, or not to use them for the purpose of any trade.[1] Such a covenant would be broken by the erection of a studio and classroom for pupils,[2] the presence of a notice signifying that the premises included an office,[3] the taking in of lodgers or paying guests,[4] or the garaging of a taxi which was used by the tenant in his business.[5] A covenant for private residence in the occupation of one household only, has been held not to be broken where one paying guest was taken in as a member of the family.[6]

In business leases, covenants against particular trades or for no trade other than a particular trade may be found, but the latter does not oblige the tenant to carry on that trade. The prohibited businesses or trades may be specific or the covenant may prohibit only noisy, offensive or dangerous trades, or it may disallow the sale of certain types of product, such as goods not usually sold in

---

19 The Lands Tribunal may modify obsolete restrictive covenants in the case of leasehold land held under a term for over 40 years under Law of Property Act 1925, s 84.
20 This does not apply to a scheme for division of adjoining terraced houses into flats, each of which would extend beyond the original houses: *Josephine Trust Ltd v Champagne* [1963] 2 QB 160, [1962] 3 All ER 136, CA.
 1 Some leases require the tenant not to cause a nuisance to the landlord, his tenants and to adjoining occupiers: if the covenant extends to 'annoyance' it is much wider than a common law nuisance (see *Tod-Heatly v Benham* (1888) 40 Ch D 80; *Chorley Borough Council v Ribble Motor Services Ltd* [1996] EGCS 110, CA).
 2 *Patman v Harland* (1881) 17 Ch D 353.
 3 *Wilkinson v Rogers* (1863) 3 New Rep 145.
 4 *Thorn v Madden* [1925] Ch 847.
 5 *Jones v Christy* (1963) 107 Sol Jo 374, CA.
 6 *Segal Securities Ltd v Thoseby* [1963] 1 QB 887, [1963] 1 All ER 500; also *Falgor Commercial SA v Alsabahia Inc*, supra.

a food supermarket.[7] The onus of proving a breach will be on the landlord. The enforcement of clauses in leases of shops which require the tenant to keep the premises open for trade throughout the lease has recently arisen. In one case, the tenant of a supermarket in a precinct closed down his shop – in breach of covenant – and removed all fittings. He was subjected to an order of specific performance which required him to observe his obligation to keep the premises open for trade until the expiry of his lease, even though it could be said that the effect of so drastic an order might be oppressive.[8] However, as has been pointed out,[9] an injunction will not necessarily be granted in every case of breach of a covenant to trade and moreover, although in the case of shop premises, damages for breach of a 'keep open' covenant may be hard to assess, the process is possible.[10]

Where the covenant is for business purposes only or a particular business only, it is a matter of construction whether residence on the premises will be allowed, but the past history of the premises, prior to the execution of the lease, is irrelevant; the nature of the premises and their suitability for use as a dwelling are both relevant to the construction of the user covenant.[11]

Mention may lastly be made of tying covenants, ie undertakings by the tenant of, notably, a public house or petrol station to sell only the beer or petrol (and perhaps related products) supplied by the landlord brewer or oil company. Subject to the regulation of the length of the tie, which is governed by the doctrine of restraint of trade, and so is outside the scope of this book, a tying covenant is enforceable at common law against the lessee currently in occupation.[12] However, in two cases the question was raised, but not decided conclusively, as to whether a tying covenant relating to beer products was void, as contravening the free trade policies of article 85 of the Treaty of Rome. The courts ruled that even if the covenants had been void, they would have been clearly severable, applying domestic legal principles, from the rest of the leases, especially as in one case it was in terms provided in the lease that the invalidity of one provision did not affect the validity of the rest of the lease.[13]

VIII OPTIONS IN THE LEASE

1 PRINCIPLES COMMON TO OPTIONS

Leases may allow the tenant an option to renew, to terminate the lease early and to purchase the landlord's reversion. Some principles are common to these

7 *Basildon Development Corpn v Mactro Ltd* [1986] 1 EGLR 137, CA.
8 *Co-operative Insurance Society Ltd v Argyll Stores (Holdings) Ltd* [1996] Ch 286, CA; see HW Wilkinson (1996) 146 NLJ 757; J Martin [1996] Conv 329.
9 By HW Wilkinson, supra.
10 See eg *Transworld Land Co Ltd v J Sainsbury plc* [1990] 2 EGLR 255, where liability in damages but not their amount had been agreed.
11 *City and Westminster Properties (1934) Ltd v Mudd* [1959] Ch 129, [1958] 2 All ER 733.
12 *Cleveland Petroleum Co Ltd v Dartstone Ltd* [1969] 1 All ER 201; *Total Oil Great Britain v Thompson Garages (Biggin Hill)* [1972] 1 QB 318, [1971] 3 All ER 1226, CA.
13 *Inntrepeneuer Estates (GL) Ltd v Boyes* [1993] 2 EGLR 112, CA; *Inntrepreneuer Estates (GL) Ltd v Mason* [1993] 2 EGLR 189; Frazer [1994] Conv 150.

options. Firstly, both options for renewal and to purchase (but not to break) must be registered in the appropriate manner, depending on whether the title is registered or unregistered, in order to be capable of binding a person to whom the landlord may assign the reversion.[14] However, if the tenant is in actual occupation of registered land, his right to exercise an option to purchase (or seemingly to renew) will depend on his occupation, as against an assignee of the reversion, rather than registration.[15]

The exercise of the tenant's privilege of exercising any of these three options is normally[16] dependent on his serving a prior written notice of exercise on the landlord, normally a given number of months before the expiry date of his lease. Indeed options to renew and to purchase may well specify that unless such a notice is served strictly within the time allowed (such as within the last six months of the term) the option is not exercisable – although the landlord may be estopped from insisting in due service or waive the requirements.[17]

Options to renew and to purchase are, for the purposes of s 2 of the Law of Property (Miscellaneous Provisions) Act 1989, a conditional contract in the lease, which the lessee may convert into a concluded contract by means of his notice of exercise, provided he has complied with any conditions precedent to exercising his rights: moreover, the landlord does not have to sign this notice, since s 2 cannot be construed as having impliedly imposed so strange an additional formality on the parties.[18] The most common of these conditions is a requirement that the tenant has paid the rent due and is not in breach of covenant at the date of service of his option notice or the date of expiry of the lease, as the case may be.

2 OPTIONS FOR RENEWAL

Where a tenant seeks during the lease[19] to exercise an option to renew, if it is a condition precedent that at the relevant date he must not be in breach of covenant, even a trivial but subsisting breach at or by the date when the option is exercisable by the tenant debars the tenant from obtaining renewal, unless it is waived.[20] This is because the tenant has a conditional privilege of renewal, not a right.[1] If the breach is spent (ie it lies at some time in the past history of the

---

14 In the case of registered land, such options should be protected by a notice or caution (Land Registration Act, ss 49 and 54) and where title is unregistered, as a Class C (iv) land charge (Land Charges Act 1972, s 2(4)); as explained in *Phillips v Mobil Oil Co Ltd* [1989] 3 All ER 97, CA (renewal) and *Pritchard v Briggs* [1980] Ch 338, [1980] 1 All ER 294, CA (purchase).

15 *Webb v Pollmount Ltd* [1966] Ch 584, [1966] 1 All ER 481, applying Land Registration Act 1925 s 70(1)(g).

16 For a case where the right to renew was not dependent on prior notice see *Gardner v Blaxhill* [1960] 2 All ER 457, [1960] 1 WLR 752.

17 See *Multon v Cordell* [1986] 1 EGLR 44.

18 *Spiro v Glencrown Properties Ltd* [1991] Ch 537, [1990] 1 All ER 600.

19 A tenant holding over as yearly tenant may seemingly exercise an option to renew: *Moss v Barton* (1866) LR 1 Eq 474.

20 *West Country Cleaners (Falmouth) Ltd v Saly* [1966] 3 All ER 210, [1966] 1 WLR 1485, CA.

1 However, a condition that renewal depended on the parties agreeing a business plan did not prevent a lessee not in breach of his leasehold obligations from renewing: *Little v Courage* (1994) 70 P & CR 469, CA.

lease), the tenant will still be entitled to renew, as where in the past a tenant had twice withheld rent but owed none at the end of the lease.[2] This rule applies to all breaches of covenant, be they positive or negative.[3] The severity of these principles is illustrated by the effect on renewal rights of breaches of covenant to repair. In one case the tenant, at the operative date, had failed to carry out repairs costing a small amount of money, which would have been easy to execute, but lost the ability to renew.[4] Likewise, a tenant who had failed to complete certain interior decorations as required, by the end of the lease, costing about £800, could not renew.[5] The High Court releaxed the rule to the extent of holding that a tenant who carried out regular checks at intervals who had failed to cure some disrepair before the end of the lease would not lose the right to renew as he was not in breach until he failed, within a reasonable time, to remedy the breach.[6] However, where a tenant had twice withheld rent to pressure his landlord into carrying out repairs, but owed no rent by the end of the term and was not otherwise in breach of covenants, the right to renewal at the expiry of the term was held unaffected.[7]

In the absence of express terms of renewal, the new lease will generally be for the same period and upon the same terms as the current tenancy. The parties may agree on the rent payable under the new lease. If they do not, the rent will likely be the same as the old rent. The parties may simply agree that the new rent is such as to be agreed by some means or other, say by two valuers, one appointed by each party. If one party tries to frustrate the machinery agreed, then the court will determine what is a fair and reasonable rent.[8] Whether the parties' formula enables an arbitrator to include rent reviews in the new term is entirely a matter of construction.[9] Where an option to renew was at a rent not exceeding a specified sum, it was proper to imply a term that a fair rent was to be agreed, with the specified sum as an upper limit.[10]

3   OPTIONS TO DETERMINE

A fixed term lease may enable the landlord or tenant to determine the term prior to its original expiry date, by notice served at some specified time. So as to limit their scope, some options to determine are expressed as exercisable only by the original, named lessee: hence, where MF, so named, assigned its lease to X and later obtained a re-assignment of the term to itself, MF's right, construed as personal, to determine, was construed as not intended to survive the assignment to X.[11] The court refused to construe this lease as creating a right running with

2 *Bassett v Whiteley* (1983) 45 P & CR 87, CA.
3 *Bass Holdings Ltd v Morton Music Ltd* [1987] 2 All ER 1001, CA.
4 *Finch v Underwood* (1876) 2 Ch D 310, CA.
5 *Bairstow Eves (Securities) Ltd v Ripley* [1992] 2 EGLR 47, CA.
6 *West Middlesex Golf Club Ltd v Ealing London Borough Council* (1993) 68 P & CR 461.
7 *Bassett v Whiteley* (1983) 45 P & CR 87, CA.
8 *Sudbrook Trading Estate Ltd v Eggleton* [1983] 1 AC 444, [1982] 3 All ER 1, HL; also *ARC Ltd v Schofield* [1990] 2 EGLR 52, CA.
9 *National Westminster Bank v BSC Footwear* (1980) 42 P & CR 90, CA.
10 *Corson v Rhuddlan Borough Council* [1990] 1 EGLR 255, CA.
11 *Max Factor Ltd v Wesleyan Assurance Society* [1995] 2 EGLR 38; affd on appeal [1996] EGCS 82.

the lease which was incapable of exercise after assignment even though it could be exercised on a re-assignment to the original lessee.

An option to determine (or break-clause) is not consensual but is a type of unilateral privilege and must be exercised strictly within any time-limits laid down for its exercise, otherwise it is not validly exercised and the lease continues.[12] Hence, where a tenant purported to end a lease by notice as on 12 January, a mistake for 13 January, his notice was void, as it did not end the lease at the agreed date. The court refused to overlook or correct this unilateral error.[13] Exceptionally, if a mistake as to the date is such that the stated date is impossible, or for some reason inconceivable, so that a reasonable landlord (or tenant) could not have been misled by the notice, the court may correct the date and substitute the correct one, as where a tenant's notice mistakenly gave a year of termination which had passed by the time the notice had been served.[14]

Where a lease is measured as from a date which precedes the taking of possession by the tenant, there is a risk that the court will conclude that the time for service of a notice to break may be the relevant anniversary of the stated date of the lease, not the date the tenant took possession.[15]

If an option is exercisable only by a written notice, an oral notice will not suffice. Especially where the option is exercisable by the landlord, it may be available only in specified circumstances, such as for the landlord's own purposes, or for redevelopment or reconstruction: whether an event falls within specified circumstances is a matter of construction.[16] Where a landlord proved that he required possession at some time after the date for exercise of the option but before the original expiry date of the term, this entitled him to exercise the option, and he only had to establish that he required to occupy part of the premises, as against the whole, as he could not occupy any part without exercising his option.[17]

Ambiguous notices of purported exercise of an option to determine will be construed so as to uphold them, if possible, so that an option exercisable by not less than three months' notice in writing at any time during the term was validly exercised by a notice to the tenant to vacate the premises 'within' a three month period from the date of the notice.[18]

Where the tenancy is one to which Part II of the Landlord and Tenant Act 1954 applies, it will end at common law at the date specified in the notice, although the tenancy then continues under s 24 of the Act.[19] The landlord may

---

12   *Hankey v Clavering* [1942] 2 KB 326, CA; *United Scientific Holdings Ltd v Burnley Borough Council* [1978] AC 904 at 929, HL; *A & J Mucklow (Birmingham) Ltd v Metro-Cammell Weymann Ltd* [1994] EGCS 64.
13   *Mannai Investment Co Ltd v Eagle Star Life Assurance Co Ltd* [1995] 1 WLR 1508, CA.
14   *Carradine Properties Ltd v Aslam* [1976] 1 All ER 573, [1976] 1 WLR 442.
15   As in *Trane (UK) Ltd v Provident Mutual Life Assurance Association* [1995] 1 EGLR 33 (date by which notice must expire was 28/8/1981, 10 years from date of lease, not a date early in 1992, ten years from taking of possession).
16   *City Offices (Regent Street) Ltd v Europa Acceptance Group plc* [1990] 1 EGLR 63, CA.
17   *Parkinson v Barclays Bank* [1951] 1 KB 368, [1950] 2 All ER 936, CA.
18   *Manorlike Ltd v Le Vitas Travel Agency* [1986] 1 All ER 573, CA.
19   *Weinbergs Weatherproofs Ltd v Radcliffe Paper Mill Co* [1958] Ch 437.

serve a notice to determine the tenancy under s 25 of the 1954 Act, Part II which will take effect, if clearly so intended, as a common-law notice of determination under an option to determine.[20]

4 OPTIONS TO PURCHASE

Options to purchase the reversion are a separate agreement by the parties, which is collateral to the lease. Accordingly, an option to purchase needs to be protected against third party assignees of the reversion by registration – as noted earlier. The tenant may be unable to exercise an option to purchase if its terms provide that he must have performed the covenants of the lease. Normally, the tenant is to exercise the option by a written notice. The terms of the option may state the price payable, or they may provide, for example, for a formula, as where the price is to be a fair and reasonable price to be agreed by the parties or determined by arbitration. In one case, the parties agreed that the price was to be agreed by two valuers, one appointed by each party. However, the landlords refused to make an appointment. The options concerned had been duly exercised, and the House of Lords ordered an inquiry into the fair value of the reversion concerned, refusing to allow the landlords to frustrate the determination machinery provided by the lease.[1] The terms of the existing lease cease, in equity, to be enforceable once the relationship of vendor and purchaser has come into existence between the parties, as where the conditions precedent for exercise of the option to purchase have been satisfied and the price has been agreed.

20 *Keith Bayley Rogers & Co v Cubes* (1975) 31 P & CR 412.
 1 *Sudbrook Trading Estate Ltd v Eggleton* [1983] 1 AC 444, [1982] 3 All ER 1, HL.

Chapter 8

Rent and rent review

I DEFINITION OF RENT

Rent has been defined for modern purposes as a contractual sum which the landlord is entitled to receive from the tenant in return for the tenant's use and occupation of his land.[1] As will appear, it is usual to reserve rent out of the land, as where the land (including any premises) is leased or demised and the tenant undertakes in any form of words to pay a fixed rent, as where he covenants to pay the rent of £X for the whole term, or where the words 'yielding and paying' a stated rent follow those of demise.[2] Unless the lease expressly provides to the contrary, rent is payable in arrear.[3] As will appear, the lease should specify the dates for payment of rent (eg on the usual quarter days). Ordinarily, rent is payable in money.[4]

Because rent issues out of the whole or any part of the demised land, it is due (unless some express exception appears in the lease) even if buildings on the land are destroyed or requisitioned during the term.[5]

If the lease is frustrated, all liability to pay rent, after the frustrating event, ceases, but a frustrating event must be so grave that no substantial use is possible for the purposes permitted or contemplated by the parties, for the residue of the term, and frustration will seldom apply to relieve the tenant from his obligation to pay rent, even if his enjoyment of the demised land is severely dislocated.[6]

For the purposes of distress, a rent must be certain to be recoverable.[7] Otherwise, if a rent is certain or capable of being rendered certain at the time it is due, it is recoverable. Insufficiently certain was a rent based on as many hours' services as the landlord required from time to time,[8] but a rent calculated

---

1 *C H Bailey Ltd v Memorial Enterprises Ltd* [1974] 1 All ER 1003, [1974] 1 WLR 728, CA.
2 In *Ashburn Anstalt v Arnold* [1989] Ch 1, [1988] 2 All ER 147, CA, it was said that a reservation of rent is not essential to the creation of a tenancy; and tenancies at will may be rent-free.
3 *Coomber v Howard* (1845) 1 CB 440; and see further, Foa, pp 103–104.
4 However, a rent may validly be payable as goods or services: Co Lit 142a: *Montague v Browning* [1954] 2 All ER 601, [1954] 1 WLR 1039, CA.
5 *Paradine v Jane* (1647) Aleyn 26; *Redmond v Dainton* [1920] 2 KB 256.
6 *National Carriers Ltd v Panalpina (Northern) Ltd* [1981] AC 675, [1981] 1 All ER 161, HL.
7 *Walsh v Lonsdale* (1882) 21 Ch D 9, CA. There were two rents in this case, one fixed and one fluctuating, but when the latter amount became certain, no doubt it could have been distrained for.
8 *Barnes v Barratt* [1970] 2 QB 657, [1970] 2 All ER 483, CA.

by reference to the index of retail prices was regarded as sufficiently certain,[9] as was a sum representing 10% of the turnover of a business.[10] Many modern leases contain rent review provisions and may not reserve a rent throughout the whole term, but only a certain sum up to a given date, as from which a new rent, revised upwards, is payable. Once ascertained, this new rent is taken as substituted for the old rent.[11]

Sums may be rent even though there is no power of distress in the lease, provided they are for use and occupation.[12] Equally, service charges or insurance premiums payable by the tenant of, say, a block of flats, to the landlord, may be expressly recoverable as rent, so that they may, in default, be distrained for.[13]

II OTHER PERIODICAL PAYMENTS DISTINGUISHED

1 *Rentcharges and rent seck* A rentcharge is charged on land in perpetuity or or a term, with an express power of distress, but the owner of the rentcharge has no reversion on the land charged.[14] A rent seck is similar to a rentcharge but there is no power of distress.[15]

2 *Premiums or Fines* These are capital sums payable as a lump sum (or in instalments) at or from the commencement of a lease or on its subsequent assignment. They are not rent.[16]

III CONSTRUCTION OF A RESERVATION OF RENT

1 *Reservation of rent* Any form of words which show an intention to pay a rent (such as 'the tenant covenants to pay a rent of £X' or 'the tenant is liable to pay a rent of £X') suffices to reserve the rent out of the land concerned.

2 *Kinds of rent* Various different kinds of rent may be encountered. A *best rent* is the highest rent that can reasonably be obtained for the duration of the lease.

A *rack rent* is (as a rule) the full annual or market value of the premises at the commencement of the lease.[17] If the maximum rent lawfully recoverable is less than the market rent then the rack-rent is that lawfully recoverable.[18]

  9 *Blumenthal v Gallery Five Ltd* (1971) 220 Estates Gazette 483, CA.
 10 *Smith v Cardiff Corpn (No 2)* [1955] Ch 159, [1955] 1 All ER 113.
 11 *CH Bailey v Memorial Enterprises Ltd*, supra.
 12 *T & E Homes Ltd v Robinson* [1979] 2 All ER 522, [1979] 1 WLR 452, CA.
 13 No special form of words is required and so 'yielding and paying' sufficed to reserve certain service charges as rent in *Royton Industries Ltd v Lawrence* [1994] 1 EGLR 110.
 14 By Rentcharges Act 1977, s 2, rentcharges cannot generally be created after 22 August 1977.
 15 Such power is conferred on chargees by Law of Property Act 1925, s 121.
 16 *Regor Estates Ltd v Wright* [1951] 1 KB 689, [1951] 1 All ER 219, CA.
 17 Cf *Compton Group Ltd v Estates Gazette* (1977) 36 P & CR 148.
 18 *Newman v Dorrington Developments Ltd* [1975] 3 All ER 928, [1975] 1 WLR 1642.

A *ground rent* is less than a rack-rent, the difference having been 'capitalised' in the form of a premium taken by the landlord on the granting of the lease. It is more usual to find this method of payment under long leases, and it is commonly used in building leases.

A *peppercorn rent* is, in effect, a nominal ground rent, in fact so nominal that it is scarcely ever collected.

A *corn rent* is simply rent paid in kind. Corn rents, where they still exist, are liable to redemption under s 30(1) of the Tithe Act 1936.

A *dead rent* is the part of the rent reserved on the lease of a mine or other wasting asset which is payable throughout the term, whether or not the mine or asset is worked. It is boosted by *royalties* which are payable over and above that, in relation to the amount of coal, etc, extracted or sold.

A *variable* or *sliding scale rent* is one fixed by reference to the cost or value of some commodity which is itself variable on a recognised scale, such as the value of gold in sterling,[19] or the cost-of-living index.[20] Such modes of fixing rent were an attempt, which preceded the common use of rent review clauses, to ensure that the rent reserved keeps pace with inflation in rents throughout the term.[1]

3   *Cesser, abatement or suspension of rent clauses*   Leases sometimes contain a clause under which the tenant is not liable to pay rent for a specified or even an unspecified period, as where owing to the destruction of or damage to the premises, by an insured risk such as fire or food, the premises become totally or even partially unfit for use and occupation.[2] Where a landlord lost some £4,305 in rent owing to the operation of a suspension of rent clause, because a third party negligently crashed into the premises, rendering them unfit, he recovered this sum from the third party: the loss was reasonably foreseeable and, as relating to physical damage, was not purely economic loss.[3]

The lease may entitle the landlord to insure against loss of rent and VAT for whatever period he thinks the re-instatement of the premises might require. The fact that the lease requires the tenant to pay premiums on such a policy was held not to impose any implied liability on the landlord to abate the rent where an insured risk materialised, where there was no express abatement of rent clause.[4]

---

19   *Treseder-Griffin v Co-operative Insurance Society* [1956] 2 QB 127, [1956] 2 All ER 33, CA.
20   *Blumenthal v Gallery Five Ltd* (1971) 220 Estates Gazette 31.
 1   For an example of 'stepped rents' (annual rent increases) combined with a rent review see *Stedman v Midland Bank plc* [1990] 1 EGLR 146, CA.
 2   See eg Law Society Business Lease, cl 9.1; and the right of the tenant under cl 9.2 to determine the lease on account of non-reinstatement.
 3   *Ehlmer v Hall* [1993] 1 EGLR 137, CA.
 4   *Cleveland Shoe Ltd v Murray's Book Sales (King's Cross) Ltd* (1973) 227 Estates Gazette 987.

IV RENT REVIEW CLAUSES[5]

Introduction

(i) *General background* Rent Review clauses are common in any lease of commercial property (and sometimes appear in residential assured tenancies under Part I of the Housing Act 1988),[6] for any substantial term of years. The general purpose of a rent review clause has been stated to be to enable the landlord to obtain from time to time the market rental which the premises would command if let on the same terms at the open market rent at the review dates: the aim is thus to reflect the changes in the value of money and real increases in the value of the property during a long term.[7] Thus, in general terms, given that it is assumed that inflation will progressively erode the real value of the initially reserved rent, if the reviewed rent is a higher figure than the current level of rent, the lease will usually require the higher figure to be substituted for the old rent; if not, the old rent usually continues to be payable.

It has been judicially stated that if the tenant is not prepared to agree to regular rent reviews, few landlords in times of inflation would be prepared to commit themselves to the grant of a long term.[8] Rent review clauses are for the benefit of landlords, as is evidenced by the fact that at present most rent review clauses do not allow for the revision of the rent below the initial level of rent reserved and so are called 'upwards-only' clauses. As to the frequency (or intervals) of rent review, this is a matter for the parties to fix in clear terms.[9] Intervals between reviews of five years are common. In the absence of express provisions, however, a valuer faced with abnormally long or short rent reviews cannot assume that in a period after the current review of rent (known as the 'hypothetical lease') there will be a 'normal' pattern of five-yearly rent reviews.[10]

The topic of rent review clauses is complex. It is judicially recognised, that a decision interpreting one particular clause is no direct authority for the interpretation of another similar but not identical clause.[11] The courts strive to give effect to the intention, actual or supposed, of the parties, and thus to the words used in their factual context,[12] so emphasising that there are no special rules governing the construction of rent review clauses. The manner in which these clauses, which may be involved, are interpreted is sometimes, for that very reason, and perhaps because of a tendency to claim over-sophisticated

---

5 See Bernstein and Reynolds *Handbook of Rent Review*; Clarke and Adams *Rent Reviews and Variable Rents* and the journal *Rent Review and Lease Renewal*.
6 See eg *Precedents for the Conveyancer* Precedent 5-100; also Clarke [1989] Conv 111.
7 *British Gas Corpn v Universities Superannuation Scheme Ltd* [1986] 1 All ER 978, at 980-981, approved in *Basingstoke and Deane Borough Council v Host Group Ltd* [1988] 1 All ER 824, CA.
8 *United Scientific Holdings v Burnley Borough Council* [1977] 2 All ER 62, at 72; also *MFI Properties Ltd v BICC Group Pension Trust Ltd* [1986] 1 All ER 974 at 975.
9 So that a further review could not be presumed from the mere words 'at a rent to be agreed': *Stedman v Midland Bank plc* [1990] 1 EGLR 146, CA.
10 See *National Westminster Bank Ltd v BSC Footwear Ltd* [1981] 1 EGLR 89, CA.
11 *Equity and Law Life Assurance Society plc v Bodfield Ltd* [1987] 1 EGLR 124, 125, CA.
12 *Montross Associated Investments SA v Moussaieff* [1992] 1 EGLR 55, 56, CA.

interpretations, governed by a 'principle of reality',[13] or 'business common sense'.[14] It is to be presumed that the parties did not intend to produce an artificial result nor one which would confer on the landlord any extra benefits beyond an uplift of the current rent to that in the open market prevailing at the date of the rent review.[15] If driven to do so by the wording of a clause, the courts will enforce a term literally, even if this produces an artificial or even unfair result (such as assuming, contrary to the terms of the actual lease, that the tenant is free to use the premises for any purpose after a rent review), or that, despite the fact that as from 1988, rental values in parts of London fell dramatically, the lessee cannot in any circumstances be allowed to pay a lesser rent at review.[16] Equally, if a particular term produces a result which is unworkable or absurd, the court interprets the clause so as to produce a workable result despite its literal wording.[17]

As to the machinery of a rent review and the interpretation of rent review clauses, it is to be assumed that the provisions of clauses are in themselves comprehensive and consistent within themselves and with the other terms of the lease.[18] Where, however, a rent review clause failed to provide a suitable formula for the ascertainment of a new rent, a term was implied that, failing agreement, the reviewed rent was to be a fair market rent for the premises at the review date.[19] In this case, no rent had been reserved for the period after the first review of rent was to take place. In the absence of a claim for rectification, where the lease reserves a rent throughout, the court will not imply a rent review clause, or arbitration machinery, as business efficacy does not require this.[20] Such a lease may continue to work without a rent review clauses. If a rent review clause fails to reflect the true intentions of both parties, due to mutual mistake, the court has a jurisdiction to rectify the lease accordingly, and a provision for arbitration in default of agreement was inserted where it was unconscionable of the tenants to take advantage of the landlords' error.[1] The jurisdiction is exercisable against an assignee who cannot show that he is a purchaser for value without notice of the equity of rectification.[2]

Standard-form clauses have been produced by the Law Society and RICS in collaboration,[3] but the parties are free to modify these or use their own clauses

---

13 *Buffalo Enterprises Inc v Golden Wonder Ltd* [1991] 1 EGLR 141, 142; also eg *Commercial Union Life Assurance Co Ltd v Woolworths plc* [1994] EGCS 191.
14 *Supasnaps Ltd v Bailey* [1995] EGCS 89, CA.
15 *Basingstoke and Deane Borough Council v Host Group Ltd,* supra, at 828; also *Co-operative Wholesale Society Ltd v National Westminster Bank plc* [1995] 1 EGLR 97, CA.
16 *Secretary of State for the Environment* v *Associated Newspaper Holdings Ltd* [1995] EGCS 166, CA.
17 *Wyndham Investments Ltd v Motorway Tyres and Accessories Ltd* [1991] 2 EGLR 114, CA.
18 See eg *Postel Properties v Greenwell* [1992] 2 EGLR 130 (where internal inconsistencies were resolved to produce a sensible result).
19 *Beer v Bowden* [1981] 1 All ER 1070; [1970] 1 WLR 522n, CA.
20 Cf *Crawford v Bruce* 1992 SLT 524 (CS, Sc).
 1 See *Thomas Bates & Son Ltd v Wyndham's (Lingerie) Ltd* [1981] 1 All ER 1077, [1981] 1 WLR 505, CA; *Central and Metropolitan Estates Ltd v Compusave* [1983] 1 EGLR 60 (complete review clause inserted).
 2 *Equity and Law Life Assurance Society Ltd v Coltness Group Ltd* [1983] 2 EGLR 118 (where the assignee paid no premium and so was not a 'purchaser').
 3 Law Society/RICS Model Forms of Rent Review Clause.

as they think fit. If a given clause fails to provide expressly for a particular matter, such as what is to happen when a notice is served late, the court is free to apply its own interpretation or even to insert an implied term as business efficacy may require.[4]

(ii) *Aims of rent review clauses*   A rent review clause, whose complexity is often in direct proportion to whether it is precedent-based, adapted from precedents or one-off,[5] may deal with the following aspects.

1   The dates for review of rent and the date as from which any reviewed rent is to be paid[6] should be specified.[7] If the date at which the premises are to be valued is not expressly stated, the courts will assume that it is the same as the review date because it is contrary to the whole purpose of a rent review to fix a later date (such as the date at which the valuer decides what the premises are worth).[8] Whether a rent review operates retrospectively is a question of construction of each clause: a clear express provision is required to overcome the presumption, which penalises any delays in the process of review, that the new rent is payable from the next quarter following the award and is accordingly not payable as from the date of review in the lease.[9]

2   The manner by which a rent review is to be initiated should be indicated. One method is to require the service of a landlord's notice of review or 'trigger notice' on the tenant: ideally, the clause should indicate the method of service.[10] Equally, though less usually, the review process may be automatic, as where the clause provides for the new rent to be agreed between the parties or determined by an arbitrator at any time before the review date.[11]

3   If a notice procedure is provided for, there may be provisions as to any further notices which have to be served after a landlord's trigger notice, such as a tenant's counter-notice and also any notices requiring arbitration which have to be served by either party, if they cannot agree on a new rent within a specified time. Usually the latter type of notice requests the President of the RICS to appoint a valuer, to act as an arbitrator: such an application should in principle be in accordance with the Guidance Notes published by the RICS though minor deviations from these will not invalidate a genuine application.[12]

---

4   See eg *Henniker-Major v Daniel Smith* [1991] 1 EGLR 128; *R & A Millett (Shops) Ltd v Leon Allan International Fashions Ltd* [1988] 1 EGLR 45.
5   For an example of the difficulties caused by a one-off clause in an otherwise standard form lease see *British Railways Board v Mobil Oil Co Ltd* [1994] 1 EGLR 146.
6   See *Holicator v Grandred Ltd* [1993] 1 EGLR 135, CA, where the use in this connection of the word 'said' was deprecated.
7   It appears that some leases of business premises seek to circumvent the interim rent provisions of Part II of the Landlord and Tenant Act (ch 25) by inserting a rent review at or near the end of the contractual term: Ross, *Drafting and Negotiating Commercial Leases*, 4th edn, para 6.53.
8   *Glofield Properties Ltd v Morley (No 2)* [1989] 2 EGLR 118, CA.
9   *South Tottenham Land Securities Ltd v R & A Millet (Shops) Ltd* [1984] 1 All ER 614, [1984] 1 WLR 710.
10   Eg by express incorporation of Law of Property Act 1925, s 196(4). See *Stephenson & Son v Orca Properties Ltd* [1989] 2 EGLR 129.
11   See Law Society/RICS Model Clause, Precedent 1.
12   *Staines Warehousing Co Ltd v Montagu Executor and Trustee Co Ltd* [1987] 2 EGLR 130, CA.

4   A rent review clause may specify in relation to one or more notice procedures that time is to be of the essence (so that a failure to serve a notice on time will preclude the initiation of a review, an effective reaction to it by the tenant or the appointment of an arbitrator). If any time-limits are not specifically and clearly stated to be mandatory, then, as will be seen, a strict compliance with them will not be fatal to the validity of the notice in question and the clause will be directory only.

5   The clause should state the *basis of valuation* of the premises (and if the premises are to be different from those demised, this should be stated). The basis of valuation is, as will appear, often based on rent payable in the open market for the premises as between a willing landlord and tenant. If any matters are to be assumed to be the case in relation to the term after review, which is referred to as the *hypothetical lease* (such as the length of the term, vacant possession or compliance with tenants' repairing covenants or as to the user of the premises after review, and the existence of future rent reviews) or to be disregarded (such as any rent-free occupation by the tenant, tenants' improvements during the term or the effect of a tenant's or a sub-tenant's occupation) these should ideally be expressly set out in the clause. Otherwise, if the clause is silent or unclear, the terms of the hypothetical lease after a rent review will be assumed to be the same as those of the actual lease.[13]

Whether time is of the essence

(i)   *General presumption*   Where the rent review clause does not expressly and clearly provide that time is to be of the essence in relation to a landlord's trigger notice (or any other notice to be served during a rent review procedure), the House of Lords, holding a rent review clause to be part of a bargain in which the tenant accepted a review of rent in return for the conferral of a long term, has ruled that it is presumed that time is not to be of the essence.[14] This is despite the fact that, because time-limits in rent review clauses seem as a matter of principle to resemble other unilateral rights exercisable by non-consensual notices, notably options to determine or to purchase, there is a fair case for the view that time should be deemed, in relation to rent review trigger notices, at any rate, to be of the essence, so that late service of a notice would deprive the landlord, for example, of his right to require a review on that occasion.[15] The presumption that time is not of the essence is said to be strong and will only be rebutted by a compelling counter-indication in the lease, although it may be only a rule of construction.[16] Where, therefore, a landlord served a trigger notice

---

13   *Basingstoke and Deane Borough Council v Host Group plc,* supra.
14   *United Scientific Holdings Ltd v Burnley Borough Council* [1978] AC 904; [1977] 2 All ER 62, HL; also eg *Panavia Air Cargo Ltd v Southend-on-Sea Borough Council* [1988] 1 EGLR 124, CA.
15   GD Goldberg and PF Smith (1992) 12 LS 349.
16   *Phipps-Faire Ltd v Malbern Construction Ltd* [1987] 1 EGLR 129; cf *Pembroke St Georges Ltd v Cromwell Developments Ltd* [1991] 2 EGLR 129.

two months after the last date for service under the rent review timetable had expired, he was, despite his default, entitled to a rent review.[17]

Where there are certain steps, such as the conclusion of an arbitration (as opposed to an application for the appointment of an arbitrator) which are out of the control of either party, even apparently mandatory language such as 'as soon as practicable' or 'not later than' in relation to an arbitration notice will not render time of the essence, enabling the landlord to apply late for an appointment.[18] This aspect of the presumption reflects the reality of the case, as is shown by the fact that s 12 of the Arbitration Act 1996 allows either party to apply to the High Court to extend the time-limits provided for in a rent review clause for seeking the appointment of an arbitrator, provided that the right to apply is conferred on both parties,[19] if the conduct of one party makes it unjust to hold the other to the strict time-limits. The factors relevant to the exercise of the statutory discretion might include the length of the delay, the amount at stake, whether the landlord or his agent was at fault and whether the tenant has suffered any prejudice.[20]

Where time is not of the essence, the mere fact that the landlord has delayed beyond the review date in implementing a rent review will not of itself entitle the tenant to claim that the right to review has been lost. The tenant, in such a case, will have the difficult task of proving that the right to review has been abrogated or repudiated by the landlord (as where the landlord ignores a tenants' notice making time of the essence) or the landlord is precluded by a supervening event or estoppel[1] from invoking the right to review or to an arbitration.[2] It is not sufficient for the tenant to prove merely that the landlord has unreasonably delayed in the service of a trigger (or other) notice even if hardship is caused to the tenant, and in one case a delay of three years was therefore condoned.[3]

(ii) *Circumstances in which time is of the essence* There are a number of circumstances in which time is of the essence: where this is so, the relevant notice must either be served within the stipulated time or the right to rely on the notice will be lost. First, it is usually[4] open to the tenant to make time of the essence in relation to a trigger or arbitration notice by a clear and unambiguous

---

17 *United Scientific Holdings Ltd v Burnley Borough Council*, supra.
18 *Touche Ross & Co v Secretary of State for the Environment* (1983) 46 P & CR 187; also *Shuwa Ashdown House Corpn v Grayrigg Properties Ltd* [1992] 2 EGLR 127.
19 *Tote Bookmakers Ltd v Development and Property Holding Co Ltd* [1985] Ch 261, [1985] 2 All ER 555.
20 *Fordgate (Bingley) Ltd v National Westminster Bank plc* [1995] EGCS 97 (1950 Act).
 1 See eg *Esso Petroleum Co Ltd v Anthony Gibbs Financial Services Ltd* [1983] 2 EGLR 112, CA.
 2 *Amherst v James Walker (Goldsmith and Silversmith) Ltd* [1983] Ch 305, [1983] 2 All ER 1067, CA.
 3 *Million Pigs v Parry (No 2)* (1983) 46 P & CR 333; cf *H West & Son Ltd v Brech* [1982] 1 EGLR 113 (18 month delay); *Printing House Properties Ltd v J W Winston & Co Ltd* [1982] 2 EGLR 118 (23 months).
 4 But not if he does not need such a right, as where he can apply for the appointment of an arbitrator: *Factory Holdings Group Ltd v Leboff International Ltd* [1987] 1 EGLR 135.

notice served on the landlord which leaves him, as a reasonable businessman, in no real doubt that the tenant requires him to exercise his right to a review of the rent within the time (reasonably) specified in the notice, failing which, the right to review will be lost.[5] There is no form of notice and a letter, however informal, will suffice provided it is sufficiently clear in intent.[6]

Second, the House of Lords accepted that time is presumed to be of the essence where the rent review notice procedures are clearly interrelated with or expressly subject to, the exercise by the tenant of an option to determine the lease.[7] Especially where a gap of some months is provided for between the last date for service of a landlord's trigger notice and the exercise of the tenant's right to break, the parties are taken to have intended that the tenant is to know that a rent review is likely and to gain an idea of the possible rent to be demanded, before deciding whether to break the lease. The late service of a landlord's trigger notice will then be fatal to his right to review, as where the tenant had the right to break his lease in a period following the last date for service of the landlord's trigger notice, which the landlord failed to serve on time, thus losing his right to review.[8] A simple correlation between time-limits in a rent review clause and a tenant's option to determine is, however, not sufficient to render time of the essence, at least where the event relied on to render time of the essence is the decision of an arbitrator, in view of the disproportionate detriment which would be caused to the landlord from a loss of his right to review and because of the tenant's right to make time of the essence by notice.[9] In addition, if the tenant allows the date for exercise of a break clause to go past without exercising it, the landlord may thereafter exercise his right to invoke a rent review.[10]

(iii)   *Strength of presumption*   Obviously, if the rent review clause clearly indicates that time is of the essence in relation to all rent review procedures, a late service of any notice is of no effect. However, because of the strength of the presumption that time is not of the essence, it is not to be assumed that merely because time is expressly made of the essence in relation to one procedural step, it is *ipso facto* of the essence in relation to any other step, such as a right to require an arbitration,[11] or in relation to other rent review periods.[12] Examples of language which has in the past been held to render time of the essence include: a statement that the landlord could require an arbitration by notice within three

5   *British Rail Pension Trustee Co Ltd v Cardshops Ltd* [1987] 1 EGLR 127; *Glofield Properties Ltd v Morley* [1988] 1 EGLR 113.
6   *Prudential Property Services Ltd v Capital Land Holdings Ltd* [1993] 1 EGLR 128.
7   *United Scientific Holdings Ltd v Burnley Borough Council*, supra.
8   See the form of clause in *C Richards & Son v Karenita* (1971) 221 Estates Gazette 25; also eg *Central Estates Ltd v Secretary of State for the Environment* (1996)72 P & CR 482, CA (fact that four reviews and only one break clause made no difference).
9   *Metrolands Investments Ltd v J H Dewhurst Ltd* [1986] 3 All ER 659, CA.
10   *Edwin Woodhouse Trustee Co Ltd v Sheffield Brick Co plc* [1984] 1 EGLR 130.
11   *Amherst v James Walker (Goldsmith and Silversmith) Ltd*, supra; also *London and Manchester Assurance Co Ltd v G A Dunn Co Ltd* [1983] 1 EGLR 111, CA.
12   *King's (Estate Agents) Ltd v Anderson* [1992] 1 EGLR 121.

months from a trigger notice if the parties could not agree 'but not otherwise';[13] or where it was provided that if the landlord failed to apply for the appointment of an arbitrator, which he was required to do if the parties could not, within a specified period, reach agreement on a new rent, within an unspecified period, his trigger notice was to be void.[14] The High Court has reached inconsistent results in relation to a term in a rent review clause which expressly provided that it was a condition precedent to the right to review that the landlord served a written notice in advance of the date at which the new rent is to take effect,[15] but it is contended that time should be presumed to be of the essence in such a case as the intent of the words could scarcely be clearer.

(iv) *Finality in procedures* If the parties clearly provide for the consequences if no rent review is invoked (or other procedure, such as the service of a tenant's counter-notice or an arbitration notice is not followed) this, depending on the context and purpose of the clause,[16] may indicate that time is to be of the essence. This has arisen in the context of clauses which enable or require the landlord to state, in his review notice, a given amount of rent as the new rent payable, which will take effect as such unless challenged by the tenant within a specified period. Only if finality is clearly intended in relation to such notices will time be held to be of the essence and the question is ultimately one of construction,[17] although it has been held that if only one party is entitled to serve a deeming notice, time is not of the essence and it is if the notices are 'two-way', so that both parties have to serve them.[18] This is not necessarily a decisive test, for where the new rent had to be 'conclusively fixed' as stated in the landlord's notice, time was of the essence,[19] but not where a suggested new rent in a lessees' counter-notice was not to take effect if the lessor applied for an arbitration.[20]

Notices of review

A number of issues arise as to trigger and other notices which may be required to be served during the process of a rent review. Some trigger notices are required to specify a rent: it is a question of construction whether the wording is sufficiently strong to render the requirement mandatory, so invalidating any notice which fails to comply with it,[1] or merely directory.[2]

13 *Drebbond Ltd v Horsham District Council* (1978) 37 P & CR 237.
14 *Lewis v Barnett* [1982] 2 EGLR 127; also *Darlington Borough Council v Waring & Gillow (Holdings) Ltd* [1988] 2 EGLR 159.
15 *North Hertfordshire District Council v Hitchin Industrial Estate Ltd* [1992] 2 EGLR 121; *Chelsea Building Society v R&A Millett (Shops) Ltd* [1994] 1 EGLR 148.
16 See *Power Securities (Manchester) Ltd v Prudential Assurance Co Ltd* [1987] 1 EGLR 121.
17 *Henry Smith's Charity Trustees v AWADA Trading and Promotion Services Ltd* (1984) 47 P & CR 607, CA; *Mecca Leisure Ltd v Renown Investments (Holdings) Ltd* (1984) 49 P & CR 12, CA.
18 *Taylor Woodrow Property Co Ltd v Lonrho Textiles Ltd* [1985] 2 EGLR 120.
19 *Mammoth Greeting Cards Ltd v Agra Ltd* [1990] 2 EGLR 124.
20 *Phipps-Faire v Malbern Construction Ltd* [1987] 1 EGLR 129.
 1 As in *Commission for the New Towns v R Levy & Co Ltd* [1990] 2 EGLR 121.
 2 As in *Dean and Chapter of Chichester v Lennards Ltd* (1977) 35 P & CR 309, CA.

If the landlord serves an invalid (but on its face unambiguous) trigger notice, the question arises as to whether he is entitled to serve a second notice: as might be expected, the question is one of the construction of the rent review clause.[3] The same principle applies to tenants' counter-notices.[4] In relation to any notice served during the rent review procedure, the courts test its formal validity by asking themselves whether the document (which is often a letter) is sufficiently clear to bring home to an ordinary landlord or tenant that the notice was intending to trigger a review, challenge a suggested rent or exercise some other right,[5] or, alternatively, especially where a rent is required to be specified in the notice, whether the notice was sufficiently clear to avoid the recipient being misled by it.[6] Strict principles of legal construction do not apply, and these tests are partly subjective, since sometimes the initial reactions of the recipient to the notice, as a reasonable business person, are taken into account.[7] If the notice is qualified by the use of words such as 'subject to contract' or 'without prejudice', it may still be an effective notice if it is clear from the context that the document is a review notice,[8] but if the notice is itself couched in ambiguous language, it will be held to be a mere negotiating document and not a notice.[9]

Basis of valuation

The chief purpose of any rent review clause is to give the landlord the benefit of a market rent so as to protect him against the ravages of inflation. In interpreting the means by which this is to be ascertained, given that most rent review clauses require the rent to be fixed in accordance with the open market value of the premises (sometimes with a number of qualifications), the courts decline to make artificial assumptions about the term after review (the *hypothetical lease*)[10] unless driven to this by the express words of the clause. The parties are taken as having intended that the notional letting postulated by the rent review clause is to be a letting on the same terms (other than as to the quantum of rent) as those still subsisting between the parties to the actual existing lease.[11] The underlying purpose of a rent review clause will hence govern the way the courts construe any assumptions the clause requires the valuer to make, such as those relating to the user of the premises under the hypothetical lease, or the existence of future rent reviews. However, if and so far as the wording of a particular clause requires an artificial assumption to be made, it will be given effect to. Thus, unless the contrary is clearly required,[12] it is assumed that the tenant will

---

3   *Norwich Union Life Insurance Society v Sketchley plc* [1986] 2 EGLR 126.
4   See eg *British Rail Pension Trustee Co Ltd v Cardshops Ltd* [1987] 1 EGLR 127.
5   *Nunes v Davies Laing and Dick Ltd* (1985) 51 P & CR 310; *Glofield Properties Ltd v Morley* [1988] 1 EGLR 113.
6   *Durham City Estates Ltd v Felicetti* [1990] 1 EGLR 143, CA.
7   *Patel v Earlspring Properties Ltd* [1991] 2 EGLR 131, CA.
8   As in *Royal Life Insurance Ltd v Phillips* [1990] 2 EGLR 135.
9   *Shirlcar Properties Ltd v Heinitz* [1983] 2 EGLR 120, CA.
10 See eg *Leigh v Certibilt Investments Ltd* [1988] 1 EGLR 116 ('primitive form' of clause, requiring valuation of estate as a whole).
11 *Basingstoke and Deane Borough Council v Host Group Ltd* [1988] 1 All ER 824, at 829, CA.
12 As in *Standard Life Assurance Co v Oxoid* [1987] 2 EGLR 140, CA.

hold the same premises, as regards extent condition and state, as immediately before the rent review.[13] In addition, the valuer is assumed to be required to value the whole property, and if it is intended that he is to value only buildings on land or land without buildings, this must be clearly stated.[14]

Requirement of open market rent

(i) *Introduction* A typical formula to give the landlord the benefit, as from the review date, of a market rent, is that the demised premises are available to let on the open market with vacant possession by a willing landlord to a willing tenant, with various further assumptions to follow. Sometimes, the clause may refer to the 'best rent' or to a 'reasonable rent for the demised premises'. A reference to the 'demised premises' in the formula is important because an objective assessment, without regard to the tenant's ability to pay, is envisaged: if the rent formula merely states that the rent is to be a rent as agreed between the parties, then the rent may be treated as a rent which it would be reasonable for the given tenant to pay having regard to his particular circumstances rather than by reference to purely objective criteria.[15] Care should be taken in drafting the precise formula required: in one case, the words a 'fair yearly rent for the demised premises' was taken to require, contrary to the fact, that the premises were vacant at the review date.[16]

(ii) *Willing landlord and tenant* The aim of this formula, linked to an open market rent, is to produce an artificial situation in which the rent reflects the open market rent, and in which the actual tenant, whose occupation is generally to be ignored (because vacant possession is generally to be assumed at review)[17] is usually one notional bidder in a competition for the premises – though it is open to the parties expressly to exclude him from consideration.[18] In general, therefore, any particular circumstances which affect either of the actual parties are to be left out of account.[19] An open market formula, such as the 'full yearly market rent' by necessary implication requires the assumption both of a willing lessor and a willing lessee to be made where a rent review clause fails to mention either.[20] But it is for the valuer to decide on the strength of the assumed market, despite any assumptions thus required, such as that the tenant had access to the premises by means of a staircase, contrary to the fact.[1] Where the user of certain premises was limited to a named lessee, the user clause was remoulded for the

---

13 See *Ravenseft Properties Ltd v Park* [1988] 2 EGLR 164; *Iceland Frozen Foods plc v Starlight Investments Ltd* [1992] 1 EGLR 126, CA.
14 See *Ipswich Town Football Club v Ipswich Borough Council* [1988] 2 EGLR 146.
15 *Thomas Bates & Son v Wyndham's (Lingerie) Ltd* [1981] 1 All ER 1077, CA.
16 *99 Bishopsgate v Prudential Assurance Co* [1985] 1 EGLR 72, CA.
17 Or the premises are to be assumed available for immediate occupation: see eg Law Society/ RICS Model Clause, Precedent 1, Variation A cl 3(A)(c).
18 See *First Leisure Trading Ltd v Dorita Properties Ltd* [1991] 1 EGLR 133.
19 *F R Evans (Leeds) Ltd v English Electric Co* (1977) 36 P & CR 185. In this case, however, the actual lessee would have made no offer at all, as he would have preferred to leave.
20 *Dennis & Robinson Ltd v Kiossos Establishment* [1987] 1 EGLR 133, CA.
 1 *Jefferies v O'Neill* (1983) 46 P & CR 376.

purpose of a review of rent, so as to produce consistency within the clause as a whole, and so as to render the assumption that a number of persons might bid for the lease, so as to produce an open market rent.[2] One difficulty with the objective requirement of a willing lessee is that arguably it requires a particular lessee's profits to be left out of account. The courts so far treat the question as entirely one of construction of the clause.[3]

Assumptions and disregards to be made on review

(i)   *Introduction*   Most rent review clauses do not stop at directing that an open market rent should be arrived at. It is quite common for a valuer to be directed to make a number of assumptions and disregards in assessing the rent payable after review. However, and importantly, except and in so far as a particular clause requires specific assumptions or disregards to be made, a valuation has to be based as a matter of principle on the assumption that the hypothetical lease will be on the same terms after review as those of the existing lease.[4] Nor, as seen, do the courts allow hypothesis to be heaped upon hypothesis (unless clear language is used) so that a landlord's argument that the condition of notionally vacant premises for review purposes would have been improved by certain works which the landlord notionally could have carried out so as to improve their letting value was rejected.[5]

One of the standard rent review clauses expressly requires the assumption of the following matters: that the demised premises are available for letting on the open market with vacant possession and that the premises are vacant but fit for immediate occupation and use; that the length of the lease is the unexpired residue thereof; that the terms of the lease after review are the same, other than as to rent but including the rent review provisions, as the current lease; that the user of the premises is for any purpose permitted by the lease; that both parties have complied with their covenants; that if a rent-free period has been granted at the commencement of the term, no reduction is to be made in rent on that account.[6]

In connection with an assumption of vacant possession but fitness of premises for occupation, it appears that the valuer is to assume for rent review purposes that the premises are free from defects and ready for the lessee to use for the purposes of his business,[7] and, where relevant, in a good state of repair and condition.[8] This type of assumption may, where the premises are in fact not

---

2   *Law Land Co Ltd v Consumers' Association Ltd* [1980] 2 EGLR 109, CA; also *James v British Crafts Centre* [1987] 1 EGLR 139, CA; *Orchid Lodge UK Ltd v Extel Computing Ltd* [1991] 2 EGLR 116, CA.

3   See eg *Cornwall Coast Country Club v Cardgrange Ltd* [1987] 1 EGLR 146; *Ritz Hotel (London) Ltd v Ritz Casino Ltd* [1989] 2 EGLR 135.

4   *Basingstoke and Deane Borough Council v Host Group Ltd*, supra. For an example of a clause requiring a different, more general, user to be assumed to that permitted under the lease see *Postel Properties Ltd v Greenwell* [1992] 2 EGLR 130.

5   *Iceland Frozen Foods plc v Starlight Investment Ltd* [1992] 1 EGLR 126, CA.

6   Law Society/RICS Model Form (1985 edn) Precedent 1, Variation A cl 3.

7   *Pontsarn Investments Ltd v Kansallis-Osake-Pankki* [1992] 1 EGLR 148.

8   See eg *London and Leeds Estates Ltd v Paribas Ltd* [1993] 2 EGLR 149, CA.

in condition or are not suitable require the lessee to pay an artificially inflated rent, if the shortcomings are due to the defaults of the landlord.

With regard to rent-free periods, it may be difficult to find a form of words in a rent review clause of a lease which concedes the lessee an initial rent holiday but where the landlord wishes it to be assumed, as at the date for rent review, that the full or 'headline' market rent will be payable, with no assumed further rent-free concessionary period.[9] It now seems clear, however, that in assessing the weight of comparable rents in a valuation of the open market rent, a comparable rent which includes a element of rent-free concession cannot properly be used in assessing the reviewed rent, so as to inflate the latter sum to the landlord's advantage.[10]

(ii) *Future rent reviews* It appears that, unless the rent review clause clearly and unambiguously requires the contrary to be assumed, the existence of future rent reviews should be taken into account on a review of rent.[11] This is in accordance with the principle that artificial assumptions will not be made about the hypothetical lease.

(iii) *User of premises* In the absence of clear contrary language, it is assumed that the user permitted by the lease will be the same after review as before.[12] If an open market rent formula is required, it is not assumed that existing user restrictions will be unilaterally relaxed by the landlord: on the contrary, it is assumed that they will continue after review.[13] If a clause is to require a lawful use alone to be assumed, this must be clearly specified.[14] If a provision makes no sense, or requires the incorporation of a subsequent variation to the lease, the court will modify it to the extent sufficient to render it sensibly operable.[15] Likewise as already noted, the user to be assumed after review will be remoulded if the original user clause permits a personal user to the lessee only, where such a user is incompatible with an overriding requirement of an open market rental.[16]

(iv) *Length of the term* If the lease is silent or ambiguous as to the length of the term to be assumed for the hypothetical lease, this is generally assumed to be the unexpired residue of the lease, running from the review date.[17] As a result,

---

9 See the opposite results in *Broadgate Square plc v Lehman Bros* [1995] 1 EGLR 97, CA and *City Offices plc v Bryanston Insurance Co Ltd* [1993] 1 EGLR 126.
10 *Co-operative Wholesale Society Ltd v National Westminster Bank plc* [1995] 1 EGLR 97, CA.
11 *Arnold v National Westminster Bank plc* [1990] 1 All ER 529, CA; affd [1991] 3 All ER 41, HL.
12 *Basingstoke and Deane Borough Council v Host Group Ltd* [1988] 1 All ER 824, CA.
13 *Plinth Property Investments Ltd v Mott, Hay and Anderson* (1978) 38 P & CR 361, CA; *James v British Crafts Centre* [1987] 1 EGLR 139, CA; *SI Pension Trustees Ltd v Ministerio de Marina de la Republica Peruana* [1988] 1 EGLR 119.
14 *Daejan Investments Ltd v Cornwall Coast Country Club* [1985] 1 EGLR 77. See also *Brewers' Co v Viewplan plc* [1989] 2 EGLR 133; *Tea Trade Properties Ltd v CIN Properties Ltd* [1990] 1 EGLR 155.
15 See now *Orchid Lodge (UK) Ltd v Extel Computing Ltd* [1991] 2 EGLR 116, CA.
16 See eg *Post Office Counters Ltd v Harlow District Council* [1991] 2 EGLR 121.
17 See *Lynnthorpe Enterprises Ltd v Sidney Smith (Chelsea) Ltd* [1990] 2 EGLR 131, CA; also *Toyota GB Ltd v Legal and General Assurance (Pensions) Ltd* [1989] 2 EGLR 123, CA; *Ritz Hotel (London) Ltd v Ritz Casino Ltd* [1989] 2 EGLR 135.

the tenant pays for what he actually enjoys and no more. A clear indication that the tenant's common-law term alone is to be taken into account will be enforced,[18] because otherwise, the possibility that a business tenant may obtain a renewal of his tenancy under Part II of the Landlord and Tenant Act 1954 may be taken into consideration.[19] The question is, as usual, ultimately one of construction, so that where a hypothetical lease was to be assumed on the same terms as the actual 35-year lease, the term was assumed to be for 35 years for rent review purposes, not the much shorter residue of the actual lease.[20]

(v)   *Lessees' improvements*   The common law rule is that the question of whether improvements carried out by the lessee or a predecessor in title of his during the term but prior to the rent review are to be reflected in the rental value depends on the formula describing the reviewed rent. If it is a 'reasonable rent for the demised premises' then the rent, according to the House of Lords, is to be objectively assessed so as to reflect the effect of tenants' improvements on the premises.[1] This is because any improvements to premises become notionally part of the premises. By contrast, where an option clause (the same rule would apply to rent reviews) expressly required the new rent to be that agreed between the parties (with no reference to the demised premises) it was held that the arbitrator was required to determine a rent which it would be reasonable for the parties to agree. This subjective test meant that the current lessee would have to show that he wholly or partially contributed to the improvements before any disregard of their effect could be made.[2]

The common law principles are frequently modified. A rent review clause may expressly require the disregard of any increase in rental value of the demised premises due to any improvement carried out by the lessee or a sub-lessee before the review date during the term. The inclusion of any such clause is no simple answer to the problem of lessees' improvements, for a number of reasons. The question of whether a given improvement to the premises by a lessee prior to the commencement of the term is within a disregard clause is one of construction, which may cause uncertainty if the lessee takes possession shortly prior to the lease in order to carry out shopfitting work.[3] Also, if the tenant carries out improvements under licence and the disregard clause refers only to improvements carried out during the term, the disregard will not apply to the work.[4] It was otherwise, as a matter of construction, where a licence to improve had been granted during the term of a lease.[5] In any event, disregard clauses do not usually extend to improvements which the lessee or sub-lessee

18   *Toyota (GB) Ltd v Legal and General Assurance (Pensions Management) Ltd* [1989] 2 EGLR 123, CA.
19   *Pivot Properties Ltd v Secretary of State for the Environment* (1980) 41 P & CR 248, CA.
20   *British Gas plc v Dollar Land Holdings plc* [1992] 1 EGLR 135.
 1   *Ponsford v HMS Aerosols Ltd* [1979] AC 63, [1978] 2 All ER 837, HL.
 2   *Lear v Blizzard* [1983] 3 All ER 662; also *Dickinson v Enfield London Borough Council* [1996] 49 EG 108, 110–111, CA.
 3   *Panther Shop Investments Ltd v Keith Pople Ltd* [1987] 1 EGLR 131; *Hambros Bank Executor and Trustee Co Ltd v Superdrug Stores Ltd* [1985] 1 EGLR 99.
 4   *Euston Centre Properties Ltd v H and J Wilson Ltd* [1982] 1 EGLR 57.
 5   *Historic Houses Hotels Ltd v Cadogan Estates* [1995] 1 EGLR 117, CA.

is bound under covenant or obligation to execute.[6] Some disregard clauses incorporate s 34 of the Landlord and Tenant Act 1954, in which case it should be made clear whether the original or subsequently amended version of that provision is incorporated, since if this is not done, the question is purely one of construction.[7]

As to the actual manner in which a valuer is to operate a disregard clause, there is little guidance. A valuer may properly compare the state of the premises as they are at the date of review with some comparable but unimproved premises. If there are no comparables, he is free to adopt any appropriate valuation method which corresponds with the parties' intentions, making due allowance for the effects of inflation and the passage of time and a 'capital revaluation' method sometimes adopted has been judicially criticised.[8]

(vi) *Miscellaneous points*   A number of other matters may be required to be disregarded or taken into account on a rent review. For example, where a review to an open market rent is required,[9] any effect on rent of a tenant's breach of his covenant to repair is generally to be disregarded.[10] Equally, where a lessee was under an onerous covenant to repair and rebuild, a downward adjustment of 27.5% of the reviewed rent was upheld.[11] Where, by contrast, a 20-year secure tenancy required that a reviewed rent should be that which it was reasonable for the landlord to demand and for the tenant to pay, the fact that the tenant had a right to buy the house concerned at a discount was to be left out of account, even though had a market rent had been reviewable, the existence of the right to buy would have been taken into account so as, presumably, to increase the reviewed rent. A hypothetical new tenant might have been prepared to pay a higher market rent (as opposed to a reasonable rent) on account of the valuable right conferred by Parliament with a view to encouraging tenants to buy council properties and remove them from the public sector.[12]

Where a rent review clause stated that the hypothetical lease was to contain covenants similar to those in the actual lease, this did not impliedly require that any subsequent variations thereto should be ignored.[13] There is no presumption that a lessees' or sub-lessees' obligation to re-instate the premises at the end of the term is to be taken into account so as to reduce the reviewed rent.[14] Again, if it is intended to require any increase in value to the premises which results

---

6   *Godbold v Martin the Newsagents Ltd* [1983] 2 EGLR 128 and *Forte & Co Ltd v General Accident Life Assurance Ltd* [1986] 2 EGLR 115 (work pursuant to statutory obligation taken into account).
7   *Brett v Brett Essex Golf Club Ltd* (1986) 52 P & CR 330, CA.
8   *GREA Real Property Investments Ltd v Williams* [1979] 1 EGLR 121; *Estates Projects Ltd v Greenwich London Borough* [1979] 2 EGLR 85.
9   See however *Wallace v McMullen* [1988] 2 EGLR 143, where the basis of comparison was a hypothetical piece of equivalent freehold land.
10   *Harmsworth Pension Funds Trustees Ltd v Charringtons Industrial Holdings Ltd* [1985] 1 EGLR 97.
11   *Norwich Union Life Insurance Society v British Railways Board* [1987] 2 EGLR 137.
12   *Dickinson v Enfield London Borough Council* [1996] 49 EG 108, CA.
13   *Lynnthorpe Enterprises Ltd v Sidney Smith (Chelsea) Ltd* [1990] 2 EGLR 131, CA.
14   *Pleasurama Properties Ltd v Leisure Investments (West End) Ltd* [1986] 1 EGLR 145, CA.

from the installation of tenants' fixtures to be taken into account, clear express language is required: otherwise, if removable at the end of the term, they will be treated as tenants' fixtures with no effect on the rental value.[15] Any of the results just given as examples could be overcome by clear express language in the rent review clause concerned.

Determination procedures

(i)   *Arbitrations*   An arbitration is subject to the provisions of the Arbitration Act 1996, which replaces earlier enactments under the same name of 1950 and 1979. An appeal on an identified point of law lies to the court (at the time of writing the High Court) against an arbitration award in a rent review. The court may confirm, vary or set aside the award, or remit the award for reconsideration by the arbitrator with its opinion as to the point of law (s 69(7)). However, by s 69(2), where an appeal is made on a point of law, it requires the leave of the court unless both parties to the dispute consent. Leave is not to be granted unless the court considers the determination of the question of law could substantially affect the rights of one or more of the parties (s 69(3)). The court will only grant leave if the decision of the arbitrator is obviously wrong, or is of general public importance and the decision is open to serious doubt. The former test is the same as applies to commercial arbitrations generally. Where one party appeals, he must displace the presumption of finality by satisfying the court that he has a strong prima facie case, otherwise the court will reject the application uncermoniously.[16] In other words, there must be at least a suspicion that the arbitrator has gone wrong, as opposed to doubt whether he had been right or wrong.

A different avenue of challenge to an arbitration award is that either party may ask the court to interfere with an award on the ground of a serious irregularity affecting the tribunal, the proceedings or the award (1996 Act, s 68). The court has powers similar to those exercisable in the case of appeals in point of law.

In conducting an arbitration, an arbitrator is bound by the rules of evidence so that an arbitrator was not to use a method of evaluation not put in evidence.[17] He is entitled to form his own judgment of the evidence submitted by the parties.[18] No arbitrator, being assumed to be endowed with professional judgment, is bound slavishly to follow the precise calculations relating to comparable rents proffered by the parties.[19] He may also, if the rent review clause permits this, receive rents agreed not only at but after the review date, though the weight to be attached to the latter is for him.[20] After all, provided that

---

15   *Young v Dalgety plc* [1987] 1 EGLR 116, CA; also *Ocean Accident & Guarantee Corpn v Next plc* [1995] EGCS 187 (assumption that premises fully fitted out made no difference).
16   *Ipswich Borough Council v Fisons plc* [1990] Ch 709, applied in eg *British Railways Board v Ringbest Ltd* [1996] 30 EG 94.
17   *Unit Four Cinemas v Tosara Investment Ltd* [1993] 2 EGLR 11.
18   *Tesco Holdings Ltd v Jackson* [1990] 1 EGLR 153; *Temple & Cook Ltd v Capital and Counties Property Co Ltd* [1990] 2 EGLR 129.
19   *Lex Services plc v Oriel House BV* [1991] 2 EGLR 126.
20   *Segama NV v Penny Le Roy Ltd* [1984] 1 EGLR 109.

an arbitrator does not use a valuation method not contemplated by the lease, the parties should ordinarily abide by the result.[1] It would be improper for an arbitrator to form his own judgment on the basis of evidence acquired in other proceedings.[2]

(ii) *Determinations by an independent expert* The rent review clause may state that if the parties cannot agree on a new rent, it is to be arrived at, in default, by a valuer or surveyor[3] acting as an independent expert, in which case, the Arbitration Act does not apply. Where, under a lease, only the landlord was entitled to apply for an expert, it was held, for the first time, that the clause imposed an enforceable obligation on the landlord to apply; if he frustrated the review, fearing a lower rent, the court could direct an inquiry as to the proper level of rent.[4]

The present procedure makes for finality; but challenges to the decision of an expert are not likely to succeed. An expert is entitled to use his own expertise and to form his own judgment, although a determination will seemingly be set aside as a nullity if there is a mistake of fact or law or a discernable mistake.[5] The decision of an independent expert may be impugned as having been negligent, but in a recent case it was held, dismissing a claim, that an expert was not liable merely because he followed a valuation method which might not be followed by others in his profession, provided that, as in that case, he adopted a method which was accepted as proper by a body of competent respected professional opinion.[6] This sensible principle prevents challenges based purely on the ground that the aggrieved party disagrees with the way an otherwise competent expert has analysed the facts of his particular case.

V PAYMENT OF RENT

Time of payment

Although rent is payable in arrear at common law, the lease should provide for the intervals (or 'gales') at which rent is payable. Indeed, it is presumed, again subject to the terms of the lease, that a yearly rent is payable.[7] However, in the case of a periodic weekly or monthly tenancy, the assumption is that the rent is payable for the same periods as those of the tenancy. Where a rent is expressly payable quarterly, the quarters are calculated from the date of the lease,[8] and to get round this, the lease may well specify the usual quarter days. These are:

1 *Pupike Service Station Ltd v Caltex Oil (No 2) Ltd* [1995] EGCS 180, PC.
2 *Top Shop Centres Ltd v Danino* [1985] 1 EGLR 9.
3 Where an 'umpire' was to be appointed, he was held to act as an expert: *Fordgate Bingley Ltd v Argyll Stores Ltd* [1994] 2 EGLR 84.
4 *Royal Bank of Scotland plc v Jennings* [1995] 2 EGLR 87; affd on appeal [1996] EGCS 168.
5 *A Hudson Pty Ltd v Legal and General Life of Australia Ltd* [1986] 2 EGLR 130. See eg *Apus Properties Ltd v Douglas Farrow & Co Ltd* [1989] 2 EGLR 265.
6 *Zubaida v Hargreaves* [1995] 1 EGLR 127, CA.
7 *Turner v Allday* (1836) Tyr & Gr 819. This rule was not altered by an oral agreement to pay the rent quarterly.
8 2 Roll 450.

25 March (Lady Day); 24 June (Midsummer); 29 September (Michaelmas) and 25 December (Christmas). Rent is due on the morning of the day specified for payment, but it is not in arrear until midnight.[9]

Rent paid before the appointed day is not strictly satisfaction of the obligation, though it will be a good defence to an action by the landlord or his personal representatives on the covenant. However, such a payment is risky: it will not discharge the tenant's obligation against anyone who in the meantime acquires the landlord's reversion, unless the tenant has had no notice of the assignment before the day appointed for payment.[10]

Manner of payment

Payment must be made by the tenant to the landlord, or their duly authorised agents respectively; and payment by a stranger does not acquit the tenant of his obligation unless the payment is so authorised by him or subsequently ratified. Legislation intervenes to protect residential tenants whose landlord has assigned the reversion. By Landlord and Tenant Act 1985, s 3(1), where the landlord of premises consisting of or including a dwelling-house assigns his interest, the new landlord must give written notice of the assignment and his name and address to the tenant, not later than the next day on which rent is payable, or if that is within two months of the assignment, the end of two months. Failure to comply with this duty without reasonable excuse is an offence and the old landlord remains under a continuing liability for breaches of covenant from the assignment date until due notification (s 3(3) and (3A)). Tender by a lawful assignee is good,[11] and the landlord is bound to accept it.

The proper place at common law for payment is the land itself, since the rent issues from it, but no doubt the lease will in terms require the tenant to pay at any place appointed, or otherwise to seek out the landlord. Payment by post, therefore, is not strictly proper, and therefore, unless the tenant is instructed to send the rent by post,[12] any loss is the tenant's. The rent must be paid in lawful currency, and a reservation such as 'yielding and paying' implies payment in cash. A landlord therefore can refuse to accept payment by cheque unless by prior agreement, but if it is accepted, payment is conditional upon it being honoured.[13]

Deductions

The landlord is entitled to the rent in full, less any deductions specifically authorised by the lease or by statute. Certain sums are allowable against the rent (in the absence of agreement to the contrary) and these include payments for which the landlord, but not the tenant, is liable, but which are recoverable on

---

9   *Re Aspinall, Aspinall v Aspinall* [1961] Ch 526, [1961] 2 All ER 751.
10   *De Nicholls v Saunders* (1870) LR 5 CP 589.
11   *Re House Property and Investment Co Ltd* [1954] Ch 576 at 586.
12   *Warwicke v Noakes* (1791) Peake 68.
13   *Beevers v Mason* (1978) 37 P & CR 452, CA; and cashed: *Official Solicitor v Thomas* [1986] 2 EGLR 1, CA.

the land. These include such payments as owners' drainage rate and payments made by the tenant to avoid ouster from the land or distress.[14] A right of deduction should be distinguished from the right, notably in equity, to set off against rent arrears, which commonly arises as a tenant's remedy for landlords' breaches of repairing covenants. An established claim to set-off goes to the root of the landlord's claim to rent and is considered in chapter 9.

Abatement of rent

Apart from any express clause in the lease entitling the tenant to an abatement of rent, if the landlord promises to accept, for a limited period, or for the residue of the term, a reduction or abatement in the rent, he will be estopped from resiling from his promise, if it was intended to be and was in fact acted on, even if made for no consideration, although this doctrine of equitable estoppel is only available to the lessee as a defence.[15] If the landlord promises by deed to accept a reduction in rent for a given period, such promise is deemed to be for consideration and is enforceable at law without any recourse to equity.

VI APPORTIONMENT OF RENT

The rent due under a lease may be apportioned, ie proportionately divided up, where either the reversion is split up or severed between different landlords, or where a lease or tenancy is terminated (by surrender, forfeiture or notice, for example) during a rental period. Where the reversion is severed, any apportionment of rent between different landlords requires, at common law, the tenant's consent. Should the tenant surrender part of the land demised, he has the right to a proportionate reduction in rent, having regard to the value of the land lost.

There is no right at common law to any apportionment of rent in respect of time, as where a tenancy is terminated during a particular quarter, and so between the usual quarter days, rather than one of such days. The Apportionment Act 1870 permits time apportionment, but it does not apply both where the rent is payable in advance, and if the lease or tenancy expressly excludes its provisions. In principle, where applicable, the Act deems rent to accrue from day to day (s 2). Thus, if a tenancy is forfeited between the Christmas and Lady quarter days, only a proportionate part of the rent due for that period would be recoverable from the tenant. Should a former tenant remain in occupation after such termination, no doubt the landlord could claim mesne profits from him.

---

14 Law of Distress Amendment Act 1908, s 3. See *Rhodes v Allied Dunbar Pension Services Ltd* [1988] 1 All ER 524, 530 (reversed on appeal on different grounds [1989] 1 All ER 1161) holding that s 3 did not extend to a mortgagee or other third party taking an estate for value.
15 *Central London Property Trust Ltd v High Trees House Ltd* [1947] KB 130, [1946] 1 All ER 256n; *Dorkins v Wright* [1983] CLY 1364; *Central Street Properties Ltd v Mansbrook Rudd & Co Ltd* [1986] 2 EGLR 33.

VII   EFFECT OF NON-PAYMENT OF RENT

It may be thought that since payment is an acknowledgement by the tenant of his tenure, the effect of non-payment of rent would be to set up in him a good title to the land by limitation against the landlord. This is not so. On the contrary, the general rule is that during the currency of a lease the tenant cannot acquire title against the landlord; but this will not prevent third parties from doing so. The land must be in the adverse possession of some person in whose favour time may run. The test is objective and therefore it makes no difference that the third party occupier mistakenly believes himself to be a tenant.[16] Adverse possession, by extension, includes the receipt of the rent by a person wrongfully claiming to be the immediate reversioner.[17] A number of specific limitation rules apply to tenants and other persons.

(a) *Lease in writing*   Where a lease is in writing,[18] the tenant himself cannot begin to acquire a good title against his landlord as long as the lease continues; but when it expires, he can. It now appears that the expression 'lease in writing' is limited to a lease passing a legal estate, as opposed to a document, such as a letter, which acknowledges the terms of a tenancy. Where, therefore, a local authority tenant had signed a letter to the effect that he agreed to abide by the terms of a periodic tenancy, the document was not a 'lease in writing' and time did not run as from the expiry in 1984 of a landlord's notice to quit, but from 1977, when the tenant ceased to pay rent.[19] The only effect of non-payment of rent is to bar recovery of each instalment of rent after six years.[20] However, where the rent is £10 a year or more, payment of rent to a third person, for 12 years[1] will bar the landlord's title to the reversion against that third person.

(b) *Lease not in writing*   Non-payment of rent by a yearly or periodic tenant without a lease in writing, however, for 12 years,[2] will debar his landlord from recovering possession from him. Time begins to run from the end of the first year or other period of the tenancy, and will start to run again after any payment of rent or written acknowledgement.

(c) *Tenancies at will on sufferance*   Tenants at will are in a similar position to a yearly tenant without a lease, time beginning to run after the date of determination of the tenancy. In favour of a tenant on sufferance, time begins to run from the commencement of the tenancy.

---

16   *Lodge v Wakefield Metropolitan District Council* [1995] 2 EGLR 124, CA.

17   Limitation Act 1980, s 15(6) and Sch 1, para 8(3).

18   A rent-book is not a 'lease' in writing: *Moses v Lovegrove* [1952] 2 QB 533, [1952] 1 All ER 1279. In *Jessamine Investment Co v Schwartz* [1976] 3 All ER 521, a weekly statutory tenant was able to claim an adverse title to a mesne landlord; see also *Price v Hartley* [1996] EGCS 74, CA.

19   *Long* v *Tower Hamlets London Borough Council* [1996] 2 All ER 683. The expression 'lease in writing' follows the language of the Statute of Frauds 1677, s 1, whereas the more modern language of related provisions (LPA 1925, ss 52 and 54) follows that of the Real Property Act 1845, s 3.

20   Limitation Act 1980, s 19.

1   Ibid, s 15(6) and Sch 1, para 6.

2   Ibid, s 15(6) and Sch 1, para 5.

(d) *Licensees* If the occupier is a licensee, his possession is not adverse and time cannot run against the reversioner.[3]

VIII REMEDIES FOR NON-PAYMENT OF RENT

In what follows, we examine the three remedies available to a landlord against a tenant who fails to pay rent in breach of his obligation to do so. The first of these is distress. We then examine actions on the personal covenant to pay rent and thereafter forfeiture.

1 DISTRESS

Distress for unpaid rent is a remedy which enables a landlord to recover the rent by seizing and then selling goods on the premises sufficient to pay off the rent arrears. This remedy gives the landlord certain rights in respect of the tenant's goods, in which he has no proprietary interest, but because of the tenant's breach of obligation to pay rent. Judicial notice has recently been taken of the fact that distress may be coming back into vogue, at least in relation to business lettings.[4] The eventual abolition of the remedy has been proposed.[5] To date, no legislation has been enacted. The continuing availability of distress may seem inconsistent with the general policy of the law, which is to discourage creditors from resorting to extra-judicial remedies to enforce the recovery of debts, with their attendant dangers of violence, coupled with uncertainties as to whether a particular distress is lawful or not. It could be argued that distress might seem unnecessary or even oppressive if reforms of the civil justice system[6] have the effect of making it easier and simpler to obtain remedies for non-payment of rent in court.

Distress entitles the landlord to enter the premises as soon as rent (including where reserved as rent both service charges and insurance premiums payable by the tenant) is in arrear and then to take possession of the tenant's goods without legal process, to satisfy the amount of the rent due. Distress is extra-judicial, subject to the exceptions mentioned below. If, within five days of the seizure of the goods, the rent remains unpaid, the goods may be sold so as to pay off the rent arrears. Should the landlord himself not act as distrainor, he must employ a certificated bailiff and a company or other corporate landlord must employ a certificated bailiff.[7]

The landlord or bailiff may impound the goods, either on the premises or in another place; should the tenant then interfere with the goods he is guilty of pound-breach. The remedy of the landlord is then recapture and a civil action

---

3 *BP Properties Ltd v Buckler* [1987] 2 EGLR 168, CA.
4 *Wharfland Ltd v South London Co-operative Building Co Ltd* [1995] 2 EGLR 21, 22.
5 Law Com No 194 (1991); and see *Salford Van Hire (Contracts) Ltd v Bocholt Developments Ltd* [1995] 2 EGLR 50, 54, CA.
6 Commencing with the Courts and Legal Services Act 1990, as noted by the Law Commission, Report, para 5.5.
7 Law of Distress Amendment Act 1888, ss 7 and 8; Distress for Rent Rules 1988, SI 1988/2050.

for treble damages.[8] This method of computing damages seems to be inconsistent with the more general policy of the law that the purpose of damages is compensation, not punishment. As a limited formal protection, at the time of distress, the tenant must be given a notice of distress by the distrainor if a bailiff is employed.[9] The distrained goods may thereafter, as was seen, be sold (in the event of continued non-payment of rent) not less than five days after service of a notice of distress.[10] The landlord should get the best net price he can for the goods. Where the rent of an immediate tenant is in arrear, the superior landlord may serve a notice on any underlessee or lodger stating the amount of the arrears and requiring all future payments of rent to be paid direct to him, until such arrears are paid off. The superior landlord may give a valid receipt for such rent.[11]

If a distress is illegal, the tenant may act in one of two ways. First, he may recapture the goods, a process called rescue, but this must be done before they are impounded. Or he may bring a county court action, at any time before sale, in replevin (for return of the goods on his giving security for costs and rent arrears). Neither of these remedies is however available for an irregular or excessive distress (an irregular distress would for instance involve a sale of goods in less than five days; an excessive distress involves taking more goods than are necessary to satisfy the rent arrears). In such cases the landlord is liable for the tort of wrongful interference with goods.[12]

Distress is restricted both at common law and by statute. In particular, many goods of the tenant are privileged against distress, ie they cannot be seized at all (absolute privilege) or only if no other goods are available (conditional privilege). For example, at common law, any tenants' fixtures, wild animals, loose money, milk, fruit and things in actual use at the time of the distress, cannot be distrained against at all. Tools and implements of the tenant's trade or profession may not be distrained, nor may certain farm animals (such as sheep or stock which the tenant is fairly paid to feed and pasture) unless there are no other sufficient goods on the premises to satisfy the distress.

Statute requires the landlord to obtain the leave of the county court in a number of cases before he may levy a distress, notably, where there is a dwelling-house let on an assured tenancy,[13] and where the lessee is a company being wound up by the court.[14] In the case of agricultural holdings, distress must be made within one year of the default.[15]

---

8 Distress for Rent Act 1689, s 3.
9 Distress for Rent Act 1689; Distress for Rent Rules, supra.
10 Distress for Rent Act 1689, s 1, extended to 15 days by Law of Distress Amendment Act 1888, s 6, following a tenant's written request for security and costs.
11 Law of Distress Amendment Act 1908, s 6; see *Rhodes v Allied Dunbar Pension Services Ltd* [1989] 1 All ER 1161, CA. Under s 3 of the 1908 Act, the underlessee is given a statutory right of deduction of sums so paid.
12 Torts (Interference with Goods) Act 1977, s 1.
13 Housing Act 1988, s 19(1); a similar exception applies where a dwelling-house is let on a protected tenancy or subject to a statutory tenancy (Rent Act 1977, s 147(1)).
14 Insolvency Act 1986 s 130(3).
15 Agricultural Holdings Act 1986 s 16(1). No corresponding provision appears in the Agricultural Tenancies Act 1995 for farm business tenancies.

Third parties, such as hire-purchase companies whose goods are in the possession of the tenant, have some protection from distress under the Law of Distress Amendment Act 1908. This relates to the goods of a third party (anyone other than the tenant, such as his spouse or lodger) which are on the premises. The person in question makes a written declaration in the prescribed form[16] on the distraining landlord or bailiff once distress is threatened, to the effect that the tenant has no beneficial interest in the goods and that they are not goods excluded from the Act by s 4. An inventory of the goods is required. Service of this declaration renders illegal any future proceedings in distress against the relevant goods, and the third party will have an action for damages against the bailiff, if any, as well as the landlord.[17] The protection of the 1908 Act is not total as there are specific exclusions from it.[18]

2 ACTIONS FOR RENT AND COMPENSATION

Action for rent

An action for rent is an action by the landlord against the current tenant[19] for a debt, for the sum agreed to be paid by the lessee. The county court has unlimited jurisdiction.[20] If the value of the action is less than £25,000, the proper court is the county court; if it is between £25,000 and £50,000, the action may be tried in either the High or county court and if the value of the action exceeds £50,000, it should generally be tried in the High Court.[1] In the county court there is a speedy procedure for actions to recover rent.[2] The tenant may answer a claim for rent in various ways, such as the following: that the landlord's title has ceased since the demise; that he has been evicted by the landlord or by title paramount; and that the deed, and any covenants in it. He may also allege that the rent due has been paid or tendered,[3] or that, if goods have been taken in distress, they have been sold in satisfaction of the arrears or remain impounded. He may also claim that the landlord is estopped from claiming the contractual rent or that the claim is statute-barred. The tenant may also assert that the lease has been frustrated. If the tenant admits the claim, he may claim a set-off, as where he has an outstanding damages claim for breach of the landlord's covenant to repair – such a claim, if established, goes to the root of the landlord's claim for rent.

16 See also *Lawrence Chemical Co Ltd v Rubenstein* [1982] 1 All ER 653, [1982] 1 WLR 284, CA.
17 *Lowe v Dorling & Son* [1906] 2 KB 772, CA.
18 Law of Distress Amendment Act 1908, ss 4 and 4A (e g goods of the tenant's spouse; also goods in reputed ownership of the tenant with the consent of the true owner). See *Perdana Properties Bhd v United Orient Leasing Co Sdn Bhd* [1982] 1 All ER 193, [1981] 1 WLR 1496, PC; if the true owner withdraws consent, eg by withdrawing the tenant's continued right to possession, s 4 will not apply and the goods will thereafter be privileged against distress.
19 For the circumstances in which persons other than the current tenant may be liable for unpaid rent, see ch 5.
20 High Court and County Courts Jurisdiction Order 1991, SI 1991/724, para 7.
 1 In the first and last case there is a power in either court to transfer the action to the other court in specified circumstances.
 2 County Court Rules, Ord 24.
 3 *Morris Gore v Westbourne Hill Properties Ltd* [1982] 1 EGLR 55, CA.

Where there is no express agreement to pay interest on rent overdue, the court may, at its discretion, award interest on the arrears from the day the rent fell due to the date of judgment.[4] Interest is calculated from the date when each payment of rent fell due.

Action for compensation for use and occupation

An action for use and occupation is based on the occupation by a person who has possession with the express or implied permission of the owner. The basis of the action is that the tenant is bound to pay reasonable compensation to the landlord for the latter's loss of use of the premises. It is available to a landlord where the tenant enters and occupies land or premises where there is no ground for an action for rent. This is so where, for example, the tenant holds as tenant at will (rent-free), as tenant at sufferance, as a tenant by estoppel, or holds over after expiry of a fixed term with no express agreement as to rent, or following service of a notice to quit on the landlord by the person now in occupation after its expiry.[5] This action is also available where a person takes possession under an agreement for a lease, or where he takes possession as a purchaser prior to completion of a contract for sale which later goes off (assuming the contract does not alter this rule).[6] If the tenant has sub-let the premises, since he holds by the sub-lessee, he remains liable to pay the landlord damages for use and occupation if the sub-lessee wrongfully holds over after the expiry of the head lease, but only until the sub-lessee leaves.[7] However, if the reason why the sub-lessee does not leave is that the tenant cannot evict him at common law owing to residential or other statutory security of tenure, the tenant is not liable to the landlord for such use and occupation by the sub-lessee of the whole or any part of the premises.[8]

The action cannot be maintained against a tenant who has never entered,[9] nor against a tenant after eviction or after the landlord has served a writ for possession after the lease expires or is claiming forfeiture, so electing to treat the tenant as a trespasser.[10]

The amount of damages is fixed by the court with regard to the letting value of the premises. It may now be that, by analogy with recent authority as to mesne profits, that the basis of recovery is that the landlord is entitled to compensation for the use of his property, even if he would not have wished to re-let it, and that the concept of 'letting value' is not an abstract notion, so that the court will have regard to the cost to the tenant of comparable accommodation, at least where the tenant had enjoyed a preferential rent, as where he was a service occupier.[11] However, it still appears that any express agreement as to rent may be used as evidence of the amount of damages and so the rent under a previous tenancy is evidence of the rental value, although seemingly, if one of

4 Law Reform (Miscellaneous Provisions) Act 1934 s 3.
5 *Bird v Defonvielle* (1846) 2 Car & Kir 415.
6 *Howard v Shaw* (1841) 8 M & W 118.
7 *Ibbs v Richardson* (1839) 9 Ad & El 849.
8 *Reynolds v Bannerman* [1922] 1 KB 719; *Watson v Saunders-Roe Ltd* [1947] KB 437, CA.
9 *Lowe v Ross* (1850) 5 Exch 553.
10 *Birch v Wright* (1786) 1 Term Rep 378.
11 See *Ministry of Defence v Thompson* [1993] 2 EGLR 107, CA.

the parties proposes a higher rent, the previously-payable rent is not relevant as the parties are no longer *ad idem*.[12] The tenant has a defence if he can show that the landlord's title ceased after he went into occupation, that the tenancy has been surrendered by operation of law, that the claim has been satisfied or is statute-barred or that his occupation was adverse to the plaintiff's.

Action for mesne profits

Once the landlord has served a writ for possession on the tenant, he must claim mesne profits; until the date of service of such writ, he claims rent or sums for use and occupation.[13] This is because, once a writ claiming possession has been issued, the tenant becomes a trespasser in the eyes of the law, and mesne profits alone may be claimed from trespassers. Mesne profits are compensatory (or perhaps nowadays even restitutionary) in nature, and so, since they are a form of damages, the court may, in the absence of special factors, base its award on the letting value of the property, as evidenced by the previously-payable rent. It may equally make a finding as to what is a reasonable rent for the wrongful use of the landlord's property by the trespasser-occupier.[14] Moreover, it now appears that the basis of compensation is the benefit to the former tenant from his wrongful occupation, and this requires a close examination of the facts in any case, as where the previous tenancy was not at a commercial rent. Hence, where a service tenant's deserted wife remained in occupation of Ministry of Defence property, for which a concessionary rent had ben paid – awaiting a re-possession order against her so that she might be re-housed by the local authority – the measure of damages was the sums payable by her for comparable local authority accommodation. That sum was more than the concessionary rent, but much less than the abstract market value figure produced by the landlords, which was rejected.[15] In relation to mesne profits, the fact that the landlord might not have let the property to anyone else is irrelevant, seeing that the landlord is entitled to some compensation for the wrongful use of his land by the trespassing occupier.[16]

Statutory duty of landlords to notify tenants

Under Part VI of the Landlord and Tenant Act 1987,[17] a landlord of premises consisting of or including a dwelling[18] must comply with ss 47 and 48 of the 1987 Act.

---

12 *Dean and Chapter of the Cathedral of Christ Church Canterbury v Whitbread plc* [1995] 1 EGLR 82.
13 *Canas Property Co Ltd v KL Television Services* [1970] 2 QB 433, CA.
14 See *Inverugie Investments Ltd v Hackett* [1995] 3 All ER 841, PC.
15 *Ministry of Defence v Ashman* [1993] 2 EGLR 102, CA; see E Cooke (1994) 110 LQR 420.
16 *Inverugie Investments Ltd v Hackett*, supra.
17 In force on 1 February 1988; Landlord and Tenant Act 1987 (Commencement No 1) Order 1987, SI 1987/2177.
18 Lettings to which Part II of the Landlord and Tenant Act 1954 applies are excluded (s 46(1)) but 'premises' is wide enough to mean the subject-matter of a letting of land, including a dwelling, as part of an agricultural holding: *Dallhold Estates (UK) Pty Ltd v Lindsey Trading Properties Inc* [1994] 1 EGLR 93, CA.

Section 47(1) requires that any demand for rent or other sums payable to the landlord under the tenancy, such as service charges, must contain the landlord's name and address, and, if this is not in England and Wales, an address in England and Wales at which notices (including those in proceedings) may be served on the landlord.

If this is not done, or any notice does not contain the relevant information, any part of the amount demanded which consists of a service charge is to be treated for all purposes as not being due from the tenant to the landlord, until compliance (s 47(2)). The only exception to this is where there is a receiver or manager currently appointed, whose functions include receipt of service charges (s 47(3)).

Section 48(1) requires a landlord who lets any dwelling to furnish the tenant with an address in England and Wales at which notices (including notices in proceedings) may be served on him by the tenant. If this is not complied with, any rent or service charge otherwise due from the tenant to the landlord is treated for all purposes as not being due from the tenant to the landlord at any time before the landlord complies with the requirement (s 48(2)). This does not apply where there is an appointment of a receiver or manager whose functions include receipt of rent or service charges (s 48(3)). Because it is procedural in nature, and so not subject to any presumption against construing statutes as being retrospective, this provision applies to a tenancy in existence before it was brought into force, so depriving a landlord who ignored it, not only of rent arrears claimed after 1 February 1988, but of some £234, claimed as due prior to that date.[19]

There is no prescribed form for a s 48 notice but it must be in writing (s 54) and any relevant landlord is obliged to serve one on the tenant before he can enforce recovery of rent or service charge arrears. It makes no difference that the tenancy does not provide expressly for any written demand. However, the requirement of service is not difficult to comply with since it suffices if there is an unqualified statement of the landlord's address in England and Wales in any written tenancy agreement. If the landlord moves, a separate notice would then be required.[20]

As regards service by a tenant to whom ss 47 and 48 apply of a notice on the landlord is concerned, s 196 of the Law of Property Act 1925 is amended, so as to include an address furnished by the landlord under s 48 or that last furnished under s 47 (s 49).

3   FORFEITURE

The landlord may elect to forfeit the lease for non-payment of rent. If he does so, assuming he has not waived the breach and proceeds in the High Court, equity has an ancient jurisdiction to grant relief against forfeiture, both to the lessee and to under-lessees and mortgagees.[1] The object of a forfeiture clause

19 *Hussein v Singh* [1993] 2 EGLR 70, CA.
20 *Rogan v Woodfield Building Services Ltd* [1995] 1 EGLR 72, CA.
 1 *Belgravia Insurance Co Ltd v Meah* [1964] 1 QB 436, 443; *Billson v Residential Apartments Ltd* [1991] 3 All ER 265, 276.

in a lease is to secure the payment of rent or money sums such as service charges reserved as rent. Equity therefore normally grants relief if the tenant or other applicant fully compensates the landlord.[2] Equity's inherent jurisdiction to grant relief for non-payment of rent did not extend to other breaches of covenant, but statute has intervened to confer such a jurisdiction on the courts. That jurisdiction applies to any case of forfeiture which is not for non-payment of rent alone or, by extension, for non-payment of service charges reserved as rent or deemed to be rent without being in terms so reserved in the reddendum.[3]

No right of forfeiture may be exercised unless the lease expressly reserves a right of re-entry for breach of covenant to pay rent,[4] but such a reservation is surely commonplace today. However, in the case of the High Court jurisdiction, statute confirms the continued existence of an equitable jurisdiction to grant relief.[5] This jurisdiction extends to any periodical sums, such as service charges payable as rent, for which distress may be levied, a principle which may be of advantage to a mortgagee whose lessee has fallen into arrear with such payments, but not necessarily with the rent proper.[6] The county court has a separate jurisdiction, under the County Courts Act 1984, s 138, which is entirely self-contained, and to the complete exclusion of any parallel High Court jurisdiction, in equity or otherwise.[7]

At common law, as an ancient limitation on forfeitures, no right of re-entry for non-payment of rent arises unless and until a formal demand has been made for the rent, by the landlord or his agent, at the place specified in the lease for payment or otherwise on the land, before and until sunset, on the last day for payment and for the sum due for the last rental period. These conditions are so inconvenient that the lease will almost certainly expressly dispense with them. Thus the lease may well state that the landlord may re-enter and determine the lease for non-payment of rent once rent is in arrear for over a stated period, whether formally demanded or not. In any case, there is no need for a formal demand in the case of High Court proceedings[8] if the right of re-entry is between landlord and tenant, one half-year's rent is in arrear, no sufficient distress is found on the premises to pay off all the arrears due and the lease expressly reserves a right of re-entry for non-payment of rent.[9] If the landlord in fact levies a distress, he apparently does not waive his right to re-enter under the 1852 Act.[10]

---

2 *Ladup Ltd v Williams and Glyn's Bank plc* [1985] 2 All ER 577, 584, [1985] 1 WLR 851, 860.
3 *Escalus Properties Ltd v Robinson* [1996] QB 231, CA; for new statutory restrictions applicable to service charges, see ch 13.
4 Unless payment of rent is expressly made a condition.
5 Supreme Court Act 1981, s 38.
6 *Escalus Properties Ltd v Robinson* [1996] QB 231, CA (even though the sums were not reserved as rent).
7 *Di Palma v Victoria Square Property Ltd* [1986] Ch 150, [1985] 2 All ER 676, CA; *United Dominions Trust Ltd v Shellpoint Trustees Ltd* [1993] 4 All ER 310, CA.
8 For a similar rule in the case of county court proceedings see County Courts Act 1984, s 139(1).
9 Since both s 210 of the 1852 Act and s 139(1) of the 1984 Act refer respectively to 'serve a writ' and 'the commencement of the action', neither exclude a formal demand in the case of physical re-entry by the landlord.
10 *Brewer d Lord Onslow v Eaton* (1783) 3 Doug KB 230.

4   RELIEF AGAINST FORFEITURE

There are two separate sets of rules governing the grant of relief against forfeiture to lessees and other applicants such as underlessees and mortgagees. One set applies to High Court actions, and is based on the ancient equitable practice and jurisdiction of the Court of Chancery, which fundamentally differentiates this form of relief from all others.[11]

Applications for relief by lessees and other applicants to the High Court must be made within six months of the landlord's actual entry under a court order for possession.[12] Where the landlord re-enters the premises without a court order, there is a rough time-limit of six months, by analogy with statute, on relief applications.[13] In the case of applications to the county court for relief, there is a self-contained statutory code is based on suspended orders for possession.

Relief in the High Court

1   *Automatic stay*   If the tenant pays into court or to the landlord at any time, before judgment is given,[14] all rent arrears and costs, he obtains an automatic stay on proceedings.[15] This applies only if at least half a year's rent is in arrear,[16] but is available if the landlord is also proceeding on other grounds and enables relief to be given where the landlord has re-entered the premises without a court order.[17]

2   *Applications for relief*   The court's power to grant or refuse relief is discretionary but only exceptionally[18] will relief be refused (assuming the application is within the six-month time-limit) where all the rent and costs have been paid before judgment or if the tenant pays off the rent arrears and costs, and undertakes, where relevant, to perform the covenants in the lease.[19] The arrears and costs must be paid within a time-limit set by the court (which no doubt in suitable cases may be extended after application).[20] On the other hand, where it is inequitable to grant relief, then it will be refused, as where the landlord, after judgment for possession, had reasonably re-let the premises to a third party.[1] The effect of relief, if given, is that no forfeiture is deemed to have taken place. The lessee is re-instated, as s 38(2) of the Supreme Court Act 1981

---

11   *Belgravia Insurance Co v Meah*, supra.
12   Common Law Procedure Act 1852, s 210.
13   *Thatcher v C H Pearce & Sons (Contractors) Ltd* [1968] 1 WLR 748.
14   See *Gill v Lewis* [1956] 2 QB 1, [1956] 1 All ER 844, CA.
15   Common Law Procedure Act 1852 s 212.
16   *Standard Pattern Co v Ivey* [1962] Ch 432, [1962] 1 All ER 452.
17   *Howard v Fanshawe* [1895] 2 Ch 581.
18   *Public Trustee v Westbrook* [1965] 3 All ER 398, [1965] 1 WLR 1160, CA.
19   *Belgravia Insurance Co v Meah*, supra; *Re Brompton Securities Ltd (No 2)* [1988] 3 All ER 677.
20   *Barton, Thompson & Co v Stapling Machines Co* [1966] Ch 499, [1966] 2 All ER 222.
 1   *Silverman v AFCO (UK) Ltd* [1988] 1 EGLR 51, CA, applying *Stanhope v Haworth* (1886) 3 TLR 34, CA.

refers to his holding the demised premises 'without the necessity for a new lease'.[2] The power to grant relief cannot be excluded by a term in the lease which operates as a disguised forfeiture clause.[3]

Underlessees and mortgagees may apply for relief in the same way as a lessee provided that they do so within the six-month limit. The effect of this form of relief is retrospectively to revive the head lease[4] so that while rent arrears are payable in full, no mesne profits are due (even if the latter would exceed any rent arrears), which would have been the case if the effect of a relief order had not been held to be retrospective. The grounds on which relief will be given are as for lessees.[5] They may also apply for a new lease under statute[6] provided the application is made before the landlord actually regains possession under a court order.[7] Where the landlord has peaceably re-entered without a court order, it would seem that there is no time-limit other than the discretion of the court.[8] It is arguable that if an application under statute is excluded[9] an application could be made by an underlessee or mortgagee by invoking the inherent equity jurisdiction of the court,[10] which may still exist in parallel to the statutory rule.

Relief in the county court

The county court's jurisdiction to grant relief is under s 138 of the County Courts Act 1984 as amended. If the tenant, or, by necessary implication, any underlessee or mortgagee,[11] pays rent arrears (or, where appropriate, any sums due as additional rent such as service charges) into court not less than five clear days before the return day, s 138(2) entitles him to automatic relief.[12] If this is not done, then the jurisdiction of the county court is based on suspended possession orders. By s 138(3), if the court is satisfied that the landlord is entitled to forfeit, it must order possession to be given not less than four weeks from the date of the order, the length of the suspension being at the court's discretion. If during the suspension period the tenant (or any underlessee or mortgagee) pays into court all the arrears and costs then the order does not take effect and then he gets automatic relief. The court has a discretion to extend the

---

2   *Dendy v Evans* [1910] 1 KB 263, CA; *Escalus Properties Ltd* v *Robinson* [1996] QB 231, CA.
3   *Richard Clarke & Co Ltd v Widnall* [1976] 3 All ER 301, [1976] 1 WLR 845, CA.
4   *Escalus Properties Ltd* v *Robinson*, supra.
5   *Belgravia Insurance Co v Meah*, supra.
6   Law of Property Act 1925, s 146(4).
7   *Rogers v Rice* [1892] 2 Ch 170, CA.
8   *Billson v Residential Apartments Ltd* [1992] 2 AC 494, [1992] 1 All ER 141 (dealing only with s 146(2) of the 1925 Act).
9   Eg by wrongful failure by the landlord to notify an underlessee or mortgagee, of whom he knows, of pending forfeiture proceedings, contrary to RSC, Ord 6, r 2.
10 See *Abbey National Building Society v Maybeech Ltd* [1985] Ch 190; *Ladup Ltd v Williams & Glyn's Bank plc* [1985] 2 All ER 577.
11 *United Dominions Trust Ltd v Shellpoint Trustees Ltd* [1993] 4 All ER 310, CA. Underlessees and mortgagees are entitled, if known to him, to be notified by the landlord of the service of his writ for possession by CCR, Ord 6, r 3.
12 This does not apply where the landlord is proceeding to forfeit on any other grounds as well as non-payment of rent.

suspension period – at any time before possession is recovered by the landlord (s 138(4)). If within this extended period the tenant pays off the rent arrears and costs, then again the tenant or other relevant applicant obtains automatic relief (s 138(5)).

If the tenant, or any underlessee or mortgagee applicant fails during the original and any extended period of suspension to pay off all the rent arrears and costs, then by s 138(7) the order will be enforced and so long as it is unreversed and subject to what follows, the tenant will be barred from all relief. This means just that: where a tenant's lease was forfeited for service charges rent arrears of £299, and the order was enforced, it was held that she could not, in view of the plain language of s 138(7), obtain any relief either in the county court, where the order was made, or in the High Court.[13]

Where the landlord recovers possession of the land at any time after the making of the court's order for possession, the tenant, or any underlessee or mortgagee, may, at any time within six months from the date of the recovery of possession[14] apply to the court for relief (s 138(9A)). The same relief is extended to any underlessee or mortgagee (s 138(9C)). Because the effect of relief granted to a mortgagee is retrospective, just as it is where relief is granted to a lessee under s 146(2) of the Law of Property Act 1925, where a mortgagee was granted a new reversionary lease, the registered title to a forfeited lease having been deleted, it was entitled to a £48,000 premium paid by a new lessee in possession to the landlord.[15]

In connection with underlessees or mortgagees, who are entitled by necessary implication to avail themselves of the right to apply for relief in s 138(2) and (5), as well as the present further extended period, it has now been held that where a mortgagee, who had been duly notified of the landlord's application for possession for non-payment of rent, failed to avail himself of any of the original or extended opportunities conferred by the 1984 Act to apply for relief, he had no right to apply for relief to the High Court, applying the principle that the 1984 Act formed a comprehensive code.[16] In any case, since the time-limits for applications had been extended by the legislature, there would seem no good reason for encouraging delays in pursuing rights and in promoting uncertainty in landlords' titles.

13 *Di Palma v Victoria Square Property Ltd* [1986] Ch 150, [1985] 2 All ER 676, CA.
14 Despite the wording of s 138(9A) it is clear that the landlord is not entitled personally to enforce a court order for possession: see *Haniff v Robinson* [1993] 1 All ER 185, CA.
15 *Bank of Ireland Mortgages* v *South Lodge Developments* [1996] 1 EGLR 91.
16 *United Dominions Trust Ltd v Shellpoint Trustees* [1993] 4 All ER 310, CA.

Chapter 9

Repairing obligations[1]

Most leases for any length of time impose express obligations to repair or for work extending beyond repairs on either the landlord or the tenant. There have been cases where the lease is silent as to the repairing obligations of either party, and, particularly in the case of short residential leases, Parliament has intervened. This chapter examines both implied and express repairing obligations, and also the range of remedies available to both parties. The chapter concludes with an examination of the control by local authorities of dilapidated residential premises and the use of statutory powers to compel owners to remedy disrepair which constitutes a 'statutory nuisance'. The importance of repairing and related obligations has been recognised by the fact that reform of the subject has been considered on four separate occasions since 1945. In this chapter, we examine in various places the latest set of reform proposals produced by the Law Commission,[2] who say[3] that there is a public interest in seeing that there is an adequate stock of usable rented property, which is why they consider that the present, to their mind untidy and haphazard state of the law, is in need of reform by the enactment of a new statute.

I LANDLORD'S IMPLIED OBLIGATIONS

The common law traditionally refused to imply any repairing obligations against a landlord who is not under any express obligations.[4] Thus, he is not under any general obligation to put the demised premises into repair at the commencement of the lease.[5] The landlord offers no implied warranty to the tenant that the premises are, or will be kept, fit for human habitation or suitable for any other purpose at the commencement of, or during the term.[6] There appears to be no general implied contractual duty on a landlord to keep in repair

1 See further Thornton, *Property Disrepair and Dilapidations* and *West's Law of Dilapidations*.
2 Law Com No 238 (1996) *Responsibility for State and Condition of Property*.
3 *Report*, para 1.27.
4 *Cockburn v Smith* [1924] 2 KB 119; *Duke of Westminster v Guild* [1985] QB 688, [1984] 3 All ER 144, CA.
5 *Gott v Gandy* (1853) 2 E & B 845.
6 *Hart v Windsor* (1844) 12 M & W 68; *Sutton v Temple* (1843) 12 M & W 52.

any premises he retains adjoining the demised premises even though, if his premises are in disrepair, this may well damage those of the lessee.[7]

The harsh traditional rule was based on the notion that a lessee could inspect the premises prior to taking a lease and must take them as he finds them. More recently, perhaps owing to the intervention of statute (see below) in the private residential sector, the Court of Appeal invoked the contractual principle of business efficacy so as to imply, as essential to make the tenancy work, a term into a periodic statutory tenancy of a terraced house that the landlord was liable to repair the exterior. The tenant was under an express obligation to keep the interior in repair, which she could not sensibly perform, owing to extensive water penetration from the exterior.[8] It is not clear whether this principle extends beyond residential leases which are in some way defective – as many leases will be expressly drafted to provide for comprehensive repairing obligations. It could be said that the main ground on which repairing obligations ought to be implied is where the landlord (or possibly the tenant) should be placed under a correlative obligation to one already undertaken by the other party, as was the position in the case just mentioned.[9] In any case, statute may impose obligations if the tenancy is residential and for less than seven years, so limiting the number of occasions of use of the power to imply repairing duties. Where this is so, there would appear to be no scope for any implied obligations, even to fill in gaps not thought of by the parties.[10] Thus, the court refused to imply against a landlord a duty to keep in repair a drain on his land, which served the tenant's adjoining premises, since the tenant's lease made fully comprehensive provisions and indeed gave him access to the landlord's land for the purpose of repairs to the drain.[11] Even in the case of residential leases, the requirement of business efficacy limits the scope for implying terms, so that no term could be implied into a lease of a flat that, should the managing company default in its obligations to repair, the landlord must take these over. There was no necessity for the term, first, because the lease expressly provided that in the case of default, the landlord might take over, but did not have to, and secondly, because the tenant could have invoked a statutory right to apply for the appointment of a manager.[12]

There are certain well-established cases where the courts have implied repairing and related obligations against a landlord.

1   *Houses in the course of erection*   In a lease of a dwelling-house which is still in the course of erection at the date of the lease, there is an implied warranty that it will be built with proper materials in a workmanlike manner, and that when it is completed, it will be fit for human habitation.[13]

---

7   *Tennant Radiant Heat Ltd v Warrington Corpn* [1988] 1 EGLR 41, CA. However, the landlord was liable in nuisance and negligence.
8   *Barrett v Lounova (1982) Ltd* [1990] 1 QB 348, [1989] 1 All ER 351, CA.
9   See also eg *Barnes v City of London Real Property Co* [1918] 2 Ch 18 (tenant undertook to pay a specified sum for repairs so impliedly obliging landlord to undertake these).
10   See *Demetriou v Poolaction Ltd* [1991] 1 EGLR 100, CA (business premises and no correlative obligation on the landlord).
11   *Duke of Westminster v Guild* supra; and see P Jackson [1985] Conv 66.
12   *Hafton Properties Ltd v Camp* [1994] 1 EGLR 67.
13   *Perry v Sharon Development Co Ltd* [1937] 4 All ER 390, CA.

2   *Landlord builder*   If the landlord builds an unfurnished dwelling-house or flat to his own design and specification (where he is a local authority for instance), he will be liable in negligence for dangerous defects causing personal injury to occupiers – as where a tenant was injured by a defective glass panel. The scope of the duty is to see that the occupiers, such as the tenant and his family, are reasonably safe when the premises are let from personal injury due to dangerous defects; and the duty is not avoided by the mere fact that the person to whom it is owed knows of the danger unless it would be reasonable to expect him to remove or avoid it.[14] If the landlord is not the builder then there remains no liability at common law for dangerous defects.[15] In such cases, recourse must be had (if any) to the Defective Premises Act 1972, but liability under s 4 of that Act depends on proof of disrepair by the tenant, which may leave him without a remedy if there is merely a design fault in the premises, but no disrepair.

3   *Furnished houses*   There is an implied condition in a tenancy of a furnished house or flat that the premises shall be fit for habitation at the commencement of the tenancy.[16] If on the day the tenancy commences, the premises are not fit for human habitation, the tenant may repudiate the lease – or he may elect to keep the lease and sue for damages.[17] The implied condition is very limited. It does not oblige the landlord to keep the premises fit for human habitation during the tenancy.[18] Infestation with bugs,[19] and defective drainage,[20] are examples of breaches of this implied condition.

4   *Miscellaneous*   There are a number of cases where an obligation to repair has been implied against a landlord which may be explained on the ground that, without an implication, the lease would be unworkable. Where the landlord retained possession and control of the common parts of a block of flats, such as the common stairways, rubbish chutes, lifts and lighting, he was under an implied duty to take reasonable care in all the circumstances to repair and maintain these parts.[1] Similarly, where a tenant enjoyed a right of way over a path which she used as an essential means of access to the premises, the landlord was under an implied duty to maintain the path.[2] More generally, in relation to premises not let to the tenant, but whose maintenance in proper repair is necessary for the protection of the demised premises or the safe enjoyment of

---

14   *Rimmer v Liverpool City Council* [1985] QB 1, [1984] 1 All ER 930, CA. The defective glass panel was standard-design and built-in: so the tenant could not remove or avoid it. Also *Targett v Torfaen Borough Council* [1992] 1 EGLR 275, CA.

15   *Cavalier v Pope* [1906] AC 428, HL; *McNerny v Lambeth London Borough Council* [1989] 1 EGLR 81, CA; PF Smith [1989] Conv. 216.

16   *Smith v Marrable* (1843) 11 M & W 5; *Collins v Hopkins* [1923] 2 KB 617.

17   *Wilson v Finch Hatton* (1877) 2 Ex D 336.

18   *Sarson v Roberts* [1895] 2 QB 395, CA.

19   *Smith v Marrable*, supra.

20   *Wilson v Finch Hatton*, supra; also *Collins v Hopkins* [1923] 2 KB 617.

 1   *Liverpool City Council v Irwin* [1977] AC 239, [1976] 2 All ER 39, HL.

 2   *King v South Northamptonshire District Council* [1992] 1 EGLR 53, CA. Also *Dunster v Hollis* [1918] 2 KB 795.

them by the tenant, there is an implied obligation of uncertain scope on the landlord to take reasonable care that these retained parts are not in such a state as to cause damage to the tenant or the premises.[3] Where the tenant had to pay for the cost of external repainting, which the landlord had not expressly undertaken to do, the landlord was under an implied obligation to do the work in question.[4] The implication of an obligation is not automatic and much will depend on the circumstances of the case: the fact that if no obligation is implied, neither party may be liable for repairs of a given type is not of itself enough to warrant any implication of liability against the landlord.[5]

Certain conditions and undertakings are implied against a landlord letting a *small house at a low rent* by s 8 of the Landlord and Tenant Act 1985. The landlord is subject to an implied condition that the house is fit for human habitation, which is defined by a statutory standard (s 10) at the commencement and (in contrast to furnished lettings) during the tenancy. However, the rent levels are an annual level of £80 in London and £52 elsewhere. It has long been recognised judicially that, thanks to these low levels, s 8 must now have very little application.[6] According to the Law Commission, a proper revision of these rent limits (which was abandoned in 1957) would have increased the upper limit to some £3,000 per annum.[7] The statutory obligation as to fitness for human habitation is lower in degree than an obligation to keep in repair: it requires the landlord to see to it that the house is decently fit for humans to live in.[8] Even if a house is within s 8 and is unfit as prescribed, the landlord is only subject to liability, by s 10, if it is so far defective in respect of one of the prescribed matters (such as repair, freedom from damp, or ventilation) that it is not reasonably suitable for occupation in that condition.

The Law Commission has proposed the introduction of a new statutory implied obligation as to fitness for human habitation, which would apply to any lease of a dwelling-house for a term of less than seven years – corresponding to the tenancies to which the existing statutory implied obligation to repair applies. The lessor would be subject to an implied covenant that the dwelling-house was fit for human habitation at the commencement of the tenancy. He would have to keep it in that state during the lease.[9] The obligation would be subject to a requirement of notice (as with the present statutory obligation to repair) and so would not be absolute, although the fitness criteria would be updated. If this proposal is ever implemented, and it would be expensive to do so, as many short lettings are by local authorities,[10] tenants would benefit from an obligation to ensure fitness for habitation to correspond to the existing landlords' obligation to keep dwelling-houses let on short leases in repair.

3   *Hargroves, Aronson & Co v Hartopp* [1905] 1 KB 472; *Cockburn v Smith* [1924] 2 KB 119.
4   *Edmonton Corpn v WM Knowles & Son Ltd* (1961) 60 LGR 124.
5   See *Demetriou v Poolaction Ltd*, supra.
6   *Quick v Taff-Ely Borough Council* [1986] QB 809 at 817, [1985] 3 All ER 321 at 324, CA.
7   *Report* (1996) para 4.12.
8   *Jones v Geen* [1925] 1 KB 659.
9   *Report* (1996), para 8.35.
10 Even though the proposal would only apply to tenancies entered into after the new obligation came into force.

II TENANT'S IMPLIED OBLIGATIONS

In the perhaps unlikely event of the lease or tenancy agreement failing to impose any express repairing or maintenance obligations on the tenant, there are circumstances in which he is subject to a liability not to commit waste (which may also be relevant where the lease fails to prohibit structural alterations). In addition, a tenant is subject to limited implied obligations to repair.

1 WASTE

Three types of waste

There are three types of waste. *Voluntary waste* is committed by any deliberate or negligent act of the tenant's which causes permanent damage, such as ploughing up pasture, felling or maiming trees or shrubs, overloading the floor of premises so as to cause it to collapse,[11] or altering or converting the premises without the landlord's prior permission. This latter point is further examined below.

Ameliorating waste is voluntary waste which improves the value of the land, buildings or premises, such as by building on land or extending premises. *Permissive waste* is based on allowing, by negligence, a building to fall down for lack of repairs. However, if a house is in a poor condition at the commencement of a lease, as where it has no roof, the tenant is not liable in permissive waste for allowing the house to collapse.[12]

A tenant's obligation not to commit waste is founded in tort, and is independent of any contractual obligation in the lease, whether express or implied. If the lease contains an express covenant to repair or against alterations, the landlord may elect to sue in waste.[13]

Liability for waste and remedies

Not all tenants are liable for waste or all kinds of waste. Tenants holding a lease for a term certain are liable both for voluntary and permissive waste. A tenant from year to year and for a shorter period is liable for voluntary but not for permissive waste.[14] A weekly tenant is also liable only for voluntary waste.[15] A tenant at will is not liable for either voluntary or permissive waste, but an act of voluntary waste terminates the tenancy and renders him liable in trespass.[16]

A tenant against whom an action for waste is brought has a defence if he shows that the damage resulted from the ordinary, reasonable and proper use of the premises,[17] or that the damage was caused by an Act of God, such as floods or lightning or fire.

---

11 *Manchester Bonded Warehouse Co v Carr* (1880) 5 CPD 507.
12 Co Litt 53a.
13 *Mancetter Development Ltd v Garmanson Ltd* [1986] QB 1212, [1986] 1 All ER 449, CA.
14 *Torriano v Young* (1833) 6 C & P 8.
15 *Warren v Keen* [1954] 1 QB 15, CA.
16 *Countess of Shrewsbury's Case* (1600) 5 Co Rep 13b.
17 *Manchester Bonded Warehouse Co v Carr* supra.

If waste is proved, on the other hand, the landlord may claim damages or an injunction. The measure of *damages* is the loss in value to the landlord's reversion.[18] This may be the cost of making good the damage to the buildings or land concerned, as where a damages award was based on the cost of making good holes left in the building by a careless removal of tenants' trade fixtures.[19] In this case, the tenant was liable even though he was entitled to remove the fixtures, because he could not exercise that right without making good the damage to the building.[20] The landlord may claim damages despite the expiry of the lease,[1] and also where the tenant holds over.[2]

The landlord may sue for an *injunction*, as where he claims a negative injunction to restrain alterations to the building. An injunction is not considered appropriate if the acts of waste are too trivial to warrant the grant of this discretionary remedy.[3] On the other hand, the fact that an alteration might also amount to a breach of covenant in the lease is no absolute bar to relief.[4] An injunction might, at discretion, be appropriate restrain the conversion of a house into a shop, so altering the whole character of the premises.[5] An injunction might also be granted to restrain further acts of waste (in such a case damages would not be an adequate remedy and could not be quantified, but damages could be awarded to compensate the landlord for any past injury).[6]

2 TENANT-LIKE USER

There is a contractual duty on a lessee to use the premises in a tenant-like manner, and to deliver up possession to the landlord at the termination of the tenancy in the same condition as when the tenant took them, fair wear and tear excepted.[7] The duty, sometimes referred to as an obligation to use in a tenant-like manner, is narrow and minimal. It does not oblige the tenant to carry out substantial repairs, as shown by the examples given in the leading case: if the tenant goes away in winter, he may, if this is reasonable, have to turn off the water and empty the boiler and do minor repairs. The tenant must not wilfully or negligently damage the house – nor must his family or guests, and he must replace any breakages. He is not bound to execute any repairs caused by items, such as windows, wearing out or decaying due to old age.[8] This obligation does not compel the tenant to lag internal water-pipes as a precaution against freezing in winter, nor to turn off the stop-cock or drain the water system, unless

18 *Whitham v Kershaw* (1886) 16 QBD 613, CA.
19 *Mancetter Development Ltd v Garmanson Ltd*, supra.
20 In *Mancetter Development Ltd v Garmanson Ltd* supra, a director of an occupying company, who had procured the removal of the fixtures, was personally liable to the landlords in damages.
1 *Kinlyside v Thornton* (1776) 2 Wm Bl 1111.
2 *Burchell v Hornsby* (1808) 1 Camp 360.
3 *Doherty v Allman* (1878) 3 App Cas 709, HL.
4 *Countess of Shrewsbury's Case* (1600) 5 Co Rep 13b.
5 *Marsden v Edward Heyes Ltd* [1927] 2 KB 1, CA.
6 See *West Ham Central Charity Board v East London Waterworks Co* [1900] 1 Ch 624.
7 *Marsden v Edward Heyes Ltd* [1927] 2 KB 1, CA.
8 *Warren v Keen* [1954] 1 QB 15, [1953] 2 All ER 1118, CA.

the circumstances, such as the severity of the cold, the conditions in the premises and the length of the tenant's absence, it would be reasonable to expect this.[9]

Almost any properly-drafted lease or tenancy will make express provisions as to the repairing obligations of the tenant. However, a covenant to leave premises in repair does not, apparently, exempt a tenant from an implied duty to use the premises in a tenant-like manner.[10]

The Law Commission consider that the current rules of waste and tenant-like user are inadequate and imprecise. They would replace both sets of rules with a statutory duty, which would, in particular, require the tenant to take proper care of the premises and to make good any wilful damage to them.[11]

III LANDLORD'S STATUTE-IMPLIED OBLIGATION TO KEEP IN REPAIR DWELLING-HOUSES AND FLATS

Since 1961 statute has imposed on landlords limited obligations[12] to keep dwelling-houses and flats held on short leases in repair. Short residential tenants are in a vulnerable position[13] and it would be perhaps unfair to expect such tenants, who may well have to pay a market rent, to live in premises which are out of repair, as it would be unreasonable to require them to carry out remedial work to the premises at their own expense. The statutory obligations of the landlord are in some respects not very onerous: they depend on notice of the want of repair and are in part subjective, owing to the fact that factors such as the age of the property are expressly relevant to the compliance with the statutory obligations (s 11(3)). Under the general law, the landlord cannot be required to cure unfitness which is not a disrepair. However, where the landlord is subjected to the extended obligation in the case of flats (so that he has to keep in repair for example a common roof not demised to any tenant) his duty is absolute and does not depend on prior notice from lessees. Hence a landlord who failed to remedy a damaged roof which allowed water ingress into a top-floor tenant's flat was liable in damages as from the date the disrepair first caused damage, as opposed to the time at which he eventually put in hand repairs.[14]

Application of 1985 Act

Section 11 of the Landlord and Tenant Act 1985 imposes repairing obligations on landlords of dwelling-houses or flats, where the lease is for a term of less than

---

9 *Wycombe Health Authority v Barnett* (1982) 47 P & CR 394, CA (short absence, tenant not liable when pipe burst); cf *Mickel v McCoard* 1913 SC 896 (long absence in mid-winter, tenant liable).
10 *White v Nicholson* (1842) 4 Man & G 95.
11 *Report*, para 10.37.
12 See *Newham London Borough Council v Patel* (1978) 13 HLR 77, 84.
13 As perhaps implicity recognised by the Law Commission in Law Com No 238 (1996) p 64 note 36.
14 *Passley* v *London Borough of Wandsworth* (24 May 1996, Unreported), CA.

seven years.[15] Excluded from the 1985 Act are any leases granted on or after 3 October 1980 to a local authority and certain other public sector bodies (s 14(4)). Tenancies to which Part II of the Landlord and Tenant Act 1954 applies are also excluded from the 1985 Act (s 32(2)), as are leases granted to the Crown (s 14(5)).[16]

A lease is caught by the Act where it is determinable at the landlord's option before seven years from the commencement of the term (s 13(2)(b)).[17] If the lease contains a tenant's option to renew which, if exercised, would prolong the lease over seven years, the Act does not apply (s 13(2)(c)). Any part of the term falling before the date of the grant of the lease is ignored in computing the statutory period which starts from the date of the grant or agreement for a lease (s 13(2)(a)).[18] This is to counter artificial backdating of leases with a view to extending the term beyond seven years. If the landlord obtains and accepts a registered rent on the basis that he is responsible for structural repairs under the 1985 Act, when in fact he is not, because the lease is for a term over seven years, as long as he demands the full rent, or rent arrears, he will be estopped from denying liability under the 1985 Act.[19]

Scope of landlord's duty

Section 11(1) implies a covenant by the landlord:

(a) to keep in repair the structure and exterior of the dwelling-house (including drains, gutters and external pipes) (s 11(1)(a)); and
(b) to keep in repair and proper working order the installations in the dwelling-house for the supply of water, gas and electricity, and for sanitation (including basins, sinks, baths and sanitary conveniences but not other fixtures, fittings and appliances for making use of the supply of water, gas or electricity) (s 11(1)(b)) and installations for space heating and heating water (s 11(1)(c)).

If the lease is of a flat – or any other 'dwelling-house' forming part only of a building – the duty in s 11(1)(a) extends to any part of the structure or exterior of the building in which the landlord has an estate or interest (s 11(1A)(a)). An example would be the common parts or the roof, if these are not demised to the individual lessees.

In the case of installations, where the landlord lets only part of the building (again for example, where flats are let and the landlord retains the common parts and/or the roof), the landlord must keep in repair and proper working order an installation which directly or indirectly serves the flat, provided that

---

15 Landlord and Tenant Act 1985, s 13(1). The date of grant must be on or after 24 October 1961.
16 Nor is the Crown bound by the 1985 Act where it is landlord: *Department of Transport v Egoroff* [1986] 1 EGLR 89, CA.
17 *Parker v O'Connor* [1974] 3 All ER 257, [1974] 1 WLR 1160, CA (lease for over seven years with right to determine lease on death of landlord outside this provision as right to determine not unfettered).
18 *Brikom Investments Ltd v Seaford* [1981] 2 All ER 783, [1981] 1 WLR 863, CA.
19 *Brikom Investments Ltd v Seaford*, supra.

the installation is in part of a building in which the landlord has an estate or interest or which is owned or controlled by him (s 11(1A)(b)).

The extended obligations only apply if the disrepair or failure to maintain affect the tenant's enjoyment of the flat or common parts (s 11(1B)).[20] If, in order to comply with the extended repairing covenant, the landlord needs to carry out works or repairs otherwise than in, or to an installation in, the dwelling-house and has no sufficient right in the part of the building or installation concerned to enable him to carry out the required repairs, it is a defence for the landlord to prove that he used all reasonable endeavours to obtain such right as would be adequate to enable him to carry out the works or repairs, but he was unable to do so (s 11(3A)).

Any covenant by the tenant for the repair of the premises (including any covenant to put in repair or deliver up in repair, to paint, point or render or to pay money in lieu of repairs by the tenant or on account of repairs by the landlord) is nullified (s 11(4)), in so far as it relates to matters covered by s 11(1).

Exceptions

Section 11(2) expressly absolves the landlord from liability:

(a) for repairs attributable to the tenant's failure to use the premises in a tenant-like manner;
(b) to rebuild, or reinstate the premises as a result of damage by fire, tempest, flood or other inevitable accident; or
(c) to repair or maintain any tenants' fixtures.

Thus, a liability to undertake responsibility for any of these matters, or to pay for their cost, may legitimately be cast on the tenant (s 11(4)).

Section 11(3) provides that in determining the standard of repair required to satisfy the obligations, regard is to be had to the age, character and prospective life of the house and the locality in which it is situated.[1]

The landlord's obligation is coupled with a right of entry, conferred on the landlord or a person authorised by him in writing, to view the state of repair of the premises, exercisable at reasonable times of the day and on giving 24 hours' written notice (s 11(6)).

No contracting out

Covenants by the tenant which purport to apply to the tenant the landlord's statute-implied duties are of no effect (s 11(4)). Accordingly, a covenant by the tenant to pay service charges or money in lieu of repairs[2] is nullified in so far as

---

20 The definition of 'common parts' in the Landlord and Tenant Act 1987, s 60(1) is expressly applied.
1 This adopts the standard of repairs in *Proudfoot v Hart* (1890) 25 QBD 42, CA; *Jaquin v Holland* [1960] 1 All ER 402, [1960] 1 WLR 258, CA; also *McClean v Liverpool City Council* [1987] 2 EGLR 56, CA.
2 Including any express covenant to carry out exterior redecorations: *Irvine v Moran* [1991] 1 EGLR 261.

it relates to landlords' statutory obligations (s 11(5)).[3] Express contracting out of the landlord's statute-implied duties is forbidden by s 12(1), except under the procedure laid down in s 12(2) by way of a joint application to the county court, prior to the granting of the lease. The court may, with the consent of the parties, authorise the inclusion in the proposed lease or in an agreement collateral thereto, of agreements excluding or modifying these statutory obligations, if, having regard to the other terms of the lease (such as an adjustment in rent) and in all the circumstances of the case, it is reasonable to do so.

Meaning of structure, exterior and installations

Structure and exterior   The High Court has ruled that the 'structure' of a dwelling-house consists of those elements of the house which give it its essential appearance, stability and shape. Windows are part of the structure even if not load-bearing. The expression 'structure' does not include fittings, decorations, an internal plaster finish and the like.[4] However, by extension, steps and a path giving access to the dwelling-house concerned were held to be part of the exterior[5] but not a path at the back not giving access.[6] Any part of the structure[7] and exterior of a house which does not form part of the demise to the tenant, such as drains or gutters on adjacent land, lies outside the statute-implied obligations of the landlord and any obligations on him in relation to those parts must be expressly imposed if at all.[8]

Installations   Sanitary conveniences are 'installations' within s 11(1).[9] Otherwise the term includes such things as pipes, radiators, boilers, or even refrigeration equipment. The landlord is bound to keep installations of the prescribed type in repair 'and proper working order' so that while he is not thereby obliged to lag water-pipes,[10] the landlord must see to it that the installation is in such condition that it works properly as an installation.[11] In addition to the statutory duties of landlords with regard to installations, landlords who own a gas appliance (such as a heater or cooker) must ensure that such appliance is maintained in a safe condition to prevent the risk of injury to any person. The landlord must ensure that each appliance is checked for safety at intervals of not more than 12 months by an approved person.[12]

3   Or a tenants' covenant to spend a stated sum annually on repairs and decorations, in so far as caught by s 11(1) of the 1985 Act: see *Moss' Empires Ltd v Olympia (Liverpool) Ltd* [1939] AC 544, [1939] 3 All ER 460, HL.
4   *Irvine v Moran*, supra.
5   *Brown v Liverpool Corpn* [1969] 3 All ER 1345, CA.
6   *Hopwood v Cannock Chase District Council* [1975] 1 All ER 796, [1975] 1 WLR 373, CA.
7   See *Irvine v Moran* [1991] 1 EGLR 261.
8   *Peters v Prince of Wales Theatre (Birmingham) Ltd* [1943] KB 73, [1942] 2 All ER 533, CA. In the case of leases of *flats*, s 11(1A), above, would appear to reverse this result, in relation to parts of the demised premises retained by the landlord in the same building, though not, presumably, in relation to adjoining land of his.
9   *Sheldon v West Bromwich Corpn* (1973) 25 P & CR 360, CA.
10   *Wycombe Health Authority v Barnett* (1982) 47 P & CR 394, CA.
11   *Liverpool City Council v Irwin* [1977] AC 239, [1976] 2 All ER 39, HL.
12   SI 1994/1886, in force from 31 October 1994. A record, open to tenants' inspection, must be kept of the appliance, the date of inspection, and any defects identified and remedial action.

Limits on landlord's duty

In the case of lettings of flats, the landlord's obligation was judicially limited. 'Exterior' referred to the exterior of the particular flat and not the exterior of the whole building. The same limit applied to 'structure'.[13] This has been reversed by statute (s 11(1A)). Whether the roof of a top-floor flat falls within the landlord's obligation under s 11(1) is a question of fact: if the ceiling and roof are an inseparable unit then they may well both be within s 11(1).[14] If not, then s 11(1A) of the 1985 Act would require the landlord to keep the roof of a building containing flats, where this was retained by the landlord, in repair in any case.

The landlord is not bound to undertake to insert any new thing, by way of an *improvement*, which was not there before, so that he is not liable under s 11(1) to instal a new damp-proof course where the 'dwelling-house' never had one.[15] Nor is he bound to improve the design of the house, or to cure inherent defects, provided that the actual items which the tenant is trying to force the landlord to replace are themselves in repair: hence a local authority landlord was held not bound to replace metal windows nor to insulate lintels so as to cure severe condensation in a house where neither item was out of repair.[16] In this case, it had been conceded that the house was built according to the requirements of the then current building regulations. By contrast, where a rotten door whose lack of repair had caused damage was replaced by a self-sealing aluminium door, this amounted to a repair and the landlord was liable for damage due to water penetration.[17]

The question of how much work is required to satisfy s 11 is thus a question of fact: in one case, piecemeal repairs to the roof of an old terraced house sufficed even though, no doubt, the whole roof might one day have to be replaced.[18] Where a landlord replaced the front and rear elevations of a house, and its roof structure and rainwater disposal system, at a cost of £10,718, extending its life by some 30 years, he was not bound to make good the interior decorations[19] because the work went beyond a repair.[20]

Notice requirement

Where a landlord has expressly covenanted to keep the premises, or the structure, exterior and main roof and walls of a building in repair, he is liable to put right any defect which falls within his covenant, as soon as physical

---

13 *Campden Hill Towers Ltd v Gardner* [1977] QB 823, [1977] 1 All ER 739, CA.
14 *Douglas-Scott v Scorgie* [1984] 1 All ER 1086, [1984] 1 WLR 716, CA.
15 *Wainwright v Leeds City Council* (1984) 82 LGR 657, CA.
16 *Quick v Taff-Ely Borough Council* [1986] QB 809, [1985] 3 All ER 321, CA.
17 *Stent v Monmouth District Council* [1987] 1 EGLR 59, CA. If the only defect in the door had been that it did not keep out the rain, and it had not been rotten, the landlord would not have been liable to replace it. Cf *Staves v Leeds City Council* [1990] 2 EGLR 37, CA.
18 *Murray v Birmingham City Council* [1987] 2 EGLR 53, CA.
19 For which, otherwise, he may be liable: see *Bradley v Chorley Borough Council* [1985] 2 EGLR 49, CA.
20 *McDougall v Easington District Council* [1989] 1 EGLR 93, CA.

damage manifests itself. Liability is strict,[1] the landlord having undertaken that the premises will not fall into disrepair. Advance notice from the tenant is not a condition precedent to liability to carry out the work or in damages, except in relation to a defect occurring in the demised premises themselves, in which case notice is required.[2] Therefore, where a landlord let parts of a house, but retained the remainder of the premises, and undertook to keep (in particular) the gutters in good tenantable condition, he was liable, without need for notice, for damages to the tenant caused by a roof gutter overflowing.[3]

It is, however, an implied condition precedent to a landlord's liability to keep in repair under s 11 of the 1985 Act, that he must have actual and advance notice of the defect or want of repair, where the defect occurs in the demised premises.[4] This condition is justifed by a need to avoid the landlord having constantly to exercise vigilence over the property.[5] The fact that the tenant has exclusive possession of the house or flat has been also advanced as a reason for the condition, since the tenant is best able to report to the landlord about disrepair within the premises.[6] Yet the notice exception extends to defects in existence prior to the commencement of the term,[7] which it is not likely that a short residential tenant, at all events, could know or be expected to find out about. It makes no difference that the landlord has an implied right to inspect and so to enter and repair under s 11(6) of the 1985 Act, in contrast to the position with s 4 of the Defective Premises Act 1972, where such a right triggers a landlord's liability without any need for notice.

The tenant must give the landlord such information as would make him, as a reasonable landlord, inquire into the position, whether by letter or report.[8] The type of defect is irrelevant, be it patent or latent. In the case of latent defects, the result of the notice rule may be to deprive the tenant of damages owing to a defect suddenly manifesting itself without warning, so that where a ceiling fell in on the tenant, injuring him, owing to an unknown defect, the landlord, who had no notice, was not liable in damages.[9] Though at one time, it appeared that the tenant had to give notice personally, the rule has been relaxed so that notice may now be given by a third party such as a landlord's rent-collector (or agent) or officer or employee.[10]

Except in relation to any parts of premises not demised to the lessee but which fall within s 11(1A) of the 1985 Act, where his obligation to keep in repair is absolute, the landlord is only in breach of covenant under s 11 if, after a reasonable time from his being given notice, he fails, following any necessary

1   *Bishop v Consolidated London Properties Ltd* (1933) 102 LJKB 257 (where the landlord carried out regular inspections).
2   *British Telecommunications plc v Sun Life Assurance Society plc* [1995] 4 All ER 44, CA; PF Smith [1997] Conv 59.
3   *Melles & Co v Holme* [1918] 2 KB 100.
4   *McCarrick v Liverpool Corpn* [1947] AC 219, HL; *O'Brien v Robinson* [1973] AC 912, HL.
5   See *McCarrick v Liverpool Corpn*, supra.
6   *Makin v Watkinson* (1870) LR 6 ExCh 25; also *Tredway v Machin* (1904) 91 LT 310 (both cases on a landlord's express obligation).
7   *Uniproducts (Manchester) Ltd v Rose Furnishers Ltd* [1956] 1 All ER 146, [1956] 1 WLR 45.
8   Eg a valuation report to the landlord: *Hall v Howard* [1988] 2 EGLR 75, CA.
9   *O'Brien v Robinson* [1973] AC 912; [1973] 1 All ER 583, HL.
10 *McGreal v Wake* [1984] 1 EGLR 42, CA; *Dinefwr Borough Council v Jones* [1987] 2 EGLR 58, CA.

inquiries, to carry out the necessary works to cure any defects.[11] What is a reasonable time is a question of fact and it will be short in the case of urgently required repairs.[12] Any notice of disrepair need not give details, but it must state in general terms what is required of the landlord.[13]

IV CONSTRUCTION OF EXPRESS COVENANT TO REPAIR

Scope of express covenants

It is in the interest of the landlord to see to it that his building or premises are kept in a proper state of repair and maintenance during the lease. Where special statutory rules do not apply, the allocation and extent of the liability for repairing and other work is for the parties to determine. Both factors may vary with the nature and intended use of the building. Thus, where there is a newly-built or mature office block or block of flats in the occupation of many tenants, it may be more convenient for the landlord to undertake liability for at least structural and major repairs and maintenance and for the tenants to contribute to the cost of the work – so making the landlord's obligation a right of recovery.[14] In the case of a single building or unit such as a factory, the tenant may undertake a general obligation to repair the demised premises.

Liability under a covenant to repair, or to keep in repair, runs as from the date of the lease. Therefore, if a head lease and subsequently granted sub-lease contain identical covenants to repair, the standard expected from the two leases may be different even if the language of each covenant is identical.[15]

It may still be the case, as a matter of general principle, that a landlord's covenant to keep in repair (or more unusually, merely to repair) is construed in the same way as would be a tenant's obligation.[16] In the absence of a term in the lease rendering it unnecessary, no notice is required to the landlord before he is liable under a covenant to keep in repair, save in relation to the premises demised to the tenant.[17] The landlord is under an absolute obligation in relation to any non-demised premises. By contrast, where notice is exceptionally required, he is liable to the tenant only if he fails within a reasonable time of notice to carry out the necessary work.

However, some landlords' obligations may be construed more widely than might similar obligations of tenants. Thus the landlord of a new office building who expressly undertook to 'maintain repair amend renew ... and otherwise keep in good and tenantable condition' certain exterior and structural parts of

---

11 *Porter v Jones* [1942] 2 All ER 570, CA (landlord who failed for eight months from notice to remedy disrepair held liable in damages); also *Morris v Liverpool City Council* [1988] 1 EGLR 47, CA (a few days' wait for emergency repairs not on facts unreasonable).
12 *McGreal v Wake*, supra (eight weeks from repair notice held a reasonable time on facts).
13 *Al Hassani v Merrigan* (1987) 20 HLR 238, CA.
14 *Plough Investments Ltd v Manchester City Council* [1989] 1 EGLR 244, 247.
15 *Ebbetts v Conquest* [1895] 2 Ch 377, CA.
16 *Torrens v Walker* [1906] 2 Ch 166.
17 *British Telecommunications plc v Sun Life Assurance Society plc* [1995] 4 All ER 44, CA; see Wilkinson (1995) 145 NLJ 1793.

the building was obliged by this covenant to replace inherently defective external cladding, even though the work went well beyond repair.[18] By contrast, a mere obligation to keep in repair did not oblige a landlord to replace metal frame windows by wooden-frame windows, where the former were not damaged, in order to alleviate severe condensation in a house.[19] There was no condition of disrepair. Likewise, the tenants of an office building who were under a general covenant to repair, were held not liable to waterproof the basement, to protect it from its propensity, caused by an inherent design fault, to allow water penetration, where at the date of the hearing the basement was dry and apparently undamaged by an earlier entry of water. The fact that the basement suffered from an inherent design fault made no difference.[20] It appears therefore that a general covenant to repair does not require the tenant to improve the premises in any way, save in so far as incidentally required as part of a repair.

The common law places limits on the scope of a tenant's general covenant to repair. As well as declining to hold a tenant liable for major improvements to the premises, it holds that he is only liable for subordinate renewal, and not for the complete rebuilding of the premises. Three questions have been posed in determining on which side of this difficult dividing line work fell: (i) whether an alteration went to substantially the whole of the structure or only to a subsidiary part; (ii) whether the effect of the alterations was to produce a building of a wholly different character to that let; and (iii) as to the cost of the works in relation to the previous value of the building and their effect on its value and lifespan.[1]

In the end, much depends on the exact words of covenant and the context in which they appear. Thus, the tenant of a building with a rusty steel frame at the date of the lease was held not liable to pay for the cost of extensive work to eliminate the rusting, but only to cure the immediate, visible, damage produced by that defect.[2] By contrast, a lessee under a general covenant to repair was bound, as part of repairing defective stone cladding, to pay for the insertion of new expansion joints, as these formed a trivial part of the whole building and no competent engineer would have allowed the work to be done without these joints.[3] The former work affected the whole structure and design of the building; the latter only a subsidiary part of it. However, where a lease in terms envisaged that the lessees of an office building would have to contribute to renewals or replacements as well as to repairs, a lessee could not escape paying his share of the cost of installing a new roof with a better, more storm-resistant design, merely on the ground that the design was an improvement on that of the old roof.[4]

---

18 *Crédit Suisse v Beegas Nominees Ltd* [1994] 4 All ER 803.
19 *Quick v Taff-Ely Borough Council* [1986] QB 809, [1985] 3 All ER 321, CA (obligation under s 11 of Landlord and Tenant Act 1985).
20 *Post Office v Aquarius Properties Ltd* [1987] 1 All ER 1055, CA, PF Smith [1987] Conv 224. As a result, no-one was liable at that stage to cure the defect.
1 *McDougall v Easington District Council* [1989] 1 EGLR 93, CA.
2 *Plough Investments Ltd v Manchester City Council* [1989] 1 EGLR 244.
3 *Ravenseft Properties Ltd v Davstone (Holdings) Ltd* [1980] QB 12, [1979] 1 All ER 929.
4 *New England Properties plc v Portsmouth New Shops Ltd* [1993] 1 EGLR 84.

Meaning of particular covenants

Some leases impose merely an obligation to repair on the landlord[5] or tenant. Others may go further and require the covenantor to put or keep the premises in repair or even in a specified condition. A breach of an obligation by a landlord, to keep premises not demised to the tenant in repair, has been held to take place as soon as the premises fall out of repair, so that damages were calculated as running from a date some two years before the repairs to cure disrepair to a floor of premises not demised to the tenant were put in hand by his defaulting mesne landlord.[6]

To put in repair

A covenant by the tenant to put the demised premises into repair, at the commencement of the lease[7] or within a reasonable time thereafter, which is appropriate where the premises are dilapidated at the date of the demise, may specify a particular standard of repairs. If not, the standard is that required to render the premises fit for the particular purpose for which they are let, and no more.[8] If the premises are dilapidated at the date of the demise, a covenant to keep them in repair impliedly involves a covenant first to put them into repair in any event.[9] In relation both to a covenant to put and to keep in repair, however, if the landlord cannot prove a condition of disrepair, ie deterioration from a former better condition, this particular rule has no application.

To keep in repair

A covenant by the tenant (or a landlord) to keep premises in repair is an absolute covenant, and so presupposes that the premises have first been put by him, where they are dilapidated at the commencement of the term, into repair, and thereafter the tenant must keep them in repair throughout the term.[10] A covenant to keep in repair also necessarily requires the tenant to deliver up the premises in repair at the end of the lease. The standard of repairs is either that laid down in the lease, or that under the general law and if a schedule of condition of the premises at the date of the demise is drawn up, it may be a guide to the required standard. Similar principles apply to a landlord who has undertaken to keep a building in a specified state and condition. He must undertake works required to put the premises in that condition, even if they have never been in that state, as where a landlord of an office building built with defective external cladding had to do the necessary works to prevent water ingress.[11]

---

5   According to Nicholls LJ in *British Telecommunications plc v Sun Life Assurance Society plc* [1995] 3 WLR 622, 630, a landlord's obligation merely to repair premises is something of a rarity in modern leases.
6   *British Telecommunications plc v Sun Life Assurance Society plc supra*, CA.
7   Ie within a reasonable time: *Doe d Pittman v Sutton* (1841) 9 C & P 706.
8   *Belcher v McIntosh* (1839) 2 Mood & R 186.
9   *Proudfoot v Hart* (1890) 25 QBD 42, CA.
10 *Proudfoot v Hart, supra*; also *Luxmore v Robson* (1818) 1 B & Ald 584.
11 *Crédit Suisse v Beegas Nominees Ltd supra*.

To leave in repair

A separate obligation may be imposed on a tenant to leave the premises in repair, whether or not an obligation to keep in repair has been imposed. If only an obligation to leave in repair is imposed, then until the lease ends, the landlord cannot make any claim against the tenant for dilapidations.[12]

Fair wear and tear excepted

An exception for fair wear and tear is sometimes found in tenants' covenants to repair, particularly in short leases. The basic effect of this exception is to relieve the tenant from liability for disrepair arising both from the normal action of time and the elements, and from the normal and reasonable use of the premises by the tenant for the purpose for which they were let.[13] Therefore, an exception for fair wear and tear will excuse the tenant from liability for any repairs required solely due to the passage of time, but not from liability for repairs necessitated as the result of abnormal or extraordinary phenomena such as lightning, storm, flood, earthquake, fire or accident. A limit has been placed on the scope of a fair wear and tear exception, because otherwise a tenant could claim that it excused him from virtually all liability, where damage originally due to ageing or weathering, led to further, indirect damage to the demised premises. Therefore, an exception for fair wear and tear applies only to direct damage which the tenant proves is the result of the reasonable use of the premises and the ordinary operation of natural forces, and the tenant must see to it that the premises do not suffer more than the operation of time and nature would produce. If further dilapidations result from a cause which may ultimately be traceable back to fair wear and tear, the tenant is not excused from doing repairs necessary to cure the indirect damage.[14] Thus, while he might not be liable merely because a worn-out slate fell off the roof, he could not escape liability by pleading a fair wear and tear exception for water ingress into the premises through the resulting hole, and so his best remedy might be to replace the slate.

Standard of repair

The standard of repair required may be laid down in terms in the covenant to repair. The length of the lease is a relevant factor, and a lower standard of repairs may be expected under a short lease as opposed to a long lease. However, in one case, it was held that the tenant could not rely on his own neglect to comply with his repairing obligations so as to reduce the standard of repairs.[15] By contrast, a tenant's obligation to keep the interior of a flat held on a three-month protected tenancy obliged the tenant only to use the premises in a tenant-like manner.[16]

---

12 A breach of a covenant to leave in repair gives a separate cause of action to the landlord, even if the tenant covenanted to keep in repair: *Ebbetts v Conquest* (1900) 16 TLR 320.
13 *Terrell v Murray* (1901) 17 TLR 570; *Gutteridge v Munyard* (1834) 1 Mood & R 334.
14 *Haskell v Marlow* [1928] 2 KB 45, approved in *Regis Property Co v Dudley* [1959] AC 370, [1958] 3 All ER 491, HL.
15 *Ladbrooke Hotels Ltd v Sandhu* [1995] 2 EGLR 92 (rent review).
16 *Firstcross Ltd v Teasdale* (1982) 47 P & CR 228.

In the case of a long lease, the proper standard, if none is laid down in the lease, is that arrived at by assuming that the tenant has kept the premises in the same condition as a reasonably-minded owner would have kept them in, with full regard to the age of the building, its locality, the class of occupying tenant, and the maintenance of the property in such a way that an average amount of annual repair only was necessary.[17]

In the case of a short lease, the rule is derived from a case where a house was let for three years and the tenant was under an express obligation to keep the premises in good tenantable repair.[18] This required such repair as, having regard to the age, character and locality of the house, would make it reasonably fit for the occupation of a reasonably-minded tenant of the class who would be likely to take it. It was said that the age of the house must be taken into account because a 200-year-old house would not be expected to be in the same condition as a new house. Its locality was relevant because houses in Grosvenor Square required a wholly different standard of repair to those in Spitalfields. The character of the house was relevant, because repairs appropriate for a palace would not be so for a cottage. If a reasonably-minded incoming tenant would not require redecorations, then these need not be done; however, if damp had caused the paper to peel off the walls, it would have to be replaced. The quality of decorations need not be better than the original quality. The standard of repair imposed by this case is a subjective one, in the sense that it may be that, during the life of the lease, the requirements of incoming tenants will be greater or lower than those prevailing at the start of the lease. This obligation only requires the court to 'have regard to' the matters mentioned and it does not directly relate the standard of repair to the intended use, if any, of the premises, and it requires the standard of repair to be decided as at the commencement, and not the termination, of the lease.

Interpreting covenants to repair

Compliance with a covenant to keep in repair or to repair will involve work of subordinate renewal. The question to ask in deciding the extent of such covenant is whether the work is, as a matter of fact and degree, properly described as repair or whether it involves substantially renewing the whole, or almost the whole, of the demised premises.[19] The answer essentially depends on interpreting the intentions of the parties as expressed in the repairing covenant.[20]

The circumstances to be taken into account in a particular case may include all or some of the following: (i) the nature of the building; (ii) the terms of the lease; (iii) the nature and extent of the defect; (iv) the nature, extent and cost of proposed remedial works; (v) at whose cost the works are to be done; (vi) the value of the building and its expected lifespan; (vii) current building practice; (viii) the likelihood of a recurrence if one remedy rather than another is

---

17 *Anstruther-Gough-Calthorpe v McOscar*, supra.
18 *Proudfoot v Hart* (1890) 25 QBD 42, CA.
19 *Ravenseft Properties Ltd v Davstone (Holdings) Ltd* [1980] QB 12, [1979] 1 All ER 929.
20 *Lurcott v Wakely and Wheeler* [1911] 1 KB 905, CA.

adopted; (ix) the comparative cost of alternative remedial works and their impact on the use and enjoyment of the building by the occupants.[1]

No liability to execute any remedial work can arise unless there is proved to be a condition of disrepair in the premises in relation to the item or items concerned. To overcome the general law, the parties may agree to exclude or limit any liability they might otherwise be under to cure inherent design faults in the structure of the premises, where newly-built: express words are required to achieve this.[2] Otherwise, liability to cure *design faults* is a question of interpretation of the particular covenant to repair. If a design fault produces a condition of disrepair, and the only sensible way of executing the work is, in the process, to cure the design fault, then a repairing covenant will require the party subject to it to pay for all the remedial work, though to some minor extent he is improving the design of the premises. Accordingly, a landlord was held liable to replace a worn-out (and originally defectively-designed) front door with a new one of a different design as the only sensible way of complying with his repairing covenant,[3] but not liable to replace metal-frame windows or to insulate lintels, neither of which items were out of repair, in order to cure a design fault in a council house, which produced severe condensation.[4]

The *extent of repairs* is a question of fact: sometimes a repair will involve replacing the whole of the damaged article, say the whole roof,[5] but sometimes mere patching-up of an admittedly old roof or other item will suffice.[6] As already noted, it may be that the covenant extends to cover significant renewals, such as the replacement of an old roof which had been blown away in a severe storm with a new roof of a better design.[7]

Repair and renewal

Repair involves, in law, the renewal of subordinate parts of the premises so as to leave the damaged article so far as possible as though not damaged.[8] Repair therefore may involve replacing a worn-out or damaged article with one which is brand new, corresponding as closely as possible to the original. A tenant subject to a general covenant to repair is not required to give back at the end of the lease premises different in kind from the original subject matter of the demise, such as a house with properly-built foundations where it had poorly-built ones formerly. Equally, the mere fact that remedial work involves the replacement of a faultily-constructed *subordinate* part of the premises, is no defence to liability to pay for the full cost of the remedial work.[9]

1 *Holding and Management Ltd v Property Holding and Investment Trust plc* [1990] 1 All ER 938, CA.
2 See eg *Precedents for the Conveyancer* (Sweet & Maxwell) Vol 1, 5-66.
3 *Stent v Monmouth District Council* [1987] 1 EGLR 59, CA.
4 *Quick v Taff-Ely Borough Council* [1986] QB 809, [1985] 3 All ER 321, CA.
5 As in *Elite Investments Ltd v T I Bainbridge Silencers Ltd* [1986] 2 EGLR 43.
6 *Murray v Birmingham City Council* [1987] 2 EGLR 53, CA.
7 *New England Properties plc v Portsmouth New Shops Ltd* [1993] 1 EGLR 84.
8 *Anstruther-Gough-Calthorpe v McOscar* [1924] 1 KB 716, CA. Thus, the replacement of electrical wiring fell within a lessee's covenant: see *Roper v Prudential Assurance Co Ltd* [1992] 1 EGLR 5.
9 *Ravenseft Properties Ltd v Davstone (Holdings) Ltd*, supra.

The exact *scope* of a general covenant to repair may be difficult to determine. For this reason, perhaps, some leases have attempted to set out in precise detail the obligations of the landlord or tenant, in such a way as to extend beyond the concept of repairs. Thus in one case the landlord undertook to 'maintain repair amend renew ... and otherwise keep in good tenantable condition' the structure of certain new office premises.[10] The result of the case has been noted earlier. The High Court refused, in holding the words to extend the landlord's obligations beyond mere repairs, to give anything other than a natural meaning to these (wide) words. It did not treat them as though contained in a standard form of covenant or contract.

Returning to a general covenant to repair, in relation to older premises, it has been held that a covenant to repair does not bind a party to give back totally new premises, but only premises in proper repair, allowing for the effects of time.[11] The terms of the covenant and the age of the premises are relevant factors.[12] If, therefore, the result of work of renovation would be to give the landlord premises totally different in kind from those let at the outset, such works lie outside the scope of repairs. This defence results from a case[13] where the tenants of a 100-year-old house on a seven-year lease covenanted that they 'when and where and as often as occasion shall require will sufficiently and substantially repair, uphold, sustain, maintain, amend and keep' the premises. The house was demolished at the end of the lease due to its dangerous condition. To have saved it would have required – in place of the old foundations which were a timber platform resting on muddy ground – underpinning of the house with new and proper foundations through 17 feet of mud to solid ground. The tenant was held not liable to pay for the costs of re-building the house. In no case, held the Court of Appeal, is a tenant bound under repair, to pay for work which would give back to the landlord a new and different thing from the premises as let at the start of the tenancy.

Similarly, a landlord has been held not liable under repair, to rid an old house of damp, which was built without a damp course.[14] A tenant, likewise, was held sufficiently to have complied with a covenant to repair by replacing an elaborate but unsafe bay window with a new window, flush with the main walls: he was not obliged to provide new supports where the old were improperly built in the first place.[15] This is because, as noted, neither the landlord nor the tenant is bound, under a covenant to repair, to improve the design of the premises or items in it such as fixtures. Accordingly, a landlord who replaced wooden windows with double-glazed windows, where the old windows could, at half the cost, have been repaired, failed to recover any part of the cost of the work from

---

10 *Crédit Suisse v Beegas Nominees Ltd* [1994] 4 All ER 803, 817-818.
11 *Lister v Lane and Nesham* [1893] 2 QB 212 at 216-217, CA.
12 *Gutteridge v Munyard* (1834) 1 Mood & R 334.
13 *Lister v Lane and Nesham* [1893] 2 QB 212; also *Sotheby v Grundy* [1947] 2 All ER 761 and *Halliard Property Co Ltd v Nicholas Clarke Investments Ltd* [1984] 1 EGLR 45.
14 *Pembery v Lamdin* [1940] 2 All ER 434, CA; also *Wainwright v Leeds City Council* (1984) 82 LGR 657, CA (council house); but cf *Elmcroft Developments Ltd v Tankersley-Sawyer* [1984] 1 EGLR 47, CA (defective damp-course to be replaced with proper course at cost of landlord under general covenant).
15 *Wright v Lawson* (1903) 19 TLR 510, CA.

the tenant.[16] If a covenant enables work going beyond mere repairs to be carried out, the basic design of the premises or part may be improved.[17]

Equally, the mere fact that remedial work is shown to involve substantial but subordinate renewal, will not of itself take the matter out of a general covenant to repair. Whether one is dealing with older or new premises, the issue is to be decided by taking into account the matters already discussed. This is ultimately a matter of fact and degree.[18] The view has been expressed that the cost of the work rather than the value of the building as repaired should be stressed if the two are seriously divergent.[19] Any repair involves subordinate renewal, and if at the completion of the work, what is done has left the premises substantially the same as when let, then the work normally falls on the repair side of the line. In a leading case,[20] the front wall of a 200-year-old house had to be demolished following a dangerous structure notice, and it was re-built from ground level, in compliance with modern requirements, but it was a similar wall to that it replaced. The tenants had to pay for the cost: what was done being the renewal or replacement of a defective part. The covenant in that case was very strong, requiring the tenant to repair and keep in thorough repair and good condition: this meant that if need be, the tenant must replace part after part until the whole was, in due course, replaced.

Further, while the age and nature of a building may qualify the meaning of a covenant, of themselves they cannot relieve a tenant (or landlord) from his obligation. Where, however, a structure has been built for a special use, and is now obsolete, it has been said that the lessee could plead the Leasehold Property (Repairs) Act 1938 to avoid liability to repair it.[1]

The possible extent of liability is shown by the fact that a tenant under a general and unqualified covenant to repair was held liable to pay for the cost of replacing a defective outside stone cladding with new and properly constructed stone cladding, the cost of this being only a small fraction of the total replacement cost of the whole building.[2] In addition, a long lessee's repairing obligation was construed as not limited to work needed to preserve for the 15 year 'commercial life' a defectively-built structure, rather than much more costly work to provide for a properly-built edifice for the duration of the lease.[3] It may be possible for a tenant to escape liability by showing that the defectively-built part of the premises cannot be saved and that it is a separate entity, so that to rebuild it would lie outside the scope of his covenant, as where a tenant was held not liable to replace to correct standards an unstable and 'jerry-built' structure built after the main premises had been constructed, which had collapsed.[4]

In view of the financial risk to which tenants of new buildings are exposed, it has been suggested either that the tenant obtains a covenant from the landlord

16 *Mullaney v Maybourne Grange (Croydon) Management Co Ltd* [1986] 1 EGLR 70.
17 *Sutton (Hastoe) Housing Association v Williams* [1988] 1 EGLR 56, CA (old windows could be replaced, accordingly, with windows of a better design).
18 *Brew Bros Ltd v Snax (Ross) Ltd* [1970] 1 QB 612, [1970] 1 All ER 587, CA.
19 *Elite Investments Ltd v T I Bainbridge Silencers Ltd* [1986] 2 EGLR 43.
20 *Lurcott v Wakely and Wheeler* [1911] 1 KB 905, CA.
 1 *Ladbrooke Hotels Ltd v Sandhu* [1995] 2 EGLR 92 (a rent review dispute).
 2 *Ravenseft Properties Ltd v Davstone (Holdings) Ltd* [1980] QB 12, [1979] 1 All ER 929.
 3 *Ladbrooke Hotels Ltd v Sandhu* supra.
 4 *Halliard Property Co Ltd v Nicholas Clarke Investments Ltd* [1984] 1 EGLR 45.

to remedy any inherent defect in the building, so limiting the repairing obligation, or that he demands the landlord provide him a collateral warranty from the building contractor and all persons involved in the design and supervision of the work.[5] However, as the learned author concedes, the collateral warranty method is untested and would require proof by the tenant of negligence, as well as continuing solvency on the part of the persons subject to the warranty. By contrast, the benefit to a tenant of a landlord's structural design guarantee was shown by the result of a case in which the landlord of a restaurant covenanted to keep the main walls and roof in good structural repair and condition throughout the lease and to make good all defects due to faulty materials or workmanship (the tenant being under a general covenant to repair as qualified by the landlord's obligation). The foundations had been faultily built so that extensive remedial work became necessary, for which the landlord was liable under his unqualified obligation, the work being within the contemplation of the parties when the lease was entered into.[6]

Apart from work to cure latent inherent defects, extensive and costly work may be required by a general covenant to repair, as where the roof of an old industrial unit had to be replaced (as the only way to repair it) at a cost of some £84,000, the value of the building with a new roof being about £140,000. After the work was done, the landlords would not get a different building, but the same building, with the roof in repair.[7]

Repair involving painting

The tenant may expressly undertake a separate obligation to repaint the exterior and interior of the demised premises, at say five or seven yearly intervals, in the case of long leases, or at the end of the term, in the case of short leases. An obligation to paint in a specific year operates as soon as that year commences.[8]

Even where the tenant is not under a specific obligation to paint, but only a general covenant to keep in good tenantable repair (or some similar obligation), he will be obliged to carry out whatever painting is necessary to preserve the woodwork and decorations from decay, to a standard sufficient for the requirements of reasonably-minded incoming tenants, bearing in mind the standard of the locality of the premises.[9]

V LANDLORD'S REMEDIES FOR BREACH OF TENANT'S COVENANT TO REPAIR

The landlord has various remedies to enforce the tenant's covenant to repair, namely, entering and executing the repairs, forfeiture, and claiming damages.

---

5 Ross, para 8.16.1.
6 *Smedley v Chumley and Hawke* (1981) 44 P & CR 50, CA.
7 *Elite Investments Ltd v T I Bainbridge Silencers Ltd* [1986] 2 EGLR 43; PF Smith [1987] Conv 140.
8 *Kirklinton v Wood* [1917] 1 K B 332; if the EU regulations referred to in chapter 4 apply to leases, obligations to paint at specified times might be within their ambit.
9 *Proudfoot v Hart* (1890) 25 QBD 42, CA.

Right of entry to do landlords' repairs

There would be little point in statute conferring repairing obligations on, notably, landlords of short residential lessees, and not conferring correlative rights of entry, inspection and repair. For example, s 11(6) of the Landlord and Tenant Act 1985 implies a covenant by the lessee that a landlord who is subject to s 11 may 'at reasonable times of the day and on giving 24 hours' notice in writing to the occupier, enter the premises ... for the purpose of viewing their condition and state of repair'.[10] The landlord of, notably, business or long residential tenants, has an implied licence, where he has no express right of entry and repair, to execute repairs for which he is liable.[11] This right is limited to what is strictly required to enable the work to be done, and no more. A right of entry to execute landlords' repairs is implied in the case of weekly tenancies,[12] because it must be in the contemplation of both parties that the tenant will not do such repairs; but in any case, a right of entry is implied if required to make the lease work, as where the landlord of a periodic tenant was held to have an implied right to enter and was thus, owing to s 4 of the Defective Premises Act 1972, liable for the repair of a defective step.[13] The exclusive possession of the tenant is emphasised by the fact that an entry to carry out repairs which is not expressly or impliedly allowed, or permitted by statute, is illegal, even if the landlord himself could lose his own head lease if the repairs are not executed.[14]

Leasehold Property (Repairs) Act 1938

Special rules imposed by the Leasehold Property (Repairs) Act 1938 apply both to forfeiture actions and to damages claims against the tenant for breach of covenant to repair.[15]

The original object of the 1938 Act was to prevent speculators buying up small property in an indifferent state of repair and serving schedules of dilapidations on the tenants, with which the tenants could not comply. The 1938 Act applies to most commercial and residential property, but it does not apply in four instances:

1   to a lease of an agricultural holding within the Agricultural Holdings Act 1986 nor to a farm business tenancy (s 7(1));
2   where the original length of the term is less than seven years (s 7(1));
3   where at the date of service of the notice under s 146(1) of the Law of Property Act 1925, less than three years of the term are unexpired (s 1(1));
4   to a breach of covenant or agreement which imposes on the lessee an obligation to put the premises into repair which is to be performed on the

---

10   This carries with it an implied right to execute repairs. Rights of access and repair in the case of protected and statutory tenancies are conferred by Rent Act 1977, ss 148 and 3(2) and for assured tenancies by Housing Act 1988, s 16.
11   *Granada Theatres Ltd v Freehold Investment (Leytonstone) Ltd* [1959] Ch 592, [1959] 2 All ER 176, CA.
12   *Mint v Good* [1951] 1 KB 517, [1950] 2 All ER 1159, CA.
13   *McAuley v Bristol City Council* [1991] 2 EGLR 64, CA.
14   *Stocker v Planet Building Society* (1879) 27 WR 877. Such entry may be restrained by an injunction: *Regional Properties Ltd v City of London Real Property Co Ltd* [1981] 1 EGLR 33.
15   See Blundell (1938/9) 3 Conv (NS) 10; PF Smith [1986] Conv 85.

lessee taking possession or within a reasonable time thereafter (s 3), so excluding an obligation to put into repair premises which are dilapidated at the commencement of the lease.

By s 1(1), where the landlord serves on the tenant a notice under s 146(1) of the 1925 Act which relates to a breach of covenant or agreement to keep or put in repair any of the demised premises, the tenant may within 28 days from that date serve a counter-notice on the landlord, claiming the benefit of the 1938 Act. At the date of service of the notice, three years or more of the term must remain unexpired.

Similarly, by s 1(2), a right to claim damages for such a breach of covenant cannot be enforced by action commenced at any time when the lease has an unexpired residue of three years or more to run, unless the landlord serves on the tenant not less than one month before the commencement of the action a s 146(1) notice. Again, the tenant may then by a 28 day counter-notice claim the benefit of the 1938 Act.

By s 1(4) of the 1938 Act, in the case both of damages and forfeiture, the requisite s 146(1) notice must, on pain of invalidity, contain a statement, in characters not less conspicuous than those used in any other part of the notice[16] to the effect that the tenant is entitled to serve on the landlord within 28 days of service of the s 146(1) notice, a counter-notice claiming the benefit of the 1938 Act; and the s 146(1) notice must also state a name and address for service of the counter-notice on the landlord.[17] The effect of service within the 28-day period of a counter-notice by the tenant is that no proceedings by action or otherwise may be taken by the landlord for the enforcement of any right of re-entry or forfeiture or for damages without the leave of the court (s 1(3)). In the absence of any authority, it is believed that a notice served outside the 28-day period would be invalid as the 1938 Act affects the landlord's substantive rights and is not simply procedural.

By s 1(5), there are only five grounds under which leave may be given:

(a) that the immediate remedying of the breach is requisite for preventing substantial diminution in the value of the reversion, or that the value thereof has been substantially diminished by the breach;

(b) that the immediate remedying of the breach is required for giving effect in relation to the premises to the purposes of any enactment, or of any by-law or other provision having effect under an enactment, or for giving effect to any order of a court or requirement of any authority under an enactment or any such by-law or provision as aforesaid;

(c) where the tenant is not in occupation of the whole premises as respects which the covenant or agreement is proposed to be enforced, that the immediate remedying of the breach is required in the interests of the occupier of those premises or of part thereof;

(d) that the breach can be immediately remedied at an expense that is relatively small in comparison with the much greater expense which would probably

---

16 I e equally readable or equally sufficient: *Middlegate Properties Ltd v Messimeris* [1973] 1 All ER 645, [1973] 1 WLR 168, CA.

17 Law of Property Act 1925, s 196 applies to the service of a 1938 Act counter-notice.

be occasioned by postponement of the necessary work; or
(e) special circumstances which in the opinion of the court render it just and equitable that leave should be given.

The terms of leave, if granted, are at the discretion of the court (s 1(6)). The House of Lords has ruled that a landlord who applies for leave to proceed must prove his case to the ordinary civil standard of proof, that one (or more) of the leave requirements has been satisfied. Where, therefore, a landlord could not prove any substantial damage to his reversion, he failed to obtain leave, even though the premises, a redundant dock, were very seriously dilapidated. If the landlord cannot prove a ground within s 1(5) of the 1938 Act, his application will be dismissed as of right and the threat of forfeiture will be removed. Should he establish a ground, the court may, at its discretion, adjourn or dismiss the application (again lifting the threat of forfeiture) on condition that the requisite repairs are carried out, under s 1(6), or grant relief on terms under s 146(2) of the 1925 Act or forfeit the lease.[18] Thus the 1938 Act is an integral part of the forfeiture process in the case of dilapidations and, according to the House of Lords, where leave is applied for, unless the parties otherwise agree, the forfeiture action is to be fought out under the 1938 Act, and any leave application by the tenant must thereafter be dealt with, where necessary. There are some limits to the scope of this Act.

1   Certain persons cannot claim the benefit of the 1938 Act, notably, mortgagees or chargees of the lessee's interest in the premises.[19] However, an assignee in possession is entitled to claim the 1938 Act.[20]

2   A landlord's claim for costs and expenses in the preparation and service of a s 146 notice is a claim for a contract debt, where the tenant is under express covenant to pay these costs, and is outside the 1938 Act.[1]

3   If the landlord has the right to enter and execute repairs under the lease, but no express right to charge the tenant with their cost, no part of the cost will be recoverable unless, prior to acting, the landlord serves a s 146 notice on the tenant, which will allow him to claim the 1938 Act. This is because the landlord's claim is for damages.[2]

4   If the lease enables the landlord, following a notice to repair to the tenant, to enter, execute the work and charge the tenant with the cost, the costs of the repairs may be now be treated as contract debt, as the landlord may recover the costs without having to concern himself with the restrictions of the 1938 Act.[3] The landlord cannot resort to such a clause in order to enter and then charge the tenant for any work not within the exact scope of his

---

18 *Associated British Ports v CH Bailey plc* [1990] 2 AC 703, [1990] 1 All ER 929; PF Smith [1990] Conv 305.
19 *Church Comrs for England v Ve-Ri-Best Manufacturing Co Ltd* [1957] 1 QB 238, [1956] 3 All ER 777.
20 *Kanda v Church Comrs for England* [1958] 1 QB 332, CA.
 1 *Bader Properties Ltd v Linley Property Investments Ltd* (1967) 19 P & CR 620, approved in *Middlegate Properties v Gidlow-Jackson* (1977) 34 P & CR 4, CA.
 2 *SEDAC Investments Ltd v Tanner* [1982] 3 All ER 646, [1982] 1 WLR 1342; PF Smith [1983] Conv 72. The repairs were urgent, and the conclusion was reached with 'surprise and regret'.
 3 *Jervis v Harris* [1996] Ch 195, [1996] 1 All ER 303, CA.

covenant to repair - any entry beyond that allowed by the clause without the tenant's licence renders the landlord a trespasser.[4]

5   The 1938 Act applies only to repairing covenants, not, for example, to a covenant to cleanse,[5] nor to a covenant to lay out insurance moneys of the premises, if these are destroyed by fire.[6]

6   Because the courts strive where possible to uphold formal notices, a s 146 notice which contains the statements required by s 1(4) of the 1938 Act will be valid even if it refers to alleged breaches of non-existent covenants.[7] If a s 146 notice is bad for want of compliance with the 1938 Act, but is good as respects other alleged breaches of covenant, it will be severed and valid as respects the latter breaches.[8]

Law of Property Act 1925, s 147

Where a s 146 notice served on a tenant relates to internal decorative repairs, the tenant may apply to the court for relief, and if, having regard to all the circumstances, including in particular the length of the tenant's unexpired term, the court is satisfied that the notice is unreasonable, it may, by order, wholly or partially relieve the tenant from liability for these repairs.

If any of the four following exclusions apply, the relieving power of s 147(1) is excluded. These are, by s 147(2):

1   where the liability arises under an express covenant or agreement to put the property into a decorative state of repair, which has not been performed;

2   where any matter is necessary or proper for putting or keeping the property in a sanitary condition, or for the maintenance or preservation of the structure;

3   to any statutory liability to keep a house in all respects reasonably fit for human habitation;

4   to any covenant or stipulation to yield up the house or other building in a specified state of repair at the end of the term.

Where s 147 applies, the tenant may apply to the court immediately he receives the notice concerned, and the court may relieve him completely from liability for internal decorative repairs. Section 147 does not apply to a tenant's covenant to carry out regular exterior redecoration at stated intervals.

Landlord and Tenant Act 1927, s 18

At common law, a lessee against whom the landlord brought an action for damages at the end of the lease was liable to pay for the reasonable cost of putting the premises into repair, so as literally to comply with his covenant to

4   *Plough Investments Ltd v Manchester City Council*, supra; also *McDougall v Easington District Council*, supra.
5   *Starrokate Ltd v Burry* [1983] 1 EGLR 56, CA.
6   *Farimani v Gates* [1984] 2 EGLR 66, CA.
7   *Silvester v Ostrowska* [1959] 3 All ER 642, [1959] 1 WLR 1060.
8   *Starrokate v Burry*, supra.

repair.[9] It made no difference that the landlord might, on regaining possession, wish to put the premises to a different use to that of the tenant.

Section 18(1) of the Landlord and Tenant Act 1927 limits the maximum amount of damages recoverable. It is not clear whether this provision is any more than declaratory of the present common law principle that damages are recoverable only for a party's actual loss.[10] At all events, the courts have striven to interpret s 18(1) in the main so as to produce this result though, as will appear, in some cases it has had the unhappy effect of fortuitously depriving a landlord of damages.

The first part of s 18(1) provides:

'Damages for a breach of covenant or agreement to keep or put premises in repair during the currency of a lease, or to leave or put premises in repair at the termination of a lease, whether such covenant is expressed or implied, and whether general or specific, shall in no case exceed the amount (if any) by which the value of the reversion (whether immediate or not) in the premises is diminished owing to the breach of such covenant or agreement'.

Section 18(1) has no effect on the computation of damages, although it fixes a ceiling on the maximum amount recoverable, to that extent modifying the common law.[11] Accordingly, a tenant could not set off against a damages award any sum to take into account the fact that the landlord had regained possession earlier than the original expiry date of the lease.[12] Yet s 18(1) may restrict a damages award where the landlord claims compensation during the lease, since it seemingly requires the court to assess the difference between the value of the landlord's reversion with the premises in repair and with them in a dilapidated state.

Where, however, the landlord claims damages after the lease has expired, the basic measure of damages remains compensatory in nature, subject to the ceiling imposed by s 18(1). The cost of repairs may be the best *prima facie* evidence of loss to the reversion. Where a tenant left a house in a poor condition at the expiry of a short residential lease, the landlord was awarded £36 as the cost of putting the premises into a condition suitable to re-let them for the same purposes to a new tenant.[13] Similarly, a landlord had to pay an incoming lessee some £690,000 as an inducement to bring the premises into a standard of repair which met with the landlord's standards. The High Court held that the already negative value of the reversion had been inflated by the former tenant's breach. However, since the cost of repairs as shown by a dilapidations schedule was the best guide to the assessment of damages, the lesser sum of £295,321 was awarded.[14] A similar principle applied where a landlord proved that a market

---

9 *Joyner v Weeks* [1891] 2 QB 31, CA.
10 The Law Commission (*Report*, 1996, para 9.36ff) think that s 18(1) need not be altered as it is probably declaratory of the common law; for a review of the provision see DN Clarke (1988) 104 LQR 372.
11 *Shortlands Investments Ltd v Cargill* [1995] 1 EGLR 51.
12 *Hanson v Newman* [1934] Ch 298, CA.
13 *Jones v Herxheimer* [1950] 2 KB 106, [1950] 1 All ER 323, CA.
14 *Shortlands Investments Ltd v Cargill plc* supra.

existed for his premises, which he sold out of repair at a reduced price: the loss to his reversion exceeded the cost of repairs (some £175,000) and this latter sum was recoverable in full.[15] However, where damage to the saleability of the reversion cannot be shown, s 18(1) may reduce any damages award to a nominal sum only, as where a landlord had been able to sell the premises for conversion into flats, for a good price, and could not prove that the price had been reduced because of the dilapidations.[16]

Section 18(1) has operated to reduce or eliminate damages in other cases which might be said to be fortuitous. For example, lessees who were entitled to obtain a renewal of their tenancies under Part II of the Landlord and Tenant Act 1954 had committed breaches of their covenants to repair, but no damages could be recovered since the reversion had not suffered loss, since a market rent was payable for the new tenancies under statute.[17] The rent had to be fixed on the assumption that the premises were in repair, otherwise the tenants could take advantage of their own wrong to reduce the rent.[18] Likewise, a landlord who re-let the premises concerned, which were badly out of repair, to a new lessee who undertook to carry out improvements failed to prove any loss to his reversion from the former tenant's breach and so failed in a claim to damages.[19]

Moreover, any damages otherwise recoverable by the landlord may be reduced if he does not intend to re-let the premises for the same purpose as those of the previous tenant, or where such re-letting is not, as where planning restrictions supervene, possible. In such a case the damages awarded will have regard to the intended or lawful future user of the premises.[20]

So as to reverse the common law, s 18(1) also provides that no damages shall be recovered for breach of any covenant to leave or put in repair at the termination of the lease, if it can be shown that the premises in whatever state of repair they might be, would at or shortly after the termination of the tenancy have been or will be pulled down or such structural alterations made as to render valueless the repairs in question. Where a local authority resolves before the end of the lease to acquire the premises compulsorily, the landlord cannot claim any diminution in value even though the compulsory purchase order is not made until afterwards.[1]

The date for determining the landlord's intention to demolish etc is the termination of the lease; and the intention must be definite and not conditional;[2] and if definite at the relevant time, it is irrelevant that the landlord's intention is later set at naught.[3] The second limb of s 18(1) contemplates a demolition rendering repairs nugatory, as opposed to acts by a tenant (and local authority) whose compulsory purchase of the premises could reward them for their breaches of covenant.[4]

15 *Culworth Estates Ltd v Society of Licensed Victuallers* [1991] 2 EGLR 54, CA.
16 *Landeau v Marchbank* [1949] 2 All ER 172.
17 *Family Management v Gray* [1980] 1 EGLR 46, CA.
18 *Crown Estate Comrs v Town Investments Ltd* [1992] 1 EGLR 61, at 63.
19 *Mather v Barclays Bank plc* [1987] 2 EGLR 254.
20 *Portman v Latta* [1942] WN 97.
 1 *London County Freehold and Leasehold Properties Ltd v Wallis-Whiddett* [1950] WN 180.
 2 *Cunliffe v Goodman* [1950] 2 KB 237, [1950] 1 All ER 720, CA.
 3 *Salisbury v Gilmore* [1942] 2 KB 38, [1942] 1 All ER 457, CA.
 4 *Hibernian Property Co Ltd v Liverpool Corpn* [1973] 2 All ER 1117, [1973] 1 WLR 751.

Some concluding points may be made. First, the date down to which damages for breaches by the tenant of his covenant to repair is measured is, in the case of forfeiture, the date of service of the writ claiming forfeiture, which effects notional re-entry, as opposed to the date when the landlord eventually recovers possession of the premises.[5] Second, s 18(1) does not apply to a covenant by the tenant to spend a stated sum on repairs, nor to a covenant to pay the landlord the difference between the stated sum and any amount actually expended.[6] Third, s 18(1) only limits landlords' damages claims in relation to the covenant to repair: it does not affect the measure of damages in other cases, such as covenants not to alter the internal planning of the premises,[7] or building leases.[8]

VI　TENANT'S REMEDIES FOR BREACH OF LANDLORD'S COVENANT TO REPAIR

Tenants have a wide range of remedies both at common law, such as damages, and in equity, such as to specific performance, against landlords in breach of their covenants to repair. This developing area is next considered.

Damages

Section 18(1) of the Landlord and Tenant Act 1927 has no application to breaches by a landlord of the covenant to repair. Therefore, the ordinary rules of compensation apply. The object of awarding damages to the tenant is, accordingly, to restore him to the position he would have been in had there been no breach by the landlord of his covenant to repair. Therefore, the tenant is entitled to recover damages for any losses which the landlord ought to have realised were not unlikely to result from the breach, as being not very unusual and easily foreseeable.[9] This applies to landlords' express and statute-implied covenants alike. If the tenant has realised his lease by sale, the measure of damages is prima facie the amount of any loss in value of his interest due to the disrepair. If the tenant remains in occupation, he may, for example, recover the cost of occupying alternative premises if the demised premises become uninhabitable, also for the personal inconvenience in living in premises out of repair, and for the cost of restoring decorations and of storing furniture pending repairs.[10] The tenant may also claim for injury to health; a tenant also recovered for loss of sub-letting income owing to disrepair.[11] The landlord may be able, as a defence, to prove that the cause of damage is subsidence or some other

5　*Associated Deliveries Ltd v Harrison* (1984) 50 P & CR 91, CA.
6　*Moss' Empires Ltd v Olympia (Liverpool) Ltd* [1939] AC 544, [1939] 3 All ER 460, HL.
7　*Eyre v Rea* [1947] KB 567, [1947] 1 All ER 415.
8　*Lansdowne Rodway Estates Ltd v Potown Ltd* [1984] 2 EGLR 80.
9　*Mira v Aylmer Square Investments Ltd* [1990] 1 EGLR 45, CA.
10　*Calabar Properties Ltd v Stitcher* [1983] 3 All ER 759, [1984] 1 WLR 287, CA; *McGreal v Wake* (1984) 13 HLR 107, CA.
11　*Mira v Aylmer Square Investment*, supra.

cause which has nothing to do with a breach of his covenant; if this is so, he will not be liable for damages.[12] However, an award of damages will be disturbed only if erroneous in principle or so grossly excessive or insufficient as to demonstrate an error of law.[13]

Because of his common law duty to mitigate losses, the tenant must give prompt notice of a want of repair to the landlord,[14] at least where the damage occurs in the demised premises, who must then remedy the breach within a reasonable time, failing which the tenant may claim damages or do the repairs himself and claim the cost from the landlord. Damages will be calculated on the basis of reasonably required repairs as opposed to extravagant repairs: extravagance means that nothing will apparently be recoverable. Prior to acting, the tenant must allow the landlord a reasonable opportunity to act himself and, since he must act reasonably, if he refuses access to the landlord, nothing is recoverable.[15] Where a landlord was liable because of the disrepair of adjoining premises of his, which caused damage by water ingress to the tenant's premises, notice was not necessary, as these premises were not demised to the tenant and liability in damages ran from the date of the breach.[16]

Set-off of cost of repairs from rent[17]

At common law, where a landlord is in breach of covenant to repair and the tenant carries out the repairs, he may set off the cost of repairs against his future liability for rent. Where occupiers spent £630 on repairs for which the landlord was liable, it was held that they could recoup themselves out of future rents for the sum spent.[18] The right is narrow in scope since any sum must be certain for the right, which is at common law, to exist; and it must be unchallenged or unchallengeable, e g awarded in arbitration; and any excess over a proper amount will be disallowed; and the sum must be spent only on matters falling within the landlord's covenant to repair, where he has notice and is in breach.[19]

Equity, following the law, still insists that there must be an existing debt or claim for an equitable right to set-off to arise.[20] But equity has relaxed the common law insistence that the relevant claim must be certain: the tenant may set off an estimated sum representing the cost of landlords' repairs as a defence to a landlord's claim for rent arrears against him. Moreover, in contrast to the common law rule, the tenant need not prove that he has spent any money of his

---

12 *Minchburn Ltd v Peck* [1988] 1 EGLR 53, CA.
13 *Chiodi's Personal Representatives v De Marney* [1988] 2 EGLR 64, CA; *Davies v Peterson* [1989] 1 EGLR 121, CA.
14 Where prompt notice was not given, a small reduction in damages for distress and discomfort was made: *Minchburn Ltd v Peck*, supra.
15 *Granada Theatres Ltd v Freehold Investment (Leytonstone) Ltd* [1959] Ch 592, [1959] 2 All ER 176, CA.
16 *Loria v Hammer* [1989] 2 EGLR 249; *British Telecommunications plc v Sun Life Assurance plc* [1995] 4 All ER 44, CA.
17 See Waite [1981] Conv 199; Rank (1976) 40 Conv (NS) 196.
18 *Lee-Parker v Izzet* [1971] 3 All ER 1099, [1971] 1 WLR 1688.
19 *British Anzani (Felixstowe) Ltd v International Marine Management (UK) Ltd* [1980] QB 137, [1979] 2 All ER 1063; *Asco Developments v Gordon* [1978] 2 EGLR 41.
20 *Barribal v Everitt* [1994] EGCS 62, CA.

own on repairs as a condition precedent to claim an equitable set-off.[1] Both these principles may be explained on the ground that the claim to set-off goes to the foundation of any claim to rent arrears: hence, a landlord's bailiffs were restrained by injunction from executing a distress against a tenant claiming equitable set-off.[2]

It would appear that both the common law and equitable rights to set off against rent arrears may be excluded by a clause which provides for payment of rent in full without any deduction or set off whatever. It was also held that such an 'anti set off clause' was not subject to the test of reasonableness imposed by s 3 of the Unfair Contract Terms Act 1977. The statutory exclusion of any contract 'so far as it relates to the creation . . . of an interest in land' (Sch 1, para 1(b)) was given a wide interpretation.[3] An argument that a covenant to pay rent did not strictly relate to the creation of an interest in land, so that the 'anti set off clause' would be subjected to the statutory reasonableness test, was rejected. Nevertheless, the Court of Appeal has insisted that the equitable right of set-off is important. Clear words of exclusion are required to displace it: the expression 'without any deduction' did not suffice to do so since the word 'deduction' was ambiguous.[4]

Specific performance

General equity jurisdiction   Subject to the overriding discretion of the court to refuse relief, the court may, in its equity jurisdiction, order a landlord who is in clear breach of a covenant to repair to comply with his covenant by carrying out the work specified in the order. Thus, a landlord was ordered to replace a balcony which he had covenanted to repair, but it was not demised to the tenants. It had partially collapsed. As there was no doubt as to the work to be done, and the breach was plain, the court's discretion would be exercised in favour of granting an order.[5] In one case an order of specific performance was made against a landlord, requiring him to keep lifts in working order, even though the landlord was insolvent.[6] An order was granted against landlords of a block of flats who had seriously neglected their obligations to repair the property, to such an extent that the tenants had been forced to leave the premises concerned.[7] The equity jurisdiction applies to all types of premises – although it is unclear whether it is superceded where the specific jurisdiction conferred by statute applies. It is also possible that, in contrast to the statutory jurisdiction, equity has no power to order specific performance (or for that matter a mandatory injunction) where the item sought to be replaced is situated within the confines of the demised premises, as the landlord is excluded from these by the very fact of his having granted a lease. The equity and also the

1   *Melville v Grapelodge Developments Ltd* (1978) 39 P & CR 179.
2   *Eller v Grovecrest Investments Ltd* [1994] 2 EGLR 45, CA.
3   *Electricity Supply Nominees Ltd v IAF Group Ltd* [1993] 3 All ER 372.
4   *Connaught Restaurants Ltd v Indoor Leisure Ltd* [1994] 4 All ER 834, CA.
5   *Jeune v Queen's Cross Properties Ltd* [1974] Ch 97, [1973] 3 All ER 97.
6   *Francis v Cowlcliffe* (1976) 33 P & CR 368.
7   *Gordon v Selico Co Ltd* [1986] 1 EGLR 71, CA.

statutory jurisdiction may be exercised not only by the High Court but also by a county court judge sitting as a small claims arbitrator.[8] Ordinarily, equity holds that for this remedy to be available, it must be capable of being awarded to both parties to a dispute. However, there is authority, which seems obsolescent and inconsistent with principle, that landlords may not claim specific performance against tenants.[9]

If damages are an adequate remedy, then specific performance is debarred; but since the latter award ensures, seeing that it is a contempt of court for a landlord to refuse to comply with it, that the work will be done, it may be that this defence is not especially formidable an obstacle. It is probably no longer a bar to an award of specific performance that constant supervision by the court might be required to enforce the order.[10]

Statutory jurisdiction　Section 17 of the Landlord and Tenant Act 1985 confers a specific jurisdiction to award specific performance against a landlord of tenants of dwellings (which is defined so as to include houses and flats and premises ancillary thereto such as yards). The landlord must be in breach of his repairing obligation, which receives a wide definition in s 17(2)(d).[11] The jurisdiction allows the court to make an order even where the disrepair relates to a part of the premises not let to the tenant, such as where a common roof to a number of flats has collapsed or is seriously damaged. The court is thus empowered to make an order against both landlords who are in breach of their statutory obligations to keep in repair, and those who have express obligations to repair and maintain a block of leasehold flats.

Reform　The Law Commission, after an exhaustive examination of the position, have now recommended that specific performance should be reformed and based on a general statutory jurisdiction. The remedy should be stripped of technical defences such as the constant supervision rule, or the fact that landlords may doubtfully obtain it. The basis of the proposed new jurisdiction would be the discretion of the court, and so whether the remedy was appropriate.[12] Since, to judge by the Commission's findings, the courts already make considerable use of the current statutory jurisdiction under s 17 of the 1985 Act, this reform seems useful, as developing, simplifying and extending to non-residential tenancies an established practice.

Appointment of a receiver

Under s 37 of the Supreme Court Act 1981, the High Court has a general jurisdiction to appoint a receiver in all cases where it appears just and

---

8　*Joyce v Liverpool City Council* [1996] QB 252, [1995] 3 All ER 110, CA; and see SE Murdoch [1995] 29 EG 118.
9　*Hill v Barclay* (1810) 16 Ves 402.
10　See *Jones v Liverpool City Council*, supra, for an analysis of the means by which this supposed bar may be overcome.
11　The definition goes beyond repairs and includes a covenant to maintain, renew construct or replace any relevant property.
12　*Report* (1996), para 9.31 et seq.

convenient to do so. A receiver was accordingly appointed under this jurisdiction over residential blocks of flats, in one case, where the premises were seriously out of repair, due to the landlord's neglect to collect and apply to repairs service charges from the tenants, and in other cases, simply to support the covenant to repair, of which the landlord was in serious breach.[13] Such an order is capable of being protected by a caution against the landlord's title under s 54 of the Land Registration Act 1925 – a means, effectively, of blighting the landlord's ability to dispose of his interest in the premises while a receivership is in force.[14]

Appointment of a manager

Under Part II of the Landlord and Tenant Act 1987, which has been amended so as to enlarge the jurisdiction and to make it more difficult for landlords to regain control over the property once an order is made,[15] a manager may be appointed by the county court (or, as from a date to be ordered by statutory instrument, a leasehold valuation tribunal) on the application of a tenant. The following deals with the position as amended by Part III of the Housing Act 1996.

There must be a lease of residential flats (whether a purpose-built block with at least two flats or a house converted into flats). This specific jurisdiction – aimed at landlords who seriously neglect their repairing and related obligations – excludes that of equity (s 21(6)). It was enacted as part of a more general policy of improving the remedies of tenants of residential flats against landlords who neglected their repairing and related obligations, such as in relation to insurance policies or the maintenance of the common parts. It was considered that the general equity jurisdiction was not sufficiently precise.[16]

In what follows we confine ourselves to an examination of this jurisdiction to the case of breaches of covenant to repair or maintain.

1   The application must be against the immediate landlord and it may be made by one or more tenants. A management order may be made if, in particular the landlord is in breach of a management obligation or he would be in breach but for the fact that it has not been reasonably practicable for the tenant to give him the requisite preliminary notice (s 24(2)(a)). In this case, it must be just and convenient[17] to make the order.

2   No order may be made unless the tenant or tenants have served on the landlord a notice which complies with s 22 of the 1987 Act. Such notice resembles a statutory forfeiture notice. In particular, a s 22 notice must specify the grounds on which an order is being requested. It must require the landlord to remedy the breach within a specified and reasonable time,

13   *Hart v Emelkirk Ltd* [1983] 3 All ER 15, [1983] 1 WLR 1289; *Daiches v Bluelake Investments Ltd* [1985] 2 EGLR 67; *Blawdziewicz v Diadon Establishment* [1988] 2 EGLR 52.
14   *Clayhope Properties Ltd v Evans* [1986] 2 All ER 795, [1986] 1 WLR 1223, CA.
15   As amended by Housing Act 1996, ss 85 and 86 and as set out in ibid, Sch 5. In force from 24 September 1996 (s 232(2)).
16   See Hawkins [1985] Conv 12 for a review of the background.
17   These words invite eg a consideration of such matters as whether delays in serving relevant notices or the onset of winter might preclude relief: see *Howard v Midrome Ltd* [1991] 1 EGLR 58.

by specified steps. The degree of particularisation will seemingly be related to the terms of the lease: thus, if redecoration at intervals is required, it might suffice to say that the property was last redecorated in a given year. The amount of time to be allowed may be governed by the conduct of the landlord to date: a landlord who showed no intention of complying with his obligations could not say that a 28-day period for compliance was too short.[18]

3　A landlord who remedies the breaches (by analogy with forfeiture, this may mean all of them) within the reasonable time allowed will avert the making of a management order. If made, an order displaces the landlord from the management of the property and, if the functions of a receiver are given to the manager, from the rent. While an order may be varied or even discharged on the application of the landlord, such an order may only be made if the landlord shows either that to accede to the application will not result in recurrence of the circumstances which led to the making of the order or it is just and equitable to vary or discharge the order (s 24(9A)).[19]

Once a management order has been in force for two years, the tenants may apply to compulsorily purchase out the landlord's interest under Part III of the 1987 Act (see chapter 20).

Repudiation

In an interesting county court decision,[20] tenants holding a three-year assured shorthold tenancy were entitled to accept a landlord's 'repudiatory breach' of his statutorily implied repairing covenants, by leaving the house concerned during the tenancy and giving back the keys. The landlord had refused to remedy serious disrepairs such as an uninhabitable bedroom due to a collapsed ceiling, rainwater penetration in the sitting-room, a damp hall wall and an unusable outside toilet. The tenants were awarded substantial general damages.

In one sense, the landlord's refusal to perform his implied repairing covenants, no doubt a primary obligation, could be said to have deprived the tenant of substantially the whole benefit which the parties intended him to obtain from the contract – a short tenancy of a house which he might expect would be kept in repair by the landlord as required by statute. The county court flew in the face of a previous denial by one member of the Court of Appeal that repudiation could ever apply to an executed lease, as passing an estate in land.[1] The court claimed, however, that contractual principles had been held by the House of Lords to allow a lessee to assert that an executed lease could be frustrated, and that the House of Lords had held in a leading rent review case that a lease could not now be considered to be essentially different from other contracts, so undermining the authority of the earlier Court of Appeal ruling.

18　*Howard v Midrome Ltd* supra.
19　As inserted by Housing Act 1996, s 85(6).
20　*Hussein v Mehlman* [1992] 2 EGLR 87, noted Bright [1993] Conv 71; Harpum [1993] CLJ 212.
　1　*Total Oil Great Britain Ltd v Thompson Garages (Biggin Hill) Ltd* [1972] 1 QB 318, 323–324 (Lord Denning MR).

Indeed, one member of the Court of Appeal has now spoken of forfeiture by a landlord as being a form of repudiation of a lease,[2] lending weight to the view that repudiation and acceptance afford a new means of terminating tenancies.

If a tenant may invoke the principles of repudiatory breach so as to treat his tenancy as being at an end, and so terminate his own obligations under it, as from his acceptance of his landlord's repudiation, landlords may be able to claim that a tenant in serious breach of covenant – eg grave and persistent default with rent – could invoke the same principle to put an end to the lease and then claim damages for loss of future rent. These and related issues are further discussed in chapter 12 of this book.

VII LOCAL AUTHORITY CONTROL OF DISREPAIR

Despite the wide range of remedies available to residential tenants against landlords who are in breach of their repairing obligations, it is considered that in this field some intervention on the part of local authorities against landlords who are responsible for dilapidated housing is called for. It is therefore appropriate briefly to examine the two areas of control: repair notices and the statutory nuisance powers.[3]

Repair Notices

Part VI of the Housing Act 1985 confers wide discretionary powers on local authorities to serve notices compelling the landlord of unfit housing or flats to carry out work to put the premises into a fit state. Local authorities are required to consider the housing conditions in their district, paying regard to guidance published by the Secretary of State.[4] The authority may serve a repair notice, a notice which relates to a house in serious disrepair, or, if the house or premises cannot be made fit for human habitation then demolition or closing may be ordered.

A repair notice served under s 189 is a notice compelling the 'person having control of the house' under s 207, who is likely to be a freeholder or long leaseholder. However, a repair notice served on the freeholder of long lessees of flats was invalid as the freeholder was not in receipt of a rack (or market) rent. The notice could validly have been served on long leaseholders.[5]

The notice specifies works which will bring the house in the opinion of the authority into a state fit for human habitation and it must state that in the opinion of the local authority, the house will be rendered fit once the works are completed, leaving it open to the person on whom it is served to claim that the premises are incapable of being rendered fit by the works. The standard in question is set out in s 604 of the 1985 Act. A house is presumed fit for human

---

2 *Kingston-upon-Thames Royal London Borough Council* v *Marlow* [1996] 1 EGLR 101, 102K-L.
3 See further Arden and Hunter, chs 12 and 13.
4 Housing Act 1985, s 605; current guidance is in Circular 6/90, Annex F.
5 *Pollway Nominees Ltd v Croydon London Borough Council* [1987] AC 79, [1986] 2 All ER 849, CA.

habitation unless it fails to meet one or more items of the statutory list of matters.[6] Therefore, merely for a house to be out of repair without being unfit in this sense is not a ground for service of a s 189 notice.

A repair notice must require the person concerned to execute the relevant works within a reasonable time (not less than seven days from the operative date of the notice)[7] specified in the notice (s 189(2)). The works must be completed within a time specified, which again must be reasonable.

Local authorities may also serve, as a different course of action, a serious disrepair notice on the person having control of the house or premises concerned under s 190 of the 1985 Act. This provision was enacted so as to prevent an owner of dilapidated premises from claiming that the state of the property had fallen into such decay that it could never be made fit for human habitation. The power to serve a s 190 notice applies to houses, and houses in multiple occupation such as flats. It arises where the authority is satisfied, following a complaint from an occupying tenant or licensee, that the premises are in such a state of disrepair that their condition materially interferes with the personal comfort of any occupying tenant or licensee (s 190(1)(b)).

Statutory nuisances

With the passing of the Environmental Protection Act 1990, an apparently comprehensive and revised set of procedures for the elimination of statutory nuisances came into force. If a complaint is made to the appropriate local authority about the condition of premises, they are under a duty to investigate; in any case they have to periodically inspect their locality so as to be able to enforce the 1990 Act, where required.

The result of the procedures may be the institution of criminal proceedings against offending landlords.[8] It appears by necessary implication that the statutory code does not confer any right on the tenant to claim damages, even though he may have suffered ill-health as a result of the condition of the premises.[9]

However, the definition of a 'statutory nuisance' does not quite correspond to that of a disrepair and this, in the present state of the law, in which the implied duty of landlords to make and keep fit houses fit for human habitation is a dead letter,[10] exposes a lacuna in the remedies offered to lessees arising out of property disrepair.[11]

Within the 1990 Act, the premises must be 'prejudicial to health or a nuisance' (s 79(1)). Premises which are out of repair or condition satisfy this

---

6 The list includes structural stability, freedom from serious disrepair, freedom from dampness, and basic facilities such as for washing and cooking and for the supply of hot and cold water.

7 A repair notice is operative when 21 days from service without an appeal being lodged against it expire (s 189(4)), so that appealing against a notice puts off its operation until the appeal is determined.

8 The authority may, alternatively, themselves abate a statutory nuisance which has not, in defiance of a notice, been abated (s 81(3)).

9 *Issa v Hackney London Borough Council* [1996] EGCS 184, CA.

10 As judicially recognised in *Issa v Hackney London Borough Council* supra.

11 The statutory nuisance legislation and the unfitness legislation were originally enacted at the same time (Public Health Act 1936 and Housing Act 1936).

test if there is a threat of disease or vermin.[12] However, the courts have limited the extent of liability by holding that the condition of the premises must amount to a nuisance at common law,[13] which is a narrower concept than statutory unfitness for human habitation or disrepair within a repairing obligation, statutory or express.

If the local authority believes that the state of premises – this, by s 79(1) is not confined to houses or flats – is within the definition of a statutory nuisance, it must serve an abatement notice on the person responsible for the statutory nuisance – the landlord or, if he is a mesne landlord, the owner of the premises. If the nuisance arises from any structural defect on the premises, however, the owner – there is no statutory definition of this word – must be served with the notice (s 80). The notice may require the abatement – or termination – of the nuisance. It may alternatively require the carrying out of works and steps necessary to abate the nuisance or to prevent its recurrence. The time for compliance need not necessarily be shown in the notice. Should a landlord on whom a notice is served prove that the condition of the premises is owing to the tenant's fault, he escapes liability.[14] It is also a defence to show that reasonable efforts have been made to abate the nuisance where the premises are commercial – this defence is not available where they are residential (s 87(1)).

VIII   REFORM

Various bodies charged with law reform have examined the present rules and have concluded that reforms are required. Earlier reports[15] have not been implemented. In 1992, the Law Commission published a Consultation Paper.[16] It suggested imposing on all landlords a duty to maintain demised premises by reference to the safe, hygienic and satisfactory use of the property for its intended purpose. The proposal was criticised. One ground was that it might turn out to be redundant, since many commercial landlords might at least attempt to pass on the burden of the maintenance obligation to their lessees, which the proposal itself envisaged.[17]

The Commission produced a final Report in 1996.[18] Many of the individual recommendations have already been noted in this chapter. The Report repays careful study. The thrust underlying the proposals as a whole, which are incorporated in a draft Bill, is to create a coherent and principled code regulating the responsibilities of the parties to a lease.[19] The Commission are

---

12 *Coventry City Council v Cartwright* [1975] 2 All ER 99.

13 See eg *National Coal Board v Thorne* [1976] 1 WLR 543.

14 As where a tenant makes use of a central heating system for which it was not designed: *Dover District Council v Farrar* (1980) 2 HLR 32.

15 Leasehold Committee Final Report (1950) Cmnd 7892 and Law Com No 67 (1975).

16 No 123 Responsibility for the State and Condition of Property.

17 PF Smith [1994] Conv 186.

18 Responsibility for State and Condition of Property (No 238); see (1996) 146 NLJ 397; Bridge [1996] Conv 342.

19 *Report*, para 6.22.

not complimentary about the present law. To them, it provides a patchwork of private and public law remedies which overlap at times and which provide no remedies on other occasions – as where a house is unfit but not out of repair.

The Commission, seemingly owing to the critical reception in some quarters of the proposed duty to maintain, have abandoned that scheme. They do think that the parties to a lease must be compelled, in the public interest in seeing properly maintained leasehold property, to address the issue of liability for repairs when negotiating a lease. They propose a general implied statutory covenant by the landlord to keep the demised premises, their common parts and any premises whose disrepair might affect the tenant's premises, in repair and to make and keep them fit for human habitation.[20] The covenant could be contracted out of, and would not apply to short residential leases, where specific compulsory obligations would be imposed.

20 *Report*, paras 7.7–7.10.

Chapter 10

Rights and liabilities as between landlord or tenant and third parties

I ON THE PART OF THE LANDLORD

1 RIGHTS AGAINST THIRD PARTIES

During the term of a lease, the tenant is entitled to bring actions for the recovery of possession of the land, as where he is dispossessed by a squatter, and is subject to various liabilities to third parties, whether in nuisance or negligence. The landlord retains a separate right of action for injuries to his reversion. In this chapter, we summarise the principal rights and liabilities of both parties to a lease to third parties.

Adverse possession

A person who acquires a squatter's title under the Limitation Act 1980, by adverse dispossession of the tenant for 12 years, does not by this means acquire a title against the landlord. This is due to the fact that the landlord's right of action to recover the land is deemed to accrue only when his reversion falls into possession.[1] Therefore, time begins to run against the landlord from the termination of the lease, and the landlord's title is only barred after the expiry of 12 years from that date.[2] If the landlord begins proceedings for the recovery of possession of the land before the expiry of the 12-year limitation period, his right of action will be unaffected by any subsequent expiry of the 12-year period while the proceedings are pending: any judgment for possession given after the expiration of the 12-year period will be enforceable for a further 12 years from the date of the judgment before a title can be acquired by the tenant in adverse possession.[3]

If a squatter acquires title against the whole, or part, of premises demised to a tenant, and title is unregistered, the estate of the tenant is not, as against his landlord, destroyed. Therefore, the tenant may validly surrender his lease to the landlord, and time will begin to run for limitation purposes, against the

1 Limitation Act 1980, s 15(6) and Sch 1, para 4.
2 Limitation Act 1980, s 15(1).
3 *BP Properties Ltd v Buckler* [1987] 2 EGLR 168, CA.

landlord, only as from the date the lease is determined by the surrender. Accordingly, the landlord is entitled to take possession proceedings against the squatter, provided he brings his action within the statutory period of 12 years from the date of the surrender.[4] In the case of registered land, once a squatter acquires title, the lessee's estate is not extinguished but is held by the lessee on trust for the squatter, without prejudice to the 'estates and interests of any other person interested in the land whose estate or interest is not extinguished'.[5] The squatter is then entitled to apply to be registered as proprietor in place of the documentary lessee.[6] Such registration has the same effect as a registration as first proprietor.[7] Where a squatter applied for registration of a possessory title of registered land, and the title of the paper lessee was closed as a result, a subsequent surrender by the lessee in favour of the landlord could not defeat the squatter's registered title, first, because the surrender was not a registered disposition by a proprietor within s 69(4) of the 1925 Act; second, the squatter had acquired the paper lessee's registered title and was entitled to be registered as proprietor in her place. However, during the pre-registration period, the paper lessee might have been able validly to surrender her title to the lessor.[8]

Prescription

In general, a third party cannot claim to acquire an easement by any method of prescription against land which has at all material times been in the occupation of a lessee, because a prescriptive user must be against the fee simple owner.[9] It is otherwise if, at the start of the prescriptive period, the land was held in fee simple.[10] In the case of a claim to light, a third party who has actually used the right for 20 years next before the action without interruption obtains an absolute and indefeasible right to light even if the land has been occupied by a lessee throughout.[11]

Trespass

For a landlord to be able to maintain an action for trespass, he would have to show injury to the reversionary interest, ie injury of such a permanent nature as to affect the value of his reversion adversely.[12] Alternatively, he might be entitled to claim any loss from the tenant under a covenant, express or implied, for redelivery, if the tenant cannot deliver up the land as it was at the commencement of the tenancy, even without there being any negligence on his part.[13]

---

4 *Fairweather v St Marylebone Property Co Ltd* [1963] AC 510, [1962] 2 All ER 288, HL. A lessee's renewal option was inoperative against a successful squatter: *Chung Ping Kwan v Lam Island Development Co Ltd* [1997] AC 1.
5 Land Registration Act 1925, s 75(1).
6 Ibid, s 75(2).
7 Ibid, s 75(3).
8 *Spectrum Investment Co v Holmes* [1981] 1 All ER 6, [1981] 1 WLR 221.
9 *Kilgour v Gaddes* [1904] 1 KB 457; but see Delaney (1958) 74 LQR 82: Sparkes [1992] Conv 167.
10 *Pugh v Savage* [1970] 2 QB 373, [1970] 2 All ER 353, CA.
11 Prescription Act 1832, s 3. See *Simper v Foley* (1862) 2 John & H 555.
12 See *Jones v Llanrwst UDC* [1911] 1 Ch 393.
13 *Phillimore v Lane* (1925) 133 LT 268 (damage by burglars).

Nuisance

The same principles apply in respect of nuisance, so that the cause of the nuisance will be actionable only by the tenant unless some permanent injury has been caused to the reversion. Smell and noise are not normally permanent, though a landlord has been granted an injunction against a third party against carrying on works which caused structural damage to the property let.[14] Although the claim is based on the damage to the reversion, the extent of that loss where the nuisance is continuing, is not the measure of damages, but as much as is necessary to ensure abatement of the nuisance.[15]

2   LIABILITY TO THIRD PARTIES

Any claims by third parties in respect of the land are maintainable against the tenant, and not against the landlord except where the landlord has himself caused the injury, and under certain statutory provisions.

Nuisance

Where the landlord lets property abutting the highway in a derelict or ruinous state, he will be liable to any third party injured as a result,[16] unless he had no reason to suspect that it was in fact dangerous;[17] so, too, if the lease expressly contemplates acts which will inevitably result in a nuisance.[18] Liability is strict, and still, it seems, does not depend on proof, ordinarily required as a condition precedent to liability in tort, that injury to the plaintiff was reasonably foreseeable as a result of the condition of the premises.[19]

The landlord is liable even if the nuisance was in fact created by a tenant under a previous tenancy and he re-lets, and even though he has no right to enter on the land to remove it.[20] If a latent defect in the premises manifests itself during the lease, the landlord will only be liable in nuisance in respect of it, if the third party proves that he was aware of the existence of the defect at the date of the lease.[1]

In the case of a public nuisance, where injury is caused to a third party user of the highway as a result of a landlord's failure to repair, whether he has agreed to repair,[2] or merely reserved a right to enter and repair,[3] he will be liable in damages to the third party. On the ground of business efficacy, the landlord is

14 *Shelfer v City of London Electric Lighting Co* [1895] 1 Ch 287, CA.
15 *Battishill v Reed* (1856) 18 CB 696.
16 *Sampson v Hodson-Pressinger* [1981] 3 All ER 710, CA; cf *Guppys (Bridport) Ltd v Brookling* [1984] 1 EGLR 29, CA.
17 *St Anne's Well Brewery Co v Roberts* (1928) 140 LT 1, CA.
18 *Harris v James* (1876) 45 LJQB 545.
19 *Cambridge Water Co Ltd v Eastern Counties Leather plc* [1994] 2 AC 264, [1994] 1 All ER 53, HL.
20 *Thompson v Gibson* (1841) 7 M & W 456.
 1 *Brew Bros v Snax (Ross) Ltd* [1970] 1 QB 612, [1970] 1 All ER 587, CA.
 2 *Wringe v Cohen* [1940] 1 KB 229, [1939] 4 All ER 241, CA.
 3 *Heap v Inde Coope and Allsop Ltd* [1940] 2 KB 476, [1940] 3 All ER 634, CA.

conferred an implied right of entry against the tenant to carry out necessary repairs.[4]

Damage by third parties – landlord's liability

If the tenant's premises are damaged due to the vandalisation of adjoining premises controlled by the landlord (as where these latter are vacant), a high degree of probability of injury as a result of the landlord's inaction must be shown, to render the landlord liable in negligence to the tenant for resulting losses. In one case, it was held that, where the landlords allowed a house next to the plaintiff tenant's to collapse, leading to serious damage by vandals to the plaintiff's house, the landlords were liable in damages – but negligence liability was admitted.[5] By contrast, where the action of vandals in a flat above the tenant's caused flooding in the tenant's flat, the landlords, who were held unable to take effective steps to defeat the vandals, were not liable in negligence to the tenant.[6]

Negligence

At common law, express contractual liability apart, a landlord is under no liability to his tenant in respect of the safety or condition of unfurnished premises at the commencement of the tenancy;[7] the doctrine of caveat emptor applies and the tenant cannot sue on any implied covenant for loss, nor in fact for any injury. A fortiori, a third party injured on the premises is at common law precluded from suing the landlord in negligence, so that the daughter of a tenant was unable to recover damages for injuries suffered as a result of the landlord's breach of his statutory obligations as to fitness for human habitation.[8] Thus, where a tenant failed to prove that his flat, which suffered from condensation, was in disrepair or dangerous, the landlord was held to be under no general duty in tort to see to it that the premises were habitable.[9] It is otherwise if the landlord is responsible for the design and building of the premises.[10] Two statutory provisions have modified the common law rules.

Under s 2 of the Occupiers' Liability Act 1957, the occupier of premises owes to all his visitors the 'common duty of care', ie a duty to see that the visitor will be reasonably safe in using the premises for the purposes for which he is invited or permitted by the occupier to be there. Where the landlord lets off premises in their entirety, this duty will fall on the tenant as 'occupier' unless it is cast back upon the landlord by s 4 of the 1972 Act. However, if he retains control over any part of the premises, such as the entrance hall, staircase, lift,

4 *Mint v Good* [1951] 1 KB 517, [1950] 2 All ER 1159, CA (weekly tenancy).
5 *Ward v Cannock Chase District Council* [1986] Ch 546, [1985] 3 All ER 537.
6 *King v Liverpool City Council* [1986] 3 All ER 544, [1986] 1 WLR 890, CA; see also *Smith v Littlewoods Organisation Ltd* [1987] 1 All ER 710, HL.
7 *Bottomley v Bannister* [1932] 1 KB 458, CA.
8 *Ryall v Kidwell & Son* [1914] 3 KB 135, CA.
9 *McNerny v London Borough of Lambeth* (1988) 21 HLR 188, applying *Cavalier v Pope* [1906] AC 428, HL.
10 *Rimmer v Liverpool City Council* [1985] QB 1, [1984] 1 All ER 930, CA.

forecourt, lavatories or other common parts, he will be under that duty as occupier. If the occupier is bound under contract to allow strangers to the contract (see s 3(3)) to enter or use the premises, his duty to them as visitors cannot be restricted or excluded by the contract but includes the duty to perform his obligations under the contract whether undertaken for their protection or not (subject to any contractual provision to the contrary) in so far as those obligations go beyond obligations otherwise involved in that duty (s 3(1)). Generally, however, any exclusion of liability clause for visitors must by ss 1 and 2(1) of the Unfair Contract Terms Act 1977[11] be shown by the landlord etc to be reasonable and he cannot purport to exclude liability for death or personal injury. In relation to other loss or damage, the landlord may only restrict his negligence liability by notice if it satisfies a statutory requirement of reasonableness (s 2(2) of the 1977 Act). The 1977 Act, however, applies to business liability only, and a purely domestic occupier is free to restrict, modify or exclude his liability for negligence.[12]

The degree of care required to satisfy the duty is relative to the particular visitor so that he must be prepared for children to be less careful than adults, for example, but he is entitled to expect that a person, in the exercise of his calling, will appreciate and guard against any special risks ordinarily incident to it (s 2(3)).

The duty is to take reasonable care to see that the visitor will be reasonably safe from injury, and his goods from damage. In the case of a known defect which is potentially dangerous, he can often discharge it by giving the visitor adequate warning, eg by means of prominent notices. Any warning, however, is not to be treated without more as absolving him from liability, unless in all the circumstances it was enough to enable the visitor to be reasonably safe (s 2(4)(a)). Moreover, he is regarded as having discharged the duty if the danger has been caused as a result of the faulty work of an independent contractor employed by him in carrying out any construction, maintenance or repairs, provided that he can show that he had taken such steps as could reasonably be expected of him in order to satisfy himself that the contractor was competent and that the work had been properly done (s 2(4)(b)). The Act mentions specifically only these two factors for consideration in determining whether he has discharged his duty; but regard must be had to 'all the circumstances'. Whether the landlord knew or ought to have known of the danger and how long it has existed, must both be relevant factors.

Under s 4 of the Defective Premises Act 1972, the landlord is under the following duties as from 1 January 1974. Where premises are let on a tenancy which puts on the landlord an obligation to the tenant for the maintenance or repair of the premises, the landlord owes to all persons who might reasonably be expected to be affected by defects in the state of the premises 'a duty to take such care as is reasonable in all the circumstances to see that they are reasonably safe from personal injury or from damage to their property caused by a relevant

---

11   As modified by Occupiers' Liability Act 1984, s 2 to allow exclusion of liability for persons obtaining access for recreational or educational purposes unless these are within the business purposes of the occupier.

12   See Mesher [1979] Conv 58.

defect' (s 4(1)). This duty is owed, by s 4(2), if the landlord knows (whether as the result of being notified by the tenant or otherwise) or ought in all the circumstances to have known of the 'relevant defect'. The latter term means (s 4(3)) a defect in the state of the premises existing at or after the material time,[13] and arising from, or continuing because of, an act or omission by the landlord which constitutes or, if he had notice of the defect would constitute, a failure by him to carry out his obligations to the tenant for the maintenance or repair of the premises.

Where premises are let under a tenancy which expressly or impliedly gives the landlord the right to enter the premises to carry out any description of maintenance or repair of the premises,[14] as from the time when the landlord first is, or by notice or otherwise can put himself in that position, he is treated for the purpose of liability under s 4 as under an obligation for that description of maintenance or repair (s 4(4)). No duty is owed as a result of this rule if the defect in the premises arises from or continues because of a failure to carry out an obligation expressly imposed on the tenant by the tenancy (s 4(4)). Section 4 applies to any right to occupy given by a contract or statute which amounts to a tenancy, e g a statutory tenancy (s 4(6)) and it applies to all types of tenancy (s 6(1)) and cannot be contracted out of (s 6(5)).

Liability under s 4 is accordingly triggered if the tenancy expressly or impliedly gives the landlord a right of entry to do repairs – even if he is not expressly liable to repair.[15] Similarly, liability to repair under statute (such as s 11 of the Landlord and Tenant Act 1985) may trigger a liability against the landlord. If a right to enter to repair is implied as a matter of business efficacy, as in the case of a weekly periodic tenancy[16] or other periodic tenancies, depending on the circumstances,[17] a corresponding liability under s 4 will arise. This implication, which extends the liability of the landlord, is not, it seems, automatic, but it is not necessarily confined to residential tenancies, as the 1972 Act applies to all types of tenancy. By contrast, if a condition of disrepair cannot be proved, s 4 does not apply, as where premises are simply unfit for human habitation.[18]

II ON THE PART OF A TENANT

1 RIGHTS AGAINST THIRD PARTIES

As stated above, it is generally the tenant who has any right of action against a third party for the infringement of rights in respect of the land, by virtue of his

---

13 This means the time when the tenancy was entered into and various other times as specified in s 4(3).

14 Obligations imposed on the landlord by statute are treated for the purposes of s 4 of the 1972 Act as imposed by the tenancy (s 4(5)).

15 *Smith v Bradford Metropolitan Council* (1982) 44 P & CR 171, CA.

16 *Mint v Good* [1951] 1 KB 517, [1950] 2 All ER 1159, CA.

17 As in *McAuley v Bristol City Council* [1991] 2 EGLR 64, CA.

18 *McNerny v Lambeth London Borough Council* (1988) 21 HLR 188, CA; PF Smith [1989] Conv 216.

possession, except as regards permanent damage to, or jeopardy of, the reversion. So, for example, if a trespasser cuts down trees, or damages landlords' fixtures and fittings, the tenant can sue in trespass, but he can recover only the loss of their amenity value to him; he cannot recover damages for their intrinsic value, for property in them is vested in the reversion. The same is true for actions in negligence or nuisance. As regards squatters, there is only a tenant's title at risk if he is dispossessed, and it is for him to bring an action for possession, in order to prevent any one acquiring a good title to the leasehold interest by adverse possession.

Easements

An easement cannot be acquired against the demised premises by prescription during the term, as the user is not against a fee simple owner, as already noted.

Conversely, a tenant can acquire easements and profits over other land in fee simple. He can do so for a term of years by express grant only from the owner of the *servient* land, or in fee simple by prescription; and in either case, such rights may give rise to an action against third parties. Thus, a long lessee claimed rights of light to certain windows on his premises over an adjacent, vacant, site; but he was defeated by the registration of an obstruction notice under the Rights to Light Act 1959.[19]

In claiming the right by prescription by virtue of his own user and enjoyment only, the tenant is necessarily claiming it for the benefit of the owner in fee simple of the *dominant* land, ie the landlord.[20] A tenant cannot therefore acquire an easement over adjacent land owned by the landlord,[1] for the landlord cannot acquire rights against himself. Because the doctrine of prescription requires acquisition by and against a fee simple owner, with his presumed acquiescence, a tenant cannot acquire an easement by prescription at common law,[2] by lost modern grant,[3] or, it seems, under the Prescription Act 1832, against neighbouring land occupied by another leaseholder from the same landlord.

If the lease grants the tenant an easement, for example, a right of way over adjoining land demised by the same landlord to other tenants, an injunction against the landlord will not be an appropriate remedy to enforce the right of way because by demising the adjoining land, the landlord has put it out of his power to interfere with the tenant's easement. Naturally, an injunction against the adjoining tenants, if they interfere with the relevant easement, is entirely appropriate.[4]

---

19 *Bowring Services Ltd v Scottish Widows' Fund & Life Assurance Society* [1995] 1 EGLR 158 (the user, having been interrupted for over 12 months from the first registration of the notice, was defeated).
20 He is not required to plead the landlord's title: Prescription Act 1832, s 5.
 1 *Gayford v Moffat* (1868) 4 Ch App 133.
 2 *Kilgour v Gaddes* [1904] 1 KB 457, CA.
 3 *Simmons v Dobson* [1991] 4 All ER 25, [1991] 1 WLR 720, CA.
 4 *Celsteel Ltd v Alton House Holdings Ltd* [1986] 1 All ER 608, [1986] 1 WLR 512, CA.

Defective Premises Act 1972, s 1

By s 1 of the Defective Premises Act 1972, anyone who takes on work for or in connection with the provision of a dwelling, is under a duty to see that the work taken on is done in a workmanlike or, as the case may be, a professional, manner, with proper materials, so that, as regards that work, the dwelling will be fit for habitation when completed. The plaintiff does not have to await the completion of the work before bringing an action, and so a long lessee was entitled to sue builders who, during conversion work, failed to install a damp proof course.[5]

The duty, which falls primarily on builders, developers and the like,[6] is owed to any person to whose order the dwelling is provided and also to any person acquiring any interest, legal or equitable, in the dwelling. For the purposes of limitation, time begins to run from the completion of the dwelling (s 1(5)); or, if the person who originally undertook work carries out further work of rectification, then time begins to run from the completion of that work. Section 6(3) prohibits any contracting out of any of the above duties.

2 LIABILITIES OF TENANTS TO THIRD PARTIES

Except to the extent that the landlord may be liable, eg for breach of statutory duty in certain cases, it is generally the tenant as occupier, upon whom is likely to fall any liability under the general law in respect of the land let.[7] So, if the tenant interferes with an easement of a third party over the land, or if he creates a nuisance, he can be restrained by injunction or sued for damages by the third party. Whether or not the tenant may have obligations to third parties under covenants entered into between the landlord and owners of other land (ie positive and restrictive covenants affecting the freehold) and covenants contained in any lease superior to his own, depends on a number of important distinctions which should be noted.

Liability to owners of other land

The tenant will be liable to observe a covenant at the instance of a third party owner of adjacent or neighbouring land.[8] if that owner is entitled to the benefit of the covenant and the tenant's land is burdened with it, which latter condition is satisfied if the covenant is negative in substance,[9] and provided that the covenant is duly registered – see below.

---

5 *Andrews v Schooling* [1991] 3 All ER 723, [1991] 1 WLR 783, CA.
6 But not where the builder is a member of the National House Builders' Registration Council and the work is guaranteed by them on completion (s 2).
7 *Sampson v Hodson-Pressinger* [1981] 3 All ER 710, CA.
8 See *LCC v Allen* [1914] 3 KB 642, CA.
9 A positive covenant (such as to repair) cannot be enforced against any successor in title to the burdened freehold land, whether that land is demised to a tenant or not: see *Rhone v Stephens* [1994] 2 AC 310, HL; unless, perhaps, the tenant in such a case takes the benefit of eg drainage, without being prepared to pay for it: *Halsall v Brizell* [1957] Ch 169, [1957] 1 All ER 371.

A tenant who takes a lease of registered land which is in fact subject to a restrictive covenant entered into or created after 1925 will be deemed to be affected with notice of the covenant if it is protected by entry of a notice.[10] In the case of unregistered land, the tenant will be bound by a post 1 January 1926 restrictive covenant if it is registered as a land charge.[11] It is indeed provided in the case of registered land that the title is subject to any post 1 January 1926 restrictive covenant,[12] and in the case of unregistered land, registration is equivalent to actual notice of the incumbrance.[13] By contrast, in the case of registered and unregistered land alike, if such a restrictive covenant is not duly registered, the tenant may ignore it, even if he has actual notice of its existence.[14]

Where a lessee contracts under an open contract for sale for a lease, he is not entitled to inspect the freehold title; similarly, a sub-lessee is not entitled to call for the superior leasehold title.[15] However, in the case of unregistered land, a lessee who intends to take a lease and who cannot call for the superior title is not deemed to be affected with notice of any matter or thing of which, had he contracted that such title would be furnished, he might have had notice. The lessee takes the lease without notice of the restrictive covenant and it does not bind him, unless the lessee has actual notice of the existence of the covenant. This apparently draconian rule, which means that a lessee without notice is entitled to ignore the covenant, and which applies to any pre-1926 restrictive covenant,[16] is abrogated in the case of restrictive covenants entered into on or after 1 January 1926, since the registration of a restrictive covenant as a land charge constitutes actual notice of its existence to the lessee. The lessee is placed in a difficult position, since he may not necessarily be able to discover by a search of the freehold title presented to him whether and if so what restrictive covenants bind the land, as where a restrictive covenant was made by a previous freeholder.

In the case of a sub-lessee of unregistered land, in principle a restrictive covenant in a head lease is binding on a sub-lessee. A sub-lessee is not bound, in relation to a post 1 January 1926 restrictive covenant in a lease, unless he has actual or constructive notice of it. Since an intending under-lessee who omits to inspect the head lease cannot invoke the protection of s 44(5) of the Law of Property Act 1925, yet may under an open contract be unable to call for the head lease, he risks being bound by a restrictive covenant of which he is ignorant.

In the case of registered land, it would seem that as from 3 December 1990,[17] an intending lessee should be able to search the registered freehold title even without the landlord's authority, owing to the fact that any person is in

---

10   Land Registration Act 1925, s 50(1) and (2).
11   Land Charges Act 1972, s 2(5) (Class D(ii)).
12   Land Registration Act 1925, ss 20(1) and 50(2).
13   Law of Property Act 1925, s 198(1).
14   Land Registration Act 1925, s 59(6) (registered land); Law of Property Act 1925, s 199(1)(i) (unregistered land).
15   Law of Property Act 1925, s 44(2) and (4).
16   *Shears v Wells* [1936] 1 All ER 832.
17   When Land Registration Act 1925, s 112, as substituted by Land Registration Act 1988, s 1, came into force.

principle entitled to inspect the Register. Likewise, if there is a separate registered leasehold title, no doubt an intending sub-lessee could inspect this title, for the same reason. In neither case could a lessee or sub-lessee ignore a covenant whose existence proper inspection would have disclosed.

Access orders

The common law provides only limited rights of access from one piece of land to neighbouring premises for the purpose of carrying out repairs or maintenance work. Access might be gained by the tenant or his landlord if the neighbour gives his permission or licence (which, however, might be easy to revoke on proper notice), or the demised premises may enjoy easements or similar rights in respect of the neighbouring land, allowing the tenant or his landlord in default to enter the neighbouring land for specific purposes. The same principles applied in reverse, where a neighbour of a tenant wished to gain access to the demised land so as to repair, say, a flank wall accessible only from the tenanted land. Not only might the tenant refuse permission; the landlord's consent to access might have to be sought and it might be given only for money payments and on terms which might be unsatisfactory.

The Law Commission examined the position and decided that it was unsatisfactory.[18] After an attempted reform received criticism because of its possibly dangerous width and for having been not properly thought through, the government procured delays, and revised the measure somewhat. It was passed as the Access to Neighbouring Land Act 1992. Its overall effect is to confer a general right of access to neighbouring owners to each other's land, subject to a number of safeguards, in particular, the requirement to obtain a court order, which may be made subject to conditions designed to safeguard the position of the owner who must submit to an access to his land which he by definition has refused to give voluntarily, and which he will no doubt find intrusive. The price of the safeguards is to create a complex measure.

A tenant and his landlord alike may be subject to orders under the Access to Neighbouring Land Act 1992, and as a 'person' within the Act, the tenant and his landlord could obtain an access order against a neighbouring recalcitrant owner.

If an applicant is refused access to neighbouring land or premises, for the purpose of carrying out work to his own land, but needs such access, he may ask the county court to make an access order. Such an order, whose precise terms are fixed by the court, allows the applicant to gain access, to the extent prescribed by the order, to the subject premises to carry out 'basic preservation works', notably repairs (s 1(4)). The court must be satisfied that the works are reasonably necessary for the preservation of the whole or any part of the 'dominant land' – ie the applicant's land.

Moreover, the works must be shown to be incapable of being carried out, or substantially more difficult to carry out, without entry to the demised or 'servient' land (s 1(2)). Once an applicant satisfies the court of the need for the works, he creates a presumption that these are necessary to preserve the land.

18 Law Com No 151 (1985), *Rights of Access to Neighbouring Land*.

The Act does not allow access for the purpose of works of improvement or alteration, unless these works are incidental to basic preservation works (s 1(5)). Drawing a distinction between these two classes of case may not be easy.

In view of the obvious danger of abuse of access rights, as where an entering owner remains for too long on the premises, or trespasses into land not required for accessing the work, an access order should specify the works in question and may contain conditions with which the entering applicant must comply, and he must leave the land and make good once the period of his access is at an end (s 3(2)). An access order may entitle the owner to bring materials, plant and equipment on to the part of the premises to which access is allowed (s 1(4)), and so carry out the works permitted, without the consent of the respondent.

There are a number of bars to the making of an access order, notably, where the consent, perhaps in the form of a licence, of the respondent tenant to the entry has been given, or where unreasonable interference with the occupation of the respondent or any other person is shown, or, similarly, hardship to such persons. However, once made, an access order, if registered, will, where appropriate, bind both the tenant and his landlord, if the latter has been joined in the application (s 4(1)).

Chapter 11

Devolution of title

In this chapter, we consider the formalities and related rules governing the devolution of title from the lessor or lessee to another person. These are: by act of the parties, by operation of law, and owing to execution on the demised premises.

I DEVOLUTION BY ACT OF THE PARTIES

Introduction

All rights and interests in leasehold land may be disposed of by the lessee,[1] so that he may assign or sub-let the premises as he thinks fit, unless the terms of the lease preclude or restrict his right to do so. In addition, a lessee may assign a lease to himself jointly with another person, and two or more persons holding a lease, who may hold as trustees or personal representatives, may assign a lease to one or some of themselves only.[2] A lessee or lessor may assign the lease or reversion to himself (i e where he holds the estate in one capacity, e g as trustee, he may assign it to himself in another, e g personally).[3] However, an assignment of the residue of a leasehold term by the original tenant will not rid him of his contractual liability to the landlord for the time being to observe and perform the covenants in the lease, in the absence of express release or waiver by the landlord.[4] In what follows, 'assignment' means an out and out transfer by the lessee of his whole leasehold estate, as opposed to the granting of a sub-lease.

Contract to assign

1 The formalities for a contract to assign the residue of a leasehold term are akin to those which apply to a contract for the grant of a lease, considered earlier.[5] Thus, a contract for an assignment of a lease entered into on or after 27 September 1989 must comply with the Law of Property (Miscellaneous Provisions) Act 1989, and so it must be in writing and incorporate all the

1 Law of Property Act 1925, s 4(2). Assignments of the reversion are discussed in ch 5.
2 Law of Property Act 1925, s 72(1) and (4).
3 Law of Property Act 1925, s 72(3), as interpreted in *Rye v Rye* [1962] AC 496, [1962] 2 All ER 146, HL; Baker (1962) 78 LQR 175.
4 See ch 5 unless the Landlord and Tenant (Covenants) Act 1995 applies, ibid.
5 See ch 4.

terms which the parties have expressly agreed in one document, or in each where the parties have exchanged contracts (s 2(1)). In order to be enforceable against any third party purchaser of the land concerned, the contract must be registered as a land charge in the case of unregistered land,[6] or protected by notice or caution where title is registered.

2   An intending assignee is not entitled to call for the production of the title to the freehold reversion,[7] but this rule yields to a contrary statement of intention in the contract to assign. The intending assignee is to assume, unless the contrary appears, that the lease was duly granted and, on production of the receipt for the last payment due for rent before the date of completion, he is to assume, unless the contrary appears, that all covenants of the lease have been performed up to the date of actual completion of the assignment.[8]

3   There are various grounds on which an intending assignee is entitled, having exchanged contracts for an assignment, to object to the lessee's title and so to rescind the contract. Thus, if the assignee has not had a fair opportunity of ascertaining for himself, by inspection, the terms of any onerous and unusual covenants, he is not affected by constructive notice of these, and may refuse to complete as a result.[9] Where the terms of a contract for an assignment of what in fact was an underlease were open to the reasonable interpretation that the assignee was purchasing a lease, he was entitled to rescind on the ground that no good title had been made by the lessee.[10] A contract under which the assignee was deemed to have bought with notice of the contents of the lease, which were stated to be available for inspection at the vendors' solicitors' office, was nonetheless entitled to rescind where he discovered that he would purchase the lease subject to a narrow restrictive user covenant which was not disclosed in particulars of sale which overrode a special condition of sale by claiming that the premises were 'valuable business premises'.[11] Where a lessee failed to make title prior to the date fixed for completion, as the landlord had forfeited the lease, time being of the essence, the assignee was entitled to rescission despite a pending application for relief against forfeiture.[12] Similarly, a prospective assignee is entitled to rescind (or 'repudiate') a contract for assignment where, although the landlord has consented, his lessee has unreasonably delayed, as where an assignee had tried for some three years to procure an assignment of the lease concerned and was entitled to rescind after serving a 20-day notice to complete on the lessee.[13] Where a lessee contracts to obtain the lessor's consent to a proposed assignment 'if necessary' this is not an absolute obligation and requires him only to use his best endeavours,[14] and in other

6   Land Charges Act 1972, s 2(4) (Class C(iv)).
7   Law of Property Act 1925, s 44(2).
8   Law of Property Act 1925, s 45(2); as to under-leases, see ibid, s 45(3).
9   *Reeve v Berridge* (1888) 20 QBD 523, CA; *Re White and Smith's Contract* [1896] 1 Ch 637.
10   *Re Russ and Brown's Contract* [1934] Ch 34, CA.
11   *Hunt (Charles) Ltd v Palmer* [1931] 2 Ch 287.
12   *Pips (Leisure Productions) Ltd v Walton* (1980) 43 P & CR 415.
13   *Frost v Walker* [1994] NPC 60, CA.
14   See eg *Bickel v Courtenay Investments (Nominees) Ltd* [1984] 1 All ER 657.

cases it is a question of construction of the contract whether the lessee's obligation is absolute or not.[15]

Assignment of the term

1 Although in theory a tenant is entitled to assign the lease to any person he likes, he may well be subject to an absolute or fully qualified prohibition against assignments (see chapter 7). However, an assignment in breach of covenant is nonetheless effective to transfer the title to the land, except that the assignee will face possible forfeiture proceedings by the landlord.[16]

2 In order to transfer the legal estate held by the lessee to the assignee, a deed must be employed to effectuate the assignment,[17] no matter how short the residue of the lease may be, and even if it was created orally or in writing.[18] If no deed is used, but the assignment is evidenced in writing, it will take effect as a contract to assign.

3 Since an assignment by deed is a 'conveyance',[19] the assignee will obtain, by it, the benefit of all easements and related rights enjoyed with the land at the time of the assignment,[20] and, if the contact so provides, and is after 1 July 1995, the benefit of the limited or full guarantee of title by the assginor (see chapter 4 above).

4 Although at common law the tenant is under no obligation to notify the landlord of an assignment,[1] it is often the case that the terms of the lease will require him to notify the landlord of any assignment, usually in writing, and often within a short time of the assignment taking place.

5 An assignment must be distinguished from the grant of a sub-lease, ie the grant of a term for a shorter period than that enjoyed by the lessee. If the tenant purports to grant a sub-lease for a period which exceeds that of what would otherwise be his leasehold reversion, this operates as an assignment by operation of law, even if the grant is not by deed.[2] However, where, by mistake, a business tenant entitled to statutory continuation under Part II of the Landlord and Tenant Act 1954 unfortunately granted an underlease for a period exceeding by one month the duration at common law of his own term, it was held that the underlease did not take effect as an assignment by operation of law since the lessees had a term which would continue indefinitely under Part II of the 1954 Act, defeasible only by a statutory notice, which sufficed to support the underlease.[3] It also appears that a tenant from year to year has a reversion sufficient to enable him to sub-let for a term of years.[4]

---

15 See eg *Fischer v Toumazos* [1991] 2 EGLR 204; Crabb [1992] Conv 213.
16 See *Old Grovebury Manor Farm Ltd v W Seymour Plant Sales & Hire Ltd* [1979] 3 All ER 504.
17 Law of Property Act 1925, s 52(1).
18 See *Crago v Julian* [1992] 1 All ER 744, [1992] 1 WLR 372, CA (weekly tenancy).
19 Within Law of Property Act 1925, s 205(1)(ii).
20 Law of Property Act 1925, s 62(1).
 1 In the case of perpetually renewable leases, the assignor is subject to an implied covenant to register every assignment with the landlord as provided by Law of Property Act 1922, s 145 and Sch XV, para 10(1)(ii).
 2 *Milmo v Carreras* [1946] KB 306, [1946] 1 All ER 288, CA.
 3 *William Skelton & Son Ltd v Harrison & Pinder Ltd* [1975] QB 361, [1975] 1 All ER 182.
 4 *Oxley v James* (1844) 13 M & W 209.

II   BY OPERATION OF LAW

Bankruptcy of the landlord

Together with all the other property belonging to the landlord, a reversion upon a lease vests, by virtue of ss 283, 306 and 436 of the Insolvency Act 1986, in his trustee in bankruptcy. If the reversion is a liability, rather than an asset, the trustee may disclaim it under s 314 and Sch 5 as being land burdened with onerous covenants; and on such disclaimer the tenant would be entitled to have the reversion vested in him.

Bankruptcy of the tenant

It is common for the landlord to insert in the lease a proviso for re-entry or forfeiture in the event of the tenant becoming bankrupt and such a covenant is perfectly valid, but it is not a 'usual' covenant. The way in which the proviso is framed, however, is important, for as with all provisos for re-entry, it will be construed against the landlord. So where the proviso is reserved 'if the tenant or his assigns become bankrupt', there can be no forfeiture if the tenant becomes bankrupt after he has assigned the tenancy,[5] for it is assumed that it was intended to operate only on the bankruptcy of the tenant for the time being.

In the absence of a proviso for re-entry for forfeiture, the lease will vest, under s 306 of the 1986 Act, automatically in the bankrupt's trustee from the time of his appointment taking effect.[6] The trustee then becomes liable on the covenants until he disposes of the lease.

One of the duties of a trustee in bankruptcy is to realise the assets of the bankrupt, by sale of his property. This may raise a problem if the lease contains a covenant against assignment.

The trustee himself takes the lease by operation of law, which involves no breach of a covenant against assignment, but when he assigns it, the problem is to know whether such an assignment is a breach of the covenant. The law is not certain on this point. In some cases a trustee in bankruptcy has been held entitled to assign without the landlord's consent, even where it would otherwise be required.[7] But it would be dangerous to suppose that this can be stated as a general proposition of law, for such cases can usually be explained by reference to the precise wording of the covenants used. For example, a covenant expressed to bind the tenant and his assigns has been held to bind his trustee in bankruptcy.[8]

The landlord is apparently entitled, under s 345 of the 1986 Act to apply to the court for rescission of the lease, on such terms as to payment of damages for non-performance of covenants under the lease as may seem equitable.

---

5   *Smith v Gronow* [1891] 2 QB 394.
6   This automatic vesting applies to a protected tenancy under the Rent Act 1977: *Smalley v Quarrier* [1975] 2 All ER 688, [1975] 1 WLR 938, CA; but not, since it is purely a personal right of occupation, to a statutory tenancy thereunder: *Sutton v Dorf* [1932] 2 KB 304; also *Eyre v Hall* [1986] 2 EGLR 95, CA.
7   *Doe d Goodbehere v Bevan* (1815) 3 M & S 353.
8   *Re Wright, ex p Landau v Trustee* [1949] Ch 729, [1949] 2 All ER 605.

If, on the other hand, the bankrupt tenant's lease is onerous, unprofitable, unsaleable, or not readily saleable, the trustee may disclaim it under s 315 of the 1986 Act and the Insolvency Rules 1986[9] within 12 months of his appointment as trustee.

The trustee may, on giving notice in the prescribed form, disclaim an onerous lease[10] or an unprofitable contract for a lease, without the leave of the court, notwithstanding that he has taken possession, endeavoured to sell the property or otherwise exercised rights of ownership over it (s 315(1)). Any disclaimer puts an end to the onerous obligations of the lease (such as to pay rent) and to the interest of the bankrupt in the lease itself, so exposing an original tenant to liability for unpaid rent.[11] In relation to a tenancy granted on or after 1 January 1996, the landlord may validly require the tenant to guarantee the assignee's performance and if the latter's lease is disclaimed, the tenant may be required by that agreement to take a new lease of the premises.[12]

A copy of the disclaimer must, in principle, be served on every person claiming under the bankrupt tenant as mortgagee or under-lessee. If such a copy if not served, the disclaimer is ineffective (s 317(1)). The mortgagee or under-lessee may apply to the court for an order under s 320, with a view to having the lease vested in him. However, the court may nonetheless direct that the disclaimer is to take effect. In such a case, and also where an order under s 320 is made, the court may make any order it thinks fit with regard to fixtures, tenants' improvements and other matters (s 317(2)). Special rules apply to disclaimers of leases of dwelling-houses (s 318).

A liquidator winding up a company has a similar power of disclaimer under ss 178-182 of the 1986 Act, to that of a trustee in bankruptcy.

The liquidator must sign a notice of disclaimer and as against underlessees and mortgagees, a disclaimer does not take effect unless a copy of the notice of disclaimer has been duly served on all underlessees or mortgagees of whom the liquidator is aware (s 179(1)) and no application has been made for a vesting order within 14 days from the date of service of the last notice of disclaimer. The court is empowered to vest the property concerned in any one applicant (s 181(2)). Other persons who may be liable to the landlord are not released by a vesting order.

Disclaimer has the same effect as surrender, but is different in nature because the landlord's consent is not necessary. Its effect is to extinguish the right and liabilities between the landlord and the trustee.[13]

In the case of companies, by s 178(4) of the Insolvency Act 1986, a disclaimer operates to determine, as from the date of disclaimer, the rights, interests and liabilities of the current lessee company in respect of the lease. But

---

9   SI 1986/1925 as amended.
10 I e a lease subject to onerous covenants by the tenant, such as to repair or restricting the user of the premises: see *Eyre v Hall*, supra.
11 *MEPC plc v Scottish Amicable Life Assurance Society* [1993] 2 EGLR 93, CA; for a detailed account of disclaimer see McLoughlin, ch 6.
12 Landlord and Tenant (Covenants) Act 1995, s 16(5)(c).
13 But the trustee remains liable for rent until notice of disclaimer is served on the landlord: *Re H H Realisations Ltd* (1975) 31 P & CR 249.

no other person is released, at least where the lease was entered into before 1 January 1996, when the Landlord and Tenant (Covenants) Act 1995 came into force. Therefore, a guarantor of the insolvent tenant, as well as an original lessee, if the insolvent tenant was an assignee, remain liable to the landlord in relation to a lease granted before 1 January 1996 for unpaid rent and other sums. This is, it appears, because the purpose of s 178(4) of the 1986 Act has been stated by the House of Lords to be to facilitate the winding up of an insolvent company's affairs, but so as to have only the least possible effect on liabilities, so that those of other persons remain untouched by the winding up.[14]

Under s 347 the landlord may distrain for up to six months' rent. If on sale of the tenant's goods seized, he realises *more* than the six months' due, he will have to hand over the surplus to the trustee in bankruptcy, even if the rent is more than six months in arrears. For the difference, he must prove in pari passu with the other creditors, and therefore gets no priority. Alternatively, he can forego his right to distrain altogether and bring an action for *all* arrears like all other creditors.

Death of the landlord

On the death of the landlord, his reversion will vest, together with all his other property, in his personal representatives, under the Administration of Estates Act 1925, ie the executors of his will.[15]

Once a lease has vested in personal representatives, they are in the same position as was the deceased landlord, and may, for example, sue the tenant for breaches of covenant committed before the landlord's death. When they come to dispose of the reversion in accordance with the will or under the law of intestate succession, they do so by simple 'assent' in writing (s 36).

Death of the tenant

A deceased tenant's lease similarly vests in his personal representatives under the Administration of Estates Act 1925. They are liable to the landlord in respect of any liabilities under the lease, but only to the extent of the value of any assets. The landlord has no priority over other creditors. When they have satisfied all the deceased tenant's debts and claims, the personal representatives should vest the remainder of his property in the person beneficially entitled under his will or by virtue of his intestacy. Vesting of the lease is by simple 'assent' in writing. As in the case of bankruptcy, it is a matter of construction whether a covenant against assignment will bind the personal representatives.

---

14 *Hindcastle Ltd v Barbara Attenborough Associates Ltd* [1997] AC 70, [1996] 1 All ER 737, overruling *Stacey v Hall* [1901] 1 KB 660, CA, which had decided the contrary. See Crabb (1996) 9 Insolvency Intelligence 57–59, 68–69.
15 Should a landlord die intestate after 1 July 1995, his reversion vests in the Public Trustee until the grant of administration (Administration of Estates Act 1925, s 9 as substituted by Law of Property (Micellaneous Provisions) Act 1994, s 14).

III EXECUTION UPON LEASEHOLDS[16]

Fieri facias

If the tenant fails to satisfy a judgment debt, the sheriff, under a writ of *fieri facias* may levy the debt on his land or goods, and so may seize his leasehold interest. The leasehold may be sold, whereupon title will be transferred from the tenant to the purchaser by an assignment executed by the sheriff.[17] If a purchaser cannot be found to take the fixtures with the leasehold, they must be sold separately.[18]

Execution under the writ of *fieri facias* results in an assignment by order of the court. The original tenant remains liable on all the covenants for the rest of the term as assignor, but by the same token, he is indemnified against future breaches by the purchaser.

Charging order

The court has the power to impose a charging order (in two phases, an order nisi and an order absolute) under the Charging Orders Act 1979, on any leasehold interest of the debtor, whether such interest is legal or equitable. The aim of the charge is to secure the payment of any moneys due or to become due under a judgment or order. The details of the 1979 Act lie outside the scope of this book; but a charging order absolute must be protected by registration. In the case of registered land, this is achieved by either a creditor's notice or a caution (s 59 of the Land Registration Act 1925). In the case of unregistered land, a charging order must normally be registered in the register of writs and orders affecting land (s 6 of the Land Charges Act 1972). In either case, failure to register renders the charging order in principle unenforceable against third parties.

16 For a detailed account see Halsbury Vol 17, paras 462–497 and 547–555.
17 *Playfair v Musgrove* (1845) 14 M & W 239.
18 *Barnard v Leigh* (1815) 1 Stark 43.

PART C
TERMINATION OF TENANCIES

Chapter 12

Introduction

I TERMINATION AT COMMON LAW

Part C of this book is concerned with an examination of the methods by which, at common law, a fixed-term lease or periodic tenancy may be terminated, notably by forfeiture, a process under which the landlord is able to put a premature end to the lease. However, the mere fact that a lease may have expired or have been put to an end by the landlord at common law does not necessarily mean that he is able, without more, to regain the physical control of the premises.

This is because in the case of residential and business tenancies in particular, statute imposes certain restrictions on the length of notices to quit or on the grounds under which re-possession may be gained, as well as giving business tenants a qualified right of renewal of their tenancies. Consequently, if a question arises as to the termination of a tenancy, one must first discover the class of tenancy and then the date it was entered into, owing to the fact that different statutory regimes apply to the same class of tenancy depending on the date of the commencement of the Act.[1] Armed with this information, one is then able to discover whether and if so which statutory restrictions apply to the landlord before he is able to re-possess the premises. These matters form virtually half the text of this book, but a short overview here is not out of place, if only to emphasise that, despite recent moves away from rigid statutory controls, in the case of private residential and agricultural tenancies, the common law and statutory rules as to termination must be understood together.

Thus, under Part II of the Landlord and Tenant Act 1954, a landlord of a business tenant is only entitled to re-possess the premises on certain grounds, such as serious breaches of covenant or his wish to redevelop the premises or to use them for his own business. If none of these grounds applies, the tenant is entitled not only to retain possession under the Act despite the tenancy having expired at common law, but is also entitled to claim a new tenancy from the court. In the case of private sector residential tenancies, however, the basic position is more complex. This is because the policy of the legislature towards tenants of this class has moved from the conferral of almost absolute protection

---

1 Thus, to give but one example, the Rent Act 1977 governs private residential tenancies entered into before 15 January 1989; as from that date the Housing Act 1988 applies to 'assured' tenancies; as from the commencement of Part III of the Housing Act 1996, an amended regime applies to assured shorthold tenancies.

against eviction, save in exceptional circumstances (epitomised by the Rent Acts, discussed in chapter 17), to the restoration to landlords of a right to regain possession, albeit following court proceedings if the tenant resists, on the ground that the tenancy (which is likely to be an 'assured shorthold tenancy') has expired. A similar movement from the security to insecurity of agricultural tenants has taken place, for reasons which will appear.

Termination at common law may result from an offer by the tenant to surrender the tenancy, which, if accepted by the landlord, terminates the estate granted to the tenant as from the operative date of the surrender. To illustrate the complexity of statute, this method is in principle preserved as a means of terminating a business tenancy if by the tenant[2] but in the case of an assured tenancy in the residential sector, although the tenancy ceases to be secure if the tenant ceases permanently to reside in the premises,[3] no mention is made of surrender at common law, perhaps because the method appears to have been superseded by the statute in question.

A related method of termination is repudiation and acceptance, which now seems to have become part of the common law, and which was examined in relation to repairs (chapter 9) and is also discussed in this chapter. The key to this method of ending a lease or tenancy might be that one party has committed such a serious breach of covenant that he thereby shows the other party that he no longer intends to be bound by the lease, as where a landlord under covenant to keep a house in good repair lets the premises in a completely dilapidated condition, or where there is a furnished letting of a house which in fact is uninhabitable. The tenant accepts the landlord's repudiation in such cases by returning the keys and abandoning possession, as he would if he were offering to surrender the premises to the landlord. However, in this case the tenant may also maintain an action for damages if he has suffered loss from the landlord's breach. It may now be no objection of principle to repudiation that its effect is to put an end to a leasehold estate in land, seeing that the House of Lords have accepted that an executed lease is capable of being frustrated, and this method is next examined.

II FRUSTRATION

Frustration is one means by which it is possible that an executed lease may be brought to an end, if a frustrating event takes place during the currency of the lease.[4] In the present context, frustration is some event, such as the total destruction of the land itself, or the rendering of the land totally or substantially unusable for a mutually contemplated purpose throughout the lease, which destroys the whole basis of the relationship of landlord and tenant.[5] Should

2 Landlord and Tenant Act 1954, Part II, s 24(2).
3 Housing Act 1988, s 1(1)(b).
4 For an exhaustive analysis see Treitel, ch 11.
5 *National Carriers Ltd v Panalpina (Northern) Ltd* [1981] AC 675, [1981] 1 All ER 161, HL. Frustration may also apply to a contract for a lease: *Rom Securities Ltd v Rogers (Holdings) Ltd* (1967) 205 Estates Gazette 427.

frustration take place, the tenant is relieved thereafter from any liability to pay rent. The lease is terminated. It is not certain what events, other than perhaps an earthquake or flood which destroyed the demised land, might frustrate the estate granted to a lessee, because these events alone could be said to render the bare legal estate in the land useless, as opposed to making performance of the tenant's obligations less convenient or more expensive. It has therefore been said, in defence of a narrow doctrine of frustration, that in the case of a long lease, the lessee takes upon himself the risk, by accepting a long term, of changes in circumstances which he could not have foreseen at the date of the grant of the lease, even though the burden of his obligations may be thereby increased.[6]

The following events supervening after the grant of a lease have been insufficiently serious to frustrate it: destruction of buildings on the land; utter impossibility of building on the land due to wartime regulations;[7] the fact that some part of the land could not be used at all for quite a significant part of the lease, or that there will be severe disruption to the user of the demised premises for the purpose or purposes contemplated in the lease, for part of the term.[8]

The fact that a supervening event, such as temporary impossibility of building on land due to regulations, may suspend the performance of an obligation of a lessee cannot of itself mean that the whole lease is frustrated, at least where it was granted for a long term; however, the possibility has now been canvassed of 'frustratory mitigation'.[9] If this principle were to be invoked, it might temporarily relieve a lessee from the performance of a specific obligation, without freeing him from the need to comply with the rest of his covenants. Thus, a lessee who could not, due to planning restrictions not foreseen at the time the lease was granted, build on his land, might be able to avert forfeiture for non-compliance with that obligation – unless and until the planning position changed – but could not avoid paying rent.

III REPUDIATION

An assured shorthold tenant was held to have been entitled to accept his landlord's repudiation of the tenancy occasioned by the latter's complete refusal to comply with his repairing obligations.[10] In relation to a tenant who vacated the premises and handed back the keys in an uncontested forfeiture, one member of the Court of Appeal referred to the repudiation of the lease involved in the landlord's forfeiture claim.[11]

---

6 Treitel, loc cit, para 11-008; but the application of this doctrine to say, a five-year tenant of furnished premises should these be destroyed is less easy to defend.
7 *Cricklewood Property and Investment Trust Ltd v Leighton's Investment Trust Ltd* [1945] AC 221, [1945] 1 All ER 252, HL.
8 *National Carriers Ltd v Panalpina (Northern) Ltd*, supra.
9 See Morgan [1995] Conv 74, noting *John Lewis Properties plc v Viscount Chelsea* (1993) 67 P & CR 120.
10 *Hussein v Mehlman* [1992] 2 EGLR 87; Bright [1993] Conv 71; Harpum [1993] CLJ 212. In *Re Olympia and York Canary Wharf Ltd (No 2)* [1993] BCC 159, 166, this case was assumed to be correct.
11 *Kingston upon Thames Royal London Borough Council v Marlow* [1996] 1 EGLR 101, 102K-L.

Assuming that the party in breach has notified the innocent party that he does not intend to comply with a given obligation, repudiation may now be available where a serious breach of covenant is established. In the case of a landlord, his persistent refusal to comply with a statutory or express covenant to keep in repair would seem a candidate for the application of the doctrine; in the case of tenants, a total abandonment of the premises without paying any further rent might suffice. A tenant could not (if he persisted in his attitude) expect relief against forfeiture. Any application of repudiation to him in such a case would seem just and equitable.

To carry any application of repudiation beyond fairly narrow but as yet unascertained limits might, however, risk depriving tenants of the right to apply to the court for relief against forfeiture. Indeed, should repudiation be applied to an executed lease, since its effect, where invoked by the landlord, is to allow him to re-possess the premises, he should be required to point to a re-entry clause in the lease, as a condition precedent of the exercise of his option to repudiate, whereupon the tenant could claim the protection of the statutory notice and relief provisions applicable to forfeitures. It is by no means clear that such an application would literally fall within the statutory scheme,[12] but the courts would surely strive to avoid their jurisdiction to grant relief from being evaded.

To justify applying the contractual principles of repudiation to contracts for leases and executed leases, it could be said that the House of Lords have more than once treated the interpretation of covenants in leases as being governed by contractual principles,[13] so that the legal estate created by an executed lease may be determined by repudiation as much as by frustration, as is now possible – albeit only in the most exceptional circumstances. Whatever might be thought of the aptness of the analogy drawn by their Lordships between rent review trigger notices and time-limits in vendor-purchaser contracts, the courts have applied for some time other contractual doctrines such as rescission for fraud to leases and tenancies (see chapter 1), so opening the way to the application of other contractual principles.

There is, it appears, a limit. Repudiation of an executed lease would resemble forfeiture where relief was refused, in that it would only be in the case of a fundamental breach of the whole lease that it could be invoked as freeing the other party from his own obligation to perform all its covenants himself, allowing him to terminate the lease and sue for damages. This idea seems to be borne out in the authorities. So, in a leading Canadian case, the tenant abandoned premises held on a 15-year lease, despite his covenant to carry on his business continuously for the whole lease. The precinct was adversely affected. The landlord was entitled to accept the tenant's repudiation of the contract and to sue for loss of future rent for the unexpired term of the lease, having mitigated his losses by re-letting to other tenants at lower aggregate rents

12 It is unclear whether Law of Property Act 1925, s 146(7) preserves a tenant's right to apply for relief after acceptance of his repudiation by the landlord: the provision seems to be directed at a term in a lease that it will continue only so long as the tenant does not commit a breach of covenant: Megarry & Wade, p 678.
13 See *United Scientific Holdings Ltd v Burnley Borough Council* [1978] AC 904, HL.

than that reserved from the ex-tenant.[14] In this respect, repudiation, being anticipatory breach, because the injured party does not have to wait until the lease expires before bringing an action in respect of it, has advantages to landlords not present where they accept an implied surrender, where no similarly based claim could seemingly be formulated.

A further example, already mentioned, of breach of covenant serious enough to raise the application of repudiation would be a complete abandonment of the premises by the tenant,[15] or a tenant's outright refusal to pay any rent. It is significant that the High Court of Australia has seemingly been reluctant to place a wide interpretation on the circumstances in which repudiation is available. It has thus held that even persistent breaches of a covenant to pay rent, in the absence of express stipulation, would not go to the root of the contract, at least where the tenant intended to pay in due course.[16] In a further decision, where the tenant holding an unregistered agreement for a lease failed to pay rent because of his baseless claim that the landlord had failed satisfactorily to complete certain works, the High Court of Australia did hold that the tenant had by conduct repudiated the lease, exposing him to a landlord's action for loss of rent.[17] However, the court recognised that a lease was not an ordinary contract. It passed an interest in property. Therefore, an isolated or insignificant breach of covenant would not trigger a right of either party to claim that the whole lease had been repudiated.

In conclusion, it appears that, although there has yet to be a formal ruling on the issue from the Court of Appeal, repudiation and acceptance has begun to find its way into the common law of England and Wales as one of a number of methods of terminating a leasehold estate and the obligations undertaken in the lease by both parties. This may be as well, despite the inevitable uncertainties resulting from a reform by evolution. The Law Commission have abandoned their interesting scheme for tenants' termination orders. Instead, they have advocated a one-sided reform: the modernisation of a landlord's right to forfeit leases.[18] If, however, landlords are to benefit from a modernised right to terminate tenancies, then it seems only fair that tenants should have recourse to a doctrine such as repudiation, allowing them to put an end to their obligations under a lease where their landlord has flagrantly and persistently disregarded his own undertakings.

14 *Highway Properties Ltd v Kelly, Douglas & Co Ltd* (1971) 17 DLR (3d) 710. A landlord cannot, after forfeiture, claim damages for loss of rent for the rest of the forfeited term of the lease: *Jones v Carter* (1846) 15 M & W 718.
15 As in eg *Buchanan v Byrnes* (1906) 3 CLR 704 and as envisaged in *Kingston upon Thames Royal London Borough Council v Marlow*, supra.
16 *Shevill v Builders Licensing Board* (1982) 149 CLR 620.
17 *Progressive Mailing House Pty Ltd v Tabili Pty Ltd* (1985) 157 CLR 17.
18 Law Com No 221 (1994) *Termination of Tenancies Bill*.

Chapter 13

Modes of termination

I INTRODUCTION

Common law and statute contrasted

A fixed-term lease expires by effluxion of time and so ends automatically, without the need for any proceedings by the landlord, at the date fixed for the expiry of the tenancy. By contrast, a periodic tenancy continues unless or until one party or the other decides to end it by notice to quit. In this chapter, we examine various means by which a lease or tenancy may be ended, most notably by notice to quit, surrender or forfeiture. The fact that the landlord may be able to terminate a tenancy at common law does not necessarily mean that he will be able as a direct result to obtain physical possession of the premises.

The extent to which statute restricts the landlord's common law right to possession varies with the type of tenancy granted. In the case of a business tenancy within Part II of the Landlord and Tenant Act 1954, for example, the tenancy is continued by the Act and the tenant may renew it, unless the landlord proves that he wishes to redevelop the property or occupy it personally or for his own business. On the other hand, the 1954 Act (s 24(2)) expressly preserves forfeiture as a valid means of terminating a business tenancy and of granting the landlord a possession order. Reference should be made to Parts D to F of this book for a discussion of the extent to which statute precludes a landlord from regaining possession notwithstanding the ending of a lease or tenancy at common law. At present the trend is towards making it easier for landlords of private residential or farming tenants to regain possession of the premises after the ending of the tenancy.

II NOTICE TO QUIT

General principles

A notice to quit is a statement, usually in writing, by either the landlord or the tenant that he has decided to put an end to a periodic tenancy at the date of termination given in the notice.[1] A periodic tenancy continues only for as long

---

1 There is nothing to prevent the landlord offering the tenant a new tenancy in a notice to quit: *Ahearn v Bellman* (1879) 4 Ex D 201, CA.

as both the landlord and the tenant or all joint tenants agree that it is to continue. A bilateral right to serve a notice to quit is therefore fundamental at common law to the validity of a periodic tenancy. If no notice to quit is served at the expiry of the period agreed for a tenancy, it will continue, at common law, for the same period as that originally agreed.

The parties to a periodic tenancy will have agreed on the length of the tenancy – either expressly or by implication. The tenancy may be for one week, one month, quarterly, for six months or yearly. Unless the parties otherwise agree, the *length* of a notice to quit must be the same as that of the initially agreed duration of the tenancy. Thus, a weekly tenancy requires a week's notice, a monthly tenancy a month and so on. In this, 'month' means a calandar month: a months's notice ends in the corresponding date in the appropriate subsequent month, no account being taken of the fact that some months are longer than others.[2] In the case of a yearly tenancy, six months' notice to quit is required, to expire on the anniversary date of the creation of the tenancy.

The length of notices to quit must be considered having regard to the intervention of statute. In the case of premises let as a dwelling, by s 5(1) of the Protection from Eviction Act 1977, no notice by a landlord or a tenant is valid unless it is in writing and contains prescribed information.[3] Such notice must be given not less than four weeks before the date on which it is to take effect.

A valid notice to quit puts an end to the right to occupy of the tenant under that tenancy as from its expiry date. Again, statute may affect the validity of notices to quit, as by limiting the landlord to certain grounds (as with assured and protected tenancies and tenancies of agricultural holdings) or by only allowing him to serve a notice to terminate which complies with statute (as is the case with business tenancies). Where the landlord of a tenant of an agricultural holding made statements in his notice to quit, as to the falsity or truth of which he was reckless, the notice was vitiated by fraud and could not be relied on.[4]

At common law, where a periodic tenant serves a valid 'upwards' notice to quit on his landlord, the notice automatically puts an end to any sub-tenancy granted by the tenant. Any periodic sub-tenancy falls with the ending of the superior tenancy on which it depends.[5] The Court of Appeal regarded the right of a periodic tenant to terminate his tenancy by notice to quit as being 'precisely equivalent' to that of a fixed-term tenant to end his tenancy by means of an option to determine, as the effect of both actions was to put an end to the tenancy; but they are not similar in all respects, owing to the stricter rules for formal validity of notices which apply to the latter type of termination.[6]

At common law, a notice to quit does not have to exclude the date of the giving of the notice and the date of its expiry. However, the tenancy may specify

---

2 *Dodds v Walker* [1981] 2 All ER 609, [1981] 1 WLR 1027, HL.
3 Ie as prescribed in Notices to Quit (Prescribed Information) Regulations 1988, SI 1988/2201.
4 *Rous v Mitchell* [1991] 1 All ER 676, CA. The same principle applies to business tenancies (see *Marks v British Waterways Board* [1963] 3 All ER 28, [1963] 1 WLR 1008) and tenancies under the Rent Acts (*Lazarus Estates Ltd v Beasley* [1956] 1 QB 702, [1956] 1 All ER 341).
5 *Pennell v Payne* [1995] QB 192, [1995] 2 All ER 592, CA.
6 For some other matters arising out of *Pennell v Payne* supra, see Luxton & Wilkie [1995] Conv 263.

that clear notice must be given. Unless this is so, a notice given to terminate a weekly tenancy which commences on, say, Saturday 1st of a month may be validly given to expire on Saturday 8th.

There are a number of technical rules governing the *expiry date* of a notice to quit. Even though a periodic tenancy strictly expires at midnight of the day before the anniversary, a notice will be valid if it is expressed to expire either on the anniversary of the commencement of the tenancy or on the previous day,[7] whether the tenancy is a yearly, monthly, or weekly tenancy.[8] A notice to quit at noon, however, is bad at common law, by virtue of the strict rule as to expiry.[9] Although a notice to quit should therefore expire on a rent day, the parties may contract out of this by sufficiently clear language.[10]

The courts try to avoid holding notices to quit void on technical grounds. Hence, a notice to quit need not specify the date of expiry, provided that the date is clearly identifiable, as for example 'at the expiration of the present year's tenancy'.[11] Moreover, if the date of the commencement of the tenancy is uncertain, it may be advisable for the notice not only to specify what is thought to be the proper date of expiry, but also to provide further that if that is not the proper date, the notice will expire on the first date thereafter upon which the tenancy could lawfully be terminated.[12]

Notice to quit by a joint tenant

We have seen that a notice to quit is a unilateral document: it does not require the consent of the recipient to be validly served nor to take full effect, assuming it is otherwise valid. The House of Lords has ruled that where a periodic tenancy is held by two or more joint tenants, any one of the joint tenants may serve a notice to quit on the landlord, without first obtaining the consent of any of the others.[13] In this case, cohabitees were granted a joint weekly tenancy of a council flat, but fell out and one of the pair then served a four week notice to quit, as required by statute, on the landlord, without consulting the other ex-cohabitee. The notice was upheld. The House of Lords applied contractual principles and held that where joint periodic tenants had agreed to a tenancy for one year initally, therafter from year to year unless terminated by notice, neither joint tenant had bound himself for more than one year. Hence, once the initial period of one week had expired in the present case, either joint tenant could put the tenancy to an end by serving a notice to quit on the landlord. Another way of putting the same point is that, if there is to be a renewal of any periodic tenancy, all parties must agree to it: so, by serving a notice to quit, one joint tenant makes

7 *Sidebotham v Holland* [1895] 1 QB 378; *Yeandle v Reigate and Banstead Borough Council* [1996] 1 EGLR 20, CA; Cooke [1992] Conv 263.
8 *Crate v Miller* [1947] KB 946, [1947] 2 All ER 45, CA.
9 *Bathavon RDC v Carlile* [1958] 1 QB 461, [1958] 1 All ER 801, CA.
10 *Harler v Calder* [1989] 1 EGLR 88, CA.
11 *Doe d Gorst v Timothy* (1847) 2 Car & Kir 351.
12 *Addis v Burrows* [1948] 1 KB 444, [1948] 1 All ER 177 but see *P Phipps & Co (Northampton and Towcester Breweries) Ltd v Rogers* [1925] 1 KB 14, CA.
13 *Hammersmith and Fulham London Borough Council v Monk* [1992] 1 AC 478, [1992] 1 All ER 1; see Goulding [1992] Conv 279; cf Webb [1983] Conv 194.

it clear to the landlords and to the other joint tenants, who share the whole tenancy with him, that he does not consent to the renewal.[14] There is no reason why, therefore, a joint landlord cannot serve a notice to quit on the tenant without consulting his co-landlord.

This case has certain limits, partly owing to the danger of a landlord reaching an agreement with one joint tenant whose relationship with his partner may have broken down to accept a notice to quit served by him alone, so as to circumvent the protection of s 5(1) of the Protection from Eviction Act 1977, which requires a minimum period of four weeks' notice from both landlord or tenant.[15] Where joint tenants were entitled to give a notice to terminate a tenancy agreement with immediate effect, a notice served by one alone – with a view to allowing the landlord to regain possession against the other joint tenant – was invalid, as the notice was not to quit, since the notice did not take effect at once.[16]

The Court of Appeal has, however, refused to circumvent the generality of the House of Lords ruling. It rejected an argument that because a joint tenancy creates a trust for sale, the provisions of s 26(3) of the Law of Property Act 1925 applied, so as to require a joint weekly council tenant first to consult her estranged husband before serving a notice to quit.[17] Nor was the court prepared to cut down the width of the general principle by creating a special exception to it in the case of lettings by local authorities and similar bodies to residential tenants. The principles of this ruling seem to apply with equal force to a trust of land arising after the commencement of the Trusts of Land and Appointment of Trustees Act 1996.[18]

Errors in notice to quit

A notice to quit which states the wrong date of expiry, without any further qualification, is invalid.[19] However, the courts strive to uphold ambiguous notices, and so a notice to quit on or before a specified date is valid and entitles the tenant to leave sooner if he wishes.[20] Exceptionally, an error in a notice to quit which is due to an obvious slip, such as a typing mistake, may be ignored and the court has the power to substitute the correct date provided that it would have been clear to a reasonable tenant from the terms of the lease, what the correct date should have been.[1] A notice to quit business premises which failed to mention part of the premises was, nevertheless, held to apply to the whole.[2] The tenant must, however, be given sufficient information as to what he is

14 *Greenwich London Borough Council v McGrady* (1982) 46 P & CR 223, CA, approved by the House of Lords in the *Monk* case.
15 And the service of prescribed information (SI 1988/2201).
16 *Hounslow London Borough Council v Pilling* (1993) 25 HLR 305, CA.
17 *Crawley Borough Council v Ure* (1995) 27 HLR 524.
18 There is a similar requirement of consultation of beneficiaries under s 19 which, like s 26(3) of the 1925 Act, is capable of being excluded.
19 *Doe d Spicer v Lea* (1809) 11 East 312.
20 *Dagger v Shepherd* [1946] KB 215, [1946] 1 All ER 133, CA.
 1 *Carradine Properties Ltd v Aslam* [1976] 1 All ER 573, [1976] 1 WLR 442; *Germax Securities Ltd v Spiegal* (1978) 37 P & CR 204, CA.
 2 *Safeway Food Stores Ltd v Morris* [1980] 1 EGLR 59.

required to quit, and a notice which failed to mention storage and other facilities to which the tenant was entitled under his lease was held bad.[3]

Service of notice

A notice to quit may be given either by the landlord or by the tenant, or by their authorised agents. If served personally, it need not be directed to the party served, by name, and if sent to him, it may be addressed to him by description. It is sufficient to leave the notice with the addressee's wife or servant, provided that the recipient is made to understand that it should be delivered, whether or not it ever is.[4] A notice which is just left on the premises, eg under the door of the tenant's house, will be validly served if it can be shown that it came into his hands in time.[5]

Leases may incorporate the provisions of s 196 of the Law of Property Act 1925. A lease or tenancy may expressly provide for the omission of this special set of service rules – as allowed by s 196(5). This particular method of service cannot be implied into a tenancy agreement, as where a weekly tenancy was silent as to service of notices and a notice to quit served on an absent tenant was invalid as it was not proved to have come to his attention.[6] Section 196, which is for the benefit of landlords, provides that a notice:

1 must be in writing;
2 is sufficient if addressed by designation and not by name;
3 is sufficiently served if it is left at the last-known place of abode or business in the United Kingdom of the addressee, or in the case of notice served on the tenant, if it is affixed or left for him on the land or any house or building comprised in the lease;
4 is sufficiently served if sent by registered post or recorded delivery and not returned undelivered; and
5 if so posted, is deemed to have been delivered at the time it would, in the ordinary course of post, be delivered.

III SURRENDER

A surrender of a lease is essentially the giving up of the tenant's estate to the immediate landlord, which causes the lease to be destroyed by mutual agreement.[7] Surrender, whose effect is, in principle, to put an end to all liability to pay rent and to perform other covenants in the lease as from the date of surrender may be either express or by operation of law.

3 *Herongrove Ltd v Wates City of London Properties plc* [1988] 1 EGLR 82. Likewise invalid was a notice which failed to identify the correct landlord: *Divall v Harrison* [1992] 2 EGLR 64, CA.
4 *Tanham v Nicholson* (1872) LR 5 HL 561.
5 *Lord Newborough v Jones* [1975] Ch 90, [1974] 3 All ER 17, CA.
6 *Wandsworth London Borough Council v Attwell* [1996] 1 EGLR 57, CA; also *Enfield London Borough Council v Devonish* (1996) Times, 12 December, CA.
7 Co Litt 337b; as to the basis of surrender see Wade (1962) 76 LQR 541, Elliott (1964) 80 LQR 244, Hopkins [1996] Conv 284.

Express surrender

Any express surrender of a lease, no matter how short or long, must be by deed, on pain of invalidity.[8] No particular form of words is required,[9] but 'surrender and yield up' or 'assign and surrender' suffice. An express surrender must operate immediately and cannot be expressed to operate in the future.[10] A future surrender may be treated as an enforceable contract to surrender, which is valid.[11]

Implied surrender

Although no deed is required for a surrender by operation of law,[12] otherwise this method would be set at naught, it appears that a mere oral agreement to surrender is not effective, owing to s 2(1) of the Law of Property (Miscellaneous Provisions) Act 1989. In order for a landlord or tenant to rely on an implied surrender, it must be shown that possession is abandoned and also that the conduct of both parties is unequivocal and inconsistent with a continuation of the tenancy. The tenant must have unequivocally offered to surrender and the landlord to accept that surrender, or vice versa. The law recognises that parties do not always observe the formalities required for a surrender, and that at some point it would be inequitable, having regard to their conduct, to allow one party to set up the absence of formalities as a ground for resisting the ending of the lease.[13]

Where, for example, a tenant no longer lived permanently in the flat concerned, but returned regularly to feed her cats, and retained a key and her furniture there, the landlord could not claim that the fact that she was no longer permanently resident amounted to an implied offer of surrender. The conduct of both parties was too equivocal.[14] The same result followed where a landlord accepted the return of the keys to the premises for a few days but intended to accept a surrender of the tenancy only once a new lease had been granted.[15]

By contrast, where a council tenancy had been granted to the present occupier's cousins, but these had left permanently for Nigeria, and the occupier frequently and in writing claimed to the landlords that she held the tenancy, the latter accepting rent from her for some time, the only conclusion could be that a surrender of the former tenancy had been impliedly offered and accepted.[16]

The types of conduct which may be relied on to amount to an implied surrender vary. One of the commonest arises where the parties agree to alter a term of an existing lease. In such a case, it is a question of construction of the later agreement whether the parties intended to surrender the former lease and to grant a new lease, or to vary the existing lease. For example, where a 1943 tenancy of an agricultural holding was varied in 1957 by a memorandum, so that

---

8 Law of Property Act 1925, s 52(1).
9 *Weddall v Capes* (1836) 1 M & W 50.
10 *Doe d Murrell v Milward* (1838) 3 M & W 328.
11 Subject to compliance with Law of Property (Miscellaneous Provisions) Act 1989, s 2.
12 Law of Property Act 1925, s 52(2)(c).
13 *Proudreed Ltd v Microgen Holdings plc* [1996] 1 EGLR 89, CA.
14 *Chamberlaine v Scally* (1992) 26 HLR 26, CA.
15 *Proudreed Ltd v Microgen Holdings plc* supra.
16 *Tower Hamlets London Borough v Ayinde* (1994) 26 HLR 631, CA.

as from then the tenancy was held jointly, the memorandum being sewn into and cast in the same formal language and terms as the current tenancy, save that the tenancy was joint and the rent increased, the High Court concluded that the 1943 tenancy had been varied, not impliedly surrendered.[17]

However, the parties may be taken to have agreed on the grant of a new lease, which is subject to the implied condition that it is valid,[18] at a higher rent on different terms, so surrendering the existing lease.[19] If so, the landlord has no power to grant the new lease except on the footing that the old lease is surrendered: by accepting the new lease the tenant is estopped from denying the surrender of the old one.[20] The difficulty is not with this application of the doctrine of estoppel, but with applying it to particular facts.[1] For example, a tenant of business premises whose original tenancy was for seven years from 1977, at a fixed rent throughout, was found to have accepted an oral offer from his landlord of a term ending only in 1991, at the same rent, but with a rent review in 1984. The previous tenancy had been surrendered impliedly and a re-grant of a new tenancy had taken place.[2] But there must be solid evidence of an agreement for a new tenancy, and sometimes, on the facts, the court may conclude that all that the parties have done is to agree on the implied surrender of the existing tenancy.[3] It appears to be a rule of law that an extension of the current lease by supplemental deed takes effect as an implied surrender of the current lease and the re-grant of a new lease.[4] This rule is narrow since where the landlord and tenant of two adjacent agricultural holdings, the second of which had been granted later than the first, agreed for the purpose of two successive rent reviews to treat the rent for the two holdings as a single rent, the underlying estates in the land were not thereby altered and the two separate tenancies continued, as the variation in rents did not, on established principles, *ipso facto* trigger a surrender and re-grant by operation of law.[5]

Difficulties have arisen, notably with council tenancies, where a tenant abandons possession of the premises and claims that this, coupled with his intention not to resume occupation, amounts to a surrender by operation of law of his tenancy. It appears that should the tenant leave owing substantial amounts of rent, after a long absence, the court may, depending on the facts, infer that his offer so to surrender the tenancy has been impliedly accepted by the landlords.[6] Such inference would be easier to make where the landlord changes the locks of the premises and re-lets them to a different tenant.[7]

---

17 *Francis Perceval Saunders Trustees v Ralph* [1993] 2 EGLR 1: hence, the succession provisions of the relevant legislation were not operated in 1957.
18 *Barclays Bank v Stasek* [1957] Ch 28, [1956] 3 All ER 439.
19 An alternative method of achieving the objective of varying a lease is to agree on the grant of a reversionary lease, to commence on the termination of the existing tenancy.
20 *Jenkin R Lewis & Son v Kerman* [1971] Ch 477 at 496, [1970] 3 All ER 414 at 419, CA.
 1 See generally Dowling [1995] Conv 124.
 2 *Bush Transport Ltd v Nelson* [1987] 1 EGLR 71, CA.
 3 As on the facts of *Take Harvest Ltd v Liu* [1993] AC 552, [1993] 2 All ER 459, PC.
 4 *Re Savile Settled Estates* [1931] 2 Ch 210; *Baker v Merckel* [1960] 1 QB 657; see *Precedents for the Conveyancer*, Precedent 5-92 for a precedent of a right to an extended lease following notice.
 5 *JW Childers Trustees v Anker* [1996] 1 EGLR 1, CA.
 6 *Preston Borough Council v Fairclough* (1982) 8 HLR 70, CA.
 7 See *R v London Borough of Croydon, ex p Toth* (1986) 18 HLR 493.

Operation of a surrender

The effect of a surrender is to transfer to the landlord the whole of the tenant's interest, but subject to any lesser interests which the tenant may have created, eg equitable charges.[8] He cannot prejudice the rights of any sub-tenants, for example, by surrender, any more than he could by an assignment of the lease, and in effect, by s 139 of the Law of Property Act 1925, the landlord is put in the position of an assignee of the sub-lease, for the purpose of preserving the rights and obligations under it. The purpose of s 139(1) has been said to be to preserve the ability to enforce the covenants and conditions of the sub-lease for the benefit of the sub-lessee and the next vested right in the land but for the unexpired portion of the sub-lease only.[9] By s 150(1) of the 1925 Act, a lease may be surrendered with a view to the acceptance of a new lease, without any surrender of any underlease.

The effect of surrender upon liabilities for breach of covenant before the surrender is not without doubt. The tenant should remain liable, for such breaches, even after surrender;[10] nevertheless, in the case of an express surrender, it would be advisable to put the matter beyond all doubt by express agreement in the instrument.

The tenant is not entitled to recover any part of any rent paid in advance.[11] The tenant remains liable for any arrears due before the surrender under any personal covenant, if any; if not, the landlord will be able to maintain an action for use and occupation.[12]

IV MERGER

Where a term of years and the reversion immediately expectant upon it become vested in the same person, the lesser estate is merged with the greater estate, and the term is extinguished. For the two estates to be merged, however, they must be both legal or both equitable. Moreover, by s 185 of the Law of Property Act 1925, there can be no merger where formerly there would have been no merger in equity. In equity the two separate estates were preserved if it was in the interest of the party concerned to keep them separate or if it was his duty to ensure that they should not be merged. Thus, there can be no merger where the two estates vest in one person in different rights, eg one beneficially and the other as tenant for life under a trust.

Where the term is extinguished by merger, all the covenants in the lease are also extinguished. So, where in a lease a landlord entered into a covenant restricting his right to build on an adjacent plot, and the estates were subsequently

---

8 *ES Schwab & Co Ltd v McCarthy* (1975) 31 P & CR 196, CA.
9 *Bromley Park Garden Estates Ltd v George* [1991] 2 EGLR 95, 96, CA.
10 *Richmond v Savill* [1926] 2 KB 530; but see F E Farrer, *Conveyancer*, vol xi, pp 73, 81.
11 *William Hill (Football) Ltd v Willen Key and Hardware Ltd* (1964) 108 Sol Jo 482. S 3 of the Apportionment Act 1870 allows apportionment of rent accruing during a period which straddles that in which surrender takes place.
12 *Shaw v Lomas* (1888) 59 LT 477.

merged, the covenant was extinguished, and held to be unenforceable against the purchaser of the plot, in due course.[13] Surrender is just one example of merger, and the effects of the transaction as against any sub-tenant, under s 139 of the Law of Property Act 1925, have already been explained. Merger also occurs by act of the parties to a lease where the tenant exercises an option to purchase the landlord's reversion, and by statute, where the tenant has the right to acquire the freehold by enlargement or enfranchisement.

Enlargement

Enlargement by deed of a long lease, introduced in 1881 and which could be said to be the forerunner of modern leasehold enfranchisement, causes the lease to be extinguished and a fee simple to be vested in the former long lessee,[14] is possible only if narrow conditions are complied with. It is said to apply where it is practically impossible that evidence as to the title to the fee simple could exist at the expiry of the long lease.[15] The original term must be for not less than 300 years and not less than 200 years of the term are unexpired and no rent must be payable, or merely a peppercorn rent or other rent of no monetary value.[16] This exception is narrow: a rent of one silver penny if demanded, as it has no value, and does not preclude enfranchisement,[17] but arguably a rent of three shillings has a value even if the rent is not regularly collected.[18] However, the narrowness of the original provision is mitigated: a rent not exceeding the yearly sum of one pound which has not been collected or paid for the continuous period of 20 years or upwards is deemed to have ceased to be payable.[19] In addition, there must be no trust or right of redemption affecting the term in favour of the freeholder or other person entitled in reversion. No enlargement is possible if the term if liable to be determined by re-entry for condition broken nor to any term created by subdemise out of a superior term which itself could not be enlarged.

V   RECOVERY OF DERELICT RENT

Where a tenant leaves, without terminating the tenancy, and cannot be traced, the landlord will presumably wish to terminate the tenancy to enable him to re-let the premises. He may be unable to serve a notice to quit, however, unless the terms of the tenancy provide expressly for the service of notices by leaving them on the premises, as for example, by the incorporation of s 196 of the Law of Property Act 1925, into the lease.

---

13 *Golden Lion Hotel (Hunstanton) v Carter* [1965] 3 All ER 506, [1965] 1 WLR 1189.
14 The fee simple is subject to the same rights, covenants and provisions relating to user and the same obligations as was the long lease (Law of Property Act 1925, s 153(8)).
15 *Wolstenholme and Cherry,* Vol 1, p 285.
16 Law of Property Act 1925, s 153(1) and (2).
17 *Re Chapman and Hobbs* (1885) 29 Ch D 1007.
18 *Re Smith and Stott* (1883) 20 Ch D 1009n (a vendor-purchaser case).
19 Law of Property Act 1925, s 153(4).

Under s 54 of the Landlord and Tenant Act 1954, the county court may, if it thinks fit, determine a tenancy if the landlord satisfies the court:

(a) that he has taken all reasonable steps to communicate with the person last known to be tenant, and has failed to do so;
(b) that for at least six months immediately prior to the application, no one has been in occupation of any part of the property comprised in the tenancy; and
(c) that during the same period either no rent was payable, or the rent payable has not been paid.

VI FORFEITURE[20]

1 RE-ENTRY DOCTRINE

Introduction

Forfeiture is a process by which the tenant of a fixed-term lease loses his interest before the time agreed for the termination of the lease. The landlord may claim that the tenant has broken a *condition* of the lease, in which case a forfeiture is said to be incurred. The lease need not contain an express right of re-entry as a condition precedent to forfeiture for breach of a condition.[1] But the lease is not put to an end automatically, since the landlord must take steps to terminate it.

On the other hand, the tenant may have broken a *covenant* in the lease, such as to repair or to insure, and in this case, owing to the fact that forfeiture may cost the tenant his right to occupy the land, the landlord may only forfeit if the lease contains an express right of forfeiture (sometimes called a 're-entry clause'). As with forfeitures for breach of condition, the effect of a breach of covenant is not to terminate the lease automatically. On the contrary, as will appear, the landlord must decide whether he wishes to affirm the lease (a process known as waiver) or to terminate it.

As noted in chapters 9 and 12, there is authority for the view that a serious breach by the tenant of his obligations might amount to a repudiation on his part of the tenancy, thus entitling the landlord to treat the lease as being at an end. If so, it might seem inconsistent with principle to hold that fundamental breach terminated a fixed-term lease automatically.[2] It would also be remarkable if a tenant's right under statute to claim relief from forfeiture could thus be prejudiced.[3] Hence the idea that if repudiation and acceptance is now part of the common law, the landlord would need to invoke an express re-entry clause before being able to re-gain physical possession: hence he would be subject to the statutory jurisdiction of the court to grant relief to the tenant and to holders of derivative interests.

---

20 See Pawlowski, *Forfeiture of Leases* (1993); also Pawlowski and Brown, ch 8.
1 *Doe v Lockwood v Clarke* (1807) 8 East 185.
2 In Megarry and Wade, p 671, it is said that 'even a breach of covenant which the other party accepts as a repudiation will not put an end to the estate in land created by the lease'.
3 Unless Law of Property Act 1925, s 146(7) could apply to preserve the tenant's right to apply for relief.

Distinction between conditions and covenants

The importance of the difference between covenants and conditions has been reduced by the fact that no doubt most leases will contain an express right of re-entry for breaches of the terms of the lease,[4] so rendering the distinction unnecessary. However, should a lease draw a distinction between breaches of covenant and condition, it might say that it is a condition of the lease that the tenant does not commit an act of bankruptcy, or become insolvent, or that the tenant is to reside personally on the premises, or, as appropriate, is to remain in the employment of the landlord. The question of whether a particular term is a condition or a covenant is one of construction of the lease.[5]

There is a leaning against forfeiture, owing to its dramatic effects on the tenant. This is a policy which runs throughout the rules to be examined, and is shown in the present context by the strictness with which provisos for re-entry in an old-fashioned form have been construed against the landlord. For example, a proviso for re-entry to take effect if a tenant 'shall do or cause to be done any act, matter or thing contrary to and in breach of any of the covenants' did not apply to a breach of covenant to repair, which was merely an omission.[6]

Insolvency restrictions

Where the tenant is a company which is subject to an administration order under Part II of the Insolvency Act 1986, because it is actually or potentially insolvent, the effect of s 11(1)(c) of that Act is that the landlord requires the leave of the court to enforce a right of re-entry or forfeiture in proceedings by writ, but not, it now appears, where he elects peaceably to re-enter.[7] If granting leave to the lessor is unlikely to impede the purpose of the administration order, leave should normally be given: in other cases, it is said, the court has to balance the legitimate interests of the lessor and the other creditors of the company, although great importance is attached to the proprietary rights of the landlord, so that normally leave will be granted if significant loss would be caused to him by a refusal of leave. The court will, however, assess the prospective losses of the landlord and unsecured creditors who benefit from the administration order.[8] Where a winding-up order is made against a tenant company, if the landlord wishes to forfeit the lease, at least where he proceeds by writ, he again requires the leave of the court.[9]

Exercise of a right of re-entry

If the landlord wishes to forfeit the lease for breach of covenant or condition, he must, because the lease has been rendered voidable, take positive steps to show unequivocally that he intends to terminate the lease, as where a landlord

---

4 See eg Law Society Business Lease (Whole Building), cl 12 (Appendix).
5 See eg *Doe d Henniker v Watt* (1828) 8 B & C 308.
6 *Doe d Abdy v Stevens* (1832) 3 B & Ad 299; also *Doe d Spencer v Godwin* (1815) 4 M & S 265.
7 See *Re A Debtor (No 13A-10-1995)* [1995] 1 WLR 1127 (dealing with s 252(2) of the 1986 Act).
8 See *Re Atlantic Computer Systems plc* [1992] Ch 505, 541G–544H, [1992] 1 All ER 476, CA, 501-503, CA.
9 Insolvency Act 1986, s 130(2).

entered into a new, reversionary, lease of premises vacated by the lessee's administrators.[10] His right of re-entry is exercisable either by taking possession peaceably, or by bringing an action for possession. Therefore, unless a tenant in occupation is prepared to give up possession voluntarily,[11] the landlord will be obliged to commence proceedings for forfeiture by writ.

It is unlawful to enforce a right of re-entry or forfeiture otherwise than by proceedings in court while any person is lawfully residing on the premises or any part of them (Protection from Eviction Act 1977 s 2). Although it is a criminal offence for the landlord to threaten or use violence for the purpose of gaining entry to any building,[12] the landlord is able to gain entry lawfully by changing the locks to temporarily or permanently unoccupied premises,[13] which is 'peaceable re-entry', as this sort of violence to property is not contrary to this rule. The landlord must, however (except in the case of breaches of covenant to pay rent and sums expressly reserved as rent such as service charges) first serve a s 146(1) notice on the tenant and allow a reasonable time for him to remedy the breach.[14] Some landlords have been quick to realise the advantages of this perhaps cheap, and certainly rapid, method of forfeiting a lease. It was held by the Court of Appeal that where a landlord peaceably re-entered an unoccupied building early in the morning, following a s 146(1) notice, the tenant not having by then applied to the court for relief against forfeiture, the peaceable re-entry put it out of the tenant's power to apply under statute and he could not apply in equity as there was no general inherent equitable jurisdiction to grant relief outside the statute.[15] This decision was reversed by the House of Lords on the narrow ground that a landlord's peaceable re-entry meant that he did not base his physical possession of the premises on an order of court, whose effect would, once actual possession was obtained, bar any application for relief by the tenant.[16] A landlord who used the uncivilised method of peaceable re-entry would face an application for relief by the tenant after regaining physical control of the premises, and, unlike the position where he had chosen to proceed by the civilised method of serving a writ, there was no cut-off point, in theory, after which a tenant could not apply for relief (other than the discretion of the court).[17]

The issue and service of writ for possession is a conclusive indication that the landlord has irrevocably decided to treat the breach as giving rise to

10 *Re AGB Research plc* [1994] EGCS 73; also *Redleaf Investments v Talbot* (1994) Times, 5 May.
11 There is no forfeiture by peaceable re-entry of a head tenant's interest where the landlord does not challenge the continuation of any sub-lease: *Ashton v Sobelman* [1987] 1 All ER 755, [1987] 1 WLR 177.
12 Criminal Law Act 1977, s 6(1).
13 Owing to the repeal by Criminal Law Act 1977, Sch 13 of the statutes of forcible entry and detainer.
14 Otherwise the re-entry will be a trespass: see eg *Cardigan Properties Ltd v Consolidated Property Investments Ltd* [1991] 1 EGLR 64.
15 *Billson v Residential Apartments Ltd* [1991] 3 All ER 265; Goulding [1991] Conv 380; PF Smith [1992] Conv 33.
16 *Quilter v Mapleson* (1882) 9 QBD 672; *Rogers v Rice* [1892] 2 Ch 170, approved by the House of Lords infra, but confined to cases where the landlord proceeds by writ.
17 *Billson v Residential Apartments Ltd* [1992] 1 AC 494, [1992] 1 All ER 141, PF Smith [1992] Conv 273.

forfeiture.[18] The lease is notionally forfeited at the date the writ is served.[19] This is seemingly because the issuing and serving of a writ claiming possession is the equivalent in law of a landlord peaceably re-taking possession of premises.[20] At this date, all the covenants in the lease cease to be enforceable by the landlord by injunction or otherwise.[1] The tenant holds a shadowy and ill-defined interest in the premises pending any order for possession.[2] This is sufficient to enable him to claim relief against forfeiture and also to enable a sub-lessee to enforce tenants' covenants.[3] Moreover, should the tenant be granted relief, his lease is restored as though it had never been forfeited.

Waiver of forfeiture

A landlord loses his right to forfeit a lease if he waives the right to re-enter. Waiver occurs where the landlord, with sufficient knowledge of the breach, communicates to the tenant his intention not to forfeit the lease or does some unequivocal act recognising its continuing existence.[4] As soon as he has the requisite degree of knowledge, which may be imputed to him from his servants or agents,[5] the landlord must elect whether to forfeit the lease or waive the breach. The degree of knowledge is a question of fact: where relevant, as with illegal alterations, the landlord need not be aware of all the exact details of the progress of the work, provided he is aware from his observation or otherwise that it is being carried out.[6] If, therefore, the landlord, or his agent communicate[7] to the tenant a fixed intention not to forfeit (express waiver), or should he or his agent do some unequivocal act which is consistent only with the continued existence of the lease (implied waiver), then the landlord waives the breach and cannot enforce a forfeiture clause in respect of it.

An absolute and unqualified demand for rent falling due after the date of the breach, or a similar acceptance of rent,[8] amount to automatic implied waiver. It makes no difference for the landlord to claim that his action is without prejudice to any right of his to forfeit.[9] Implied waiver takes place if the landlord or his agent unequivocally affirms the lease and actions speak louder than words. Once the landlord has elected to forfeit, as by serving a writ for

18 *Serjeant v Nash, Field & Co* [1903] 2 KB 304, CA.
19 *Canas Property Co Ltd v KL Television Services* [1970] 2 QB 433, [1970] 2 All ER 795, CA; *Associated Deliveries Ltd v Harrison* (1984) 50 P & CR 91, CA; *Capital and City Holdings Ltd v Dean Warburg Ltd* [1989] 1 EGLR 90, CA.
20 *GS Fashions Ltd v B&Q plc* [1995] 4 All ER 899, [1995] 1 WLR 1088.
 1 *Wheeler v Keeble (1914) Ltd* [1920] 1 Ch 57.
 2 *Liverpool Properties Ltd v Oldbridge Investments Ltd* [1985] 2 EGLR 111, CA.
 3 *Peninsular Maritime Ltd v Padseal Ltd* [1981] 2 EGLR 43, CA.
 4 *Matthews v Smallwood* [1910] 1 Ch 777, 786, approved by Lord Diplock in *Kammins Ballrooms Co v Zenith Investments (Torquay) Ltd* [1971] AC 850, 883, HL.
 5 *Metropolitan Properties Ltd v Cordery* (1979) 39 P & CR 10, CA.
 6 *Iperion Investments Corpn v Broadwalk House Residents Ltd* [1992] 2 EGLR 235.
 7 The silence of a landlord is not, however, waiver: *West Country Cleaners (Falmouth) Ltd v Saly* [1966] 3 All ER 210, [1966] 1 WLR 1485, CA.
 8 *Central Estates (Belgravia) Ltd v Woolgar (No 2)* [1972] 3 All ER 610, [1972] 1 WLR 1048, CA; also *Welch v Birrane* (1974) 29 P & CR 102; *Van Haarlam v Kasner* [1992] 2 EGLR 59.
 9 *Segal Securities Ltd v Thoseby* [1963] 1 QB 887, [1963] 1 All ER 500.

possession,[10] this is regarded as a conclusive decision to terminate the lease.[11] However, as service of a notice under s 146(1) of the Law of Property Act 1925 is merely a preliminary to forfeiture, it cannot operate as waiver.[12] An offer to purchase the tenant's interest, if made with the requisite knowledge of the breach, may, however, amount to waiver.[13] A mere entry into negotiations cannot do so, however.[14]

Implied waiver is judged objectively: the landlord's acts and not his words or intentions count. The landlord is exposed to the risk that his agent's acts, even if unauthorised, may be imputed to him, as where the landlord wished to forfeit a lease for a breach of covenant but rent was accepted, in error, by an employee of the landlord's agent.[15]

It may be that cases of acceptance of rent fall into a specific category. In some mitigation of the exact time at which waiver of this kind may take place, it was held that rent payable into a bank account was only impliedly accepted where the landlord became aware, from bank statements, that his account had been credited with payments: he did not waive a known breach unless, within a reasonable time of his awareness, he failed to repay the money.[16] It has been said that cases other than payment or acceptance of rent, the court is free to look objectively at all the circumstances of the case, in order to decide whether a landlord's act amounts to waiver.[17] Hence, if, having become aware of circumstances which might entitle him to forfeit the lease, the landlord reasonably accepts an explanation from the tenant, his continued acceptance of rent will not prevent him from bringing a forfeiture based on the circumstances in question, if the tenant's explanation is in fact false.[18]

Any actual waiver by a lessor is limited by s 148(1) of the Law of Property Act 1925, unless a contrary intention appears, to any breach 'to which such waiver specially relates' and is not to 'operate as a general waiver of the benefit of any such covenant or condition'.

This provision does little more than to affirm the common law, since the effect of waiver in a given case depends on the type of covenant broken. In the case of rent, a fresh cause of action arises each time an instalment falls due and seemingly not before then.[19] In the case of negative covenants, such as against assignments or under-lettings, a waiver of a given breach is final in relation thereto; but not in relation to any later breach, which gives rise to a separate

---

10 By contrast, a landlord who issued a summons requiring access to certain flats once he knew of breaches of covenant waived the right to forfeit the leases: *Cornillie v Saha* (1996) 72 P & CR 147, CA.

11 *Expert Clothing Service and Sales Ltd v Hillgate House Ltd* [1986] Ch 340, [1985] 2 All ER 998, CA.

12 *Church Comrs for England v Nodjoumi* (1985) 51 P & CR 155.

13 *Bader Properties Ltd v Linley Property Investments Ltd* (1967) 19 P & CR 620 at 641.

14 *Re National Jazz Centre Ltd* [1988] 2 EGLR 57.

15 *Central Estates (Belgravia) Ltd v Woolgar (No 2)*, supra. Since the breach was once and for all, no further cause of action arose in relation to it.

16 *John Lewis Properties plc v Viscount Chelsea* [1993] 2 EGLR 77.

17 *Expert Clothing Service and Sales Ltd v Hillgate House Ltd*, CA, supra.

18 *Chrisdell Ltd v Johnson* [1987] 2 EGLR 123, CA.

19 See *Re A Debtor No 13A-10-1995* [1995] 1 WLR 1127.

cause of action.[20] Where there is a breach of a continuing covenant, such as to repair or as to user, a continuing breach after a waiver gives rise to a fresh cause of action.[1] The question as to at what, if any, point in time, a waiver comes to an end and a fresh cause of action arises, is one of fact.[2] Where a tenant was in breach of covenant to repair, and, following a s 146(1) notice, the breach was waived, but the disrepair continued, no further statutory notice was required since the condition of the premises had not changed.[3]

Where the tenant is a statutory tenant under the Rent Act 1977, the doctrine of implied waiver is less strictly applied. A demand or acceptance of rent, with knowledge of a breach, is not necessarily waiver, because a statutory tenant is entitled to retain possession unless and until his tenancy is determined by the court.[4] Thus the landlord may have no choice but to accept rent. Whether a demand or acceptance of rent then constitutes waiver is a question of fact for the county court judge.[5]

2   RESTRICTIONS ON AND RELIEF AGAINST FORFEITURE

While equity was prepared to grant relief from forfeiture for non-payment of rent, only in very limited circumstances could the courts grant relief in other cases.[6] The present-day restrictions on forfeiture and also the general power to grant relief against forfeiture are contained in s 146 of the Law of Property Act 1925, applying to all covenants other than that to pay rent. The policy of this provision may be said to be as follows.

(a) to give the tenant warning of a breach of covenant;
(b) to enable the tenant to have a reasonable opportunity to remedy the breach, where remediable;
(c) to enable the court, at its discretion, which is very wide, to relieve the tenant from forfeiture;
(d) to give sub-lessees and mortgagees special protection against loss of their respective interests where the lease is forfeited.

3   LAW OF PROPERTY ACT 1925, s 146

General

Section 146 of the 1925 Act restricts a landlord's right of re-entry or forfeiture in various ways. Generally, compliance with s 146(1) is an essential preliminary to forfeiture.

Section 146, in principle, applies to any lease which contains a right of re-entry or forfeiture under a proviso or stipulation for breach of any covenant or

---

20 Contra, *Chelsea Estates Ltd v Kadri* (1970) 214 Estates Gazette 1356 (special facts).
 1 *Penton v Barnett* [1898] 1 QB 276, CA. No new statutory notice is required in such cases. See also *Farimani v Gates* (1984) 128 Sol Jo 615, CA.
 2 See *Cooper v Henderson* [1982] 2 EGLR 42, CA.
 3 *Greenwich London Borough Council v Discreet Selling Estates Ltd* [1990] 2 EGLR 65, CA.
 4 *Trustees of Henry Smith's Charity v Willson* [1983] QB 316, [1983] 1 All ER 73, CA.
 5 *Oak Property Co Ltd v Chapman* [1947] KB 886, [1947] 2 All ER 1, CA.
 6 See eg *Hill v Barclay* (1811) 18 Ves 56.

condition.[7] The right of re-entry or forfeiture is rendered unenforceable by action or otherwise unless and until the landlord serves a s 146(1) notice on the tenant. The contents of this notice are discussed below. By s 146(12), any express stipulation to the contrary in the lease is overridden.[8]

Total exclusions of s 146

Section 146 does not apply to forfeiture for non-payment of rent (s 146(11)), though sub-lessees and mortgagees have the right to request a vesting order under s 146(4) where a lease is forfeited for non-payment of rent, as well as in the case of breaches of other covenants and conditions.

Section 146 does not apply, by s 146(9), to a condition for forfeiture on the bankruptcy of the lessee, nor on taking in execution of the lessee's interest if contained in a lease of:

(a) agricultural or pastoral land;
(b) mines or minerals;
(c) a house used or intended to be used as a public-house or beershop;
(d) a house let as a dwelling-house, with the use of any furniture, books, works of art, or other chattels not being in the nature of fixtures;
(e) any property with respect to which the personal qualifications of the tenant are of importance for the preservation of the value or character of the property, or on the ground of the neighbourhood to the lessor, or to any person holding under him.[9]

Section 146 is also excluded, by s 146(8), in two further specific cases:

(i) where there was a breach of a covenant against assignment, sub-letting or parting with possession of the demised premises before the commencement of the 1925 Act;
(ii) in the case of a mining lease, to a covenant or condition allowing the lessor to have access to or inspect books, accounts, records, weighing machines or other things, or to enter or inspect the mine or its workings.

It appears that the second exception is justified by the fact that the rent payable under a mining tenancy is usually dependent on the amount of minerals produced by a mine.[10]

Partial exception in other cases of bankruptcy

Section 146 is partially excluded, where s 146(9) does not apply, by s 146(10), whose net effect is this. Section 146 applies for one year from the date of the

---

7 This includes voluntary and involuntary acts by the lessee, and a lessee must be served with a s 146(1) notice if his surety is bankrupt: *Halliard Property Co Ltd v Jack Segal Ltd* [1978] 1 All ER 1219, [1978] 1 WLR 377. Semble, s 146 applies to breach of a implied condition or covenant: *British Telecommunications plc v Department of the Environment* (29 October 1996, Unreported), (see Commercial Leases, February 1997).
8 By SI 1991/724, art 2, the county court has jurisdiction under ss 146 and 147 of the 1925 Act whatever the amount involved or the value of any assets connected with the proceedings.
9 Cf *Earl Bathurst v Fine* [1974] 2 All ER 1160, [1974] 1 WLR 905, CA where relief against forfeiture was refused because the tenant had shown himself to be personally unsuitable.
10 Law Com No 142 (1985), Forfeiture of Tenancies, para 2.51.

tenant's bankruptcy or the taking in execution of his lease. If the tenant's interest is sold during the year referred to, the protection of s 146 continues without time limit for the new tenant. If the tenant's interest is not sold within the year, the protection of s 146 ceases completely.[11]

We now deal with the notice requirements, relief against forfeiture, recovery of costs and vesting orders for sub-tenants and mortgagees. The rules governing forfeiture for non-payment of rent, which are quite separate from the present rules, are dealt with in chapter 8.

4   RESTRICTIONS ON ENFORCEMENT OF RIGHT OF RE-ENTRY: S 146(1)

No right of re-entry or forfeiture for breach of any covenant or condition in the lease is enforceable by action or otherwise, unless and until the landlord has served on the tenant a notice complying with s 146(1) of the 1925 Act. Section 146(1) provides that the notice must:

(a) specify the particular breach complained of;
(b) if the breach is capable of remedy, require the tenant to remedy the breach (a reasonable time must be allowed for a remedy); and
(c) in any case, it must require the tenant to make compensation in money for the breach.

A letter containing the requisite points will suffice. A s 146(1) notice is required whether re-entry is by service of a writ or peaceable, due to the words 'or otherwise' in s 146(1).[12] A s 146(1) notice operates as a necessary preliminary to actual forfeiture.[13]

Any attempt to avoid s 146(1) will be invalidated by the courts, who are astute to detect disguised forfeiture clauses, and are jealous to safeguard their jurisdiction to grant relief to the tenant.[14] For example, a term under which, in the event of failure to comply with a covenant in the lease, the landlord could fill in the date on an undated deed of surrender previously executed, did not avoid the need to serve a s 146 notice prior to forfeiture proceedings.[15] Similarly, a clause enabling the landlord to terminate the lease for breaches of covenant by a three months' notice served on the tenant did not preclude the court from exercising its jurisdiction to grant relief against forfeiture.[16] Not every term entitling the landlord to terminate a tenancy is a disguised forfeiture: for example a provision in a weekly tenancy agreement enabling either party to terminate it on four weeks' notice was not treated as a disguised forfeiture clause: however, the tenancy was a weekly tenancy terminable on a minimum

---

11 The time-limit is strictly enforced as far as the tenant's interest is concerned, but it has no effect on any right of a mortgagee to apply for a s 146(4) order outside the one-year period: *Official Custodian for Charities v Parway Estates Developments Ltd* [1985] Ch 151, [1984] 3 All ER 679, CA.
12 *Re Riggs, ex p Lovell* [1901] 2 KB 16; *Billson v Residential Apartments Ltd*, supra.
13 *Church Comrs for England v Nodjoumi* (1985) 51 P & CR 155.
14 See *Meadows v Clerical, Medical and General Life Assurance Society* [1981] Ch 70, [1980] 1 All ER 454 (relief applications are part of the process of forfeiture).
15 *Plymouth Corpn v Harvey* [1971] 1 All ER 623, [1971] 1 WLR 549.
16 *Richard Clarke & Co Ltd v Widnall* [1976] 3 All ER 301, [1976] 1 WLR 845, CA.

four weeks' notice and no considerations of policy required the court to go behind the term.[17]

A s 146(1) notice must be served on the lessee in possession at the time of service;[18] this means (s 146(5)) an original or derivative under-lessee, where relevant; and all joint lessees, if any, must be served with a notice; as must any assignee, even where the assignment was in breach of covenant.[19] If the landlord serves a s 146(1) notice on the tenant which might be invalid, and serves a further notice, he is not obliged to await the determination of the validity of the first notice before serving the second.[20]

When preparing a s 146(1) notice, the landlord has two predictions to make. If he gets either wrong, any proceedings based on his notice will fail. First, he must decide whether the breach in question (or, if there is more than one, then *each* breach in question) is capable of remedy. As a rule of thumb, positive covenants, such as to repair, are capable of remedy and negative covenants are incapable of remedy. There is no absolute rule and in marginal cases difficult questions of construction arise, there being no guarantee that the landlord will be correct in law. Where a breach is capable of remedy and the landlord's notice fails to require one, it will be invalid.[1] Secondly, a reasonable time must be allowed from service of the notice for all breaches to be remedied; if the landlord issues a writ too soon then proceedings will fail.[2] The time for remedy must be allowed, even if it is an empty formality, as where it is plain that the tenant has no intention of doing anything. But a s 146(1) notice is not invalid merely because it omits to require the tenant to pay the landlord compensation, as the latter need not touch the former's money if he does not wish to.[3]

Particular breach

In relation to certain covenants (eg against sub-letting) it is necessary for the landlord to indicate no more than the particular covenant which has been broken. Breaches of other covenants, on the other hand, should be specified in greater detail. In relation to breaches of repairing covenants especially is it necessary to identify the respects in which the covenant has been broken, as by a dilapidations schedule prepared by the landlord's surveyor.[4] It was held that a notice which mentioned repairs needed under various headings, such as 'roofs', was sufficiently informative in relation to a covenant to repair in a lease

17 *Clays Lane Housing Co-operative Ltd v Patrick* (1984) 49 P & CR 72, CA.
18 *Kanda v Church Comrs for England* [1958] 1 QB 332, [1957] 2 All ER 815, CA.
19 *Old Grovebury Manor Farm Ltd v W Seymour Plant Sales and Hire Ltd (No 2)* [1979] 3 All ER 504, [1979] 1 WLR 1397, CA.
20 *Fuller v Judy Properties Ltd* [1992] 1 EGLR 75, CA. The tenant's relief application succeeded and it was granted a reversionary lease, the premises having been re-let.
 1 As in *Expert Clothing Service and Sales Ltd v Hillgate House Ltd* [1986] Ch 340, [1985] 2 All ER 998, CA (failure to reconstruct premises by certain date held capable of remedy and landlord's notice which failed to require remedy held bad).
 2 As in *Horsey Estate Ltd v Steiger* [1899] 2 QB 79, CA (two days' time held insufficient).
 3 *Rugby School (Governors) v Tannahill* [1935] 1 KB 87, CA.
 4 Owing to the fact that under Law of Property Act 1925, s 146(3), the costs of preparation of such a schedule may only be recovered if the lessee obtains relief, some leases expressly enable the landlord to recover such costs whether or not relief is granted.

of a row of six houses, without indicating which house or houses were referred to.[5] After all, the means by which a remedy should be carried out is for the tenant to decide on.[6]

Special statutory rules now exist in relation to service charges whose amount is disputed by the tenant of premises let as a dwelling or where a court or arbitral tribunal has to determine the amount of a service charge in relation to such premises. The restrictions are seemingly aimed at landlords who buy up the reversions of leasehold flats and then claim forfeiture for servive charges arrears – perhaps where large outstanding repairs are said to be needed. However, the new legislation cuts across the fact that separate rules exist for forfeiture for non-payment of rent and for breaches of other covenants. This may render the application of the new provisions less than easy, as covenants to pay service charges are not clearly on either side of this dividing line. On the one hand, some leases expressly reserve service charges as rent; some, however, do not. Yet it has been said that in the context of relief against forfeiture there is no difference between a covenant to pay rent and a covenant to pay service charges.[7] But the statutory references to s 146(2) of the Law of Property Act 1925 do not seem relevant where a landlord claims rent and service charges reserved as rent.

The provisions may thus be set out. A landlord cannot enforce a right of re-entry or forfeiture where there is such a dispute or pending determination as to the amount of a service charge. He may only serve a writ claiming forfeiture after 14 days running from the date of decision have elapsed.[8] Second, while the landlord is not prevented by a dispute with the tenant or a pending determination from serving a s 146(1) notice on the tenant, there are new special formal requirements of any s 146(1) notice. If these are not complied with, then so far as the claim relates to service charges of premises let as a dwelling, the notice is ineffective.[9] The notice must insert prescribed information as to the effect of the special rule just mentioned. The information must be in characters not less conscicious than those used in the s 146(1) notice to indicate that the tenancy may be forfeited or to specify the breach of covenant to pay service charges, whichever is the more conspicuous.[10]

If the breach is capable of remedy

The general policy behind s 146 is to give time to the lessee to remedy the breach. Breaches of a covenant against assignment or underletting are incapable of remedy[11] as are those of a covenant against illegal use of the premises.[12] To

---

5 *Fox v Jolly* [1916] 1 AC 1, HL.
6 *John Lewis Properties plc v Viscount Chelsea* [1993] 2 EGLR 77, 83–84.
7 *Khar v Delbounty Ltd* [1996] EGCS 183, CA.
8 Housing Act 1996, s 81(1) and (2). This restriction does not apply to business tenancies nor to tenancies of agricultural holdings or farm business tenancies (s 81(4)).
9 Housing Act 1996, s 82(1)–(2). In force from 24 September 1996 (s 232(2)).
10 Housing Act 1996, s 82(4).
11 *Scala House and District Property Co Ltd v Forbes* [1974] QB 575, [1973] 3 All ER 308, CA.
12 *Hoffman v Fineberg* [1949] Ch 245, [1948] 1 All ER 592; *Van Haarlam v Kasner* [1992] 2 EGLR 59.

that extent there is a difference between breaches of positive and negative covenants, and where a breach is incapable of remedy, a s 146(1) notice need not require a remedy.[13]

A breach of a covenant not to cause or permit immoral use of the premises is probably still incapable of remedy by mere cessation of the use, if the breach has cast a stigma on the premises, which is only removable by the eviction of the offending tenant.[14] The concept of a breach being incapable of remedy seems unnecessary since if the ground of complaint is irremediable damage to the landlord's interests, such considerations might properly go to the question of relief against forfeiture, where the court has a discretion, rather than to technical matters relating to the drafting of s 146(1) notices.

It now appears that the courts are reluctant to discriminate between breaches of positive and negative covenants. If compliance by the tenant with a remedy required by a s 146(1) notice, combined with payment of any compensation, puts right the harm suffered by the landlord then, save in the specific cases mentioned, a breach of a negative covenant may be remedied. It makes no difference that the precise status quo ante may not be capable of being restored. Thus, a s 146(1) notice which complained that the tenant had broken a covenant not to put up signs or to alter the property without consent was invalid, as it failed to require a remedy from the tenant – which would have been simple enough in that case, seeing that the offending sign could have been removed.[15]

Where a lessee was personally innocent, and, at the date of service of the s 146(1) notice, lacked any knowledge of the breach or breaches, and had not deliberately shut his eyes thereto, a prompt cesser of the breach, procured by his removal of offending sub-lessees, was in any case held to amount to a remedy on the facts and a s 146(1) notice which failed to require a remedy was held bad.[16]

Requirement to remedy the breach

Since most breaches of covenant, positive or negative, are capable of being remedied by the tenant, so enabling him to avert dispossession, if the landlord, after service of his s 146(1) notice, fails to allow the tenant a reasonable time to elapse in which to remedy the breach, any action based on his notice will fail. In the case of such few breaches of covenant as are as a matter of law incapable of remedy, no reasonable time at all need be allowed to elapse for any remedy and it was held in order for a writ to follow service of a s 146(1) notice in 14 days.[17]

13 *Rugby School (Governors) v Tannahill* [1935] 1 KB 87, CA.
14 *Rugby School (Governors) v Tannahill* [1935] 1 KB 87, CA (use as a brothel); *Dunraven Securities Ltd v Holloway* [1982] 2 EGLR 47, CA; *British Petroleum Pension Trust Ltd v Behrendt* [1985] 2 EGLR 97, CA.
15 *Savva v Houssein* [1996] 47 EG 138, CA.
16 *Glass v Kencakes Ltd* [1966] 1 QB 611, [1964] 3 All ER 807.
17 *Scala House and District Property Co Ltd v Forbes* [1974] QB 575, [1973] 3 All ER 308, CA (relief granted on facts).

There is no hard and fast rule as to what exactly does amount to a reasonable time for the purpose of remediable breaches, but what is quite clear is that if there are a number of remediable breaches alleged in the notice, a reasonable time, sufficient to enable each breach to be remedied, must be allowed.[18]

Service of a notice

The service of a s 146 notice is governed by the provisions of s 196 of the Act. In the case of repairs, by virtue of s 18(2) of the Landlord and Tenant Act 1927, however, delivery alone is not sufficient. In effect, that sub-section modifies s 146(1) to the extent that a right of re-entry is not enforceable unless the lessor proves that the fact that notice has been served on the tenant was known either to the tenant or certain other persons and that a reasonable time for executing the repairs has elapsed since the tenant (or other person) learned of the service of the notice. Further, if the notice is sent by registered post or recorded delivery to a person at his last known place of abode in the United Kingdom, he will be deemed to have had knowledge of the fact that the notice had been served as from the date on which the letter would have been delivered in the ordinary course of post, unless he shows proof to the contrary.

5   RELIEF AGAINST FORFEITURE

Jurisdiction to grant relief

By s 146(2) of the 1925 Act: 'where a lessor is proceeding, by action or otherwise to enforce a right of re-entry or forfeiture, the lessee may, in the lessor's action, if any, or in an action brought by himself, apply to the court for relief'. The sub-section proceeds: 'the court may grant or refuse relief, as the court, having regard to the proceedings and conduct of the parties under the foregoing provisions of this section, and to all other circumstances, thinks fit'. Should the court grant relief, s 146(2) provides that it may do so on 'such terms, if any, as to costs, expenses, damages, compensation, penalty, or otherwise, including the granting of an injunction to restrain any like breach in the future, as the court, in the circumstances of each case, thinks fit'.

The borderline between the scope of the present jurisdiction and that arising from equity of the High Court to grant relief in the case of rent default is not always easy to define, as shown by a case in which the lease did not reserve maintenance payments as rent, so that in the result the court had to consider relief under the statutory jurisdiction, whereas had the service charges been reserved as rent, the court's jurisdiction to grant relief would have presumably been based on equity.[19]

---

18   *Hopley v Tarvin Parish Council* (1910) 74 JP 209. In *Bhojwani v Kingsley Investment Trust Ltd* [1992] 2 EGLR 70, three months was said to be adequate in the case of repairs, but it was also admitted that there were no hard and fast rules. A two-month period was held not to be sufficient on the facts.
19   *Khar v Delbounty Ltd* [1996] EGCS 183, CA.

The courts are anxious not to allow the statutory jurisdiction to grant relief to be whittled down on technical grounds. So, for example, the power to grant relief arises as from the service of a s 146(1) notice on the lessee, who may thereafter apply for relief.[20] It has now been held that, despite the fact that he is not, under common law rules, in privity of estate with the lessor, an equitable assignee of an underlease may apply under s 146(2) of the 1925 Act for relief against forfeiture.[1] Similarly, the statutory jurisdiction is not excluded by the fact that the landlord chooses to forfeit the lease by the uncivilised method of peaceable re-entry, rather than by proceeding by writ against the lessee, as 'proceeding' in s 146(2) includes out of court proceedings.[2] The court has, however, no power to grant relief once the landlord has obtained an order for possession forfeiting the lease and the order has been lawfully enforced against the tenant.[3]

Indeed, not only may a head tenant, but also, having regard to the width of the expression 'lessee' in s 146(5) of the 1925 Act,[4] a person holding a lesser estate by way of underlease and a mortgagee by sub-demise may both apply for relief under s 146(2). It makes no difference that neither party is, at common law, any more than is an equitable assignee of a lease referred to above, in privity of estate with the head landlord.[5] There may be advantages to mortgagees in applying for the court to exercise its discretion under s 146(2) rather than s 146(4), since the effect of relief is to fully re-instate the lease as if it had been never forfeited, whereas the grant of relief under s 146(4) is effective only from the date of the court's order. Thus, while a landlord demanded mesne profits from a mortgagee from the date of issue of the writ (and of notional forfeiture) to that of the date of the order, the court, since the lease was granted at a premium, refused to make any such order against a mortgagee under a s 146(2) relief application.[6]

Relief is based on the notion that, if the tenant is able and willing to take effective steps within a time-limit specified in the court's order, to remedy the breach or breaches in question, forfeiture should not, ordinarily, be ordered: a forfeiture clause is regarded as a security for the compliance by the tenant with his covenants.[7] In many cases, therefore, whether the court will grant relief or

---

20 *Pakwood Transport Ltd v 15 Beauchamp Place* (1977) 36 P & CR 112, CA.
1 *High Street Investments Ltd v Bellshore Property Investments Ltd* [1996] 35 EG 87, CA.
2 *Billson v Residential Apartments Ltd* [1992] 1 AC 494, [1992] 1 All ER 141, HL.
3 *Quilter v Mapleson* (1882) 2 QBD 672; *Rogers v Rice* [1892] 2 Ch 170, as explained in the *Billson* case, supra.
4 As including 'an original or derivative underlessee' and, by analogy with s 146(4), a mortgagee by underlease or charge; as pointed out in *Escalus Properties Ltd v Robinson*, infra, this definition is wider than the definition of 'lessee' in s 14(3) of the Conveyancing Act 1881, which first conferred the statutory jurisdiction to grant relief.
5 *Escalus Properties Ltd v Robinson* [1996] QB 231, [1995] 4 All ER 852. This was the first time the point had been decided but the Court of Appeal held that s 146(5) had been drafted so as to overrule on that point *Nind v Nineteenth Century Building Society* [1894] 2 QB 226, holding the contrary; their interpretation of s 146(5) is shared by Wolstenholme & Cherry, Vol 1, p 267.
6 *Escalus Properties Ltd v Robinson* supra.
7 *Hyman v Rose* [1912] AC 623, HL; *Shiloh Spinners Ltd v Harding* [1973] AC 691, [1973] 1 All ER 90, HL.

not will depend on whether the tenant is prepared to accept or comply with the terms that the court imposes as a condition of the giving of relief: the court cannot force the tenant to accept relief on its terms.[8] Whether or not it grants relief to the tenant against forfeiture of his lease may also depend on the respective merits of the tenant and any sub-tenants involved in the proceedings.[9] The court has jurisdiction to grant relief in respect of part of the premises if physically separated from the remainder and a separately re-lettable unit.[10]

Relief in particular cases

If a covenant against immoral user is deliberately broken, generally, unless the breach is isolated, no relief will be granted.[11] Indeed, a deliberate breach of any covenant, especially a negative covenant, will prejudice the tenant's chances of relief.[12] Thus, where lessees by assignment, motivated by the wish to make a rapid profit out of short-term lettings of the altered premises, carried out flagrant breaches of a covenant against alterations, which work was also in breach of planning enforcement notices, all relief was refused despite the fact that the landlord's own recourse to a 'dawn raid' (and so to peaceable re-entry) might otherwise have prevented them from resisting the grant of relief.[13] In another case, the county court was held entitled to refuse relief to an applicant where it was not sure that he would comply immediately with a condition to put up a surgery which he had so far failed to do in breach of covenant.[14] The result of these cases well illustrates the way in which no one factor is relevant to relief applications: the attitudes of the parties as well as objective breaches may be relevant.

Nevertheless, weight may properly be attached to the financial losses which the tenant would suffer if refused relief, and it has been said that the wilfulness of a breach does not of itself preclude the court from granting relief.[15] This is especially so if no lasting damage will result from the breach to the lessor, provided that he can be adequately compensated, in money or in the terms of relief. Thus, where the tenant's sub-lessee and licensee permitted prostitution in their premises, which was contrary to covenant in the tenant's own lease, which required the use of the premises as a high-class restaurant or night club, relief was granted to the tenant, even though it was fixed with knowledge of the breach, because there was no lasting damage or stigma, as the offending occupiers had been removed, and if relief had been refused, the lessee, who held a valuable lease, would suffer a disproportionate financial loss.[16]

8 *Talbot v Blindell* [1908] 2 KB 114.
9 *Duke of Westminster v Swinton* [1948] 1 KB 524, [1948] 1 All ER 248.
10 *GMS Syndicate Ltd v Gary Elliott Ltd* [1982] Ch 1, [1981] 1 All ER 619.
11 *Borthwick-Norton v Romney Warwick Estates Ltd* [1950] 1 All ER 798, CA; *British Petroleum Pension Trust Ltd v Behrendt* [1985] 2 EGLR 97, CA.
12 *St Marylebone Property Co Ltd v Tesco Stores Ltd* [1988] 2 EGLR 40.
13 *Billson v Residential Apartments Ltd (No 2)* [1993] EGCS 155.
14 *Darlington Borough Council v Denmark Chemists Ltd* [1993] 1 EGLR 62, CA.
15 As in eg *Southern Depot Co Ltd v British Railways Board* [1990] 2 EGLR 39.
16 *Ropemaker Properties Ltd v Noonhaven Ltd* [1989] 2 EGLR 50.

Two technical limits on applicants for relief are worthy of note. In the case of joint tenants, all must apply for relief.[17] A person holding a possessory title to unregistered land cannot apply for relief.[18]

Effect of relief

If relief is granted, the effect is as if there had never been a forfeiture of the lease, which will be fully restored, so that any sub-tenant will be unaffected by the proceedings.[19] However, should possession be granted by the High Court, but the Court of Appeal reverses the forfeiture (say by ordering relief to be granted to the tenant), the clock is not totally put back, because any acts of the landlord under the order for possession, until its reversal, are considered lawful.[20] If the court imposes time-limits to comply with a condition of relief, it has an inherent jurisdiction to extend them.[1] If relief is not granted, and an order for possession is made, the lease will be treated as having been forfeited with effect from the service of the writ.

Failure to apply for relief

If the tenant fails to apply for relief under s 146(2), he cannot apply for relief in equity on any ground covered by statute, since the enactment of legislation has ousted any general inherent equity jurisdiction there might previously have been.[2] There appears, therefore, to be only a residual equitable jurisdiction in these circumstances to grant relief to the lessee applicable to cases of fraud, accident, surprise or mistake.[3] The position of under-lessees and mortgagees who do not avail themselves of s 146(4) of the 1925 Act is unclear and is discussed below. The scope and basis of the relieving jurisdiction under s 146(2) contrasts with the position with respect to non-payment of rent,[4] where the High Court's jurisdiction is based on equitable principles as modified by statute on points of detail (see chapter 8).

Costs

Under s 146(3) of the 1925 Act, the landlord is entitled to recover, as a debt due to him from the tenant, all reasonable costs he has properly incurred 'in the employment of a solicitor and surveyor or valuer, or otherwise', if the tenant is

17 *T M Fairclough & Sons Ltd v Berliner* [1931] 1 Ch 60. The Law Commission Report on Forfeiture, infra, recommended abolishing this rule: para 3.63.
18 *Tickner v Buzzacott* [1965] Ch 426 [1965] 1 All ER 131. Query whether this applies to registered titles in view of Land Registration Act 1925, s 75(1).
19 *Dendy v Evans* [1910] 1 KB 263; *Hynes v Twinsectra Ltd* [1995] 2 EGLR 69, CA.
20 *Hillgate House Ltd v Expert Clothing Service and Sales Ltd* [1987] 1 EGLR 65.
 1 *Chandless-Chandless v Nicholson* [1942] 2 KB 321, [1942] 2 All ER 315, CA.
 2 *Shiloh Spinners Ltd v Harding* [1973] AC 691, at 725, [1973] 1 All ER 90 at 102, HL; also *Official Custodian for Charities v Parway Estates Developments* [1985] Ch 151 at 155, CA; *Smith v Metropolitan City Properties Ltd* [1986] 1 EGLR 52.
 3 *Barrow v Isaacs & Son* [1891] 1 QB 417. In *Billson v Residential Apartments Ltd* supra, HL, Lord Templeman referred to this jurisdiction without specifically mentioning surprise but surprise was mentioned in *British Telecommunications plc v Department of the Environment* (29 October 1996, Unreported), (see Commercial Leases, February 1997).
 4 See also *Ladup Ltd v Williams and Glyn's Bank plc* [1985] 2 All ER 577, [1985] 1 WLR 851.

given relief, or if the breach is waived at the request of the tenant.[5] Consequently, if the tenant remedies the breach on notice and there are no court proceedings, the landlord is probably not entitled to any costs incurred, for example, in the preparation of his s 146 notice.[6] It may well be that the lease contains an express term allowing the landlord to recover these costs, whether arising in actual or contemplated proceedings.

6 PROTECTION OF SUB-LESSEES AND MORTGAGEES[7]

General principles

At common law, a sub-tenancy is destroyed automatically if the head tenancy is forfeited.[8] Section 146(4) of the 1925 Act enables any sub-lessee, and hence any legal mortgagee by demise or charge, of any part of the property to apply to the court for a vesting order, either in the forfeiture proceedings or a separate action. An order will, if granted, create a new tenancy and vest in the applicant the part of the property occupied by the sub-lessee for a term not exceeding the remaining term of the original sub-lease, the length of the term being, subject to that, at the court's discretion.

The conditions for the grant of a vesting order are at the court's discretion. Section 146(4) refers to the position immediately before forfeiture: if then a sub-lessee occupies the whole or part of the premises for business purposes, he will be entitled to a vesting order, not only in relation to the residue of his contractual term but also in respect of its continuation by Part II of the Landlord and Tenant Act 1954, after expiry of the sub-term at common law, of appropriate length.[9] The sub-section applies where the landlord is *proceeding* to enforce, by action or otherwise, a right of re-entry or forfeiture under *any* covenant, proviso, etc, in the lease, or, exceptionally within s 146 of the 1925 Act, *for non-payment of rent*, thus conferring a parallel statutory jurisdiction to that of equity.

A mortgagee by way of legal charge[10] is entitled to an order, as is a guarantor who has a right to call for a legal charge or mortgage.[11] If the words 'is proceeding' in s 146(4) bear the same meaning as in s 146(2), the fact that the landlord proceeds to forfeit by peaceable re-entry rather than by writ should not exclude the statutory jurisdiction to grant relief to under-lessees and mortgagees.[12]

---

5 If the tenant claims the Leasehold Property (Repairs) Act 1938, the landlord requires the leave of the court to recover costs under s 149(3) (1938 Act, s 2); but recovery under an express term of the lease would be outside this, as a contract debt.

6 *Nind v Nineteenth Century Building Society* [1894] 2 QB 226, which would appear not to have been overruled in *Escalus Properties Ltd v Robinson*, supra, on this point.

7 See generally S Tromans [1986] Conv 187.

8 *Viscount Chelsea v Hutchinson* [1994] 2 EGLR 61, CA.

9 *Cadogan v Dimovic* [1984] 2 All ER 168, [1984] 1 WLR 609, CA.

10 *Grand Junction Co Ltd v Bates* [1954] 2 QB 160, [1954] 2 All ER 385. An order will not *ipso facto* re-instate sub-lessees: *Hammersmith and Fulham London Borough v Top Shop Centres Ltd* [1990] Ch 237, [1989] 2 All ER 655.

11 *Re Good's Lease* [1954] 1 All ER 275, [1954] 1 WLR 309.

12 In *Billson v Residential Apartments Ltd* supra, this issue was not expressly dealt with. In *Gray v Bonsall* [1904] 1 KB 601, 607, however, Conveyancing and Law of Real Property Act 1892, s 4 (the predecessor to s 146(4)) was treated as a separate relieving provision. If so, the view in the text would not necessarily apply.

Discretion as to relief

In granting an order, on the application of a sub-lessee or mortgagee, the court has a discretion whether to grant relief,[13] and relief may be granted to an underlessee or mortgagee where there is no jurisdiction to grant it to a lessee, as where the latter is bankrupt.[14] The terms of relief are at the discretion of the court.[15] As a general rule, relief will be granted provided the applicant pays off all rent arrears owing to date, undertakes to comply with the covenants in the head lease, pays off the landlord's costs, and remedies any outstanding breaches of covenant, in relation to the premises or part to which the application relates.[16] The idea is to put the landlord back into the same position as he was in before the forfeiture took place.[17] If the circumstances warrant it, relief will be refused at discretion. For example, relief was refused where rent had not been paid to the head landlord for 22 years and it had been assumed that the sub-leases had gone.[18] The same result followed where a sub-lessee held only a monthly tenancy of a basement, which was badly out of repair: he refused to undertake admittedly onerous repairing obligations in relation thereto, which the head lease had cast on the lessee: if relief had been granted in these circumstances, the landlords would have had less extensive rights regarding repairs than originally.[19]

If the court makes an order under s 146(4), its effect, in contrast to s 146(2), is not retroactive. The forfeited interest is not revived. Any conditions attached to a vesting order are conditions precedent to actual vesting: hence, any rights accrued in the landlords prior to an order, such as to rent in the twilight period from service of the writ down to the date of a s 146(4) order, are unaffected by the order.[20] For this reason, as indicated above, it may be advantageous for a legal mortgagee to apply for relief under s 146(2). If, however, a receiver was in possession of the tenant's interest during the twilight period between notional and actual forfeiture, he is entitled to rents for that period to the exclusion of the landlord.[1]

Defects of s 146(4)

Arguably, section 146(4) suffers from certain defects, for example:

(a) it does not enable the court, for reasons explained earlier, to preserve existing tenancies, nor indeed may the landlord elect to do so. The effect of

---

13 See eg *Matthews v Smallwood* [1910] 1 Ch 777.
14 *Wardens of Cholmeley School, Highgate v Sewell* [1894] 2 QB 906.
15 *Ewart v Fryer* [1901] 1 Ch 499.
16 *Belgravia Insurance Co Ltd v Meah* [1964] 1 QB 436, [1963] 3 All ER 828, CA; *Official Custodian for Charities v Mackey (No 2)* [1985] 2 All ER 1016, [1985] 1 WLR 1308; *Grangeside Properties Ltd v Collingwoods Securities Ltd* [1964] 1 WLR 139, CA.
17 *Chatham Empire Theatre (1955) Ltd v Ultrans* [1961] 2 All ER 381, [1961] 1 WLR 817.
18 *Public Trustee v Westbrook* [1965] 3 All ER 398, [1965] 1 WLR 1160, CA.
19 *Hill v Griffin* [1987] 1 EGLR 81, CA. The applicant was not prepared to undertake onerous liabilities for repairs on a periodic tenancy, which was all the court could grant him.
20 *Official Custodian for Charities v Mackey* [1985] Ch 168, [1984] 3 All ER 689.
 1 *Official Custodian for Charities v Mackay (No 2)* [1985] 2 All ER 1016, [1985] 1 WLR 1308.

relief under s 146(4) is to create a new tenancy – as is shown by the fact that if the successful applicant is a mortgagee, he holds a substituted security;[2]
(b) subject to special considerations applicable to business tenancies, the court can never grant to the applicant a new tenancy for a longer term than he had originally under his old sub-lease. As was seen, this may work harshly where the original sub-tenancy was merely periodic, or for a short fixed term;
(c) the sub-section contains no guidelines as to the rent payable under the new tenancy, but it has been held that the court has power to vary the rent;[3]
(d) after the landlord has regained actual possession following an order of court forfeiting the lease, no applications under s 146(4) may be entertained. A landlord is under a duty, both in High Court and county court proceedings, to indorse his writ with a statement giving the name and address of any under-lessee or mortgagee, known to him, and he must then send these persons a copy of the writ.[4] There may be sub-lessees and mortgagees unknown to the landlord – not a likely situation if the lease requires due notification of any sub-leases or mortgages to the landlord. These unknown persons, if such there be, may still not be notified of pending forfeiture proceedings, and the landlord is under no implied obligation to notify them.[5] In these exceptional circumstances it is possible that the court has an inherent jurisdiction in equity to accede to an application for relief even after it has ordered forfeiture.[6] As already mentioned, this inherent jurisdiction may still exist, although it is difficult to see how it could have survived the enactment of a statutory code, of which s 146(4) is part, so ruling out any co-existing equity jurisdiction.[7] According to the High Court, a mortgagee (or sub-lessee) may apply for an executed judgment for possession to be set aside, if he has grounds for relief, but that only rarely would the court accede to the application, and merely forgetting to respond to a landlord's notification of his writ claiming forfeiture was not a case for relief.[8]

7   REFORM

Reform of the present system governing forfeiture for all breaches of covenant has been proposed by the Law Commission.[9]

2   *Chelsea Estates Investment Trust Co Ltd v Marche* [1955] Ch 328 at 339.
3   *Ewart v Fryer* [1901] 1 Ch 499, CA (higher rent commanded due to fact that premises ceased, with forfeiture of head lease, to be a tied house).
4   RSC, Ord 6 and CCR, Ord 6, as amended by SI 1986/1187 and SI 1986/1189, from 1 October 1986.
5   *Egerton v Jones* [1939] 2 KB 702, [1939] 3 All ER 889, CA.
6   *Abbey National Building Society v Maybeech Ltd* [1985] Ch 190, [1984] 3 All ER 262. A sub-lessee may invoke equitable estoppel to save his interest: *Hammersmith and Fulham London Borough v Top Shop Centres Ltd*, supra.
7   See e g *Shiloh Spinners Ltd v Harding* [1973] AC 691, HL; also *Official Custodian for Charities v Parway Estates Developments* [1985] Ch 151 at 155, CA.
8   *Rexhaven Ltd v Nurse* [1995] EGCS 125.
9   Law Com No 142 (1985) Forfeiture of Tenancies; and see eg PF Smith [1986] Conv 165, Cherryman (1987) 84 LSG 1042; Adams (1991) 17 LSG 17; Luxton [1991] JBL 42. A special notice rule in cases involving repairs would, generally, be retained, though there would be modifications: paras 8.33 et seq.

(a) There should be brought into force, in place of the current systems, a new termination order scheme. It would apply to all breaches of tenants' covenants, whether non-payment of rent or all other breaches, and to insolvency events.

(b) Certain archaic doctrines, which operate either harshly or capriciously, would be abolished. These include the doctrine of re-entry and waiver. The latter doctrine would be replaced by a new rule that the landlord would lose his right to forfeit only if his conduct would lead a reasonable tenant (and the actual tenant) to believe that he would not seek a termination order. (It might be noted that the doctrine of waiver antedates the availability of statutory relief and is a less flexible instrument designed to attain that object.)

(c) Rent would be due down to the date the court terminated the lease – not, as at present, down to the date of notional re-entry and no further.

(d) The court would have power to grant either (i) an absolute termination order, reserved for very serious and irremediable cases, or (ii) a remedial termination order, which would operate to end the tenancy unless the tenant took specified remedial action.

(e) The power to save sub-leases and the interests of mortgagees would be retained and improved. For example, the landlord would be enabled to elect to retain some, or all, of any derivative interests in the premises.

The Law Commission's scheme also proposed granting tenants a right to terminate their tenancies on the ground of landlords' breaches of covenant.

The enactment of this reform package might in some ways be advantageous. For example, the doctrine of re-entry causes uncertainty as to the position of the parties after service of a writ claiming forfeiture. Waiver is technical, and operates irrespective of the merits of the case.

The landlord would, if the scheme were adopted, be spared the necessity of guessing accurately whether a given breach was remediable and also how much time to allow the tenant to remedy the breach before serving a writ. Moreover, the separation between the rules governing rent and breaches of all other covenants, and the different schemes for relief, in the former case, between the High and county courts, seem difficult to justify.

Perhaps so as to give an impetus to their now long-standing proposals, the Commission have published their Termination of Tenancies Bill.[10] The Bill deviates from the original proposals, as it does not seek to implement the proposed tenants' termination order scheme. Although there are many unimplemented Reports in the field of landlord and tenant,[11] the Commission evidently regard forfeiture as being in special need of rapid reform by legislation.

No doubt the law of forfiture is complex in places, but the seeming view of the Commission that the law is as a whole as unsatisfactory as it was thought to be in 1985 is open to some question. We have seen that the courts have recently been at pains to clarify some of the more difficult areas of the present

10 Law Com No 221, 1994; see Peet (1994) 26 EG 132 and Wilkinson [1994] Conv 177.
11 As noted in the Commission's *Sixth Programme of Law Reform*, Law Com No 234 (1995), p 30.

law. This is shown by the recent interventions of the House of Lords both with regard to peaceable re-entry and relief for breaches of covenant to repair and of the Court of Appeal in relation to relief generally and breaches incapable of remedy. In addition, the abandonment of the proposed tenants' termination order scheme seems regrettable. The Commission had admitted in their original report that not even the worst possible conduct by the landlord gave the tenant the right to end the tenancy.[12] That view in turn may have been partly overtaken by the subsequent development of fundamental breach. Still, the concept of a one-sided reform of remedies seems inconsistent with the principle that comparable remedies ought to be available to both parties to a lease.[13]

12 Law Com No 142 (1985), paras 17.2 and 17.4.
13 The Commission in the context of repairing obligations in their Report of 1996 (Law Com No 238, para 9.19) object to the refusal of equity to allow a landlord to claim specific performance on the ground that a tenant may do so.

Chapter 14

Landlord's rights on termination

I INTRODUCTION

On the termination of a lease or tenancy, the tenant must, at common law, deliver up to the landlord peaceably the possession of the whole of the demised premises, together with all erections, buildings, improvements and fixtures, save fixtures which he is entitled to remove, and all growing crops. The lease, or the custom of the country, may provide to the contrary in relation to all or any of these matters.[1]

Moreover, at common law, if the tenant fails to remove any sub-tenant before the termination of his tenancy, he is liable to the landlord for the costs incurred by the latter in recovering possession and for any damages he has to pay for breach of contract, if he agreed to re-let the premises to a third party. This is because possession means vacant possession.[2]

The common law rules are profoundly affected by statutory protection afforded to business, residential and agricultural tenants: see the first parts of chapters 12 and 13 for some general guidance and Parts D to G of this book for further details. The effect of these codes is to put off the right of the landlord to possession until the time when the court orders possession, or the tenancy is otherwise validly determined, in accordance with the statutory code concerned.

If there is a lawful sub-tenant in occupation under the Rent Act 1977, or a sub-tenant protected by Part II of the Landlord and Tenant Act 1954, the common law rule rendering the head tenant liable in damages to the landlord, where the sub-tenant remains in occupation, cannot apply. The head tenant is liable, however, if the landlord shows that the sub-tenancy was granted in breach of covenant: it is outside statutory protection, unless the landlord waived the breach.[3]

II REMEDIES ON TERMINATION

The landlord has remedies for the recovery of damages for breaches of covenant committed by the tenant, and for waste, which have been considered and for holding over.

1 For tenants' rights to remove emblements, see ch 32.
2 See *Henderson v Van Cooten* [1922] WN 340; *Bramley v Chesterton* (1857) 2 CBNS 592.
3 *Reynolds v Bannerman* [1922] 1 KB 719; *Watson v Saunders-Roe* [1947] KB 437, CA.

Remedies for breach of obligation

The landlord may bring an action for rent accruing before the termination of the tenancy. He may also bring an action for damages for waste, mesne profits, breach of covenant and for use and occupation, as appropriate. He may also distrain for arrears of rent due before the termination of the tenancy under ss 6 and 7 of the Landlord and Tenant Act 1709, within six calendar months after termination, provided the tenant is still in occupation.

Remedies for recovery of possession

1   The landlord may bring an action for possession in the county court, which, as from 1 July 1991, has unlimited jurisdiction to hear any action for the recovery of land.[4]
2   Thanks to the repeal of the statutes of forcible entry, the landlord may physically re-enter the premises without bringing an action for possession, at least where these are vacant, as by changing the locks, but the House of Lords has done what it can to discourage this self-help remedy (see chapter 13). It is, however, a criminal offence for him or any other person such as his agent to use or threaten violence for the purpose of securing entry to the premises, provided that (a) there is someone on the premises who is opposed to the entry and (b) the person using or threatening violence knows that this is the case.[5]

III   REMEDIES FOR HOLDING OVER

It is a question of fact whether a tenant holding over after a fixed-term is to be taken to be holding as a tenant from year to year by implication of law. If so, he will hold on such of the terms of his former tenancy as are consistent with a yearly tenancy. In practice, however, statutory rights of tenants to continue in occupation will generally make it impossible to imply the creation of a new tenancy. Moreover, on the proper termination of any statutory rights it will rarely be possible to establish the mutual consent necessary for the creation of a new tenancy. Where no new tenancy is created, but the tenant stays in possession after the proper determination of his tenancy, he may do so as a tenant at will (ie with the landlord's consent), or on sufferance (ie wrongfully, without the landlord's consent), or the landlord may elect to treat him as a trespasser. In any event, the landlord has appropriate remedies if the tenant fails to give the landlord vacant possession.

Action for use and occupation

Where a tenant has been in occupation by permission or sufferance of the landlord, in the absence of an express lease or agreement for a lease at a fixed

---

4   SI 1991/724.
5   Criminal Law Act 1977, s 6(1). The mere fact that the landlord may be entitled to possession is in itself no defence (see s 6(2)).

rent, the law will imply a promise by the tenant to pay a reasonable sum for use and occupation.[6] See further chapter 8.

Action for mesne profits

Whenever a landlord brings an action for possession he is entitled in the action to claim *mesne profits* which have or might have accrued from the date of the expiration or termination of the tenancy (eg re-entry) down to the time of judgment, and thereafter down to the day of delivery of possession, under s 214 of the Common Law Procedure Act 1852. In proceedings for forfeiture, this is the appropriate action for the recovery of compensation from the date of re-entry, ie the date of the service of the writ.[7] The action is an action for damages, which may, depending on the circumstances, be the market value of the premises. The rent payable immediately prior to the termination of the tenancy may be evidence of the value of the premises, but if their value is higher or lower, the rent must be ignored.[8] In the case of a regulated tenancy, the amount would not exceed the lawfully recoverable rent.[9] The principles applicable are further discussed in chapter 8.

The landlord may, alternatively, claim *mesne profits* in a subsequent action for trespass, or bring an action for double value or double rent.

Action for double value

Under s 1 of the Landlord and Tenant Act 1730, the landlord may bring an action for double the yearly value of the premises if a tenant holds over wilfully after the landlord has given notice under the Act before (or as soon as possible after) the expiry of the tenancy requiring the tenant to give up possession. The tenant must hold over wilfully and contumaciously,[10] and not by mistake or under a bona fide claim of right, such as statutory protection. If a tenant holds over and the landlord has not made a demand for possession in writing, the statutory penalty cannot be claimed from him, as the tenant is not acting wilfully.[11]

The section applies to both tenancies for a fixed-term and to periodic tenancies of not less than year to year, and to tenancies for life or lives; it does not apply to weekly, monthly or quarterly tenancies. In the case of a yearly tenancy, a valid notice to quit in writing is sufficient for the requirements as to prior notice.

The action is for double *value*, and not for double rent. It is a penalty which cannot be distrained for, and in respect of which there can be no relief in equity. The amount payable is at the rate of double the yearly value of the premises from

---

6 See *Churchward v Ford* (1857) 2 H & N 446.
7 *Elliott v Boynton* [1924] 1 Ch 236; *Associated Deliveries Ltd v Harrison* (1984) 50 P & CR 91, CA.
8 *Clifton Securities v Huntley* [1948] 2 All ER 283.
9 See *Rawlance v Croydon Corpn* [1952] 2 QB 803 at 813, CA.
10 See *French v Elliott* [1960] 1 WLR 40 at 51.
11 *Dun & Bradstreet Software Services (England) Ltd v Provident Mutual Life Association* [1996] EGCS 62 (and see *Commercial Leases*, July 1996).

the date of termination or the date of the written notice, whichever is the later, for as long as the land is detained. No previous action for possession is necessary though the two actions may be joined.

Action for double rent

The landlord may bring an action for double rent against a tenant who gives a valid notice to quit (whether or not in writing) and holds over, whether wilfully or not, after the notice has expired under s 18 of the Distress for Rent Act 1737. Double rent is recoverable not withstanding that the tenancy is a protected tenancy.[12] In contrast to the position under the 1730 Act, double rent is recoverable no matter that no notice has been given by the landlord. The acceptance of a single rent may amount to waiver of the right to double rent.[13] It is recoverable in the same manner (ie by action or distress), and at the same time as rent would have been payable, up to the time that the tenant quits.

12   *Flannagan v Shaw* [1920] 3 KB 96, CA.
13   *Dun & Bradstreet Software Services (England) Ltd* v *Provident Mutual Life Association*, supra.

Chapter 15

Tenant's rights to fixtures

I INTRODUCTION

A fixture is a chattel which is attached to land in such a way that it becomes part of the land, even though in its original state, it could have been removed without damaging the land. The chattel, which once had a separate identity of its own, once it becomes a fixture, loses its original moveable character, and becomes part of the realty. Since 'land' is defined so as to include buildings and parts of buildings,[1] buildings cannot be fixtures. Thus a fixture is something which is affixed to the freehold as an accessory to the land or building, but does not, for example, include things which were part of a house in the course of its construction.[2] Thus, where a tenant carries out improvements to a building by installing new doors or windows, these are classified as 'landlords' fixtures' which the tenant will have to leave on quitting the premises.[3] So, heavy plate-glass windows were held to be part of the structure of a building,[4] and, by contrast, fluorescent light fittings in glass boxes fitted securely into ceiling plaster, and fitted carpets, were fixtures, being both accessories to and permanently attached to the premises.[5] Trees, shrubs, and things growing naturally on the land, cannot be fixtures.

Once a chattel becomes a fixture by reason of its attachment or annexation to the land, and so becomes part of the land, at common law, the tenant will have to leave it on the land at the expiration of the lease unless it is a trade fixture, a domestic and ornamental fixture or an agricultural fixture, in which case he has a right to remove the fixture.

II ANNEXATION TESTS

The common law utilises two tests in order to decide whether a chattel has become a fixture: the degree of annexation and the object of annexation. Although it appears that the second test is more likely to be decisive than the

---

1 Law of Property Act 1925 s 205(1)(ix).
2 *Boswell v Crucible Steel Co* [1925] 1 KB 119, CA.
3 *New Zealand Government Corpn v HM & S Ltd* [1982] 1 All ER 624 at 627, CA.
4 *Boswell v Crucible Steel Co*, supra.
5 *Young v Dalgety plc* [1987] 1 EGLR 116, CA; in *TSB Bank v Botham*, infra, fitted carpets were held incapable of being fixtures, as not being permanent.

first,[6] it cannot be said with certainty which test will apply to a particular case, especially as the first is an ancient common law test whereas the second was apparently designed to protect a tenant for life under a settlement against valuable chattels owned by him from passing with the land as fixtures where they were but lightly attached thereto.[7]

Degree of annexation

If the article is substantially attached to the land or fastened to it in such a way that its removal would injure the land, then it is deemed to be a fixture, but if the chattel merely rests on the land under its own weight, it remains a chattel. Any attachment of the chattel, however slight, will deem the article to be a fixture – unless it is shown by the person who attached the article that it was intended to be a chattel; but non-attachment gives rise to a presumption that the article was not intended to be a fixture.[8] Hence, a fireplace, an ornamental chimney-piece, pannelling and wainscoting fixed by screws, have all been held to be fixtures, because they could not be removed without injuring the land.[9] Similarly, an electric motor and dynamo sunk into a concrete bed were held to be fixtures, but not the batteries attached to the machine by wires.[10] By contrast, where an article may be removed intact without any injury to the land, and has not been attached thereto, as with a Dutch barn,[11] or a greenhouse bolted to a concrete plinth which lay on the ground and rested on its own weight,[12] the chattel concerned was held not to be a fixture.

Object and purpose of annexation

If the chattel was attached to the land with the intention merely of making a more convenient use of the article as a chattel, rather than with a view to permanently improving the land itself, then it will not become a fixture, at least provided it can easily be removed, or where the method of attachment used was necessary to enable the article to be used as a chattel in the circumstances, as where a tapestry was attached by a normal method to the wall of a drawing-room by a life tenant so that it could be viewed.[13]

In the application of this test, much depends on the facts and no clear line may be laid down and it is very difficult to reconcile all the cases. For example, seats fastened to the floor of a cinema were held to be fixtures,[14] as were statues, stone vases and garden seats which were part of an architectural scheme to

---

6 *Berkley v Poulett* [1977] 1 EGLR 86, 89, CA.
7 See *Leigh v Taylor* [1902] AC 157, HL.
8 *Holland v Hodgson* (1872) LR 7 CP 328, 335; *TSB Bank plc v Botham* [1996] EGCS 149, CA.
9 See *Buckland v Butterfield* (1820) 2 Brod & Bing 54.
10 *Jordan v May* [1947] KB 427, [1947] 1 All ER 231, CA.
11 *Elwes v Maw* (1802) 3 East 38; or wooden chalets: *Elitestone Ltd v Morris* (1995) 71 P & CR 06, CA. The pillars on which the chalets stood might be fixtures.
12 *Deen v Andrews* (1986) 52 P & CR 17; also *HE Dibble Ltd v Moore* [1970] 2 QB 181, [1969] 3 All ER 1465, CA.
13 *Leigh v Taylor*, supra.
14 *Vaudeville Electric Cinema Ltd v Muriset* [1923] 2 Ch 74; also fitted kitchen units in *TSB Bank plc v Botham* [1996] EGCS 149, CA.

improve the property concerned, even though they rested on their own weight.[15] Similarly, petrol tanks[16] and machinery fixed to concrete beds by bolts[17] were held fixtures. By contrast, a collection of stuffed birds in iron-fronted cages nailed to the walls,[18] were held to have remained a chattel. Likewise, a white marble statue of a Greek athlete, weighing half a ton and resting by its own weight on a plinth, was held merely to be a chattel.[19] Likewise, carpets, fitted or not, were not permanent and so could not as a matter of principle become part of the land; neither could light fittings, baths and gas fires only connected to a pipe running into the premises.[20] In conclusion, the subjectivity of this test is best shown by an illustration in an old case,[1] where the example of stone was taken: if a person put up a dry stone wall, this would become a fixture and so part of the land; but if he heaped the stone in a stack on the land, with the notion of storing it, it would remain a chattel.

Consequences of annexation

Once a chattel has become a fixture by annexation, the ownership of the fixture will pass with the freehold on a conveyance.[2] Since the fixture is classified as realty, it will pass under the landlord's will to any devisee under his will. No distraint will be possible against the fixture,[3] since it is part of the land and not part of the lessee's goods. If the lessee is under a general covenant to repair, this is ordinarily considered to extend to fixtures. The tenant will not be able to remove the fixture unless it is within one of three exceptional classes. These are: domestic and ornamental, trade and agricultural fixtures, all referred to as 'tenants' fixtures' in contrast to all other fixtures, which are known as 'landlords' fixtures'.

III TENANT'S RIGHTS TO REMOVE FIXTURES

Domestic and ornamental fixtures

The tenant is entitled to detach and remove articles affixed to the premises for the sake of ornament and convenience, but it seems only if the injury caused to the premises is to the decorations rather than to the fabric of the building itself.[4] Thus the tenant is entitled to remove entire articles (rather than parts of articles) such as tapestries, panelling,[5] gates, stoves, cupboards and bookcases fastened

---

15 *D'Eyncourt v Gregory* (1866) LR 3 Eq 382.
16 *Smith v City Petroleum Co* [1940] 1 All ER 260: the pumps were held to be (removable) trade fixtures.
17 *Reynolds v Ashby & Son* [1904] AC 466, HL.
18 *Viscount Hill v Bullock* [1897] 2 Ch 482, CA.
19 *Berkley v Poulett* [1977] 1 EGLR 86, CA.
20 *TSB Bank plc v Botham*, supra.
 1 *Holland v Hodgson*, supra.
 2 Under Law of Property Act 1925 s 62.
 3 Even if it is a tenants' fixture: see eg *Provincial Bill Posting Co v Low Moor Iron Co* [1909] 2 KB 344, CA.
 4 *Spyer v Phillipson* [1931] 2 Ch 183, CA.
 5 See *Spyer v Phillipson*, supra.

by ties to the wall, but not a greenhouse resting on bricks, since the whole article could not be removed in one piece.[6] On the other hand, a fixture which would constitute a permanent improvement to the premises cannot be removed, as where a permanent addition to them has been made, an example being the addition of a sun-lounge, bathroom, garage or verandah.

Trade fixtures

Trade fixtures are those fixtures which have been installed by the tenant for the purpose of his trade or business, and, to encourage tenants in the running of these, the courts have shown considerable latitude in the definition of this exception. For example, engines and boilers,[7] petrol pumps,[8] shrubs put in by a market gardener,[9] and fittings in a public house,[10] have all in the past been held trade fixtures. The tenant may, as noted, remove these at any time during the tenancy and possibly any statutory extension of the tenancy, but not once the lease has ended.[11]

In relation to structures erected by the tenant for the purposes of trade, the courts have gone some way towards resolving the problem, from the tenant's point of view, that buildings are not fixtures. No building of a substantial and permanent character which would be incapable of being removed without reducing it to its constituent parts is removable by the tenant.[12] On the other hand, a tenant has been held entitled to remove the superstructure of a shed which could readily be dismantled in sections and re-erected elsewhere, even though it was bolted to iron straps let into a concrete floor, on the grounds that the shed and the floor did not constitute a single unit.[13]

Removal of fixtures by tenants of agricultural holdings

The tenant of an agricultural holding has special rights to remove fixtures under s 10 of the Agricultural Holdings Act 1986. Two types of fixtures become the property of the tenant of an agricultural holding and are removable by him at any time during the tenancy or before the expiry of two months from its termination (s 10(1)):

(a) any engine, machinery, fencing or other fixture (of whatever description) affixed, for the purposes of agriculture or not to the holding, by the tenant; and

(b) any building erected by him on the holding.

If the tenant is in arrear with any rent or is otherwise in breach of any obligations under the tenancy, his right of removal is not exercisable (s 10(3)(a)).

6 *Butterfield v Buckland* (1820) 2 Brod & Bing 54.
7 *Climie v Wood* (1861) LR 4 ExCh 328.
8 *Smith v City Petroleum Co Ltd* [1940] 1 All ER 260.
9 *Wardell v Usher* (1841) 3 Scott NR 508.
10 *Elliott v Bishop* (1854) 10 Exch 496.
11 See *New Zealand Government Property Corpn v HM & S Ltd* [1982] 1 All ER 624, CA.
12 *Pole-Carew v Western Counties and General Manure Co* [1920] 2 Ch 97, CA.
13 *Webb v Frank Bevis Ltd* [1940] 1 All ER 247, CA.

The tenant must, both before the exercise of the right to remove and the termination of the tenancy, give the landlord at least one month's notice of his intention to remove the fixture or building (s 10(3)(b)). If the landlord, before the expiry of the tenant's notice, elects by a written counter-notice to purchase a particular fixture or building, the tenant cannot remove it (s 10(4)). The landlord is then bound to pay the tenant the fair value of the fixture of building to an incoming tenant (s 10(4)). Any disputes as to the amount payable are to be settled by arbitration under the 1986 Act (s 10(6)).

If the fixture or building was erected in pursuance of an obligation to the landlord, it cannot be removed (s 10(2)(a)): this limit on the tenant's right of removal extends to certain other cases, notably where the fixture or building replaces a fixture or building of the landlord's (s 10(2)(b)) or where the tenant is entitled to compensation under the 1986 Act in respect of the item (s 10(2)(c)).

The tenant must not, in exercising his right of removal, do any unavoidable damage, and must make good any damage he does (s 10(5)).

Section 10 may be contracted out of.[14] An agricultural tenant has the same rights to remove trade fixtures as any other tenant.

Removal of fixtures by tenant of a farm business tenancy

The tenant of a farm business tenancy, governed by the Agricultural Tenancies Act 1995, in force from 1 September 1995, is entitled to remove any fixture affixed, for the purposes of agriculture or not, to the holding, as well as any building erected by him on the holding (1995 Act, s 8(1)). This right of removal extends to fixtures or buildings acquired by the tenant (s 8(5)) – as from a predecessor in title. This right is exclusive of any other right, common law or statutory, or, in principle, by custom (s 8(6) and (7)) so, if a trade fixture has been erected by such a tenant as envisaged by the 1995 Act, his right to remove it is solely governed by the Act. The present right is exercisable at any time during the 'continuance of the tenancy' or at any time after termination, provided, in this case, the tenant remains in possession as tenant, whether under a new tenancy or holding over. So long as the tenant may remove it under s 8, the fixture or building remains his property; if he loses such right, as where he holds over as a trespasser, he forfeits, by inference, his property in the fixture or building.

If the fixture or building has been erected, or acquired, under some obligation, then it cannot be removed under this provision (s 8(2)(a)), or indeed, having regard to the previous considerations, at all, at least without the landlord's consent. The statutory right to removal is also excluded where the fixture or building had been erected in place of a landlord's fixture or building (s 8(2)(b)).[15] The right to remove a fixture or a building is also excluded in two

---

14 *Premier Dairies Ltd v Garlick* [1920] 2 Ch 17 (in contrast to the counter-notice rules: see ch 31).

15 So confirming a rule at common law that, if a tenant substitutes a non-agricultural trade fixture for one of the landlord's, he cannot remove that fixture as of right: see *Sunderland v Newton* (1830) 3 Sim 450, expressly adopted during the House of Lords Committee debate on this provision (Hansard, 12 December 1994, col 1170).

cases, so as to prevent any overlap with Part III of the Act. First, where the tenant has received compensation for the item because it is an improvement within s 16 of the 1995 Act (s 8(2)(c)). Second, where the tenant erected the fixture or building as an improvement within Part III and the landlord consented in writing, on condition, agreed to by the tenant, that he should not exercise his right of removal (s 8(2)(d)).

When exercising his right of removal, the tenant is bound not to cause any avoidable damage to the holding (s 8(3)) and must, immediately after such removal, make good all damage caused thereby (s 8(4)) – in similar fashion to the common law duty to make good damage caused by removal of trade fixtures.

In contrast to the 1986 Act right of removal, the 1995 Act right to remove is not in terms debarred where the tenant is in arrears with his rent. He does not have to give the landlord any notice of the exercise of his right. The landlord is not given a statutory right of purchase after notice – this would not preclude an agreed right.

IV   REMOVAL OF FIXTURES

Agricultural fixtures apart, the general rule is that the tenant may remove such fixtures as he is entitled to remove at any time during the lease and during such further period of possession by him as he holds the possession of premises under a right to consider himself a tenant. It seems certain that once the landlord resumes possession, the tenant's rights will be lost,[16] except where the term itself is an uncertain one (eg a tenancy at will), in which case the tenant will have a reasonable time after its termination within which to remove them. Similarly, a stipulation in the lease that the tenant may remove fixtures 'at the end of the term', will be construed as extending the time for a reasonable period thereafter.[17]

Where an existing lease expires or is surrendered, expressly or impliedly, and is then followed immediately by another lease to the same tenant, who throughout remains in possession, the tenant will not lose his right to remove tenants' fixtures and will be entitled, at the end of the new tenancy, to remove them.[18] Likewise, where the common law term expires or is surrendered but the tenant remains in possession, by holding over under the Rent Acts or Part II of the Landlord and Tenant Act 1954, it has been said that he retains his right to remove tenants' fixtures.[19] On the other hand, as was seen, failure to remove tenants' fixtures in due time extinguishes the tenant's right of removal on expiry of the relevant lease unless the landlord consents to removal, and the fixtures then become part of the freehold. Then the tenant's sole remedy is damages.

---

16 *Penton v Robart* (1801) 2 East 88; *Weeton v Woodcock* (1840) 7 M & W 14; *New Zealand Government Property Corpn v HM & S Ltd* [1982] QB 1145, [1982] 1 All ER 624, CA. See Kodilinye [1987] Conv 253.
17 *Stansfield v Portsmouth Corpn* (1858) 4 CBNS 120.
18 *New Zealand Government Property Corpn v HM & S Ltd* [1982] QB 1145, [1982] 1 All ER 624, CA.
19 Ibid, at 1160 and 630.

In removing his fixtures, the tenant must ensure that as little damage as possible is done to the premises, and any damage that is done, he is liable to repair.[20]

V REMEDIES IN RESPECT OF FIXTURES

The landlord has an action for damages for waste in respect of any fixtures wrongfully removed by the tenant,[1] as where, for example, he removes trade fixtures, such as fans and pipes, from a building, without making good the consequential damage to the structure of the building.[2] The obligation to make good such damage is regarded as part and parcel of the tenant's right to remove fixtures. Only where damages would not be an adequate remedy will a mandatory injunction be granted to replace the fixture wrongfully removed, as, for example, where a tenant was ordered to put back an Adam door which he had removed, having substituted a new one in its place.[3]

Although a tenant has no right in law to remove any fixture whatsoever belonging to the landlord, it is generally recognised that a tenant may remove a landlord's fixture and substitute for it one of his own, and may subsequently remove his own fixture provided that he replaces the landlord's fixture, or one of at least equal value, and makes good any damage caused by the substitution. The landlord cannot reasonably complain of an act committed during the tenancy which, though technically an act of waste, has resulted in no loss or damage to his reversion.

---

20 See *Mancetter Developments Ltd v Garmanson Ltd*, CA, infra.
 1 Including, it is submitted, fixtures wrongfully removed by a tenant of a farm business tenancy, where he is not acting within the terms of the 1995 Act, above.
 2 *Mancetter Developments Ltd v Garmanson Ltd* [1986] QB 1212, [1986] 1 All ER 449, CA.
 3 *Phillips v Lamdin* [1949] 2 KB 33, [1949] 1 All ER 770.

PART D
RESIDENTIAL TENANCIES

Chapter 16

Introduction to private sector residential tenancies legislation

I GENERAL

The common law imposes no direct controls over either the amount of rent which the landlord of a residential private sector tenant is entitled to charge, nor over the security of tenure enjoyed by the latter. Since 1915 there have been statutory rules affecting most private sector residential tenants. In the next two chapters, those controls which apply to private sector tenants who are not long leaseholders are examined. The origins of legislative intervention were certain wartime emergency measures passed to restrict the maximum rents payable for scarce rented accommodation. These rules are now contained in the Rent Act 1977. It consolidated a large range of controls over the maximum amount of rent chargeable from protected or statutory tenants, conferred security of tenure on the tenant under the statute despite termination of the tenancy at common law, and allowed for the succession to a statutory tenancy on the death of the original tenant.

In 1988, a distinct change took place. With the enactment of Part I of the Housing Act 1988, it became generally impossible to create tenancies to which the rules of the Rent Act 1977 applied. Only assured or assured shorthold tenancies were permitted in the private residential sector on or after 15 January 1989. The object of Parliament was to free the private sector rented sector from what were said to be the evils of rent control and security of tenure. This object has been pressed to some lengths, so that the balance of advantage seems to have shifted as much in favour of landlords, who may let at a market rent without any security of tenure after expiry of the tenancy, as it had been tilted by the Rent Acts in favour of tenants, whose rents were regulated and who might enjoy a status of irremovability after the expiry of the tenancy.

A further shift towards the removal of security for private residential tenants took place as from the commencement of Part III of the Housing Act 1996. From then on, any assured tenancy (subject to a number of exceptions, notably where the parties otherwise agree) is to be an assured shorthold tenancy. Thus, once the tenancy has expired or been brought to an end at common law by notice to quit, the tenant has no right to remain in possession without the landlord's express or implied consent. The landlord will have to ask the county court for an order for possession but he may obtain it on the ground that the tenancy has come to an end. The tenant has the limited safeguard against too rapid an eviction on the ground of expiry of the tenancy that no order for possession may take effect until six months after the shorthold tenancy was originally granted. However, if the tenant accumulates eight weeks arrears in the payment of rent, he may be dispossessed following proceedings. Although under the original assured tenancies scheme, significant rent arrears could trigger dispossession during the initial shorthold term, the new rule represents a shortening by about one-third of the period of arrears which must be shown to have accumulated before the landlord may institute proceedings.

The subjection of tenanted houses and flats to the new rules as from 15 January 1989 was not retrospective. However, as time passes, the significance in numerical terms of Rent Act tenancies will diminish. There cannot have been many new fully protected tenancies for some time before the passage of the 1988 Act, since Parliament had enabled landlords to grant tenancies under which they could fairly easily re-possess the premises, notably where the landlord was a resident landlord or an owner-occupier. However, statutory tenancies, which confer a status of irremovability, may well continue in existence into the next century, all the more so since where the original tenant dies, his spouse may succeed to the statutory tenancy – in contrast to a family member, who is awarded only an assured periodic tenancy by succession, which is less secure. In addition, some of the basic conditions precedent to the application of the various residential codes are similar, such as the requirement of a tenancy, of a dwelling-house and so on, and the phraseology of certain exemptions and grounds for possession looks similar. There is a system for rent regulation, which applies notably to statutory tenants, which differs from the rules applicable to assured tenancies. Therefore a chapter devoted to the Rent Acts has been retained in a somewhat reduced form.

Common to assured shorthold, assured and Rent Act tenancies are special statutory provisions aimed at encouraging landlords to provide information about the terms of the tenancy, and discouraging them from illegally evicting or harassing their tenants. These rules exist in parallel to the common law rules but they may prove advantageous to tenants as the way in which damages are calculated is more generous, at least for illegal eviction, than at common law, since the landlord is to be deprived of any illicit profit he may have made from the eviction: where a statutory tenant is illegally evicted and replaced with an assured tenant, the value of the landlord's reversion might be expected to rise.

Tenants holding from local authorities and certain other public sector or quasi-public sector bodies may hold a secure tenancy, which is governed by Part IV of the Housing Act 1985. Unlike the previous two codes, however, the 1985 Act also confers on secure tenants a right to buy the landlord's freehold or leasehold interest, even against his will, in much the same way as private sector long residential lessees of houses and flats have the right to enfranchise the freehold (and all intermediate leasehold interests), again even where the landlord is unwilling.

Before examining the two private sector residential codes, some general examination of them, with relevant comparisons, may assist.[1]

---

1   The subject is well served by specialist literature: see notably Martin, *Residential Security* and Megarry *Rent Acts*.

II THE TWO CODES

Rent Acts

The Rent Act 1977 was the last in a series of enactments originating in 1915. The emergency legislation of that year was replaced by the Increase of Rent and Mortgage Interest (Restrictions) Act 1920, and this Act, which extended the number of houses to which rent control and security of tenure applied, was followed by a long series of further Acts, consolidated in the Rent Act 1977 and the Protection from Eviction Act 1977. The key features of the Rent Act 1977 are:

1 The treatment of a common law tenancy of residential premises caught by the 1977 Act as a 'protected tenancy'.

2 The designation of the tenant, whose common law or 'contractual' term has expired, as a 'statutory tenant'. Both in his capacity as protected tenant (during which time he also holds an estate in land) and as statutory tenant (during whose duration he has a mere personal right to occupy) the tenant is entitled to the control of the rent payable, being designated by the 1977 Act as a 'regulated tenant'. It may be that, with the introduction of assured tenancies and a consequent de-control of rents, that the reduction in rent which a 'regulated tenant' might at one time have been able to obtain owing to the legislative rule that any scarcity of accommodation must be ignored in assessing a 'fair rent' may be no longer so readily available, at least where the premises in the immediate vicinity to that let are held by assured tenants.[2]

3 Moreover, a protected or statutory tenant is also entitled to claim statutory security of tenure, the extent of which depends on the type of tenancy he holds, but in no case is the tenant to be lawfully evicted from the premises unless the landlord proves to the satisfaction of the county court that he falls within one of a number of grounds for possession. These are divided by the Rent Act 1977 into those where the landlord is only entitled to possession if he proves the requirements of the ground and that it is reasonable to make the order ('discretionary grounds') and those where, if the landlord proves the appropriate requirements, the court must order possession (called 'mandatory grounds'). The 'mandatory grounds' had come into being, in an effort to encourage lettings, albeit at a controlled rent: for example, the 'owner-occupier' ground[3] was first introduced in 1965.[4]

4 If the landlord cannot rely on any ground for possession, he may be able to recover possession if he is able to prove that suitable alternative accommodation is available for the tenant.

5 The 1977 Act allows the transmission on death of the right to occupy the premises vested by the original tenancy agreement in a statutory tenant to

---

2 See eg *BTE Ltd v Merseyside and Cheshire Rent Assessment Committee* [1992] 1 EGLR 116.

3 Rent Act 1977, Sch 15, para 11.

4 Rent Act 1965, s 14; subsequently Rent Act 1968, Sch 3, Part II, Case 10. A differently-constructed 'owner-occupier' ground for assured tenants is conferred by Housing Act 1988, Sch 2, Part I, ground 1.

his surviving spouse or to a member of his family. The 1988 Act did away with the right of a family member to succeed to a statutory tenancy as from 15 January 1989, but preserved the right of a surviving spouse to succeed to a statutory tenancy even where the original tenant dies on or after 15 January 1989, and this may mean that Rent-Act statutory tenancies survive well into the next century.

Part I of the Housing Act 1988

In the case of assured and assured shorthold tenants alike, the landlord cannot lawfully evict the tenant without an order of the county court, and in the case of an assured tenant who is not (exceptionally after the Housing Act 1996) an assured shorthold tenant, the court is only entitled to make an order for possession if one of a number of 'mandatory' or 'discretionary' grounds are proved by the landlord. The 1988 Act rules apply to all types of residential tenancies, except those to which other legislation applies. The most noticeable differences between the 1988 Act rules and those of the 1977 Act may be summarised as follows.

1   It would appear that an assured tenant enjoys an estate in land as from the commencement of an assured tenancy until its termination by an order of court.[5] If this is so, he has an interest which he may assign or leave by will, in complete contrast to a statutory tenancy under the Rent Act 1977 which is a mere personal, non-assignable right.

2   The way in the limited security of tenure for assured tenancies arises (as opposed to assured shorthold tenancies, where there is no statutory right to remain in possession or to renewal after expiry of the contractual term) is on the surface similar to the conferral of security on business tenants by continuation. But the court has no power to order a renewal of an assured term certain if the parties fail to agree on this. Generally, once an assured fixed-term tenancy ends by effluxion of time, the assured tenant holds over under an assured periodic tenancy. The 1988 Act enables the landlord to increase the rent of this tenancy and to alter the other terms: in contrast, the landlord of a business tenant may only apply to the court for an interim rent and even the court has only limited powers to modernise a new lease. The absence of restrictions on this process of revision of an assured periodic tenancy is deliberate legislative policy. In any case, as from the commencement of the new regime of Part III of the Housing Act 1996, because most tenancies granted as from then will most likely be assured shortholds, the significance of the statutory assured shorthold tenancy which follows the contractual term of a shorthold tenancy is likely to be mainly a temporary device under which the tenant lawfully holds over pending either his eviction or renewal of his tenancy.

3   Although the landlord of an assured tenant is not entitled to evict the tenant without an order of court, the grounds on which he may do so are in general wider than those which govern Rent Act tenants. For example, the landlord

---

5   *N & D (London) Ltd v Gadsdon* [1992] 1 EGLR 112, in relation to Housing Act 1988, s 39(5) and (6).

of an assured tenant is entitled to prove that he requires the premises for the purpose of redevelopment, on a mandatory ground which is obviously borrowed from business tenancies; it is a great deal easier to evict an assured tenant for rent arrears; and the recovery of the dwelling-house by a landlord who was a former owner-occupier or who wished to live there is generally easier under the 1988 Act than it is under the 1977 Act. With the enactment of the rule that private sector residential tenancies are to be assured shorthold tenancies – save in exceptional circumstances – it seems that the main methods of recovery of possession by the landlord against the tenant are likely to be first, by proof that the initial fixed-term tenancy has expired, so that he may ask the court for possession on that ground and second, by proof of rent arrears.

Chapter 17

Rent Act protected and statutory tenancies

A POLICY OF RENT ACT PROTECTION

Introduction

Private sector residential tenancies have been subject to statutory controls since 1915. The legislation in its present form began with the Increase of Rent and Mortgage Interest (Restrictions) Act 1920, which imposed comprehensive rent controls and created statutory tenants. Since then, no less than 26 Acts in this field have been passed (excluding the Rent Act 1977) with a pattern of the imposition of comprehensive security and rent control being followed by relaxations of security and control of rent. The end result of this is a complex maze of consolidating and amending legislation. Its effects, notably in the case of statutory tenancies, will be felt for some time despite the introduction, as from 15 January 1989, of assured tenancies.

Objects of Rent Act

The objects of the Rent Act 1977 are these. First, to limit the maximum amount of rent which the landlord is entitled to charge the tenant. Second, it confers security of tenure on tenants. Third, it controls the extent to which the landlord may extort a premium as a condition of the grant of a tenancy to which the Acts apply. The control of rents is based on the right of a tenant to refer a rent he dislikes to a rent officer, who then fixes the rent in accordance with statutory guidelines. Security of tenure is achieved by requiring the landlord to obtain an order of court before physically regaining possession of the premises and then by limiting the grounds on which the landlord may obtain an order for possession to those specified in the Act.

Differing levels of protection

As mentioned in chapter 16, the Rent Act 1977 offers differing levels of protection, depending on the nature of the tenancy. Full protection is conferred on protected and statutory tenants, although the exact degree of protection depends on the nature of the tenancy itself. Even before the legislature made it impossible in most cases after 15 January 1989 to create protected tenancies, it may well, for some time before then, have been unusual for landlords consciously to grant such tenancies except where one of a number of 'mandatory' grounds for possession might apply, as in the case of owner-occupying landlords.[1]

At one time, the security of furnished tenants was much less extensive than that offered to unfurnished tenants, and the former tenants could hold only *restricted contracts*. One feature of these is rules enabling the control of the rent along similar but not, in terms, identical lines, to those applicable to protected and statutory tenancies.[2] In due course, however, furnished tenancies were brought into full protection, and restricted contracts are confined to tenancies granted by resident landlords under s 12 of the 1977 Act, or where the rent includes payment for the use of furniture or services, provided that in the latter case, the payments are for board or substantial attendance (within s 7 of the 1977 Act). In addition, there may be a restricted contract where there is a licence with the provision of furniture or services. Since it is not possible to create a restricted contract after the commencement on 15 January 1989 of the Housing Act 1988 Part I, and having regard to the limited security of tenure conferred on tenants under restricted contracts, this class of tenancy is today likely to be rare.

Tenancies granted by local authorities and by housing associations, housing trusts and the Housing Corporation are not, in any case, protected tenancies.[3] Equally, where the landlord is an 'owner-occupier', he is entitled, on compliance with certain formal notice and residence requirements, mandatorily to obtain an order for possession once the contractual tenancy has expired.

Criticisms of the Rent Acts

One of the chief difficulties with the Rent Acts is the quality of their provisions, which have been criticised for 'inadequate definition, hidden meanings, missing principles, incautious superimposition and plain mistakes'.[4] In addition, much of the legislation is couched in unsatisfactory terms. The Acts were passed almost as if the common law principles of landlord and tenant did not exist. The courts have therefore been left to make what they can of the Acts, and it has been said that they should interpret them in a reasonable and common sense way.[5] At the same time, since the Acts interfere with common law rules, the courts often limit this interference to the smallest necessary extent and may thus interpret provisions literally.[6] If there is a real difficulty which the court cannot resolve without going back through the antecedents of the legislation, it will do so, even though the Rent Act 1977 is taken at least in part, to be a consolidating Act.[7] If such difficulties cannot then be resolved, the court has the power to refer

---

1 In *White v Wareing* [1992] 1 EGLR 271, CA, it was recognised that most county court cases within the 1977 Act were statutory tenancies.
2 Rent Act 1977, s 77, enabling a reference to a Rent Assessment Committee.
3 As from 15 January 1989, any tenancy granted by a housing association or similar body must be an assured or an assured shorthold tenancy: Housing Act 1988, s 35.
4 Megarry *The Rent Acts*, p 15.
5 See eg *Remon v City of London Real Property Co Ltd* [1921] 1 KB 49, CA.
6 *Landau v Sloane* [1981] 1 All ER 705, HL; *Wilkes v Goodwin* [1923] 2 KB 86, CA.
7 *Farrell v Alexander* [1977] AC 59, [1976] 2 All ER 721, HL.

to Parliamentary debates so as to aid it, provided, that is, that a clear statement may be found by the sponsor of the legislation.[8] This latter point is of course of general application and could be relevant if a difficulty arose in interpreting, say, a provision about assured tenancies in the Housing Acts 1988 or 1996.

Replacement of Rent Acts

The legislature made a fundamental shift in its policy in relation to tenancies granted in the private residential sector by private landlords and other bodies such as housing associations, when it created, as from 15 January 1989, assured and assured shorthold tenancies. These are the only two forms of residential tenancy which may, in principle, be granted as from that date.

In connection with the enactment of the two new types of residential tenancy, Parliament enacted a number of complex transitional provisions, whose overall effect is that, if any of the following exceptions applies to a private sector residential tenant, the Rent Act 1977 will apply to his tenancy and not the Housing Act 1988 Part I, even though the date of the new tenancy is on or after 15 January 1989.

1   The tenant was a protected or statutory tenant whose tenancy was originally granted before 15 January 1989. The tenant has died, before that date, leaving a surviving spouse or family member, either of whom is entitled to claim a statutory tenancy by succession.
2   The protected or statutory tenant died on or after 15 January 1989, leaving a surviving spouse, who, in contrast to a family member, has the privilege of being able to claim a statutory tenancy by succession. Thus this type of statutory tenancy may well last well into the next century.
3   Where transitional provisions apply to the tenancy, as where, in particular, it was granted to a person (alone or jointly with others) who, immediately before the tenancy was granted, was the protected or statutory tenant and the tenancy was granted by the person who was either the landlord, or one of the joint landlords, under the previous protected or statutory tenancy.[9] The exception is designed, no doubt, to prevent landlords of existing protected or statutory tenants from persuading them to agree to accept a new tenancy of different accommodation, which tenancy could be not subject to the same degree of protection as the previous tenancy. However, there is no time-limit for the period which must elapse before a new tenancy lying outside the protection of the Rent Act 1977, is granted to the tenant. Where a protected tenant faced with a possession order agreed to accept a new protected shorthold tenancy (which has no security after expiry) and to

---

8   *Pepper v Hart* [1993] AC 593, HL – this is a point applicable to any statute, though the occasions when the power might be used remain to be seen. The county court resorted to this power in *Goringe v Twinsectra* [1994] CLY 2723, infra.
9   Housing Act 1988, s 34(1)(b), subject to s 34(2) in the case of protected shorthold tenancies. A related rule, so that the tenant does not lose security by a transfer against his will, to other accommodation, is that where the court has ordered possession on the ground of suitable alternative accommodation being available for a former protected or statutory tenant, and considers that the grant of an assured tenancy would not afford the tenant the required security of tenure, it may direct that the tenancy is to be a protected tenancy (s 34(1)(c)).

leave the flat concerned for 24 hours, he could not later claim that his new tenancy was fully protected.[10] The same result might have been reached if the tenant had voluntarily surrendered an earlier protected or statutory tenancy and in such a case it is seemingly unnecessary for the tenant to remove himself physically from the premises.[11]

It is not clear whether the premises held under the new tenancy must, for the exception to apply to the tenancy, rendering it Rent Act protected, be the same or substantially the same as those previously held. It has been held in the county court that, having regard to the policy of the exception as stated during its passage in Parliament, that the new premises do not have to be the same or substantially the same as those previously held,[12] so extending the benefit of the exception to a protected tenant who might have a new tenancy of the same house as before, minus one room.

B PROTECTED TENANCY DEFINED

I GENERAL PRINCIPLES

Section 1 of the Rent Act 1977 provides that: 'a tenancy under which a dwelling-house (which may be a house or a part of a house) is let as a separate dwelling is a protected tenancy.' A protected tenancy remains protected only during the contractual period of the tenancy, whether this is for a term certain or periodic.

As already discussed, it is not generally possible to create a protected tenancy of residential premises on or after 15 January 1989, with the advent of assured tenancies. For some years before that date, it must have been unusual for a landlord knowingly to grant a protected tenancy unless he was able to rely on a mandatory ground for re-possession of the tenant after expiry of the contractual term (as where the landlord was an owner-occupier). There may still be a number of fully protected tenancies in being, which, after their contractual term expires, or is otherwise terminated (by notice to quit in the case of a periodic tenancy or by forfeiture or surrender) automatically become statutory tenancies (by s 2(1) of the 1977 Act). These latter are the creature of the Rent Act 1977 and so confer on the 'tenant' a purely personal right of occupation, despite the fact that his previous protected tenancy has expired,[13] rather than an estate in land.[14]

---

10 *Bolnore Properties Ltd v Cobb* [1996] EGCS 42, CA.
11 Cf *Dibbs v Campbell* [1988] 2 EGLR 122, CA.
12 *Goringe v Twinsectra*, supra; see Walden-Smith (1994) 29 EG 114.
13 *Remon v City of London Real Property Co* [1921] 1 KB 49, CA.
14 *Jessamine Investment Co v Schwartz* [1978] QB 264, [1976] 3 All ER 521, CA; also *Johnson v Felton* [1994] EGCS 135, CA (so that such a tenancy cannot amount to a 'lease' within Housing Act 1985, s 317).

II   THE QUALIFYING CONDITIONS

Section 1 of the Rent Act 1977 may be broken down as follows into its various component parts. The first three of these deserve to be discussed in some detail, if only because they are also conditions precedent to the creation of assured tenancies (chapter 18).

Tenancy

There must be a contractual tenancy for there to be full protection, but 'tenancy' expressly includes a sub-tenancy (s 152(1)). If it is assigned, a protected tenancy remains protected. If it is terminated by forfeiture or notice to quit, it loses its protected status and becomes a statutory tenancy (s 2(1)(a)).

Section 1 of the 1977 Act applies to any kind of common law tenancy, so that tenants at will paying rent[15] and tenants on sufferance[16] are protected, as are tenants by estoppel, at all events as against the landlord.[17] The type of tenancy does not matter and s 1 may apply both to fixed term and to periodic tenancies of any length; and equally, it may subject legal and equitable tenancies alike to the 1977 Act. However, there are limits. If a prior legal mortgage has been created by the landlord, the tenant cannot claim any protection under the Act against the mortgagee if it sells under its title paramount.[18] The same rule applies both to a statutory tenant, whom a legal mortgagee with a title paramount may evict without being subject to s 98(1) of the 1977 Act,[19] and even where the legal mortgagee's interest or charge is created after the granting of the tenancy by the landlord.[20]

Moreover, the 1977 Act deals with premises of which the person is in a real sense the tenant of a landlord, as opposed to cases where the tenancy is a device to enable some other sort of relationship to come into existence, and so a prospective purchaser going into possession pending completion is not a protected tenant: it makes no difference that sums labelled as rent are payable.[1] Similarly, a mortgagor in possession who, in his mortgage, attorns tenant to the mortgagee is outside the scope of s 1 of the 1977 Act.[2]

A genuine licence to occupy is outside s 1 of the Act but the courts are astute to detect and frustrate artificial devices and sham transactions whose only object is to disguise the grant of a tenancy and to evade the 1977 Act (see further chapter 3). By contrast, provided the agreement is genuine and not shown by the occupier to be a sham, a tenancy may legitimately be granted to a company, even one specially bought 'off the shelf', which licences or authorises an

---

15   *Chamberlain v Farr* [1942] 2 All ER 567, CA.
16   *Artizans, Labourers and General Dwellings Co v Whitaker* [1919] 2 KB 301.
17   *Mackley v Nutting* [1949] 2 KB 55, [1949] 1 All ER 413, CA.
18   *Dudley and District Benefit Building Society v Emerson* [1949] Ch 707, [1949] 2 All ER 252, CA.
19   *Britannia Building Society v Earl* [1990] 1 EGLR 133, CA.
20   *Abbey National Building Society v Cann* [1991] 1 AC 56, [1990] 1 All ER 1085: see Goldberg (1992) 108 LQR 380.
1   *Hopwood v Hough* (1944) 11 LJCCR 80; cf *Bretherton v Paton* [1986] 1 EGLR 172, CA.
2   *Portman Building Society v Young* [1951] 1 All ER 191, CA.

individual to occupy a house or flat. On the termination of the contractual or protected tenancy, the company tenant, provided that it genuinely performs the obligations of the tenancy, enjoys no further security as statutory tenant since it cannot comply with the residence requirement of s 2 of the Act.[3] The occupier, as its licensee, is in no better a position: the fact that the letting is to a company so as to avoid the 1977 Act does not of itself entitle the court to hold that the whole arrangement is a sham device.[4]

Dwelling-house

'Dwelling-house' in s 1 includes entire houses and self-contained flats; and any permanent buildings designed or adapted for living in are capable of being a dwelling-house for present purposes. A house cannot be a 'dwelling-house' if it is constructed to consist of a number of units of habitation, all of which are to be sub-let.[5] In the end the question of whether given premises are a 'dwelling-house' is one of fact, and where premises had been converted from a warehouse into a garage with living rooms above, the living rooms fell within the Act.[6] A tenant under a letting of a barn would be outside s 1.[7] One or two rooms in a larger house, if they are self-contained, may be a 'dwelling-house'.[8] A caravan, house-boat or other mobile structure is capable of coming within s 1, but only if rendered completely immobile and, presumably, capable of being used by the tenant as his permanent home.[9]

Let as a separate dwelling

To comply with this part of s 1, the premises need not comprise a single unit: two or more physically separate units, demised together, may constitute a separate dwelling.[10] Likewise, where a house, cottage and land attached thereto were demised in one lease, the combined unit was a separate dwelling within s 1.[11] Indeed, a tenancy may be protected notwithstanding that (1) the tenant never dwells in the house or any part of it; (2) the tenancy includes land or buildings not used as a dwelling[12] and (3) the premises are (incidentally) used for business purposes.[13]

It is implicit in the statutory requirement that the premises are let as a separate dwelling, that the tenant is able to go, as of right, to all the rooms in

---

3 *Hiller v United Dairies (London) Ltd* [1934] 1 KB 57, CA; also *Carter v SU Carburetter Co* [1942] 2 KB 288, [1942] 2 All ER 228, CA.
4 *Hilton v Plustitle Ltd* [1988] 3 All ER 1051, CA; Rogers [1989] Conv 197; *Estavest Investments Ltd v Commercial Express Travel Ltd* [1988] 2 EGLR 91, CA; *Kaye v Massbetter Ltd* [1991] 2 EGLR 97, CA.
5 *Horford Investments Ltd v Lambert* [1976] Ch 39, [1974] 1 All ER 131, CA.
6 *Gidden v Mills* [1925] 2 KB 713.
7 *Epsom Grand Stand Association v Clarke* [1919] WN 170 at 171, CA.
8 *Curl v Angelo* [1948] 2 All ER 189, CA.
9 *R v Rent Officer of Northamptonshire Registration Area, ex p Allen* [1985] 2 EGLR 153.
10 *Langford Property Co Ltd v Goldrich* [1949] 1 KB 511, [1949] 1 All ER 402 (two separate flats let together); also *Grosvenor (Mayfair) Estates v Amberton* (1982) 265 Estates Gazette 693.
11 *Whitty v Scott-Russell* [1950] 2 KB 32, [1950] 1 All ER 884, CA.
12 This must be read subject to the statutory exclusions set out below.
13 *Horford Investments Ltd v Lambert* [1976] Ch 39, [1974] 1 All ER 131, CA.

the premises concerned.[14] The accommodation let must be a separate unit in which it is possible for the tenant to carry on all the major activities of life, particularly sleeping, cooking and eating: if one or more of these cannot be carried on, the tenancy is not protected.[15] If the tenant is tenant of different parts of the same house under different lettings from the same landlord, and carries on some of his living activities in one part of the house and the remainder of them in the other part of the house, neither tenancy will be protected. If there is a single composite letting of the two parts as a whole, then, as already noted, the tenancy may well be protected, but the difference between the two results is one of fact and degree.[16] Moreover, if all parts of a house, consisting of single rooms and a flat, were let by the tenant to other persons, the tenant has no protected tenancy since 'let as a separate dwelling' is confined to the singular.[17] On the other hand, a sub-letting of part of the premises by the tenant of the whole did not deny the tenant protection of the whole, since he was entitled to possession of the sub-let part.[18]

If part of a house is let, the part need not necessarily be self-contained for there to be a protected tenancy: but in any event, the tenant must have the exclusive right to use essential living rooms, which include the kitchen: sharing of other accommodation, such as a bathroom, does not of itself deprive the tenant of protection.[19] But where a tenant had exclusive possession of two rooms only in a house and shared the kitchen and other accommodation with the landlord, he fell outside protection.[20] Where the tenant shares accommodation with the landlord, if the tenancy was granted on or after 14 August 1974 and before 15 January 1989, it will be a restricted contract since the landlord will be a resident landlord.[1] Where the tenant shares accommodation with other tenants, s 22 confers protected tenancy status on the separate accommodation which the tenant holds exclusively (assuming it otherwise qualifies for protection) and has the further consequence that the tenant cannot be evicted from the shared accommodation by an order for possession unless the order also relates to the separate accommodation (s 22(5)).

Partial business use

Sometimes, the courts have had to decide whether a tenancy is subject to the Rent Act 1977 or Part II of the Landlord and Tenant Act 1954, especially where a business tenant claims to have altered the de facto user of the premises to residential purposes. If the terms of the lease clearly state or contemplate a

---

14 *St Catherine's College v Dorling* [1979] 3 All ER 250, [1980] 1 WLR 66, CA.
15 *Wright v Howell* (1947) 92 Sol Jo 26, CA.
16 *Hampstead Way Investments Ltd v Lewis-Weare* [1985] 1 All ER 564 at 568, HL; also *Kavanagh v Lyroudias* [1985] 1 All ER 560, CA.
17 *Horford Investments Ltd v Lambert*, supra.
18 *Regalian Securities Ltd v Ramsden* [1981] 2 All ER 65, [1981] 1 WLR 611, HL.
19 *Cole v Harris* [1945] KB 474, CA; *Horford Investments Ltd v Lambert*, supra.
20 *Neale v Del Soto* [1945] KB 144, [1945] 1 All ER 191, CA.
 1 As to tenancies granted prior to 14 August 1974, see Rent Act 1977, s 21 (repealed by Housing Act 1988, Sch 18).

particular purpose (eg shop user) this is the essential factor and, in the absence of the landlord's consent to, or acceptance of, a change from business to residential user, the Rent Acts cannot apply to the tenancy at any time.[2] The same principle applies if the premises are described as let for business purposes,[3] or where user covenants in the lease expressly prohibit residential user.[4] If a tenancy permits both business and residential user, the actual user of the premises is taken into account in determining which Act applies; but the Rent Act cannot apply if the business user is significant rather than purely incidental to the residential user.[5] The issue of whether business or professional user is significant is one of fact and degree.[6] It appears that the words 'let as a separate dwelling' in s 1 of the 1977 Act no longer include partial use for business purposes, or mixed residential and business user.[7]

A business tenant who abandons a business user and commences a residential user unilaterally cannot claim to have a protected tenancy, although it is different if the landlord by an express or implied consent (such as a prolonged acceptance of rent with knowledge of the change) or waiver, agrees to the change and varies the terms of the lease.[8] The same principles apply where it is asserted that the tenant of premises let as an agricultural holding within the Agricultural Holdings Act 1986 has ceased to use them for that purpose and de facto occupies them as his residence.[9]

III RENTAL AND RATEABLE VALUE LIMITS

A tenancy cannot be protected if the dwelling-house is outside certain rental value limits, where the tenancy was entered into after 1 April 1990 – not a very likely contingency in view of the enactment of Part I of the Housing Act 1988. A tenancy entered into on or after 1 April 1990 is accordingly not protected if under it the rent (defined in s 4(5)) payable for the time being is payable at a rate exceeding £25,000 a year (s 4(4)). There is a rebuttable presumption that the dwelling-house is caught by these limits (s 4(6)). Rental value limits have thus replaced the former system under which the tenancy fell outside the Rent Act 1977 if the rateable value of the house or flat was above certain fixed limits, which differed depending on the date of creation of the tenancy and on whether the premises were in Greater London or elsewhere (s 4(1)).

---

2 *Wolfe v Hogan* [1949] 2 KB 194, [1949] 1 All ER 570, CA.
3 *Ponder v Hillman* [1969] 3 All ER 694, [1969] 1 WLR 1261 ('all that shop and premises').
4 See *Levermore v Joby* [1956] 2 All ER 362, [1956] 1 WLR 697; *Cooper v Henderson* (1982) 263 Estates Gazette 592, CA.
5 *Cheryl Investments Ltd v Saldanha* [1979] 1 All ER 5, [1978] 1 WLR 1329, CA; see further ch 23.
6 *Wright v Mortimer* (1996) 28 HLR 719, CA.
7 *Henry Smith's Charity Trustees v Wagle* [1989] 1 EGLR 124, CA.
8 *Pulleng v Curran* (1980) 44 P & CR 58, CA.
9 *Russell v Booker* [1982] 2 EGLR 86, CA; and, in the absence of authority, the same principle seems to apply to a tenant of a farm business tenancy.

IV   TENANCIES EXCLUDED FROM PROTECTION

If a tenancy falls within one of the following statutory exclusions from protection, it is not a protected tenancy and cannot be a statutory tenancy.

Tenancies at a low rent

(i)   *General rule*   By s 5(1), a tenancy entered into before 1 April 1990[10] is not a protected tenancy if under the tenancy either no rent is payable or the rent is less than two-thirds of the rateable value of the dwelling-house on, in principle, 23 March 1965. By s 5(1A) a tenancy is not a protected tenancy if it is entered into on or after 1 April 1990 and under the tenancy either no rent is payable or the rent is payable at specified rates.[11] Long tenancies at a low rent are given separate protection under Part I of the Landlord and Tenant Act 1954. The relevant date for deciding whether s 5 applies is the date of the hearing; thus a progressive rent under a rent review clause might bring a tenancy originally within s 5 within s 1.[12]

(ii)   *Meaning of rent*   The word 'rent' in s 5 refers to the total money payment payable by the tenant to the landlord.[13] Capital payments such as genuine premiums or fines do not count as rent within s 5 although a capital sum which was rent in disguise would qualify as rent.[14]

(iii)   *Miscellaneous*   Service charges payable under long tenancies at a low rent (defined in s 5(5)) do not count towards the two-thirds figure for rent if expressed to be payable as service charges (s 5(4)).[15] In the case of a variable rent, as noted, the premises may enter and leave protection, depending on the level of rent at any one time. If the rent of a protected tenancy is reduced below the two-thirds level, s 5 may deprive the tenant of protection; but if the tenancy is statutory, this result is not possible.[16]

Dwelling-houses let with other land

(i)   *General rule*   By s 6 of the Rent Act 1977, a tenancy is not a protected tenancy if the dwelling-house subject to the tenancy is let together with land other than the site of the dwelling-house. This is expressly subject to s 26: and

---

10   Subject to a transitional rule for tenancies entered into after that date pursuant to contracts made before it.
11   Namely, at a rate of £1,000 or less per year for a dwelling-house situated in Greater London and £250 or less per year elsewhere.
12   *Woozley v Woodall Smith* [1950] 1 KB 325, [1949] 2 All ER 1055, CA.
13   *Sidney Trading Co Ltd v Finsbury Borough Council* [1952] 1 All ER 460 at 462; *Mackworth v Hellard* [1921] 2 KB 755, CA.
14   *Samrose Properties Ltd v Gibbard* [1958] 1 All ER 502, [1958] 1 WLR 235, CA.
15   See *Investment and Freehold English Estates Ltd v Casement* [1988] 1 EGLR 100, CA.
16   See *J & F Stone Lighting and Radio Ltd v Levitt* [1947] AC 209, [1946] 2 All ER 653, HL; *McGee v London Rent Assessment Panel Committee* (1969) 210 Estates Gazette 1431.

s 26(1) provides that any land or premises let together with a dwelling-house shall, unless it consists of agricultural land exceeding two acres, be treated as part of the dwelling-house. The effect of s 26 is that, where it applies, the whole of the composite entity, dwelling-house plus land, is protected.[17]

(ii) *General test* In order to resolve these two provisions, a dominant purpose test applies: whether the land is an adjunct to the dwelling-house or whether the dwelling-house is an adjunct to the land.[18] Where a house occupied merely one-quarter of the land, the rest of which comprised buildings used for business purposes, there was no protected tenancy,[19] nor where there was a letting of a camping site which had a bungalow on it.[20]

(iii) *Agricultural land* It has been held that if at the date of the hearing or application the land is not used for agricultural purposes[1] but is used in conjunction with the user of the dwelling-house, then the tenancy of both house and land will be protected.[2] But if the land is let for use as agricultural land, mere unilateral abandonment of such user will not of itself attract the Rent Acts.[3]

(iv) *'Let together with'* This requires a reasonably close connection between the letting of the dwelling-house and the land but the two do not necessarily have to be let at the same time in one document,[4] and the landlord of one entity need not necessarily be the same landlord as that of the other part so let.[5] The lettings would presumably have to be to the same tenant.

Tenancies with payments for board and attendance

By s 7(1) of the 1977 Act, a tenancy is not a protected tenancy if under it the dwelling-house is bona fide let at a rent which includes payments in respect of board or attendance. By s 7(2), a dwelling-house is not to be taken to be bona fide let at a rent which includes payments in respect of attendance unless the amount of the rent fairly attributable to attendance, having regard to the value of the attendance to the tenant, forms a substantial part of the whole rent. But for this, a landlord could provide services which were more of a burden than a benefit to tenants but evade the 1977 Act.[6] If substantial board is provided, not only is the tenancy not protected, it will not ordinarily be capable of being a restricted contract.

17 *Langford Property Co Ltd v Batten* [1951] AC 223, [1950] 2 All ER 1079, HL.
18 *Pender v Reid* 1948 SC 381.
19 *Pender v Reid*, supra; *Cargill v Phillips* 1951 SC 67.
20 *Feyereisel v Turnidge* [1952] 2 QB 29, [1952] 1 All ER 728, CA.
 1 Defined by Rent Act 1977, s 26(2).
 2 *Bradshaw v Smith* [1980] 2 EGLR 89, CA.
 3 *Russell v Booker* [1982] 2 EGLR 86, CA.
 4 *Mann v Merrill* [1945] 1 All ER 708; *Wimbush v Cibulia* [1949] 2 KB 564, [1949] 2 All ER 432, CA.
 5 *Jelley v Buckman* [1974] QB 488, [1973] 3 All ER 853, CA.
 6 *Woodward v Docherty* [1974] 2 All ER 844, [1974] 1 WLR 966, CA.

(i)   *General*   The rent must genuinely include payments for board or attendance.[7] The relevant date at which the conditions of s 7 are complied with is the commencement date of the tenancy.[8] The word 'rent' refers to the total monetary payment made by the tenant.[9]

(ii)   *Meaning of board*   There is no definition of 'board' but it is not confined to full board and the daily provision of a continental breakfast, with no other meals, in a dining room in the same building as the tenant's room was held to be sufficient board for the statutory purpose.[10] The provision a meal other than breakfast will suffice, subject to the de minimis principle.

(iii)   *Meaning of attendance*   The word 'attendance' refers to a service personal to the tenant performed by the landlord under covenant for the convenience of the individual tenant in his use or enjoyment of the premises.[11] Examples include the delivery of letters,[12] and the provision of a resident housekeeper who cleaned the tenant's room daily, provided weekly clean linen and a person from whom food could be obtained on request and payment.[13] Services provided to all tenants in common do not qualify as attendance, as for instance, the provision of common central heating, hot water or general porterage.

The landlord must prove that the rent includes payments in respect of attendance.[14] The court may take a broad, commonsense approach. The question is one of fact and degree. Regard is paid to the value or benefit to to the tenant of the attendance. It now appears that 10% is at the lower and 20% at the upper end of the range allowed.[15]

Lettings to students

By s 8(1) of the 1977 Act, a tenancy is not a protected tenancy if it is granted to a person who is pursuing, or who intends to pursue, a course of study provided by a specified educational institution, and the tenancy is either granted by that institution or by another specified[16] institution or body of persons. Private landlords cannot take direct advantage of s 8; but if they let to a specified institution which sub-lets the whole premises to students, the students will have no protection as against the institution and the institution will lack protection.[17]

---

7   *Palser v Grinling* [1948] AC 291, [1948] 1 All ER 1, HL.
8   *Woodward v Docherty, supra.*
9   *Wilkes v Goodwin* [1923] 2 KB 86, CA.
10   *Otter v Norman* [1989] 1 AC 129, [1988] 2 All ER 897, HL.
11   See now *Nelson Developments Ltd v Taboada* [1992] 2 EGLR 107 (where there were six itemised types of service, including taking away, washing and returning linen).
12   *Wood v Cawardine* [1923] 2 KB 185.
13   *Marchant v Charters* [1977] 3 All ER 918, [1977] 1 WLR 1181, CA; *Nelson Developments v Taboada, supra.*
14   *Woodward v Docherty, supra.*
15   *Nelson Developments Ltd v Taboada, supra.*
16   Ie specified in regulations made from time to time (s 8(2)); see eg SI 1993/559.
17   *St Catherine's College v Dorling* [1979] 3 All ER 250, [1980] 1 WLR 66, CA.

Holiday lettings

By s 9 of the 1977 Act, a tenancy is not a protected tenancy if the purpose of the tenancy is to confer on the tenant the right to occupy the dwelling-house for a holiday.[18] Out of season lettings are protected but possession is recoverable after termination of these under a mandatory ground.[19] The policy of s 9 is to deny Rent Act protection to lettings of holiday homes or flats. Yet there is no statutory definition of 'holiday' and so in one case,[20] a dictionary definition was accepted, so that 'holiday' was taken to mean a period of cessation of work or period of recreation. Therefore the question of whether a working holiday is within or outside s 9 was not directly addressed; but it was later held that the word 'holiday' meant simply a suspension of one's normal activities not necessarily implying a period of recreation.[1] Although it is open to question whether the exemption was really required, since it had been said that a holiday tenant could not comply with the statutory residence requirement,[2] the present provision is a useful device enabling landlords to avoid the 1977 Act.[3] The question is how far the courts are prepared to accept at face value a statement of purpose such as that 'it is mutually agreed that the letting hereby made is solely for the purpose of the tenant's holiday in the London area'.[4] Such a statement is evidence of the purpose of the tenancy, and it takes effect unless the tenant proves that it does not correspond with the true purpose of the tenancy, and so, being a misstatement of fact, renders the statement a sham, with the result that full protection would be conferred on the tenant.[5] Thus, where a landlord was proved by the tenants to have known that, despite a statement that the tenancy was (in effect) a holiday letting, the tenants in fact intended to occupy the premises as students, ie for work, the letting fell outside s 9.[6] By contrast, where the tenant held under a three-month tenancy which stated that it was for the purpose of the tenant's holiday in the London area, it was held that the statement had not been proved to be untrue by the tenant, so that it was taken to be genuine, and the agreement therefore stood at face value, so that s 9 applied to exclude the tenancy from protection.[7]

---

18 See Lyons [1984] Conv 286.
19 Rent Act 1977, Sch 15, Part II, Case 13.
20 *Buchmann v May* [1978] 2 All ER 993 at 995, CA.
1 *Francke v Hakmi* [1984] CLY 1906.
2 *Walker v Ogilvy* (1974) 28 P & CR 288 at 293, CA.
3 And no doubt the same will apply to the similar exclusion from assured tenancy status, see ch 18.
4 The statement of purpose in *Buchmann v May*, supra.
5 *Buchmann v May*, supra.
6 *R v Rent Officer for London Borough of Camden, ex p Plant* [1981] 1 EGLR 73.
7 *Buchmann v May*, supra. Thus, that the tenant may be foreign and the flat situated in a place not usually considered to be a holiday resort will not disentitle the landlord to rely on a statement that the letting is for the tenant's holiday unless the statement is proved to be false: see *McHale v Daneham* (1979) 249 Estates Gazette 969; also *Ryeville Properties v Saint-John* [1980] CLY 1598.

Agricultural holdings

By s 10(1) of the Rent Act 1977,[8] a tenancy is not a protected tenancy if the dwelling-house is comprised in an agricultural holding (as defined by s 1 of the Agricultural Holdings Act 1986), where the dwelling-house is occupied by the person responsible for the control (whether as tenant or as a servant or agent of the tenant) of the farming of the holding. A tenancy is also not protected if the dwelling-house is comprised in the holding held under a farm business tenancy (within the Agricultural Tenancies Act 1995) and is occupied by the person responsible for the control (whether as tenant or as servant or agent of the tenant) of the management of the holding. Where a sub-tenancy of part of a house (which is excluded by s 10 from protection) is granted, s 137(3) of the 1977 Act provides that the sub-tenancy is within the 1977 Act: there is deemed to be a separate tenancy of the dwelling-house and the sub-tenancy is not therefore ended merely because the head-tenancy has expired or been terminated by notice to quit.

If, in relation to a tenancy of an agricultural holding granted before 15 January 1989, the tenant unilaterally discontinues all agricultural user, so risking loss of the protection of the 1986 Act, the tenancy cannot fall within the Rent Act 1977, so enabling the tenant to claim security of tenure in relation to the dwelling-house. By contrast, if the previous tenancy has been expressly or impliedly superseded by a new tenancy for residential occupation, then the 1977 Act would apply if the conditions of s 1 were satisfied.[9]

Licensed premises

Section 11 of the Rent Act 1977 provides that a tenancy of a dwelling-house which consists of or comprises premises licensed for the sale of intoxicating liquors on the premises cannot be a protected tenancy.

Resident landlords

A tenancy granted by a resident landlord which falls within s 12 of the 1977 Act is not a protected tenancy, but will be a restricted contract.[10] The policy of this provision is to enable an owner of a house or flat to let rooms without conferring any security on the tenant,[11] and so with the assurance of being able to recover vacant possession at the end of the contractual tenancy with a view to selling his home with vacant possession where appropriate.[12] Only individual landlords and not companies, even where controlled by one person, may benefit from s 12.

---

8   As substituted by Agricultural Tenancies Act 1995, Sch, para 15.
9   *Russell v Booker* [1982] 2 EGLR 86, CA.
10 There is a similar exclusion from assured tenancy status where the landlord is resident (see ch 18) and the discussion in the next pages would seem relevant thereto. In this case, the tenancy may also be an excluded tenancy (i e excluded from s 3 of the Protection from Eviction Act 1977 by Housing Act 1988, s 31) in which case the tenant has no security of tenure whatever.
11 *Cooper v Tait* (1984) 48 P & CR 460, CA.
12 *Barnett v O'Sullivan* [1995] 1 EGLR 93, CA.

(i)   *The rule*   A tenancy of a dwelling-house granted[13] on or after 14 August 1974 is not a protected tenancy if three conditions apply:

1   The dwelling-house forms part only of a building and, except where the dwelling-house also forms part of a flat, the building is not a purpose-built block of flats.
2   The tenancy was granted by a person who, at the time when he granted it, occupied as his residence another dwelling-house:
   (a)   where part of a flat is let, the part occupied by the landlord forms part of the flat;
   (b)   in any other case, it also forms part of the building.
3   At all times since the tenancy was granted the interest of the landlord under the tenancy has belonged to a person who, at the time he owned that interest, occupied as his residence another dwelling-house which:
   (a)   is either part of the same flat in which the tenant resides; or
   (b)   is part of the same building in which the tenant resides.

The last two conditions are, it seems, not to be construed too narrowly, having regard to the policy of s 12, so that where a tenant holding a tenancy within s 12 moved into new accommodation nearby, into which the landlord and his family followed him, a matter of weeks after, the new tenancy was as much subject to s 12 as was the previous one, as there had been, in substance, a concerted move by all parties, despite the time-interval between the actual moves.[14]

(ii)   *'Building'*   The word 'building' is not defined but the question of what is the same building is one of fact. There must be one building at the time of the grant and termination of the tenancy, so that any conversion works to a building during the tenancy must not, as a matter of fact and degree, achieve a separation of the building into two entities.[15] If the landlord lives in an extension to the house where the tenant lives, which extension is separate from the house, having no internal communication with it, and its own separate entrance, the landlord does not live in the same building as the tenant.[16] The mere fact that there may be a continuous roof common to a number of separate units of dwelling does not of itself mean that the units all form one building, but if the appearance of the property is that it is one large continuous building with various extensions in which the landlord and tenant reside, these may be one building, at least if there is no lack of internal communications within the entity.[17] Where two flats had the appearance of being part of the same building, albeit with separate entrances, a ruling that the landlord was resident in the same building was not upset on appeal.[18]

---

13   Excluded is a tenancy granted to a sitting protected or statutory tenant, which remains fully protected or statutory as the case may be: s 12(2).
14   *Barnett v O'Sullivan* supra, CA.
15   *Lewis-Graham v Conacher* [1992] 1 EGLR 111, CA.
16   *Bardrick v Haycock* (1976) 31 P & CR 420, CA.
17   *Griffiths v English* [1982] 1 EGLR 86, CA; also *Guppy v O'Donnell* (1979) 129 NLJ 930.
18   *Wolff v Waddington* [1989] 2 EGLR 108, CA.

(iii)   *Purpose built block of flats*   A building is a purpose-built block of flats if as constructed it contained and contains two or more flats.[19] Thus a two-storey building with a shop on the ground floor and a flat above is not within the term 'purpose-built block of flats'. The exception of s 12 in any event applies where part of a flat is let even though the flat happens to be in a purpose-built block of flats. The question of whether there is a purpose-built block of flats is tested as at the date of the original design and construction of the building: if at that date, there was no purpose-built block of flats, a later conversion of a building into flats will not take a tenancy granted by a resident landlord out of the exception.[20]

(iv)   *Residence requirement*   The residential occupation by the landlord[1] must be continuous at all times since the grant of the tenancy and in another dwelling-house in the same building. A person is treated as occupying a dwelling-house if he fulfils the same conditions as are required by s 2(3) for a statutory tenant.[2] What amounts to sufficient occupation is a question of fact and degree. In one case, the fact that the landlord did not sleep on the premises did not prevent his residing there, as he lived there during the day and kept personal belongings in the subject premises.[3] If the landlord shares with the tenant essential living accommodation, he is not occupying another dwelling-house and s 12 cannot apply.[4]

(v)   *Periods of disregard*   The requirement of continuous residential occupation is relaxed so as to permit the transfer inter vivos and on death of a resident landlord's interest for interim periods of between 28 days and four years[5] without loss of the exemption.
(1) *Owner-occupier inter vivos transfer* A period of up to 28 days is disregarded, from the date when the landlord's interest becomes vested in a non-resident person; but in the case of sale, this period runs from the date of completion of the contract. Within the 28 day period, but not, it seems, after it has elapsed, the disregard period may be extended to a maximum of six months, running from the date of completion, following notice by the non-resident landlord to the tenant of his intention to occupy.[6]
(2) *Transfer to Trustees as such* If the resident landlord's interest becomes vested in trustees as such and remains so vested, there is a two-year period of

---

19 Rent Act 1977 Sch 2 para 4. 'Flat' means a dwelling-house which (1) forms part only of a building, and (2) is separated horizontally from another dwelling-house which forms part of the same building.
20 *Barnes v Gorsuch* (1981) 43 P & CR 294, CA.
1   Which includes one of two or more joint landlords: *Cooper v Tait* (1984) 48 P & CR 460, CA.
2   Rent Act 1977, Sch 2, para 5.
3   *Palmer v MacNamara* [1991] 1 EGLR 121; cf *Jackson v Pekic* (1989) 22 HLR 9, where a landlord out of occupation for three years was not 'resident'.
4   *Lyons v Caffery* [1983] 1 EGLR 102, CA.
5   If landlord A dies and his heir B dies, say, after 23 months, his personal representatives having taken advantage of the two-year suspension period, qv, C, B's heir, has up to a further 24 months in which to become a resident landlord.
6   Rent Act 1977, Sch 2, para 1.

disregard. During any period when the landlord's interest is so vested and his interest or the proceeds of sale are held in trust for a resident beneficiary, the residence requirement is satisfied and no part of this period is to be disregarded.[7] Trustees as such include bare trustees for the landlord, who may thus absent himself for up to two years and vest his interest in trustees for himself. The term also includes cases where trustees hold under a trust of land, and in addition where trustees hold under a trust arising under a will or intestacy.[8]

The effect of the disregard periods in both the above cases is that no order for possession can be made against the tenant during a disregard period save on grounds applicable to a regulated tenancy.[9] During a disregard period the tenant holds over without any right to do so, temporarily protected by the rule just mentioned from an order for possession; once the transitional period ends, two things may happen. First, the tenancy may not by then have been determined: if so the tenant becomes a protected tenant. Second, the non-resident landlord to be or the trustees may have validly determined the tenancy: if so, vacant possession may be obtained after the period of disregard.[10]

(3) *Vesting in personal representatives* Where a resident landlord dies and his interest becomes vested in his personal representatives acting as such after his death, the residence requirement is deemed to be satisfied for two years from the vesting of his interest in these persons.[11] It would appear that this provision involves rather different considerations to the disregard paragraphs just referred to, since the personal representatives acting as such are apparently deemed to be in the same position as the erstwhile resident landlord, for the two year period running from the relevant vesting in them. It is because of that deeming that the statutory ban on recovery of physical possession against the tenant during a disregard period such as that applicable to trustees as such does not appear to apply to personal representatives acting as such. If, during the two-year extension period, the tenancy expires or is determined by notice to quit, as the case may be, the latter being served by the personal representatives, possession may be recovered from the tenant without the need to prove a statutory ground for possession, not only after the end of the extension period but also, and in contrast to the rule for the two disregard periods, while the said period is continuing. If a beneficiary, during the two-year extension period, takes up residence in the dwelling-house or flat, even without a formal assent in their favour, or if the former landlord's interest is vested in such a person, during the extension period, the tenancy will be not protected for so long as the new landlord satisfies the residence requirement.[12] If the extension period

---

7 Ibid, Sch 2, paras 1(c)(ii) and 2, respectively.
8 *Williams v Mate* (1982) 46 P & CR 43, CA.
9 Rent Act 1977, Sch 2, para 3.
10 *Landau v Sloane* [1982] AC 490, HL; *Williams v Mate*, supra.
11 Rent Act 1977, Sch 2, para 2A, inserted be the Housing Act 1980, s 65.
12 *Beebe v Mason* [1980] 1 EGLR 81, CA.

expires and possession has not been recovered during it by the personal representatives and no beneficiary moves into residential occupation then the tenancy becomes protected or statutory as the case may be.[13]

Miscellaneous

Two further exclusions from protection must now be noted.[14]

1   A tenancy is not protected at any time when the landlord's interest belongs to Her Majesty in right of the Crown or belongs to a government department or is held in trust for Her Majesty for the purposes of a government department (s 13(1)(a) of the Rent Act 1977).[15] The operation of the 1977 Act as between tenants and sub-tenants is unaffected by s 13 and sub-tenancies held indirectly from the Crown, ie where the mesne landlord is not the Crown, may be protected or statutory (s 154).

2   If the immediate landlord's interest is held by one of a number of bodies as listed in ss 14-16 of the 1977 Act, such as local authorities, development corporations, a registered or co-operative housing association, the Housing Corporation and charitable housing trusts, the tenancy is not protected, although, as will appear, it may be secure. Should the landlord assign his reversion to a non-exempt landlord, the tenancy will come within the 1977 Act unless excluded for some other reason.

C   RENT REGULATION

I   INTRODUCTION

Rent regulation applies to protected and statutory tenancies alike, both of which are 'regulated tenancies'. During a protected tenancy, if no rent is registered for the dwelling-house, the parties are free to agree on any rent level. One party alone, or both jointly, may apply for the rent to be registered as a fair rent to a Rent Officer, who must act within statutory guidelines.

II   RENT LIMIT DURING THE PROTECTED TENANCY

The maximum amount of rent recoverable from a regulated tenant during the protected tenancy (referred to as a 'contractual period' by s 61(1)) varies. If

---

13   *Landau v Sloane*, supra.
14   As to the exclusion of tenancies of overcrowded dwellings, see Rent Act 1977, s 101; of tenancies of parsonage houses, Sch 15, Part II, Case 15; and as to the regulatory ministerial power to exclude by order all tenancies of dwelling-houses in a particular area from being regulated tenancies, see s 143(1).
15   If the interest of the immediate landlord is held by one of these bodies, the tenant cannot be a statutory tenant (s 13(1)(b)). If the interest of the Crown is managed by the Crown Estate Commissioners, s 13(2) allows the tenancy to be protected or statutory.

there is a previous uncancelled registered rent, by s 44(1) of the 1977 Act, the rent recoverable from the tenant is limited to the registered rent, and any excess over that figure is irrecoverable from the tenant (s 44(2)). If there is no registered rent, then the rent limit is simply the rent agreed between the landlord and tenant.

The dwelling-house originally specified for the purposes of registration of a previous rent (s 66(2)(b)) may no longer be the same as the premises let to the current regulated tenant, as where he holds a tenancy of additional or different rooms in the house or flat concerned, or where he is let the whole, as opposed to just part, of a house. In these cases, because the unit of letting is not the same, the previously registered rent will not apply to the new tenancy.[16] This principle does not necessarily apply to a re-letting of the same accommodation. Where a flat was let furnished in 1987 at a monthly rent of £450, but a fair rent of £550 a year had been registered for the premises in 1974, when unfurnished, the 1974 rent remained the sole recoverable rent. The premises had not undergone such a change in their structure as to be no longer a dwelling (s 44); the registered rent was not cancelled (s 73) and no new registration of rent had, under s 67(3), been entered.[17]

III   RENT LIMIT DURING THE STATUTORY TENANCY

In this case, the rent limit depends on examination of the position at the date of the termination of the protected tenancy. If under the last 'contractual period' of the regulated tenancy, there is no registered rent, then the rent limit is the rent recoverable for that period (s 45(1))[18] and any excess is irrecoverable from the tenant. By contrast, where there is a registered rent for the last contractual period of the regulated tenancy, the rent limit is the rent registered for that period (s 45(1)) and again, any excess is irrecoverable from the tenant.[19]

IV   APPLICATION FOR REGISTRATION OF RENT

An application for the registration of a fair rent under Part IV of the 1977 Act must be made to the Rent Officer.[20] The landlord or tenant alone may apply or

---

16 See *Gluchowska v Tottenham Borough Council* [1954] 1 QB 438, [1954] 1 All ER 408, a decision on rent control provisions under furnished lettings.

17 *Rakhit v Carty* (1990) 22 HLR 198, CA; *Cheniston Investments Ltd v Waddock* [1988] 2 EGLR 136, CA (where the landlord modernised and refurbished a flat).

18 Subject to the adjustments specified in ss 47 and 49 in respect of rates borne by the landlord and alterations in the quality or quantity of furniture provided.

19 If the amount of the registered rent under this rule exceeds the actual amount of the rent payable for a statutory period, the rent may be brought up to the registered amount by means of a notice of increase specifying the date on which the increase is to take effect, which is not earlier than the date of registration nor four weeks from service of the notice (s 45).

20 This must be in the form prescribed by Rent Act 1977 (Forms etc) Regulations 1980, SI 1980/1697 as amended.

the application may be joint (s 67). A registered rent takes effect for two years from the date of registration (s 72(1)).[1] The fact that the tenant is not in occupation will not disentitle him from applying.[2] The application form must be duly completed, or the application will be a nullity, and the amount of the proposed rent must be stated.[3] If one of a number of joint tenants applies, unless he has authority to apply for the others,[4] the application will be invalid.[5] Detailed rules govern the procedure for applications for registration of a fair rent.[6] Both parties have a right of appeal to a Rent Assessment Committee from the Rent Officer's decision; the appeal is a re-hearing. If the Committee decide on a different rent to that assessed by the Rent Officer, the registration takes effect from the date of its decision (s 72(2)). The High Court has statutory powers to review decisions of Rent Assessment Committees.

Some 'fair rents' are assessed by Committees by use of the comparables method, and so on the basis of evidence put to them of comparable rents. It may well be increasingly the case that comparables of this kind will reflect the fact that some of the tenancies of the dwelling-houses concerned have been let to assured or assured shorthold tenants. These rents are market rents and contain no allowance for the fact that accommodation may be in scarce supply. Owing perhaps to the impossibility of drawing technical distinctions between regulated rents and assured tenancy rents, the High Court has now indicated that, at least where assured tenancy comparable rents are produced, while Committees are required by statute to discount any scarcity element from these rents, evidence of a scarcity of accommodation must be demonstrated by the Committee to exist on the facts.[7] However, there remains the so far unresolved difficulty that it may not be easy for Committees to discover whether there is any inherent scarcity value in assured tenancy comparables; and it may be the case that in other respects, the premises are shown not to be comparable, as where the subject premises are old-fashioned but the comparable premises are such that the landlord provides inducements to let such as carpets and curtains.[8]

V   DETERMINATION OF A FAIR RENT

Section 70(1) of the 1977 Act provides that in determining a fair rent (which is a market rent) under a regulated tenancy, regard is to be had to all the

---

1 The landlord alone may apply for a different rent within the last three months of this period (s 67(4)).
2 *London Housing and Commercial Properties Ltd v Cowan* [1977] QB 148, [1976] 2 All ER 385; also an application may be made by a tenants' association: *Feather Supplies Ltd v Ingham* [1971] 2 QB 348, [1971] 3 All ER 556, CA.
3 *Chapman v Earl* [1968] 2 All ER 1214, [1968] 1 WLR 1315; but the prescribed particulars requirement is not mandatory: *Druid Development Co (Bingley) Ltd v Kay* (1982) 44 P & CR 76, CA.
4 As in *R v Rent Officer for the London Borough of Camden, ex p Felix* [1988] 2 EGLR 132.
5 *Turley v Panton* (1975) 29 P & CR 397.
6 Rent Act 1977, Sch 11, Part I.
7 *BTE Ltd v Merseyside and Cheshire Rent Assessment Committee* [1992] 1 EGLR 116.
8 See Pritchard (1995) 145 NLJ 210.

circumstances, but not to personal circumstances. It is apparently permissible for inflation to be taken into account in such manner as the Rent Officer or Rent Assessment Committee deem reasonable, provided cogent reasons are given.[9] Should a Committee, having given cogent reasons for so doing, adopt the 'contractor's method' (finding the sums which would represent a fair return on the landlord's capital), then any security of tenure of the tenant must be disregarded as a personal circumstance. The value of such security depends on personal factors such as his age, which has nothing to do with a return on capital. If comparable rents (both of regulated and assured tenancies) are used, which is seemingly the ordinary method, any security of tenure of the tenants under these tenancies is taken into account in assessing the rent and may well increase it.[10]

Statute directs that three particular matters must be taken into account.

1 The age, character, locality and state of repair of the dwelling-house (s 70(1)(a)).
2 The quantity, quality and condition of any furniture provided for use under the tenancy (s 70(1)(b)).[11]
3 Any premium or sum in the nature of a premium, which has been or may be lawfully required or received on the grant, renewal, continuance or assignment of the tenancy (s 70(1)(c)).

Disregards

The following matters must be disregarded.

1 *Scarcity* Any element of scarcity in the relevant neighbourhood, by assuming that the number of persons seeking to become tenants of similar dwelling-houses in the locality on terms (other than as to rent) is not substantially greater than the number of such dwelling-houses in the locality which are available for letting on such terms (s 70(2)). Scarcity is distinct from matters such as specific amenities or any inherent advantages in the particular dwelling-house, which matters may be taken into account.[12] Where there was no scarcity, however, it was held that a Rent Assessment Committee was not entitled to determine a reasonable rent, below that of the open market: it ought to have assessed a fair rent on the basis of comparable assured tenancy rents.[13] If such comparables are presented to the Committee, they must take these into account and, if they wish to make a discount from the market rent so arrived at, owing to scarcity values, they must give proper reasons for so doing. It is true that it was held by one Committee that the requirement of a market rent less any scarcity could be qualified by the requirement of a fair return on the landlord's capital, and by the fact that the

9 *Metropolitan Property Holdings Ltd v Laufer* (1974) 29 P & CR 172; *Wareing v White* [1985] 1 EGLR 125, CA; *R v London Rent Assessment Panel, ex p Chelmsford Building Co Ltd* [1986] 1 EGLR 175.
10 *Spath Holme Ltd v Greater Manchester and Lancashire Rent Assessment Committee* [1995] 2 EGLR 80, CA.
11 *R v London Rent Assessment Panel, ex p Mota* (1987) 20 HLR 159 (furniture 'provided' is available to the tenant, even if not used by him).
12 *Metropolitan Property Holdings Ltd v Finegold* [1975] 1 All ER 389, [1975] 1 WLR 349.
13 *BTE Ltd v Merseyside and Cheshire Rent Assessment Committee* [1992] 1 EGLR 116.

intervals between revisions of 'fair rents' were twice as long as those between revisions of assured tenancy rents.[14] Despite the seeming flexibility and realism of this latter approach, it may be less easy to adopt it in future since the Court of Appeal has indicated that it is preferable for Committees to evaluate comparable rents of assured and regulated tenancies. Where a Committee rejected the assured tenancy comparables, and examined only the rents of regulated tenancies in the premises, in relation to a flat in a block where there were lettings of both types of tenancy, it was held to have erred in law. It was seemingly held that if registered rent comparables had built into them an open market rent with a scarcity discount, then so too did assured tenancy rents presented by the landlord, and the latter were comparable accordingly with the former, as market rents with a scarcity discount were what the statute required to be assessed, seeing that the security offered by each type was comparable.[15] The latter assertion, having regard to the absence of statutory tenancies and the greater ease of repossession in the case of assured tenancies seems less than fully accurate but overall this ruling may simplify the position at the price of limiting the discretion of Committees.

2 *Disrepair* Any disrepair or other defect attributable to a failure by the tenant or any predecessor in title of his to comply with the terms of the regulated tenancy (s 70(3)(a)).[16]

3 *Improvements* Any improvement, including the replacement of any fixture or fitting, carried out, otherwise than in pursuance of the terms of the tenancy, by the tenant under the regulated tenancy or any predecessor in title of his (s 70(3)(b)).[17]

4 *Furniture* If any furniture is provided under the regulated tenancy, any improvement to it by the tenant or any predecessor in title of his; and any deterioration in the condition of the furniture due to any ill-treatment by the tenant and any person residing or lodging with him or any sub-tenant of his (s 70(3)(e)).

Repairs and services

(1) *Repairs* A landlord's failure to enforce a tenant's covenant to repair cannot be taken into account and the premises must be valued as at the date of the determination.[18] A low rent may be registered where the state of disrepair is not the fault of the tenant.[19]

14 *Aspley Hall Estates Ltd v Nottingham Rent Officers* [1992] 2 EGLR 187.
15 *Spath Holme Ltd v Greater Manchester and Lancashire Rent Assessment Committee* supra. If, of course, an assured tenancy rent is not comparable, at least not without deductions, it may properly be rejected: see *Curtis v London Rent Assessment Committee* (1996) 28 HLR 841.
16 See *Sturolson & Co v Mauroux* (1988) 20 HLR 332, CA. This disregard does not extend to a tenant's failure to comply with some lesser obligation eg to use furnished premises in a tenant-like manner, which neglect may properly be taken into account: *Firstcross Ltd v Teasdale* (1982) 47 P & CR 228.
17 Ie a predecessor in title to the tenant in the premises, as opposed to a person who improves them and then obtains a lease: *Trustees of Henry Smith's Charity v Hemmings* (1981) 45 P & CR 377.
18 *Metropolitan Properties Co Ltd v Wooldridge* (1968) 20 P & CR 64.
19 *McGee v London Rent Assessment Panel Committee* (1969) 210 Estates Gazette 1431 (unexplained fire); but it was held not to be obligatory to register a nil rent merely because the house was subject to a closing order: *Williams v Khan* (1980) 43 P & CR 1, CA.

(2) *Services* Services provided under covenant by the landlord are matters which should be taken into account where appropriate.[20] Since the basis of valuation is the value of the service to the tenant, if a service is insufficiently provided, however, any allowance made for it will be reduced.[1] The cost of services to the landlord may be taken into account, and, if it is, depreciation of his equipment which provides services and for his profit must be included in any allowance,[2] and in respect of the cost of replacement, based on original cost.[3]

General principles

One of the methods of assessing a fair rent is to take into account any evidence presented to the rent officer or Committee of comparable rents in the vicinity, which may be registered comparables,[4] or, increasingly perhaps, rents of local assured tenancies. It is, as seen, for the assessing body to decide whether there is a scarcity element in the comparable rents, and if there is in fact a scarcity element, as opposed to in the interests of what might seem to be fair, such element must be discounted from the rent.[5] This is because s 70(2) requires the assumption to be made that there is an equilibrium of supply and demand, so causing a discount to any comparable rent inflated by the scarcity element alone. Rent Officers and Committees are not bound to use the comparables method. They may use any lawful valuation method, such as that of basing the rent on a fair return to the landlord of his capital (the 'contractors' method), even though this was criticised in the House of Lords as being notoriously unreliable.[6]

VI REGISTRATION AND ITS RESULTS

Once a fair rent has been determined, it must be entered by the Rent Officer in an area register.[7] The registered rent includes services and furniture, if any.[8] Services should be considered separately and include insurance and depreciation to boilers and lifts, but not the insurance of the whole building.[9]

20 *R v Paddington North and St Marylebone Rent Tribunal, ex p Perry* [1956] 1 QB 229, [1955] 3 All ER 391.
1 *Metropolitan Properties Co v Noble* [1968] 2 All ER 313, [1968] 1 WLR 838.
2 *Perseus Property Co Ltd v Burberry* [1985] 1 EGLR 114.
3 *Regis Property Co v Dudley* [1958] 1 QB 346, [1958] 1 All ER 510, CA. In this and any like case, the landlord's figures ought to be considered but do not mandatorily have to be accepted: *R v London Rent Assessment Panel, ex p Cliftvylle Properties Ltd* [1983] 1 EGLR 100.
4 *Tormes Property Co v Landau* [1971] 1 QB 261, [1970] 3 All ER 653; *Mason v Skilling,* [1974] 3 All ER 977, HL.
5 *BTE Ltd v Merseyside and Cheshire Rent Assessment Panel* [1992] 1 EGLR 116.
6 *Western Heritable Investment Co Ltd v Husband* [1983] 2 AC 849, [1983] 3 All ER 65, at pp 857 and 69; but see above.
7 Rent Act 1977, s 66. As to the details of what must appear in the entry see s 71 and SI 1980/1697.
8 Rent Act 1977, s 71; see *Firstcross Ltd v Teasdale* (1982) 47 P & CR 228. As to service charges in particular, see s 71(4); if these are considered unreasonable, the correct amount may be ascertained: see eg *Betts v Vivamat Properties Ltd* [1984] 1 EGLR 95.
9 Whose cost is relevant generally: *Property Holding and Investment Trust v London Rent Assessment Panel* (1969) 20 P & CR 808.

The registration, or confirmation, of a fair rent takes effect from the date of registration by a Rent Officer or the date of a Rent Assessment Committee's decision (s 72(1)). No further single application for a registered rent may be entertained within the two years following the date when the registered rent took effect or was confirmed (s 67(3) and (5)).[10] The rent may be reconsidered within the two-year period on the application of either party (s 67(3)) if there is a change in one of four specified circumstances, namely, any change: (a) in the condition of the dwelling-house, including the making of any improvements; (b) in the terms of the tenancy; (c) in the quantity, quality or condition of any furniture provided for use under the tenancy[11] or (d) in any other circumstances taken into consideration when the rent was last registered or confirmed. Once the landlord makes out a case for a reconsideration of the fair registered rent, all the relevant circumstances may be taken into account, not just the change in condition which allowed reconsideration.[12]

A registered rent may be cancelled, without prejudice to subsequent applications, where the dwelling-house is not subject to a regulated tenancy, the two-year time bar is up and the applicant would be the landlord if there were such a tenancy (s 73(1A)).

D   GROUNDS FOR POSSESSION

I   RESTRICTIONS ON RECOVERY OF POSSESSION

A tenant whose tenancy is within the Rent Act 1977 may only be evicted from the dwelling-house concerned following proceedings in the county court taken by the landlord. The landlord is bound by the restrictions of s 98 of the Rent Act 1977, which are overriding of any contract between the parties,[13] although if the tenant concedes that s 98 does not apply, the court may order possession without reference to it.[14] The fact that a tenancy may have come to an end at common law does not enable the landlord to re-gain possession of the dwelling-house. He may only do so if he shows that he has one or more statutory grounds for doing so, and in some cases he must also satisfy the court that it is reasonable to grant him possession. Judicial notice has been taken of the fact that most cases for re-possession will be concerned with statutory tenancies, and the court is entitled to assume that a Rent Act tenancy will be statutory rather than protected.[15]

---

10   Subject to s 67(4), allowing for a landlord's application during the last three months of the two-year period, the new rent to take effect from the end of that period.
11   Excluding deterioration by fair wear and tear.
12   *London Housing and Commercial Properties v Cowan* [1977] QB 148, [1976] 2 All ER 385.
13   *Appleton v Aspin* [1988] 1 All ER 904, [1988] 1 WLR 410, CA.
14   *Barton v Fincham* [1921] 2 KB 291; *Syed Hussain v AM Abdulla Sahib & Co* [1985] 1 WLR 1392; but if the tenant does not concede his case, an order cannot be made without the landlord proving a ground and compliance with s 98(1) where appropriate: *R v Newcastle upon Tyne County Court, ex p Thompson* [1988] 2 EGLR 119.
15   *White v Wareing* [1992] 1 EGLR 271 (no notice to quit being necessary owing to the statutory restrictions on re-possession).

Section 98 distinguishes between the rules applicable where suitable alternative accommodation is available to the tenant and 'discretionary' grounds for possession, which are subject to an overriding discretion in the court to refuse an order if it thinks it unreasonable to make the order, despite the landlord's proving the ground concerned, and 'mandatory' grounds for possession, where the overriding discretion of the court is absent. This distinction is also drawn in the case of assured tenancies: the general principles concerned with the overriding discretion apply, in the absence of authority, to the 'discretionary' grounds applicable to these tenancies.

Discretionary grounds – introduction

By s 98(1) of the 1977 Act, the court must not make an order for possession of a dwelling-house let on a protected or statutory tenancy unless the court considers it reasonable to make such an order and either:

(a) the court is satisfied that suitable alternative accommodation is available for the tenant or will be available for him when the order in question takes effect, or

(b) the court is satisfied that the landlord has established one of the Cases (or grounds) for possession set out in Sch 15, Part I, which are referred to as 'discretionary grounds'.

The court's overriding discretion not to order possession despite the proof of alternative accommodation or of a 'discretionary ground' should operate as follows. The onus of convincing the court that it is reasonable to order possession is on the landlord.[16] The county court judge is required to direct his mind to the question of reasonableness and exercise his discretion judicially, having regard to the general scheme and purpose of the Act, and to the special conditions, which will largely include matters of a domestic and general character.[17] The judge is bound to take account of all the relevant circumstances as they exist at the date of the hearing in a broad common-sense way, giving whatever weight he thinks right to the various factors in the situation.[18] Even where a ground or Case itself in terms involves a requirement of reasonableness, the general issue of reasonableness must itself be separately considered.[19] Once the judge has heard the relevant evidence, it will ordinarily be assumed that he directed his mind to the overall issue of reasonableness.[20] If for some reason the judge has not done so, the Court of Appeal has exercised its own discretion.[1] However, the Court of Appeal will not interfere with any proper exercise of discretion,[2] even if it might have acted differently to the judge.

---

16 *Smith v McGoldrick* [1977] 1 EGLR 53, CA.
17 *Chiverton v Ede* [1921] 2 KB 30 at 45; *Redspring Ltd v Francis* [1973] 1 All ER 640, [1973] 1 WLR 134, CA.
18 *Cumming v Danson* [1942] 2 All ER 653 at 655; *Dawncar Investments Ltd v Plews* [1994] 1 EGLR 141, CA.
19 *Shrimpton v Rabbits* (1924) 131 LT 478 at 469 (Case 9).
20 See eg *Minchburn Ltd v Fernandez* [1986] 2 EGLR 103, CA (where the judge related reasonableness solely to the specific, not the general, issue of reasonableness).
 1 As in *Roberts v Macilwraith-Christie* [1987] 1 EGLR 224.
 2 *RF Fuggle Ltd v Gadsden* [1948] 2 KB 236, [1948] 2 All ER 160.

In the exercise of the overall discretion, the judge must consider all the relevant circumstances in relation to both the landlord and the tenant, the premises and the interests of the public.[3] It was therefore open to a judge to refuse to order possession, he having taken into account the personal attachment of the tenant to her existing flat, where she had lived for 35 years.[4] Anything which may cause hardship to either party is relevant.[5] The conduct of the parties is relevant, such as an expressed intention to continue a breach of covenant.[6] It is easier to establish reasonableness when suitable alternative accommodation is available for the tenant than when it is not, but there is no hard and fast rule.[7] Thus if the suitable alternative accommodation is part of the house which the tenant currently occupies exclusively, so precluding him from living with persons of his own choosing, it may be unreasonable to order possession.[8]

Mandatory grounds – introduction

If the landlord would be entitled to recover possession because the matter falls within one of the mandatory grounds for possession (Sch 15, Part II), the court must make an order for possession. The court has, in such cases, no overriding discretion to refuse to make an order for possession on the ground that it is not reasonable to do so, once the landlord has made out the facts of a mandatory case to its satisfaction and has proved a genuine case.[9]

II   SUITABLE ALTERNATIVE ACCOMMODATION

Statutory definitions

Subject to the overriding discretion of the court to refuse to order possession despite proof of the availability of suitable alternative accommodation, which discretion must always be separately considered,[10] the landlord may satisfy the onus of proving that suitable alternative accommodation is available to the tenant by producing a certificate of the local housing authority that they will provide such accommodation for the tenant by a date specified in the notice: it is conclusive evidence for the purpose of establishing this ground.[11]

In the absence of such a certificate, accommodation, whether offered by the landlord himself, or available otherwise, in either case at the date of the hearing,[12] will be deemed to be suitable if it consists of either:

---

3   *Cresswell v Hodgson* [1951] 2 KB 92, CA.
4   *Battlespring Ltd v Gates* [1983] 2 EGLR 103, CA.
5   *Williamson v Pallant* [1924] 2 KB 173.
6   *Bell London and Provincial Properties v Reuben* [1947] KB 157, [1946] 2 All ER 547, CA.
7   *Cumming v Danson*, supra.
8   *Yoland Ltd v Reddington* [1982] 2 EGLR 80, CA.
9   *Kennealy v Dunne* [1977] QB 837, [1977] 2 All ER 16, CA.
10 *Hill v Rochard* [1983] 2 All ER 21, [1983] 1 WLR 478, CA; *Battlespring Ltd v Gates* [1983] 2 EGLR 103, CA.
11 Rent Act 1977, Sch 15, Part IV, para 3.
12 *Nevile v Hardy* [1921] 1 Ch 404.

(a) premises comprising a separate dwelling so as to be let on a protected tenancy (other than one on which the landlord might recover possession under one of the mandatory re-possession grounds); or

(b) premises to be let as a separate dwelling on such terms as will, in the opinion of the court, afford to the tenant the same security of tenure as under a protected tenancy, other than such a tenancy with the right to mandatory re-possession.

There are additional conditions to be proved where the accommodation is not based on a local authority certificate. It must, in the opinion of the court, be reasonably suitable to the needs of the tenant and his family as regards proximity to place of work, and either:

(a) similar as regards rental and extent to the accommodation afforded by any local housing authority for persons whose needs as regards extent are, in the opinion of the court, similar to those of the tenant and of his family; or

(b) reasonably suitable to the means of the tenant and to the needs of the tenant and his family[13] as regards extent and character.[14]

If any furniture was provided for use under the protected or statutory tenancy in question, furniture is provided for use in the accommodation which is either similar to that so provided or is reasonably suitable to the needs of the tenant and his family.

Further considerations

The courts interpret the requirement that the accommodation is to be suitable objectively, without making concessions to special fads of the particular tenant but taking into account substantially adverse factors, especially related to his quality of life. Thus, the fact that the accommodation offered was unsuitable for the tenant to entertain business acquaintances and had no garden for the tenant's child has been held to be relevant,[15] as was the fact that the proposed accommodation would not enable the tenant to carry out his profession as an artist because it lacked a studio.[16] So too has the fact that it would not accommodate the tenant's furniture,[17] but not that it had no garage.[18] Shared accommodation is not suitable,[19] but the dwelling under the current tenancy *minus* one room (as where the landlord lives in the same house and requires an additional room for his own family) may be suitable, depending on the needs of the tenant;[20] indeed, where the tenant has sub-let part of the premises under

---

13 'Family', by analogy with statutory tenancies, does not include friends (*Kavanagh v Lyroudias* [1985] 1 All ER 560, CA) nor a resident housekeeper (*Darnell v Millward* [1951] 1 All ER 88, CA).

14 Sch 15, Part IV, para 5(1). A local housing authority certificate may be issued under para 5(2); see *Jones v Cook* [1990] 2 EGLR 108, CA.

15 *De Markozoff v Craig* (1949) 93 Sol Jo 693, CA.

16 *MacDonnell v Daly* [1969] 3 All ER 851, [1969] 1 WLR 1482, CA.

17 *McIntyre v Hardcastle* [1948] 2 KB 82, [1948] 1 All ER 696, CA.

18 *Briddon v George* [1946] 1 All ER 609, CA.

19 *Barnard v Towers* [1953] 2 All ER 877, [1953] 1 WLR 1203, CA.

20 *Mykolyshyn v Noah* [1971] 1 All ER 49, [1970] 1 WLR 1217, CA.

the tenancy, it would be difficult for him to show that it was not suitable.[1] 'Place of work' does not necessarily refer to a single place of work: an area in which the tenant travels to carry out his profession may itself constitute the 'place of work'.[2]

In deciding whether proposed accommodation is suitable as regards 'extent and character', the court will, for reasons just mentioned, examine the particular tenant's objective housing needs, not other ancillary advantages enjoyed with the present accommodation, nor to the tenant's own peculiar wishes and desires.[3] The court may, in dealing with 'character', objectively compare the present environment of the tenant and that offered in the alternative accommodation. Environmental factors are relevant to this question, so that accommodation was not suitable where it was situated in a busy road with a nearby hospital and fish and chip shop, in place of the tenant's quiet residential flat.[4] Such factors can only be taken into account if they relate to the character of the property itself as opposed to personal factors such as alleged loss of friends or culture due to the move away from the present accommodation.[5]

III   DISCRETIONARY GROUNDS FOR POSSESSION

The court may order possession, absolutely or conditionally,[6] in favour of a landlord who proves that the matter falls within one or more of the following 'cases', subject to its overriding discretion (s 98(1)) to refuse possession. If the court makes an order for possession, it may exercise, on the tenant's or his spouse's application,[7] extensive discretionary powers to adjourn the proceedings. It may also stay or suspend the execution of the order for possession, either at the date the order is made or at any time until it is executed.[8]

It is not for the landlord to enforce any court order for possession himself and so a landlord who ejected a statutory tenant against whom an order for possession had been made but not then executed was liable in the sum of £28,300 damages for illegal eviction, calculated in accordance with s 28 of the Housing Act 1988.[9]

1   *Thompson v Rolls* [1926] 2 KB 426; *Parmee v Mitchell* [1950] 2 KB 199, [1950] 2 All ER 872, CA.
2   *Yewbright Properties Ltd v Stone* (1980) 40 P & CR 402, CA (hence, a tenant's difficulty in travel from the proposed accommodation to various places of work was relevant).
3   *Hill v Rochard* [1983] 2 All ER 21, [1983] 1 WLR 478, CA.
4   *Redspring Ltd v Francis* [1973] 1 All ER 640, [1973] 1 WLR 134, CA.
5   *Siddiqui v Rashid* [1980] 3 All ER 184, [1980] 1 WLR 1018, CA.
6   In the case of an absolute order, the tenancy ends and cannot be succeeded to if the tenant dies before it is executed: *American Economic Laundry v Little* [1951] 1 KB 400, [1950] 2 All ER 1186.
7   Rent Act 1977, s 100(4A) and (4B).
8   Rent Act 1977, s 100(1) and (2). The court, save in the case of exceptional hardship to the tenant, or where this would otherwise be unreasonable, must impose conditions as to the payment by the tenant of arrears of rent or mesne profits, and may impose such other conditions as it thinks fit (s 100(3)).
9   *Haniff v Robinson* [1993] 1 All ER 185, CA, applying s 3 of the Protection from Eviction Act 1977 (ch 20).

Case 1: breach of obligation

Where any rent lawfully due from the tenant has not been paid or any obligation of the tenancy has been broken or not performed.

This is a difficult ground for a landlord to rely on, since no order can be made if rent is tendered before commencement of the proceedings;[10] if rent is paid after the commencement of proceedings, an order can be made, and in practice, even if arrears are still unpaid at the time of the hearing, the court will rarely make an absolute order unless the arrears are substantial or there are other special circumstances, such as the tenant's bad record for non-payment.[11] Where a tenant withheld rent because of a reasonable complaint of a landlord's breach of covenant to repair, it was not reasonable to order possession.[12] A statutory tenant by succession is not liable for arrears of rent owed by his predecessor at the time of his death.[13]

On the overriding question of reasonableness of granting an order for possession, the court will take into account the fact that the tenant has remedied the breach at the time of the hearing or that he is willing to give an undertaking in respect of it.[14] Case 1 applies to both to breaches of a continuing and of a once and for all nature. It was therefore held to apply to a breach of covenant against business user[15] and to sub-lettings, as opposed to an occupation by lodgers, without the landlord's consent.[16] It is a natural inference, in this connection, that a statutory tenant may occupy the premises with his family or extended family as licensees, without committing a breach within Case 1.[17]

A landlord cannot rely on a breach that he has waived, but the common law doctrine of waiver cannot strictly apply to a statutory tenancy; but the landlord may lose the right to rely on this ground by continued acceptance of the rent in knowledge of the breach without qualification and undue delay in commencing proceedings.[18]

Case 2: Nuisance, etc

Where the tenant or any person residing or lodging with him or any sub-tenant has been guilty of conduct which is a nuisance or annoyance to adjoining occupiers, or has been convicted of using the dwelling-house, or allowing it to be used, for immoral or illegal purposes.

10 *Bird v Hildage* [1948] 1 KB 91, [1947] 2 All ER 7, CA.
11 *Dellenty v Pellow* [1951] 2 KB 858, [1951] 2 All ER 716; the exact amounts owed must be discovered: see *Crompton v Broomfield* [1990] EGCS 137, CA.
12 *Televantos v McCulloch* [1991] 1 EGLR 123, CA.
13 *Tickner v Clifton* [1929] 1 KB 207.
14 However, s 212 of the Common Law Procedure Act 1852 does not apply to a statutory tenant: *Brewer v Jacobs* [1923] 1 KB 528.
15 *Florent v Horez* (1983) 48 P & CR 166, CA.
16 *Roberts v Macilwraith-Christie* [1987] 1 EGLR 224, CA.
17 *Blanway Investments Ltd v Lynch* (1993) 25 HLR 378, CA.
18 *Oak Property Co Ltd v Chapman* [1947] KB 886, [1947] 2 All ER 1; *Henry Smith's Charity Trustees v Willson* [1983] QB 316, [1983] 1 All ER 73, CA.

This ground for possession remains unaltered in contrast to the extension of its scope by the Housing Act 1996 in the case of assured and secure tenancies (chapters 18 and 19).

'Annoyance' has a wider meaning than 'nuisance'. Any behaviour which is likely materially to affect the peace of mind or physical comfort of an ordinary person is an annoyance, and it may be inferred without evidence from adjoining occupiers.[19] 'Adjoining' means 'neighbouring' and the premises of the complainant need not necessarily be physically contiguous to or even on the same floor as the offending tenant.[20] Conviction of immoral or illegal user is sufficient for this ground to be relied on, without evidence of nuisance or annoyance, and if the purpose of the tenant's user of the premises is illegal or immoral, a single offence is sufficient.[1] If an offence is committed on the premises accidentally, when the user itself is capable of being lawful, this is not enough to infringe Case 2.[2] Where the tenant was convicted of being in unlawful possession of cannabis resin, the drugs having been found on the premises, the Court of Appeal held that possession without knowledge did not constitute using the dwelling for illegal purposes; though presumably it would have been otherwise if it had been used for storing the drugs.[3] Even if the nuisance has abated, it may be reasonable for an order for possession to be made.[4]

Case 3: Deterioration by waste or neglect

> Where the condition of the dwelling-house has deteriorated owing to acts of waste by, or the neglect or default of, the tenant, any sub-tenant or any lodger, and if caused by a sub-tenant or lodger, the court is satisfied that the tenant has not, before the making of the order in question, taken all reasonable steps to remove him.

'Waste' includes unauthorised alterations to the premises such as putting in new doors, enlargement of rooms, etc and also demolishing any part of the premises.[5] Likewise, failure by the tenant to take reasonable precautions to look after the premises causing deterioration to them, such as deterioration due to want of firing and airing in winter[6] or due to frost damage, will presumably suffice within this ground. Where the tenant allowed the garden to grow uncontrolled for a growing season, possession was ordered but the order was suspended for a year to allow her to comply with her obligations.[7]

---

19 *Frederick Platts & Co Ltd v Grigor* [1950] 1 All ER 941n; eg substantial business user of the tenant's residential flat; *Florent v Horez* (1983) 48 P & CR 166, CA.
20 *Cobstone Investments Ltd v Maxim* [1985] QB 140, [1984] 2 All ER 635, CA; Lyons (1985) Conv 168: nor is the sub-tenant of the tenant himself included as an 'occupier': *Chester v Potter* [1949] EGD 247.
1 *S Schneiders & Sons v Abrahams* [1925] 1 KB 301, CA.
2 See *Waller & Son Ltd v Thomas* [1921] 1 KB 541 (sale, out of hours, of intoxicating liquor).
3 *Abrahams v Wilson* [1971] 2 QB 88, [1971] 2 All ER 1114, CA.
4 *Florent v Horez* (1983) 48 P & CR 166, CA.
5 *Marsden v Edward Heyes Ltd* [1927] 2 KB 1, CA.
6 *Robertson v Wilson* 1922 SLT (Sh Ct) 21.
7 *Holloway v Povey* [1984] 2 EGLR 115, CA.

Case 4: Deterioration of furniture by ill-treatment

Where the condition of any furniture provided for use under the tenancy has deteriorated owing to ill-treatment by the tenant or any person residing or lodging with him or any sub-tenant of his, and, in the case of lodgers of the tenant or any sub-tenant of his, the court is satisfied that the tenant has not, before the making of the order for possession, taken reasonable steps to remove the lodger or sub-tenant.

Case 5: Tenant's notice to quit

Where the tenant has given notice to quit, and in consequence of that notice, the landlord has contracted to sell or let the dwelling-house, or has taken any other steps as a result of which he would be seriously prejudiced if he could not obtain possession.

This ground may be relied upon where the tenant gives an undertaking that he will give up possession, though not strictly in terms of a notice to quit; it does not apply to surrender.[8] Where a contractual tenant gave a notice to quit, and after its expiry changed her mind, the Court of Appeal held that the tenant was thereupon a statutory tenant, and that since, on the facts, the landlord only intended to sell and had not contracted to sell, he could not rely on this ground.[9]

Case 6: Assignment or sub-letting

Where, without the consent of the landlord, the tenant has assigned or sub-let the whole of the dwelling-house or sub-let part of the dwelling-house, the remainder being already sub-let. This applies for most regulated tenancies, and to assignments or sub-lettings since 8 December 1965.[10]

Case 6 is available to the landlord whether the tenancy is contractual or statutory, and whether or not there is a covenant against assignment or subletting in the head tenancy.[11] Even if there is a sub-tenant who is 'lawful' within s 137, the court may order possession against the sub-tenant under Case 6.[12] The policy of Case 6 is evidently to protect the landlord against the risk of finding a person unknown to him irremovably installed in his property.[13]

'Consent', however, need not be in writing, but may be implied, but must be given to a particular tenant,[14] and it will be sufficient if it is given at any time before the proceedings are issued.[15]

---

8 *Standingford v Bruce* [1926] 1 KB 466. Nor to an agreement to surrender: *De Vries v Sparks* (1927) 137 LT 441.
9 *Barton v Fincham* [1921] 2 KB 291.
10 Special rules exist for other tenancies, in particular the relevant date for furnished tenancies being 14 August 1974.
11 *Regional Properties Co Ltd v Frankenschwerth and Chapman* [1951] 1 KB 631, [1951] 1 All ER 178, CA; also *Pazgate Ltd v McGrath* [1984] 2 EGLR 130, CA.
12 *Leith Properties Ltd v Byrne* [1983] QB 433, [1982] 3 All ER 731, CA.
13 *Hyde v Pimley* [1952] 2 QB 506 at 512, [1952] 2 All ER 102, CA.
14 *Regional Properties Co Ltd v Frankenschwerth*, supra.
15 *Hyde v Pimley* [1952] 2 QB 506, [1952] 2 All ER 102 at 105, CA.

Case 8: Dwelling required for landlord's employee

Where the dwelling-house is reasonably required for occupation as a residence for an employee or prospective employee either of the landlord or of some tenant from him, provided that the existing tenant was formerly a service tenant of the landlord or a previous landlord, but has ceased to be employed by him and the dwelling-house was let to him in consequence of that employment.

This ground may be relied upon even though another house is available for the employee.[16] Where the dwelling is required for a prospective employee, he must have entered into a contract of employment which is conditional upon housing being provided, and started work by the date of the hearing unless reasonably prevented from doing so by reason of his absence on holiday or through illness.[17] In such a case, it might be reasonable to make a suspended order in case he should give notice. The employment must be full-time, but although the former employee *ex hypothesi* must have been a service tenant,[18] it is not necessary that the person for whom the dwelling is required should take it in that capacity; and it will be sufficient if he is merely a service occupier.[19]

Case 9: Dwelling reasonably required for landlord

Under this ground for possession, the landlord must prove that the dwelling-house is reasonably required for occupation as a residence for himself, or any adult son or daughter of his, or his father or mother, or his father in law or mother in law.

The policy of this case is to allow the landlord to recover possession of the dwelling-house for the use of his or his spouse's immediate family.[20] The three obstacles imposed by Case 9 on landlords' wishes to recover possession may be contrasted with their absence from the owner-occupier ground applicable to assured tenancies and from Case 11, discussed below.

Purchase condition

Case 9 is subject to a 'purchase condition'.[1] Its aim is to prevent a sitting tenant from eviction after a house is bought over his head,[2] requires a 'purchase' in the popular sense of buying for money.[3] The purchase of a leasehold interest at a

---

16 *Lowcock & Sons Ltd v Brotherton* [1952] CPL 408, CA.
17 *R F Fuggle Ltd v Gadsden* [1948] 2 KB 236, [1948] 2 All ER 160, CA.
18 As opposed to a licensee: see *Matthew v Bobbins* [1980] 2 EGLR 97, CA.
19 *UBM Ltd v Tyler* (1949) 99 L Jo 723. As to the payment of compensation under Case 8 (and Case 9) where a landlord obtains an order for possession by misrepresentation or concealment of material facts, see 1977 Act s 102.
20 *Potsos v Theodotou* [1991] 2 EGLR 93, CA.
 1 It prevents the landlord from relying on the ground if, notably, he bought the freehold or any interest in the property after 23 March 1965 or some later date such as 24 May 1974, at which date furnished tenancies became fully protected.
 2 *Fowle v Bell* [1947] KB 242, [1946] 2 All ER 668, CA.
 3 See *H L Bolton (Engineering) Co Ltd v T J Graham & Sons Ltd* [1957] 1 QB 159, CA; also *Ammadio v Dalton* (1991) 23 HLR 332, CA.

premium is included,[4] as is a conveyance procured by the landlord to a company he controlled.[5] The acquisition of the landlord's interest by will or gift is not caught.[6] The condition does not preclude a landlord from relying on Case 9 as against a former sub-lessee, where the head tenant has been removed,[7] nor where, after the sitting tenant left, a new tenancy was granted to another person.[8] The date of 'purchase' is the date of the contract of purchase, and not completion.[9]

Reasonably required

Whether the dwelling is 'reasonably required' is a question of fact; there must be a genuine need at the time of the hearing,[10] ie something more than desire but something much less than absolute necessity.[11] The onus of proof of 'reasonably required' is on the landlord.[12] He does not have to show that he requires possession at once, provided that it is reasonably required in the ascertainable future.[13] 'Reasonably required' would include proximity to work[14] and need not necessarily involve a genuine need for the whole house.[15] The fact that the person for whom the dwelling is required already has a house is clearly relevant, but it is not conclusive.[16] However, Case 9 does not apply if a landlord's intention to reside is uncertain, as where it was not clear that she might not wish to let the property at a profit.[17] If the reversion is held by two or more joint landlords, Case 9 may be claimed only if both or all the landlords are able to prove an intention to reside in the dwelling-house.[18] This rule is not applicable where the landlord holds the legal estate as sole owner but would be bound on demand to transfer the title into the joint names of himself and another beneficiary.[19] Trustees or personal representatives cannot claim possession under Case 9 for the benefit of a beneficiary[20] but they may rely on it if able to show that they themselves intend, without breach of trust, to reside in the house.[1]

4 See *Powell v Cleland* [1948] 1 KB 262, [1947] 2 All ER 672, CA.
5 *Evans v Engelson* (1979) 253 Estates Gazette 577, CA.
6 *Baker v Lewis* [1947] KB 186, [1946] 2 All ER 592 (will); *Mansukhani v Sharkey* [1992] 2 EGLR 105, CA (gift).
7 *Cairns v Piper* [1954] 2 QB 210, [1954] 2 All ER 611, CA.
8 *Fowle v Bell*, supra.
9 *Emberson v Robinson* [1953] 2 All ER 755, [1953] 1 WLR 1129, CA.
10 *Williamson v Pallant* [1924] 2 KB 173.
11 *Kennealey v Dunne* [1977] QB 837, [1977] 2 All ER 16, CA.
12 *Epsom Grand Stand Association Ltd v Clarke* (1919) 35 TLR 525, CA.
13 *Kidder v Birch* (1982) 46 P & CR 362, CA.
14 *Jackson v Harbour* [1924] EGD 99.
15 *Kelley v Goodwin* [1947] 1 All ER 810, CA.
16 *Nevile v Hardy* [1921] 1 Ch 404.
17 *Ghelani v Bowie* [1988] 2 EGLR 130, CA.
18 *McIntyre v Hardcastle* [1948] 2 KB 82, [1948] 1 All ER 696, CA.
19 *Bostock v Tacher de la Pagerie* [1987] 1 EGLR 104, CA.
20 *Parker v Rosenberg* [1947] KB 371, [1947] 1 All ER 87, CA.
 1 *Patel v Patel* [1982] 1 All ER 68, [1981] 1 WLR 1342, CA (personal representatives also parents of infant beneficiaries).

Greater hardship

The court cannot order possession under Case 9 alone if satisfied that, having regard to all the circumstances, including specifically the question whether other accommodation is available to the landlord or the tenant, greater hardship would be caused by granting the order than by refusing it.[2]

In considering the question of greater hardship, the judge must take into account all the relevant circumstances of the case, including, for example, the financial means of both parties,[3] and whether, if any other accommodation is available to the tenant, it is Rent Act protected.[4] If the landlord has no alternative accommodation of his own, this is a relevant factor,[5] as is the fact that he has another, suitable, house.[6] It was therefore an error of law for the court not to have taken into account the disparity between the landlord and tenant caused by the former's alternative premises.[7] The judge must consider hardship to all who may be affected by the grant or refusal of an order for possession – relatives, dependents, lodgers, guests and the stranger within the gates – but should weigh such hardship with due regard to the status of the persons affected and their 'proximity' to the tenant or the landlord, and the extent to which, consequently, hardship to them would be hardship to him.[8] The judge must also have regard to the longer-term effects of a possession order, as, after all, the short-term effect is always to cause some hardship to the tenant.[9] The onus of proof of greater hardship is on the tenant.[10] The Court of Appeal will interfere if, however, it is shown that the judge misdirected himself in law, or based his decision on a finding of fact for which there was no evidence.[11] Where there is an error of law, and the Court of Appeal has sufficient evidence to resolve the issue of greater hardship, it will do so; otherwise, a remit must take place.[12] However, the mere fact that the Court of Appeal might have arrived at a different result to that of the judge is no sufficient ground for interfering with his decision.[13]

Case 10: Sub-letting of part at an excessive rent

Where the court is satisfied, in particular, that the rent charged by the tenant for any sub-let part of the dwelling-house let on a protected or subject to a statutory tenancy is or was in excess of the maximum rent recoverable for that part, having regard to Part III of the 1977 Act.

---

2   Rent Act 1977, Sch 15, Part III, para 1.
3   *Kelley v Goodwin* [1947] 1 All ER 810, CA.
4   *Sims v Wilson* [1946] 2 All ER 261, CA; *Baker v MacIver* (1990) 22 HLR 328, CA.
5   *Coombs v Parry* (1987) 19 HLR 384; *Baker v MacIver*, supra.
6   *Chandler v Strevett* [1947] 1 All ER 164, CA.
7   *Baker v MacIver* (1990) 22 HLR 328 (especially since the tenant would have less secure accommodation if he had to move).
8   *Harte v Frampton* [1948] 1 KB 73 at 79.
9   *Manaton v Edwards* [1985] 2 EGLR 159, CA.
10 *Sims v Wilson*, supra.
11 *Smith v Penny* [1947] KB 230, [1946] 2 All ER 672, CA.
12 *Alexander v Mohamadzadeh* [1985] 2 EGLR 161, CA.
13 *Hodges v Blee* [1987] 2 EGLR 119, CA.

This ground applies only where there is a sub-letting of part, which is itself a regulated tenancy within the Act; it does not apply to an arrangement for sharing living accommodation at an excessive rent,[14] nor where the part sub-let is furnished.

IV MANDATORY GROUNDS FOR POSSESSION

The landlord of a protected or statutory tenant may recover possession 'mandatorily' under Cases 11 to 20 of Part II of Sch 15 to the 1977 Act.[15] If the landlord makes out one of these grounds for possession then the court must, by s 98(2), order possession, but the onus of proof falls on the landlord as regards the basic facts of, and compliance with, a given ground, but there is no express requirement in s 98(2) that it must be reasonable to make an order for possession, and no such requirement can be implied.[16]

Should the court make an order for possession under any of the following mandatory grounds, the giving up of possession is not to be put off to a date later than 14 days after the order is made, unless exceptional hardship to the tenant would be caused, and in any event the giving up of possession cannot be put off beyond six weeks from the making of the order.[17]

The principal mandatory grounds are as follows.

Case 11: The landlord is an 'owner-occupier'

Where the person (the 'owner-occupier') who let the dwelling-house on a regulated tenancy had, at any time before the letting, occupied it as his residence, and

(a) not later than the 'relevant date' (usually the commencement of the tenancy)[18] the landlord gave notice in writing to the tenant that possession might be recovered under Case 11; *and*
(b) the dwelling-house has not, since one of three specified dates, been let on a protected tenancy not subject to a Case 11 notice; *and*

the court is satisfied that *one* of the following conditions is complied with:

(a) the dwelling-house is required as a residence for the owner or any member of his family who resided with the owner when he last occupied the dwelling-house as his residence; *or*
(b) the owner has died and the dwelling-house is required as a residence for a member of his family who was residing with him at the time of his death; *or*
(c) the owner has died and the dwelling-house is required by a successor in title as his residence or for the purpose of disposing of it with vacant possession; *or*

---

14 *Kenyon v Walker* [1946] 2 All ER 595, CA.
15 For a speedy procedure for obtaining possession under mandatory grounds see Rent Act etc Rules 1981, SI 1981/139; *Minay v Sentongo* (1982) 45 P & CR 190, CA.
16 *Kennealy v Dunne* [1977] QB 837, [1977] 2 All ER 16, CA; *Lipton v Whitworth* (1993) 26 HLR 293, CA.
17 Housing Act 1980, s 89(1), which, however, does not apply to High Court proceedings: *Bain & Co v Church Comrs* (1988) 21 HLR 29.
18 Rent Act 1977, Sch 15, Part III, para 2, which applies to all mandatory grounds.

(d) the dwelling-house is subject to a mortgage by deed granted before the commencement of the tenancy, and the mortgagee is entitled to exercise his express or statutory power of sale and requires possession to dispose of the dwelling-house with vacant possession; or

(e) the dwelling-house is not reasonably suitable to the needs of the owner, having regard to his place of work, and he requires it to dispose of it with vacant possession to use the sale proceeds to acquire a more suitable dwelling-house. [19]

So as to protect the tenant, Case 11 cannot be relied on unless a written notice is served on the tenant, not later than the grant of the tenancy. However, the court has a power to dispense with the notice requirement if it is just and equitable to do so. This dispensation power also applies to the requirement that all lettings must be under tenancies governed by a Case 11 notice. The court takes a broad view in the exercise of its dispensation power and examines all the circumstances. [20]

Where a landlord sent a Case 11 notice to the tenant but it was never received (and the tenant must receive the notice for Case 11 to be satisfied in this respect), the dispensation power was exercised in the landlord's favour because she honestly believed that due notice was given. [1] Where a landlord let on a tenancy which, at that time, he did not intend to be subject to Case 11, and later decided to rely on Case 11, he failed to invoke the dispensation power, and it was held that Case 11 only applied to lettings originally intended to fall within its terms. [2] Where a landlord gave an oral notice, the dispensation power was, exceptionally, exercised: the tenant knew the landlord was an owner-occupier. [3]

One of two joint landlords who originally let subject to it, is entitled to rely on Case 11, even though only one of them requires the dwelling-house as his residence, or for another permitted purpose within the Case, as the emphasis of Case 11 is on occupation. [4]

Case 11 may be relied on, not only by a person who was, immediately prior to the grant of the tenancy concerned, an 'owner-occupier', (there being no requirement that an 'owner-occupier' should be a freeholder or long leaseholder) [5] but also by someone who has let on a series of tenancies – provided all tenancies comply with Case 11 and are subject to the relevant notices. Case 11 does not necessarily require that the landlord must occupy the dwelling-house concerned as his only or main residence after regaining possession: if he has another home, abroad for example, all that is required is that he requires the dwelling-house for use as an intermittent residence, [6] but whether there is residence in this sense

---

19 See *Bissessar v Ghosn* (1985) 18 HLR 486, CA.
20 *Bradshaw v Baldwin-Wiseman* (1985) 17 HLR 260, CA.
 1 *Minay v Sentongo* (1982) 45 P & CR 190, CA.
 2 *Bradshaw v Baldwin-Wiseman* supra.
 3 *Fernandes v Parvardin* [1982] 2 EGLR 104, CA, as explained in *Bradshaw v Baldwin-Wiseman*, supra.
 4 *Tilling v Whiteman* [1980] AC 1, [1979] 1 All ER 737, HL.
 5 *Mistry v Isidore* [1990] 2 EGLR 97, CA.
 6 *Naish v Curzon* [1985] 17 HLR 220, CA (twice-yearly visits by landlord to UK sufficient): *Davies v Paterson* (1988) 21 HLR 63, CA (frequent visits to UK sufficient).

is ultimately a question of fact for the county court,[7] which may lead to generous results, as where a landlord of only a few weeks' residence prior to selling the house came within Case 11 on the facts.[8] But where a landlord intended to let for gain and not to return to the house, her claim failed.[9]

Case 12: Retirement home

The landlord must show that he intends to occupy as his residence the dwelling-house, when he retires from regular employment; that he let it prior to retirement, and:

(a) not later than, as a rule, the commencement date of the tenancy, he served on the tenant a notice in writing that possession might be recovered under Case 12; *and*

(b) that at no time since 14 August 1974 has the dwelling-house been let on a tenancy not subject to a Case 12 notice; *and*

(c) that owner has retired as above and requires the dwelling-house as a residence for himself, *or* that conditions (b) to (d) inclusive listed under Case 11 above, apply. The court has a power to dispense with the notice requirement[10] and also with condition (b) above.

In addition to these Cases, mandatory recovery of possession is allowed where, in particular:

1   The dwelling-house has been let at some period in the last 12 months preceding the commencement of the tenancy under a holiday let (s 9) which lies outside protection and was let off-season for a term certain not exceeding eight months. Written notice must be given to the tenant that possession might be recovered (Case 13).

2   The dwelling-house is let for a term certain not exceeding 12 months and is subject to notice from the landlord that possession might be recovered, and that at some time in the 12 months ending with the commencement of the tenancy the dwelling-house had been let to students (Case 14). The aim is to enable vacation lettings to take place of property which falls within the exemption to protection of s 8 of the 1977 Act.

3   Where the house or flat has been let subject to a proper notice after 28 November 1980 to a member of the armed forces by a landlord who now requires the property as his residence or falls within conditions (b) to (e) as stated under Case 11 above (Case 20).

---

7   *Mistry v Isidore*, supra (where it was held that, had the decision gone the other way, it would not have been upset); also *Ibie v Trubshaw* (1990) 22 HLR 191 (where a landlord who mainly lived abroad failed).

8   *Lipton v Whitworth*, supra.

9   *Ghelani v Bowie* [1988] 2 EGLR 130, CA.

10   In contrast to the position under Cases 13 to 18.

V STATUTORY TENANCIES

Statutory tenancies arise automatically as from the termination of the previous protected tenancy.[11] A succession scheme exists so that the surviving spouse or certain other relatives of the statutory tenant may succeed to the tenancy. However, as from 15 January 1989, this scheme has been curtailed and this type of statutory tenancy will eventually die a lingering death.

Statutory tenancy on expiry of protected tenancy

A protected contractual tenancy, fixed-term or periodic, automatically becomes a statutory tenancy if and so long as, from the termination of the previous protected tenancy, the tenant occupies the dwelling-house as his residence (s 2(1)(a)). The statutory tenancy will continue unless it is terminated in possession proceedings (subject to the various statutory restrictions) or unless the tenant ceases to comply with the statutory residence requirement.

If the tenant gives notice to quit but subsequently remains in occupation after the notice has expired, he becomes a statutory tenant, but the landlord may be able to terminate his occupation in proceedings.[12] If the previous protected tenancy has been forfeited, a statutory tenancy arises under s 2(1)(a), but the landlord may then establish a ground for possession which corresponds to the breach which was the basis of the forfeiture, and he then regains possession if he complies with the statutory restrictions.[13] If a protected tenant goes bankrupt, no statutory tenancy can arise.[14] Where a landlord was induced to grant a protected tenancy, which had since expired, by a fraudulent misrepresentation of the tenant, the landlord could rescind the contractual tenancy, as fraud unravels everything, and no statutory tenancy could arise.[15]

The precise nature of the rights of a statutory tenant has caused some apparent inconsistencies in the law. It was held that a statutory tenant is conferred a purely personal right of continuing occupation of the dwelling-house, provided he continues to comply with the residence requirement of s 2(1)(a); he has no estate in the land concerned.[16] Although, therefore, his rights may be in that sense personal, a statutory tenant retains a form of possession and enjoyment against all the world unless possession is ordered by the court under s 98, and so, a status of irremovability, and also the right to treat any person entering without his permission as a trespasser.[17] Moreover, it now appears that a statutory tenant has an 'interest' within the Insolvency Act 1986, s 182 to

---

11   Where two persons held a protected tenancy, but one of them alone occupied the property on its termination, that person alone was entitled to become the statutory tenant: *Lloyd v Sadler* [1978] QB 774, [1978] 2 All ER 529, CA.

12   Under Sch 15, Part I, Case 5.

13   *Tideway Investment and Property Holdings v Wellwood* [1952] Ch 791, [1952] 2 All ER 514, CA.

14   *Smalley v Quarrier* [1975] 2 All ER 688, [1975] 1 WLR 938, CA. If a statutory tenant goes bankrupt, this is not *ipso facto* a ground for possession: *Sutton v Dorf* [1932] 2 KB 304.

15   *Killick v Roberts* [1991] 4 All ER 289, [1991] 1 WLR 1146, CA.

16   *Jessamine Investment Co v Schwartz* [1978] QB 264, [1976] 3 All ER 521, CA.

17   *Keeves v Dean* [1924] 1 KB 685 at 694, CA.

apply to the court for a vesting order where the head lease is terminated as a result of the insolvency of the head lessee.[18]

The rights of occupation of a statutory tenant were also protected by the court as against a mortgagee whose claim for possession, which had nothing to do with protecting her security, was treated as unenforceable in equity.[19] Whilst any assignment inter vivos of a statutory tenancy causes the loss of security, owing to s 2(1)(a), the court has power to direct an assignment of a statutory tenancy in matrimonial proceedings.[20] A statutory tenancy may be assigned, under a statutory procedure, by a statutory tenant to another person with the (formal) agreement of the landlord.[1] Where no formal agreement had been made, but the landlord's agent had represented to the tenant that she and her daughter now held a joint (statutory) tenancy, the landlord was estopped from going back on his word, seeing that the mother had, as a result of the representation, given up her priority housing status.[2] This shows the remarkable operation of equity, since it would probably not be possible for the statutory tenant by agreement with the landlord to transfer that tenancy to herself and her daughter jointly.

The personal nature of his right to occupy is, however, shown by the fact that if a statutory tenant sub-lets the whole dwelling-house, he loses his status, as he cannot comply with the statutory residence requirement.[3] If the statutory tenant sub-lets part only of the dwelling-house, generally he retains security.[4] Loss of security also follows if the dwelling-house ceases for whatever reason to be occupied by the statutory tenant personally.[5]

Succession to statutory tenancies

There is a scheme for succession to a statutory tenancy on the death of the statutory tenant. Its operation was curtailed in relation to deaths on or after 15 January 1989.[6] There is a sharp difference between the position on the death of the original tenant and the death of a first successor.

Death of original tenant

The rules differentiate between the position of a surviving spouse, who has the privilege of succession to a statutory tenancy, and of a family member, who

18 *Re Vedmay Ltd* [1994] 1 EGLR 74 (the word 'interest' not being confined to proprietary rights).
19 *Quennell v Maltby* [1979] 1 All ER 568, [1979] 1 WLR 318, CA.
20 Matrimonial Homes Act 1983 ,s 1.
1 Rent Act 1977, Sch 1, para 13.
2 *Daejan Properties Ltd v Mahoney* [1995] 2 EGLR 75, CA.
3 *Haskins v Lewis* [1931] 2 KB 1, CA; *Skinner v Geary* [1931] 2 KB 546, CA.
4 *Berkeley v Papadoyannis* [1954] 2 QB 149, [1954] 2 All ER 409, CA.
5 *Metropolitan Properties Co v Cronan* (1982) 44 P & CR 1, CA.
6 The rules applicable where the death occurred *before* that date allowed for two successions. In the case of both, a succession could be claimed to the statutory tenancy by either the surviving spouse of the tenant, provided such spouse occupied the dwelling-house as his residence; or by a resident family member, who had to satisfy a six-month residence with the deceased tenant, ending with the death of the latter (Rent Act 1977, Sch 1, paras 2 and 6 and 3 and 7 respectively). Thus, a statutory tenancy could be subject to a double succession, one to, say, a deceased tenant's wife and then to that person's son or daughter.

succeeds, if at all, to an assured periodic tenancy by succession under the less secure assured tenancy régime of the Housing Act 1988.[7]

A *surviving spouse* of the original tenant is entitled to succeed to the statutory tenancy, provided that the claimant occupies the dwelling-house as his residence. A person living with the original tenant (eg as his cohabitee) as his or her wife or husband is treated as a surviving spouse.[8] Until this change in the law, a cohabitee would have had to claim as being a member of the deceased tenant's 'family'.[9]

A *member of the family* of the deceased statutory tenant cannot take the tenancy by succession if there is a surviving spouse. Subject to that, the family member claimant cannot obtain a succession unless he or she has resided in the dwelling-house immediately before the original tenant's death and for a minimum period of two years immediately before then.[10] The family member, whether the succession is a first or a second succession, the latter following the death of a successor surviving spouse, obtains an assured tenancy by succession, whose terms are governed by statute, and which are in principle the same as those of the tenancy held by the predecessor immediately before his death, except that the tenancy is converted by s 39 (5) and (6) of the Housing Act 1988 from being a statutory tenancy into an assured periodic tenancy by succession. This assured periodic tenancy by succession is an estate in land, but it is probable that the burdens of the previous statutory tenancy would continue to bind the successor tenant, but not the original rent, if the rent for the previous tenancy was fixed on assumptions which do not apply to the fixing of a rent under an assured tenancy. Hence, where a registered rent had been calculated without paying any regard to the tenant's breaches of repairing covenant, it was held that a rent assessment committee were entitled, in determining the open market rent, to reduce the rent in order to take the breaches of covenant of the predecessor tenant into account.[11]

Death of first successor

If on the death of the first successor, the first successor was still a statutory tenant,[12] the succession of any claimant is to be to an assured periodic tenancy of the dwelling-house by succession.[13] A person who was a member of the original tenant's family immediately before that tenant's death and also a member of the first successor's family immediately before the first successor's death, is entitled to claim an assured periodic tenancy by succession. The

---

7   Such a tenancy is, however, an assured and not an assured shorthold tenancy even if it arises under the 1996 regime (discussed in ch 18): Housing Act 1988, Sch A, para 7 (inserted by Housing Act 1996, Sch 7).
8   Rent Act 1977, Sch 1, para 2(2). If there is more than one such person, the claimant is to be decided by agreement, or by the court in default of agreement: ibid, para 2(3).
9   As in eg *Dyson Holdings Ltd v Fox* [1976] QB 503, [1975] 3 All ER 1030, CA.
10 Rent Act 1977, Sch 1, para 3.
11 *N & D (London) Ltd v Gadsdon* [1992] 1 EGLR 112.
12 This will be impossible if the first successor was a member of the original tenant's family and the death of the original tenant took place on or after 15 January 1989, whereupon the succession will be to an assured tenancy by succession, which is a single succession.
13 Rent Act 1977, Sch 1, para 5.

claimant must have resided in the dwelling-house with the first successor at the time of, and for the period of two years immediately before the first successor's death.[14]

Further principles applicable to succession

Where a claimant had a permanent home elsewhere, the claim to succeed to a statutory tenancy failed, and the residence of the claimant in the tenant's home was found to be transient, given that the claimant continued to maintain her other home.[15] Under the rules applicable to deaths on or after 15 January 1989, the residence must simply be in the same house as the tenant, so that it need not necessarily be shown that the claimant was part of the latter's household.

The term 'family' is, it is thought, still to be interpreted in the popular sense and is not confined to blood relatives: accordingly, it has been held to include not just adopted children, but also those accepted into the tenant's family.[16] An adult who is in no sense related to the tenant may well find it hard to claim a succession, as long residence is insufficient by itself.[17] Therefore, a person treated by the tenant as her so-called 'nephew', and who formed part of her household, failed in a succession claim,[18] as did a resident housekeeper.[19]

Succession under the 1977 Act takes precedence over the rights of any person entitled under the deceased tenant's will,[20] or in his intestacy. If a person entitled to succeed is also entitled to inherit the contractual tenancy, there is a presumption that he takes the latter by inheritance.[1]

VI   TERMS AND CONDITIONS OF STATUTORY TENANCIES

By s 3(1), so long as he retains possession, a statutory tenant is bound to observe and is entitled to the benefit of all the terms and conditions of the protected tenancy existing immediately beforehand, so far as consistent with the provisions of the Act. It is a condition of a statutory tenancy (s 3(2)) that the tenant must afford to the landlord access to the dwelling-house and all reasonable facilities for executing any repairs which he is entitled to execute.

Section 3(1) imports into the statutory tenancy all express obligations which run with the land and, indeed, any covenant which is of any benefit to the parties as such, for example, for the provision of personal services to the tenant.[2] Therefore, express and implied repairing obligations of either party are

---

14 Rent Act 1977, Sch 1, para 6. If there is more than one claimant, the question is either resolved by agreement or the court.
15 *Swanbrae Ltd v Elliott* (1986) 19 HLR 86, CA.
16 *Brock v Wollams* [1949] 2 KB 388, [1949] 1 All ER 715, CA.
17 *Sefton Holdings Ltd v Cairns* [1988] 2 FLR 109, CA (almost 50 years insufficient).
18 *Carega Properties SA (formerly Joram Developments Ltd) v Sharratt* [1979] 2 All ER 1084, [1979] 1 WLR 928, HL.
19 *Darnell v Millward* [1951] 1 All ER 88, CA.
20 *Moodie v Hosegood* [1952] AC 61, [1951] 2 All ER 582, HL.
 1 *Whitmore v Lambert* [1955] 2 All ER 147, [1955] 1 WLR 495, CA.
 2 *Engvall v Ideal Flats Ltd* [1945] KB 205, [1945] 1 All ER 230, CA.

carried into the statutory tenancy, as are landlords' statute-implied repairing obligations under ss 11-16 of the Landlord and Tenant Act 1985 and his obligations under the Defective Premises Act 1972. So as not unduly to burden the landlord, purely personal covenants which are collateral to the protected tenancy are not carried into a statutory tenancy, but an obligation to pay £40 towards redecoration on quitting was held capable of running with the land and so of binding a statutory tenant.[3]

Statutory tenants are subject to special consent rules in relation to improvements: absolute prohibitions on these are banned, and the landlord cannot unreasonably withhold his consent to an improvement. If he does withhold his consent, he must prove that he had reasonable grounds for doing so.[4]

If the terms of the statutory tenancy do not expressly prohibit it, a statutory tenant may, without loss of security, sub-let part of the dwelling-house, but not if he has already sub-let the remainder.[5] If the tenant sub-lets part, but retains part of the premises and may at some future date re-occupy the parts sub-let, he will not lose security.[6]

VII TERMINATION OF STATUTORY TENANCIES

A statutory tenant retains his status only, by s 2(1)(a), 'if and so long as he occupies the dwelling-house as his residence'. There are three main ways in which the status of statutory tenant may be lost by non-compliance with the residence requirement and each of these is examined in what follows.[7]

Occupation by tenant's spouse or ex-spouse

Where the tenant ceases permanently to occupy the dwelling-house, occupation by his wife has been held to be sufficient for the purposes of s 2(1)(a), and the tenant remains statutory tenant, even if the parties are separated.[8] This will not apply if the house was never the matrimonial home.[9] Therefore, where a statutory tenant left, and eventually returned, leaving his wife in occupation of the house in between, he retained his statutory tenancy, in the absence of evidence of a surrender of it.[10]

If the parties are divorced, or judicially separated (in either case by court order) an occupation by that statutory tenant's ex-wife is not his occupation,

---

3 *Boyer v Warbey* [1953] 1 QB 234, [1952] 2 All ER 976, CA.
4 Housing Act 1980, ss 81-83.
5 *Crowhurst v Maidment* [1953] 1 QB 23, [1952] 2 All ER 808, CA (where the tenant never resided and never intended to reside, in the premises sub-let).
6 *Berkeley v Papadoyannis* [1954] 2 QB 149, [1954] 2 All ER 409, CA.
7 The onus of proof in each case is on the landlord: see eg *Roland House Gardens Ltd v Cravitz* (1974) 29 P & CR 432, CA.
8 *Brown v Draper* [1944] KB 309, [1944] 1 All ER 246, CA; *Hoggett v Hoggett* (1979) 39 P & CR 121; see now Matrimonial Homes Act 1983, s 1(6).
9 *Hall v King* [1988] 1 FLR 376, CA.
10 *Hulme v Langford* (1985) 50 P & CR 199, CA.

and if he is out of occupation, with no intention to return, security is lost.[11] The same rule applies in the case of a statutory tenant's mistress.[12] The occupation of a wife is deemed to be that of the tenant; that of a divorced wife etc, cannot be so deemed, and the occupier is a mere licensee. In the case of wives, the court has power in divorce, nullity or judicial separation proceedings, to transfer a statutory tenancy to the wife.[13]

Permanent absence of tenant

Where a landlord proves that the tenant is permanently absent from the dwelling-house with no intention to return, the tenant ceases to be a statutory tenant.[14] A sufficiently prolonged absence, without any objective evidence of the necessary intention, such as the presence of the tenant's furniture, will enable the court to infer an abandonment of occupation, but it is open to the tenant to show an intention to return, backed by objective indicia such as the occupation of the house by his relatives (see below).[15] The question of intention to return is one of fact, and does not depend merely on the number of years concerned, but there must be a real hope of return coupled with a practical possibility of its fulfilment within a reasonable time.[16] Thus, where a tenant who moved out of her accommodation pending refurbishment did not, for some six months after the completion of the works, definitely indicate to the landlord that she intended to resume her residence there, her intention to return was held to be too contingent; she lost a statutory tenancy as a result.[17] In one case,[18] a tenant who was absent for seven years and who also held the freehold of other premises, was held to have lost his status of statutory tenant. However, a finding that a tenant had a genuine intention to return after ten years enabled him to retain his statutory tenancy.[19] It is not too much to conclude from this that if a county court judge makes a finding of fact that the tenant genuinely intends to return, the Court of Appeal will interfere with his decision only if it is perverse. Moreover, there is a difference between cases where the tenant is voluntarily absent, and those where he is absent due to factors he cannot control, or where he is away for, say, an extended but finite absence.[20] In the latter instances, it may be easier for the tenant to retain security, as the court

---

11 *Metropolitan Properties Ltd v Cronan* (1982) 44 P & CR 1, CA.
12 *Colin Smith Music Ltd v Ridge* [1975] 1 All ER 290, [1975] 1 WLR 463, CA, where the statutory tenant had, effectually, surrendered the tenancy.
13 Matrimonial Homes Act 1983, Sch 1. If the tenancy was subject to a suspended possession order, this infirmity will equally affect the tenancy transferred to the spouse: *Church Comrs for England v Alemarah* (1996) 72 P & CR D45, CA.
14 The following considerations (in the absence of authority) might also govern the residence requirement of assured tenancies (ch 18).
15 *Brown v Brash and Ambrose* [1948] 2 KB 247, [1948] 1 All ER 922, CA.
16 *Gofor Investments Ltd v Roberts* (1975) 29 P & CR 366, CA.
17 *Robert Thackray's Settled Estates Ltd v Kaye* [1989] 1 EGLR 127, CA; Bridge [1989] Conv 450.
18 *Duke v Porter* [1986] 2 EGLR 101, CA.
19 *Gofor Investments Ltd v Roberts*, supra; also *Brickfield Properties Ltd v Hughes* (1987) 20 HLR 108, CA (eight-year absence not sufficient to cost tenant security where he satisfied judge that he might well retire to the dwelling-house concerned); Bridge [1988] Conv 300.
20 See eg *Richards v Green* [1983] 2 EGLR 104, CA.

may more readily infer a genuine intention to return. For example, a tenant retained his statutory tenancy despite being in prison,[1] and also while detained in hospital due to insanity.[2] In all cases, as said, there must be some objective evidence of intention to return, such as retained furniture, or the presence of a relative in the premises to look after them, to back up the tenant's inward intention to return.[3] It need hardly be said, in view of the foregoing, that a statutory tenant will not lose his status merely if he is temporarily absent.

Two-home tenants

A third way in which security may be lost is if the landlord is able to prove that the tenant has another home and he is using the house of which he is statutory tenant as a convenient resort only.[4] But the fact that the tenant has another home is, apparently, certainly not enough of itself to deprive him of his statutory tenancy.[5] Even though it might be supposed that it cannot really have been the policy of the Rent Act 1977 to protect a person in his occupation of a second, rented home, some generous results have been reached. It seems that a person may even occupy his own home for most of the time and the house held under a statutory tenancy more rarely or for a limited purpose: where this is so, it is a question of fact and degree whether the second house is occupied as his second home and, therefore, whether it remains held under a statutory tenancy.[6] Where, therefore, a tenant occupied a flat for some six years and then returned to his home abroad, making only occasional trips to the UK, he failed to retain his statutory tenancy as it was impossible to say that he occupied the flat as a home: his visits were too infrequent even by the two homes tenant standard.[7]

If, by contrast, the tenant holds two adjoining houses, originally from the same landlord, and lives in one and sleeps in the other (or divides his living activities in some other way between the two houses), it is a question of fact whether he, as s 2(1)(a) requires, resides in both houses as one complete unit, in which case he has security, or whether each unit is self-contained and occupied separately, in which case the tenant has no statutory tenancy in respect of either unit of habitation.[8]

Surrender and termination by tenant's notice

A statutory tenant may surrender his statutory tenancy by express or implied surrender, and the common law rules as to this apply. If the premises are destroyed and the tenant has no intention to return to them, the statutory tenancy ends.[9]

1   *Maxted v McAll* [1952] CPL 185, CA.
2   *Tickner v Hearn* [1961] 1 All ER 65, [1960] 1 WLR 1406, CA.
3   See *Brown v Brash and Ambrose*, supra.
4   As in *Regalian Securities Ltd v Scheuer* (1982) 47 P & CR 362, CA.
5   *Langford Property Co v Tureman* [1949] 1 KB 29, CA.
6   *Hampstead Way Investments Ltd v Lewis-Weare* [1985] 1 All ER 564; Wilkinson (1985) 135 NLJ 357; PF Smith [1985] Conv 224.
7   *D J Crocker Securities (Portsmouth) Ltd v Johal* [1989] 2 EGLR 102, CA.
8   *Wimbush v Cibulia* [1949] 2 KB 564, [1949] 2 All ER 432, CA; *Kavanagh v Lyroudias* [1985] 1 All ER 560, CA.
9   *Ellis & Sons Amalgamated Properties Ltd v Sisman* [1948] 1 KB 653, [1948] 1 All ER 44, CA.

The tenant also has the right to terminate the statutory tenancy by a written notice of the requisite length, which means a notice sufficient to terminate his previous protected tenancy (s 3(3)) and the minimum period of the notice must be four weeks, by s 5 of the Protection from Eviction Act 1977. Where the landlord obtains possession by an order of court, no notice to quit to the statutory tenant is required (s 3(4)). If no notice was required under the protected tenancy, because it was fixed-term, then the tenant may terminate the statutory tenancy by a notice of not less than three months (s 3(3)).

E PROTECTION OF SUB-TENANCIES

General rules

So as to reverse the common law principle that the termination of a head tenancy entails automatically the ending of any sub-lease derived out of it, by s 137(1) of the Rent Act 1977, the determination in proceedings for possession of a head tenancy of a dwelling-house let to a protected or statutory tenant will not automatically determine any lawful sub-tenancy of the whole or any part. By s 137(2), where a head tenancy of a dwelling-house is determined in possession proceedings by the court, any lawful sub-tenant of the dwelling-house or any part is deemed to hold directly from the head landlord on the same terms as if the head 'statutorily protected tenancy' had continued.[10]

Where there is a sub-tenancy of a dwelling-house which forms part only of the premises let as a whole under a superior tenancy which is not a statutorily protected tenancy, on termination of that superior tenancy, the sub-tenant will, in principle, retain such protection as s 137 offers him, by the statutory fiction that the dwelling-house subject to the sub-tenancy is deemed to be let separately from the remainder of the premises at a rent equal to the just proportion of the rent under the superior tenancy (s 137(3)). The notional separate lettings are taken as made to the superior tenant. The protection of s 137(3) is limited. It only applies if the head tenant, whose tenancy is determined, is tenant of a dwelling-house within the Rent Acts.[11] Therefore, where a sub-tenant of a flat held over as a statutory tenant and his landlord, a head lessee, surrendered his term, which was a business tenancy, the sub-tenant fell outside s 137(3) as the head lease, the relevant lease, was not protected by the 1977 Act.[12]

---

10 'Statutorily protected tenancy' is defined by s 137(4) as meaning: (a) a protected or statutory tenancy under the 1977 Act; (b) a protected occupancy or statutory tenancy under the Rent (Agriculture) Act 1976; (c) a tenancy of an agricultural holding within the Agricultural Holdings Act 1986; (d) a farm business tenancy within the Agricultural Tenancies Act 1995; and most long tenancies are within s 137 by s 137(5).
11 *Cow v Casey* [1949] 1 KB 474, CA; *Maunsell v Olins* [1975] AC 373, [1975] 1 All ER 16 (reversed where the head tenancy is an agricultural holding by s 137(3)).
12 *Pittalis v Grant* [1989] 2 All ER 622; Martin (1989) 139 NLJ 1260; see also *Bromley Park Garden Estates Ltd v George* [1991] 2 EGLR 95; PF Smith [1991] Conv 393.

Further aspects

Section 137(1) protects sub-tenants of Rent Act protected tenants where the court orders possession against the head tenant on one of the discretionary grounds. If it orders possession on a mandatory ground, s 137(1) has no application, and any sub-tenancy falls with the head tenancy.

If the head tenant sub-lets the *whole* dwelling-house at a time when he is *statutory* tenant, then, as the residence requirement of s 2(1) of the 1977 Act is not satisfied, the sub-tenancy cannot be statutorily protected at all and so s 137 will not apply to it.[13] The same result follows, where for some other reason, such as the sub-tenant holding under a head tenant who is a resident landlord, there is no protected (sub-) tenancy in the first place. While a sub-letting of the whole dwelling-house causes a statutory tenancy to cease, the sub-tenancy, if 'lawful', falls within s 137 but it is subject to Case 6 of Sch 15, Part I to the 1977 Act.[14] However, there must be some doubt as to whether a statutory tenant is entitled lawfully to sub-let, so as to create a term binding on the landlord, as he has no proprietary interest in the land.

By s 137(2) where the head tenant's protected tenancy is determined, in proceedings based on discretionary grounds, by the landlord, any lawful sub-tenant continues to be 'tenant' under the 1977 Act, and his position must be considered separately. He is still vulnerable to a discretionary order for possession under s 98(1) and Sch 15, Part I.[15] Therefore, if the tenant has gone, the landlord will have to prove any such grounds separately against the sub-tenant. If a statutory head tenancy has been determined, as by forfeiture, s 137(2) deems any sub-tenant to hold as statutory tenant, to avoid the latter being given a more valuable right in the premises than his erstwhile landlord held.[16]

Requirement that sub-tenancy must be lawful

No part of s 137 applies unless the sub-tenancy itself is lawful. This matter is by no means free from difficulty, but it imposes a significant limit on the scope of the provision.

A sub-letting in breach of an absolute covenant in the head tenancy is not lawful.[17] If the head tenancy prohibits any sub-letting merely in a fully qualified form, a sub-letting which amounts to a breach, ie to which the landlord could reasonably object, is unlawful. If the covenant is in form absolute and contains a limited exception, it is a matter of construction in the light of the surrounding circumstances whether the sub-letting concerned is lawful, by falling within the exact terms of the exception, or unlawful. For example, an absolute covenant

---

13 *Stanley v Compton* [1951] 1 All ER 859 at 863, CA. The date at which the status of the sub-tenant is decided is that of the determination of the head tenancy: *Jessamine Investment Co v Schwartz* [1978] QB 264, [1976] 3 All ER 521, CA.
14 *Henry Smith's Charity Trustees v Willson* [1983] QB 316, [1983] 1 All ER 73 at 333 and 87, CA.
15 *Leith Properties Ltd v Springer* [1982] 3 All ER 731 at 736, CA; Martin [1983] Conv 155.
16 *John Lyon Grammar School v James* [1995] 4 All ER 740, CA.
17 *Oak Property Co Ltd v Chapman* [1947] KB 886, [1947] 2 All ER 1, CA.

against sub-letting allowed only consensual sub-lettings for a term not exceeding six months in any year: it was held that any sub-lettings apart from these must be unlawful, including a six-month periodic sub-tenancy.[18] Likewise, where sub-lettings of part were absolutely prohibited, except on terms providing for a substantial part of the rent to represent payments for furniture, a sub-letting without sufficient furniture to enable the place to be lived in was unlawful.[19] As part of the surrounding circumstances, the court in one case examined the quality of furniture provided with a view to ascertaining whether it was within a requirement for high-class furnished sub-lettings only.[20]

An initially unlawful sub-letting in breach of covenant could become lawful by the date of the hearing, if the landlord by then has waived the breach. The strict common law doctrine of waiver is not applied in the case of s 137 where the head tenancy is statutory; and so a rent demand on the head tenant for future rent is not necessarily waiver, even if the landlord has full knowledge of the breach, as he has no choice but to accept the rent, owing to the effect of s 3(3) of the 1977 Act, and so the demand is not regarded as unequivocal. If any danger of waiver is to be avoided when making a rent demand, the landlord must make it clear at the time of the demand that it is without prejudice to his right to ask for possession; and he should follow up his demand with a summons for possession within a reasonable time. This is because the question of whether the acts of the landlord amount to a condonation of the absence of consent and an unequivocal affirmation of the sub-tenancy is one of fact.[1] In the case of protected head tenancies, the manner in which waiver is judged, and the requisite degree of knowledge required to be imputed to the landlord, correspond more nearly to those at common law.[2]

F   OTHER PROVISIONS

Distress

No distress for rent of any dwelling-house let on a protected or statutory tenancy is permitted except with the leave of the county court (s 147(1)) which has wide powers of adjournment and the like (s 100).

Premiums

The Rent Act 1977 prevents the landlord, on the grant of a protected tenancy, from charging a premium (or capital sum) to the tenant, and so evading the rent control provisions of the Act. It is an offence for any person[3] to require the

---

18 *Henry Smith's Charity Trustees v Willson* [1983] QB 316, [1983] 1 All ER 73, CA.
19 *Patoner Ltd v Alexandrakis* [1984] 2 EGLR 124, CA.
20 *Patoner Ltd v Lowe* [1985] 2 EGLR 154, CA.
 1 *Oak Property Co v Chapman*, supra; *Henry Smith's Charity Trustees v Willson* supra.
 2 See eg *Metropolitan Properties Ltd v Cordery* (1979) 39 P & CR 10, CA; *Chrisdell Ltd v Johnson* [1987] 2 EGLR 123, CA.
 3 Whether the landlord or eg his agent: see *Farrell v Alexander* [1977] AC 59, [1976] 2 All ER 721, HL; *Saleh v Robinson* [1988] 2 EGLR 126, CA.

payment of any premium (as widely defined in s 128(1)) in addition to rent, as a condition of the grant, renewal or continuance of a protected tenancy.[4] There are also provisions aimed at deterring the taking of a premium on assignment of a protected tenancy.[5] It is also an offence for any person (such as an agent) to receive such a premium in addition to rent (s 119(2)). While a lump sum in cash would amount to a premium, the prohibition appears also to include any consideration expressed in money conferring a benefit on the landlord and a detriment to the tenant.[6] There are no provisions to prohibit the taking of a premium on the grant of a statutory tenancy, as such tenancies arise under the Act. Certain rules restrict the sums a statutory tenant may require from an assignee in those cases where a statutory tenancy is assigned.[7]

G   AGRICULTURAL TIED COTTAGES

Scope of rules

Agricultural workers who occupy agricultural tied cottages under a tenancy or exclusive licence are governed by a specific code, the Rent (Agriculture) Act 1976, if the occupation arose under an agreement entered into before 15 January 1989.[8] It is still appropriate to note the pre-15 January 1989 code, in view of the possibility of continuing statutory tenancies after that date and because there may be some surviving spouses who succeeded to a 1976-Act agreement before or after that date whose agreements are still running.

The 1976 Act applies only to a 'protected occupier': a person who qualifies has the protection of the 1976 Act during the period of his tenancy or licence and, once this is terminated, he automatically becomes a statutory tenant (s2(4)) subject to a residence condition (s 4(1)).[9]

By s 2(1), a protected occupier is a qualifying worker, or a person who has been such a worker at any time during the licence or tenancy. The worker must be or have been employed in agriculture or forestry.[10] Part business user by an occupier of the premises, who qualified as a protected occupier, did not automatically preclude his coming within the scope of the 1976 Act.[11]

The 1976 Act protects any contract, be it a tenancy or licence, entered into before 15 January 1989, under which the relevant protected occupier occupies

---

4   Any term in a contract requiring the payment of a prohibited premium is void; and the court has powers to enable the tenant to recover the payment of such sums (s 125(1)).

5   Rent Act 1977, s 120.

6   *Elmdene Estates Ltd v White* [1960] AC 528, [1960] 1 All ER 306, HL (where a prospective tenant was required to sell his house to a named third party connected to the landlord for less than its market value, as a condition of obtaining a protected tenancy).

7   Rent Act 1977, Sch 1, Part II, paras 12 and 14.

8   Where the occupation is under an agreement on or after 15 January 1989, the tenancy or licence is treated as an assured agricultural occupancy (ch 18).

9   A statutory tenancy also arises following a notice of increase of rent (1976 Act, s 16).

10   As defined in s 1 so as to include eg dairy farming, production of consumable produce and using land for grazing, but not eg sporting activities or matters related to these such as raising pheasants for shooting: *Earl of Normanton v Giles* [1980] 1 All ER 106, [1980] 1 WLR 28, HL.

11   *Durman v Bell* (1988) 20 HLR 340, CA (though he might have been in breach of Sch 5).

a dwelling-house exclusively as a separate dwelling (Sch 2, para 1). The same qualifying conditions apply to tied cottages where protected status is claimed as apply to the Rent Act 1977, though there are certain necessary modifications to the usual conditions applicable.

Where a protected occupier dies on or after 15 January 1989, leaving a surviving spouse, the latter may succeed to the tenancy or licence and it will be within the 1976 Act (ss 3 and 4). By contrast, if the only successor in such a case is a family member, then, as is the case with Rent Act statutory tenancies, the family member succeeds to an assured agricultural occupancy.[12]

There are strict rules which must be satisfied before the occupier is protected. These relate both to the time worked in agriculture and as to the nature of the work. Thus, for example, full-time work in agriculture is generally required.[13]

Terms of agreement

The rent is that agreed between the parties, and without an agreement as to rent the occupier is not liable to pay any rent. If the tenancy is a weekly statutory tenancy, rent is payable in arrears (s 10(3)). The fair rent provisions of the Rent Act 1977 apply (s 13). If a rent is registered, that amount is the maximum amount recoverable from the occupier (s 11(4)). If the rent payable is less than the registered rent, a notice of increase may be served (s 14) so as to increase the rent to that level, and the notice converts the occupier's status into that of statutory tenant.

Where the occupier holds as statutory tenant, the terms of the 1976 Act (Sch 5) apply. Although in principle, all benefits and burdens of the original contract continue to apply to the statutory tenancy, there are specific modifications. Thus the tenancy may be subject to the repairing obligations of s 11 of the Landlord and Tenant Act 1985 and is incapable of assignment or of sub-letting. Where the original contract makes no provision as to tenants' notices to quit, the tenant must give the landlord a minimum four weeks' notice.[14]

Security of tenure

The security of tenure offered to protected occupiers is similar to that offered to protected or statutory tenants under the Rent Act 1977, so that proof of one or more of a number of specific statutory grounds by the landlord is a pre-requisite of obtaining possession against a protected occupier of a tied agricultural cottage (s 6 and Sch 4).[15] As is the case with the Rent Act 1977, the court cannot

---

12 Provided the family member satisfies a two-year residence condition: Housing Act 1988 Sch 4, Part I, para 11, amending 1976 Act, s 4.

13 1976 Act, Sch 3, para 1. Certain periods are discounted, however, eg periods of illness or incapacity.

14 The parties may by agreement vary the statutory terms, but not, notably, those as to repairing obligations.

15 Sub-tenants are subject to the same general rules by s 9 of the 1976 Act as would be sub-tenants of protected or statutory tenants; thus, a sub-tenant lawfully sub-letting the dwelling-house or any part of it, who qualifies for protection under the 1976 Act, holds directly from the landlord where the mesne tenancy has been determined (s 9(2)).

make an order for possession unless it is reasonable to do so, where any of a number of discretionary grounds applies (s 7(2)).[16] However, Case III (breaches of obligation) includes not just breaches of the terms of the tenancy or licence, but also, as might be expected, breaches of the statutory tenancy. As with the Rent Act 1977, there are a number of mandatory grounds for possession, such as an owner-occupier ground (Case XI) and a retirement ground (Case XII). In the case of these latter grounds, there is no discretion in the court to refuse to order possession if the ground is made out (s 7(1)).

Again as with the Rent Act 1977, the landlord is able to recover possession, subject to the overriding discretion of the court, if he proves that suitable alternative accommodation is available to the tenant: the general requirements of suitability are akin to those of the 1977 Act. In addition, however, a landlord who wishes to obtain possession of an agricultural tied cottage with a view of housing an employee of his in agriculture may apply to the relevant housing authority (usually a local authority) under s 27.[17] If the authority ought, in the interests of efficient agriculture, to provide such accommodation, they may seek the advice of an agricultural dwelling advisory committee for the area (s 28). Following a special procedure, the authority may decide to provide accommodation and, if the tenant declines a written offer from the authority, or, notably, the tenant accepts no offer and is taking an unreasonable attitude, the landlord may bring proceedings under Sch 4, Case II to the 1976 Act.

H   PROTECTED SHORTHOLD TENANCIES

I   GENERAL RULES

The Housing Act 1980 created what was then an innovation, short fixed-term 'protected shorthold tenancies' – residential tenancies which came within the protection of the Rent Act 1977 during the term of the tenancy, but which were mandatorily terminable by the landlord after the expiry of the term certain. Protected shorthold tenancies (PSTs) have to all intents and purposes been superseded by assured shorthold tenancies, the creature of Part I of the Housing Act 1988. However, a short account of them may still be useful, if only to enable the two types of tenancy to be compared.

A protected shorthold tenancy is a protected tenancy which, in contrast to assured shorthold tenancies, must be granted for a term certain of not less than one nor more than five years (s 52(1) of the 1980 Act). The initial term certain of a PST must be incapable of being brought to an end by the landlord before its expiry date except by a provision for forfeiture or re-entry (s 52(1)(a)). A tenant holding a PST has an absolute right, which cannot be fettered by any penalty clause, to terminate

---

16   *Burgoyne v Griffiths* [1991] 1 EGLR 14 (fact that judge did not expressly refer to reasonableness did not imply that he did not consider it).
17   This provision applies also to lettings of houses which are subject to the assured agricultural occupancy rules (Housing Act 1988, s 26(1)).

it by notice in writing (s 53 of the 1980 Act). The notice, whose effect is to terminate the initial protected shorthold tenancy and to turn it into a statutory tenancy,[18] must be one month in length if the shorthold term was for two years or less and for three months if its duration was above this period. No corresponding right is conferred on a tenant who holds an assured shorthold tenancy. It will also be seen that under the reforms of the Housing Act 1996, an assured shorthold tenancy does not have to be fixed term and does not have to last for a minimum or maximum period: in other words, the process of liberalisation commenced by the PST scheme has been taken a few steps further by the legislature.

II RECOVERY OF POSSESSION BY THE LANDLORD

The landlord is entitled to recover possession against a protected shorthold tenant in proceedings, under the mandatory Case 19 in Sch 15, Part II to the Rent Act 1977 (s 55(1) of the 1980 Act). Case 19 applies where either of the following conditions is present:

(a) there has been no grant of a further tenancy of the dwelling-house since the end of the shorthold tenancy; or
(b) if there has been such a grant, it was to a person who was not, immediately before the grant, in possession as protected or statutory tenant.

The landlord must have served a prescribed warning notice on the tenant[19] before the grant of the protected shorthold tenancy. If not, the tenancy will not be within Case 19; but this requirement may be dispensed with by the court. Where an initial shorthold term certain expires, and is followed by a periodic tenancy, the latter is a protected tenancy (s 52(5)) but it is terminable under Case 19. The notion that if a tenancy commences life as a shorthold, it continues as such until it is ended is continued in the assured shorthold tenancy regime.

The landlord must give at least three months' advance notice of his intention to bring proceedings, and also must show that he has served an *appropriate notice* on the tenant, and commence proceedings not later than three months after its expiry. If these time-limits, which cannot be waived by agreement, are not strictly complied with by the landlord, the court has no jurisdiction to act under Case 19. The general prohibition on the making of possession orders under s 98(1) of the Rent Act 1977 then applies.[20]

Appropriate notice requirements

There are a number of requirements which must be met if a notice is to be appropriate for Case 19 purposes. These are:

(a) it must be in writing and state that after its expiry, Case 19 proceedings may be brought; and

18 *Griffiths v Renfree* [1989] 2 EGLR 46, CA.
19 Protected Shorthold Tenancies (Notice to Tenant) Regulations 1987, SI 1987/267.
20 *Ridehalgh v Horsefield* (1992) 24 HLR 453, CA.

(b) it must expire not earlier than three months after it is served; and
(c) if, at the date of service, the tenancy is periodic, the notice cannot be served
    to expire any earlier than the periodic tenancy could have been terminated
    by a common law notice to quit served on the same day.

In addition, the landlord's appropriate notice must be served in principle within
the three months period immediately before the expiry date of the initial
shorthold term. If not, and where the date has passed, it must be served within
the three months immediately before any anniversary date of such expiry. One
special rule applies to past notices. If a previous but lapsed appropriate notice
was served by the landlord, a further notice is capable of being subsequently
served and of being appropriate for Case 19, if it is served not earlier than three
months after the expiry date of the stale and previous notice.

Chapter 18

Assured tenancies

A INTRODUCTION

I TWO FORMS OF PRIVATE SECTOR RESIDENTIAL TENANCY

Part I of the Housing Act 1988 created two forms of new tenancy for the private residential sector: assured and assured shorthold tenancies.[1] When the scheme was originally conceived, unless the landlord elected to grant the tenant an assured shorthold tenancy, the tenancy was an assured tenancy. An assured tenant may only be removed against his will from the house or flat concerned if the landlord is able to prove a statutory ground for possession against him. Some grounds, such as rent arrears, allow the landlord to procure the removal of the tenant during the assured tenancy itself; but in some cases, such as redevelopment, this is not generally possible and the court may only order possession as from the expiry of the tenancy, if the ground is proved. However, under an assured tenancy the landlord may charge the market rent for the premises. It is also generally easier to re-possess the property let on an assured tenancy than on a Rent Act statutory tenancy, if only because the number of mandatory grounds for possession is larger in the case of an assured tenancy.

Assured tenancies have not been very popular with landlords. The government thought that by 1996 some 70% of private sector tenancies were assured shorthold.[2] As from the commencement of Part III of the Housing Act 1996, a tenancy which satisfies the criteria required to be an assured tenancy is presumed by statute, subject to a number of exceptions, to be an assured shorthold tenancy.[3] Such a tenancy has the advantage for the landlord that, although he must seek an order for possession, he may do so on the simple ground that the tenancy has expired. Moreover, in accordance with the general government policy of deregulation, the formalities required to create an assured shorthold tenancy have been simplified. Thus, it is no longer a requirement that an assured shorthold tenancy should have a minimum fixed term of at least six months, although the landlord cannot ask for an order for possession against

---

1 Subject to transitional provisions to prevent a protected or statutory tenancy under the Rent Act 1977 being replaced by an assured or assured shorthold tenancy (1988 Act, s 34).
2 House of Lords Committee on Housing Bill 1996, *Hansard* 12 June 1996, col 1854 (Lord Mackay of Ardbrecknish). Driscoll, (1996) 146 NLJ 1699, citing research findings, states that there may currently be about 880,000 assured shortholds.
3 Housing Act 1988, s 19A, (added by Housing Act 1996, s 96). The relevant provisions (ss 6–104 and ss 148–151) came into force, with transitional savings, on 28 February 1997: SI 1997/225.

any assured shorthold tenant until six months after the beginning of the tenancy.[4] The landlord need not any longer precede the grant of an assured shorthold tenancy with a prescribed form warning notice.[5] All the landlord has to do is to submit to a demand for a statement of the written terms of the tenancy, if these do not deal with particular matters. While the 1988 Act regulates certain terms of all assured tenancies, such as in relation to assignments, the parties are generally free to agree on the type of tenancy, the terms and the rent (subject to rights of reference of an excessive shorthold tenancy rent and in the landlord to increase the rent). If the tenancy is for a term of less than seven years, it will be appreciated that the repairing obligations of s 11 of the Landlord and Tenant Act 1985 will apply to the landlord.

In what follows, for the sake of ease of exposition and simplicity, the rules given are applicable as from the commencement on 28 February 1997 of the relevant provisions of the 1996 Act, beginning with the general requirements common to both assured and assured shorthold tenancies.

II GENERAL REQUIREMENTS

The following principles are common to assured and assured shorthold tenancies alike. Section 1(1) of the Housing Act 1988[6] provides that an assured tenancy is a tenancy under which a dwelling-house is let as a separate dwelling. Because there must be a tenancy, a licence to occupy which is not a sham is not capable of being an assured shorthold or assured tenancy. Since no security is conferred after its expiry by the former type of tenancy, there seems little point in a property owner with no immediate use for a house or flat in risking the uncertainties involved in creating a licence to occupy, when he may easily, subject to a few easily complied with formalities, let the property subject to an assured shorthold tenancy. The expression 'tenancy' includes a sub-tenancy (s 45(1)) and the sub-tenant may validly be granted an assured shorthold or assured tenancy even if the head tenancy is not assured or assured shorthold.

The requirement of a dwelling-house would presumably be interpreted so as to require a letting of a house or flat (see s 45(1)) to be lived in, in much the same way as would have applied to the Rent Acts. If a tenant shares accommodation with the landlord, the tenancy is not assured or assured shorthold, owing to the operation of the resident landlord exclusion, considered later on. However, two additional specific conditions apply. If at any time during the tenancy these are not satisfied, it cannot be assured or assured shorthold.

4 Housing Act 1988, s 21(5)(c), inserted by Housing Act 1996, s 99. The 'beginning of the tenancy' seems to refer to the date of its commencement: *Sidebotham* v *Holland* [1895] 1 QB 378, CA.

5 Save where an assured tenancy ends and a new tenancy is granted to replace it to the same tenant: if it is to be a shorthold tenancy, then it must be preceded by a prescribed form notice (Housing Act 1996, Sch 7, para 4).

6 Hereafter, unless otherwise stated, all references to statutory provisions are to Part I of the 1988 Act as amended by Part III of the Housing Act 1996 where appropriate.

The first such condition is that the tenant, or each of the joint tenants (where applicable), is an individual (s 1(1)(a)). The second is that the tenant or at least one of a number of joint tenants occupies the dwelling-house as his only or principal home (s 1(1)(b)).

Owing to s 1(1)(b), therefore, if a tenant is granted, say, an assured shorthold tenancy and he permanently abandons the property with no intention of returning, as where he buys his own house and lives there, the landlord would be able to regain possession from the tenant without recourse to any ground for possession, unless the tenancy is claimed by the tenant's wife in divorce, nullity or judicial separation proceedings. In that case the court has power to transfer the tenancy to the tenant's wife.[7] The same result would follow if a tenant occupies a house as his only or principal home, but for a period of time occupies another house in that capacity.[8] It appears that assured shorthold or assured tenants are not, in contrast to Rent Act statutory tenants, to be allowed the luxury of, say, having a holiday home held on a tenancy within Part I of the 1988 Act. Indeed, if this is right, one may doubt the need for the specific exclusion from the 1988 Act regime of holiday lets.[9]

Only an individual may hold an assured tenancy, so that a residential tenancy held by a company is not capable of being assured, and if the company licenses a person to occupy the dwelling-house, he will hold as a mere licensee. If a tenancy of residential property is granted to an individual and a company as joint tenants, neither party has any kind of assured tenancy, owing to s 1(1)(a), which requires that *each* joint tenant must be an individual. However, provided that, in the case of a tenancy granted to two or more joint tenants, each tenant is an individual, the effect of s 45(3) appears to be that only one of a larger number of joint tenants needs at any one time to comply with the residence requirement of s 1(1)(b). If L grants an assured shorthold tenancy for one year certain to A, B and C as joint tenants, and A resides alone in the premises for the first six months and B and C reside there for the second six, L cannot, it seems, terminate the tenancy early merely because at no time in the year were A B and C resident together in the property.

B   TENANCIES WHICH CANNOT BE ASSURED OR ASSURED SHORTHOLD TENANCIES

General principles

There is a statutory list of tenancies which cannot be assured or assured shorthold. It resembles the list of exclusions from Rent Act 1977 protection. If a tenancy falls within any of the following categories, and is precluded from

---

7   Matrimonial Homes Act 1983, Sch 1, as extended by Housing Act 1988, Sch 17, para 34.
8   It is not clear whether, if a married couple had two homes, and divided their time between that let on an assured tenancy and their other residence, H could claim that the tenanted property was his only or principal home while W's was their other premises; nor whether the parties could make an election to treat H's premises as their only or principal home.
9   Housing Act 1988, Sch 1, para 9.

being assured shorthold or assured, it may be a business or farm business tenancy if the conditions of application which govern those tenancies govern the tenancy concerned. However, if a residential tenancy is within an excluded class of tenancy, then once the tenancy expires, the tenant has virtually no statutory protection of his occupation. However, if the tenancy is not an excluded tenancy (as to which see chapter 20), s 3 of the Protection from Eviction Act 1977 will apply to the tenant, so that the landlord will have to enforce his right to possession in court proceedings if the tenant is not willing to leave of his own accord, but no grounds for possession would need to be shown.

The statutory exclusions

The specific statutory exclusions, which apply in addition to the non-operation of Part I of the 1988 Act for failure to comply with s 1, are as follows.

Pre-commencement tenancies

A tenancy which was entered into before, or under a contract made before Part I of the 1988 Act came into force, which was on 15 January 1989.[10]

Dwelling-houses with high rental or rateable values

A tenancy entered into on or after 1 April 1990 (except where the dwelling-house had a rateable value on 31 March 1990, in pursuance of a contract made before 1 April 1990) and under which the rent for the time being is payable at a rate exceeding £25,000 a year is outside Part I of the 1988 Act. A tenancy entered into before 1 April 1990, or on or before that date in pursuance of a contract made after that date, cannot be an assured tenancy if the rateable value for the time being of the dwelling-house exceeds £1,500 if the house is in Greater London or £750 if it is elsewhere.[11]

Tenancies at a low rent

A tenancy under which for the time being no rent is payable is excluded from Part I of the 1988 Act, as is a tenancy entered into on or after 1 April 1990[12] and under which the rent payable for the time being is payable at a rate, in the case of a dwelling-house situated in Greater London, of £1,000 or less a year, and elsewhere of £250 or less a year.[13]

---

10   Housing Act 1988, Sch 1, para 1. Also excluded are protected tenancies within the Rent Act 1977, a housing association tenancy within Part VI of that Act, a secure tenancy and a relevant tenancy of a protected occupier within the Rent (Agriculture) Act 1976 (para 13).
11   Sch 1, para 2. Rateable values are to be ascertained under Sch I, Part II: para 15 of which is akin to Rent Act 1977, s 25 but the 'appropriate day' base for ascertainment of RVs has gone.
12   Subject to an exception for a tenancy entered into after 1 April 1990, in pursuance of a contract made before that date where the dwelling-house had a rateable value on 31 March 1990.
13   Housing Act 1988, Sch 1, paras 3 and 3A. In the case of a tenancy entered into before 1 April 1990, subject to a transitional provision where a contract therefor was entered into before that date, it is not assured if the rent payable is less than two-thirds of the rateable value of the dwelling-house on 31 March 1990, ascertained in accordance with the formula for para 2, above.

Business tenancies

A tenancy to which Part II of the Landlord and Tenant Act 1954 applies cannot be an assured shorthold or an assured tenancy.[14]

No guidance is given in the 1988 Act as to determining whether a mixed residential and business user tenancy is assured or within Part II of the 1954 Act. It is thought, because the present exclusion resembles the Rent Act 1977, s 24(3), that similar considerations would apply here as apply to protected tenancies: please refer to the discussion in chapter 17. Presumably, as with the Rent Act 1977, if an assured tenant sub-lets part of the premises wholly for business purposes, the sub-tenancy is not protected by the 1988 Act vis-à-vis the head tenant.

Licensed premises

A tenancy under which the dwelling-house consists of or includes premises licensed for the sale of intoxicating liquors for consumption on the premises is outside Part I of the 1988 Act.[15]

Tenancies of agricultural land

A tenancy under which agricultural land, exceeding two acres, is let together with the dwelling-house, is excluded from the assured tenancies rules.[16]

This exclusion must be read with s 2(1) of the 1988 Act,[17] under which, where a dwelling-house is let together with[18] other land:

(a) if and so long as the main purpose of the letting is the provision of a home for the tenant (or at least one of a number of joint tenants) the other land is treated as part of the dwelling-house;

(b) if and so long as the main purpose of the letting is not the provision of a home as above, the tenancy is not assured.

Therefore, if agricultural land exceeding two acres is let together with a dwelling-house, the tenancy is outside Part I of the 1988 Act. If a dwelling-house is let together with other land, as an adjunct to the house, the tenancy will be assured only if and so long as the purpose of the letting is the provision of a home for the tenant or at least one joint tenant. In that case, the land is treated as part of the house (s 2(1)(a)). If the purpose of the tenancy is not to provide a home as above, the tenancy cannot be assured (s 2(1)(b)), as where a dwelling-house and land are let for non-residential purposes. This may require the court to discover the purpose of the tenancy from the terms of the lease, or, if this is not possible, from the intentions of the parties and the circumstances at the date of the tenancy or that when the issue arises, if different. Unlike s 26(1) of the Rent Act 1977, there is no presumption that agricultural land under 2 acres let

---

14 1988 Act, Sch 1, para 4.
15 1988 Act, Sch 1, para 5.
16 Ibid, para 6(1). 'Agricultural land' is as defined by s 26(3)(a) of the General Rate Act 1967.
17 Which is subject to Sch 1, para 6 above (s 2(2)).
18 This expression presumably has the same meaning as in ss 6 and 26 of the Rent Act 1977.

with a dwelling-house is within the 1988 Act. If the letting is mainly for residential purposes, the tenancy will fall within the 1988 Act even though subsidiary agricultural activities are carried out on the land. If residential occupation is abandoned, during the tenancy, since the residence condition of s 1(1) will not be complied with, the tenancy will cease to be an assured shorthold or assured tenancy.

Tenancies of agricultural holdings

A tenancy under which the dwelling-house is comprised in[19] an agricultural holding as defined in the Agricultural Holdings Act 1986 cannot be an assured or assured shorthold tenancy if the dwelling-house is occupied by the person responsible for the control (as tenant, servant or agent of the tenant) of the farming of the holding. A tenancy under which the dwelling-house is comprised in the holding let under a farm business tenancy and which is occupied by the person responsible for the control (as above) of the management of the holding is excluded from Part I of the 1988 Act.[20] Tenancies of these types fall either within the Agricultural Holdings Act 1986 or the Agricultural Tenancies Act 1995, depending on the date of their creation.

Lettings to students

A tenancy granted to a person following or intending to follow a course of study provided by a specified educational institution, granted by that institution or by another specified institution is outside Part I of the 1988 Act.[1] This exclusion corresponds to s 8 of the Rent Act 1977.

If a specified, or any other, landlord lets out of term time, he will be able to recover possession from any assured or assured shorthold tenants under a mandatory ground, provided the landlord complies with a notice requirement and the tenancy is for a fixed-term not exceeding 12 months.[2]

Holiday lettings

A tenancy whose purpose is to confer on the tenant the right to occupy the dwelling-house for a holiday is not an assured or assured shorthold tenancy.[3] This exclusion corresponds to s 9 of the Rent Act 1977 (see further chapter 17). A holiday letting is an excluded tenancy.[4] As a result, s 3 of the Protection from Eviction Act 1977 does not apply to the tenant. It is therefore lawful for the landlord to recover possession, once the tenancy has expired, without an order of court.

---

19 As to 'comprised in' see *Lester v Ridd* [1989] 1 All ER 111, CA (where a long lease was partitioned without the lessor's consent so that one partner obtained a house and some land, the other the remaining land, but this did not create two separate holdings).
20 Housing Act 1988, Sch 1, para 7, as substituted by Agricultural Tenancies Act 1995, Schedule, para 34.
1 Sch 1, para 8(1). See Assured and Protected Tenancies etc Regulations 1988 SI 1988/2236, as amended.
2 Sch 2, Part I, ground 4, which is governed, as from 1 November 1993, by the rapid repossession rules in SI 1993/2175.
3 Sch 1, para 9.
4 Protection from Eviction Act 1977, s 3A(7).

Where the landlord lets off-season, he may recover possession mandatorily,[5] provided he complies with a notice requirement and the letting is for a term certain not exceeding eight months.

Resident landlords

A tenancy granted by a resident landlord cannot be an assured or assured shorthold tenancy.[6] Certain conditions must, however, be complied with: if they are not followed, the tenancy will be within Part I of the 1988 Act. If the date of grant of such a non-complying tenancy was before the commencement of s 96 of the Housing Act 1996, then the tenancy will be an assured tenancy. If the relevant date fell as from such commencement, it seems that the tenancy is presumed to be an assured shorthold tenancy.

The present exemption allows a landlord to let off part or parts of his house while being reasonably sure that he will be able easily to regain possession, without having to prove any statutory grounds, and without needing to resort even to the procedures of s 21 of the 1988 Act, as from the expiry or determination of the tenancy at common law.

The conditions for application of the exemption are in most respects identical to those which apply under s 12 of the Rent Act 1977, and similar rules to those in Sch 2 to the 1977 Act apply where the resident landlord sells his reversion to another person, or where, following the death of a resident landlord, his executors sell the reversion to a third party.[7]

Accordingly, reference should be made to the discussion in chapter 17 of s 12 and Sch 2 to the 1977 Act, which applies to the present exception, subject to the modifications below, and to its construction. This is particularly so, it is thought, with regard to the meaning of the word 'building'; and the operation in law of the statutory disregard periods (which are the same in length as for s 12 of the 1977 Act).

Some rules under the present exception differ from the position under the Rent Act 1977 and these must be examined.

1   In the first place, the resident landlord, described as an 'individual', must occupy the house or flat concerned as his only or principal home at the time the tenancy was granted.[8] If the landlord has another house where he resides permanently, it may be impossible for him to claim that, for the purposes of the exception, a convenience residence on occasions in the house or flat concerned is sufficient – in which case, since the condition is not complied with, the tenancy falls within Part I. If he has two residences and divides his time between the two, it will presumably be a question of fact and degree, whether the residence in the tenanted premises is in his 'only or principal home' for the purposes of this exemption: if it is not, then any tenancies he grants of the latter premises will be assured or assured shorthold.

---

5   Sch 1, Part I, ground 3, which is subject, from 1 November 1993, to the rapid re-possession procedures of SI 1993/2175.
6   Sch 1, para 10.
7   Housing Act 1988, Sch 1, Part III.
8   As opposed to 'as his residence' in s 12(1)(b) of the 1977 Act.

2   The rule for joint tenants is that if the reversion is held by two or more persons as joint tenants, only any one of them need satisfy the residence requirement at the date of the grant of the tenancy.[9] The same applies to the requirement that the landlord must be a resident landlord throughout: it needs only to be satisfied by any one of a number of joint landlords. If A and B are joint landlords and A is resident in the statutory sense at the date of the grant of a tenancy to X and later B becomes resident and A leaves, the tenancy remains non-assured because the residence requirement at the date of the grant was satisfied by A and later by B.

3   Where a resident landlord dies and the executors vest the reversion within the two-year period in a further resident landlord, where the landlord is a joint landlord, of whom at least one must be an individual, the tenancy is not assured provided that at least one of the joint landlords occupies the house or flat as his only or principal home.[10]

4   Where the reversion is held under a trust of land, while disregard periods apply during the occupation of a beneficiary, occupation by any one of a number of beneficiaries will qualify. If an occupying beneficiary dies, a two-year period of disregard runs from the date of his death until another beneficiary occupies, during which the tenancy is not assured.[11]

An advantage to landlords of a tenancy falling within the resident landlord exemption is that it may also be an excluded tenancy, so that, once the tenancy has expired, the landlord may lawfully recover possession without needing to take court proceedings. However, certain conditions need to apply. If the landlord or a member of his family share accommodation (ie use it in common) with the tenant, then the tenancy may be excluded, as to which see chapter 20. Sharing of a kitchen will suffice. Sharing of storage areas, or a staircase, passage or corridor, is, however, insufficient.[12] Where a flat is occupied by a resident landlord and tenant, it will commonly be an excluded tenancy and also not assured; where different self-contained accommodation in the same building is so occupied, the tenancy will simply not be assured. In the latter case put the landlord will still need to go to court in order to lawfully evict a tenant who will not voluntarily leave once his tenancy expires (owing to the application of s 3 of the Protection from Eviction Act 1977).

Crown tenancies

Tenancies under which the interest of the landlord belongs to the Crown or to a government department or is held in trust for the Crown by a government department cannot be assured or assured shorthold tenancies. If the interest of the Crown is managed by the Crown Estate Commissioners, the tenancy may be assured.[13] This particular exclusion is akin to s 13 of the Rent Act 1977.

9   Sch 1, para 10(2).
10   Sch 1, Part III, para 17(1) and (2).
11   Sch 1, para 18(1), (2) as amended by the Tursts of Land etc Act 1996, Sch 4.
12   Protection from Eviction Act 1977, s 3A.
13   Sch 1, para 11.

Local authority etc tenancies

Tenancies granted by the following landlords fall outside Part I of the 1988 Act: local authorities,[14] the Commission for the New Towns, the Development Board for Rural Wales, an urban development corporation, a development corporation, waste disposal authorities, a residuary body, a fully mutual housing association and a housing action trust established by the Part III of the Housing Act 1988.

C RULES SPECIFIC TO ASSURED SHORTHOLD TENANCIES

I GENERAL CONSIDERATIONS

Introduction

Assured shorthold tenancies are the main form of assured tenancy (AST) as from the commencement on 28 February 1997 of s 96 of the Housing Act 1996. The tenancy is presumed to be an assured shorthold unless one of a number of exceptions apply.[15]

The following are the main exceptional cases where an assured and not an assured shorthold tenancy will be taken to have been granted to the tenant – provided all other conditions are satisfied.

1   The tenancy is a periodic tenancy arising under s 5 of the 1988 Act, following on the ending of an assured fixed-term tenancy granted before the commencement of s 96 of the 1996 Act. The periodic tenancy so arising is assured.
2   Where a notice is served before the assured tenancy is entered into by the landlord on the tenant. It must state that the tenancy is not to be an assured shorthold tenancy. A notice may also be served to the like effect after the tenancy has been entered into.
3   Where the tenancy contains express provision to the effect that the tenancy is not an assured shorthold tenancy.
4   Where there is an statutory assured periodic tenancy to which, under s 39 of the 1988 Act, a person whose predecessor held a Rent Act 1977 statutory tenancy may succeed.[16]
5   Where, following the transfer of local authority housing containing secure tenancies, the tenancies in consequence losing their secure status, the tenants affected then hold as assured tenants from their new landlord.
6   Where an assured tenant is offered a new tenancy by the landlord. Although ordinarily, the new tenancy is to be assured, there is a provision under which

14 As listed in Sch 1, para 12(2).
15 Housing Act 1988, s 19A and Sch 2A (added by Housing Act 1996, s 96 and Sch 7).
16 Except that if the landlord could have recovered possession against a statutory tenant who succeeded to a contractual protected shorthold tenancy, the tenancy following it is an AST (Housing Act 1988, Sch 2A, para 4).

if the tenant serves a prescribed form notice on the landlord stating that the replacement tenancy is to be an assured shorthold, then the present exception does not apply. The replacement tenancy is accordingly an AST.[17] There is nothing in this notice provision to prevent the landlord presenting the tenant with a prescribed form notice for signature – and no statutory safeguards against abuse of the provision against existing assured tenants.

If an assured, as opposed to an assured shorthold, tenancy is granted or conferred as a result of the operation of one of the above exceptions, it is not terminable merely on account of the fact that, whether it is fixed-term or periodic, it has expired, and once that happens, the tenancy will be followed by a statutory periodic assured tenancy.

Advantages of assured shortholds

An assured shorthold tenancy (AST) in the latest form allows the landlord all the advantages of an assured tenancy, such as the right to charge a market rent. The landlord may invoke mandatory Ground 8 of the grounds for possession if he wishes to regain possession from the tenant on account of rent arrears during any initial fixed term of an AST. Once that term has expired, the landlord may obtain possession, again only after proceedings, under s 21 of the 1988 Act provided he complies with a simple possession notice requirement.

There are but few restrictions on the landlord's otherwise dominant position, which is emphasised by the fact that there is no statutory right for a shorthold tenant holding a fixed term tenancy which has expired to renew, even though the landlord cannot recover possession against an assured shorthold tenant save by court proceedings. Nor has such a tenant holding a fixed-term assured shorthold tenancy any statutory right, as was available to protected shorthold tenants, to terminate the fixed term early by notice.[18] If the tenant is granted a periodic AST it is true that the landlord cannot ask the court to re-possess the property for the first six months but the tenant will face a statutory review of the rent under s 13, as the tenancy is periodic, subject to a right of reference under s 14. It may therefore be asked whether any landlords will grant assured, as opposed to assured shorthold, tenancies in the future.[19]

Definition and conditions of grant

An assured shorthold tenancy is an assured tenancy. Under the revised regime, it may be fixed term or periodic. Contrast the position prior to the 1996 Act: to qualify as a shorthold tenancy, a residential tenancy had to be granted for a

---

17 Sch 2A, para 7(2). Some of the dangers of draft notices prepared in connection with this provision, especially of its possible oppressive use against an estimated remaining 310,000 Rent Act tenants, are discussed by Driscoll, loc cit.

18 The government resisted an Opposition amendment to include such a right on the ground that allowing the right would deprive the landlord of the expectation of a rent during an initial fixed term: *Hansard*, HC Standing Committee G, 7 March 1996, col 256.

19 See further Driscoll, loc cit.

term certain of not less than six months (s 20(1)(a)). If the landlord had a power to determine the tenancy, it could not be exercisable during the first six months of the tenancy (s 21(1)(b)).

Where an AST has been granted before the commencement of s 96 of the Housing Act 1996, a preliminary statutory notice must have been served by the landlord before the tenancy is entered into (s 20(1)(c))

The penalty for non-compliance with the prescribed notice rule is that the tenancy is an assured tenancy. Landlords seem at times to have fallen foul of this provision[20] and the requirement of a preliminary notice was abandoned. It was replaced by the statutory presumption of the creation of an AST already mentioned.

Where service of the preliminary warning notice in relation to a tenancy granted under the original scheme of the 1988 Act had been left to the last minute before the tenancy was granted, difficulties arose. A tenant was given a prescribed form notice on the morning of December 18, for a six-month tenancy as from that day and took possession that afternoon. His claim to an assured tenancy on the ground that he did not have the full six-month term required by the Act was dismissed on the ground that the fraction of the first day that he was not in possession was to be ignored as being unimportant; the tenancy was, by the narrowest of margins, a shorthold tenancy.[1]

The landlord's preliminary warning notice, where required, may be in a form substantially to the like effect as a prescribed form notice, but reliance on this limited concession covers trifling mistakes or deviations in the notice which could in no sense mislead the tenant. Where a landlord in a non-prescribed form notice gave 6 May as the termination date of the tenancy when in fact he had granted the tenant a tenancy terminating on 7 November, one year from the commencement date, his notice, which was stigmatised as being obtuse, failed the required test of substantial compliance and was invalid.[2]

Although an assured shorthold tenant of a tenancy granted as from the commencement of the new rules has no right to a preliminary notice, he may by notice in writing request[3] the landlord[4] to supply him with a written statement of certain terms of the tenancy, if these have not been already evidenced in writing, be this in the tenancy agreement or elsewhere. New-style ASTs may be both periodic and informal. Thus the present right may be useful. It is deemed important enough for Parliament to have made it a criminal offence for a landlord to fail without reasonable excuse to comply with the tenant's request for 28 days as from receipt of the notice (s 20A(4)).

The terms which fall within this requirement are basic. They are:

(a) the date the tenancy began or came into being;
(b) the rent payable and the dates on which it is payable;

20 The government regarded the notice procedure as a trap: House of Lords Committee on Housing Bill 1996 *Hansard* 12 June 1996 col 1851.
1 *Bedding v McCarthy* [1994] 2 EGLR 40, CA. On the facts, the notice was held to have been given before the granting of the tenancy.
2 *Panayi v Roberts* [1993] 2 EGLR 51, CA; PF Smith [1993] Conv 301.
3 Under Housing Act 1988, s 20A, inserted by Housing Act 1996, s 97.
4 Where appropriate, this means any joint landlord (s 20(A)(7)).

(c) any term providing for an express rent review;
(d) if the tenancy is fixed term, its length (s 20A(2)).

The statement provided is not conclusive evidence of what was agreed (s 20A(5)) so that the tenant may always challenge its accuracy, as where he refers the rent as being excessive.

II   RECOVERY OF POSSESSION

Once a new-style AST has terminated, the landlord will, in principle, be able to regain possession of the premises once he satisfies a few simple formal conditions. If a fixed-term AST has been granted, the landlord may terminate it during the term certain under statutory grounds applicable also to assured tenants, notably that relating to rent, which has been amended so as to make it easier for landlord to invoke it.

Repossession for rent arrears under Ground 8

The landlord of an assured shorthold tenant may obtain a mandatory order for possession against an assured shorthold tenant on the ground of rent arrears, under Ground 8 of Sch 2 to the Housing Act 1988.[5] This is one of the grounds under which an assured shorthold tenancy may be terminated before the end of the contractual term of the tenancy: the other is Ground 2, relating to mortgagees, discussed in relation to assured tenancies. The statutory bar on the court making an order for possession to take effect during the first six months of an AST (s 21(5)(a)) does not apply to orders for possession made under Ground 8.

As a condition precedent to invoking Ground 8, the landlord must have served a s 8 notice on the tenant, which specifies the rent arrears and gives the amounts alleged to be owed. The notice must be in the prescribed form and must comply with a number of further requirements listed below in relation to assured tenancies, notably that proceedings must be stated in the notice to begin not earlier than two weeks from the date specified in the notice. A s 8 notice relying on rent arrears, whether or not in the prescribed form must give full particulars to the tenant if it is to be valid.[6]

This particular ground is likely to be the main reason invoked by the landlord of an assured shorthold tenant for possession during the period of the tenancy. During the passage of the Housing Bill 1996, the government claimed that although the periods of rent arrears which must exist at the date of the hearing had been reduced, given that it might take some 12 weeks for a matter to reach court, the total time allowed for a responsible tenant to put his affairs in order seemed reasonable.[7]

---

5   If the landlord wishes to levy a distress on the premises as an alternative to use of Ground 8, he must obtain the leave of the county court: Housing Act 1988, s 19(1), which applies equally to assured tenancies.

6   *Mountain* v *Hastings* [1993] 2 EGLR 53, CA.

7   House of Lords Committee, 12 June 1996, *Hansard*, col 1883 (Lord Mackay of Ardbrecknish).

Ground 8, as amended, provides as follows:

Both at the date of service of the s 8 notice and at the date of the hearing:
(a) at least eight weeks' rent is unpaid, where rent is payable weekly or fortnightly;
(b) at least two months' rent is unpaid, where the rent is payable monthly;[8]
(c) at least one quarter's rent is more than three months in arrears, where the rent is payable quarterly;
(d) at least three months' rent is in more than three months' arrears, where the rent is payable yearly.

'Rent' means rent lawfully due from the tenant. Having regard to s 48 of the Landlord and Tenant Act 1987, which requires the landlord to supply the tenant with a suitable name and address as a condition precedent to recovery of rent (see further chapter 8), unless and until such a notice has been served on the tenant, Ground 8 cannot be relied on.[9] This potential trap for landlords has been alleviated because s 48 does not have to be complied with by means of a formal notice – a statement of the requisite information, say with a notice under s 8 of the 1988 Act, suffices. The amount of rent alleged to be due may be specified in the landlord's s 8 notice, but it appears that it suffices if he gives the tenant sufficient information to enable him to work out what is owed, as where a tenant who had paid no rent since a given date had been told that at that date he owed a specified sum.[10]

The present ground is mandatory, and if rent arrears are proved within the above requirements, the court has no discretion to refuse to make an order for possession. The periods of rent arrears to be proved as a condition precedent to obtaining possession were shortened by the Housing Act 1996, as part of a policy of strengthening the position of the landlord of what will be presumed, in post-1996 Act tenancies, to be an assured shorthold tenancy.

However, the rent must be in arrears in the prescribed sense both at the date of service of the s 8 notice and at the date of the hearing, and so, if the tenant repays all the arrears and (presumably) costs, between the date of service of the s 8 notice and that of the hearing, the landlord cannot regain possession on this ground, irrespective of the tenant's past record.

Repossession on expiry of tenancy

There is also a specific procedure for the recovery of possession against an assured shorthold tenant. This arises once the initial tenancy has expired and no further assured tenancy, shorthold or not, exists for the time being, other than a statutory periodic tenancy which, it will be remembered, comes into being automatically as from expiry of the contractual term of an AST, but which is deemed to be a shorthold tenancy (s 21(1)(a)). The landlord, or at least a number of joint landlords, must have given the tenant a written notice of not

8 These periods are given as substituted by Housing Act 1996, s 101 as from 28 February 1997 (SI 1997/225); the previous, longer, intervals were thirteen weeks and three months respectively.
9 *Marath* v *MacGillivray* (1996) 28 HLR 484, CA; see M Jones (1996) 146 NLJ 1517.
10 *Marath* v *MacGillivray*, supra.

less than two months stating that he requires possession (s 21(1)(b)). The notice requiring possession may not only be given, once any term certain has expired; it may be given before or on the expiry date notwithstanding the fact that on the coming to an end of the fixed-term or periodic contractual tenancy a statutory periodic tenancy arises (s 21(2)). A landlord may time his termination notice so that it may expire on the contractual termination date of an initial term certain, provided it is served not less than two months before then. If a valid s 21 notice is served on the tenant, it may also do service as a notice to terminate the tenancy under a contractual break clause which requires one month's advance notice to the tenant, since once possession is obtained, the tenancy comes to an end.[11] In the case of a periodic assured shorthold tenancy, there is a further restriction. The court cannot order possession unless the landlord has specified, in his notice, the date when possession is required. This date must be the last day of a period of the tenancy. It must also be earlier than two months after the date the notice was given (s 21(4)).[12]

Provided the landlord has complied with the relevant notice requirements, the court, following the landlord's application, must make an order for possession, and has no discretion to refuse to make the order, if it is satisfied that the shorthold term has come to an end, and no further assured tenancy other than a shorthold tenancy, whether statutory or not, is in existence.

No order for possession may be made as from the commencement of an amended s 21, so as to take effect earlier than six months after the beginning of an AST granted after the commencement of the 1996 Act rules.[13] If the landlord has granted the tenant a new or 'replacement' tenancy of the same or substantially the same premises as those let under the first tenancy, the six month period runs from the commencement of the first-mentioned tenancy.[14] Thus, if a tenant is granted in say 1997 a monthly periodic assured (shorthold) tenancy, and it is ended by valid common law notice to quit after three months, the tenant will have a further three months in the premises, if he wants them, as a statutory periodic tenant – unless he has, for example, fallen seriously into arrear with his rent.

Where possession is ordered, any statutory periodic tenancy coming into being on expiry of the initial term certain ends automatically (without further notice and regardless of the period) on the day the order takes effect (s 21(3)). There is no prescribed form of termination notice. Indeed, it appears that the specific notice procedures of s 21 are not to be subjected to a further requirement of service on the tenant of a notice under s 8 of the 1988 Act.[15]

---

11   *Fawaz* v *Alyward* (1996) Times, 15 July, CA.
12   See *Lower Street Properties Ltd v Jones* (1996) 28 HLR 877, CA.
13   Housing Act 1988, s 21(5)(a), inserted by Housing Act 1996, s 99.
14   Ibid, s 20(5)(b).
15   *Panayi v Roberts*, supra.

III SHORTHOLD TENANCY RENTS

An assured shorthold tenant may refer the rent for the tenancy[16] to a rent assessment committee (s 22(1)).[17] This must be by an application in the prescribed form.[18] The committee must then determine the rent which, in its opinion, the landlord might 'reasonably be expected to obtain'. The rent cannot be referred by the tenant of a new-style shorthold tenancy if more than six months have expired since the beginning of the tenancy (s 22(2))[19] – that period being the time during which the landlord cannot ask the court to implement an order for possession. If a rent has previously been determined under s 22, the tenant cannot in any case refer the rent (s 22(2)(a)).

The committee cannot make a determination unless, by s 22(3), they consider that:

(a) there is a sufficient number of similar dwelling-houses in the locality let on assured tenancies (shorthold or not); and
(b) the rent payable under the assured shorthold tenancy is 'significantly higher' than the rent which the landlord might reasonably be expected to be able to obtain under the tenancy, having regard to the level of rents payable under the tenancies in the locality of similar dwelling-houses.[20]

A rent as determined takes effect from whatever date the committee direct, but no earlier than the date of the application (s 22(4)(a)). Any excess rent over that determined is irrecoverable from the tenant as from the date the determination takes effect (s 22(4)(b)).[1] The landlord cannot serve a notice of increase of rent under s 13(2) until one year from the date of the determination taking effect (s 22(4)(c)).

If there is a scarcity of dwellings let on assured tenancies, the committee cannot consider any application for a reduction in the rent, even if it is very high for that reason (s 22(3)(a)). This, it is said, contrasts with referrals of the rents of assured periodic tenancies, as a discount for scarcity might be proper, as there is no security of tenure for assured shorthold tenants.[2]

In any case, the limited right to refer is shown by the fact that the landlord will only have to face a determination if the tenant can prove that the rent is significantly higher than the landlord might reasonably obtain under the tenancy, regard being had to the general rent level in the locality (s 22(3)(b)). This is, therefore, a provision designed to counteract overcharging by landlords

---

16 In contrast to the position with fixed-term assured tenants, where such reference is impossible.
17 The Secretary of State has power, by regulations, to order that s 22 is not to apply to specified cases or tenancies of dwelling-houses in such areas or other circumstances as may be specified (s 23).
18 See Assured Tenancies etc (Forms) Regulations 1988, SI 1988/2203.
19 As amended by Housing Act 1996, s 100(1).
20 By s 22(5); s 14(4), (5) and (8) apply to a determination under s 22.
1 The information, procedural and publicity of determinations rules apply to ASTs as to any assured tenancy (ss 41 and 42).
2 Davey, *Residential Rents*, p 226.

above that level which the Committee find to be the general level of rents for comparable assured tenancies in the area. If the general rent level is forced up by the market in a given case, then it is more than arguable that a landlord could reasonably expect to obtain a rent reflecting the scarcity factor, against which a shorthold tenant is given no shield at all, this being the reverse of the position which, it has been held, applies to regulated tenants.[3]

D   STATUTORY RULES GOVERNING SPECIFIC TERMS OF ASSURED TENANCIES

The following rules apply to assured shorthold and assured tenancies alike.

Prohibition on dispositions

Any periodic assured tenancy, but not a fixed-term tenancy, is subject to a specific statutory prohibition on assignments or sub-lettings of the tenancy, which applies instead of the general statutory rule.[4] By s 15(1), it is an implied term of any periodic assured tenancy and also of any statutory periodic tenancy that, except with the consent of the landlord, the tenant cannot:

(a) assign the tenancy (in whole or in part); or
(b) sub-let or part with the possession of the whole of any part of the dwelling-house let on the tenancy.

The implied prohibition of s 15(1) does not apply, by s 15(3)(a), if there is a 'provision (whether contained in the tenancy or not) under which the tenant is prohibited (whether absolutely or conditionally) from assigning or sub-letting or parting with possession' or is permitted (absolutely or conditionally) to assign, sub-let or part with possession.[5]

Therefore, while the statutory prohibition on assignments, etc, applies in all circumstances to a statutory periodic tenancy (as where a periodic tenancy arises under s 5 of the 1988 Act, after the expiry of a previous fixed-term tenancy), it is apparently open to the parties to a periodic tenancy to exclude the terms of s 15. What is not so clear, as has been pointed out,[6] is whether an express term in a less comprehensive form than the statutory implied prohibition would suffice to exclude the statutory implied term, as where there is an express prohibition on assignments or sub-lettings of the whole, but not in terms of any part of the dwelling-house. However, if the parties have inserted an express term, this surely evinces an intention wholly to exclude s 15, even though the terms of the statute may be wider than those of the express exclusion. Because statutory periodic tenancies are subject to the full force of s 15, which cannot be derogated from by the parties, if a previous fixed-term tenancy contained a

3   *Western Heritable Investment Co Ltd v Husband* [1983] 2 AC 849, [1983] 3 All ER 65, HL.
4   1988 Act, s 15(2), excluding Landlord and Tenant Act 1927, s 19(1).
5   Nor does the statutory implied prohibition apply where a premium is required to be paid on the grant or renewal of the tenancy (s 15(3)(b)).
6   Megarry, *Rent Acts*, Vol 3, p 105.

narrower prohibition on dispositions than that of s 15, the landlord will benefit from the fact that the periodic tenancy arising after the fixed-term tenancy determines will be subject to a wider prohibition than any originally agreed.

Repairs

It is an implied term of every assured tenancy (and so of assured shorthold, assured fixed-term, assured periodic and statutory periodic tenancies alike) that the tenant is bound to afford access to the landlord to the dwelling-house concerned and all reasonable facilities for executing therein any repairs which he is entitled to execute (s 16). The landlord's agents and servants are not expressly entitled to access under s 16, which applies to work classified as repairs or subordinate renewal, but not full-scale renewals. There is nothing in s 16 to prevent the landlord from inserting into a fixed-term assured tenancy an access right in wider terms than those implied by s 16. Where this is so, it is presumed that such a term would be carried forward by s 5(3)(c) into any statutory assured tenancy arising after the termination of the former fixed-term tenancy.

Sub-tenancies

At common law, where a tenant sub-lets, and his own leasehold interest comes to an end by forfeiture or landlords' or tenants' notice to quit, any sub-tenancies granted by the tenant are determined by operation of law. In the case of a residential sub-tenant, proceedings may be required to evict him (see chapter 20).

Section 18 of the 1988 Act modifies the common law rule that a sub-tenancy is in principle dependent for its continued survival on an immediately superior leasehold interest. It applies only if the interest of the sub-tenant's immediate landlord is not such that the (sub) tenancy could not be assured (s 18(2)). Thus, if the sub-tenancy was granted by a local authority landlord, the Crown or a resident landlord, s 18 is excluded and the common law rule applies. Thus the protection of a residential sub-tenant depends on the status of the landlord at the time of the grant and if the leasehold reversion becomes vested in a landlord who cannot grant assured tenancies, the protection of the provision is lost.

The protection of s 18(1) applies if, at any time, three conditions are satisfied. Where these are satisfied, the sub-tenancy continues in existence, despite the termination of the intermediate tenancy, held direct from the landlord of the person who granted the sub-tenancy. The conditions are:

(a) a dwelling-house is 'for the time being lawfully let on an assured tenancy' (which therefore includes a letting on an assured shorthold tenancy)
(b) the landlord is himself a tenant holding a superior tenancy;
(c) the superior tenancy has come to an end.

The requirement that the letting of the house or flat concerned must be 'lawful' disqualifies a sub-tenancy which was granted in breach of an absolute or qualified prohibition in his landlord's own lease from being preserved under s 18. Similar considerations would seem to apply as govern s 137 of the Rent Act 1977 (chapter 17).

The granting of reversionary tenancies as a means of avoiding s 18 is defeated by s 18(3). Thus, if the landlord, having granted a fixed-term tenancy, grants a reversionary tenancy to commence as from, or after, the date of the previous contractual tenancy[7] ends by effluxion of time, and the fixed-term tenancy continues under s 5 as a statutory periodic tenancy, the reversionary tenancy is subject to the statutory periodic tenancy. A similar rule applies where the first-mentioned tenancy is periodic. Were it not for s 18(3), the superior tenancy mentioned in s 18(1)(c) would not have come to an end, so that the protection of the provision could not be claimed by any sub-tenant.

E   REPOSSESSION RULES

I   GENERAL PRINCIPLES

An assured shorthold tenant has, as we have seen, no statutory security at all once his contractual term has expired. He may hold over as a periodic shorthold tenant but his landlord is entitled to ask the court for possession under the specific procedures of s 21, which have already been examined.

By contrast, the position of an assured tenant is more secure as the following matters demonstrate.

1   The fixed term cannot in principle be terminated by the landlord before it expires (s 5(1)). An assured tenancy may allow the landlord to exercise a contractual right to terminate it for a specified reason (eg redevelopment) before the end of the fixed term. Section 5(1) of the 1988 Act preserves such a right as being efficacious (if properly exercised at common law). If such a break clause is duly operated by the landlord, the fixed term tenancy ends on the date specified in the landlord's notice and a statutory periodic tenancy comes into being. That tenancy is terminable solely in accordance with the proof by the landlord of one or more specified grounds for possession. So, in the case of exercise of a break clause on the ground of redevelopment, the landlord would also, to be sure of obtaining possession, need to prove that the requirements of ground 6 applied. There is a risk that if a contractual right to terminate is exercisable for breach of covenant, it may be held to be equivalent to a forfeiture clause, so rendering it not effective to put a premature end to the assured fixed term tenancy in question.[8]

2   The tenant is entitled to remain in possession after the expiry of the fixed term as a statutory periodic tenant. The terms of this type of tenancy, which may after the 1996 Act become a rare creature, are governed by statute but they may be varied by the landlord under a statutory procedure. If the tenant dies while holding a statutory periodic tenancy under the 1988 Act, provision is made under s 17 for a single succession to the tenancy. This may

---

7   As defined in s 18(4).
8   See Megarry, *Rent Acts*, Vol 3, p 136.

be by the tenant's spouse or sex partner (s 17(4)) if that person occupied the dwelling-house concerned as his only or principal home.

3 The landlord may in cases of breaches of covenant by an assured tenant ask the court to put an end to the tenancy prior to its contractual expiry date, as by invoking mandatory Grounds 2 (nuisance), or 8 (rent arrears), or discretionary grounds other than 9 or 16 (s 7(6)).

4 Once a fixed term assured tenancy has expired and has been followed by a statutory periodic tenancy, the latter may be terminated by the landlord proving to the satisfaction of the court the existence of facts within one or more grounds relating to breach of covenant by the tenant or other matters such as owner-occupation (s 7). We have already noted that these grounds apply to an assured shorthold tenancy whose initial fixed term has expired, but the landlord would no doubt prefer to have recourse to s 21, in such a case, to remove a tenant who declined to leave voluntarily.

5 Any assured tenancy may be terminated by the tenant surrendering it (provided the surrender is accepted by the landlord) or by 'some other action' of his (s 5(2)(b)). It might be argued that conduct such as leaving the house or flat concerned, without paying rent, which might not necessarily amount to an implied surrender, could be treated as falling within this part of s 5(2)(b) by the landlord and so entitling him to possession without the need for proceedings.

II STATUTORY PERIODIC TENANCY

A statutory periodic tenancy is an interim device. It bears the same general nature as the tenancy preceding it: if it was assured, the statutory periodic tenancy will be assured; if not, then the periodic tenancy arising is shorthold. It comes into being once the contractual term of the previous tenancy comes to an end by effluxion of time or notice to quit. The general principle is therefore that, as postulated by s 5, the terms of the statutory periodic tenancy are the same as those of the tenancy which immediately preceded it. They may be varied by the landlord within the first complete year of the statutory periodic tenancy coming into being under s 6 of the 1988 Act – a provision seemingly mainly apt for assured as opposed to assured shorthold tenancies.

The tenant may prevent the coming into being of a statutory assured tenancy, if the contractual tenancy was fixed term, by surrendering the latter (a method preserved by s 5(2)(a)). This statutory tenancy will continue until:

1 The landlord, if he can, obtains from the court an order for possession under s 21.

2 The landlord obtains an order for possession under a statutory ground for possession.

3 A new assured or assured shorthold tenancy is granted to the tenant of the same or substantially the same dwelling-house (s 5(4)).

III REPOSSESSION BY LANDLORD AGAINST ASSURED PERIODIC OR STATUTORY TENANTS

Basic rules

The following principles apply where the relevant tenancy is an assured periodic tenancy as opposed to an assured periodic shorthold tenancy. A periodic assured tenancy may only be ended if the landlord is able to prove one or more statutory grounds (s 7 of the 1988 Act) and it cannot be brought to an end by a common law notice to quit: a special notice under s 8 must be served on the tenant.

These rules would also apply to the landlord of an assured shorthold tenant who was granted a fixed term which has not expired, so that s 21 is not available to the landlord but where he wishes to rely on the mandatory ground applicable to rent arrears.

Notice procedure

A special notice procedure (s 8) applies to the contractual tenancy, and to the statutory periodic tenancy which follows it. If a s 8 notice is served when the dwelling-house is let on a fixed-term tenancy, or in relation to events occurring during an expired fixed-term tenancy, it is effective even though the tenant holds or held under a statutory periodic tenancy (s 8(6)). This is to save the landlord the necessity of serving two notices.

The s 8 notice must be in the prescribed form.[9] If s 8 is ignored, or no prescribed form notice is served, or the court takes the view that the notice, although not prescribed, is also not in a form substantially to the like effect, the court cannot entertain the possession proceedings (s 8(1)). The court has a power to dispense with the notice requirement if it considers it just and equitable to do so (s 8(1)(b)). Where on the facts the tenant had sufficient time in which to remedy the breach of covenant complained of, despite the absence of a s 8 notice, the power of dispensation was exercised. It was, however, pointed out that, as with the Rent Acts, each case would depend on its facts.[10] The dispensation power is not available in the case of serious rent arrears (s 8(5)). Section 8 imposes the following requirements.

1   The landlord, or at least one joint landlord, must have served due notice on the tenant, and proceedings must be begun within the time-limits given in the notice (s 8(1)(a) and (3)).
2   The notice must specify the ground or grounds and particulars of it or them; the landlord may, with the leave of the court, alter or add to specified grounds which appear in a valid notice,[11] but, subject to that, if a ground and particulars are not specified in a s 8 notice, the court cannot order possession on that ground (s 8(2)).

---

9   Assured Tenancies etc (Forms) Regulations 1988, SI 1988/2203 as amended.
10 *Kelsey Housing Association v King* (1995) 28 HLR 270, CA.
11 It appears from *Mountain v Hastings*, supra, that if the notice is void, as where it is not in a form sufficiently like the prescribed form, this power cannot be exercised by the court.

3   The notice, as seen, must be in the prescribed form or a form substantially to the like effect and it must inform the tenant, by s 8(3):
   (a)   that the landlord intends to bring proceedings for possession on one or more grounds specified in the notice;
   (b)   proceedings will begin not earlier than a date specified in the notice which, generally, must be not earlier than two weeks from the date of service of the notice and not later than twelve months from the service thereof.

4   If the notice specifies certain grounds[12] the date for beginning proceedings must not, by s 8(4),[13] be earlier than two months from the date of service of the s 8 notice; and if, in this, the tenancy is periodic, as well as the two months requirement, the s 8 notice cannot specify a date for beginning proceedings any earlier than the earliest lawful date for determination of the tenancy by a common-law notice to quit. In all other cases except domestic violence, the specified date may be two weeks from the date of service of the notice.

Should the landlord rely on a notice which is not in the prescribed form, he is only entitled to claim that the notice is within the concession allowing for notices to be valid if substantially to the like effect if his notice closely follows the wording of s 8 and the relevant form, so as to avoid any danger of misleading the tenant. So, where a landlord served a non-prescribed form notice, followed by a written statement 'ground 8, at least three months rent is unpaid', this notice was invalid, as not giving full particulars to the tenant.[14]

The court has a number of discretionary powers in possession proceedings, but these do not apply to mandatory grounds for possession nor where the court is asked to order possession after an assured shorthold tenancy has expired (s 9(6)). The powers, in s 9, resemble closely those conferred by Rent Act 1977, s 100.

Where the tenant has the right under his tenancy to share some accommodation with other persons, but not the landlord, (i e where s 3 applies) the court cannot order possession of the shared accommodation unless it orders possession of the accommodation which the tenant occupies exclusively (s 10(2)). The court may, on the landlord's application, order the termination or modification of the tenant's right to occupy shared non-living accommodation (s 10(3)) except where the tenancy itself enables this to be done (s 10(4)).

F   GROUNDS FOR POSSESSION

In what follows we examine the statutory grounds for possession and are not concerned with the specific right of the landlord of an assured shorthold tenant whose tenancy has ended to resort to s 21 as a means of regaining possession of the premises.

---

12   Ie where the landlord was owner-occupier, a mortgagee seeks vacant possession, occupation for a minister of religion, redevelopment, devolution of periodic tenancy, suitable alternative accommodation and employee-tenant whose employment has ceased.
13   As amended by s 151 of the Housing Act 1996.
14   *Mountain v Hastings* [1993] 2 EGLR 53, CA.

I INTRODUCTION

The court cannot make an order for possession of a dwelling-house let on an assured tenancy, nor on an assured shorthold tenancy whose initial fixed term has not expired, except on one or more of a number of grounds in Sch 2 to the 1988 Act (s 7(1)). The grounds for possession are divided into mandatory and discretionary grounds. In all cases, the onus of proving a ground is on the landlord. In the case of a mandatory ground the court must order possession if it is established (s 7(3)). If the dwelling-house is, at the relevant time, let on an assured fixed-term tenancy, the court cannot make a possession order take effect on a mandatory ground before the end of the tenancy, unless ground 2 or ground 8 is made out (s 7(6)), and the terms of the tenancy make provision, by a forfeiture clause or in some other way, for the tenancy to be brought to an end on the ground concerned – ie re-possession by a mortgagee or for serious rent arrears. In other cases, where there is a fixed-term assured tenancy, the earliest date on which an order for possession will be able to take effect is a date after the contractual expiry date of the tenancy (s 7(7)).

Once a mandatory ground has been made out, and subject, in the case of fixed-term tenancies, to the above, the court will have no overriding discretion to refuse an order for possession. By contrast, in the case of discretionary grounds, the court has powers of adjournment and the like conferred by s 9. The court also, in the case of discretionary grounds, has an overriding discretion to refuse to order possession, since it may only make an order if it is reasonable to do so (s 7(4)). Similar principles govern the matter, as would apply to s 98(1) of the 1977 Act. Therefore, the issue of reasonableness must be given separate consideration by the court, and merely because it may be reasonable for a landlord to require possession, it does not follow that it is reasonable for the court to gratify his wish. If the judge acts in a broad, commonsense way, taking all relevant factors into account, it may be assumed that the weight of any given factor is for him alone,[15] and it would be reasonable, if appropriate, to take into account personal, environmental and domestic factors. For some further considerations, refer to chapter 17. Even apart from s 5(1), no power in an assured tenancy which would, if exercised, deprive the tenant of his tenancy for breach of obligation, can be enforced except following an order of the court.[16]

Grounds 1 to 5 inclusive in the mandatory grounds depend on prior and specific notices from the landlord to the tenant, which may be presumably incorporated into the terms of the tenancy itself. Any notice must be in writing, and must, where there are joint landlords, be given by at least one of them.[17] In these grounds, the notices have to be given 'not later than the beginning of the tenancy': this means 'not later than the day the tenancy was entered into'.[18] Where a landlord gives a notice as required, the notice has

---

15 Cf *Cumming v Danson* [1942] 2 All ER 653, CA.
16 *AG Securities v Vaughan; Antoniades v Villiers* [1990] 1 AC 417, HL.
17 Sch 2, Part IV, para 7.
18 Ibid, paras 8 and 11, overriding s 45(2).

effect in relation to any later tenancy which starts immediately after the ending of the earlier tenancy.[19]

Under s 12, where a landlord obtains an order for possession under a ground for possession and subsequently it is proved that the order was obtained by misrepresentation or concealment of material facts, the court must order the landlord to pay to the former tenant 'such sum as appears sufficient as compensation for the damage or loss sustained by that tenant as a result of the order'. The section does not give any further guidance, so it may be assumed that the quantum of an award is entirely at the discretion of the court: one wonders if it could legitimately order the landlord to pay to the tenant the value of the tenant's interest as sitting tenant, or his 'nuisance value'. One remedy which the tenant does not have, under s 12, is re-instatement in the premises.

II MANDATORY GROUNDS FOR POSSESSION

With the alteration in the balance between assured and assured shorthold tenancies in favour of the latter type of tenancy having been made by Chapter II of Part III of the Housing Act 1996, it may be in the future that the main ground on which the landlord of a private sector tenant will invoke as a means of putting an end to the tenancy during its initial fixed term will be Ground 8. The principal mandatory grounds are here set out even though it may be that as time passes, assured tenancies as opposed to ASTs may become increasingly rare animals.[20]

Ground 1 – Owner occupation

Not later than the beginning of the tenancy the landlord gave the tenant notice in writing that possession might be recovered on this ground[21] and:

(a) at some time before the beginning of the tenancy,[1] the landlord seeking possession or, in the case of joint landlords, at least one of them, occupied the dwelling-house as his only or principal home; or

(b) the landlord seeking possession or, in the case of joint landlords, at least one of them, requires the dwelling-house as his or his spouse's only or principal

---

19 Ibid, para 8(1). The tenant must be the same as the immediately preceding tenant, and the dwelling-house must be 'substantially the same' (para 8(2)). This rule does not apply if the landlord serves a further written notice on the tenant that the ground concerned is not applicable: para 8(3).

20 Those not discussed are: Ground 4, which relates to vacation lettings of student accommodation, and which is like Rent Act 1977, Sch 15, Part II, Case 14; Ground 5, which is appropriate to houses let to a Minister of religion; and Ground 7, which ensures that the sole way an assured tenancy devolves after the death of the tenant is by s 17.

21 The court may dispense with the notice requirement if it is just and equitable to do so; see *Boyle v Verrall* [1997] 04 EG 145, CA (all relevant circumstances are to be taken into account: the tenant failed to draw the landlord's attention to her mistaken non-service of a notice despite her known intention to do so and notice was dispensed with).

1 Ie not later than the day on which the tenancy is entered into (Sch 2, Part IV, para 11). It may be advisable for *any* private landlord letting on an assured tenancy to serve a Ground 1 notice.

home *and* neither the landlord nor any one joint landlord (where appropriate) nor any person deriving title under the landlord who gave the notice acquired the reversion on the tenancy for money or money's worth.

Some points of construction arise out of this ground, which applies once any fixed-term assured tenancy has come to an end.

1　'At some time before the beginning of the tenancy' appears to indicate that occupation by the landlord concerned need not necessarily have been immediately before the beginning of the tenancy – an occupation several years previously would presumably suffice. The quality in which the landlord previously occupied is of no relevance, so that a previous occupation as a lessee or licensee suffices.

2　Once sufficient previous occupation is proved within para (a), the landlord does not have to prove that he requires to occupy the house personally, as with the owner-occupier grounds in the 1977 Act.

3　The previous occupation by the landlord must have been as his only or principal home. A tenant who could show that, at the relevant time, the landlord had a second home, which he treated as his principal home, might be able to defeat a claim based on para (a): but presumably in such a case, an alternative claim could be made under para (b).

4　Where the landlord was not previously an owner-occupier, he will have to rely on para (b) of ground 1, which is mandatory, unlike a similar discretionary ground in the 1977 Act (Case 9), but it is narrower with regard to the types of person whom the landlord can claim for.[2] Unlike Case 9, the strict joint landlord rule does not apply the present ground, as only one joint landlord need require occupation as a residence.

As is the case with the similar Rent Act ground for possession, it has been judicially recognised that this particular ground gives the court no discretion to refuse to order possession. The landlord need not show that his requirement of the house is reasonable: it need only be shown to be bona fide intention to use the premises as a residence for him and his spouse.[3]

Ground 2 – Repossession by mortgagee

The dwelling-house is subject to a mortgage or charge granted before the beginning of the tenancy,[4] and:

(a) the mortgagee (or chargee) is entitled to exercise a power of sale conferred by the mortgage or by s 101 of the Law of Property Act 1925; and

(b) the mortgagee requires possession of the dwelling-house to dispose of it with vacant possession; and

(c) either notice was given as mentioned in ground 1 or the court is satisfied that it is just and equitable to dispense with the requirement of notice.

2　A reasonable requirement of occupation by certain members of the landlord's family is sufficient for Case 9. There is no equivalent to Cases 12 and 20 of the 1977 Act.

3　*Boyle v Verrall* [1997] 04 EG 145, CA, applying the Rent Act decision of *Kennealy v Dunne* [1977] QB 837, [1977] 2 All ER 16, CA.

4　Defined, Sch 2, part IV, para 11, above.

If the landlord has given a notice under Ground 1, it will thus suffice for a mortgagee within Ground 2. If not, the mortgagee must presumably either give a notice which states that possession might be required under Ground 2, not later than the beginning of the tenancy, or invoke the court's dispensation power.

Ground 3 – Out of season lettings

The tenancy is a fixed-term tenancy for a term not exceeding eight months and:

(a) not later than the beginning of the tenancy[5] the landlord gave notice in writing to the tenant that possession might be recovered on this ground; and
(b) at some time within the period of twelve months ending with the beginning of the tenancy,[6] the dwelling-house was occupied under a right to occupy it for a holiday.

This ground is to enable a landlord who lets houses or flats on holiday lettings, which are not assured tenancies, to let on a fixed-term assured tenancy or series of fixed-term assured tenancies not exceeding eight months in all and recover possession mandatorily. If a notice is served as required before the first tenancy, and a second or subsequent tenancy is granted, the notice will be effective for that tenancy, if it is off-season, and the beginning of the tenancy is deemed to run from the beginning of the tenancy for which the notice was actually given.[7]

Ground 6 – Redevelopment by landlord

Under this ground, the landlord[8] or, if the landlord is a registered housing association or charitable housing trust, a superior landlord, intends to demolish or reconstruct the whole or a substantial part of the dwelling-house or to carry out substantial works on the dwelling-house or any part thereof or any building of which it forms part, and:

(a) the intended work cannot reasonably be carried out without the tenant giving up possession of the dwelling-house because:
   (i) he is not willing to agree to a variation of the terms of his tenancy so as to give access or other facilities to permit the intended work to be carried out; or
   (ii) the nature of the intended work is such that no such variation is practicable; or
   (iii) the tenant is not willing to accept an assured tenancy of a reduced part of the dwelling-house leaving the landlord in possession of so much of the dwelling-house as would be reasonable to enable him to carry out

5 Sch 2, Part IV, para 11 above.
6 Ie by Sch 2, para 11, the day on which the tenancy was entered into, disapplying s 45(2).
7 Sch 2, Part IV, para 10. The same rule applies to Ground 4, below.
8 Described as the 'landlord who is seeking possession' so as to enable one of joint landlords to rely on the ground.

the intended work and would give access and other facilities over the reduced part to permit the work to be carried out, or

(iv) the nature of the work is such that such a tenancy is not practicable; and

(b) either the landlord acquired his interest in the dwelling-house before the grant of the tenancy[9] or his interest was in existence at the time of the grant and neither the landlord or any joint landlord nor any other person who has acquired the landlord's interest since the grant of the tenancy acquired it for money or money's worth; and

(c) the assured tenancy did not come into being under a succession to a former statutory tenancy under the Rent Act 1977 or the Rent (Agriculture) Act 1976.

The purchase condition will not prevent a landlord who acquires the reversion under a will or intestacy or by surrender for no consideration from relying on this ground. This ground enables a landlord or superior landlord with redevelopment plans to regain possession mandatorily of a dwelling-house let on an assured tenancy for, presumably, a substantial period.[10] If the tenancy is fixed-term, however, because the court cannot make an order for possession take effect until the contractual expiry date of the tenancy, a landlord intent on redevelopment will not be able to evict the tenant until after that date. If the fixed-term tenancy contains a break clause entitling the landlord to determine it for redevelopment, then, by analogy with Part II of the 1954 Act, the clause, if duly exercised, will be effective to determine the fixed-term tenancy, and an order for possession may thereafter be sought on ground 6.[11] Where the court orders possession under this ground, the landlord must pay the tenant his reasonable removal expenses (s 11(1)).[12]

Ground 8, which deals with rent arrears, has already been discussed in relation to assured shorthold tenancies, even though it equally applies to an assured tenant.

III DISCRETIONARY GROUNDS FOR POSSESSION

There are a number of grounds which, if they apply, enable the court to make an order for possession only at its discretion. The court may only evict the tenant if it considers it reasonable to do so (s 7(4)). The following grounds are noted for the sake of completeness.

The court has power to make an order for possession take effect before the expiry date of an assured fixed-term tenancy in the case of most discretionary grounds (s

---

9 If the tenant (or any joint tenant) was in possession under an earlier assured tenancy, this means the grant of the earlier tenancy.

10 The policy of this ground is similar to that of Landlord and Tenant Act 1954, s 30(1)(f); a similar ground exists in relation to secure tenancies (Housing Act 1985, Sch 2, ground 10), whose policy is similar to that of s 30(1)(f): *Wansbeck District Council v Marley* (1987) 20 HLR 247, CA.

11 Cf *Weinbergs Weatherproofs v Radcliffe Paper Mill Co* [1958] Ch 437, [1957] 3 All ER 663.

12 If the parties cannot agree an amount, this will be determined by the court (s 11(2)) and in any event the sum is recoverable as a civil debt (s 11(3)). It has been argued (Megarry, *Rent Acts* Vol 3, p 158/9) that any expenses reasonably incurred by the tenant as a direct and natural consequence of the removal are recoverable.

7(6)) provided that the terms of the tenancy enable the landlord to terminate the tenancy on that ground, by forfeiture or otherwise (see further above).

Ground 9 – Suitable alternative accommodation

Suitable alternative accommodation is available for the tenant or will be available for him when the order for possession takes effect.

This ground is similar in most material respects to the corresponding provision in the Rent Act 1977.[13] One new feature of the present ground is that where the landlord obtains possession, he is bound to pay the tenant's reasonable removal expenses (s 11(1)). Otherwise, reference should be made to the appropriate parts of chapter 17.

Ground 10 – Rent lawfully due

Some rent lawfully due from the tenant is unpaid on the date on which the proceedings for possession are begun and is in arrears at the date of service of a s 8 notice, except where service of a s 8 notice is dispensed with.

This corresponds in material respects to Case 1 of Sch 15 to the Rent Act (chapter 17).

Ground 11 – Persistent delay

Whether or not any rent is in arrears on the date on which proceedings are begun, the tenant has persistently delayed paying rent lawfully due.

Under this ground, the tenant's past record may be examined: even if he is currently punctual with his rent payments, if his past record is bad enough, the landlord may obtain possession.

The ground is in many respects akin to s 30(1)(b) of Part II of the 1954 Act, though in this precise form it is new for private sector tenancies, and hence, reference may be made to the discussion in chapter 26.

Ground 12 – Breach of obligation

Any obligation of the tenancy (other than as to rent) has been broken or not performed.

In general, this ground is akin to Case 1 of Sch 15 of the Rent Act 1977.

Ground 13 – Waste, neglect, etc

The condition of the dwelling-house or any of the common parts[14] has deteriorated owing to acts of waste by, or the neglect or default of, the tenant or any other person residing in the dwelling-house and, in the case of an act of waste by, or the

---

13 It is supplemented by Sch 2, Part III.
14 Ie parts of the building which the tenant is entitled, under the terms of the tenancy, to use, in common with other dwelling-house occupiers of, in effect, the same landlord.

neglect or default of, a lodger of the tenant or a sub-tenant, the tenant has not taken such steps as he ought reasonably to have taken for the removal of the lodger or sub-tenant.

While in most respects this ground corresponds to Case 3 of Sch 15 to the Rent Act 1977 (chapter 17), Ground 13 refers, in addition, which is new, to the common parts, so that if the tenant or those claiming under him actively injure a common staircase or damage the lighting in common passageways, for example, the landlord could invoke the present ground.

Ground 14 – Nuisance, annoyance, etc[15]

The tenant or any other person residing in the dwelling-house has been guilty of conduct which was, or is likely to have been, a nuisance or annoyance to a person residing, visiting or otherwise engaging in a lawful activity in the dwelling-house, or has been convicted of using the dwelling-house or allowing it to be used for immoral or illegal purposes or an arrestable offence has been committed in, or in the vicinity of, the dwelling-house.[16]

Ground 15 – Deterioration of furniture

The condition of any furniture provided for use under the tenancy has, in the court's opinion, deteriorated owing to ill-treatment by the tenant or any other person residing in the dwelling-house and, in the case of ill-treatment by a lodger or sub-tenant, the tenant has not taken reasonable steps for the removal of the lodger or sub-tenant.

Ground 16 – Employee of landlord

The dwelling-house was let to the tenant in consequence of his employment by the landlord or a previous landlord under the tenancy and the tenant has ceased to be in that employment.

This ground is based on the same general idea as Case 8 of Sch 15 to the Rent Act 1977, but is greatly simplified. The landlord seeking possession will have to prove either that the assured tenancy was granted by him to the tenant, as his former employee, or that the tenant was the former employee of any predecessor in title. The tenancy must be in consequence of the employment, but the tenant need not necessarily be occupying the house for the better performance of his duties. No doubt, if alternative accommodation is available for the tenant, it will be easier to persuade the court to order possession in its overriding discretion.

---

15 The ground is given as substituted by s 148 of the Housing Act 1996, which also (by s 149) created a Ground 14A, allowing specific landlords, notably a charitable housing trusts, to evict a husband or wife or partner who has driven out the other party by domestic violence; special rules as to service of notices (s 8A, added by 1996 Act, s 150) apply.

16 It is assumed in the absence of authority that this ground would be construed in like manner to Housing Act 1985, Sch 2, ground 2 (ch 19).

Ground 17 – False statement inducing grant of tenancy[17]

The tenant was the person, or one of them, to whom the tenancy was granted and the landlord was induced to grant the tenancy by a false statement made knowingly or recklessly by the tenant or a person acting at the tenant's instigation.

Since at common law it is possible for a landlord to rescind a statutory tenancy on the ground of fraudulent or reckless misrepresentation, the need for this new ground may be doubted.

G RENT PROVISIONS

I GENERAL RULES

One of the most important reasons, it was said, for the enactment of the assured tenancies scheme was the fact that private sector residential landlords would be able to grant new tenancies free of the shackles of rent controls, and so at whatever rent the landlord of a particular house or flat could extract from the tenant.

Section 13 of the 1988 Act applies where a periodic assured or, after the commencement of s 96 of the 1996 Act, periodic assured shorthold tenancy, is granted, as also where an assured or assured shorthold tenancy granted for a fixed term expires.

Fixed term tenancies

Under a fixed-term tenancy, the parties may agree on any rent they like, which cannot be referred, and the tenancy may include rent reviews.[18] Subject to that, if the landlord wishes to increase the original rent, he will have to await the end of the fixed-term tenancy and the automatic coming into being of a periodic tenancy following the assured shorthold tenancy or of a statutory periodic tenancy following the assured tenancy. On that event, he will be able to proceed with a notice of increase. In the case of a statutory periodic tenancy, the general requirements as to the service of a notice apply, but the landlord does not have to delay the start of the period for the proposed new rent for one year from the commencement of the periodic tenancy -which he must do where he granted a periodic tenancy (s 13(2)(b)). All he must do is to serve his notice during the final year of the fixed-term assured tenancy, giving a minimum period for the coming into effect of the new rent, which will depend on the intervals at which rent is payable under the tenancy (s 5(3)(d)). Further increases in rent will be governed by the provisions which apply to periodic tenancies.

---

17 Inserted by Housing Act 1996, s 102.
18 Unless such provisions fall foul of SI 1994/3159 (ch 4).

The landlord may increase the rent of a periodic or statutory periodic assured tenancy by a notice under s 13. If there is a rent review provision in a periodic tenancy, however, it will govern rent increases to the exclusion of the statutory procedure (s 13(1)(b)). The statutory procedure is without prejudice to the right of either party to vary the rent by agreement (s 13(5)). It allows for an annual increase in rent.

The notice must be in the prescribed form,[19] proposing a new rent (s 13(2)). The new rent may take effect as from a 'new period of the tenancy specified in the notice' – so if it is not specified, presumably, though the section does not so state, the notice is void. The minimum periods below, run as from the date of service of the notice (s 13(2)(a)).

The 'minimum period', by s 13(2) and (3), from which the new rent begins, is not to begin earlier than:

(a) in the case of a yearly tenancy, six months;
(b) in the case of a tenancy where the period is less than a month, one month;
(c) in any other case, the period of the tenancy.

Each of the above runs from the date of service of the s 13 notice. In addition, no new rent period can begin except from the end of the first anniversary of the date in which the first period of the tenancy began (s 13(2)(b)), but this does not apply where a periodic tenancy follows a fixed-term tenancy, in which latter case the rent increase may be sought as from the expiry of the term certain. If the rent has been previously increased by a s 13 notice or a s 14 determination by a rent assessment committee, no further notice of increase can be served until one year after the increased rent takes effect (s 13(2)(c)).

Once the period specified in the notice expires, unless the tenant has referred the notice to a rent assessment committee, by an application in the prescribed form,[20] or the parties have agreed on a different rent, the new rent takes effect as specified in the notice (s 13(4)). The tenant must refer the notice, if he is going to do so, before the beginning of the 'new period' specified in the notice: if he does not, and a different rent has not been agreed, then he will have to pay the new rent, however steep an increase has been proposed. Whether this is a reasonable result, may be questioned, except that a periodic tenant who dislikes a new rent may always, by a notice to quit, determine his tenancy.

If the tenant is served an invalid notice, as where it is not in the prescribed form or a form substantially to the like effect, he may presumably ignore the notice, and while there is no express right to recover excess overpayments of rent from the landlord, nor is there a provision that the increase is irrecoverable from the tenant,[1] such a right must be implied by necessary implication of law.

---

19 Assured Tenancies and Agricultural Occupancies (Forms) Regulations 1988, SI 1988/2203.
20 Assured Tenancies and Agricultural Occupancies (Forms) Regulations 1988, SI 1988/2203. As to the duties of a rent assessment committee on a reference, see Rent Assessment Committee etc Regulations 1988, SI 1988/2200, amending SI 1971/1065.
 1 As there is in the case of determinations of an excessive rent of an assured shorthold tenancy, see s 22(4)(b).

II DETERMINATION BY RENT ASSESSMENT COMMITTEE

General

Where a tenant refers a rent increase notice to a rent assessment committee, which must be in a prescribed form application and before the beginning of the period from which the new rent is to commence (s 13(4)) the committee must consider the reference under s 14. Committees have powers to obtain information from both landlord and tenant (s 41). Specified information must be kept by the president of every rent assessment panel as to rents of assured and assured shorthold tenancies (s 42).[2] Both parties may, by written notice, withdraw a reference (s 14(8)). Rent does not include a service charge (s 14(4)),[3] but the committee must consider, nevertheless, sums payable for furniture and also sums payable for services, repairs, maintenance or insurance or the landlord's costs of management whether or not these sums are separate from the sums payable for the occupation of the dwelling-house concerned or are payable under separate agreements.[4]

The rent assessment committee must then determine the rent at which they consider the dwelling-house might reasonably be expected to be let in the open market by a willing landlord under an assured tenancy on the following assumptions (s 14(1)).

(a) The tenancy is periodic with the same periods as the current tenancy.
(b) It begins at the beginning of the period from which the new rent is payable, specified in the notice.
(c) The terms are those of the current tenancy (other than as to rent).
(d) Notices under Sch 2 grounds 1 to 5 have, where relevant, been given to the tenant.

The rent determined by a rent assessment committee takes effect as from the beginning of the period specified in the landlord's s 13 notice, and so retrospectively, unless the committee are satisfied that the application of this rule would cause undue hardship to the tenant, in which case a later date may be substituted by them, which cannot be any later than the date of their determination of the rent (s 14(7)). Thus the landlord is not to be deprived of any rent increase sanctioned by a committee by a tenant's reference.

Statutory disregards

While the rent must be determined as a market rent, the committee must make the following disregards (s 14(2)):

(a) Any effect on rent of there being a sitting tenant.
(b) Any increase in the value of the dwelling-house or flat attributable to certain improvements carried out by the person who, at the time he carried them

---

2 Assured Tenancies etc (Rent Information) Order 1988 SI 1988/2199; and a new rent may be proposed to take into account the tenant's liability to council tax (s 14A and SI 1993/654).
3 As defined by Landlord and Tenant 1985, s 18.
4 As to rates borne by the landlord or a superior landlord, the determination is made as if these were not so borne (s 14(5)).

out, was the current tenant. Any improvement must have been carried out otherwise than under an obligation to the immediate landlord, or carried out under an obligation to the immediate landlord, following a consent to the improvement. Moreover, the improvement cannot be disregarded unless it was either carried out during the current tenancy, or unless the conditions are satisfied which closely resemble those imposed by s 34(2) of the Landlord and Tenant Act 1954 (s 14(3)).

(c) Any reduction in the value of the dwelling-house attributable to a failure by the tenant to comply with the terms of the tenancy. Where a person became an assured tenant by succession under s 39 of the 1988 Act, a Rent Assessment Committee could properly disregard a failure by his predecessor to comply with the terms of his tenancy, thus greatly reducing the rent payable, the premises being out of repair, as s 14(2)(c) applied only to the defaults of the current tenant.[5]

H ASSURED AGRICULTURAL OCCUPANCIES

Part I of the Housing Act 1988 created a new regime for agricultural workers, assured agricultural occupancies. The main rules are outlined below.

By contrast to the position which applies to private residential tenancies, if an assured tenancy is to be a shorthold tenancy as from 28 February 1997, the landlord must, ordinarily, before the tenancy is entered into, serve the tenant with a prescribed form notice. This must state that the tenancy is to be a shorthold tenancy.[6]

The present regime is designed to exclude all others. Hence, a tenancy or licence granted to an agricultural worker on or after 15 January 1989 cannot, with a limited number of exceptions,[7] be within the Rent (Agriculture) Act 1976. A tenancy or licence within the 1988 Act is an assured agricultural occupancy.[8] If the tenant has a tenancy of an agricultural holding or a farm business tenancy then the Agricultural Holdings Act 1986 or the Agricultural Tenancies Act 1995 will apply to his tenancy and not the 1988 Act.[9]

Modifications of assured tenancies scheme

The assured tenancies scheme has a number of special modifications in the case of assured agricultural occupancies.

5 *N & D (London) Ltd v Gadsden* [1992] 1 EGLR 112. This is because it was held that s 39 vests a new estate in the new tenant.

6 Housing Act 1988, Sch 2A, para 9(2) (inserted by Housing Act 1996, s 96 and Sch 7). If the agricultural worker condition is at any time, then or later, fulfilled, it seems the tenancy is assured: para 9(1).

7 Housing Act 1988, s 34(4): the exceptions are (a) pre-commencement contracts and (b) the grant of a tenancy or licence to a sitting 1976 Act occupier.

8 In particular, s 14 (determinations of rent by a rent assessment committee) is specifically applied (s 24(4)).

9 Housing Act 1988, s 24(3) as amended by Housing Act 1996, s 103(3).

1   A tenancy may be an assured agricultural occupancy even though it is at a low rent.
2   A licence will qualify as an assured agricultural occupancy provided it is exclusive and provides for the occupation of a dwelling-house as a separate dwelling.
3   If no rent is payable under a fixed-term tenancy or licence, then, when a statutory periodic tenancy arises under s 5, the periods of the tenancy will be monthly beginning on the day following the coming to an end of the fixed-term tenancy (s 25(1)(b)).
4   If the tenant gives notice to terminate his employment, notwithstanding anything in the occupancy agreement or otherwise, the notice is not a notice to quit the assured agricultural occupancy (s 25(4)).

Agricultural worker condition

In all cases, the occupier must comply with a specific agricultural worker condition. If this condition is at any time not complied with, the occupier ceases to hold an assured tenancy. The same rules as those which apply under the Rent (Agriculture) Act 1976, apply in the case of assured agricultural occupancies, to determine whether a person is a qualifying worker, whether he is incapable of whole time work in agriculture, and whether the dwelling-house is in qualifying ownership.[10]

The agricultural worker condition itself is governed by specific rules, which may be summarised as follows.

1   The condition is satisfied if the dwelling-house has been in qualifying ownership at any time during the current tenancy or licence, and the occupier, or, where there are joint occupiers, at least one of them, is or was a qualifying worker at any time during such tenancy or licence.[11]
2   The above condition is also fulfilled if the qualifying occupier died, and the new occupier is the occupier's qualifying widow/widower or a qualifying member of his or her family.[12]
3   The agricultural worker condition is satisfied if the tenancy or licence was granted to the occupier in consideration of his giving up possession of another dwelling-house where he, or he and other joint occupiers, held that house under a qualifying tenancy or licence, and, immediately before giving up possession, the agricultural worker condition was fulfilled.
4   If an occupier is granted a new tenancy or licence of the same dwelling-house and he, solely or as one of a number of joint occupiers, immediately beforehand satisfied the agricultural worker condition, the condition will be satisfied under the new tenancy or licence and, for as long as it continues to be satisfied, the tenancy remains assured.

10   Housing Act 1988, Sch 3, para 1.
11   Housing Act 1988, Sch 3, paras 2 - 5.
12   Broadly, this requires, in the case of a widow etc, occupation of the dwelling-house as a residence immediately before the previous occupier's death; in the case of a family member, occupation at death and for two previous years is required. Only one family member may be taken into account.

Chapter 19

Secure tenancies

I INTRODUCTION

General aspects

The Housing Act 1985 confers security of tenure on certain tenants, known as secure tenants, who hold from a public-sector landlord, such as notably a local authority, or whose tenancies are held from quasi-public sector or publicly funded bodies, notably certain registered housing associations. The rules form a 'tenants' charter' and were first introduced in 1980, along with the right of secure tenants to buy the house or flat in which they live.

   The basic operation of the security of tenure rules is that, as with other statutory codes of protection in the residential sector, common law methods of termination of the tenancy, whether it is fixed-term, or, as is more likely in this sector, periodic, do not suffice to end the tenancy and it must be terminated within Part IV of the 1985 Act. There are, however, a number of exclusions from security, as specified in the Act, but licensees holding an exclusive licence fall within the protection of the scheme.

Introductory tenancies

Part V of the Housing Act 1996 has enabled local authorities to elect to grant new periodic tenants (and licensees thanks to s 126) an introductory tenancy rather than a secure tenancy. This type of tenancy lasts for an initial or 'trial' period of one year in principle. The trial period runs, where the tenancy is entered into by a local housing authority or housing action trust, from the date of entering into the tenancy or if later, the date when the tenant is first entitled to possession (s 125(2)).[1] It is prevented from being a secure tenancy.[2] Once the trial period comes to an end, the tenancy becomes a secure tenancy (s 125(1)). This will not apply if the landlord has begun possession proceedings before the end of the one-year trial period and obtains possession during or outside the first year of the tenancy (as envisaged by ss 127 and 130) or if one of the events in s 125(5) apply, notably that a person or body other than a local housing authority or housing action trust becomes landlord.

---

1 Periods under which a tenant granted an introductory tenancy had held under an assured shorthold tenancy from a registered social landlord count, in principle, towards the one-year trial period (s 125(3)). Sections 124–128 came into force on 12 February 1997: SI 1997/66.
2 Housing Act 1985, Sch 1, para 1A, added by Housing Act 1996, Sch 14, para 5.

Since an introductory tenancy has the potential to become, at the end of the intial year, a secure tenancy, it has some resemblances to a secure tenancy. A succession is allowed to the tenancy on the death of the original tenant by a member of his family subject to similar conditions to those applicable to secure tenancies (ss 131–134). The express assignment of an introductory tenancy is prohibited with certain exceptions (s 134). The secure tenants' repair scheme may be extended to introductory tenancies by subordinate legislation (s 135).

If the local authority does not deem the tenant suitable for the grant of a secure tenancy, it may seek possession without having to prove that a ground for possession exists, which would have to be done in the case of a secure tenancy. The landlord must bring an introductory tenancy to an end by obtaining an order for possession from the court (s 127(1)) and not, say, by means of a notice to quit. The landlord is bound to comply with a preliminary notice procedure, or possession cannot be ordered (s 128(1)). Thus, a notice must set out the landlord's reasons for seeking possession (s 128(3)) which enables the tenant to request him to review his decision to seek possession (under s 129). A tenant dissatisfied with reasons given by an authority for its decision would be able to challenge these by seeking a review under regulations.[2a] A landlord's notice must specify a date for the beginning of proceedings, which must be no earlier that that of a common law notice to quit (s 128(4)). A landlord may seek possession during the trial period. Provision is made for a case where it is sought during that period and then the one year initial period expires without an order having been made: during the whole period in question, the tenancy remains an introductory tenancy (s 130(2)).

The security offered by an introductory tenancy is thus limited. It is deemed important to ease the removal of those introductory tenants whom the landlord considers to be anti-social, partly in the landlord's own interest, partly in the interest of other tenants in the vicinity. Provision is made for the loss of introductory status if any landlord other than a local authority or a housing action trust holds the landlord's interest (s 125(5)).

II SCOPE OF SECURE TENANCY PROVISIONS

By s 79(1) of the 1985 Act, 'a tenancy under which a dwelling-house[3] is let as a separate dwelling is a secure tenancy' at any time when the landlord condition and the tenant condition are satisfied. The scheme envisages, therefore, that a tenancy may move into or out of the Act as and when either condition is satisfied or not applicable. This principle was applied with unfortunate results to a council landlord, whose business lessee, in breach of covenant, sub-let part of the premises on a weekly tenancy as a residential flat. The council obtained a surrender of the head lease without previously terminating any rights of the sub-

2a Introductory Tenants (Review) Regulations 1997, SI 1997/72.
3 Which, as with the Rent Act 1977 and Part I of the Housing Act 1988, may be a house or part of a house (1985 Act, s 112(1)); similarly, land let together with the dwelling-house is within the 1985 Act unless it is agricultural land exceeding two acres (s 112(2)).

lessee by notice, and the latter held a secure tenancy as a result.[4] Compliance with these conditions is not only important for the attaining of secure tenancy status: only a secure tenant, save in those cases mentioned later in this chapter, is entitled to exercise the 'right to buy' conferred by Part V of the 1985 Act.

Landlord condition

The landlord condition relates to the type of landlord holding the interest out of which the tenancy is granted. This interest must, at all times, belong to a local authority, a new town corporation, an urban development corporation, the Development Board for Rural Wales, and certain housing co-operatives (1985 Act, s 80(1)).[5] The landlord condition is satisfied if one of two joint landlords comply with it: both do not have to do so.[6] However, if the landlord's interest becomes transferred to a landlord who is outside those listed as satisfying the landlord condition of s 80, the tenancy ceases to be secure.

Tenant condition

The tenant condition requires, by s 81, that the tenant is an individual who occupies the dwelling-house as his only or principal home. In principle, these latter expressions carry the same meaning as in relation to the Rent Act 1977 (chapter 17). Thus, if all that the tenant has is a room in certain premises with the right to share kitchen and other facilities with others, he has no secure tenancy or relevant licence, by analogy with the Rent Act 1977.[7] Two houses may be occupied at the same time as a home and actual physical occupation is not, it seems, always necessary to satisfy the tenant condition.[8] In the case of a joint tenancy, each of the tenants must be an individual and at least one of them must occupy the dwelling-house as his or her only or principal home.

If any of these requirements ceases to be applicable, the tenancy ceases without more to be secure as the tenant condition is no longer satisfied. So, too, where the landlord proves that the tenant has abandoned his occupation permanently, which occupation alone confers on him the statutory right to security. Thus, on the one hand, where a tenant had abandoned the premises permanently, leaving no possessions, and the landlords peaceably re-entered, changing the locks, security was lost[9] but, by contrast, a secure tenant who was imprisoned but who intended to return on release, was held to retain his occupation because he left his furniture on the premises as well as an occupying licensee.[10] The tenant condition therefore may be lost by an intention to yield

4   *Basingstoke and Deane Borough Council v Paice* [1995] 2 EGLR 9, CA.
5   Until 15 January 1989, most housing associations were able to grant secure tenancies; but these bodies are not longer within the landlord condition, and may only grant assured tenancies.
6   *R v Plymouth City Council, ex p Freeman* (1987) 19 HLR 328, CA.
7   *Central YMCA Housing Association Ltd v Saunders* (1990) 23 HLR 212, CA.
8   *Crawley Borough Council v Sawyer* (1987) 20 HLR 98, CA.
9   *R v London Borough of Croydon Council, ex p Toth* (1987) 20 HLR 576, CA.
10 *Notting Hill Housing Trust v Etona* [1989] CLY 1912.

up the tenancy, even if the actual transaction concerned is ineffective, as where a tenant ceases to hold a secure tenancy because of an ineffective assignment to another person.[11]

If the tenant has, at the date of the letting, a tenancy under which he may both carry on a significant amount of business user and also reside on the premises, he cannot hold a secure tenancy.[12] Moreover, a secure periodic tenancy is a personal right of occupation (much as is a statutory tenancy under the Rent Acts) so that it cannot be an asset forming part of the estate of a bankrupt.[13]

Secure licences

Section 79(3) provides that the security provisions apply to a licence to occupy a dwelling-house (whether granted for a consideration or not) as they apply to a tenancy. By s 79(4) this rule does not apply, and there is no security, where there is a licence granted as a temporary expedient to a person who entered the dwelling-house as a trespasser (whether or not before the grant, another licence to occupy that or another dwelling-house had been granted to him).

As is the case with agricultural holdings, s 79(3) is narrow in scope, although it certainly brings a licence which confers exclusive possession within the secure tenancies rules.[14] It appears that s 79(3) has not altered the general law, and so where a single homeless person occupied a hostel room, and his 'licence to occupy' provided that he might have to change his allotted accommodation without notice, he held a licence outside s 79(3) as he lacked the requisite exclusive possession, which was retained by the landlord who, in the circumstances, needed it genuinely so as to control and supervise the hostel inmates.[15] Similarly, short-term arrangements in the form of licences from a developer, with a view to providing temporary accommodation, before the developer commenced redevelopment, were outside s 79(3).[16] On the other hand, where a council granted a licence of a self-contained flat, in premises awaiting redevelopment, to an occupier, and retained a duplicate set of keys, but the occupier had apparently exclusive possession, she held a secure tenancy as the basic requirements of s 79(3) were satisfied.[17] The difference between these two cases is seemingly that the occupier had no direct legal relations with the owner of the property in the first case, unlike in the second, and also the clear understanding of the occupiers was that they had temporary rights of occupation only. For further considerations, see chapter 3 of this book.

---

11 See *Westminster City Council v Peart* (1991) 24 HLR 389, CA.
12 *Webb v Barnet London Borough Council* (1988) 21 HLR 228, CA: hence, a cesser of business activities at the date of the hearing, made no difference.
13 *City of London Corpn v Bown* (1989) 22 HLR 32, CA. Thus it will lie outside Insolvency Act 1986, s 306.
14 *Family Housing Association v Miah* (1982) 5 HLR 94, CA; also *Kensington and Chelsea Royal Borough Council v Hayden* (1984) 17 HLR 114, CA.
15 *Westminster City Council v Clarke* [1992] 1 All ER 695, HL.
16 *Shepherd's Bush Housing Association v HATs Co-operative* (1991) 24 HLR 176, CA.
17 *Family Housing Association Ltd v Jones* [1990] 1 All ER 385, CA.

Tenancies which cannot be secure

As is the case with both the other residential tenancies codes, Part IV of the Housing Act lists a group of tenancies which cannot be secure; and if a tenancy is excluded from Part IV of the 1985 Act, the tenant cannot, not being a secure tenant, exercise the right to buy conferred by Part V.

Long leases

A long tenancy, defined as a tenancy granted for a term certain exceeding 21 years whether or not terminable before the end of the term by a tenant's notice or by forfeiture is not secure.[18]

Premises occupied in connection with employment

If the tenant is the employee of certain landlords, notably of a local authority, and where his contract of employment requires him to occupy the dwelling-house for the better performance of his duties, the tenancy is not secure. Once a dwelling-house has been let on a tenancy within this exclusion, it may be re-let to any person for a period or periods not exceeding three years.[19] By this means, it is possible for a local authority to let employee accommodation for short periods to non-employees without granting a secure tenancy to the tenant.

The construction of the present exclusion is not easy. If a tenancy of employment tied accommodation were held to become secure as soon as the employment ended, the landlord would lose the accommodation for use of future employees. It might also have to act harshly against any former employees in the accommodation.[20] Thus, the status of a tenancy is not necessarily fixed as not secure, even if the conditions for exclusion are then satisfied, immutably at its commencement. If circumstances of the tenant alter, it may become secure.

Indeed, the exception may apply to a tenant who originally was not required by his contract of employment to occupy in the required sense, but whose contract is later varied so as to incorporate such a requirement.[1] The court may imply a term that the employee is in occupation for the better performance of his duties, as where a school caretaker's terms of employment required him to live in school accommodation where possible, and he was allowed by the landlord authority to occupy a house near the relevant school.[2] In this particular case, a local authority regained possession from a tenant whose employment had ceased not long before the service of the notice to quit. The exception for tied accommodation was construed, by extension, to apply to a tenant provided that his occupation was referable to his employment. By contrast, where at the date of a notice to quit the tenant, a former school caretaker, had been made

---

18   Sch 1, para 1 and s 115(1). Also excluded are tenancies with a right to perpetual renewal (s 115(1)(b)).
19   Sch 1, paras 2(1) and 2(4).
20   *Greenfield* v *Berkshire County Council* (1996) 28 HLR 691, CA.
 1   *Elvidge* v *Coventry City Council* [1994] QB 241, [1993] 4 All ER 903, CA.
 2   *South Glamorganshire County Council* v *Griffiths* (1992) 24 HLR 334, CA.

redundant some 14 months earlier, and had been allowed to remain in the house pending the availability of tied accommodation with his new employers, all connection with his former employment was held to have been severed. He therefore obtained a secure tenancy even though his tenancy, when it began, was not secure.[3]

If the occupation in that particular property is not essential for the better performance of the duties of the employee, the exemption is not applicable, so that a head teacher whose employment terms did not expressly require his residence in a specific house was outside the exemption, as no requirement to that effect needed to be implied to give business efficacy to the contract.[4] Where the exemption does not apply, the tenant will be able to exercise the right to buy and remove the house concerned from the local authority's housing stock.

Land acquired for development

A tenancy is not secure if the dwelling-house is on land which has been acquired for development and the dwelling-house is used by the landlord, pending development of the land, as temporary housing accommodation.[5] This exception, whose policy is to avoid land awaiting redevelopment from being sterilised and removed from the housing stock in the interim, does not impliedly require that the landlord be the person who acquired the land for development, so that where a housing association held a flat under an agreement with a government department for use as temporary housing, and the former body granted a temporary weekly licence to occupy, the association was entitled to re-possess for rent arrears and the agreement fell within the exception.[6]

Accommodation for homeless persons

A tenancy granted to certain classes of homeless persons is not secure for the first twelve months from notification of a decision on homelessness or threatened homelessness, unless before the expiry of the twelve months, the landlord notifies the tenant that the tenancy is to be regarded as secure.[7] The relevant date for the purpose of this exclusion runs from the date of written notification of the decision of the authority whether the occupier is intentionally homeless, and an oral notification will not, having regard to the importance of such decisions to homeless persons, suffice.[8]

A person who is let into exclusive occupation under this exclusion occupies as a tenant and not a licensee, and so s 79(3) cannot apply, converting it into a secure tenancy, as the tenancy was never secure when granted (though it may subsequently

---

3 *Greenfield* v *Berkshire County Council*, supra.
4 *Hughes* v *London Borough of Greenwich* (1992) 24 HLR 605, CA.
5 Sch 1, para 3(1); see *Lillieshall Road Housing Co-operative Ltd* v *Brennan* (1991) 24 HLR 195, CA.
6 *Hyde Housing Association* v *Harrison* [1991] 1 EGLR 51, CA; Fox LJ pointed out that the identity of the acquirer was left at large by para 3, and the fact that there might be an overlap with para 6 was treated as immaterial.
7 Sch 1, para 4.
8 *Swansea City Council* v *Hearn* (1990) 23 HLR 284, CA.

become so).[9] In any event, s 79(3) did not convert a non-exclusive licence to occupy into a tenancy so as to enable the occupier to claim a secure tenancy.[10]

Temporary accommodation for persons taking up employment

A tenancy is not secure for one year from its grant, unless before the expiry of that year the tenant has been notified by the landlord that the tenancy is to be regarded as a secure tenancy, if it is granted to a person not previously resident in the local housing authority's district, and who, prior to the grant of the tenancy, obtained employment or an offer thereof in the district or in the area of any district surrounding it. The tenancy must be granted to enable the person to meet his need for temporary accommodation in the district or its surrounding area in order to work, and to enable him to find permanent accommodation there. The landlord must notify the tenant in writing of the circumstances of the application of this exception.[11]

Short-term arrangements

If the dwelling-house has been leased to the landlord itself, by a landlord who cannot grant secure tenancies, with vacant possession, for use as temporary housing accommodation and the head lessor is able to obtain vacant possession from the landlord on the expiry of a specified period or when required by it (say pursuant to a break clause in the head lease) and the head landlord has no interest in the dwelling-house other than as lessor or mortgagee, the tenancy is not secure.[12] It appears, so as to avoid unnecessary technicalities, that if the person granting the tenancy or licence to the immediate occupier in terms reserves himself the right to vacant possession, this exemption will still apply; and moreover, where a licence was terminable on seven days' notice, this requirement was sufficient to enable recovery within this exclusion.[13] Where a licensee was permitted to occupy premises in circumstances which in fact fell within this exclusion, it was held that he had no security on the termination of his licence, even though the exclusion is in terms confined to tenancies.[14] Were it otherwise, a licensee would be in a better position than a tenant.

Temporary accommodation pending works

A tenancy is not a secure tenancy if the dwelling-house has been made available to the tenant or to a predecessor in title of his for occupation by him while works are carried on a dwelling-house previously occupied as his home, and the tenant or, seemingly, any, predecessor was not a secure tenant of that dwelling-house at the time when he ceased to occupy it as his home.[15]

---

9   *Eastleigh Borough Council v Walsh* [1985] 2 All ER 112, [1985] 1 WLR 525, HL.
10   *Kensington and Chelsea Royal Borough Council v Hayden* (1984) 17 HLR 114, CA.
11   Sch 1, para 5.
12   Sch 1, para 6.
13   *Tower Hamlets London Borough Council v Abdi* [1993] 1 EGLR 68, CA.
14   *Tower Hamlets London Borough Council v Miah* (1992) 24 HLR 199, CA.
15   Sch 1, para 7. The aim of this is presumably to stop a claim to security merely on account of the enforced temporary move.

Other exclusions

Tenancies or licences of the following classes cannot be secure: agricultural holdings or farm business tenancies,[16] licensed premises,[17] student lettings,[18] business tenancies within Part II of the 1954 Act,[19] and licences to occupy almshouses.[20]

III ASSIGNMENTS, LODGERS AND SUB-LETTINGS

Assignments

A secure tenancy agreement may contain an express prohibition on the assignment of the tenancy, but Part IV of the Housing Act 1985 contains specific and seemingly, to the extent of the application of the statute, overriding rules as to assignments. Neither a secure periodic tenancy and nor a secure fixed-term tenancy granted on or after 5 November 1982[1] may be assigned (s 91(1)). It appears that a secure tenancy which is rendered non-assignable by s 91 is treated, for the purposes of assignments by operation of law, as a mere personal contract. Hence, such a tenancy cannot pass to the tenant's trustee in bankruptcy as part of his estate.[2]

There are three exceptions to the statutory prohibition on express assignments. It now appears that, while to be valid at common law, an assignment within these exceptions must be by deed,[3] it may be that the courts would accept as valid an informal or equitable assignment, to save the parties the unnecessary trouble and expense of drawing up a deed.[4]

1   *Assignments under s 24 of the Matrimonial Causes Act 1973 (s 91(3)(b)).*[5]   Such an assignment causes the statutory succession provisions to operate if the other party to the marriage was a successor (ss 91(3) and 88(2)). The relationship between s 24 of the 1973 Act and the express terms of a secure tenancy held by one sole tenant has not been examined in recent authorities. While the court

---

16   Sch 1, para 8, as substuted by Agricultural Tenancies Act 1995, Sch, para 30. The dwelling-house must be occupied by the person responsible for the control of the farming or management of the holding, as the tenant, or as his servant or agent.
17   1985 Act, Sch 1, para 9. This corresponds to Rent Act 1977, s 11 and Housing Act 1988, Sch 1, para 5.
18   1985 Act, Sch 1, para 10. Specific notification rules apply.
19   1985 Act, Sch 11: this is akin to Rent Act 1977, s 24(3) and Housing Act 1988, Sch 1, para 4.
20   Sch 1, para 12.
 1   Such a tenancy granted before that date ceases, unless any exception of s 91(3) applies, to be secure after its assignment.
 2   *City of London Corpn v Bown* (1990) 22 HLR 32, CA.
 3   *Crago v Julian* [1992] 1 All ER 744, [1992] 1 WLR 372, CA.
 4   *Westminster City Council v Peart* (1991) 24 HLR 389, CA (where the point was left open); but such assignment would need to comply with Law of Property Act 1925, s 53(1)(c), and so be in writing, save where a resulting, implied or constructive trust had been created on the facts.
 5   Where a suspended possession order was made and the tenant failed to comply with its terms, from that moment, the tenancy ended and there was nothing for s 24 of the 1973 Act to operate on: *Thompson v Elmbridge Borough Council* [1987] 1 WLR 1425, CA.

would presumably be prepared to exercise its powers to transfer the tenancy under s 24 of the 1973 Act if the tenancy did not in terms prohibit assignments, it has been said that it would not exercise its jurisdiction if the order would be defeated by an express prohibition on assignments in the tenancy agreement,[6] perhaps because, as was said, the court had the same power only as the tenant would have had to assign the tenancy.[7] However, if a secure tenancy is jointly held by a couple whose marriage ends in divorce, the court has the statutory power to order the transfer of the tenancy to the sole name of the spouse still in occupation.[8] If a secure tenancy is held by a husband as sole tenant and the parties are divorced by decree absolute, it could be argued that the court cannot use this latter power since the occupation of the wife, if she was not the secure tenant, was through her husband until the divorce and after it, her occupation does not satisfy, as a result, the tenant condition of s 81.[9]

2   *An assignment to a person who would be qualified to succeed to the tenancy had the tenant died immediately prior to the assignment (s 91(3)(c)).*   The statutory succession provisions are operated by an assignment of this type and, on the death of the person to whom the tenancy has been assigned, there may be no further succession (s 88(1)(d)). Therefore, a secure tenant may use this exception as a way of preventing or pre-empting disputes as to who is entitled to succeed after his death by assigning to his spouse or resident family member. Such an assignment renders the tenancy secure in the hands of the successor-assign (provided this person is qualified to succeed, eg the tenant's husband or wife or son or daughter). The present exception overrides any term of the tenancy prohibiting assignments; but, curiously, if the tenancy prohibits assignments, the landlord may proceed against the successor for the previous tenant's assignment contrary to covenant.[10] Where a claimant relied on cohabitation in order to claim that a purported assignment to her by the secure tenant of the tenancy of a flat fell within the present exemption, it was held that the relevant date for determining whether the parties lived together as husband and wife was the date of the assignment, and so the twelve month period required for residence by a family member ran back from that date. On the facts, the parties had at best intermittently cohabited (as the claimant, the tenant's ex-wife, retained a secure tenancy of a different flat throughout the relevant period).[11]

3   *Assignments by way of exchange (s 91(3)(a)).*   A secure tenant may, under s 92, assign the tenancy by way of exchange with another secure tenant, or with an assured tenant. The statutory succession provisions only operate if the

6   *Thompson v Thompson* [1975] 2 All ER 208, CA.
7   *Hale v Hale* [1975] 2 All ER 1090, CA: in this and the preceding case, the tenancy contained no prohibitions and the court exercised its power to order a transfer to the tenant's ex-wife after a divorce.
8   Matrimonial Homes and Property Act 1981, Sch 2, para 2.
9   See *Old Gate Estates v Alexander* [1950] 1 KB 311; the issue was unresolved in *Lewis v Lewis* [1985] AC 828, HL.
10   *Peabody Donation Fund v Higgins* [1983] 3 All ER 122, [1983] 1 WLR 1091, CA.
11   *Westminster City Council v Peart* (1991) 24 HLR 389, CA.

tenant receiving an assignment of a tenancy was a successor in relation to the tenancy he himself assigned (s 88(3)).

The tenant must obtain the written consent of the landlord (s 92(2)) which may be withheld only on the grounds set out in Sch 3 of the 1985 Act. A consent withheld on any other ground is treated as given (s 92(3)).[12] The landlord cannot rely on any Sch 3 ground unless, within 42 days from the tenant's application for consent, he has served a notice on the tenant specifying the ground and giving particulars of it (s 92(4)). The landlord cannot subject his consent to any conditions (s 92(6)).[13] These grounds may be summarised as follows.

(a) The tenant or proposed assignee is obliged to give up possession of the dwelling-house concerned under a court order, or will be so obliged at a date specified in the order.
(b) Proceedings for possession of the dwelling-house of which the tenant or proposed assignee is secure tenant have begun on one or more of Grounds 1 to 6 of Sch 2; or a s 83 notice, which is still in force, has been served on either party which specifies one or more of these grounds.
(c) The accommodation afforded by the dwelling-house is substantially more extensive than is reasonably required by the proposed assignee.
(d) The extent of the accommodation afforded by the dwelling-house is not reasonably suitable to the needs of the proposed assignee and his family.
(e) The dwelling-house forms part of or is within the curtilage of a building which is held mainly for purposes other than housing purposes and consists mainly of accommodation other than housing accommodation, or is situated in a cemetery, and was let to the tenant or his predecessor as an employee of the landlord, a local authority or other specified landlord.[14]
(f) The landlord is a charity and the proposed assignee's occupation of the dwelling-house would conflict with its objects.
(g) The dwelling-house has features which make it substantially different from others, and is suitable for occupation by a disabled person; or the landlord is a housing association or housing trust which lets to persons whose non-financial circumstances make it specially difficult for them to satisfy their need for housing; and in either case, if the assignment were made, there would no longer be a disabled or disadvantaged person residing in the dwelling-house.[15]
(h) The dwelling-house is subject to a management agreement managed by a housing association, where at least half the tenants are subject to the

12 According to the *Encyclopedia of Housing Law*, notes to s 92 of the 1985 Act, the tenant cannot simply (as he could at common law) assign if the landlord fails to give due consent or delays beyond the 42-day period, and would have to seek an injunction or declaration.
13 Where the tenant is in arrears with rent or has broken the terms of his tenancy, this is not a ground for refusing consent, but the landlord may impose a condition requiring repayment of the arrears or remedy of the breach concerned (s 92(5)).
14 Ie a housing corporation, a housing action trust, a new town corporation, the Development Board for Rural Wales, an urban development corporation or the governors of an aided school.
15 Similarly there is a ground (Ground 9) which applies where the dwelling-house is one of a group of premises for letting by the landlord to 'special needs' tenants.

agreement and members of the association but the assignee is not willing to become a member of the association.

Lodgers and sub-lettings

Specific statutory rules are provided to deal with the taking in of lodgers and sub-lettings. First, it is a statutory (implied) term of every secure tenancy that the tenant may allow lodgers to reside in the house or flat in question (s 93(1)(a)).[16]

By contrast, no secure tenant may, except with the landlord's written consent, sub-let or part with the possession of part of the house or flat.[17] Should the tenant part with the possession or sub-let the whole of the 'dwelling-house', or sub-let part and then the remainder, the tenancy ceases to be secure and cannot subsequently become secure, as where the sub-tenancy is terminated (s 93(2)). Therefore, on termination of the head (and, where s 93(2) applies, non-secure) tenancy, the sub-tenancy is equally not secure as against the head landlord, applying common law principles already discussed.[18] A secure tenant who, for some intermittent periods, had ceased to occupy a flat, had not parted with possession in favour of the premises in the permanent and illegal sense required by s 93.[19]

The landlord is bound not to unreasonably withhold his consent (s 94(2))[20] – as to which see chapter 7. The landlord must show that consent was not unreasonably withheld if his decision is challenged. He may give his consent following any action (as for a declaration by the tenant) – so reversing the common law (s 94(4)). If the tenant applies in writing for consent, if the landlord refuses consent, it must give the tenant a written statement of the reasons for the refusal, and if he neither gives nor refuses consent within a reasonable time, consent is taken to have been withheld (s 94(6)).[1]

IV STATUTORY SUCCESSION SCHEME

Introduction

Part IV of the Housing Act 1985 allows for a single succession to a secure fixed-term or periodic tenancy by a person qualified to succeed, who is either the secure tenant's spouse or a resident family member. However, where a landlord

---

16 'Lodgers' mean a specific type of licensee: see further ch 3.

17 These rules apply to the exclusion of Landlord and Tenant Act 1988 (1988 Act, s 5(3)).

18 According to the *Encyclopedia of Housing Law*, note to s 92(2), no secure tenant could argue that, because a sub-tenancy contravened the provision, the sub-tenancy was not binding on him.

19 *Hussey v London Borough of Camden* (1994) 27 HLR 5, applying *Lam Shee Ying v Lam Shes Tong* [1975] AC 247.

20 Two factors are listed as material for the purpose, viz, the likelihood of overcrowding or the effect of works which the landlord proposes to carry out on the accommodation to be offered to the proposed sub-tenant (s 94(3)).

1 By analogy with the Landlord and Tenant Act 1988, the 'reasonable time' allowed to the landlord is likely, save in exceptional cases of complexity, to be a few weeks at most.

agreed to grant a new secure tenancy to a deceased intestate tenant's widow, the statutory succession scheme was not operated, and on her own death the secure tenancy could be transmitted to a member of her family.[2]

A *secure periodic tenancy*[3] devolves under statute as follows. After the death of the secure tenant, if there is a person qualified to succeed, the tenancy vests by operation of law, under s 89(1), in that person. Should there be more than one such person, as where there is both a spouse and a resident family member, preference is to be given to the tenant's spouse. If there should be no spouse, but two or more family members in competition for the succession, since only one person may succeed to the tenancy solely, the preference is to be by agreement or, failing agreement, by selection of the landlord (s 89(2)).

Should there be no person qualified to succeed, and the tenancy is then vested or otherwise disposed of in the administration of the tenant's estate, the tenancy ceases to be secure, and cannot become secure subsequently.[4]

Persons who may succeed

A person is qualified to succeed if he occupied the dwelling-house as his only or principal home at the time of the tenant's death and is either the tenant's spouse or another member of the tenant's family (s 87). The family member must reside with the tenant throughout the 12 months ending with the tenant's death. However, this twelve-month period may be interrupted temporarily, without costing the claimant a right to succeed. Whether a period of interruption is temporary is a question of fact, to be settled by analogy with loss of residence issues in the case of statutory tenancies. Hence, a person who resided with his grandmother for all but ten weeks of a year, living for the ten weeks with his spouse in a friend's home, did not lose his right to succeed as his absence was purely temporary.[5]

The expression 'family' is defined in s 113(1) as including a person living with the tenant as husband or wife, the tenant's parent, grandparent, child, grandchild, brother, sister, aunt, nephew or niece. Moreover, a stepchild is treated as a child and an illegitimate child as legitimate, for statutory purposes.[6]

'Reside with' means to spend a significant part of one's time with the person concerned.[7] The statutory residence rule does not impliedly involve the further requirement that the claimant to a succession should have resided in the same dwelling-house with the tenant for the full 12 month period: thus, where a

---

2 *Epping Forest District Council v Pomphrett* (1990) 22 HLR 475, CA; none of the 'triggers' in s 88 of the succession scheme applied.

3 A similar provision is made for secure fixed-term tenancies by s 90. The tenancy is secure until it vests under the succession provisions in the successor, as a secure tenancy, or, if there is no such person, the tenancy ceases to be secure when it is vested or disposed of elsewhere or as soon as it is known that when so vested etc it will not be secure.

4 Housing Act 1985, s 89(3) and (4), subject to a limited exception in favour of disposals under property adjustment orders under s 24 of the Matrimonial Causes Act 1973.

5 *Camden London Borough Council v Goldenberg* (1996) 28 HLR 727, CA.

6 See *Reading Borough Council v Ilsley* [1981] CLY 1323; also *Harrogate Borough Council v Simpson* [1986] 2 FLR 91 (lesbian co-resident with tenant not a member of her 'family').

7 *Peabody Donation Fund (Governors) v Grant* [1982] 2 EGLR 37; otherwise the term 'reside with' bears a similar meaning to that under the Rent Act 1977 scheme (ch 17).

secure tenant and his brother, having lived in the same premises for two-and-a-half years, moved to a different house, both properties being held on secure tenancies, and the tenant died within 10 days of the move, the House of Lords upheld the brother's claim to succeed: he had resided with the deceased for well over double the statutory period and it made no difference that the residence was in different premises.[8]

Position after death of successor

After the death of any successor to a secure tenancy, there is no further succession under the statute and the tenancy ceases to be secure. The word 'successor' is accordingly defined by s 88(1)(a) as including a person in whom the tenancy vested under a statutory succession. The succession provisions are operated where a joint secure tenant becomes the sole tenant.[9] They are also operated if the tenancy arose after the ending of a fixed term secure tenancy and that first tenancy had been granted to another tenant, or to that person and another person jointly (s 88(1)(c)), and also where the tenant became a secure tenant by an assignment,[10] and where the tenant becomes tenant by vesting in him of the tenancy on the death of the previous tenant (s 88(1)(d) and (e)), and finally where the tenancy had previously been an introductory tenancy and he had succeeded to it on the death of the original tenant (s 88(1)(f)).

V   REPOSSESSION BY THE LANDLORD

General rules

Part IV of the 1985 Act restricts the extent to which the landlord is entitled to terminate a secure fixed-term tenancy, and in the case of both this type of tenancy and secure periodic tenancies, requires that the landlord obtains an order of court on one or more statutory grounds. The first thing to note, however, is that once a secure fixed-term tenancy comes to an end, a periodic tenancy arises under s 86(1).[11] The periodic tenancy arising on the determination of the fixed-term tenancy is on the terms of s 86(2) and, in particular, the rental periods are the same as those for which rent was payable under the previous tenancy. The other terms of the tenancy are those of the former tenancy, provided these are compatible with those of a periodic tenancy, and excluding

---

8   *Waltham Forest London Borough Council v Thomas* [1992] 2 AC 198, [1992] 3 All ER 244, HL.
9   *Bassetlaw District Council v Renshaw* [1991] 2 EGLR 254, CA: for this rule to operate, the tenant must have been first a joint tenant and then a single tenant under the *same* tenancy: thus where T held a joint tenancy with X, which X terminated by notice to quit, and T was granted a new tenancy, and later died, a succession to the *second* tenancy was still possible.
10   Subject to the exceptions mentioned in s 88(2) and (3), relating to assignments under property adjustment orders or by exchange, where the succession provisions are operated by the assignment only if the assignor was a successor.
11   This is automatic, unless the tenant is granted another fixed-term or periodic tenancy of the same dwelling-house to begin when the first tenancy ends.

forfeiture provisions. This statutory periodic tenancy is terminable only in accordance with the procedures of the 1985 Act.[12]

If the landlord should decide to take proceedings for possession against a secure fixed-term tenant, rather than awaiting the ending of the term and then terminating the periodic tenancy arising, he cannot rely on any forfeiture clause, genuine or disguised,[13] to put an end to the tenant's right to occupy the house or flat. He must serve a statutory notice on the tenant under s 83, which notice will, however, apply to any statutorily arising periodic tenancy arising once the fixed-term tenancy has come to an end (s 83(6)).[14]

Possession will only, however, be ordered by the court if the landlord is able to prove one or more of the statutory grounds which must be established against secure tenants (s 82(1)(b)). The court cannot, indeed, order possession as a result of the operation of any forfeiture clause in the fixed-term tenancy, but if it would, but for the 1985 Act, have ordered possession under common law principles already discussed (chapter 13), it must terminate the fixed-term tenancy on the date specified in its order (s 82(3)). In this event, the statutory periodic tenancy arises under s 86. The powers of the court to grant relief to the tenant (but not to a sub-tenant) apply to proceedings under any forfeiture clause, as does the general doctrine of waiver (s 82(4)).

Termination of periodic tenancies

By s 82(1), a weekly or other periodic tenancy, whether arising under the Act or originally granted to the tenant, cannot be brought to an end by a landlord's notice to quit.[15] The landlord must obtain an order for possession (in the county court (s 110)) and the tenancy ends on any date specified in that order.

The landlord must, if he wishes to recover possession, serve a statutory notice on the tenant, who is thus entitled to advance warning of pending possession proceedings and as to the claims he will face. The court may dispense with the need to serve a statutory notice if it is just and equitable to do so (s 83(1)(b)). Any notice must, with the exception of proceedings based on Ground 2 (s 83(4)), state a date after which proceedings may be begun.[16] A notice ceases to be in force twelve months after that date (s 83(4)). The specified date is of critical importance since the county court cannot allow the landlord to bring a claim for possession until after the specified date has passed where the notice remains in force (s 83A(1)).[17] Moreover, the specified date cannot be sooner than the earliest date the tenancy could be brought to an end

---

12 See *Hammersmith and Fulham London Borough v Harrison* [1981] 2 All ER 588 at 597-598, CA.
13 As considered in eg *Clays Lane Housing Co-operative Ltd v Patrick* (1984) 49 P & CR 72, CA.
14 See note 17, infra.
15 The landlord must put an end to the periodic tenancy by a notice which complies with the requirements of Protection from Eviction Act 1977, as well as the common law rules (inference from s 83(3)). Any notice must be in the prescribed form: SI 1987/755, as amended.
16 In the case of Ground 2 proceedings, the notice must specify the date at which the landlord wishes the tenant to give up possession (s 83(2)).
17 Substituted for s 83 of the 1985 Act by Housing Act 1996, s 147(1) as from 12 February 1997, SI 1997/66.

by a common law notice to quit, though it may presumably correspond with that date. The protection given to a weekly or monthly secure tenant by this latter rule is not great although statute entitles him to a minimum four weeks' notice (see chapter 20).

In accordance with the warning function assigned to termination notices, such notices must specify and give particulars of the ground on which the court will be asked to make an order for possession of a dwelling-house let under a secure tenancy (s 83(2)). Otherwise the court cannot entertain the proceedings. Giving particulars seems to require that landlords give some details of the alleged breaches, such as the amount of rent allegedly in arrear, or as to alleged items of disrepair -otherwise the notice risks being invalid.[18] A s 83 notice is – perhaps resembling statutory forfeiture notices – a warning shot accross the bows of the tenant, warning him that unless he puts right the alleged breaches, he faces dispossession.[19] In any case, where the court may refuse possession in its general discretion (as with grounds based on allegations of tenant misconduct), a tenant may therefore improve his chances of resisting an order for possession by discontinuing the offending conduct as from receipt of the s 83 notice. If his record has in the past been bad, this would presumably be one factor to be taken into account in assessing whether the court would exrcise its discretion to refuse possession; but a remedied breach at the time of the proceedings being heard cannot presumably afford the landlord a ground for possession.

The above rules as to notices have no application to tenants' notices to quit: if a tenant serves a notice to quit, he cannot later rely on the security provisions,[20] and the same principle would appear to apply if one of a number of joint tenants serves a notice to quit, without having consulted his co-tenants, as the joint tenancy would be at an end after expiry of this notice.[1] If, moreover, a secure tenant permanently leaves the premises, whether or not owing rent, he loses security, having ceased to comply with the statutory residence requirement imposed by the tenant condition.[2]

Grounds for possession – general

The court cannot make an order for possession against a secure tenant except on proof by the landlord of one or more grounds for possession as laid down in Sch 2 to the 1985 Act. If a ground is not specified in the landlord's statutory notice, the court cannot make an order for possession based on that ground (s 84(3)).[3] This particular provision states that 'the grounds so specified may be altered or added to with the leave of the court'. The power has been widely

---

18   *Torridge District Council v Jones* [1985] 2 EGLR 54, CA.

19   Ibid, 56J.

20   *Greenwich London Borough Council v McGrady* (1982) 81 LGR 288, CA.

  1   *Hammersmith and Fulham London Borough v Monk* [1992] 1 All ER 1, HL, as applied in *Crawley Borough Council v Ure* (1995) 27 HLR 524, CA.

  2   *Preston Borough Council v Fairclough* (1982) 8 HLR 70, CA; also *R v Croydon London Borough Council, ex p Toth*, supra.

  3   As substituted by Housing Act 1996, s 147(2). The court cannot make an order for possession requiring the tenant to give up possession before any date specified in a s 83 notice (s 84(4) as substituted).

construed. The court may alter a specified ground, and add a new ground, and also, though the particulars of a ground are not in terms mentioned by s 84(3) in its former or altered form, it may even alter or add to these latter, as they may be said to be part and parcel of a ground. The protection of the tenant seems to lie in the discretion of the court and the power of the Court of Appeal to review the exercise of that discretion by a lower court.[4] The court cannot, however, order possession to take effect any earlier than the date specified in the landlord's s 83 notice (s 84(4)).

Grounds 1 to 8, as listed below, are subject to an overriding requirement that it must be reasonable to make an order for possession (s 84(2)(a)). The court exercises this overriding discretion in much the same way as it might under the Rent Act 1977.[5] The courts do not take a restrictive view of this legislation, and all relevant circumstances have to be taken into account as at the date of the hearing, taking a broad, common-sense view, giving weight to the various relevant factors.[6] It is a material factor that, for example, a tenant is continuing with conduct which amounts to a nuisance or annoyance at the date of the hearing, so showing no wish to mend his ways.[7] However, the mere fact that a term of the tenancy agreement may have been broken, although no doubt a relevant matter, is not the sole factor, so that a judge was entitled to conclude that it was not reasonable to order possession against a tenant who had taken no active part in a fire caused by visitors to his flat, although the terms of his tenancy had been broken.[8]

Grounds 9 to 11, listed below, are subject to a requirement that when the order takes effect, suitable alternative accommodation will be available to the tenant and his family (s 84(2)(b)).[9] These grounds are, however, mandatory in the sense that there is no overriding discretion to refuse possession, if the alternative accommodation condition and the basic requirements of the ground have been proved. So as to protect such persons, the court cannot make an order for possession under s 84(2)(b) if a member of the tenant's family living in the premises, such as his estranged wife, has not been joined as a party to the proceedings.[10]

Grounds 12 to 16 are subject to *both* the overriding discretion of the court to refuse possession on the ground that it would not be reasonable to order it and to proof by the landlord of the alternative accommodation condition (s 84(2)(c)).

---

4 *Camden London Borough Council v Oppong* (1996) 28 HLR 701, CA.
5 See *Woodspring District Council v Taylor* (1982) 4 HLR 95, CA; *Second WRVS Housing Society v Blair* (1986) 19 HLR 104, CA (personal factors relevant); *Islington London Borough Council v Reeves* [1997] CLY 436.
6 *Haringey London Borough Council v Stewart* [1991] 2 EGLR 252, CA.
7 *Woking Borough Council v Bistram* (1993) 27 HLR 1, CA.
8 *Wandsworth London Borough v Hargreaves* (1994) 27 HLR 142, CA.
9 See Housing Act 1985, Sch 2, Part IV; cf Rent Act 1977, Sch 15, Part IV; and see *Enfield Borough Council v French* (1984) 83 LGR 750, CA.
10 *Wandsworth London Borough Council v Fadayomi* [1987] 3 All ER 474 (where a consent order for possession made where the tenant's wife had not been allowed to intervene was set aside). The principle as to consent orders is applicable to the whole of s 84 and is by analogy with the Rent Acts.

'Discretionary' grounds

Ground 1 – Tenant's breach of covenant

Rent lawfully due from the tenant has not been paid or an obligation of the tenancy has been broken or not performed.

This ground is similar (albeit in a simpler form) to the corresponding Rent Act 1977 ground. Under it, the court is to take into account, as under the Rent Acts, all relevant circumstances as they exist at the hearing: thus where a tenant in serious rent arrears made no proposals as to his paying these off, it was held correct, exceptionally, not to suspend an order for possession.[11] Where the tenant breaks a condition of his tenancy agreement, he cannot argue, it seems, that only if the conduct amounts to a nuisance or annoyance is the court able to order possession against him.[12]

Ground 2 – Nuisance, etc[13]

The tenant or a person residing in or visiting the dwelling-house has been guilty of conduct which was, or is likely to have been, a nuisance or annoyance to a person residing, visiting or otherwise engaged in a lawful activity in the vicinity of the dwelling-house, or has been convicted of using the dwelling-house or allowing it to be used for immoral or illegal purposes or an arrestable offence committed in, or in the locality of, the dwelling-house.[14]

The expression 'nuisance or annoyance' must apparently bear the meaning it has in the general law. The term 'annoyance' therefore means something which materially affects the peace of mind or physical comfort of ordinary sensible people.[15] Ground 2 in its original form had been held to cover nuisance by noise, and also abusive and foul language directed at neighbouring tenants over a long period.[16] Certainly, fault by the tenant personally does not need to be shown: it would suffice, if a son of the tenant who was too young to be evicted by his family caused neighbouring tenants a nuisance or annoyance by his indiscipline or bad behaviour – indeed this was held to be the position prior to the 1996 amendments.[17]

Ground 2A – Domestic violence by partner[18]

Under this new ground, introduced seemingly because of the new policy of enabling landlords to remove unsocial tenants from the premises, the landlord

---

11 *Harringey London Borough Council v Stewart* [1991] 2 EGLR 252, CA.
12 *Sheffield City Council v Green* [1993] EGCS 185, CA.
13 This ground is given as amended by Housing Act 1996, s 144. A possession order cannot here be refused solely because no suitable alternative accommodation is available: *Darlington Borough Council v Starling* [1997] CLY 435, CA.
14 Special rules apply to s 83 notices in the case of this ground (s 83(3) as substituted by Housing Act 1996, s 147(1)), notably, owing to the policy of the new ground, that the notice is to state that possession proceedings may be begun immediately.
15 *Chorley Borough Council v Ribble Motor Services Ltd* [1996] EGCS 110, CA.
16 *Woking Borough Council v Bistram* (1993) 27 HLR 1, CA.
17 *Kensington and Chelsea Royal London Borough v Simmonds* [1996] 3 FCR 246, CA.
18 Inserted by Housing Act 1996, s 145 from 12 February 1997: SI 1997/66. Special requirements as to the service of a s 83 notice apply in this case, notably, service of a copy of the notice on the partner who has left.

is enabled to recover possession from a tenant or his partner where the tenant or his partner has left because of the violence of one to the other or to a child residing with the person leaving immediately before that person left. The court must be satisfied that the partner who left is unlikely to return and also that the accommodation offered by the house or flat is more extensive than is reasonably required by the person remaining there.[19]

Ground 3 – *Deterioration in condition of dwelling-house*

The condition of the dwelling-house or of any of the common parts has deteriorated owing to acts of waste by, or the neglect or default of the tenant or a person residing in the dwelling-house and, in the case of an act of waste by, or the neglect or default of a lodger of the tenant's or a sub-tenant of his, the tenant has not taken such steps as he ought reasonably to have taken to remove the lodger or sub-tenant.[20]

Ground 4 – *Deterioration in condition of furniture*

The condition of furniture provided by the landlord for use under the tenancy, or for use in the common parts, has deteriorated owing to ill-treatment by the tenant or a person residing in the dwelling-house. In the case of a lodger or sub-tenant, the tenant has not taken such steps as he ought reasonably to have taken for the removal of the lodger or sub-tenant.[1]

Ground 5 – *Inducement to grant tenancy*

The landlord was induced by the tenant, as the person, or one of them, to whom the tenancy was granted, to grant the tenancy by a false statement made knowingly or recklessly by the tenant or a person acting at the tenant's instigation.

This ground reflects a wider principle. It is a ground for rescinding a statutory tenancy that the tenant has induced the landlord to grant the protected tenancy from which it is derived by a fraudulent statement.[2]

Ground 6 – *Premium paid on permitted assignment*

The tenancy was assigned under s 92 by 'exchange' to the tenant or to a predecessor in title who is a member of his family, and a premium[3] was paid in connection with that assignment or the previous assignment.

---

19 As with Ground 2, a special rule applies to s 83 notices served by the landlord (s 83A(3))) notably that if the leaving partner is not the tenant, the landlord has served a copy of the notice on that person or has taken all reasonable steps to do so.
20 Subject to the omission of the words 'before the order in question', these words are the same as Rent Act 1977, Sch 15, Case 3, discussed in ch 17.
 1 These words correspond to Rent Act 1977, Sch 15, Case 4 (ch 17).
 2 *Killick v Roberts* [1991] 4 All ER 289, [1991] 1 WLR 146, CA.
 3 As widely defined so as to include capital payments and any other pecuniary consideration in addition to rent.

Ground 7 – Dwelling-house within building used for non-housing purposes

The dwelling-house forms part of a building[4] which[5] is held mainly for purposes other than housing purposes and consists mainly of accommodation other than housing accommodation. The dwelling-house was let to the tenant or a predecessor in title of his in consequence of the tenant or predecessor being in the employment of the landlord or the employment of certain bodies[6] and the tenant or a person residing in the house has been guilty of conduct such that, having regard to the purpose for which the building is used, it would not be right for him to continue in occupation of the dwelling-house.

Ground 8 – Temporary occupation during works

The dwelling-house was made available for occupation by the tenant (or a predecessor in title of his) while works were carried out on the dwelling-house previously occupied by him as his only or principal home. The tenant or predecessor held a secure tenancy of the other property at the date he ceased to occupy it (owing to the works). The tenant or predecessor accepted the tenancy of the dwelling-house of which possession is sought on the understanding that he would give up occupation when, on completion of the works, the other dwelling-house was again available for occupation under a secure tenancy. The works have been completed and the other dwelling-house is available for re-occupation.

Grounds where possession must be ordered on proof of suitable alternative accommodation

Ground 9 – Overcrowding

The dwelling-house is overcrowded, within Part X of the Housing Act 1985, in such a way as to render the occupier guilty of an offence.

Ground 10 – Redevelopment

The landlord intends, within a reasonable time of obtaining possession of the dwelling-house:

(a) to demolish or reconstruct the building or part of the building comprising the dwelling-house, or

(b) to carry out work on that building or on land let together with, and thus treated as part of, the dwelling-house,

and cannot reasonably do so without obtaining possession of the dwelling-house.[7]

---

4 Or is within its curtilege, as to be understood in the narrow sense discussed above.
5 Or, to the extent that the landlord holds part of the building, as where it is sub-divided, that part.
6 Notably, a local authority, new town corporation, housing action trust and the governors of an aided school.
7 Under Ground 10A, possession may be recovered mandatorily if the dwelling-house is within the area of a redevelopment scheme under Part V of Sch 2 to the 1985 Act.

The landlord is expected to prove the same definite and settled intention under this ground as would apply to s 30(1)(f) of the Landlord and Tenant Act 1954. Thus, where the only evidence of work said to be required to a cottage adjacent to a countryside park, so as to incorporate it into the latter, was oral evidence by an officer of the local authority concerned, rather than any relevant minutes of the authority, which would have been better evidence, it was held that the evidence was not sufficient to meet the statutory requirement, but, even if it had been, the authority had not produced evidence to show that the work could not be done without possession of the cottage.[8] It will be noted that the tenant lacks the protection of any equivalent to s 31A of the Landlord and Tenant Act 1954.

Ground 11 – Landlord is a charity

The landlord is a charity and the tenant's continued occupation of the dwelling-house would conflict with the objects of the charity.

'Discretionary' grounds where suitable alternative accommodation must be available

Where any of the following grounds applies, the landlord must overcome both the overriding discretion of the court and show that suitable alternative accommodation will be available for the tenant when the order for possession takes effect (s 84(2)). It is convenient to discuss briefly the requirements as to suitability which must be shown by the landlord.

The general criteria which the landlord must prove to the satisfaction of the court as to the suitability to the needs of the tenant[9] are similar to those which govern the Rent Act 1977 (see chapter 17). The types of tenancy which qualify for suitability, if the first hurdle is passed, are: lettings as a separate dwelling under a secure tenancy[10] or an assured tenancy, in which latter case the tenancy must not be an assured shorthold tenancy or an assured tenancy subject to recovery of possession on any of the five relevant mandatory grounds.[11]

Ground 12 – Mainly non-housing accommodation and premises reasonably required for landlord's employee

The dwelling-house forms part of, or is within the curtilege of, a building (or part) which is held mainly for non-housing purposes and consists of mainly non-housing accommodation, or is situated in a cemetery. It was let to the tenant or a predecessor in title of his in consequence of either or both being in the landlord's employment, or that of certain bodies, such as a local authority, new town corporation, or the governors of a grant-aided school. The relevant employment has ceased and the landlord reasonably requires the dwelling-

---

8 *Wansbeck District Council v Marley* (1987) 20 HLR 247, CA.
9 1985 Act, Sch 2, Part IV.
10 Or, where appropriate, a protected tenancy under the Rent Act 1977, where possession cannot be recovered on any mandatory ground.
11 Housing Act 1985, Sch 2, Part IV, para 1.

house for occupation as a residence for some employee of his, or of one of the bodies listed (such as a local authority) with whom a contract of employment has been entered into conditional on such housing being provided.

Ground 13 – Special features to dwelling-house

The dwelling-house has features which are substantially different from those of ordinary dwelling-houses and which are designed to make it suitable for occupation by a physically disabled person who requires accommodation of the kind provided by the dwelling-house and:

(a) there is no longer such a person residing in the dwelling-house; and
(b) the landlord requires it for occupation (whether alone or with members of his family) by such a person.

Ground 14 – Lettings to tenants whose circumstances are difficult

A housing association or housing trust landlord lets housing only to tenants whose circumstances (other than merely financial) make it especially difficult for them to satisfy their need for housing. The house or flat must have no such tenant residing there or he must have received an offer of accommodation from the local housing authority for a tenancy of premises to be let under a secure tenancy, and the landlord requires the subject property for occupation by tenant of the kind they let housing to.

Ground 15 – Special needs tenants

The dwelling-house is one of a group of properties which it is the practice of the landlord to let for occupation by persons with special needs. A social service or special facility is provided in close proximity to the group of dwelling-houses in order to assist persons with special needs. There is no longer a person with such needs residing in the particular dwelling-house, and the landlord requires it for occupation, alone or with family members, by a person having such special needs.

Ground 16 – Accommodation too extensive

The ground provides that the accommodation in the dwelling-house is more extensive than that reasonably required by the tenant, but only applies where the tenant obtained the dwelling-house by succession under s 89, and had succeeded as a family member of the deceased secure tenant.[12] Apart from matters to be taken into account in the general discretion of the court, this ground specifies specific matters, notably the age of the tenant and the period he has occupied the dwelling-house as his only or principal home.

---

12 Notice of proceedings for possession must have been served under s 83 more than six but less than twelve months after the date of the previous tenant's death, or the ground is not applicable.

Possession orders

In relation to the discretionary grounds, s 85 confers on the county court wide powers of adjournment, staying or postponement in relation to any order for possession.[13] The court may, under s 85(1), adjourn the proceedings for such period or periods as it thinks fit. Under s 85(2), the court may, if it makes an order for possession, stay or suspend execution of the order, or postpone the date of possession, for such perior or periods as it thinks fit. This power is exercisable at any time up to the date of execution of the order. If the court exercises its powers under s 85(1) or (2), it must impose conditions on the tenant for the payment of rent arrears or in respect of mesne profits, and may impose such other conditions as it thinks fit (s 85(3)). This provision has been recently examined in depth by the House of Lords.[14]

It was held,[15] adopting the analysis in an earlier decision,[16] that although under s 85(2) the court could order possession, this was not necessarily final, owing to the power of s 85(2) to postpone the date for possession. That date was the crucial one for the tenant. The power of postponement, for example, was exercisable even after the date for possession specified in the court's order, and so even after the tenancy had terminated, thanks to s 85(2). Section 85(3)(a) supported this view. It referred to the imposition of a condition as to the payment of mesne profits. The court could revive a defunct tenancy if the relevant condition was complied with.

By contrast, once a warrant for possession has been made against a secure tenant, it can only be set aside on narrow grounds, as where the order for possession is itself set aside, or the warrant has been obtained by fraud, or there has been an abuse of the process of the court or oppression in the execution of the warrant.[17]

It has further been held by the House of Lords that a former secure tenant against whom a final order for possession had been made was best described as a tolerated trespasser.[18] The old tenancy was in limbo and no new tenancy could be inferred.[19] The old tenancy could be revived under s 85(3) on an application by the tenant, which in that case seemed unlikely as the tenant would have needed some 14 years in which to discharge the rent arrears which had formed the basis of the order of possession. The local council there were entitled, owing to her failure to comply with an arrangement entered into days before an order for possession was due to be enforced, to procure the tenant's eviction by

---

13 As from any failure by the tenant to comply with a suspended possession order, it becomes effective to terminate the tenancy: *Thompson v Elmbridge Borough Council* [1987] 1 WLR 1425, CA.
14 *Burrows v Brent London Borough Council* [1996] 4 All ER 577, [1996] 1 WLR 1448.
15 Per Lord Browne-Wilkinson [1996] 1 WLR 1448 at 1452-1453, [1996] 4 All ER 577, 581-582, Lords Keith, Goff and Steyn agreeing; also Lord Januncey, ibid, 1457 and 588.
16 *Greenwich London Borough Council v Regan* (1996) 28 HLR 469, CA.
17 *Hammersmith and Fulham London Borough Council v Hill* [1994] 2 EGLR 51, CA.
18 *Burrows v Brent London Borough Council* [1996] 4 All ER 577, [1996] 1 WLR 1448.
19 Lord Jauncey said, 1457, 588,that s 85(4) was inconsistent with the creation of a new tenancy as a discharge of a possession order would work only if the old tenancy had not been superceded by a new tenancy.

executing the original order for possession by warrant issued over two years after the order. Had their Lordships decided that the parties had impliedly agreed to a new tenancy, local authorities might become unwilling to make concessionary arrangements in favour of tenants whose personal circumstances had changed for the worse.[20] This would be because with any implied new tenancy, new possession proceedings, in an overstretched court system, would have to be commenced against the tenant.

The statutory restrictions on making an order for possession assume that the tenant is a secure tenant and has not lost that status, as by ceasing to comply with the tenant condition of residence. If, for example, he concedes that he has abandoned possession, the court may make a consent order for possession on the ground that the tenant no longer occupies the dwelling-house as his only or principal home. While clear evidence is required, it would be hard for the tenant to persuade an appellate court to revoke such an order if he had originally admitted that the protection of the 1985 Act, Part IV did not apply.[1]

VI   SECURE TENANTS' IMPROVEMENTS AND REPAIRS

Part IV of the Housing Act 1985 provides specific rules for the consent of the landlord to improvements by secure tenants, as well as a limited scheme for improvements compensation after the secure tenancy ends, and provides enabling provisions for secure tenants' repair schemes. These rules are summarised as follows.

Improvements

1   Special *consent rules* apply to improvements[2] by secure tenants.[3] By s 97(1), it is a term of every secure tenancy that the tenant will not make any improvement without the written consent of the landlord. Consent cannot be unreasonably withheld: if it is, it is treated as given (s 97(3)). If the tenant applies in writing for a consent, the landlord must give a written statement to the tenant of his reasons for refusing it, if applicable, and is treated as withholding consent if he does not consent or refuse consent within a reasonable time (s 98(4)). The onus of proving the reasonableness of a withholding of consent is on the landlord (s 98(1)).[4] However, the landlord has a power, when giving consent, to impose a reasonable condition (s 99(1)), and failure to comply with such a condition is treated as a breach of

---

20   [1996] 4 All ER 577, 583, [1996] 1 WLR 1448, 1454 (Lord Browne-Wilkinson).
1   *Bruce v Worthing Borough Council* (1993) 26 HLR 223, CA.
2   As widely defined so as to include not only alterations or additions to the dwelling-house but also eg additions or alterations to landlords' fittings and external decorations (s 97(2)), neither of which might constitute an improvement at common law, as well as the provision of services, eg central heating, which would; cf ch 7.
3   The rules of s 19(2) of the Landlord and Tenant Act 1927 do not, therefore, apply: s 97(4).
4   As to the matters to be taken into account by the court in determining reasonableness, see s 98(2).

the secure tenancy obligations (s 99(4)). The landlord must show that any condition is reasonable (s 99(3)) and the imposition of an unreasonable condition is equivalent to refusing consent (s 99(2)).

2   Limited provision is made for compensation to be paid to a former secure tenant, or, if appropriate, another 'qualifying person'[5] such as his successor, where the secure tenancy comes to an end and was held, at that time, of a local authority landlord.[6] The improvement will not qualify unless the landlord or its predecessor must have given written actual, or deemed, consent. The scheme is supplemented by regulations.[7]

Repairs

Under s 96 of the Housing Act 1985[8] new regulations have been made,[9] which apply to most secure tenants holding from local authority landlords, so that secure tenants of such bodies as housing associations are outside the scheme. This is a repair scheme under which minor repairs may be required to be carried out following a tenant's notice. The work must then be put out to a private contractor by the authority. There are default provisions available to the tenant who may require the landlord to procure the work to be done by a different contractor, and if the latter defaults, there is a provision for compensation to the tenant, with a right of set-off in the landlord if the tenant owes rent arrears.

Miscellaneous

No doubt secure tenants will hope to hold their premises under a written tenancy agreement. If so, the terms of the agreement may only be varied within the limits of s 102 of the 1985 Act, superceding the common law. These methods include agreement between the landlord and tenant, or under s 103, which allows the landlord to vary the terms of a secure periodic tenancy by notice.[10] Part IV of the 1985 Act contains a number of provisions about management matters, such as a requirement that every body letting under secure tenancies is to publish information about the express terms of its tenancies and about the right to buy (s 104), as well as a requirement of consultation about certain matters of housing management (s 105), housing allocation (s 106), and there is a provision limiting the right of landlords of secure tenants to recover heating charges (s 108).[11]

5   As defined in 1985 Act, s 99B(2), added by Leasehold Reform, Housing and Urban Development Act 1993, s 122.
6   Thus, if the reason for the cesser of secure tenancy status is that the landlord condition is not satisfied, as where the reversion passes to a private landlord, the compensation rules may apply (s 99A(8)), inserted by 1993 Act, s 122.
7   Secure Tenants of Local Authorities (Compensation for Improvements) Regulations 1994, SI 1994/613, in force from 1 April 1994.
8   As substituted by s 121 of the Leasehold Reform, Housing and Urban Development Act 1993.
9   Secure Tenants of Local Authorities (Right to Repair) Regulations 1994, SI 1994/133, in force from 1 April 1994, extended to introductory tenancies by SI 1997/73. See further *West*, pp 200-202.
10   But cf *Palmer v Metropolitan Borough of Sandwell* (1987) 20 HLR 74, CA (holding that statements in a booklet which differed from terms of tenancy did not bind landlord).
11   Note that the special provisions about assignments repairs, improvements and management do not apply where the landlord is a housing co-operative association (s 109).

VII   THE RIGHT TO BUY

Introduction

Secure tenants whose landlords hold the freehold of their homes, or whose landlords[12] are long leaseholders, have the right to buy ('RTB') the landlord's interest in their 'dwelling-house' on terms set out in Part V to the Housing Act 1985.[13] These terms include a substantial discount from the purchase price, which may have to be repaid if the former tenant disposes too rapidly of his property, having exercised the right to buy. The rules are subject to a number of exemptions, where policy dictates that the right should be withheld, but, in principle, as with private sector enfranchisement, a landlord against whom a right to buy is claimed has no choice but to submit to its exercise, provided the tenant complies with the various statutory procedures and conditions.

The legislature has placed but few formal obstacles to a secure tenant claiming the right, which has been judicially recognised as having the deliberate purpose of inducing secure tenants to buy their homes (and to take them out of the public sector).[14] This generosity is shown by the following matters: the narrow scope of the exemptions to the RTB (see below); the entitlement of the tenant to a generous discount and, as will appear, the fact that, while he is under an obligation to repay it if he re-sells or re-assigns, the obligation is of short duration (three years from the acquisition of his title). Moreover, it is provided that any provision in a lease held by the landlord which prohibits or restricts the grant of a lease under the RTB (or under rent to mortgage terms) is void – so protecting the RTB of the secure (sub) tenant.[15] Although a secure tenant is required to serve his notice claiming the RTB in a prescribed form, 'a notice served by a tenant ... is not invalidated by an error in, or omission from, the particulars which are required by regulations ... to be contained in the notice'.[16] Moreover, the Secretary of State has wide powers of intervention against a landlord whom he considers to be, in effect, unduly slow in allowing his secure tenants to exercise the RTB and has sweeping powers to repeal any local Act passed before the RTB was introduced as from 8 August 1980 which appear to him to be inconsistent with the present set of provisions.[17]

Nevertheless, it has been said that because the provisions of Part V of the 1985 Act give a secure tenant considerable benefits and result in corresponding disadvantages to the landlord, its provisions should, where appropriate, be construed strictly. In particular, a person claiming the right to buy but who, on investigation, has in fact lost it during one of the stages to obtaining the grant

---

12   Although the present provisions are aimed at public sector landlords such as local authorities, where the tenant's interest comes to be held by a private landlord, his right to buy is preserved where ss 171A-171H apply.

13   References to the provisions of Housing Act 1985, Part V are as amended or substituted by Leasehold Reform, Housing and Urban Development Act 1993, Part II, Chapter I. The expression 'dwelling-house' is defined in s 183.

14   *Dickinson* v *Enfield London Borough Council* [1996] 49 EG 108, 111, CA.

15   Housing Act 1985, s 179.

16   Ibid, s 177(1).

17   The powers are in Housing Act 1985. ss 164 and 182 respectively.

of the freehold or a lease, is precluded from pursuing his claim any further.[18] By contrast, once the right to buy is fully established, and a binding contract has been entered into, the tenant is entitled to an injunction under s 138(1) to enforce the landlord's duty to convey him the property. The court will not refuse the remedy on the ground of general considerations of hardship.[19] Parliament intended to block all opportunities to reluctant landlords to preclude the acquisition of the premises by tenants. Even where it was alleged that the tenant (who had satisfied all the statutory steps leading to the right to buy) was involved in a serious criminal offence, the Court of Appeal refused to interfere with the reluctant grant of an injunction to the tenant.[20]

Conditions for right to arise

The right to buy is conferred by the 1985 Act on secure tenants, so that if the tenancy is excluded from being secure, the right to buy is also incapable of arising (s 118(1)). In the case of a house, where the landlord is the freeholder, the right is to acquire the freehold. If the premises are a flat, the RTB is to obtain a long lease, as is the case where the landlord of a house does not own the freehold (s 118(1)).

If the secure tenancy is joint, the right to buy belongs to the tenants jointly or to such one of them as may be agreed (s 118(2)). The requirement of residential occupation of the house or flat (which is a condition precedent to secure tenancy status) is relaxed because a joint tenant who does not reside in the house or flat as his only or principal home may still exercise the RTB. However, in the case of an agreement that one (or more) of a number of joint tenants is to exercise the RTB, at least one of these persons must satisfy the statutory residence requirement (s 118(2)).

A qualifying period of residence is imposed on the tenant[1] as a condition precedent to the RTB arising (s 119(1)). It need be satisfied, where relevant, by only one joint tenant (s 119(2)). The statutory period to be taken into account for the purpose of this condition is two years.[2] Although this concept also relates to the amount of permitted discount on sale (see below), it is best dealt with here. Thus, for example, a period of occupation as a secure tenant or as a spouse of a secure tenant (if they were living together at that time) counts as a qualifying residential period, if, before the date of service of the tenant's notice of claim to exercise the RTB, the tenant was a public sector tenant.[3]

Where right to buy does not arise

There are a number of cases in which the right to buy does not arise in any event and these may be summarised as follows. The first two sets of exclusions relate

---

18 *Muir Group Housing Association Ltd v Thornley* (1992) 25 HLR 89, CA.
19 *Taylor v Newham London Borough Council* [1993] 1 WLR 444; also *Dance v Welwyn Hatfield District Council* [1990] 3 All ER 572, [1990] 1 WLR 1097, CA.
20 *Bristol City Council v Lovell* [1996] EGCS 140, CA.
 1 Who must be an individual and who must comply with the residence condition, see below.
 2 In accordance with Housing Act 1985, Sch 4.
 3 As defined Sch 4, para 6(1).

to the status of the landlord (as where he has been grant-subsidised out of public monies), or to specific houses or flats where their sale under the RTB would be undesirable in the general interest. The last exclusion may be explained on the ground that the landlord against whom the RTB is exercisable is the secure tenant's immediate landlord.

1   *Status of landlord*   The landlord is a charitable housing trust or a housing association, or is a co-operative housing association or is a housing association which at no time has received grants under specified legislation.[4] The RTB does not arise where the landlord holds a tenancy from the Crown, even if it would be sufficient, but for the exemption, to support the grant of a long lease to the tenant.[5]

2   *Certain types of houses or flats*   A small class of premises are excluded from the RTB owing to policy considerations.

Letting in connection with tenant's employment: where the dwelling-house 'forms part of, or is within the curtilage of' a building or that part held by the landlord which building is held mainly for non-housing purposes and consists mainly of accommodation other than housing accommodation, or is situated in a cemetery. The accommodation must have been let to the tenant in 'consequence of the tenant or his predecessor' being in the landlord's employment.[6] The word 'curtilege' might extend the amount of exempt premises, were it not for the fact that it appears that a restrictive meaning must be applied, namely, the ordinary meaning, which refers to a small area forming part of the house and attached to it: hence, a cottage let to a college lecturer which was within but on the edge of the college grounds, and fenced off from the rest of the grounds, albeit with pedestrian access to them, was not within the 'curtilege' of the college buildings and the RTB was not excluded.[7]

Certain houses for the disabled: where the dwelling-house has 'features which are substantially different from those of ordinary dwelling-houses and are designed to make it suitable for occupation by physically disabled persons'.[8] It appears

---

4   Housing Act 1985, Sch 5, paras 1 and 2 respectively; as to the meaning of 'housing trust' see *Hounslow London Borough Council v Hare* (1990) 89 LGR 714 (provisions of a will created a housing trust in required sense, by providing gifted premises to a local authority to house old people).
5   Ibid, para 12. However, the exemption does not apply where the landlord is entitled to grant a lease under the 1985 Act without the agreement of the appropriate authority, eg the Crown Estate Commissioners, as where such authority notifies the landlord that as respects the Crown's interest, consent will be granted to the grant of a lease under the RTB.
6   Ibid, para 5; or in that of a local authority and certain other bodies such as, notably, the governors of an aided school.
7   *Dyer v Dorset County Council* [1989] QB 346, CA; also *Barwick and Barwick v Kent County Council* (1992) 24 HLR 341, CA (where a house situated near a fire station did not fall within the curtilege of the main fire station building; adjacent garages would have fallen within the 'curtilege' of the latter building).
8   Ibid, para 7. The narrowness of this exemption is shown by the requirement that the house or flat must be one of a group of dwellings which it is the practice of the landlord to let for occupation by physically disabled persons and a special service or special facilities must be provided in close proximity so as to aid or assist those persons.

that the exemption is to be narrowly construed, as contemplating structural design features not found in ordinary dwellings, wherever situated, such as a ramp, lift or other mechanical contrivance, rather than the fact that, in one case, the house had a specially-designed, additional, ground-floor WC, owing to the fact that the secure tenants' daughter suffered from spina bifida, and so had difficulty mounting stairs.[9]

Certain houses for pensioners: this exemption relates to a house or flat which is one of a group of dwellings which are particularly suitable, having regard to their location, size, design, heating systems and other features, for occupation by elderly persons, and which it is the practice of the landlord to let for occupation by persons aged 60 or over, or to those and physically disabled persons. However, so as to restrict the exemption, special facilities must be shown to be provided wholly or mainly to assist those persons.[10]

3 *Landlord's reversion insufficient* The right to buy cannot arise unless the landlord owns the freehold, or has a leasehold interest which suffices to enable him to grant a lease within Part V of the 1985 Act for a term exceeding 21 years in the case of a house and for a term of not less than 50 years in the case of a flat.[11]

Where right to buy cannot be exercised

So as not to allow undesirable or financially insecure tenants to exercise the RTB, it cannot be exercised if the tenant is obliged to give up possession of the house or flat concerned under a court order for possession or will be so obliged at a specified date (s 121(1)). Nor can the RTB be exercised where the tenant has a bankruptcy petition pending against him, a receiving order pending against him, or in two similar cases (s 121(2)).[12]

Tenant's claim to exercise right to buy

The Court of Appeal has recognised that there are four stages to the exercise of the right to buy. The first stage is the tenant's claim to exercise the right. The last stage is the grant of the relevant interest, and the intermediate stages are the establishment of the right and the agreement, or in default, determination, of the terms of the grant.[13] These stages are now examined.

A secure tenant who wishes to exercise the RTB must do so by a written notice served on the landlord (s 122(1)).[14] The claim notice is to be in the

---

9 *Freeman v Wansbeck District Council* (1984) 82 LGR 131, CA.
10 Ibid, Sch 5, para 10, as amended. The relevant facilities are defined in para 10(2). There is also an exemption in para 11, as substituted by s 106(2) of the 1993 Act, which relates to individual dwelling-houses for elderly persons, but which relates only to lettings on or after 1 January 1990.
11 Ibid, para 4. The measurement of the leases commences as from the date of the tenant's notice of claim to exercise the right to buy.
12 Ie where he is an undischarged bankrupt or has made a non-fulfilled composition or arrangement with his creditors.
13 *Muir Group Housing Association Ltd v Thornley* (1992) 25 HLR 89.
14 The notice may be withdrawn at any time by a further written notice (s 122(3)).

prescribed form, or in a form substantially to the like effect.[15] The right to buy is not, however, 'exercised' (within s 121) once and for all when the tenant serves his notice of claim. On the contrary, it is 'exercised' at each of a number of separate steps, and may be lost at each hurdle leading to the conveyance or grant of a new lease, because, after all, the secure tenancy is continued until the latter event.[16] The RTB may extend to any land let together with the dwelling-house treated as part of the dwelling-house, and may be included in the notice of claim, unless it is agricultural land exceeding two acres (s 184(1)).[17]

Where the tenant has members of his family (widely defined in s 186(1)) who are not secure tenants but who occupy the dwelling-house as their only or principal home, up to three of these may be included by him in the notice of claim (s 122(1)).[18] However, the benefit of this extension is limited since although the tenant may insist, no matter what the landlord's wishes, in including in his claim notice his spouse or a family member, such as his cohabitee, who has been residing with him throughout the 12 month period ending with the giving of the notice, in the case of any other family member, the landlord must consent to the inclusion of that person (s 123(2)). Where a secure tenant validly required by notice that her daughter should be included in the RTB with her, and died before the completion of the purchase, the daughter, as deemed sole tenant, was as much entitled to require completion under s 138 (below) as would her mother have been, if still alive.[19] By contrast, where a sole secure tenant, who had claimed the RTB, died before she was able to execute a conveyance, the RTB had been lost, since a binding contract had been concluded, so that none could vest in her estate in favour of her daughter.[20]

Should the identity of the secure tenant change, prior to any contract of sale,[1] but after the giving of a notice claiming the RTB, otherwise than under an exchange permitted by s 92, the new tenant is in the same position as if he had given the notice and in all other respects[2] as the tenant who gave the

---

15   The prescribed form is Form No 1 in the Housing (Right to Buy) (Prescribed Forms) Regulations 1986, SI 1986/2194, as amended.

16   *Enfield London Borough Council v McKeon* [1986] 2 All ER 730, CA; hence, there is nothing in Part V of the 1985 Act against a landlord claiming re-possession of the house or flat during the statutory buy-out procedures.

17   Land outside s 184(1) may be included in the tenant's claim to the RTB if he serves a separate, revocable, written notice on the landlord and it is reasonable in all the circumstances for the land to be included (s 184(2) and (3)).

18   The effect of such inclusion, if valid, is that for the purposes of the RTB the tenant and the included family members are treated for RTB purposes (including therefore the conveyance of the property) as joint tenants (s 123(3)).

19   *Harrow London Borough v Tonge* (1992) 25 HLR 99, CA; the effect of death on the RTB is reviewed by Brierley [1995] Conv 114.

20   *Bradford Metropolitan City Council v McMahon* [1993] 4 All ER 237, CA; it appears that no notice had been served under s 136(1) by the daughter at the stage the notice to claim has been served, and none could have been served, it appears, once the binding contract had been concluded.

1   As will appear, once a binding contract of sale is entered into, this ends the secure tenancy and it cannot thereafter be succeeded to: see *Cooper v City of Edinburgh District Council* (1991) 23 HLR 349, HL.

2   Including, therefore, the amount of the discount allowed to the new claimant: see *McIntyre v Merthyr Tydfil Borough Council* (1989) 21 HLR 320, CA.

notice of claim (s 136(1)).[3] A similar rule applies where the identity of the landlord is passed to another landlord after the service of notice of claim on the former landlord (s 137(1)). However, where the new landlord is an exempt landlord (such as a charitable housing trust) then, as the RTB ceases to be exercisable, both sides to the claim must, so far as possible, take steps to see to it that the position is restored to the pre-claim circumstances (s 137(2)).

Procedures after claim notice

1   After a secure tenant has served a RTB claim notice, the landlord must serve a written notice of reply on the tenant, within four weeks, unless the two-year residence period of the tenant included a period of residence under another landlord, in which case the period is eight weeks (s 124(1) and (2)). The notice is in the prescribed form,[4] or in a form substantially to the like effect, and it must either admit the right to buy or deny it. If the latter, the reasons for the non-existence of the right to buy, in the landlord's opinion, must be given.[5]

2   Where the landlord admits the RTB, or it is otherwise established, as in proceedings, the landlord must serve a *notice of the purchase price* under s 125, within eight or twelve weeks, depending on whether the right is to a freehold or long lease (s 125(1)). This notice must, among other things, set out all matters relevant to the eventual conveyance or grant of a long lease, which pertain to the premises, such as a description of the dwelling-house and the price to be paid in the landlord's opinion,[6] including, notably, the amount of the discount to which the tenant is entitled (s 125(2)).[7] Where, in the case of the grant of a lease to the tenant, the landlord would be enabled, in the terms of his notice, to recover from the tenant either service charges or contributions to improvements, the notice must contain estimates and certain other information about these charges (s 125(4)).[8]

3   The same result follows where the tenant who gave a notice of claim when holding a fixed-term secure tenancy holds a secure periodic tenancy under s86 after the expiry of the former tenancy (s 136(2)(b)); and in either case, the original notice of claim would be applicable to any subsequent changed secure tenant (s 136(7)) although in all cases, if the original tenant did not claim to exercise the RTB for family members, his successors cannot alter the notice of claim in that respect (s 136(6)).

4   1986 Regulations, Form No 2.

5   Where a landlord's notice has been served and the tenant changes, the new tenant is bound to serve a notice under s 125D, notably within 12 weeks of his becoming secure tenant (s 136(2)).

6   The tenant must be informed in the s 125 notice of his right to require the price to be determined by the district valuer under s 128 (s 125(5) as substituted).

7   In addition, the notice must set out the value of the house at the date of the notice of claim (s 122(2)), certain tenants' improvements to be disregarded in determining that value (within s 127).

8   The required information about these matters is set out in s 125A and 125B. The notice must also describe any structural defect known to the landlord affecting the premises (s 124(4A)).

3   Following service of the landlord's purchase price notice, the tenant must[9] serve a written notice on the landlord stating either that he intends to pursue the claim to the RTB or that he withdraws it (s 125D).[10]

Price of house or flat

The price payable for the house or flat is governed by the Act and not by the voluntary agreement of the parties, and is made up to two elements:

(a) its value as determined in accordance with s 127;
(b) less the discount to which the tenant is entitled (s 126).

The most important rule is that the *value of the house or flat*, determined as at the date of the notice of claim to the RTB, so that subsequent increases or falls are left out of account, is that the value is the 'price which at that time it would realise if sold on the open market by a willing vendor' but upon certain statutory assumptions (s 127(1)). So as to prevent the secure tenant from paying for the effect of his own improvements, the effect of these is to be disregarded (s 127(1)(b)).[11] The assumptions differ as between conveyances of the freehold and grants of a lease.

In the case of a freehold conveyance, the main assumptions are that the vendor is selling for an estate in fee simple with vacant possession and that neither the tenant nor a resident member of his family wanted to buy (s 127(2)).[12] In the case of the grant of a lease, the main assumptions are that a lease is being granted with vacant possession (see further below) and at a ground rent not exceeding £10 per annum – otherwise they are similar to those for the conveyance of a freehold (s 127(3)).

The *discount due to the tenant* is a percentage applied to reduce the purchase price, by reference to the periods to be taken into account under the Act.[13] In principle,[14] the discount is 32% plus 1% for each complete year by which the qualifying period exceeds two years, with a maximum of 60%, in the case of a house. In the case of a flat, the lowest and highest percentages are 44% and 70% (s 129(2)).[15] A conveyance of the freehold or lease must contain a covenant binding on the secure tenant, which in principle lasts for three years from the

---

9   On penalty of receiving a landlord's default notice under s 125E requiring the service of a s 125D notice within 28 days or the deemed withdrawal of the RTB.
10   He may alternatively serve a notice that he claims to exercise the right to acquire on rent to mortgage terms under s 144 of the Act (s 125D).
11   See *Dickinson v Enfield London Borough Council* [1996] 49 EG 108, CA. The disregard extends to improvements made by any person who was a secure tenant before the secure tenant (whether, therefore, under that or a different tenancy, unless the applicant tenant has a secure tenancy by exchange) and to those made by a member of the applicant tenant's family who, immediately before his secure tenancy was granted, held a secure tenancy of the same dwelling-house (s 127(4)). Any failure by any of these persons to keep the premises in good internal repair is, to any extent relevant, disregarded.
12   The house or flat is to be conveyed with the same rights etc as under Part V of the Act.
13   1985 Act, s 129(1), referring to Sch 4.
14   Subject to the floor set by s 131.
15   These percentages may be varied up or down by regulations (s 129(2A) and 129(2B); and where a previous discount has been given, see s 130.

disposal,[16] to repay the discount if he makes certain types of disposal, notably if he re-conveys the freehold or assigns the lease, and in certain other cases,[17] although disposals to the former secure tenant's spouse or to a resident family member are not caught, nor are disposals under property adjustment orders in divorce proceedings (s 160).[18]

Contract to completion

The Act says little about the position once all the terms have been agreed or determined by the parties other than that the landlord is then under a duty to complete (s 138(1)). If the tenant fails within a reasonable time of receiving a landlord's offer to reply to it, the right to buy lapses, as where a tenant failed for one year to reply to such an offer and had moved to other premises.[19]

Completion duty

As with private-sector enfranchisement schemes, an unwilling landlord against whom the right to buy has been established has no choice but to sell or grant a lease of the property concerned, and on terms as laid down in the Act. Thus, it is provided that once the right to buy has been established by a secure tenant, as soon as all matters relating to the grant have been agreed or determined, the landlord is bound to grant to the tenant the fee simple absolute, in the case of a house, of which the landlord holds the freehold. He is similarly bound to grant a lease of the house if he does not own the freehold or the property is a flat (s 138(1)).[20] The statutory duty is 'enforceable by injunction' (s 138(3)).[1] This duty is almost absolute, and arises after the four stages of the RTB have been successfully passed by the secure tenant, who, once he has become entitled to a conveyance (or lease)[2] has an equitable interest in the house concerned, and so entitled to an injunction, in much the same way as would a purchaser of land not under statutory compulsion be entitled to seek a decree of specific performance.[3] Once the conveyance or lease has been made, pursuant to Part V of the 1985 Act, the secure tenancy comes to an end (s 139(2)).[4]

---

16 And which takes effect as a legal charge on the house or flat: s 156(1).
17 Housing Act 1985, s 155(1); the 'relevant disposals' are listed in s 159(1). The amount to be repaid is reduced by one-third for each complete year elapsing after the RTB was exercised (s 155(2)).
18 See *R v Rushmoor Borough Council, ex p Barrett* [1988] 2 All ER 268, CA.
19 *Sutton London Borough Council v Swann* (1985) 18 HLR 140, CA.
20 While landlords may be entitled, for the sake of administrative convenience, to use standard-form leases, the court reserves the power to strike out unreasonable terms, such as a reservation to a local authority of a right to deal with any land or building near the flat as it thought fit: *Guinan v Enfield London Borough Council* [1996] EGCS 142, CA.
 1 It is not avoided where the tenant has failed to pay rent or other payments such as service charges, due from him as tenant, for a period of four weeks after lawfully demanded, although the landlord is not bound to comply with his duty to convey or lease until the whole of the sums due have been paid (s 138(2)).
 2 Cf *Guinan v Enfield London Borough Council*, supra.
 3 *Dance v Welwyn Hatfield District Council* [1990] 3 All ER 572, [1990] 1 WLR 1097, CA.
 4 Subject to the application of Law of Property Act 1925 s 139 to any sub-tenant.

The Act makes specific provision, in the form of a landlord's first and second notice to complete, so as to require the tenant to complete, once all relevant matters have been agreed or determined.[5] It makes similar provisions enabling the tenant to serve an initial and a further notice of delay on the landlord where he has failed to serve a notice under s 124 or 125 or where he considers that delays of the landlord are preventing him from expeditiously exercising his right to buy (s 153A).

The courts have concluded that the reference in s 138(1) to a 'secure tenant' requires that the tenant must be a secure tenant not only at the date of his claim notice, but throughout the whole period running from then, during negotiations and ending with the date of the conveyance.[6] Thus, where a sole secure tenant had, before any completion date had been agreed, sub-let the whole premises, the right to buy was lost.[7]

Terms of conveyance or lease

The terms of the conveyance or lease are not as negotiated between the parties, but, as might be expected in a scheme such as this, which is weighted in favour of the secure tenant, are those terms laid down in Sch 6 of the Act in detailed provisions which, in the case of the grant of the fee simple, are designed to secure to the tenant the full benefit of that grant. Thus, the tenant is entitled to the benefit of s 62 of the Law of Property Act 1925, as well as to rights of support, passage and related matters which are, as far as possible, as equivalent to the rights he enjoyed with the property as secure tenant.[8] The title to the freehold, and to any lease, whether for not less than 40 years or not, is to be registered, even if the title to the land at that time had not been registered (s 154).

The same policy of maximising benefits for the acquiring secure tenant is seen in the case of leases. So, if at the time of the grant the landlord's leasehold interest is not less than a lease for a term of which more than 125 years and five days are unexpired, the appropriate term is a term of not less than 125 years.[9] Similarly, rights enjoyed in common by the former secure tenant with other tenants are to be inserted in the lease granted under the Act to the same extent.[10] So as to protect the loss of the new lease by the landlord's neglect to comply with his own obligations to his superior landlord, the landlord is under an implied obligation to pay his own rent and to discharge his own leasehold obligations.[11] Since the legislature aims to favour the free transfer of leases granted under

---

5   1985 Act, ss 140 and 141; see *Milne-Berry v Tower Hamlets London Borough Council* [1995] EGCS 86 (notices not void merely by referring to wrong version of Act).
6   *Jennings v Epping Forest District Council* (1992) 25 HLR 241, CA; also *Bradford Metropolitan City Council v McMahon* [1993] 4 All ER 237, [1994] 1 WLR 52, CA.
7   *Jennings v Epping Forest District Council*, supra.
8   1985 Act, Sch 6, para 2. Similarly, the tenant is entitled to the grant of any rights of way within the landlord's power to grant that are necessary for the reasonable enjoyment of the dwelling-house (para 3).
9   Sch 6, para 12(1). Otherwise, the appropriate lease is in principle for a term expiring five days before the term of the landlord's own lease (para 12(2)).
10   Sch 6, para 13.
11   Sch 6, para 15.

these rules, generally speaking, terms purporting to prohibit or restrict the assignment or sub-letting of the lease are void.[12]

In the case of the grant of a long lease, however, the landlord is under a covenant to keep in repair[13] the structure and exterior both of the flat itself and of the building in which it is situated and to make good any defect affecting that structure.[14] Although the tenant is under an implied covenant, which may be varied by the parties, to keep the house in good repair or the interior of the flat in such repair, as the case may be,[15] the width of the landlord's own obligation is such that it could easily extend to the complete rebuilding of the building containing the flat even if the cause were to be an inherent defect unknown at the date the premises were constructed, or at the date of the lease being granted. However, the landlord is entitled to insert service charges clauses in the new lease so as to enable him to recover from the tenant a 'reasonable part' of the costs incurred in complying with his repairing, rebuilding and insuring obligations.[16] While the 1985 Act contains various controls (akin to those which apply to private sector tenants) on the recovery of variable service charges, so that the tenant is not faced with unpredictable levels of future charges, these controls may be avoided by a service charge which is initially fixed and which is subject only to an indexed escalation clause, so as to protect the landlord from the consequences of, for example, rising building costs.[17]

Rent to mortgage scheme

There may be some secure tenants who would like to exercise the right to buy a house or flat but who have not sufficient resources to be able to afford more than an initial deposit.[18] This possibility was foreseen at the time the legislation was introduced, and a right to a mortgage was introduced. So as further to widen the access of this class of tenant to the right to buy, Parliament has abolished the right to a mortgage and replaced it with a 'rent to mortgage' scheme.[19]

The essence of the scheme is as follows.[20] The tenant must first serve a notice of claim to the RTB, and his notice of exercise must still be in force at

---

12 Sch 6, para 17 (1).
13 To which there is linked an implied duty to rebuild or reinstate the premises in the case of damage by fire or other insurable risk (para 14(3)).
14 Sch 6, para 14(2). The county court may authorise the exclusion or modification of these duties (para 14(4)). The duty extends to any property over which the tenant has rights under Sch 6, and the landlord is also bound to ensure, so far as practicable, that services provided by him are maintained at a reasonable level.
15 Sch 6, para 16.
16 Sch 6, para 16A. The tenant's liability is limited for the first five years from the grant of the lease (para 16B).
17 *Coventry City Council v Cole* [1994] 1 All ER 997, [1994] 1 WLR 398, CA.
18 However, a secure tenant who has received housing benefit at any time in, notably, the last 12 months ending with the day of service of notice exercising the rent to mortgage right cannot in fact claim that right (s 143A).
19 The new rules are in Housing Act 1985, Part V, ss 143-151 as substituted or amended by Leasehold Reform, Housing and Urban Development Act 1993, ss 108-117, from 11 November 1993.
20 For a detailed analysis, see Matthews & Millichap, *A Guide to the Leasehold Reform, Housing and Urban Development Act 1993*, ch 9.

the time he claims the rent to mortgage right (s 143(1)). Once the tenant has by notice claimed to exercise the right to rent on mortgage terms, and receives a landlord's notice admitting the claim, the tenant has 12 weeks from service of the landlord's reply notice to inform the landlord that he opts to exercise the right to buy, or to proceed with the rent to mortgage scheme, or to withdraw entirely from both (s 146A).

Should the tenant in fact be able to pay most of the purchase price out of his own resources, either outright, or where the rent payable would be the equivalent of notional mortgage repayments by instalments, the right to rent to mortgage is excluded.[1] However, if the tenant is entitled to proceed with the exercise of a right to rent to mortgage, the rules envisage that, once he pays his initial deposit, the whole of the remaining price of the house or flat concerned is left outstanding. Subject to the same conditions as apply to the RTB, the tenant obtains a conveyance of the house or a lease of the flat concerned (s 150).

Since the tenant has not paid the whole purchase price, he is entitled to leave the balance of the price outstanding, and the conveyance (or lease) must include a covenant to repay the outstanding amount where the house or flat is disposed of to a person who is not the spouse of the secure tenant or is left in the secure tenant's will or is transferred in divorce proceedings. This covenant binds him and his successors in title.[2]

---

1   The statutory formulae for calculating these limits are in Housing Act 1985, s 143B and appropriate regulations.
2   Housing Act 1985, Sch 6A, para 1; however, the secure tenant and his successors in title may repay the amount outstanding at any time, following a notice procedure (para 2). This contingent liability to repay must be secured by a mortgage (s 151B).

Chapter 20

Special residential tenancies provisions

I GENERAL INTRODUCTION

Statute does not merely provide security of tenure to certain residential tenants. Parliament has provided a battery of rules aimed at combatting particular types of abuse by landlords of their superior bargaining strength in the residential sector. These specific rules may be termed information rules (about rent books and the like), anti-eviction rules, buy-out enabling provisions, and provisions aimed at overcharging for services.

Thus, statute gives short residential tenants, who pay the rent weekly, and who may be specially vulnerable, the right to information about the rent payable and the terms of their tenancy, by requiring the landlord to provide a rent book. In addition, both residential tenants and licensees are entitled, even if they may not have any security of tenure, to a notice to quit both for a minimum four week period, and in a prescribed form, so preventing the landlord from serving an oral notice or a written notice which might be unclear as to the date for quitting. Parliament has not been content to leave the protection of residential tenants against illegal eviction or harassment to the common law implied covenant for quiet enjoyment (see chapter 6). It has enacted two codes which give statutory protection against illegal eviction and harassment, one of which imposes criminal penalties on the landlord, and the more recent of which provides for a specific (and penal) statutory method of calculation of damages for illegal eviction. This is designed to rob the landlord of any profit he may have made from his illegal eviction, as where a landlord evicts a Rent Act protected or statutory tenant and replaces him with an assured tenant.

Residential tenants, especially of flats, may hold their leases under a scheme whereby the landlord is responsible for major structural repairs and for outside decoration, and is entitled under the lease to collect service charges from individual tenants, sometimes through the medium of a management company. The lease may also entitle the landlord to impose service charges for services such as lifts, cleaning of common parts, grounds maintenance and the like. There is a clear danger that a landlord or his managing agent[1] might exploit the

---

1 The Statute also gives recognised tenants' associations consultation and information rights where the landlord proposes to employ a managing agent as well as where such is employed (Landlord and Tenant Act 1985, s 30B, inserted by the Landlord and Tenant Act 1987, s 44).

privilege of recovery of charges, by overcharging, and the courts interpret service charges clauses strictly so as to combat such abuses, and they are astute to prevent landlords from charging for work not literally within the scope of a clause. Statute provides for consultation procedures for most work which is not trivial in nature.

Long lessees of flats may invoke the Landlord and Tenant Act 1987, Part I of which allows them to claim and exercise a statutory right of first refusal if the landlord sells, mortgages or otherwise disposes of his freehold interest. Part III provides for a compulsory buy-out of the landlord, notably where he has seriously and persistently neglected his repairing obligations, to the detriment of the value, and so the marketability, of individual flats. The 1987 Act had been passed as a result of the deliberations of the Nugee Committee[2] which had reported into management problems in the case of certain long leasehold flats – such as gross neglect by landlords to comply with their repairing obligations or failure to collect service charges and so build up a fund to pay for repairs and related work. It should now be read in the light of the more recent enactment of Part I of the Leasehold Reform, Housing and Urban Development Act 1993, enabling the buy-out of the freeholder by a majority of long lessees, even where there has been no attempt by the freeholder to dispose of his interest (see chapter 21). Whichever complex statute the lessees act under, they will acquire the building in its then state and condition, however dilapidated.

II   INFORMATION RULES

Provision of rent book

Where a tenant has the right to occupy premises as a residence in consideration of a rent payable weekly, the landlord must, by s 4(1) of the Landlord and Tenant Act 1985, provide a rent book or similar document.[3] 'Tenant' includes a statutory tenant and a person with a contractual right to occupy the premises (s 4(3)). Therefore, the statutory duty applies to occupation of a residence at a weekly rent whether under a common-law tenancy, or statutorily protected tenancy including protected or assured tenancies, secure tenancies and also under licence.

However, the rent must be payable weekly, or the duty does not apply, but the length of the tenancy need not necessarily be weekly, so that if a tenant holds under a monthly tenancy with the rent payable weekly, the duty applies; if it happens that the rent is payable monthly, it does not. If there is a term of years and the rent is payable weekly, then the duty to provide a rent book applies. The operation of the duty is thus quite fortuitous and it is difficult at first blush to see why the present obligation is confined to tenancies with a rent payable weekly, as opposed to those where the rent may be monthly or quarterly.

---

2   Analysed by Hawkins [1986] Conv 14.
3   This duty does not, by s 4(2) of the 1985 Act, apply where the rent includes a payment in respect of board where the value thereof forms a substantial proportion of the whole rent. Any failure to comply with the various statutory duties is an offence (s 7).

A rent book must state the name and address of the landlord (s 5(1)). If the tenancy is a protected or statutory tenancy or an assured tenancy then particulars must be given of the rent and of the matters prescribed by regulations.[4]

Prescribed form of notice to quit

By s 5(1) of the Protection from Eviction Act 1977, no notice by a landlord or a tenant to quit any premises let as a dwelling is valid unless it is in writing and is given not less than four weeks before the date on which it is to take effect. Moreover, the notice, if served[5] by either side, must contain prescribed information.[6] By s 5(1A), the same rule applies to periodic licences; but not to a licence which is expressed to be terminable with the licensee's employment.[7] It does not apply to excluded tenancies or licences, nor to tenants at will.[8]

III PROTECTION AGAINST UNLAWFUL EVICTION, HARASSMENT AND EVICTION[9]

Unlawful eviction

By s 1(2) of the Protection from Eviction Act 1977, it is an offence if any person unlawfully deprives a residential occupier of his occupation of the premises or of any part thereof, or for that person to attempt to do so.[10] It is a defence if the person evicting the occupier proves that he believed, and had reasonable cause to believe, that the residential occupier had ceased to reside in the premises. To amount to an offence, a deprivation of occupation must have the character of eviction: an exclusion from premises for a day and a night was outside s 1(2).[11] However, it seems that an offence may be constituted even though the eviction may not be permanent, if there is an intention to deprive the occupier of his occupation by eviction.[12] The person accused has a defence if he is able to prove that he believed with reasonable cause that the residential occupier had ceased to reside on the premises.

---

4 Rent Books (Forms of Notice) Regulations 1982, SI 1982/1474 as amended.
5 In *Wandsworth London Borough Council v Atwell* [1995] EGCS 68 it was held that where a tenancy agreement did not expressly incorporate s 196 of the Law of Property Act 1925, the landlord could serve a notice to quit by leaving it at the tenancy address and failed to prove service, the tenant being absent from the premises.
6 Notices to Quit (Prescribed Information) Regulations 1988, SI 1988/2201.
7 *Norris v Checksfield* [1991] 4 All ER 327, CA.
8 *Crane v Morris* [1965] 3 All ER 77, [1965] 1 WLR 1104, CA.
9 For a comprehensive analysis of the criminal law principles applicable see ATH Smith, *Property Offences*, ch 16.
10 Civil remedies remain available to a residential tenant who is unlawfully evicted or harassed: s 1(5) of the 1977 Act.
11 *R v Yuthiwattana* (1984) 80 Cr App Rep 55, CA.
12 ATH Smith, para 16-10, noting that if L evicts T in that sense and then repents, he could still be convicted under s 1. There is, indeed, no provision in s 1 comparable to that of Housing Act 1988, s 27(7), allowing for mitigation of a damages award if the landlord repents and re-admits the tenant to occupation.

The wide term 'any person' means that s 1 applies both to landlords and licensors, which is no doubt deliberate. The term 'residential occupier' is defined (s 1(1)) as a person occupying the premises as a residence, whether under a contract, statute or rule of law. It therefore includes tenants, licensees, lodgers and statutory tenants under the Rent Act 1977, assured and excluded tenants under the Housing Act 1988 and secure tenants. It seems, though the point is not settled, that the protection of s 1 may extend to the tenant's wife, where she does not hold the tenancy jointly with him, as her occupation is through that of her husband.[13]

Damages for occupier

A residential occupier (a term to be understood as for s 1 of the Protection from Eviction Act 1977) has a right to claim damages in two cases, by s 27 of the Housing Act 1988. These provisions may deter landlords from procuring an unlawful eviction of a residential tenant whose presence on the premises is inconvenient to the landlord, as where he has a statutory or assured tenant and prefers to be able to re-let to the same or a different tenant on what is now a wholly insecure assured shorthold tenancy. The purpose of the legislation has been said to be to deprive the landlord of any profit that his wrongful eviction has released, but the Act does not intend to fine the landlord.[14]

The first case is where a landlord (referred to as the 'landlord in default') or any person acting on his behalf unlawfully deprives the occupier of his occupation of the whole or part of the premises (s 27(1)). 'Landlord' is defined (s 27(9)(c)) as the person who, but for the occupier's right to occupy, would be entitled to occupation of the premises and any superior landlord under whom he derives title. This definition was held to include, on a beneficial construction, a landlord-purchaser entitled in equity to the immediate reversion pending completion.[15] It also appears to extend to the wife of a landlord who occupies parts of the premises through her husband as his licensee.[16] The words 'any person acting on behalf of the landlord in default' cannot however extend the scope of the Act to agency and employment by the landlord: a person employed to evict the tenant or to manage the property in such a way as to procure his departure was thus not liable with the landlord as a joint tortfeasor. The statutory language made it clear that the landlord alone is liable.[17]

The second case applies where these persons are guilty of an attempt unlawfully to deprive the occupier of his occupation, or are guilty of knowing harassment, as a result of which the occupier gives up occupation of the

---

13 See ATH Smith, para 16-09: s 1 might extend to any occupying member of the tenant's family.

14 *Melville v Bruton* [1996] EGCS 57, CA; it was said that with the increasing use of assured shorthold tenancies, the incentive on landlord to use illegal evictions might decrease; *sed quaere*: some tenants may hold assured tenancies. The replacement provisions of Housing Act 1988, Sch 2A, para 7(2) may be open to abuse (ch 18).

15 *Jones v Miah* [1992] 2 EGLR 50, CA: the fact that, as against the vendor, the landlord, pending completion, held only a revocable licence made no difference.

16 *Sullman v Little*, Current Law Week, 1993, Issue 29, p 2 (Cty Ct).

17 *Sampson v Wilson* (1995) 70 P & CR 359, CA.

premises as a residence (s 27(2)). The acts of harassment are described as acts calculated to interfere with the peace or comfort of the residential occupier or members of his household, or persistent withdrawal or withholding of services. The acts must be done with an intent akin to that required for the offence of harassment (below). The sort of conduct here envisaged might include intimidation of the kind which is also capable of constituting a breach of the implied covenant for quiet enjoyment.

If the former occupier is reinstated as residential occupier before proceedings to enforce the liability are finally disposed of, there is no statutory liability (s 27(6)(a)).[18] This is also the case where the court, at the request of the occupier, orders his reinstatement (s 27(6)(b)). Re-instatement has been held not to consist in handing the tenant back a key to a lock which did not work and allowing her to resume occupation of a totally wrecked room; if the tenant does not wish to be re-instated, it is difficult to see how s 27(6) can apply.[19] The court, by s 27(7), may reduce the damages to such amount as it thinks appropriate, if:

(a) prior to the event concerned, the conduct of the occupier or a person living with him is such that it is reasonable to mitigate the damages for which the landlord is liable;[20] or
(b) before proceedings were begun, the landlord offered reinstatement and it was unreasonable for the occupier to refuse it, or, if offered alternative accommodation before that offer, that it was unreasonable to him to refuse the offer if he had not obtained the accommodation.

Where there is liability, the landlord is liable to pay the former occupier damages 'in respect of his loss of the right to occupy[21] the premises in question as his residence' (s 27(3)). Liability is in the nature of a tortious liability, and is additional to any other liability in contract or tort (s 27(4)). But damages cannot be awarded for the same loss both under s 27 and under common-law liability (s 27(5)). This has been taken to mean that the claimant may pursue two claims, but that the lesser sum awarded will be deducted from the larger sum.[1] The person liable has a statutory defence similar to that as under s 1 of the Protection from Eviction Act 1977 (s 27(8)).

Damages are based, by s 28(1), on the difference in value, as at the time immediately before the residential occupier ceased to occupy the premises as his residence, between:

(a) the value of the landlord's interest[2] on the assumption that the occupier has a continuing right of occupation; and
(b) the value of the landlord's interest on the assumption that the occupier ceased to have that right.

---

18 See *Murray v Aslam* (1994) 27 HLR 284, CA.
19 *Tagro v Cafane* [1991] 2 All ER 235, [1991] 1 WLR 378, CA.
20 Eg non-payment of rent without prior notice or justification: *Regalgrand Ltd v Dickerson* [1996] 3 EGCS 182, CA
21 This term expressly includes, by s 27(9)(b), any restriction on the right of any person to recover possession of the premises.
1   *Mason v Nwokorie* [1994] 1 EGLR 59, CA.
2   Ie the landlord's interest in the building (s 28(2)), not just the part occupied by the occupier, if less extensive.

Valuations for the purpose of assessing damages are to be based on objective criteria set out in s 28(3), which are: that the landlord is assumed to be selling his interest on the open market to a willing buyer, that neither the occupier nor any member of his family[3] wishes to buy, and that any substantial development (defined by s 28(6)) or demolition of the building is unlawful.

The comparisons are between the value of the landlord's interest incumbered and unincumbered by the tenant's interest, owing to the aim of the Act. It is to rob the landlord of any illegitimate profit made from an illegal eviction. The valuations must be factual and not notional. Otherwise the landlord would be paying a fine. So where a set of valuations had been reached assuming vacant possession, ignoring the fact that the evicted tenant had only an assured shorthold tenancy and that there remained other tenants in the premises, an award of damages of £15,000 was reduced to £500 on appeal.[4] By contrast, where a valuer with local knowledge concluded that a business tenancy held by a mesne landlord who had illegally evicted a residential tenant should be valued on the basis that it 'could go on virtually for ever', even though theoretically it could be terminated on one month's notice, an award of £31,000 damages, though high, was not disturbed on appeal.[5] It was held correct in law for a judge to value the landlord's interest on the basis of what he paid for his interest with vacant possession, and then to take into account the value of each individual tenant's interest.[6]

Harassment

Under s 1(3) of the Protection from Eviction Act 1977, it is an offence, if any person with intent to cause the residential occupier (as defined above) of any premises either:

(a) to give up the occupation of the premises or any part thereof; or
(b) to refrain from exercising any right or pursuing any remedy in respect of the premises or part thereof

does acts likely to interfere with the peace or comfort of the residential occupier or members of his household, or persistently withdraws or withholds services reasonably required for the occupation of the premises as a residence. An act of harassment may constitute an offence under s 1(3) even if it is not an actionable wrong, if done with the purpose or motive of causing a residential occupier to give up his occupation.[7]

It is an offence under s 1(3A) for the landlord (defined in s 1(3C)) of a residential occupier or his agent to:

(a) do acts likely to interfere with the peace or comfort of the residential occupier of members of his household; or

---

3　As defined in Housing Act 1985 s 113, applied by s 28(5).
4　*Melville v Bruton* [1996] EGCS 57, CA.
5　*Tagro v Cafane* [1991] 2 All ER 235, CA; however it appears that the landlord did not challenge the evidence which formed the basis of the valuation.
6　*Jones v Miah* [1992] 2 EGLR 50, CA.
7　*R v Burke* [1991] 1 AC 135, [1990] 2 All ER 385, HL.

(b) persistently to withdraw or withhold services reasonably required for the occupation of the premises as a residence

and in either case he knows or has reasonable cause to believe that the conduct is likely to cause the residential occupier to give up the occupation of the whole or part of the premises or to refrain from exercising any right of pursuing any remedy in respect of the whole or part of the premises.[8]

The penalties for harassment are the same as for unlawful eviction (see above) and, similarly, civil remedies in respect of it are expressly preserved (s 1(5)). For example, there may be a contractual action for breach of the covenant, express or implied, for quiet enjoyment; and an occupier may even be granted a mandatory injunction to ensure access to and occupation of the premises, pending trial of the main action.[9]

Restriction on re-entry without due process of law

Section 2 of the 1977 Act provides that, where any premises are let as a dwelling on a lease which is subject to a right of re-entry or forfeiture, it is unlawful to enforce that right save by proceedings in court, while any person is lawfully residing in the premises or part of them.

Prohibition on eviction without due process of law

Under s 3(1) of the 1977 Act, where any premises have been let as a dwelling under a tenancy which is *not* a statutorily protected tenancy (defined s 8(1)) nor an excluded tenancy[10] and:

(a) the former tenancy has come to an end, but
(b) the occupier continues to reside in the premises or part of them

then it is unlawful for the owner to enforce against the occupier his right to regain possession of the premises, otherwise than by proceedings in court. The term 'occupier' is widely defined (s 3(2)) so that it means any person lawfully residing in the premises at the termination of the former tenancy; and, by s 3(2A), the above restriction is extended to a restricted contract under the Rent Act 1977 which creates a licence. By s 3(3), the general prohibition of s 3(1) applies where an owner has the right to recover possession after the death of a statutory tenant under the Rent Act 1977 or the Rent (Agriculture) Act 1976, as the case may be.

These rules apply to residential licences, provided that the licence is not excluded but whether entered into before or after the commencement of Part I of the Housing Act 1988 (s 3(2B)).[10a]

---

8 Under s 1(3B) if the person proves that he had reasonable grounds for his actions, he is not liable.
9 *Luganda v Service Hotels Ltd* [1969] 2 Ch 209, [1969] 2 All ER 692, CA.
10 This includes, for example, a protected tenancy under the Rent Act 1977, but not a statutory tenancy. Thus, where a landlord obtained an order for possession against a statutory tenant, the protection of s 3 applied until the court bailiff duly executed the court's order: see *Haniff v Robinson* [1993] 1 All ER 185.
10a But an occupier of an hotel room, lacking exclusive possession of his room, was not within s 3(2B): *Brillouet v Landless* (1995) 28 HLR 837, CA.

Section 3 does not apply to any excluded tenancy or licence. The result is to render it easier for landlords to recover possession of residential premises which are shared with the occupier by himself or his family. This is because no security is enjoyed as an excluded tenancy cannot be assured, since the landlord must be resident, and s 3 of the 1977 Act is also not applicable. Eviction without a statutory requirement of legal process is possible in the case of excluded tenancies and licences.

By s 3A(2) and (3) a tenancy or licence is excluded if, under its terms:

1   The occupier shares any accommodation with the landlord or licensor and, immediately before the grant and when the tenancy or licence ends, the landlord occupied as his only or principal home the shared accommodation, or that plus other accommodation.[11]

2   The occupier shares any accommodation with a member of the landlord's or licensor's family (as defined in s 3A(5)) and, immediately before the grant and also when the tenancy ended, the family member occupied as his only or principal residence premises of which the whole or part of the shared accommodation formed part, and, immediately before the grant of the tenancy etc and when it ends, the landlord occupied as his only or principal home premises in the same building. If the building is a purpose-built block of flats (defined as for the resident landlord exclusion from assured tenancies) the tenancy etc is not excluded. An occupier 'shares' accommodation if he has the use of it in common with another person (s 3A(4)). Certain other types of tenancy or licence are excluded from the 1977 Act, such as a right to occupy the premises for a holiday or gratuitously (s 3A(7)) even though there may be no sharing.

If the landlord flouts s 3 of the 1977 Act, as where he resorts to forcible or peaceable re-entry without a court order, or where, after 9 June 1988, following an order of the court, he forcibly ejects the tenant, he will face a potentially heavy liability in damages under s 27 of the Housing Act 1988.[12]

IV   LONG TENANT'S RIGHT OF FIRST REFUSAL

Introduction

Part I of the Landlord and Tenant Act 1987[13] confers on qualifying tenants of residential flats a right to a first refusal where the landlord disposes of his interest in the premises. The aim of this legislation is to allow such tenants to buy out the transferring or the new landlord. However, the attainment of this object is weakened by the sheer complexity of the Act. Part I of the 1987 Act

---

11   Accommodation within these rules does not include storage areas, passages, corridors or other areas of access, nor staircases.

12   As in *Haniff v Robinson*, supra, where an award of £28,300 damages for forcible ejection of a statutory tenant, computed under s 28 of the 1988 Act, was upheld.

13   Parts II and VI are discussed in chs 9 and 8. For critiques of the Act, see Percival (1988) 51 MLR 97; Rogers [1988] Conv 122; PF Smith (1992) 12 LS 41.

has been judicially stigmatised as ill-drafted, complicated and confused.[14] In a more recent case, it was said that the legal profession appeared to be the main beneficiaries of this Act, which had also been said to allow no room, by reason of the complexity of its provisions, for arguments based on common sense.[15] It will therefore be appreciated that it is only possible in what follows to give some essential matters in relation to Part I of the 1987 Act.

Scope of Part I

The statutory right of first refusal applies only to tenants holding long leases of residential flats occupied for residential purposes, as opposed to, notably, business or assured tenancies. In particular, the premises must consist of the whole or part of a building containing two or more flats held by qualifying tenants. To prevent a minority of tenants buying out the landlord, the number of such flats must exceed half the total number of flats in the premises (s 1(2)). Essentially, a qualifying tenant is a tenant of a flat holding under a long lease (s 3). Where an estate had been registered under two titles, the claim of the long lessees of one block of flats in the estate could nevertheless be dealt with on its own merits, as the expression 'premises' referred to that block and not to the whole estate.[16]

The most frequent type of disposal which will trigger the right of first refusal is, no doubt, a sale, grant of a reversionary lease (for perhaps a longer period than that of the leases of individual tenants of the flats) or a mortgage by the landlord. Certain types of disposal fall outside Part I of the 1987 Act, notably, disposals under a will or in insolvency, or gifts to a member of the landlord's family or to an associated company of the landlord (s 4). The policy of these exclusions seems to be that voluntary disposals for a substantial money consideration, especially as these might be deliberately intended to evade the statutory right of first refusal, are to be caught but not those which are involuntary or for no or no substantial consideration.

Operation of Part I

Part I of the 1987 Act works by means of a series of notices, one to be served by the landlord who wishes to dispose of his interest, as by selling or leasing it and then followed by an acceptance notice from the tenants, who then appoint a nominee purchaser, who deals on their behalf with the landlord and who, it is hoped, acquires the landlord's interest under a contract within the Act. There are also provisions, which were probably originally intended as fall-back devices, to cover cases where the landlord disposes of his interest in defiance of the Act to a purchaser or lessee.

An attempt has been made by amendments in the Housing Act 1996 both to streamline the 1987 Act procedures and to impose penalties for non-

---

14 *Denetower Ltd v Toop* [1991] 3 All ER 661, 668, CA.
15 *Belvedere Court Management Ltd v Frogmore Developments Ltd* [1996] 1 All ER 312, 331, CA (Sir Thomas Bingham MR).
16 *Kay Green v Twinsectra Ltd* [1996] 4 All ER 546, CA.

compliance with the rules or for delays. It remains to be seen whether these will draw the sting from the criticisms of the Act. The principal rules may be summarised as follows.

1   Where the landlord proposes to make a disposal, such as by sale or lease of his interest, which will often be the freehold, he is supposed to serve an offer notice under s 5 of the Act. It must be served on all, or at least 90%, of the qualifying tenants of the flats concerned (s 5(1) and (4)(a)). If there are fewer than ten qualifying tenants, a notice should be served on all but one of them (s 5(4)(b)). The notice must comply with formalities. It must include particulars of the principal terms of the proposed disposal, the property to which it relates and the estate or interest proposed to be disposed of and the consideration required by the landlord. It should give a minimum two-month period for acceptance of the offer and specify a further two-month period after the end of the acceptance period, for nomination by the qualifying tenants of a person to acquire the landlord's interest (s 5(2)).

2   The notification requirement has sometimes been flouted. It is now an offence punishable on summary conviction with a fine at level five on the standard scale, for a landlord without reasonable excuse not to comply with s 5.[17] The deterrent effect of this type of penalty may be doubted as it remains to be seen how often prosecutions are brought for contravention of this provision.

3   In any case, there is an alternative route to the exercise of a right to buy out the landlord's interest. First, where s 3 of the Landlord and Tenant Act 1985 applies (see chapter 5) not only must the purchaser-landlord give any qualifying tenant within Part I of the 1987 Act notice of the assignment: he must serve a further notice complying with s 3A of that Act.[18] The object of this requirement is to make sure, if possible, that the assignee informs the tenant concerned that the disposal falls within Part I of the 1987 Act (if indeed it does). The tenant is entitled to information about the disposal and to be told that he may acquire the purchasing landlord's interest, as well as about the time he may have to do so. Failure to comply without reasonable excuse with this requirement within the time allowed for service of s 3 notices (usually by the next rent day) is a criminal offence punishable on summary conviction with a fine not exceeding level 4 on the standard scale.

In any case, upon receipt of notification of assignment or a rent demand from the new freeholder, the qualifying tenants may serve a purchase notice, which must be in writing, on him under s 12 requiring the sale to them of his interest, although if a notice omits one flat this will not in itself prejudice its validity. This provision has been held to be mandatory since, first, it has sufficient language to support that result by necessary implication (notably the use of the expression 'required') and second, it would frustrate the

17   Landlord and Tenant Act 1987, s 10A (inserted by Housing Act 1996, s 91 as from 1 October 1996: SI 1996/2212). This penalty applies also to landlords' contraventions of ss 6 to 10 of the 1987 Act.
18   Inserted into Landlord and Tenant Act 1985 by Housing Act 1996, s 93, in force on 1 October 1996: SI 1996/2212.

purpose of Part I of the 1987 Act if such were not the result.[19] Since ss 47 and 48 of the 1987 Act require the new landlord to supply particulars of his name and address to the tenants on pain of non-recovery of rent, and of service charges, this particular procedure may also be of importance to tenants of flats who wish to buy out the new landlord who obtained his interest in contravention of Part I of the 1987 Act. A person considering purchasing an interest who might then be caught by a tenant's right of first refusal has the right to serve on any persons who might be entitled to exercise statutory rights an information notice under s 18, so safeguarding himself and allowing himself the possibility of withdrawal from any draft contract with the landlord.

4   The requisite majority of qualifying tenants may serve an acceptance notice on the landlord if he has served a s 5 notice on them.[20] The notice must be served within the period specified for acceptance in the landlord's offer notice (s 6(1)). That period is a minimum period of two months from date of service of the s 5 notice. During the time allowed for service of an acceptance notice, the landlord cannot dispose of the interest in question (s 5(2A)). All qualifying tenants who wish to accept the landlord's offer must sign any s 6 notice and where one such tenant withdrew his consent to a s 6 notice, so reducing the number of accepting tenants below the minimum level to qualify for purchase, no valid notice had been served.[1] It made no difference that the tenant concerned had agreed not to withdraw. Moreover, for all its complexity, the 1987 Act did not impose a formal requirement on any expression by a qualifying tenant of a desire to withdraw.

5   Once validly served by the tenants, an acceptance notice precludes the landlord from disposing of the 'protected interest' (ie the interest he proposes to dispose of, such as his freehold interest by assignment) from the date of service of the acceptance notice until either of two dates. One is the end of the period specified by the landlord's offer notice for appointing a nominated person (s 6(2)(a)). The other is that, if a person is nominated, for that period plus a further three months (s 6(2)(b)).[2] If no timely acceptance notice is served on the landlord, he has a twelve month period in which he may dispose of the interest concerned outside Part I of the 1987 Act (s 7).

6   Let us suppose that the landlord has served his offer notice on the tenants and they have replied with an acceptance notice. The landlord may then serve a further notice on the nominee purchaser of the tenants, who it is hoped will by then have been appointed to act for them. In that notice the landlord may state his intention to withdraw from the relevant disposal. Alternatively, he must send to the nominee purchaser a 'requisite contract'. This is a contract for the acquisition by the latter of the landlord's interest

---

19   *Kay Green v Twinsectra Ltd* [1996] 4 All ER 546, CA.
20   The requisite majority is ascertained by s 5(6), and is, essentially, 50% or more of the qualifying tenants – one vote per flat.
1   *Mainwaring v Henry Smith's Charity Trustees (No 2)* [1996] EGCS 152, CA.
2   The landlord must use his best endeavours to obtain any necessary consents to the disposal (s 6(7)).

(s 8). The policy of Part I of the 1987 Act, as revised, is to make for speed and finality. Hence, the nominee purchaser has only two months from the date of the sending of this contract in which to offer an exchange of contracts to the landlord. In this case the nominee purchaser signs the statutory standard form contract and pays a 10% deposit. Alternatively, he himself may serve notice of intention not to proceed (s 8(4)). If the latter option is adopted, the landlord is free to dispose of the interest concerned – but not of any other interest – for a twelve month period from the expiry of the nominee purchaser's notice, outside the 1987 Act (s 8(5)).

7   Supposing that the landlord disposes of his interest where Part I applies, without complying with it, the requisite majority of qualifying tenants have the right to serve a notice on the new landlord, whom they will find out about once he has demanded rent or service charges or both, if not sooner, requiring information as to the disposal (s 11). Thereafter, they may operate a purchase notice procedure (s 12), as noted above, which requires the assignee to transfer the interest concerned to a person nominated by the tenants. In this way, it is hoped, flouting of the Act is circumvented. A tenant's purchase notice may include not only the bricks and mortar of the actual building housing the flats, but any garden and appurtenances demised with them.[3] Where flats in different blocks are held as part of one scheme, a single s 12 notice appears to suffice for the whole scheme.[4]

Disputes under Part I are regulated as follows. A rent assessment committee has jurisdiction to determine 'any question arising in relation to any matters specified in a purchase notice' – such as the price payable for the freehold or any other terms of the disposal (s 13(1)).[5] By contrast, the county court has jurisdiction to determine the extent of any property which the nominee purchaser is entitled to acquire, as a preliminary step to determining the validity of a purchase notice.[6]

V   COMPULSORY ACQUISITION

Part III of the 1987 Act enables long residential tenants[7] of a block of flats, or a majority of them, to buy out the landlord's interest compulsorily, by court order, made on account of the landlord's gross neglect of his repairing and related obligations. The tenants must serve a preliminary notice of warning and intention (s 27) on the landlord as a condition precedent to applying to the court. This notice, which resembles a statutory forfeiture notice, must allow the landlord a reasonable time to remedy the breaches alleged, and the landlord must have failed within that time to comply with it, which latter may not be a

---

3   *Denetower Ltd v Toop* [1991] 3 All ER 661, [1991] 1 WLR 945, CA.
4   *30 Upperton Gardens Management Ltd v Akano* [1990] 2 EGLR 232 (LVT).
5   See eg *Cousins v Metropolitan Guarantee Ltd* [1989] 2 EGLR 223; *Gregory v Saddiq* [1991] 1 EGLR 237; *Newman v Kay* [1991] 2 EGLR 237; *Nolan v Eagle Wharf Developments Ltd* [1992] 2 EGLR 223 (LVT).
6   *Denetower v Toop*, supra; *Saga Properties v Palmeira Square Nos 2-6 Ltd* [1995] 1 EGLR 199.
7   Ie those holding terms certain exceeding 21 years (s 59(3)).

difficult condition to satisfy if the landlord has seriously defaulted to date. The court order provides for the acquisition by a nominee purchaser, such as a tenant-controlled off-the-shelf company, of the landlord's interest on terms as agreed by the parties or determined, in default, by a leasehold valuation tribunal (s 30). The court may only make an order if one of two conditions has been satisfied.

1 The landlord is in breach of any obligation under the leases relating to the repair, maintenance, insurance or management of the premises or any part; that the breaches are likely to continue (s 29(2)).[8]
2 At the date of the making of the application and for three years (from 1 October 1996, when s 88 of the Housing Act 1996 commenced[8a] this period will be shortened to two years) immediately preceding that date, an appointment of a manager under Part II was in force (s 29(3)).

VI VARIATION OF LONG LEASES OF FLATS

Part IV of the 1987 Act enables the county court to make an order varying the provisions of an individual long lease of a flat (defined as for Part III) on various grounds, where the lease fails to make satisfactory provision with respect to:

(a) the repair or maintenance of the flat or of the building containing the flat or of any land or building let to the tenant under the lease or in respect of which rights are conferred on him under it (s 35(2)(a));
(b) the insurance of the flat or building or land (s 35(1)(b));
(c) the repair or maintenance of any installations (in the same building as the flat or not) which are reasonably necessary to ensure that occupiers of the flat enjoy a reasonable standard of accommodation (s 35(1)(c));
(d) the provision or maintenance of services necessary to ensure the above standard (s 35(1)(d));
(e) the recovery by one party from another of expenditure incurred or to be incurred by him for the benefit of that party or him and others (s 35(1)(e));
(f) for the computation of service charges (s 35(1)(f)).

No application may be made if Part II of the Landlord and Tenant Act 1954 applies to the long lease in question (s 35(7)).

An application may be made by one party or by two or more parties in respect of their leases – as opposed to an individual application under s 35. In this case, the leases need not be in the same building, nor drafted identically (s 37(2)). To protect other tenants, the application cannot be made unless a majority of the tenants concerned consent.

The court has a general power to vary the lease (or leases) the subject-matter of the application, whether individual or collective, in such manner as specified in the order (s 38(1)). If grounds are established for some but not all leases, then the court only has power to vary the leases in respect of which

8 See *Gray v Standard Home and Counties Properties Ltd* [1994] 1 EGLR 119.
8a SI 1997/2212.

grounds have been established (s 38(4)). As an alternative to variation orders, the court may direct the parties to vary the lease as specified (s 38(8)). If the variation would be likely to prejudice any respondent or any person not a party and an award of financial compensation under s 38(10) would not be adequate, the court cannot order variation (s 38(6)). Special rules limit the power of the court in relation to any variation of the insurance provisions of the lease (s 38(7)).

A variation order will bind third parties and their predecessors in title (s 39(1)) and any surety who has guaranteed performance of any leasehold obligation (s 39(2)).

The service of notices on respondents and on any person whom the applicant knows or has reason to believe will be affected by the application are governed by rules of court (s 35(5)). If a person entitled to a notice does not receive one, he is both entitled to an action for damages for breach of statutory duty and to apply to the court for cancellation or modification of the variation (s 39(3)).

In the case only of insurance and the recovery of insurance costs, where a long lease of a dwelling fails to make satisfactory provision for these matters, Part IV applies with certain modifications (s 40(1)); the scope of this provision is limited since it does not apply to flats,[9] which are however within s 35(1).

Part IV of the 1987 Act is presumably intended to enable the curing of defects in the repairing or maintenance obligations under leases, which are necessary in the interests of the proper management of the block of flats as a whole.

VII   CONTROL OF LEVYING OF SERVICE CHARGES

Common law

Service charges are sometimes levied against lessees of flats by landlords, who may use a managing agent or surveyor to collect the sums from each lessee. Sometimes, the charges are reserved as rent, so that their non-payment incurs a forfeiture, and the right to distrain for them. The charges may be paid in advance or in arrear and the exact items of work to be recovered for are a question of fact depending on the terms of each clause. It is not unusual to specify a right to recover in respect of repairing, maintenance and insurance costs incurred by the landlord, as well as any costs incurred in the provision of specified services such as lifts, cleaning of common parts and garage user. There may be a sweeping up clause, such as a right to charge for 'beneficial services', but in one case, such words did not of themselves entitle the landlord to charge for repairs or decorations.[10]

In order to counteract the obvious dangers posed by the landlord's privilege of levying service charges, notably the twin traps of overcharging and of charging for non-recoverable items, the courts insist that, provided that sense

9   *John Lyon School Governors v Haysport Properties Ltd* [1995] EGCS 171.
10   *Lloyds Bank plc v Bowker Orford* [1992] 2 EGLR 44.

can be made of a clause, it will be construed as covering the items listed and no others not literally specified or within the general intent of the words used. Thus, a clause entitling a landlord to recover for legal and other costs incurred in obtaining service charges from any tenant, from lessees generally, was confined to costs incurred in individual litigation, not those arising out of a consent order made as part of a settlement between the landlord and the generality of lessees, which related to the future management of the property.[11]

The policy of counteracting abuses is furthered by the principle that it is implied into any service charges clause that costs must be reasonably and properly incurred prior to their recovery.[12] By extension, if a basis of calculation of charges, originally fair, becomes, during the lease, unfair and unreasonable, the landlord is limited to recovery of what are deemed to be reasonable amounts.[13] This sort of matter might now be the subject of an application for a variation order (see above).

In interpreting the meaning of individual items in a service charges clause, the courts employ the ordinary canons of construction, so that a clause which enabled the recovery of repairing costs did not enable the landlord to charge for the replacement of one design of windows with a new, improved, design.[14] Similarly, where a landlord was required, before carrying out major or substantial works, to submit a copy of the estimates to the lessees, who had a right to comment, but failed to do so, he failed to recover any part of the £36,707 spent by him, having not complied with a condition precedent to recovery.[15]

Service charges clauses cannot be construed in isolation from the other relevant terms of the lease: hence, where external windows were not demised to lessees, a service charge did not apply to them.[16] Moreover, such clauses are not construed as entitling the landlord to recover for costs not within the reasonable contemplation of the parties, so that a power to increase sums payable in respect of heating costs extended only to fuel cost increases and not to central heating costs as a whole,[17] and a clause entitling the landlord to recover for services required in the interests of efficient management allowed the landlord to charge in respect of an improved method of window-cleaning,[18] but not for exterior repairs, on the facts.[19]

The landlord cannot evade these controls by providing in the lease that a surveyor's or agent's certificate is to settle the amount (and by implication the

---

11 *Morgan v Stainer* [1993] 2 EGLR 73.
12 *Finchbourne v Rodrigues* [1976] 3 All ER 581, CA.
13 *Pole Properties Ltd v Feinberg* (1981) 43 P & CR 121 (floor area basis unfair and tenant charged for actual heating use).
14 *Mullaney v Maybourne Grange (Croydon) Management Co* [1986] 1 EGLR 70; cf *Sutton (Hastoe) Housing Association v Williams* (1988) 20 HLR 321, CA, where the words were wide enough to enable such a charge.
15 *Northways Flats Management Co (Camden) v Wimpey Pension Trustees Ltd* [1992] 2 EGLR 42; also *Yorkbrook Investments Ltd v Batten* [1985] 2 EGLR 100 and *CIN Properties Ltd v Barclays Bank plc* [1986] 1 EGLR 59, CA.
16 *Reston Ltd v Hudson* [1990] 2 EGLR 51.
17 *Jollybird Ltd v Fairzone Ltd* [1990] 1 EGLR 253.
18 *Sun Alliance and London Insurance Co Ltd v British Railways Board* [1989] 2 EGLR 237.
19 *Jacobs Isbicki & Co Ltd v Goulding & Bird Ltd* [1989] 1 EGLR 236.

right to recover a sum) conclusively, as the courts insist on their jurisdiction to go behind any such certificate if challenged.[20]

Statutory controls

Four sets of controls are mentioned. It will be apparent that in the last ten to fifteen years the legislature has been increasingly anxious to combat absuses by landlords of lessees of flats in relation to the payment of service charges.

First, to safeguard funds against landlord insolvency, in the case of tenants of two or more dwellings, including flats, s 42(2) and (3) of the Landlord and Tenant Act 1987 require that service charges paid to the landlord or some person such as his managing agent must, together with all other service charges, be held by the payee as a single fund or as separate funds, on trust to pay for the matters covered; subject to this, on trust for the contributing tenants for the time being. The fund is not claimable in whole or in part, by any tenant whose lease ends (s 42(6)); it is held on trust for the benefit of tenants from time to time and if there are no remaining contributing tenants, the fund will vest in the landlord or payee for his own use and benefit (s 42(7)).[1]

The second set of controls entitle certain tenants to consultation before the incurring of certain works, although they cannot use these rules to stop their being executed once the consultation has been carried out. Sections 18 to 30 of the Landlord and Tenant Act 1985 impose duties on landlords with respect of costs and estimates, on which service charges will be based, which apply to tenants of dwellings, including flats. 'Relevant costs' cannot be recovered unless reasonably incurred; and only if the works or services concerned have been provided to a reasonable standard (s 19(1)).[2] The rights of tenants to exercise control over service charges have been strengthened because they, as well as the landlord, now have a right to apply to a leasehold valuation tribunal to determine such matters as whether costs were reasonably incurred or whether works are to a reasonable standard. Indeed, a party may apply to a leasehold valuation tribunal to obtain a ruling as to whether certain costs incurred for services or repairs of any specified description are reasonable (s 19(2A). The exercise of this jurisdiction will involve, perhaps, scrutiny of detailed factual evidence as to the efficacy of certain precise repairing or maintenance work.

Estimated costs and management charges, if these comply with these two conditions, are recoverable. Where the cost of certain 'qualifying works' (s 20(2)) exceeds prescribed amounts, currently £25 multiplied by the number of dwellings, or £500, whichever is the greater, the excess over these amounts is only recoverable by the landlord if he complies with certain requirements, unless these are dispensed with by the court (s 20(1)). The extent of the

---

20 *Re Davstone Estates Ltd's Lease* [1969] 2 Ch 378, [1969] 2 All ER 849; *Rapid Results College v Angell* [1986] 1 EGLR 53, CA.

 1 If the terms of the lease provide differently for the destination of the fund, these prevail (s 42(8)) but otherwise, s 42 overrides the lease except in the case of express trusts created prior to its commencement (s 42(9)).

 2 What is 'reasonable' is a question of fact and degree: *Russell v Liamond Properties Ltd* [1984] 1 EGLR 37.

requirements depends on whether the tenant is represented by a recognised tenants' association or not. If he is, the landlord must give the secretary of the association a notice with a detailed specification of the works and each represented tenant is entitled to a brief description of the works and to summaries of the estimate (s 20(5)). Any tenant also has the right by notice to require the landlord to supply him with a written summary of costs incurred in the 12 months to the date of the request (s 21). To aid them in any dispute, a recognised tenants' association may appoint, under a new statutory right, a surveyor to advise it on any matters relating to or which may give rise to service charges. The surveyor has wide powers of entry and inspection.[3]

The third set of controls relates to forfeiture, which is still apparently actively in use in this field, as where landlords buy up flats in a poor state of repair and then, hoping to re-possess the premises, serve heavy service charge demands on lessees which they may not be able to meet.[4] As from 24 September 1996, where premises are let as a dwelling, the landlord is not entitled to re-enter or forfeit for non-payment of service charges if the amount is not agreed or admitted by the tenant. Either party may refer the disputed amount to the county court or to an arbitral tribunal (s 81). This provision is further considered in chapter 13.

Lastly, the tenant may apply to the court, or, once juridisction is transferred, to a leasehold valuation tribunal, for the appointment of a manager under Part II of the Landlord and Tenant Act 1987. The ground of such an application is that unreasonable service charges have been made, or are proposed or are likely to be made.[5] It must be just and convenient to make the order. A service charge passes the test of being unreasonable if its amount is unreasonable having regard to the items for which it is payable; or if the items for which it is payable are of an unnecesarily high standard; or if these items are of an insufficient standard so that additional service charges are or may be incurred.[6] The effect of the exercise of this jurisdiction has already been set out in chapter 9; the policy of the new rules may be to prevent landlords from making any profit out of service charges, while ensuring that proper repairs and maintenance takes place.

---

3 Housing Act 1996, s 84 and Sch 4, in force from 1 October 1996: SI 1996/2212.
4 Housing Bill 1996 Standing Committee G, 28 March 1996, col 881.
5 Landlord and Tenant Act 1987, s 24(2)(ab), inserted by Housing Act 1996, s 85(3).
6 Ibid, s 24(2A), inserted by Housing Act 1996, s 85(4) as from 24 September 1996 (s 232(2)).

Chapter 21

Protection of long residential tenants and enfranchisement

I INTRODUCTION

It has for some time been the policy of Parliament to provide special legislative rules applicable to long residential tenancies. The first set considered in this Chapter, those of Part I of the Landlord and Tenant Act 1954 and of a modified assured tenancies scheme, operate by extending a long residential tenancy at a low rent, as from the termination date, but enable the landlord to procure the revision of the terms of the continuing tenancy. There are, at the time of writing, two sets of rules because the old rules, of the 1954 Act Part I, apply where a long residential tenancy was granted before 1 March 1990, prior to the introduction of the new rules, which apply to long residential tenancies granted on or after that date. However, if any long residential tenancy granted before 1 March 1990 is still in being as at 15 January 1999, the new modified assured tenancy scheme will as from then apply to the tenancy, after its expiry.

The necessity for some protection of long residential lessees whose leases were coming to an end raises the question of why long leases of residential houses or flats had been granted as from the latter part of the nineteenth century. It will be appreciated, however, that it is not in principle possible to enforce covenants to repair or other positive covenants, such as to pay for repairs, against any successor in title to freehold land burdened with that type of covenant.[1] Hence, developers of residential flats may prefer to grant long leases of the units.

By the latter part of the twentieth century, however, Parliament was not slow to realise the political advantages in enacting legislation allowing for the enfranchisement or purchase out, against the landlord's will, of his freehold interest in the premises, and we now have two major (and complex) statutes which enable long lessees of houses and of flats to acquire the freehold, and any intermediate leases, for themselves. These Acts, the Leasehold Reform Act 1967 (applicable to houses) and Part I of the Leasehold Reform, Housing and Urban Development Act 1993 (applicable to flats) also provide for extensions of the lessee's interest where it is not desired to purchase the freehold.

---

1 *Rhone v Stephens* [1994] 2 AC 310, HL.

The enfranchisement legislation could be said to be adverse to the interests of landlords, since they cannot ultimately refuse to convey the freehold or grant a new long lease to a claimant lessee or lessees who have established their right within the relevant Act. Equally, some long lessees seem to take the view that the presence of the landlord's freehold interest is at best a nuisance and at worst a source of difficulty, especially where there is a poorly-maintained block of long leasehold flats, or where a leasehold interest has diminished in length below the point where it can be used as security for a mortgage, so rendering it almost unassignable.

A still more recent twist to the resolution of the conflicting interests of the parties was exposed by amending legislation, applicable from 15 January 1999, aimed at discouraging failed end of tenancy applications to enfranchise houses or flats as a means of avoidance of a market rent. As from that date, the rent payable under a long tenancy which continues after expiry under statute is a market rent. If, however, prior to the reform, enfranchisement was claimed at the very end of the lease, not only is the tenancy continued on an interim basis: the old ground rent continued to be payable for the time being. The new rules apply where an enfranchisement claim is made during the last two years of the leasehold term but it fails. Broadly, the landlord is entitled to statutory compensation, designed to give him the difference between the ground rent and a market rent for the period concerned.[2] This aspect deserves mention if only to illustrate the complexity of the legislation applicable in this field.

Though in this chapter we summarise the principal aspects of the two sets of rules, it will be appreciated that the enfranchisement legislation is a detailed subject in itself, about which specialist works exist.[3]

A   PROTECTION OF LONG TENANCIES UNDER PART I OF LANDLORD AND TENANT ACT 1954

II   APPLICATION OF THE 1954 ACT

To qualify for protection under Part I, the tenancy must be a long tenancy at a low rent and must satisfy the *qualifying condition* (s 2). The 1954 Act rules, which confer Rent-Act style protection on long residential lessees after termination of the contractual lease, will cease to apply to any long tenancy still in being on 15 January 1999. The rules may be noted as follows.

1   *Long tenancy* –This is a tenancy originally granted for a term exceeding 21 years[4] whether or not it has subsequently been extended by the parties or by any enactment (s 2(4)). The tenant must be entitled to remain as tenant for an initial period of over 21 years.[5] If the tenant has held a qualifying long

---

2   Housing Act 1996, s 116 and Sch 11, in force 1 October 1996: SI 1996/2212.
3   Notably Hague, *Leasehold Enfranchisement*.
4   Which is not terminable by landlords' break clause before the end of the term (s 2(4)).
5   *Roberts v Church Comrs for England* [1972] 1 QB 278, [1971] 3 All ER 703, CA, subject to his being entitled to terminate the lease himself.

tenancy, and is granted a new tenancy for a term of less than 21 years, he is still within Part I.[6]

2   *At a low rent* – The 1954 Act Part I only applies where the rent[7] payable annually is less than two-thirds of the rateable value.[8] The policy of the Act is to catch tenancies where a ground rent is payable solely in recognition of the landlord's superior title.

3   *Qualifying condition* – Because the protection of Part I is styled on the Rent Act 1977, the qualifying condition is that the tenant must, on termination of the long tenancy, have been entitled to retain possession subject to the same requirements as apply to a Rent Act statutory tenant (s 2(1)). There must therefore have been a tenancy of a separate dwelling occupied by the tenant as his residence.[9] Since the Act does not necessarily apply to the whole of the premises originally let, questions may arise as to whether the tenant is entitled to possession of the whole dwelling, whether this is a single entity or sub-divided into flats; and, where part has been sub-let, with the tenant in occupation of the rest at the term date, the qualifying condition is satisfied, so long as the tenant remains in possession of the whole just before the term date, or, if he occupies part, then intends to regain eventual possession of the whole.[10] The tenant must further be in occupation at the time a notice to terminate takes effect.[11] If, immediately before the term date of the tenancy, the qualifying condition is satisfied, and during continuation it ceases to be, as where the tenant ceases permanently to reside in the premises, the tenancy continues unless and until it is terminated under statutory procedures.

III   CONTINUATION AND TERMINATION OF TENANCIES

Continuation

A qualifying long tenancy is automatically continued by the 1954 Act Part I beyond the contractual expiry date (or 'term date') unless or until it is terminated in accordance with the provisions of the Act. The extent of the premises which qualify for continuation corresponds to those which the tenant could have occupied as a statutory tenant, but for the fact that the tenancy is at a low rent, so that he must continue to comply with the residence condition

---

6   This rule may apply to any number of successive tenancies, including a periodic express or implied tenancy (s 19(2)).

7   There is a special rule for a progressive rent in s 2(5), basing it on the maximum rent but excluding, eg lessees' service charges (Rent Act 1977, s 146(1)).

8   Which is defined as that within Rent Act 1977, s 5.

9   *Haines v Herbert* [1963] 3 All ER 715, [1963] 1 WLR 1401, CA. See also *Grosvenor Estates Belgravia v Cochran* [1991] 2 EGLR 83; PF Smith [1991] Conv 393 (where a sub-lease of a flat assigned by operation of law failed to qualify).

10   *Herbert v Byrne* [1964] 1 All ER 882, [1964] 1 WLR 519, CA; *Regalian Securities Ltd v Ramsden* [1981] 2 All ER 65, [1981] 1 WLR 611, HL.

11   If the landlord wishes to deter a tenant out of residence from resuming it in the fag-end of the tenancy, during its last 12 months, he may apply to the court for a declaration under s 2(2) that the tenancy is outside Part I of the 1954 Act.

imposed by the Act on a contractual tenancy. The continuing tenancy is an indefinite statutory extension of the contractual tenancy[12] upon the same terms, and therefore at the same rent as before the term date, where the whole of the premises qualify for protection (s 3(2)(a)).[13]

Termination by tenant

A tenancy which is protected by Part I of the 1954 Act, whether a continuation tenancy or not, may be terminated by the tenant, either by surrender, or by not less than one month's notice in writing given to his immediate landlord to expire on the term date or any date thereafter, regardless of the fact that the landlord has already served on him a notice to terminate on some later date (s 5). Any agreement (apart from surrender by the tenant) purporting to contract out of Part I is void (s 17).[14]

Termination by landlord

Part I of the 1954 Act provides specific machinery for the termination of long tenancies within it.[15] The landlord[16] may accordingly terminate the tenancy either on the term date or any later date by giving not more than 12 but not less than 6 months' notice before the 'termination date', or contractual expiry date of the tenancy, to the tenant in one of the two forms prescribed (s 4(1) and (2)).[17] Both forms of notice must invite the tenant to notify the landlord within two months whether he is willing to give up possession and specify the premises which the landlord believes to be, or to be likely to be, the premises qualifying for protection. The two forms of notice are as follows.

1 *Notice to resume possession* – this notice must inform the tenant that if he is not willing to give up possession the landlord proposes to apply to the court for possession on any one or more of the grounds under s 12 (s4(3)(b)).[18] The tenant is invited within two months of the landlord's notice to notify him whether he is willing to give up possession, and, if he is not willing to do so, the landlord is then entitled to ask the court for possession. If he fails to establish a ground for possession, his notice will lapse, and the tenancy will continue. If he fails to establish a ground, he may serve on the tenant a notice proposing a statutory tenancy (s 14).

---

12 If the tenant holds from an intermediate landlord whose interest comes to an end during statutory continuation, he holds direct from the superior landlord (s 65(2)).

13 Provision is made for continuation of part only of the premises if the tenant has sub-let part, with consequential apportionment of the rent (s 3(2)(b)).

14 See *Re Hennessey's Agreement, Hill v Davison* [1975] Ch 252, [1975] 1 All ER 60 (option to purchase in landlord following notice procedure struck down).

15 Hence, the landlord's right to enforce a forfeiture clause in the tenancy is limited as provided in s 16.

16 If the tenant is a sub-tenant, the landlord is the next superior landlord whose interest will last at least five years longer than that of the tenant (s 21(1)).

17 Landlord and Tenant (Notices) Regulations 1957, SI 1957/1157.

18 The grounds, set out in Sch 3, correspond to Sch 15, Part I to the Rent Act 1977, Cases 1 to 9 and a ground that, where the landlord is a local authority or certain other types of public landlord, that he proposes to redevelop the premises on the termination of the tenancy.

2   *Notice proposing a statutory tenancy* – this notice must contain the landlord's proposals for a statutory tenancy. The protection of the tenant is emphasised by the fact that if the parties cannot reach agreement about five specified matters within two months from the termination date stated in the notice, and within these two months the landlord has not applied to the county court to determine them, the landlord's notice lapses and the tenancy continues unaltered (s 7(2)).[19]

The court has a wide discretion in determining terms not agreed.[20] The state of affairs existing at the date of the hearing is of primary importance, and while the terms of the contractual lease will be considered, they will not necessarily be incorporated into the statutory tenancy, in view of the latter's potentially indefinite life. Hence, a tenant's future intention to sub-divide the house and use it as a source of income was disregarded, and a power enabling him to do so in the contractual lease was not incorporated into the statutory tenancy.[1] A prohibition in qualified form against assignment, sub-letting etc by the tenant was replaced by an absolute prohibition in the statutory tenancy order, for the landlord's protection against any sub-tenancy; but a prohibition on sharing proposed was disallowed as being unreasonable, new and imprecise, on the facts.[2]

Generally, once the statutory tenancy starts, all liability of the tenant under the former tenancy is extinguished (s 10) except for liability to pay rent, rates or for insurance in particular. However, liability is not extinguished where it relates to property other than the dwelling-house, and thus a service charge contribution, to the extent that it covered matters outside the demise of a flat, continued to be recoverable despite s 10.[3]

Terms of statutory tenancy

Subject to an interim continuation of the long tenancy,[4] the statutory tenancy takes effect by virtue of s 6(1) as a statutory tenancy under the Rent Act 1977, as if the former tenancy had been a tenancy of the dwelling-house on the terms agreed between the parties or agreed by the court. There can be no statutory tenancy, however, if after two months after the landlord's notice was served, the qualifying condition was not satisfied unless the tenant had elected to retain possession (s 6(2)).

B   PROTECTION OF LONG TENANCIES UNDER MODIFIED ASSURED TENANCIES SCHEME

With the supercession of Rent Act protection by the assured tenancies scheme, and subject to the transitional provisions already explained, a long residential

---

19   The five matters are, briefly: the premises, the rent and rental periods, the carrying out and payment for initial repairs, the responsibility for repairs during the statutory tenancy and any other terms proposed.
20   There is, however, detailed guidance as to the terms relating to initial repairs in s 9.
1   *Lagens Properties Ltd v Bandino* [1965] EGD 69.
2   *Etablissement Commercial Kamira v Schiazzano* [1985] QB 93, [1984] 2 All ER 465, CA.
3   *Blatherwick (Services) Ltd v King* [1991] 2 All ER 874, CA.
4   Under 1954 Act, s 64.

tenancy at a low rent granted on or after 1 March 1990, is subject after its coming to an end to a form of protection akin to that offered to assured tenants whose tenancies have expired.[5] This scheme works in a similar way to the previously-discussed rules of Part I of the 1954 Act, with due modifications. The principle is that the long tenancy is continued unless the landlord is able to terminate it on one or more statutory grounds, or, alternatively, until the landlord serves a notice proposing an assured tenancy on the tenant.

The statutory definitions of long tenancy and of low rent are similar to that applicable to long tenancies covered by Part I of the 1954 Act.[6] There is also a *qualifying condition* applicable. This, as might be expected, is that the tenancy must be such that, were it not for the fact that it is at a low rent, it would be an assured tenancy within Part I of the Housing Act 1988.[7]

The landlord is entitled to terminate a long residential tenancy which has expired at common law but which is continued by statute by a notice served on the tenant. The notice may propose an assured monthly periodic tenancy: if different terms to those of the previous long tenancy are to be proposed, they must be specified in the notice. Alternatively, the notice must state that if the tenant is not willing to give up possession at the date of termination, the landlord proposes to apply to the court for possession, in which case he must state the ground or grounds on which he intends to rely. The tenant must be required to notify the landlord in writing within two months from the date of service whether he wishes to remain in possession or give up possession.[8]

Where the tenant elects to retain possession after a notice to resume it from the landlord, the latter may apply for possession to the county court. His application is, as with 1954 Act applications, subject to a strict statutory timetable, so that, notably, it must be made within two months from the date of any tenants' election to retain possession.[9] If he fails to apply within this deadline, his notice to resume possession ceases to have effect, but he is then entitled to serve a notice proposing an assured tenancy.[10]

To obtain an order for possession, the landlord must rely on one of a number of statutory grounds, provided he specifies the ground concerned in his notice. These include most of the discretionary grounds applicable to assured tenancies, and a number of other grounds, including two modified redevelopment grounds, one of which is that applicable to assured tenancies,[11] and a ground under which the landlord reasonably requires the premises or part of them for occupation as a residence for himself or his close relatives.

Where, by contrast, the landlord by notice proposes an assured tenancy, he may also serve a notice proposing an interim monthly rent to be payable during continuation of the tenancy.[12] Once a long residential tenancy is terminated by

---

5 By Local Government and Housing Act 1989, Sch 10, hich is excepted from the presumption that new assured tenancies are assured shortholds: Housing Act 1996, Sch 2A, para 6.
6 1989 Act, Sch 10, para 2(3) (long tenancy) and 2(4) (low rent).
7 Ibid, para 1(1).
8 Ibid, para 4.
9 Sch 10, para 13(2). If the tenant makes no such election, the landlord has four months from the date of service of his notice in which to apply to the court.
10 Ibid, para 15(2) and (4).
11 Which does not apply if the tenancy was a former 1954 Act, Part I tenancy: Sch 10, para 5(2).
12 Sch 10, para 6.

a landlord's notice proposing an assured tenancy, the tenant is entitled to remain in possession under an assured periodic tenancy arising under the 1989 Act.[13] The terms of this tenancy may be those of the previous long tenancy, but the landlord may propose different terms (and he must propose a rent) and the tenant may by further notice propose a different rent and different terms to those proposed in the landlord's notice.[14]

C ENFRANCHISEMENT OF LONG LEASES OF HOUSES UNDER LEASEHOLD REFORM ACT 1967

1 INTRODUCTION AND APPLICATION OF 1967 ACT

The Leasehold Reform Act 1967 gives a tenant[15] under a long lease of a house at a low rent, either the right to acquire the freehold or an extended lease. As already noted, the policy of the Act, which has been amended over the years so as to ease the tenant's position still further, is to allow him to resort to the statutory machinery against an unwilling landlord, who is forced to convey the freehold to the tenant (provided he holds it) provided the tenant complies with the Act in all respects, on terms laid down by the Act.[16] The landlord may be able to stop the process by proving that the conditions of the Act do not apply, or that the tenant has served incorrect notices, for example, but cannot resist the ultimate acquisition by the tenant of the freehold solely on the ground that he does not wish to part with his interest.

The 1967 Act is limited to houses because of the fact that it is not possible to enforce the running of positive covenants against freehold land.[17] Section 1 of the 1967 Act confers on 'a tenant of a leasehold house, occupying the house as his residence, a right to acquire on fair terms the freehold or an extended lease of the house and premises' where the following conditions are satisfied:

 (i) the tenancy is a long tenancy at a low rent;
(ii) at the relevant time (ie when the tenant gives notice under the Act of his desire to have the freehold or to have an extended lease, as the case may be), he has been a tenant of the house under a long tenancy at a low rent, and occupying it as his residence, for the last three years or for periods amounting to three years in the last ten years.

13 As to the terms thereof, see Sch 10, para 9.
14 Sch 10, para 10. Thereupon the dispute is to be referred to a rent assessment committee (paras 11 and 12).
15 Including a tenant whose landlord's forfeiture action had been dismissed, so re-instating him: *Hynes v Twinsectra Ltd* [1995] 2 EGLR 69, CA.
16 The determination of Parliament to promote enfranchisement of houses is shown by the treatment of devices such as 'Prince of Wales clauses', which were designed to avoid the 1967 Act, but which have now been nullified, seemingly, by the combined effect of s 1B and 3 of the 1967 Act.
17 A fact judicially recognised in *Duke of Westminster v Birrane* [1995] QB 262, CA, noted [1995] Conv 166.

These conditions are complicated by the fact that they must each be satisfied at different times. The second condition is more complicated still, because it must be satisfied at all times throughout the three-year qualifying period, during which time there may well have been more than one tenant and more than one tenancy; and there may have been changes not only in the rent and the rateable value but also in the premises comprised in the tenancy.

Financial limits

In principle, the house must fall within the relevant financial limits on the appropriate day, or the right to enfranchise is blocked. So as to ease the path of tenants, a house whose value, as so measured, is too high to qualify for enfranchisement will still be within the 1967 Act if these limits are the sole reason why the tenant cannot exercise his statutory rights (s 1A).[18]

Where the tenancy was entered into before 1 April 1990, the financial limits are based on ascertaining the rateable value of the house on the appropriate day.[19] Where a long tenancy was entered into on or after 1 April 1990, rateable value limits do not apply and the value of the premises is calculated by a formula based on the premium paid as a condition for the grant of the tenancy and on its length when granted (s 1(1)).

'Tenant'

There must be a 'tenancy', which is defined by s 37 as including a legal or equitable tenancy, but not a tenancy at will or a mortgage term.[20] 'Tenant', however, is not as such defined, but is given specific meanings in various provisions of the Act. Under s 1(1) it is 'the tenant' who must satisfy the condition as to occupation and who has the right to claim the rights under the Act. Normally they will be the same person, but not necessarily. Thus, under s 5, a tenant who has established a right under the Act, by giving a notice of intention, may assign that right together with the tenancy, and the assignee will be entitled to enforce that right without himself having to satisfy the condition as to occupation; so too may executors or administrators of a tenant who dies after establishing his right. Similarly, trustees of land have the same rights as a beneficiary under the trust of land would have had if he had been the tenant (s 6); and the widow (and certain other members of a deceased tenant's family), who succeeds to the tenancy, will be treated as having been the tenant during any period before the tenant's death when she was resident in the house during which the tenant was in occupation of the house as his residence (s 7). Members of the tenant's family who so qualify include his or her spouse, parents-in-law, son, daughter, son-in-law, daughter-in-law, step-children, illegitimate and adopted children and their respective spouses.

---

18 Inserted by Leasehold Reform, Housing and Urban Development Act 1993, s 63.
19 These differ depending on the rateable value of the dwelling-house on a number of different days, eg where a tenancy had been rated on or after 1 April 1973, the limits are £750 except in Greater London and £1,500 in Greater London.
20 Mortgage term means a subsisting term, not one sold to the tenant under the mortgagee's power of sale: *Re Fairview, Church Street, Bromyard* [1974] 1 All ER 1233, [1974] 1 WLR 579.

A sub-tenant may qualify for rights under the Act unless his sub-tenancy was unlawfully granted out of a superior tenancy, which was not itself a tenancy at a low rent, and that breach has not been waived (s 5(4)).

'Long tenancy'

By virtue of s 3(1) this means a tenancy (or sub-tenancy unless created out of a tenancy which was not itself a long tenancy) granted for a fixed-term exceeding 21 years,[1] whether or not it was terminable within that time by notice (ie a break-clause exercisable by either party), by re-entry, forfeiture or otherwise, except on death or marriage with special provisions in this latter case. Where a long lease provided that it should cease in certain events, including the lease not being held by a member of a certain housing association, it was held still to be within s 3(1) as 'terminable' therein includes (a) determination by act of the parties and (b) determination by a specified event prior to the term date.[2] A tenancy continuing under s 3 or s 24 of the 1954 Act is within the definition (s 3(5)),[3] but not a statutory tenancy under that Act. Where the original tenancy was not for more than 21 years (with a covenant for renewal without premium but not for perpetual renewal) and by one or more renewals the total term exceeds 21 years, the Act applies as if from the outset there had been a long tenancy (s 3(4)). Where the tenant takes a new tenancy of the property (or part of it) at the end of a long tenancy at a low rent, the later tenancy (and any later tenancy) will be deemed to be a long tenancy irrespective of its terms (s 3(2));[4] and where the tenant takes a new long tenancy (whether or not by virtue of s 3(2)) of the property, or part of it, on the coming to an end of a long tenancy, the Act will apply, as if there had been a single tenancy beginning with the earlier tenancy and expiring with the later tenancy (s 3(3)).[5] Where the tenant holds parts of a house (any of which may include other premises occupied with the house) under separate tenancies from the same landlord, the separate parts and other premises will be treated as being under a single tenancy corresponding to the duration of the tenancy comprising the house (s 3(6)).

'Low rent'

The tenant cannot claim the benefit of the 1967 Act unless the tenancy is at a low rent. Where the financial limit applicable is referable to the rateable value of the house, the rent must not exceed two thirds of that value on the relevant appropriate day. Where, notably in the case of a tenancy granted on or after 1 April 1990, the financial limit is the rental value of the house, the rent must be not over £1,000 in Greater London and £250 elsewhere (s 4(1)).[6]

---

1 See *Roberts v Church Comrs for England* [1972] 1 QB 278, [1971] 3 All ER 703, CA.
2 *Eton College v Bard* [1983] Ch 321, [1983] 2 All ER 961, CA.
3 As is a long tenancy continued under Local Government and Housing Act 1989 Sch 10.
4 Section 3(2) applies also to assigns of the tenant: *Austin v Dick Richards Properties Ltd* [1975] 2 All ER 75, [1975] 1 WLR 1033, CA.
5 See *Bates v Pierrepoint* (1978) 37 P & CR 420, CA (two leases granted in 1961 and 1973 at same rent treated as single term).
6 There is an exception (s 4(1)) where the tenancy, if not a building lease, was granted between the end of August 1938 and the beginning of April 1963: the low rent test is then applied with

However, the rent test has been recently relaxed, apparently so as to counteract devices such as providing in the lease for the payment of a rent outside the relevant financial limits.[7] There is an alternative low rent test where the rent in the initial year following the commencement of a tenancy is too high to qualify (s 4A).[8] It postulates a figure for the rent payable during the first year of the tenancy, which, if exceeded, precludes enfranchisement. The most notable rule relates to a tenancy entered into on or after 1 April 1990, £1,000 in Greater London and £250 elsewhere. Thus, if the rent level is set below these figures during the first year but rises above it during a second or subsequent year, the tenancy will not be disqualified. In relation to applications made after the commencement of s 106 of the Housing Act 1996, the low rent test need not be satisfied in the case of certain tenancies, most notably, a tenancy for a term certain exceeding 35 years (whether or not terminable by a landlord's break clause or forfeiture). The same exemption from the low rent test applies to a tenancy which, although not originally granted for 35 years, now exceeds that period owing to one or more renewals.[9]

Section 1(1)(b) requires that the condition as to low rent be satisfied – where it still applies – not only at the 'relevant time' (ie when the tenant serves his notice of intention) but also throughout the qualifying period of three years. The tenant cannot make up the relevant period of years by adding to an insufficient period of occupation at a low rent, earlier periods at a rack rent.[10] If during this time the property comprised in the tenancy (whether or not that includes a new tenancy under s 3(3)) has remained the same, no problem arises in applying the test, since the rateable value will not have changed, though an increase in rent under a variable rent clause may have taken the rent reserved above the two-thirds limit.

'House'

The policy of the 1967 Act is to allow the enfranchisement of separate dwellings, such as detached houses, and of houses which are vertically separated, such as terraced houses, but not to allow for the purchase of the freehold in horizontally divided premises such as flats.[11] A house to which the Act applies is thus defined by s 2(1) as including any building designed or adapted for living in and reasonably so called,[12] notwithstanding that the building is not structurally

reference to the rent and 'letting value' at the beginning of the tenancy; as to 'letting value' see *Manson v Duke of Westminster* [1981] QB 323, [1981] 2 All ER 40, CA; *Johnston v Duke of Westminster* [1986] AC 839, [1986] 2 All ER 613, HL.

7 See Matthews and Millichap, para 5.5.
8 Inserted by Leasehold Reform, Housing and Urban Development Act 1993, s 65.
9 1967 Act, s 1AA (inserted by Housing Act 1996, Sch 9, making an identical amendment in the case of long leases of flats).
10 *Harris v Plentex Ltd* (1980) 40 P & CR 483.
11 Enfranchisement of leasehold flats is provided for by Part I of the Leasehold Reform, Housing and Urban Development Act 1993, considered below.
12 See *Malpas v St Ermin's Property Co Ltd* [1992] 1 EGLR 109 (building which looked like a house, but with two separate front and back doors, where each floor occupied by different families, a house reasonably so called); but, seemingly, several freestanding buildings could not be a 'house reasonably so called' since 'building' is used in s 2(1) in the singular: *Dugan-Chapman v Grosvenor Estates* [1997] 10 EG 152, (Cty ct).

detached, or was or is not solely designed or adapted for living in,[13] or is divided horizontally into flats or maisonettes, and:

(a) where a building is divided horizontally, the flats or other units into which it is so divided are not separate 'houses', though the building as a whole may be; and
(b) where a building is divided vertically the building as a whole is not a 'house' though any of the units into which it is divided may be.

Section 2(1) has been said to recognise that not every building is within the enfranchisement rules, even though the building could be lived in, otherwise office or factory buildings with some living accommodation could be caught.[14]

A house which is not structurally detached, and of which a material part lies above or below a part of the structure not comprised in the house, is excluded from the above definition by s 2(2). By this provision, the Act ensures that, for example, a long tenant who holds a lease of a house and a basement, the latter being underneath neighbouring freehold premises, cannot enfranchise, since a material part of the whole premises lies under other premises.[15]

'Structurally detached' means detached from any other structure: where part of a tenant's rooms were above garages sub-let by him, the rooms fell outside s 2(1) since they were not detached from the rest of a structure not comprised in the house.[16] A house above an archway which gave access to mews behind was held not to be structurally detached.[17]

Because the essential requirement of s 2 is that these should be a building, which is designed or adapted for living in, and which can be called a house in the broad sense by a reasonable man, a purpose-built shop with living accommodation above it may fall within the notion of 'house' as tenants of such premises are fully within the intendment of the 1967 Act; and the question is not just one of fact. Thus, a mixed-user building which may reasonably be called a house (and this is a question of law) falls within the 1967 Act unless exceptional circumstances are shown.[18] A building consisting of two floors, with a flat on each floor, there being access between the two floors, which was used as a single dwelling, was held to be a 'house'.[19] However, it was recently held that the statutory residence test and the requirements of s 2(1) of the Act were quite distinct. The tenant must show that he satisfies the residence requirement and that he has a building designed or adapted for living in, and that it must be reasonable to call that building a house.[20]

---

13 See *Lake v Bennett* [1970] 1 QB 663, [1970] 1 All ER 457 where part of the building had been converted into business premises.
14 *Tandon v Trustees of Spurgeon's Homes* [1982] AC 755, [1982] 1 All ER 1086, HL.
15 As in *Duke of Westminster v Birrane* [1995] 2 WLR 270, CA.
16 *Parsons v Viscount Gage (Trustees of Henry Smith's Charity)* [1974] 1 All ER 1162, [1974] 1 WLR 435, HL.
17 *Cresswell v Duke of Westminster* [1985] 2 EGLR 151, CA.
18 *Tandon v Trustees of Spurgeon's Homes*, supra.
19 *Sharpe v Duke Street Securities NV* [1987] 2 EGLR 106, CA.
20 *Duke of Westminster v Birrane*, supra (the fact that the tenant claimed not to use the basement concerned residentially was irrelevant as it formed part of the premises demised to him, so that he could not enfranchise).

'Premises'

Where the qualifying conditions have been satisfied, a claim under the Act may be made in respect of the 'house and premises'. 'Premises' means any garage, outhouse, garden, yard and appurtenances which are let to the tenant with the house and are occupied with, and used for the purposes of, the house or any part of it by him or by another occupant (s 2(3)). A strip of land at the back of a house was not part of the premises, where it was let separately and was not closely connected with the lease of the house;[1] the term 'appurtenances' includes land let with the house; what falls within that is a question of fact.[2]

In addition to premises which the tenant occupies, there may be other premises under the tenancy which, because he does not occupy them, he is not entitled to claim. Section 2(4) entitles the landlord to require that they be treated as part of the house and premises. Conversely, s 2(5) entitles him to have excluded from the house and premises any part of them lying above or below other premises (not consisting only of underlying mines or minerals). As regards underlying minerals, the landlord can require them to be excluded, if proper provision is made for the support of the house and premises.

'Occupying'

Occupation of the house by the tenant as his residence is a condition to be satisfied not only at the time when he serves his claim notice, but also throughout the qualifying period of three years. He must be in occupation of the house as his only or main residence (whether or not he uses it for other purposes) by s 1(2). Tenants of houses comprised in agricultural holdings, however, are in effect precluded from acquiring rights under the Act by such occupation under s 1(3)(b). Occupation 'in part only' is sufficient, and this requirement has been held by the Court of Appeal to have been satisfied by the tenant occupying a basement flat, the remaining three floors being sub-let unfurnished as separate flats.[3] The part occupied, however, must be viewed in relation to the whole, for under the definition of 'house' (see above) the building must be what could reasonably be called a house; moreover, under s 1(3)(a), a tenant cannot acquire rights under the Act by occupying a house let with land or premises to which the house is ancillary. Whether the house is the tenant's only or main residence is a question of fact;[4] and it has been held that a husband and wife can each have a main residence.[5] The condition must normally be satisfied by the tenant personally, and accordingly, under s 37(5), no company or other artificial person, nor any corporation sole is capable of occupation.[6] He

---

1 *Gaidowski v Gonville and Caius College, Cambridge* [1975] 2 All ER 952, [1975] 1 WLR 1066, CA.
2 *Methuen-Campbell v Walters* [1979] QB 525, [1979] 1 All ER 606, CA (paddock not within s 2(3) on facts, though a valuable amenity).
3 *Harris v Swick Securities Ltd* [1969] 3 All ER 1131, CA.
4 *Byrne v Rowbotham* (1969) 210 Estates Gazette 823; *Baron v Phillips* (1978) 38 P & CR 91, CA.
5 *Fowell v Radford* (1969) 21 P & CR 99, CA.
6 If the occupation by the tenant is as bare trustee for a company but with its permission, then, though he has the legal estate as against the landlord, he is not within s 2(1) as he does not have the right to occupy as a residence; the 1967 Act does not extend to a company: *Duke of Westminster v Oddy* [1984] 1 EGLR 83, CA.

must normally occupy *qua* tenant, but there are exceptions in the case of assignment (s 5), trusts of land (s 6) and succession of certain members of the tenant's family on his death (s 7). Where the tenant is temporarily absent, he will not for that reason cease to be in occupation; prolonged absence with no intention to resume physical occupation, or absence due to legal inability to do so, disqualifies the tenant.[7]

II   LIMITATIONS ON RIGHTS UNDER THE ACT

In addition to the cases, mentioned above, of tenants who cannot acquire any rights under the Act, eg tenants of agricultural holdings, companies, corporations sole, etc, there are a number of special cases where the rights under the Act are either excluded entirely or are restricted, even though all the conditions above have been satisfied.

(a) *Special categories of landlord*   Tenants of the National Trust cannot enfranchise (s 32). Specific but narrow exemptions, the details of which lie outside this book, deal with special landlords, who cannot be the subject of enfranchisement, either because of their privileged position, such as the Crown (s 33), or for policy reasons, as with reservation of development and other rights by local authorities (ss 28 and 29), or where the landlord is, subject to certain conditions, a charitable housing trust (s 1(3A)),[8] seeing that charities often enjoy exemptions of this kind. If a landlord cannot be traced, there is a special rule that, after a claim procedure, the court deals in effect with the enfranchisement process (s 27). Tenancies granted by local authorities, or registered housing associations, at a premium are, subject to conditions, outside the 1967 Act.[9]

(b) *Loss of rights by the tenant*   Any claim by a tenant is void under s 22 and the Third Schedule, if he has already given notice to terminate the tenancy (eg by notice to quit, or a notice under ss 5, 26 or 27 of the 1954 Act), or if he has been granted a new tenancy under s 28 of that Act. Conversely, such a notice is of no effect if it is given whilst a claim under the 1967 Act subsists. Second, a tenant loses his rights under the Act, if within two months of being given notice to terminate by the landlord, he does not himself give notice of his intention to claim enfranchisement or an extension under the Act. Third, he may serve a notice under s 9(3)[10] within one month of the price being fixed stating that he is unable or unwilling to take the freehold at that price; he will thereupon be liable for the landlord's costs, and will not be entitled to make another claim to enfranchise within the next three years. Finally, a tenant's rights may be lost by forfeiture, but after notice of a claim has been given, forfeiture proceedings may be commenced only with the

---

7 *Poland v Earl Cadogan* [1980] 3 All ER 544, CA.
8 Inserted by Leasehold Reform, Housing and Urban Development Act 1993, s 67(3).
9 Housing Act 1980, s 140 and Housing (Exclusion of Shared Ownership Tenancies) etc Regulations 1982, SI 1982/62.
10 The tenant may instead claim an extension.

leave of the court, and leave will not be granted unless the court is satisfied that the claim was not made in good faith,[11] ie in order to avoid forfeiture.[12] Once a tenancy has been extended, the tenant has no further rights under the 1954 or 1967 Acts.

(c) *Landlord's claim for possession* Where the tenancy is extended, or the tenant claims an extension, the landlord may apply to the court for possession under s 17(1) (not more than one year before the term date of the original tenancy) on the grounds that he intends to redevelop the whole, or a substantial part, of the premises; in certain circumstances, the tenant will then have a right to claim enfranchisement. Also, where the tenant has claimed enfranchisement or an extension, the landlord may apply to the court for possession under s 18 on the ground that he reasonably requires possession for occupation either by himself or an adult member of his family. The court shall not make an order for possession under s 18 if having regard to all the circumstances of the case, including the availability of other accommodation for the landlord or the tenant, the court is satisfied that greater hardship would be caused by making an order than by refusing an order for possession. The landlord cannot seek possession on this ground if he acquired his interest in the house after 18 February 1966. In both cases, the tenant is entitled to compensation.

III ENFRANCHISEMENT

Where the necessary conditions are satisfied, and the tenant has duly notified the landlord of his desire to acquire the freehold, the landlord is bound to make, and the tenant to accept, a conveyance of the freehold of the house and premises at a price to be fixed in accordance with the Act (s 8).

The tenant's notice[13]

The tenant's notice of intention may be served[14] on the landlord at any time, provided that all the conditions have been satisfied. He may serve it even though the original contractual tenancy has come to an end, as with a tenancy continuing under s 3 of the 1954 Act. If the house has been beneficially occupied by two joint tenants under a trust for sale, one joint tenant having left, the sole remaining occupying joint tenant is not, seemingly, entitled to serve a s 8 notice alone, in his capacity as a trustee of land (as envisaged by s 6(3)), unless he has obtained the authority of his co-joint tenant to serve the notice on his or her behalf. Thus, where a husband and wife held a long lease under a trust

---

11 1967 Act, Sch 3, para 4(1).

12 See *Central Estates (Belgravia) Ltd v Woolgar; Liverpool Corpn v Husan* [1972] 1 QB 48, [1971] 3 All ER 647, CA.

13 For provisions where the tenant is a sub-tenant, see Leasehold Reform Act 1967, Sch 1, identifying the 'reversioner' as the person with whom the sub-tenant deals.

14 In the form prescribed by the Leasehold Reform (Notices) Regulations 1967, SI 1967/1768.

for sale as beneficial joint tenants, the wife having left the premises permanently, a s 8 notice served by the husband alone was invalid.[15]

Once validly served, the tenant's notice creates a binding contract of sale (in effect).[16] Time runs, for limitation purposes, for 12 years from the service of the s 8 notice.[17] The tenant may, after service of a s 8 notice, abandon or contractually release the right to enfranchise; but mere failure to pursue a disputed claim following a s 8 notice is not sufficient for this purpose, because any release has to be mutual, and arise out of mutual contract, representation or estoppel.[18] The 1967 Act contains detailed procedural rules as to s 8 (and other notices) required to be served by the tenant.[19]

The price

1   *Houses with rateable values below £1,000 or £500*

The level of rateable values for the purposes of price determination, is that at the date of service of the tenant's notice.[20] The general principles on the calculation of the price are laid down in s 9(1). The price is the amount which at the date of the notice, the house and premises might be expected to realise, if sold in the open market by a willing seller, with the tenant and members of his family residing in the house, not buying or seeking to buy. The following statutory assumptions must be made (s 9(1)):

(a) that the vendor is selling an estate in fee simple subject to the tenancy; that the Act did not confer a right to acquire the freehold; that the tenancy was extended by the tenant for 50 years subject to the landlord's right to resume possession under s 17 (for redevelopment purposes);

(b) that, apart from the incumbrances for which the tenant would be liable until the determination of the tenancy, it is being sold subject to the same rent charges as in the sale to the tenant;

(c) that it is being sold subject to the same rights and burdens as in the sale to the tenant.

The general principles of valuation which result from the above assumptions are that there is a hypothetical sale in the open market by a willing seller of the freehold reversion upon a lease which is deemed to be extended for 50 years under s 14 of the 1967 Act. In addition, the following factors govern the ascertainment of the value of the reversion:

(a) the value of the present rent;

(b) the value of the ground rent for the site only;[1]

---

15   *Wax* v *Viscount Chelsea* [1996] 41 EG 169 (Cty Ct).

16   The terms are governed by Leasehold Reform (Enfranchisement and Extension) Regulations 1967, SI 1967/1874.

17   *Collin* v *Duke of Westminster* [1985] QB 581, [1985] 1 All ER 463, CA.

18   *Collin* v *Duke of Westminster*, supra.

19   Leasehold Reform Act 1967, Sch 3, esp para 6. See eg *Dymond* v *Arundel-Timms* [1991] 1 EGLR 109, CA.

20   Leasehold Reform Act 1967, s 9(1) and (1A)(i).

1   See *Official Custodian for Charities* v *Goldridge* (1973) 26 P & CR 191, CA.

(c) the value of the right to resume possession under s 17 for redevelopment purposes;

(d) the value of the freehold reversion in possession at the end of the (deemed) 50 years' extension lease;

(e) the length of the existing term.[2]

No allowance is to be made under s 9(1) valuations for 'marriage value', that is, the benefit to the landlord of other adjacent or neighbouring sites owned by him, even though enfranchisement will preclude him from comprehensive redevelopment which would enhance the value of each individual site.

By contrast, if the tenant is able to enfranchise only as a result of the recent relaxations in the relevant conditions, namely, the extensions to the financial limit tests or the rental value tests, the valuation of the house is to be under s 9(1A), in which case any marriage value is to be taken into account, but up to a maximum of 50 per cent (s 9(1C) and 9A).[3] The 1967 Act rules are thus rendered, to that extent, consistent with the rules for enfranchisement of leasehold flats.

2 Houses with rateable values above £1,000 or £500[4]

In this case the principles differ somewhat. First, there is no assumption that the tenant is granted a 50 year extension lease; and secondly, s 9(1A) involves, in particular, the following special assumptions in calculating the price payable:

(a) there is a deemed continuation of the tenancy under Part I of the 1954 Act;[5]

(b) it is to be assumed that the vendor is selling the freehold subject to the tenancy, but that the Act did not confer a right to acquire the freehold or an extended lease, and, where the tenancy has been extended under the 1967 Act, that the tenancy will terminate on the agreed date;[6]

(c) that the tenant is assumed to have no liability to carry out any repairs, maintenance or redecorations at any time;

(d) the price must be treated as diminished by any increase in the value of the house and premises due to an improvement carried out by the tenant or his predecessors in title at their own expense.

Otherwise the general assumptions to be made are the same as those laid down in s 9(1) for the lower rateable values. In valuing the price, however, an allowance may be made for 'marriage values'[7] so that an allowance may be made for the higher bid which the sitting tenant would make (as compared to any investor) due to the extra value to him of buying the reversion.

2 See *Gallagher Estates Ltd v Walker* (1973) 28 P & CR 113, CA.

3 Inserted by Leasehold Reform, Housing and Urban Development Act 1993, s 66. No doubt this amendment was to compensate landlords for the easing of the relevant conditions.

4 These rules also apply where on 31 March 1990 the house had no rateable value limit and its value is above the statutory valuation formula: Reference to Rating etc Regs 1990, SI 1990/434, para 9.

5 The same is required to be assumed in the case of a long tenancy continued under the Local Government and Housing Act 1989.

6 1967 Act s 9(1A) as amended by Housing and Planning Act 1986, s 23, reversing *Mosley v Hickman* [1986] 1 EGLR 161, CA.

7 See *Norfolk v Masters, Fellows and Scholars of Trinity College Cambridge* (1976) 32 P & CR 147 (LT).

3   *Miscellaneous*

In the event of any dispute as to the price payable, it being initially supposed that the parties are to agree to it, the price must be determined by the leasehold valuation tribunal, which has jurisdiction also to determine any ancillary questions such as the terms of the conveyance (s 21).

The tenant has the right to resile by notice to the landlord once the price has been determined (s 9(3)) but this ends his rights under the relevant notice and no further rights may be claimed under the 1967 Act for three further years (s 9(3)).

The conveyance

The landlord's obligation under s 8(1) is to convey to the tenant the house and premises in fee simple, subject to the tenancy and incumbrances on the leasehold interest created by the tenant (eg sub-tenancies, mortgages etc), but otherwise free from incumbrances. Incumbrances attaching to the freehold (eg rights of beneficiaries under a trust of land) are to be overreached, and for that purpose, the tenant is, in any event, to be treated as a purchaser for valuable consideration. Rights binding upon the land, such as easements and restrictive covenants, cannot be defeated, except by virtue of the general law, and the liability of the tenant is expressly preserved in relation to burdens originating in tenure and burdens in respect of the upkeep or regulation for the benefit of any locality of any land, building, structure, works, ways or water courses.[8]

Unless the tenant agrees otherwise, or they are excluded to protect the landlord's existing interest in tenants' incumbrances, the rights under ss 62 and 63 of the Law of Property Act 1925, will be implied in the conveyance (s 10(1)). Additionally, the tenant is entitled to have the benefit, so far as the landlord is capable of granting them, of easements that he had under the tenancy (including rights of support, light and air, the passage of water or gas, sewage, drainage, and the use of maintenance of electricity, telephone or television cables; and conversely the burden of such easements may be imposed on the tenant for the benefit of other land (s 10(2)). Rights of way necessary for the reasonable enjoyment of the house by the tenant (or of other property retained by the landlord) are to be included in the conveyance (s 10(3)), as are covenants restrictive of user for the purpose of ensuring that existing covenants remain enforceable, of indemnifying the landlord in respect of any breaches, or of enhancing the value of the house of the tenant or land of the landlord (s 10(4)).

The tenant is liable for the landlord's legal and other professional fees and incurred in verifying the tenant's claim, having the house valued and executing the conveyance (s 9(4)). The landlord has a lien in respect of the purchase price, his costs, arrears of rent and any other sums due under the tenancy up to the date of the conveyance (s 9(5)).

---

8   While the tenant acquires any intermediate interest superior to his (s 5(4) and Sch 1), if he holds the freehold already, he is not given the right to acquire intermediate leasehold interests: *Gratton-Storey v Lewis* [1987] 2 EGLR 108, CA.

Rights of assigns

The rights of a tenant to enfranchise or to an extended lease, after a tenant's notice, are, by s 5(2), assignable with, but not apart from, the tenancy of the entire house and premises. An assignment without the benefit of the notice nullifies the notice, as does an assignment of the tenancy of one part only of the house and premises, to another person.

IV EXTENSION OF THE LEASE

The tenant's right to claim a single extension of his lease for 50 years under s 14 is dependent upon all the conditions having been satisfied and the service of a valid notice of intention by the tenant.

The 50-year extension runs from the date on which the existing tenancy would have come to an end (i e the term date). In effect, the new tenancy will be substituted for any rights of continuation under Part I of the 1954 Act. The Rent Act 1977 does not apply to an extended lease (s 16(1A)). Nor is it an assured tenancy or an assured agricultural occupancy within Part I of the Housing Act 1988.[9] The tenant is liable to pay the landlord's legal and other professional fees and costs incurred in verifying the tenant's claim, executing the lease, and valuing the house and premises for the purpose of fixing the rent (s 14(2)), and the landlord is not bound to execute the lease until such costs have been paid, together with any arrears of rent or other sums due under the existing tenancy (s 14(3)).

Where he would otherwise have had the right, the tenant may claim enfranchisement at any time before the term date of his existing tenancy, even though he first claimed an extension, but once the extended tenancy has commenced, he loses all further rights under the Act, and any rights he would have had under the 1954 Act, or under the Rent Act 1977 (s 16(1)): and a sub-tenancy granted by a tenant under an extended lease cannot acquire any rights under the Act (s 16(4)), nor under the 1954 Act, nor under Part VII of the Rent Act 1977 (s 16(1)).

Terms of the extended tenancy

Section 15(2) provides in effect that the rent payable under the extended tenancy shall be a modern ground rent for the site only, to be determined not more than 12 months before the new rent becomes payable. A rent review clause exercisable after 25 years, on notice, may be inserted, if the landlord so requires. In fixing the rent, regard must be had to any changes in the property to be comprised in the new tenancy, or in the terms of the new tenancy; further, costs of services, repairs, maintenance, etc, may be added (s 15(3)).

The other terms of the tenancy will generally be the same as under the existing tenancy, except in so far as they need to be modified as a result of

---

9 Leasehold Reform Act 1967, s 16(1A).

changes in the property, etc (s 15(1)). Options to purchase and options to renew contained in the existing lease or in a collateral agreement will not be included, however, nor any right to terminate the tenancy before the term date other than for breach of covenant (s 15(5)). Either party may under s 15(7) require the modification or exclusion of any terms under the existing tenancy that it would be unreasonable to include unchanged in view of changed circumstances since they were imposed. The landlord's right to resume possession under s 17 must be reserved (s 15(8)).

D   RIGHT OF LONG LESSEES OF FLATS TO COLLECTIVE ENFRANCHISEMENT OR TO NEW LONG LEASE

I   INTRODUCTION

General principles

Part I of the Leasehold Reform, Housing and Urban Development Act 1993 confers, as from 1 November 1993,[10] two new rights on long lessees of flats: a right to collectively buy out the freehold and all intermediate leasehold interests, and a right, on an individual basis, to a new long lease. The two rights exist in parallel. The provisions of Part I of the 1993 Act are complex, perhaps unneccessarily so.[11]

There seem to have been a number of reasons behind the enactment of this legislation. Two of these may be mentioned. Firstly, as appears from the enactment of measures such as the Landlord and Tenant Act 1987, considered in chapter 20 of this book, there has for some time been dissatisfaction with the rights and remedies available to long leaseholders of flats, at all events where they are saddled with a neglectful or absentee landlord, to the detriment of the repair and general well-being and so to the value on the market of the long leases of each flat-owner. Second, as has been mentioned earlier in this chapter, the purchase collectively of the freehold of flats cannot be the last step, since the enforcement of obligations to repair and maintain, and to pay for the cost of such works, cannot be enforced against any person who is a successor in title to freehold land.

Part I of the 1993 Act seemingly represents a step as adverse to the interests of landlords as the Leasehold Reform Act 1967 had seemed to them to be. Some might regard the 1993 Act enfranchisement provisions as being in some degree confiscatory. However this may be, the Court of Appeal have indicated that Part I of the 1993 Act must be construed fairly, and with a view, if possible, to making it effective to confer on tenants the advantages which Parliament must have intended them to enjoy.[12] The legislation is, after all, tenants' legislation

---

10 At which date it was brought into force by SI 1993/2314.
11 For reviews of the Act see Clarke [1994] Conv 223; also PF Smith [1994] 12 PM 34; for a policy evaluation, Bright [1994] Conv 211.
12 *Cadogan v McGirk* [1996] 39 EG 175, 177, CA.

and recognition of this principle by the judiciary may ease some of the technical complexities surrounding it.

Outline of collective enfranchisement scheme

The scheme of the 1993 Act is to enable the long lessees of residential flats who are qualifying tenants, holding a lease originally granted for over 21 years, to in effect rid themselves of their freeholder, against his will, provided they can surmount the various procedural obstacles of the Act. The expression 'freeholder' is now to be understood as, where appropriate, a term of art, where the freehold to one or more flats is owned by a different person to he who owns the freehold of the rest of the block.

There is a complex procedure which must be followed, which is started by preparation and service of a notice of claim by the tenants who wish to participate – since not all lessees are obliged to do so. There follows a procedure for the giving of information by and to the freeholder and the tenants must appoint a nominee purchaser, normally no doubt a company, which will acquire the freehold on their behalf, as well as all intermediate leasehold interests. The cost of service of various notices and of setting up the nominee purchaser falls on the participating tenants. On the other hand, the freeholder may have no choice but to sell his freehold, unless he is able to resist the claim by use of one or more of the limited exemptions within the scheme, or he is able to question the validity of notices on such grounds as that sufficient of the participating tenants are not resident, as required by the Act, to invalidate the claim notice. The limited power of resistance of a freeholder who cannot point to one or more of the exemptions in the Act is shown by the fact that, as with the enfranchisement of houses, he cannot refuse to reply to a tenant's claim notice and if the parties cannot agree about the terms of the acquisition, these must be settled by a leasehold valuation tribunal. The price for the freehold is to be settled in accordance with statutory rules, as is the case with the enfranchisement of houses, although in all cases the freeholder and any intermediate lessors bought out are entitled to share in the 'marriage value' arising from the acquisition of the freehold by the leaseholders.

The Act, once its procedures have been followed, presupposes the continued operation of the leasehold system as between the flat-owners after the buy-out, with the difference that, formerly, the freehold was controlled by a landlord who might have had no real concern for the good of the building, whereas the freehold, after the buy-out, is held by the participating lessees.[13] The fact that in this way, two tiers of flat lessees might be created, viz, those who participate in a buy-out and who control the freehold, and those who did not so participate, did not seem to worry Parliament; and individual flat-lessees who do not participate in collective enfranchisement may at any time demand of their new freeholder a right to a new long lease, so mitigating the otherwise undesirable consequences of such discrimination between different classes of flat lessee.

---

13 They may well hold the freehold by means of a management company, which grants the tenants who participated in collective enfranchisement long leases, eg of 999 years.

II PRECONDITIONS FOR EXERCISE OF RIGHT TO COLLECTIVE ENFRANCHISEMENT

There are a number of conditions which must be satisfied before the present right may be exercised. There must be qualifying tenants, the premises must not be excluded, and even premises which seem to qualify must comply with specific tests.

Qualifying tenants

The right to collective enfranchisement is exercisable by *qualifying tenants* who hold long leases of flats (1993 Act, s 1(1)). No flat is to have more than one qualifying tenant at any one time (s 5(3)) but where the lease is held by joint tenants, they together constitute the tenant for the purposes of Part I (s 5(4)(b)). The policy of the Act is to confer the right to collective enfranchisement on the person in residence, provided he otherwise qualifies, as is shown by the fact that if a flat is let subject to two long leases, the lessee with the superior leasehold interest is excluded from the right to collective enfranchisement (s 5(4)(a)). However, the right cannot be exercised in pluralist form: a tenant holding a long lease of two or more flats cannot claim or exercise the right to collective enfranchisement, even if they might have so qualified had they held one single lease (s 5(5)). Therefore, where, as sometimes happens, a person has bought up a number of leases of flats, and lets say two and resides in one further flat, that person cannot participate in the right to collective enfranchisement. This exclusion was deliberate, as otherwise, largely or entirely absentee lessees could have collectively exercised the present right, to the possible detriment of the resident lessees.

Long lease at low rent

In order to qualify, a tenant must be the tenant of a flat under a *long lease at a low rent* (s 5(1)). The expression 'long lease' is defined as a lease for more than 21 years certain, whether or not terminable before expiry.[14] However, a business tenancy is excluded from the right to collective enfranchisement.[15] Although a flat lessee whose lease qualifies for the right to collective enfranchisement is not subject to a residence qualification, such is imposed as a condition precedent to the right to participate in a buy-out.

There is a statutory low rent test, which is satisfied if no rent was payable under the lease during the first year from the commencement of the lease (s 8(2)(a)). This test is the same, therefore, as now applies to the enfranchisement of houses, and, alternatively, the test may be satisfied where a lease, in its initial year, is at a rent not above specified amounts.[16] However, so as to avoid loss of

---

14 1993 Act, s 7(1), which includes four other types of lease, notably, a lease granted under the right to buy conferred on secure tenants.
15 1993 Act, s 5(2)(a), as defined by s 101(1); also excluded, so emphasising the privileged position of such bodies, is a lease granted by a charitable housing trust in pursuance of its charitable housing purposes (s 5(2)(b)).
16 Eg in the case of a lease entered into on or after 1 April 1990, £1,000 if the flat is in Greater London and £250 elsewhere: 1993 Act, s 8(1)(c).

the right to collective enfranchisement arising where a long lease at a low rent comes to an end, and the tenant remains in possession under a subsequent tenancy (as where it is continued as an assured periodic tenancy), he may still claim the present right (s 7(3)). In relation to certain types of long tenancy, notably terms certain exceeding 35 years, the low rent test need not be satisfied as from the commencement of s 106 of the Housing Act 1996.

Specific exclusions

There are a small number of narrow exclusions from the right to collective enfranchisement.

1 Small premises, which contain not more than four units, with a *resident landlord* are outside the right (s 4(4)).[17]
2 There is no right to collective enfranchisement if the tenant holds a lease which itself had been created out of a superior lease in *breach of covenant* – unless the superior lease in question was itself a long lease at a low rent (s 5(1)(c)).
3 Since Part I only applies to residential flats, it does not apply if more than 10% of the internal floor area of any structurally detached premises is occupied for *non-residential purposes* (s 4(1)).[18] It has been said that this might suffice to exclude blocks of residential flats above a row of shops unless there are nine storeys of flats.[19]

Premises within Part I

While the object of Parliament throughout this legislation is to make the exercise of the right to collective enfranchisement as easy as possible for lessees, the definition of the premises which qualify is complex, because it is the policy of Part I of the 1993 Act to extend this right not only to, say, lessees in a single block of flats, but also to those holding flat leases in part of a building which may be considered as separate from the rest of the building, even though it shares a common roof or foundations with the rest of the building. There are therefore three conditions which must be satisfied before the right may apply to particular premises.

1 The premises must be a *self contained building or part of a building* (s 3(1)). The building must be structurally detached (s 3(2)).[20] The requirement of being self-contained is satisfied if the building has been vertically divided

---

17　'Resident landlord' is widely defined in s 10(5); in addition, to fall within this narrow exemption, the premises must not be in or included in a purpose-built block of flats, and there is a minimum 12-month residence limit at any one time. This exemption does not apply to the right to a new long lease.

18　In computing the 10% figure, any common parts of the disputed premises are left out of account and also, parts used or intended to be used in conjunction with a flat or flats such as garages or parking and storage areas are treated as residentially occupied (s 4(2)).

19　Matthews and Millichap, para 2.11.

20　As with a single independent block of flats; less so, where a row of terraced houses was converted into flats, but according to Clarke, p 26, some but not all might qualify (eg houses 1 and 2, being vertically separated, but not 1 and 4, not being physically linked).

and the rest of the building is such that it could be redeveloped independently of the remainder of the building (s 3(2)(a)). However, in this, it must be shown that services provided by means of pipes, cables or other fixed installations are provided independently of the same services provided for other occupiers of the remainder of the building (s 3(2)(b)(i)).[1] As originally enacted, s 3 of the 1993 Act required that the freehold must be owned by the same person, so making it possible for a freeholder to sell the freehold in one or more flats to, say, a company controlled by him. This would preclude collective enfranchisement. This loophole has now, it seems, been plugged.[2] The 1993 Act has therefore been amended throughout so as to allow collective enfranchisement to be exercised against one or more persons owning different freehold interests in the building concerned.

2   The premises must contain at least *two flats* held by qualifying tenants (s 3(1)(b)). Thus, a tenant with a flat above a shop is excluded from the right to collective enfranchisement, but not from that to a new long lease.

3   The total number of flats held by qualifying tenants must be at least two-thirds of the total number of flats contained in the premises over which the present right is claimed (s 3(1)(c)). This condition was adopted so as to ensure, it was said, that the block was occupied by a majority of qualifying tenants and that a majority of those tenants wished to buy out the freeholder under Part I of the Act.[3]

This last condition is linked to a requirement that a tenants' initial notice of claim to exercise the right to collective enfranchisement must be given by not less than two-thirds of the total qualifying tenants of the flats in the premises, ascertained as at the date of the notice, and the notice must relate to not less than half of the flats in the premises (s 13(1)). Otherwise, the right to collective enfranchisement is debarred for the time being. Suppose that a block of ten flats contains four long lessees who qualify for the exercise of the right to buy out the freeholder. Clearly, they cannot serve a notice of claim; but if there were seven out of ten qualifying tenants, and twelve flats in the block, the notice could indeed be served. However, having regard to the *residence requirement* of the Act, which requires that at least half the qualifying tenants must reside in the statutory sense[4] at the date of giving the notice of claim so as to participate in the right to collective enfranchisement (s 13(2)), a landlord faced with the seven qualifying tenants in our example might prevent the exercise of the right to collective enfranchisement if he shows that four of the tenants signing the notice of claim failed to comply with the residence test.

---

1   This condition is alternatively satisfied if the services could be provided without involving the carrying out of works likely to result in a significant interruption of any such services for occupiers of the remainder of the building (s 3(2)(b)(ii)).

2   Housing Act 1996, s 107 and Sch 10 (making consequential amendments to the 1993 Act) as from 1 October 1996: SI 1996/2212.

3   Lord Strathclyde, Hansard, 11 May 1993, col 1225.

4   Ie for periods amounting to 12 months before the notice or three years out of the last ten years (s 6) and in any case, as the tenant's only or principal home; but periods of occupation under a licence or short tenancy may count towards the residence rule (s 6(3)(b)).

III PRINCIPLES OF PROCEDURE FOR CLAIMING AND EXERCISING RIGHT TO COLLECTIVE ENFRANCHISEMENT

The following is a necessarily brief consideration of the complex procedures of the 1993 Act, which must be followed before the freehold is bought out. The persons who wish to exercise the right to acquire the freehold will need to inform themselves as to who is the freeholder (or, if need be, who are the various holders of freehold interests[5]) and the holders of any of leasehold interests in the premises, and provision is made in Part I of the Act for the service of appropriate notices designed to obtain that information (s11).[6] The nominee purchaser must be constituted by the tenants who wish to buy out the freehold and he must procure, at their expense, a valuation of the property which the tenants wish to acquire, as well as any ancillary premises as well as of any specified leasehold interests (s 13(6)).[7] After the completion of this unavoidable first step, the Act provides for the procedure leading to the conveyance of the freehold, by means of a series of notices.

1   *Initial notice*   This notice of claim is served under s 13 of the 1993 Act. As already noted, it may only be served if there are sufficient tenants of flats, and where the residence requirement is complied with by at least half the tenants who give the notice. There is a list of formal matters which a s 13 notice should contain,[8] such as a specification of the premises which are to be acquired, as well as any appurtenant property (such as garages), which is likewise claimed.[9] Since details of each tenant serving the notice must be given – such as the giving of particulars of his residence, the landlord will be able to see if he is able to reduce the number of tenants below the requisite minimum numbers, so as to defeat a s 13 notice and so a claim, on that occasion, to the right to collective enfranchisement. This notice must also inform the freeholder of the identity of the nominee purchaser, as it is to this latter person that the freeholder's own notice in response is to be given. The initial notice must specify such matters as the purchase price for the premises to be acquired – which will have been discovered by the survey.

2   *Persons disqualified to serve initial notice*   There is a statutory list of persons, whose participation would be obviously undesirable and so who

---

5   In such a case, all freeholders are subject to the enfranchisement process (s 9(2A) and may be identified by Sch I, Part 1A, added (by Housing Act 1996, Sch 10, para 15) to the 1993 Act.
6   For further details, see Matthews and Millichap, paras 3.1–3.7. They note that there is no direct sanction against a freeholder for non-response to information notices; but indicate that in their view, where title is registered, an application to the (now open) Land Registry might do just as well from the lessee's point of view.
7   The valuation so made must conform to Sch 6 of the 1993 Act.
8   However, so as to ease the path of tenants, any inaccuracy in the relevant particulars or any misdescription of the relevant property do not of themselves invalidate a s 13 notice (1993 Act, Sch 3, Part III, para 15(1); but a failure to enclose a plan of the property rendered a s 13 notice invalid as a failure to comply is not an inaccuracy: *Mutual Place Property Management Ltd v Blaquiere* [1996] 28 EG 143.
9   If it is proposed to acquire any intermediate leasehold interests, these must be specified in the notice (hence the importance of the information notices already referred to).

cannot participate in service of a s 13 notice of claim, such as a tenant who might otherwise qualify but who has given notice to terminate his long lease, and likewise, a tenant against whom there are pending forfeiture proceedings.[10]

3   *Freeholder's response*   Any freeholder must, within the time stated in the s 13 notice,[11] serve a counter-notice on the nominee purchaser (s 21(1)). If he fails to do so, the court has default powers on the application of the nominee purchaser to determine the terms of the acquisition.[12] The counter-notice must do one of three things. It may admit the right of the tenants' to participate in collective enfranchisement; it may deny the right for reasons stated or it may indicate that the landlord intends to redevelop the premises, and to apply for a court order under s 23 that therefore the right to collective enfranchisement is not possible.[13] Where the notice admits the right to collective enfranchisement, it must then state which of the tenants' proposals in the initial notice it accepts and which it does not, putting forward alternative proposals in the latter case(s 21(3)). Thus the freeholder may reject the price and also the premises suggested for acquisition and suggest alternatives.[14]

If any landlord would, thanks to the exercise of the right of collective enfranchisement, be left with property which would, in particular, cease for all practical purposes to be of use and benefit to him then he may in his counter-notice require that this property is included in the premises to be acquired by the nominee purchaser on behalf of the participating tenants (s 21(4)).

IV   TERMS AND PRICE OF ACQUISITION

Following the service of the above notices, the parties may be able to agree on the terms of the acquisition, but, if they cannot, or cannot agree on some of them, then either side may apply to the leasehold valuation tribunal to resolve the disputed terms, within two months of the giving of a freeholders' counter-notice (s 24(1)).[15]

---

10 1993 Act, Sch 3, paras 2 and 3. By contrast, once a notice of claim is served, and is current, no landlords' or tenants' notice to terminate the lease has any effect on the claim (para 5).
11 Ie not less than two months of the date of the service of the tenants' notice of claim.
12 1993 Act, s 25(1), provided the application is within six months of the last date for the giving of the freeholder's notice. The terms will be those as set out in the initial notice under s 13.
13 The landlord may use this means of defeating a claim only if two-thirds of the relevant long leases are due to expire within five years of the date of service of the initial notice (s 23(2)(a)). The landlord must also show that the work intended is akin to that required by s 30(1)(f) of the Landlord and Tenant Act 1954, Part II.
14 The freeholder also may to require the lease-back of part of the premises from the nominee purchaser, eg mandatorily where any flat is held on a secure tenancy and where the freeholder is his landlord (1993 Act, s 36 and Sch 9).
15 If no application is made on time to the tribunal, the whole procedure is deemed to have been withdrawn (s 29(2)). The terms include the purchase price (s 24(8)): *Moore v Escalus Properties Ltd* [1997] 07 EG 149, (LUT).

Price of freehold

The price of the freehold and of any intermediate leasehold interests is determined by a statutory formula[16] and not by the agreement of the parties. The main rule is that the price payable by the nominee purchaser, for the tenants, for the freehold and also for intermediate leasehold interests is the open market price payable as between a willing landlord and a willing tenant. There are a number of assumptions, so that it is assumed that the nominee purchaser acquires the freehold incumbered by the existing leases – otherwise, presumably, the price would rise greatly in some cases. Tenants' improvements to any flat held by a participating tenant are to be left out of account. If there is more than one freeholder concerned, as where flying freeholds on flats A and B are held by one person and the rest of the building is owned in freehold by a different person, the nominee purchaser must pay a separate price for the freehold of these parts, calculated in accordance with a specific formula.[17]

An important concession to the freeholder and, where relevant, to intermediate leaseholders being bought out is that they are entitled to share in the marriage value of the premises. This means the increase in value resulting from the fact that the person acquiring will be able to obtain a new long lease without paying any premium and for an unlimited length of time. Moveover, a separate price must be paid for each intermediate leasehold interest.

Completion

The whole procedure of collective enfranchisement, which commenced with the preliminary inquiry notice, and was followed by the tenants' initial notice and reversioners' counter-notice, is followed, once the price has been determined and the other terms agreed or determined, by a conveyance to the nominee purchaser of the freehold of the specified premises or part or of any other property (s 34(1)). The nominee purchaser's fee simple absolute is stripped of all intermediate leasehold interests, if any. Moreover, the effect of the conveyance is in principle to discharge the property from any mortgage (s 35). The conveyance must be conformity to the statutory rules.[18] After due conveyance, the nominee purchaser will apply for registration of title to the Land Registry.

V RIGHT TO NEW LONG LEASE

Introduction

There may be a number of long lessees of flats who are not able to participate in collective enfranchisement, because they are excluded from it, or because

---

16 1993 Act, s 32 and Sch 6 as amended by Housing Act 1996, s 109 as from 1 October 1996: SI 1996/2212.
17 1993 Act, Sch 6, para 5A, inserted by Housing Act 1996, Sch 10, para 18(5).
18 1993 Act, Sch 7. This is for example to ensure, so far as possible, that the nominee purchaser, and so the acquiring lessees, enjoy the same rights of support, access and so on as were enjoyed up until the conveyance with the premises. The conveyance must contain the statement required by SI 1993/3045.

there are insufficient other lessees interested in exercising that right. At the same time, it appears that a residential long lease which has an unexpired term of less than 60 years is difficult to assign or to mortgage. At all events, the legislature has enacted a right to obtain a new, and individual, long lease. The procedures for the exercise of this right, with due modifications, are those which govern collective enfranchisement. The right is exercised as against the landlord, ie a freeholder or a long leaseholder whose reversion is sufficient to enable him to grant a new long lease (s 40(1)).[19] If successfully exercised, the lessee obtains a substituted lease at a peppercorn rent for the term of his current unexpired lease plus 90 years (s 56(1)). The right to a new long lease may be exercised again, after expiry of the new term. The new lease is paid for by a premium calculated in accordance with the 1993 Act.

The tenant, if his claim succeeds, obtains a new lease of a 'flat' – which expression bears an extended statutory definition (s 62(2)), and so includes any garage, outhouse, gardens, yard and appurtenances 'belonging to or usually enjoyed with' the flat. Unlike the position with the Leasehold Reform Act 1967 s 2(3), where any appurtenance, for example, must be within the curtilage of the house,[20] owing perhaps to the difficult questions of degree which might otherwise arise, in the case of new long leases of flats, it suffices if the appurtenant property is within the premises of which the flat forms part.[1] Hence, the tenant of a second-floor flat was entitled to have included in his new long lease a box attic room situated on the sixth floor of the building.

Conditions for exercise of right

The right to an individual long lease is conferred on a 'qualifying tenant' holding a long lease at a low rent.[2] The individual concerned[3] must comply with a residence condition, which is occupation of the flat as his only or principal home for the last three years or for periods amounting to three years in the last ten years (s 39(2) and (3)). Provided the tenant is able to show periods of residence amounting in a ten year maximum period to three years, it makes no difference that at some periods, he has sub-let the whole of the flat. Moreover, residence for the relevant periods in part of the flat concerned is sufficient (s 39(5)(a)), so that if a lessee who has resided in a flat for the last three years has sub-let part of the flat for that period, retaining the rest, the residence qualification will be satisfied.

---

19 If a claim to collective enfranchisement is made before or after a claim to an individual new long lease is made, the former claim suspends the latter, which is then to be disposed of once the collective buy-out has succeeded or failed (1993 Act, s 54).
20 *Methuen-Campbell* v *Walters* [1979] QB 525, [1979] 1 All ER 606, CA.
1   *Cadogan* v *McGirk* [1996] 39 EG 175, CA.
2   These expressions are defined as for collective enfranchisement (s 39(3)(b) and (c)).
3   In the case of joint tenants, only any one of them needs to comply with the residence requirement (s 39(6)) and, by s 42(4), the three year total residence may be made up out of the residence periods of different joint tenants, so that if A and B are joint tenants of a flat and A resides there for 12 months and B for 24, in total, in the last 5 years, the requirement is satisfied.

Outline of procedure

As with collective enfranchisement, the process is commenced by the tenant making preliminary inquiries (s 41). This may then be followed by a tenant's notice under s 42. This notice is given to the landlord and to any third party to the lease. However, a notice served in certain cases is of no effect, in particular, if it is given after the tenant has by notice terminated the lease of the flat,[4] or if it is given more than two months after a landlord's notice to terminate the lease.[5] In addition, if the landlord is able to show to the satisfaction of the court that, where the tenant's lease is due to terminate within five years from the service of his notice of claim, he intends to redevelop the whole or a substantial part of the premises in which the flat is contained, he can defeat the exercise of the right to a new long lease.[6]

It must give certain details, such as sufficient particulars of the flat to identify the property in question, as well as such particulars of the tenant's lease as identify it, and show that it is a lease at a low rent. The notice must supply particulars of the relevant periods of residence within the ten years preceding the service of the notice. The tenant's notice must also specify the premium he is prepared to pay for the new lease as well as his proposals for the other terms of the new lease.[7]

Once served, the notice continues to run until the right to a new lease is established, or the claim is withdrawn, or the claim fails (s 42(8)). If a notice is given and then withdrawn, no further notice may be given with respect to that flat for a further 12 months from the date of withdrawal (s 42(7)).[8] The effect of a s 42 notice is that the rights and obligations arising from the notice of both parties enure for their benefit and that of their successors in title 'as rights and obligations arising under a contract for leasing freely entered into between the landlord and tenant' (s 43(1)). Thus, the tenant is treated, from that time, as being entitled, in equity, to the grant of a new long lease, provided he complies with such requirements as the payment of a premium.[9]

Once a s 42 notice has been given, the existing lease cannot be terminated during the currency of the claim and for three months after then by effluxion of time, or by a notice from the tenant's immediate landlord, or by termination of any superior lease.[10]

---

4 Or where the tenant is obliged to give up possession of the flat under a court order: 1993 Act, Sch 12, para 3.
5 Under Part I of the 1954 Act or Sch 10 to the Local Government etc Act 1989, as the case may be: 1993 Act, Sch 12, para 2.
6 By specifying this intention in his counter-notice (s 47(1)). The conditions are specified in s 47(2) and are akin to those applicable to collective enfranchisement. If the landlord's application to court fails, the court must order him to serve a fresh counter-notice on the tenant (s 47(4)) so recommencing the statutory procedure.
7 The date for service of the landlord's counter-notice must be specified (s 42(3)(f)), which must be not less than two months after the giving of the notice (s 42(5)).
8 As noted by Matthews and Millichap, para 4.24, a purchaser of a flat subject to a s 42 notice ought to take an assignment of the benefit of this notice (and so profiting from s 43(1)).
9 But if the lease is assigned without the benefit of the notice, the notice is automatically withdrawn (s 43(3)).
10 1993 Act, Sch 12, para 5(1). Similarly, by para 6, during the currency of a claim, forfeiture proceedings against the lessee require the leave of the court, which is only to be granted if the notice was given for the purpose of averting a forfeiture.

The landlord is entitled, as from the giving of the tenant's claim notice, to gain access to the flat concerned for valuation purposes (s 44) and he must, within the time-limit allowed by the tenant's notice, serve a counter-notice (s 45). The purpose and, as modified for the lease renewal scheme, contents, of this notice are similar to those of the landlord's counter-notice in the case of collective enfranchisement.[11]

Steps to obtaining new lease

If the landlord's counter-notice does not admit the right of the tenant, he may prevent the exercise of the right going further by applying to the court for a declaration to that effect (s 46(1)) but if the application is dismissed, the landlord's counter-notice will be declared to be of no effect and he will be required to serve a further counter-notice (s 46(4)).[12]

However, if the landlord accepts the right to a new long lease but disputes some of the terms, or the landlord proposes terms which the tenant does not accept, and they cannot resolve their differences, then either party may apply to a leasehold valuation tribunal to resolve them (s 48(1)).[12a] The application must be made within two months of the giving of the landlord's counter-notice (s 48(2)). The landlord cannot evade the granting of a new long lease by failing to serve a counter-notice, for, in this case, the tenant may apply to the court to determine the terms of the new long lease (s 49).

Terms of new lease

The new lease is for a substituted term of 90 years from the expiry date of the existing lease, and at a peppercorn rent (s 56(1)).[13] A premium must be paid as calculated in accordance with the Act, so as to take into account any diminution in the value of the landlord's interest in the flat, based on market values subject to statutory assumptions. The landlord is entitled to a share in the marriage value.[14] The tenant has to pay the rent due up to the date of the new lease (s 56(3)).

The other terms of the new lease are the same as those of the existing lease which it replaces.[15] If the terms of the old lease did not contain any provision for variable service charges, or indeed for any service charges, the terms of the new lease must provide for the payment of such charges and for suitable enforcement provisions (s 57(2)).[16] Were it not for this provision, the landlord

---

11 Thus, the counter-notice must admit the claim, or state that the landlord denies it, for stated reasons, or, in either case, that he intends to apply for an order under s 47 because of his intention to redevelop any premises in which the flat is situated; as to this ground and to the procedure generally, see Matthews and Millichap, paras 4.21–4.36.

12 However, applications relating to redevelopment are saved from this provision (s 46(5)).

12a See *Hordern v Viscount Chelsea* [1997] 07 EG 144 (LUT).

13 Any prohibition in a superior lease which prohibits absolutely or in a qualified way the granting of a new long lease is overridden (s 56(5)).

14 1993 Act, Sch 13 as amended, Part III of which provides for the payment by the tenant of compensation to the holders of any intermediate leaseholds affected by the grant of the new lease.

15 Subject to any modifications as specified in s 57(1), eg that the new lease is of the flat only and not of other premises in the former lease.

16 The parties may otherwise agree (s 57(6)).

could not, it appears. have asked the court to insert a new or revised service charges clause in the new lease, as such a modification might only have been capable of being imposed on an unwilling tenant if the landlord offered some compensations: Either party may require the other to modify the terms of the existing lease in so far as necessary to do so to remedy a 'defect' in the existing lease or in view of changes occurring since the commencement of the existing lease which affect the suitability of the provisions of the lease (s 57(6)). It seems that, so far, the word 'necessary' is treated as limiting the power of the landlord to vary the terms of a lease and it will not suffice to show that it might be convenient, or in accordance with modern practice, to revise the disputed term.[17] The new lease is not subject to any statutory security of tenure provisions but it may be further renewed at any time (s 59(1)). In this respect, the position of long lessees of flats who obtain a substituted new long lease is much better than those lessees of houses who cannot enfranchise, since they only obtain a single 50 year term, which is not renewable.

17 *Waitt v Morris* [1994] 2 EGLR 224, LVT (where a new suggested term about notification of mortgagees by the landlord prior to forfeitures was rejected).

PART E
BUSINESS TENANCIES

Chapter 22

Introduction

The relationship of landlord and tenant of business premises is governed by the general law until the contractual tenancy expires, or the landlord serves a notice to quit or otherwise terminates the tenancy at law. Thereafter, Part II of the Landlord and Tenant Act 1954 applies, and it is only possible to regain possession as laid down in the Act.

The following is a summary of the main effects of the 1954 Act.

1   Business tenants are given security initially by the continuation, despite termination of the contractual term, of the tenancy (s 24).
2   Continuation is on the same terms as the contractual tenancy: and may be prevented or terminated only as provided in the 1954 Act.
3   The landlord may prevent, or set in motion, the termination of continuation by a strict notice procedure (s 25): if he wishes to regain possession where the tenant is unwilling to give it up, he may do so only on the grounds in s 30. This procedure generally overrides the common law methods: certain of these are specially preserved (s 24(2)) such as forfeiture and tenants' notice to quit.
4   If the landlord has not served a s 25 notice, the tenant may request by notice a new tenancy (ss 26 and 24(1)(b)). If the landlord has served a s 25 notice, the tenant must first, if he wishes a new tenancy, state his unwillingness to give up possession and then apply to court for a new tenancy (ss 24(1)(a) and 29(2)). In both cases the landlord may resist the new tenancy on one of a number of grounds in s 30.
5   In the event that the court orders a new tenancy (on the basis of guidelines in ss 32-35) the tenancy may be for up to 14 years and is for a term certain.
6   Should the landlord make out a ground of opposition to the grant of a new tenancy and the tenant quits, he may be entitled to compensation for quitting and also for qualifying improvements (these latter being dealt with by Part I of the Landlord and Tenant Act 1927).

These procedural rules have to be carefully followed and yet it is thought that a key policy of Part II of the 1954 Act is to encourage the parties to agree on matters out of court, although if the parties negotiate 'subject to contract' beyond the strict time-limits for a tenants' application to court for a new tenancy, the tenant loses his right to claim a new tenancy under the Act if the landlord exercises his right to resile prior to the conclusion of a final agreement.[1]

---

1   See *Saloman v Akiens* [1993] 1 EGLR 101, CA; the same rule would apply where it is the tenant who resiles: see *Derby & Co Ltd v ITC Pension Trust Ltd* [1977] 2 All ER 890.

It is for this reason alone that the time-limits laid down in the Act must be strictly adhered to. In any event, these are imposed so as to require some speed of decision from both parties, once the statutory processes have been commenced by either side.

The policy of Part II of the 1954 Act has been described as follows by the Law Commission.[2] Part II recognises that a business tenant stands to lose any goodwill he has built up, and much of the value of his equipment and stock, if he has to leave when his tenancy expires. So, as a rule, he is able to obtain a renewal of his tenancy, or, failing that, compensation.

Part II of the 1954 Act is thought to work well, but some difficulties on particular points of detail may be noted.

1   In the case of joint tenants, all must together apply for a new tenancy under the Act, otherwise the application will fail.[3] This rule has been modified for partnership tenancies (s 41A of the 1954 Act).
2   Difficulty has been experienced in balancing the interests of landlord and tenant where the terms of a new tenancy are reviewed by the court. It is generally thought that the House of Lords' decision in *O'May v City of London Real Property Co Ltd*[4] precludes any modernisation of the form of the lease by the court under s 35. The Law Commission doubted[5] whether there was any need to amend the legislation, despite the view of some critics that the *O'May* principle is weighted against landlords.
3   The compensation provisions applicable where the landlord succeeds on one of any of three mandatory grounds for possession under s 30, are linked to the rateable value of the premises concerned. It has been said that they should be linked to the tenant's actual loss.[6]
4   A tenant holding a lease of business premises personally may lose security under the 1954 Act Part II if he incorporates his business, although he might be able to avert this result if he is able to assign the lease to the relevant company, which might require the landlord's consent. Where tenants ran a business and held the lease in their personal names, and later they incorporated the business, the lease continued to be held by them personally.[7] As a result, it was held that since the tenants traded through a company, they could not obtain a renewal of the lease under the Act, as they were not in occupation within s 23.[8]

The Law Commission have recommended a number of specific improvements to the workings of Part II of the 1954 Act.[9] The Report does not propose a fundamental overhaul of the Act but it lists a number of reforms which are

2   Law Com No 141 (1985), para 7.22.
3   *Jacobs v Chaudhuri* [1968] 2 QB 470, [1968] 2 All ER 124, CA.
4   [1983] 2 AC 726, [1982] 1 All ER 660, HL.
5   Report, infra, para 3.35.
6   Law Com No 162 (1987), para 4.58.
7   *Cristina v Seear* [1985] 2 EGLR 128, CA.
8   Occupation by trust beneficiaries is treated as within the Act by s 41 and groups of companies are specially treated by s 42.
9   *Landlord and Tenant: Business Tenancies: A Periodic Review of the Landlord and Tenant Act 1954 Part II* Law Com No 208 HC 224.

significant, if technical.[10] It bears in mind three general principles: (i) the need to maintain the present fair overall balance between landlord and tenant; (ii) the retention of the present renewal procedure (with adjustments of detail); and (iii) the need not to require the taking of court proceedings as a routine part of the procedure.[11]

The Report does not, however, call into question a basic rule that when the court orders a new tenancy, it should not revise the terms of the contractual tenancy against the wishes of either party unless the party claiming change proves that the change is justified and reasonable. As this is a heavy onus of proof, the usual assumption is that the principal terms of the contractual tenancy will not be revised without the agreement of both parties.[12]

There is, at the time of writing, a possibility of further legislation in this field, because during the summer of 1996, the Department of the Environment produced a consultation paper. In essence, it favours the implentation by legislation of the Law Commission recommendations with only a few minor modifications.[13] The recently-produced Code of Practice in relation to commercial tenancies[14] has now enabled the present government to say that the time is right for reforms, most notably so as to make it possible to contract out of Part II of the 1954 Act without any need to seek the approval of the court.

The main recommendations of the Law Commission may be summarised as follows.

1   An individual and the company he controls should be treated as the same entity for the purposes of the renewal procedure. At present, as noted, if an individual tenant incorporates, he loses the right to renew the lease if the company so formed occupies the premises.[15] (See also 3 below.)
2   Companies controlled by one individual should be treated as members of groups of companies for the purposes of the Act.[16]
3   The tenant should retain his right to renew under the Act even if the premises are occupied by a company controlled by the tenant, or the individual occupying the premises controls the tenant company.[17]
4   Where the landlord is a company, it should be able to oppose a new tenancy (under s 30(1)(g) below) even though the property is to be occupied by the company for business purposes and the business is to be carried on by the individual who controls the company, or another company in the same group.[18]
5   Where an individual acquires control of a landlord company within five years of the date of the tenant's application to the court for a new tenancy, he should not be able to oppose the application under s 30(1)(g) where the

10 For a critique of the Report and of the Act generally see Haley (1993) 13 LS 225.
11 *Report*, para 1.9.
12 *Report*, para 3.32-3.33.
13 See passim Martin [1996] 34 EG 86.
14 See the Appendix to this book, note to Precedent 1.
15 Para 2.7.
16 Para 2.8.
17 Para 2.9.
18 Para 2.10.

tenancy existed when he assumed control. This would extend the protection of the five year rule (s 30(2)) to corporate control.[19]

6   The Law Commission proposes to revise the contracting-out procedures so that certain formalities would have to be observed by both parties for any agreement to contract out of the right to renew to be effective.[20] However, if these new formalities were followed, with the idea of ensuring that the tenant had full information as to his position, contracting out would become possible without the need, as at present, to seek the approval of the county court.

7   The statutory information procedures would be revised. For example, both parties would be placed under a duty to give information to each other within the last two years of the term of the lease, a breach of which duty would be actionable in damages. The duty would include a duty within six months of supplying any information, to update that information. This duty would bind any assignee, to the exclusion of the original landlord or tenant who served the notice. The information covered would include a statement as to whether the tenant occupies the whole or part of the property for business purposes, and details of any sub-letting, in the case of tenants, and, as regards landlords, as to whether he is a freeholder or mortgagee and the identity of any reversioner of a severed part of the reversion.[1]

8   A landlord who serves a s 25 notice terminating the tenancy would have to include his proposals for a new tenancy. The tenant would not have to serve a counter-notice, once a s 25 notice had been served on him. Both parties should be entitled to apply for renewal of the tenancy. The tenant would no longer be forced, as at present, to wait for two months from service of a s 25 notice, before applying for a new tenancy.[2]

9   There would be a number of reforms of the interim rent scheme, most notably that the date for payment of interim rent should be moved to the date specified in the landlord's s 25 notice to terminate the tenancy or the first date which he could have specified – with the same rule to apply where the tenant has served a s 26 new tenancy request. The amount of the interim rent should be at least equal to that payable initially under the new lease.[3]

10 The maximum length of the term allowed to be ordered would go up to the more convenient figure of 15 years – not 14 as it now is.[4]

11 Compensation for disturbance should in future be payable *inter alia* where the landlord withdraws his action to terminate the lease, which is not the case at the moment. On the other hand, it would be calculated for each part of the property occupied by the tenant, if he occupied different parts for a different length of time.[5]

---

19 Para 2.11.
20 Thus the tenant would have to declare in the agreement that he read and understood the terms of the prescribed form agreement and statement (para 2.14-2.16 and 2.20).
 1 Paras 2.24-2.32.
 2 Paras 2.34-2.39.
 3 Paras 2.61-2.75.
 4 Paras 2.76-2.79.
 5 Paras 2.81-2.84.

Chapter 23

Application of Part II of the 1954 Act

I TENANCIES PROTECTED BY PART II

Section 23(1) provides that Part II of the Landlord and Tenant Act 1954 'applies to any tenancy where the property comprised in the tenancy is or includes premises which are occupied by the tenant and are so occupied for the purposes of a business carried on by him or for those and other purposes'.

Tenancy

There must be a *tenancy* before Part II applies. The expression 'tenancy' is defined by s 69(1) as including a tenancy created either immediately or derivatively out of the freehold, by lease or underlease, and also includes an agreement for a lease or underlease or by a tenancy agreement or under any enactment, including Part II. Thus it makes no difference whether the agreement for a tenancy is by deed, written or oral, but licences are excluded from Part II.[1] Express or implied tenancies at will are excluded from Part II.[2] Where it is not clear whether the parties have agreed on a tenancy, the presence of Part II security if a tenancy is granted impliedly is a relevant factor in assessing the parties' intentions: where a person was granted a series of extensions to his current tenancy, which excluded ss 22 to 28 of the 1954 Act, Part II, pending negotiations for a new tenancy, which failed, it was held that even though, in the interim, rent was paid and accepted, the occupier was, from expiry of his old agreement, merely a tenant at will and outside Part II: he was not a periodic tenant by implication of law.[3]

Occupation: the premises and the holding

Part II of the 1954 Act confers statutory renewal rights only on a business tenant who is in occupation of the 'holding' for the purposes of his business, which may include ancillary purposes, such as his residence. The Act distinguishes

---

1 *Shell-Mex and BP Ltd v Manchester Garages Ltd* [1971] 1 All ER 841, [1971] 1 WLR 612, CA; *Dresden Estates Ltd v Collinson* (1987) 55 P & CR 47, CA; see further ch 3.
2 *Manfield & Sons Ltd v Botchin* [1970] 2 QB 612, [1970] 3 All ER 143; *Hagee (London) Ltd v Erikson and Larson* [1976] QB 209, [1975] 3 All ER 234, CA (express); *Wheeler v Mercer* [1957] AC 416, [1956] 3 All ER 631, HL (implied).
3 *Cardiothoracic Institute v Shrewdcrest Ltd* [1986] 3 All ER 633, [1986] 1 WLR 368; also *Javad v Aqil* [1991] 1 All ER 243, [1991] 1 WLR 1007, CA.

between the premises as designated by the contractual tenancy and the 'holding'. It continues the whole contractual tenancy as from the common law expiry date under s 24(1). However, renewal under Part II is only possible for a tenant who is in personal occupation of the 'holding'. By s 23(3), the 'holding' is the part of the property comprised in the contractual tenancy, excluding any part not occupied by the tenant for the purposes of his business.

It is therefore important to bear in mind that, to obtain the benefit of continuation under the Act as well as statutory renewal rights, the tenant must satisfy the occupation test of s 23(1) and also occupy the 'holding', personally or through a servant or agent. Therefore, if the tenant has sub-let the whole of the premises to a sub-tenant, he no longer occupies a 'holding' for business purposes and cannot claim renewal rights under Part II. This is because, according to the House of Lords, the policy of Part II of the 1954 Act is not to protect a mesne landlord's rental income, but to confer renewal rights on an occupying business tenant. In our example, the occupying sub-tenant may claim renewal from the head landlord in respect of his 'holding' (owing to the combined operation of ss 23(3) and 44 of the Act).[4]

In addition, difficulties may arise where the tenant has sub-let part of the property and retains part. In such a case, depending on the facts, the tenant would only occupy for renewal purposes a 'holding' which amounted to the parts he occupied at the date of the court order for a new tenancy (which is the relevant date). The sub-tenant could claim renewal for the parts he occupied for business purposes at that date. It may be that the tenant has sub-let most of the premises: in such a case only the sub-tenant may claim renewal if the tenant could not run a business solely in the retained parts. In one case, a tenant sub-let most of a market trading area to sub-tenants. He retained an office in the premises and provided services to the sub-tenants. Since it was held that Part II of the 1954 Act does not permit the simultaneous occupation by two persons of a 'holding', the sub-tenants were held to occupy their 'holdings' to the exclusion of the tenant and could alone exercise renewal rights.[5]

Occupation: existence in fact

Turning now to the existence of the occupation requirement for continuation and renewal purposes, the question is ultimately a question of fact and degree and no hard and fast rule may safely be laid down.[6] The Court of Appeal has emphasised that s 23 shows that occupation for business purposes is essential, and that this provision recognises that the occupation may change from time to time while a tenancy continues.[7] Dealing with cases where a dispute arises whether a tenant, who has not sub-let any part of the premises, is in occupation, as well as where it is a sub-tenant who claims to be in occupation, a continuity or thread of occupation must exist, but it is not necessary for the tenant to be

---

4 *Graysim Holdings Ltd v P & O Property Holdings Ltd* [1996] AC 329, [1995] 4 All ER 831, HL, approving *Bagettes Ltd v GP Estates Co Ltd* [1956] Ch 290, [1956] 1 All ER 729, CA.
5 *Graysim Holdings Ltd v P & O Property Holdings Ltd*, supra.
6 As recognised by Lord Nicholls in *Graysim Holdings Ltd v P & O Property Holdings Ltd* supra.
7 *Esselte AB v Pearl Assurance plc* [1997] 02 EG 124.

continuously in physical occupation: thus, premises capable only of seasonal occupation may fall within Part II.[8] Similarly, the fact that the tenant had temporarily abandoned occupation but intended to resume it if granted a new tenancy,[9] or that he temporarily abandoned occupation after a fire, with the intention of resuming it, leaving certain fittings and fixtures,[10] did not prevent the tenant from retaining the right to apply for a new tenancy. The thread of continuity was held to have been broken where the tenants ceased their business activity at the premises, began it at other premises and merely wished, if so allowed by the Gaming Board, to resume it at the subject premises if granted a new tenancy.[11] Likewise, a tenant who, some ten days before the contractual expiry date of the tenancy, had removed all its equipment from the premises, had ceased to 'occupy' for statutory purposes on expiry of the tenancy and the tenancy did not continue under s 24(1) of the Act, owing to the requirement, read into s 24(1), of continuing occupation by the tenant at the expiry date.[12]

Sometimes, a tenant cannot be said, owing to his nature, to be in personal occupation, as where he is a company or unincorporated association: in such cases, occupation by the tenant's employees (such as managers) or agents suffices, if they maintain a sufficient degree of management and control over the premises, which is itself a question of fact and degree. For example, the Board of Governors of a hospital were capable on the facts of complying with the requirement.[13] So was a Secretary of State, owing to the day-to-day control exercised over the premises – employee flats.[14] Where a local authority's servants regularly exercised control over the premises, a piece of land used for the purposes of leisure and recreation, and carried out work on the land from time to time, it was held that the occupation requirement was satisfied.[15] Should the premises be only occupied by the tenant's servants, only if this is a necessary part of their contractual duties will such occupation be ancillary to the occupation of the tenant, and so within Part II.[16] In all of these cases, the court looks through the occupation of the servants, managers or agents to the tenant itself, which differentiates the position from the exclusive occupation by a sub-tenant.

By contrast, where the tenant carried on the business of proprietor of lock-up garages and sub-let most of them, retaining merely a nominal presence on the land, he failed to satisfy the occupation test as the degree of control he exerted was insufficient on the facts.[17] Although a tenant who let most of the

---

8 *Teasdale v Walker* [1958] 3 All ER 307, [1958] 1 WLR 1076, CA (where the tenant was not in occupation, having made a fictitious management agreement with a third party).

9 *I & H Caplan v Caplan (No 2)* [1963] 2 All ER 930, [1963] 1 WLR 1247.

10 *Morrison Holdings Ltd v Manders Property (Wolverhampton) Ltd* [1976] 2 All ER 205, [1976] 1 WLR 533, CA.

11 *Aspinall Finance Ltd v Viscount Chelsea* [1989] 1 EGLR 103.

12 *Esselte AB v Pearl Assurance plc* [1997] 02 EG 124, CA.

13 *Hills (Patents) Ltd v University College Hospital Board of Governors* [1956] 1 QB 90, [1955] 3 All ER 365, CA; also *Groveside Properties Ltd v Westminster Medical School* [1983] 2 EGLR 68.

14 *Linden v Department of Health and Social Security* [1986] 1 All ER 691, [1986] 1 WLR 164.

15 *Wandsworth London Borough v Singh* [1991] 2 EGLR 75, CA.

16 See *Groveside Properties Ltd v Westminster Medical School* (1983) 47 P & CR 507, CA; *Methodist Secondary Schools Trust Deed Trustees v O'Leary* [1993] 1 EGLR 105, CA.

17 *Trans-Britannia Properties Ltd v Darby Properties Ltd* [1986] 1 EGLR 151, CA.

premises as furnished rooms was held to be in occupation, as a resident director of the tenant was on the premises, having a sufficient degree of control,[18] this case would now seem to depend on its special facts.[19]

Partial business user of whole premises

Where the tenant uses business premises for residential purposes, or residential premises for business purposes, the question arises whether Part II of the 1954 Act continues to apply. A number of principles are relevant. If the premises are let on a tenancy to which Part II of the 1954 Act initially applies, it ceases to do so if the premises are no longer occupied by the tenant for any business purposes.[20]

If, however, premises have been let for residential purposes, and thus fall within the Rent Act 1977 (or Part I of the Housing Act 1988) but during the tenancy, significant business user begins and is continued, the tenancy ceases to qualify for residential protection and is then brought within Part II of the 1954 Act, apparently even if the landlord does not consent to the change of user.[1] If any business user is merely incidental to the residential user, the relevant residential code will continue to apply to the tenancy.[2]

If the user of the premises intended at the commencement of the tenancy is a wholly business user, but later, the user becomes part business and part residential, Part II of the 1954 Act will continue to apply to the tenancy.[3] However, if the tenant of business premises, without the landlord's knowledge or consent, discontinues all business activity but resides on the premises, he cannot for this reason alone claim to be protected by either residential code.[4]

Personal occupation

While personal occupation by a tenant is ordinarily a condition precedent to the exercise of renewal rights under Part II, there are three specific statutory relaxations to this principle.

(a) Section 41(1) provides that where a tenancy is held on trust,[5] beneficial occupation by all or any of the beneficiaries under the trust for business purposes is to be treated as equivalent to occupation by the tenant.
(b) Section 41A enables, subject to a number of conditions, two or more joint tenants (eg partners in a firm) in whom the tenancy is vested to apply for a new tenancy where the same partnership no longer exists.
(c) Section 42(2) provides that where a tenancy is vested in one member of a group of companies (as defined in s 42(1)), occupation by any member of the same group of companies is to be treated as equivalent to occupation.

18 *Lee-Verhulst (Investments) Ltd v Harwood Trust* [1973] QB 204, [1971] 3 All ER 619, CA; also below.
19 After *Graysim Holdings Ltd v P & O Property Holdings Ltd* [1996] AC 329, 337G–338A, [1995] 4 All ER 831, 837–838, HL.
20 *Henry Smith's Charity Trustees v Wagle* [1989] 1 EGLR 124, CA.
 1 *Cheryl Investments Ltd v Saldanha* [1979] 1 All ER 5, [1978] 1 WLR 1329, CA.
 2 *Gurton v Parrott* [1991] 1 EGLR 98, CA.
 3 *Cheryl Investments Ltd v Saldanha*, supra.
 4 *Pulleng v Curran* (1980) 44 P & CR 58, CA.
 5 As in *Morar v Chauhan* [1985] 3 All ER 493, [1985] 1 WLR 1263, CA.

Business

The statutory definition of 'business' (s 23(2)) is wide and non-exclusive as it is stated to include a trade, profession or employment and also any activity carried on by a body of persons whether corporate or unincorporate. Despite this, the words 'trade, profession or employment' have been held to be exhaustive of the meaning of 'business' in relation to an activity carried on by a single person, and in one case it was consequently held that a tenant who took in lodgers carried on no trade.[6] Because the definition requires an activity, a mere casual user such as dumping or storing waste on the premises concerned is not within it,[7] but an activity is not sufficient: thus the gratuitous running of a Sunday School by an individual was outside Part II.[8] It appears that a spare-time activity which does not reap a commercial profit, even if it could be described as a business activity, will not bring the tenancy within Part II.[9]

On the other hand, the width of business activities capable of falling within s 23(2) is considerable and they include use for offices, shops, garages, warehouses, factories, laboratories, hotels, cinemas, a doctor's or dentist's surgery and members' clubs.[10] Moreover, because the words of definition of 'business' are not exhaustive in the case of a body corporate, the non profit-making running of a hospital by a board of governors fell within Part II,[11] as did the provision of offices for Crown servants.[12]

While business user is a condition precedent to renewal, the occupation condition must also be satisfied by the tenant. Hence, a property company tenant ran a business of sub-letting residential flats in a block, retaining only the common parts, but was not in 'occupation' and could not renew.[13] This result, according to the House of Lords, illustrates a general and fundamental principle that the business for which the tenant is in occupation must not be terminated by the process, at the date of the court order for a new tenancy, of ascertaining the holding. Since the only occupiers in that case were the sub-tenants, and the tenant could not run his business of sub-letting flats from the retained parts, he was denied renewal by the very nature of Part II itself.[14]

A business carried on in breach of a general prohibition of use for business purposes covering the whole premises is outside Part II unless the immediate landlord or his predecessor in title consented to the breach, or the immediate landlord acquiesced (s 23(4)).[15] This exclusion does not apply to a business

6 *Lewis v Weldcrest Ltd* [1978] 3 All ER 1226, [1978] 1 WLR 1107, CA.
7 *Hillil Property and Investment Co Ltd v Naraine Pharmacy Ltd* (1979) 39 P & CR 67, CA.
8 *Abernethie v AM & J Kleiman Ltd* [1970] 1 QB 10, [1969] 2 All ER 790; but not in the case of a body corporate: *Parkes v Westminster Roman Catholic Diocese Trustee* (1978) 36 P & CR 22, CA (a case on s 30(1)(g)).
9 *Lewis v Weldcrest Ltd*, supra.
10 As to the latter see *Addiscombe Garden Estates Ltd v Crabbe* [1958] 1 QB 513, [1957] 3 All ER 563, CA.
11 *Hills (Patents) Ltd v University College Hospital Board of Governors* [1956] 1 QB 90, [1955] 3 All ER 365, CA.
12 *Town Investments Ltd v Department of the Environment* [1978] AC 359, [1977] 1 All ER 813, HL.
13 *Bagettes Ltd v GP Estates Co Ltd* [1956] Ch 290, [1956] 1 All ER 729, CA.
14 *Graysim Holdings Ltd v P & O Property Holdings Ltd* [1996] AC 329, [1995] 4 All ER 831.
15 See *Bell v Alfred Franks & Bartlett Co Ltd* [1980] 1 All ER 356, [1980] 1 WLR 340, CA; *Methodist Secondary Schools Trust Deed Trustees v O'Leary*, supra.

carried on despite a prohibition of use for the purposes of a specified business, or of its use for purposes of any but a specified business (s 23(4)).

II   TENANCIES EXPRESSLY EXCLUDED FROM PROTECTION

A number of tenancies are prevented by the 1954 Act Part II from being protected, notably because they are within a different statutory code or because the tenancy does not qualify, or due to the character of the tenant.

Agricultural holdings

A tenancy of an agricultural holding is excluded from Part II, as is a tenancy which would be such a tenancy but for the fact that it is excluded by s 2(3) of the Agricultural Holdings Act 1986; a tenancy of agricultural land which has been approved by the Minister is likewise excluded, as is a farm business tenancy within the meaning of the Agricultural Tenancies Act 1995 (s 43(1)(a)).

Mining leases

A tenancy created by a mining lease[16] is excluded from Part II (s 43(1)(b)). Thus, a tenant who had the right to extract sand and gravel fell outside the Act.[17]

Residential tenancies

Exclusively residential tenancies are excluded from Part II.[18] See the discussion above as to the position where a tenant uses the premises partly for business and partly for residential purposes.

Tenancies of on-licensed premises

With certain exceptions, notably tenancies of restaurants and hotels with a licence to sell intoxicating liquor on the premises and where a substantial proportion of the business consisted of transactions other than the sale of alcohol,[19] a tenancy of on-licensed premises granted before 11 July 1989 was excluded from Part II (s 43(1)(d)). This has altered. A tenancy entered into on or after 11 July 1989 of premises licensed for the sale of intoxicating liquor on the premises is within Part II of the 1954 Act.[20]

---

16   As defined by Landlord and Tenant Act 1927, s 25(1), applied by s 46 of the 1954 Act, Part II.
17   *O'Callaghan v Elliott* [1966] 1 QB 601, [1965] 3 All ER 111, CA.
18   If the tenancy is an assured tenancy, it cannot be within Part II: see Housing Act 1988, s 1 and Sch 1, para 4; likewise with a protected or statutory tenancy within the Rent Act 1977, s 24(3)).
19   See *Grant v Gresham* [1979] 2 EGLR 60, CA; *Ye Old Cheshire Cheese Ltd v Daily Telegraph plc* [1988] 3 All ER 217, [1988] 1 WLR 1173.
20   Landlord and Tenant (Licensed Premises) Act 1990, s 1(1). Section 1(2) and (3) enable a tenancy of on-licensed premises granted before 11 July 1989 or on or after 11 July 1989 under a contract entered into prior to that date to be terminated prior to 11 July 1992: such tenancy subsisting after that date will fall within Part II of the 1954 Act.

Service tenancies

A tenancy granted by reason of the fact that the tenant was the holder of an office, appointment or employment from the grantor thereof and continuing only so long as the tenant holds the post, or terminable by the grantor on his ceasing to hold it, or coming to an end at a time fixed by reference to the time when the tenant ceases to hold it, is excluded from Part II of the 1954 Act (s 43(2)). A tenancy granted after 1 October 1954 (when Part II of the 1954 Act commenced) is only excluded from Part II if the tenancy was granted by an instrument in writing which expressed the purpose for which the tenancy was granted.

Short tenancies

By s 43(3), Part II of the 1954 Act does not apply to a tenancy granted for a term certain not exceeding six months unless:

(a) the tenancy contains provision for renewing the term or for extending it beyond six months from its beginning; or
(b) the tenant has been in occupation for a period which, together with any period during which any predecessor in title in the carrying on of the business carried on by the tenant was in occupation, exceeds twelve months.

Periodic tenancies are not mentioned in s 43(2) and they are capable of falling within Part II.

III   TENANCIES IN WHICH PART II IS EXCLUDED BY AGREEMENT

In a number of cases, of which the two mentioned are the most important, Part II of the 1954 Act cannot apply.

Exclusions authorised by the court

The county court is empowered (s 38(4)(a)) on the joint application of the intending landlord and tenant in relation to a term certain which would otherwise be within Part II, to authorise an agreement excluding in relation thereto sections 24 to 28 of the Act.

Agreement for a new tenancy

Where the landlord and tenant agree, in writing (s 69(2)), for the grant to the tenant of a future tenancy of the holding, or of the holding with other land, on terms and from a date specified in the agreement, the current tenancy is to continue until that date but no longer, and Part II does not apply to the future tenancy (s 28). This provision applies only to an unconditional enforceable contract.[1] The 'landlord' referred to is, in most cases, the tenant's immediate

---

1   *RJ Stratton Ltd v Wallis Tomlin & Co Ltd* [1986] 1 EGLR 104, CA.

landlord; if the latter is not 'the landlord', within s 44 for the purposes of Part II, the 'landlord' in question is a superior landlord: if so, the agreement would be capable of being specifically enforced against him.[2]

IV   TENANCIES WHICH HAVE COME TO AN END

In certain cases, the contractual or continuing tenancy has come to an end by permitted common law or certain other means within the 1954 Act, leaving the the tenant with no security.

Notice to quit

The giving of a valid notice to quit by the tenant will terminate his periodic tenancy at common law and will remove any protection he might have under Part II. To ensure that the notice is given voluntarily, s 24(2)(a) precludes the tenant from giving an effectual notice to quit until he has been in occupation in right of the tenancy for at least one month.

Surrender

If the tenant voluntarily surrenders the tenancy, he loses any security he might have had under Part II. If the instrument of surrender[3] is executed, or, where appropriate, the instrument was executed in pursuance of a prior agreement, before the tenant had been in occupation in right of the tenancy for one month, the surrender will not deprive the tenant of security under Part II.[4]

Forfeiture

A tenancy within Part II may be terminated by forfeiture of the tenancy or of a superior tenancy (s 24(2)). If there is a pending application for relief in respect of a forfeited tenancy, the Act continues to apply to the tenancy, since relief applications are part of the process of forfeiture.[5]

Termination by tenant

By s 27(1), a tenant holding under a tenancy for a term of years certain to which Part II applies may give his immediate landlord, not later than three months before the date at which the tenancy would come to an end by effluxion of time, a notice in writing that he does not desire the tenancy to be continued. Such

---

2 See *Bowes-Lyon v Green* [1963] AC 420, HL, where differences of opinion as to the correct 'landlord' within s 28 were expressed.
3 This does not include a notice pursuant to an option to purchase: *Watney v Boardley* [1975] 2 All ER 644, [1975] 1 WLR 857.
4 An agreement caught by this provision may be authorised by the court where s 38(4) applies.
5 *Meadows v Clerical, Medical and General Life Assurance Society* [1981] Ch 70, [1980] 1 All ER 454. Likewise, s 24(2) will not exclude s 24(1), and continuation, where a vesting order could have been made under Law of Property Act 1925, s 146(4): *Cadogan v Dimovic* [1984] 2 All ER 168, [1984] 1 WLR 609, CA.

notice will, unless given before the tenant has been in occupation in right of the tenancy for one month, prevent continuation under s 24 in relation to that tenancy. A continuing tenancy for a term of years certain may be brought to an end on any quarter day by not less than three months' notice in writing given by the tenant to the immediate landlord, subject to the one-month occupation restriction just mentioned (s 27(2)).

A number of points have recently arisen in relation to this provision and its relationship to the occupation conditions of sections 23(1) and 24(1). If a business tenant is no longer in occupation of the premises at the contractual expiry date of the tenancy, he is not impliedly required to serve any notice under s 27(2) to put an end to continuation: no continuation arises if he is out of occupation at such expiry date.[6] The Court of Appeal ruled that statutory continuation did not apply where a tenant had in the past been in occupation but was not at the expiry at common law of the tenancy, owing to the fact that s 24(1) reproduces in shorthand form the conditions of s 23(1) of the Act. The court refused to follow an earlier decision of its own, as being *per incuriam*.[7] The ground for this was that a number of authorities, from which it was a necessary inference that a requirement of occupation by the tenant for business purposes at the contractual expiry date of the tenancy applies as much to s 24(1) as it does to s 23, had not been cited to the Court of Appeal in that previous case.[8]

In the result, a tenant who had abandoned occupation before the contractual expiry date did not have to pay any rent as from then. By necessary inference, if a landlord serves a s 25 termination notice on a tenant, who ceased to occupy the property at such date, the tenant may quit without formality and is not liable for rent or under the covenants of the tenancy until any later expiry date of the s 25 notice.[9] However, it is thought that the right of a business tenant to serve a s 27(2) notice to terminate during continuation, whether or not he has received a s 25 notice from his landlord, is not affected.[10]

A question not resolved arises as to a business tenant who continues to occupy after the contractual expiry date and so falls within s 24(1) and then decides to quit. Owing to the fact that once continuation starts it is only terminable within the terms or circumstances envisaged by Part II of the 1954 Act, it might be held that he cannot simply quit and is bound to terminate the continuing tenancy only in accordance with Part II of the 1954 Act, as by serving a s 27(2) notice on the landlord.[11] However, the Court of Appeal have

6 *Esselte AB v Pearl Assurance plc* [1997] 02 EG 124, CA.
7 Ie *Long Acre Securities v Electro Accoustic Industries Ltd* [1990] 1 EGLR 91.
8 These included *Morrison Holdings Ltd v Manders Property (Wolverhampton) Ltd* [1976] 2 All ER 205, [1976] 1 WLR 533, CA, in which Scarman LJ approved a passage from the judgment of Cross J in *I&H Caplan v Caplan (No 2)* [1963] 2 All ER 930 at 936, [1963] 1 WLR 1247 at 1254-1255 to the effect that if the occupation condition ceased at any time to be fulfilled by a tenant, he could not claim a new tenancy under Part II.
9 *Cheryl Investments Ltd v Saldanha* [1979] 1 All ER 5, at 13, [1978] 1 WLR 1329 at 1338, as cited in *Esselte AB v Pearl Assurance plc*, supra.
10 In the *Longacre* case the tenant having received a s 25 notice was able to cut short the date of expiry of that notice by means of a s 27(1) notice; but was held, it now seems erroneously, liable for rent for a few months into what would have been a continuation if he had not abandoned the premises a few days into such continuation.
11 See Legal Notes, *Estates Gazette*, November 30, 1996, p 153.

interpreted ss 23, 25 and 27 as imposing a requirement of continuing business occupation on the tenant as essential if he is to retain the protection of the 1954 Act, Part II.[12] Moreover, as noted in that case, s 24(3)(a) assumes that a fixed-term tenancy will end unless continued by s 24(1). Section 24(3)(b) – enacted to prevent a tenant from claiming the protection of the Act by re-occupying premises which he did not occupy at the date of service of a landlord's notice to quit – makes the same assumption as to continuing occupation as a condition prececent to statutory protection. It could be inferred therefore that continuing occupation during statutory continuation is required not only for the purposes of claiming a new tenancy, but in relation to the need for any statutory notice from the landlord under s 25 or the tenant under s 27(2). Thus a tenant who quits during continuation would, if this is correct, be entitled, at least in theory, to do so without any need to notify the landlord under s 27(2).

Tenant's failure to comply with s 29(2)

Where the landlord serves a notice to terminate the tenancy under s 25, the tenant is required by s 25(5) to notify the landlord within two months whether or not, at the date of termination, he will be willing to give up possession of the premises.[13] If the tenant fails to comply strictly with the two-month time limit then, waiver by the landlord and estoppel apart, the tenant will lose any right, thanks to s 29(2), to apply to the court for a new tenancy, and the effect of the s 25 notice will be to put his rights under the current tenancy to an end.

Tenant's failure to comply with s 29(3)

The court cannot, by s 29(3), entertain any application for a new tenancy unless the application is made not less than two nor more than four months after a landlord's s 25 notice or a tenant's request for a new tenancy under s 26 is given. These time-limits are procedural, being for the benefit only of one party, the landlord, who may waive them expressly or impliedly, if so minded.[14] The court cannot extend these time limits either way.[15]

---

12   *Esselte AB v Pearl Assurance plc* supra.
13   No special form of notice is required from the tenant: *Lewington v Trustees of the Society for the Protection of Ancient Buildings* (1983) 45 P & CR 336, CA.
14   *Kammins Ballrooms Co Ltd v Zenith Investments (Torquay) Ltd* [1971] AC 850, [1970] 2 All ER 871, HL.
15   *Dodds v Walker* [1981] 2 All ER 609, [1981] 1 WLR 1027, HL.

Chapter 24

Restrictions on contracting out

Although the 1954 Act Part II confers only qualified security of tenure on business tenants, because of the ability of the landlord to oppose the grant of a new tenancy, especially if he wishes to redevelop the premises or to occupy them for the purposes of his own business, in principle it is not possible for the tenant voluntarily to contract out of the Act.

I SECURITY OF TENURE

Any agreement (whether contained in the instrument creating the tenancy or not) is rendered void by s 38(1) in so far as it purports to preclude the tenant from requesting or applying for a new tenancy, or provides for the termination or surrender of the tenancy in the event of his making such application or request or for the imposition of any penalty or disability on the tenant in that event.[1] 'Purports' in s 38(1)[2] means 'has the effect of precluding the tenant' and so caught an agreement for a tenancy under which the tenant agreed to give up possession by a certain date, thus precluding him from applying for a new tenancy under Part II.[3] Where a tenant held on a lease with a fully qualified prohibition on assignments which provided that, if the tenant wished to assign, he must first offer the landlord a surrender of the lease, s 38(1) rendered the agreement to surrender void:[4] as with the previous case, if the agreement had been carried out (in fact the tenant withdrew from it) the tenant would in fact have been precluded from applying for a new tenancy. Similarly a letter stating that the tenant would quit within 28 days, released from rent arrears, was caught by s 38(1) as part of a contract for a surrender enforceable in equity.[5] However, s 38(1) is limited to agreements to surrender, and was held not to apply to an actual surrender of a tenancy pursuant to a consent order in

---

1 See *Stevenson & Rush (Holdings) Ltd v Langdon* (1978) 38 P & CR 208 (payment of all landlord's costs clause a penalty).
2 Which has been characterised as a declaratory anti-avoidance provision in *Nicholls v Kinsey* [1994] 1 EGLR 131, CA.
3 *Joseph v Joseph* [1967] Ch 78, [1966] 3 All ER 486, CA.
4 *Allnatt London Properties Ltd v Newton* [1981] 2 All ER 290, affd on this aspect [1984] 1 All ER 423, CA.
5 *Tarjomani v Panther Securities Ltd* (1982) 46 P & CR 32.

repossession proceedings.[6] Nor does s 38(1) invalidate surrender-back clauses in covenants against assignments.[7]

The above prohibition has no effect on the ability of the tenant to give a notice to quit the holding or a notice that he does not desire to continue the tenancy.[8] The tenant may also validly execute an instrument of surrender, but s 24(2)(b) precludes this from being executed before the tenant has been in occupation in right of the tenancy for one month or under an agreement entered into before such occupation. Such instrument must be immediately effective as a contract for a future surrender is caught by s 38(1).[9]

The court (normally the county court) is empowered by the 'loophole' in s 38(4)(a) to authorise, on the joint application of the parties,[10] agreements to be granted for a term of years certain[11] which exclude ss 24 to 28 of the Act. It also has power, under s 38(4)(b), to authorise agreements for the surrender of the tenancy on such date or in such circumstances as may be specified in the agreement and on such terms as may be specified. The agreement must be contained in or endorsed on the instrument creating the tenancy or other instrument specified by the court. To come within s 38(4)(a), any lease must be granted conditionally on the court's approval of the relevant contracting out: an unconditional grant, with blanks to be filled in for the date of the order and other matters, conferred full security on the tenant.[12] An agreement authorised by the court took effect, however, even though it was not contained in or indorsed on a formal lease, since the tenant continued in possession and paid an increased rent under the terms of the new agreement, which were accordingly enforceable in equity.[13] It has been claimed that the county court will invariably approve s 38(4) applications by business persons who act with legal advice.[14]

However, the scope of s 38(4) is narrow, because it has been held that an agreement is only saved by it, despite the wide prohibition of s 38(1), if (1) there is a prospective tenancy for a term of years (2) the court has authorised an agreement excluding the relevant provisions of the Act in relation to that tenancy and (3) the agreement is made under that authorisation. Thus, where

---

6   *Hamilton v Sengray Properties* (6 March 1987, unreported), CA.

7   *Allnatt London Properties Ltd v Newton*, supra: the tenant was refused a declaration that he was entitled, for so long as Part II applied to the tenancy, freely to assign it.

8   See 1954 Act, Part II, ss 24(2)(a) and 27 (discussed in ch 23).

9   *Tarjomani v Panther Securities Ltd* (1982) 46 P & CR 32.

10 Cf *Cardiothoracic Institute v Shrewdcrest Ltd* [1986] 3 All ER 633, [1986] 1 WLR 368, where a tenant holding over under interim extensions, paying rent, had no security as it was intended that the parties would resort to s 38(4) but failed to do so.

11 In *Re Land and Premises at Liss, Hants* [1971] Ch 986, [1971] 3 All ER 380, accepted in *EWP Ltd v Moore* [1992] 2 EGLR 4, CA, 'term of years certain' was held to include, in the context of the 1954 Act Part II, a term of six months certain. Query where a tenancy includes a landlords' or tenants' break clause.

12 *Essexcrest Ltd v Evenlex Ltd* (1987) 55 P & CR 279, CA; Sparkes [1988] Conv 445.

13 *Tottenham Hotspur Football and Athletic Co Ltd v Princegrove Publishers Ltd* [1974] 1 All ER 17, [1974] 1 WLR 113. In view of Law of Property (Miscellaneous Provisions) Act 1989, s 2, it is possible that this result cannot apply to any similar tenancy entered into on or after 27 September 1989.

14 *Hagee (London) Ltd v AB Erikson and Larson* [1975] 3 All ER 234 at 236, CA.

a court order in relation to a tenancy for 12 months, thereafter from year to year, purported to exclude ss 24–28, the order was void, as the tenancy was not for a term certain.[15]

II   RIGHTS TO COMPENSATION

The right to compensation conferred by s 37 (see chapter 27) may be excluded or modified by agreement (s 38(3)). Where, during the whole of the five years immediately preceding the date on which the tenant was to quit the holding, the business has been carried on by the occupier on the holding or part of it, any agreement whether contained in the tenancy agreement or not and whether made before or after the termination of the tenancy, which purports to exclude or restrict compensation under s 37 is void to that extent. If during those five years there was a change of occupier of the premises, the person who was the occupier immediately after the change was a successor to the business, an agreement as above purporting to exclude or restrict compensation is likewise void (s 38(2)). In that s 38(2) is not directed at agreements as to accrued rights to compensation, an agreement as to the amount of any compensation under s 37 which is made after the right thereto has accrued is not invalidated (s 38(2)).

---

15   *Nicholls v Kinsey* supra.

Chapter 25

Continuation and termination of business tenancies

It is provided that a tenancy to which Part II of the 1954 Act applies is not to come to an end unless terminated in accordance with the provsions of Part II (s 24(1)). This is the principle of statutory continuation of a business tenancy, but three common law methods of termination, where applicable, are preserved from the principle that continuation is only terminable within Part II of the 1954 Act (s 24(2)). Those methods are: a tenant's notice to quit, surrender and forfeiture. However, if the tenant is not in occupation in the sense required by s 23(1) at the contractual expiry date of the tenancy then there is no continuation of the tenancy under s 24(1), since a past, as opposed to a present, occupation will not suffice to trigger the operation of s 24(1).[1] Thus, as mentioned in chapter 23, if a tenant permanently abandons his occupation of business premises before the contractual expiry date, he may quit without having to serve a s 27(1) notice on the landlord. If he continues to occupy at and for a time, after such expiry date, but then abandons occupation permanently, it is not clear whether he would have to serve a s 27(2) notice of termination on the landlord. This issue is further discussed in chapter 23.

The 1954 Act, Part II enables a continuing tenancy to be brought to an end by a landlord's notice of termination under s 25 or a tenant's request for a new tenancy under s 26, and this chapter considers both these methods.

I STATUTORY CONTINUATION

But for s 24(1), the contractual term of a business tenancy would expire by effluxion of time. Section 24(1) continues the contractual term of a tenant in occupation at that date indefinitely,[2] despite its having reached its common law expiry date, unless or until it is terminated in accordance with Part II of the 1954 Act.

---

1 *Esselte AB v Pearl Assurance plc* [1997] 02 EG 124, CA.
2 By s 65(2), a sub-tenancy continued beyond the term of a superior tenancy, is kept alive for the duration of its term, and is then deemed to have been surrendered under Law of Property Act 1925, s 139(1), so that the sub-tenant holds directly under the head landlord.

A continuation tenancy is apparently an extension of the contractual term with a statutory variation as to the mode of termination.[3] The current tenant therefore has an estate in the land, not merely a personal right to occupy, and is subject to the burdens and benefits of the contractual tenancy. A right to remove tenants' fixtures extends into continuation.[4] Any liability of an original tenant to pay rent, if it is expressed to last for the term of the lease, does not extend into any period of continuation, where the original tenant has assigned the term before its contractual expiry date. The contractual obligations of the original tenant are not independently continued by s 24(1). Thus, if the original tenant is to be liable,[5] clear words of extension of his contractual liability under the lease into statutory continuation are required.[6] Moreover, it was not possible for a landlord who had terminated the contractual term before its expiry date of 2000, pursuant to a break clause, to invoke a rent review during continuation, where the term was assumed for review purposes to run until 2000.[7] (In any case, a landlord is entitled to seek an interim rent under s 24A during continuation.) In the absence of clear words, however, a guarantor's liability in respect of rent arrears does not, in principle, extend into continuation.[8]

A landlord's notice to quit or notice to determine the contractual tenancy are effectual to put an end to the contractual term, if otherwise valid, and continuation will commence as from the date of the expiry of the notice.[9] The landlord may serve a statutory notice to terminate the continuing tenancy under s 25; or he may serve a single notice, which will, if it complies both with s 25 and common law rules, suffice to terminate the contractual tenancy and continuation under Part II.[10]

Where, during continuation, a tenancy ceases to be a business tenancy, it may be determined by the landlord, subject to the terms of the contractual tenancy, on not less than three nor more than six months' written notice (s 24(3)(a)). If the landlord gives a notice to quit to a periodic tenant who enjoys no security of tenure (and so no continuation rights) under Part II, the operation of the notice is not affected by the fact that after the giving of the notice, the tenancy becomes one to which Part II applies (s 24(3)(b)). But for

3   See eg *Weinbergs Weatherproofs Ltd v Radcliffe Paper Mill Co* [1958] Ch 437; *Cornish v Brook Green Laundry Ltd* [1959] 1 QB 394, [1959] 1 All ER 373, CA; *GMS Syndicate Ltd v Gary Elliott Ltd* [1982] Ch 1, [1981] 1 All ER 619.

4   *New Zealand Government Property Corpn v HM & S Ltd* [1982] QB 1145, [1982] 1 All ER 624, CA; as to rights of way enjoyed under the contractual tenancy: *Nevill Long & Co (Boards) v Firmenich & Co* (1983) 47 P & CR 59, CA.

5   As to the effect of the Landlord and Tenant (Covenants) Act 1995 on such liabilities, see ch 5.

6   *City of London Corpn v Fell* [1994] 1 AC 458, [1993] 4 All ER 968, HL. Where an original lessee was, under an express clause, liable to pay rent into continuation, this liability did not as a matter of construction extend to a liability to pay an interim rent fixed under s 24A between the landlord and the assignee.

7   *Willison v Cheverell Estates Ltd* [1996] 1 EGLR 116, CA.

8   *Junction Estates Ltd v Cope* (1974) 27 P & CR 482; *A Plesser & Co v Davis* [1983] 2 EGLR 70.

9   *Weinbergs Weatherproofs Ltd v Radcliffe Paper Mill Co*, supra.

10 *Keith Bayley Rogers & Co v Cubes* (1975) 31 P & CR 412; also *Aberdeen Steak Houses plc v Crown Estates Comrs* [1997] EGCS 14 (single notice validly served under break clause and s 25 under which landlord desired to demolish etc premises).

this provision, the tenant might try to occupy the premises for business purposes during the currency of a notice and then claim the benefit of statutory continuation.

II   TERMINATION BY THE LANDLORD

Notice under s 25

The landlord may terminate a tenancy to which Part II of the 1954 Act applies solely by giving the tenant a statutory or s 25 notice[11] to terminate the tenancy.[12] If the landlord serves a valid notice, it cannot be withdrawn; if his notice is invalid, and the tenant does not waive the defect, the landlord may withdraw the invalid notice and serve a new, valid, notice.[13] The requirement of a notice applies to all periodic tenancies and tenancies for a fixed term exceeding six months, whether the tenancy is continuing or not. The following requirements apply to the landlord's notice.

1   It must be both in writing and in the prescribed form,[14] or in a form substantially to the like effect. In particular, the notice must require the tenant, within two months after it is given, to notify the landlord in writing whether or not he is willing to give up possession (s 25(5)). If the tenant fails to serve a counter-notice on time, he generally loses his right to apply to the court for a new tenancy (s 29(2)) unless the landlord is estopped by his conduct from taking the point.[15] If the tenant replies in time, however, the effect is to enable him to apply under s 24(1) for a new tenancy. No special form is prescribed for the tenant's s 25(5) notice which must express unequivocally the tenant's intentions.[16]

2   Although it is best to follow strictly the most up to date prescribed form available,[17] a notice which omits certain immaterial details, such as notes to the prescribed form, will be upheld.[18] Likewise an otherwise correct notice

---

11   Thus a common law notice is ineffectual: *Commercial Properties Ltd v Wood* [1968] 1 QB 15, CA.

12   Service of both s 25 and s 26 notices (and all notices under Part II) is governed by Landlord and Tenant Act 1927, s 23 (s 66(4)), so that a notice sent by recorded delivery or registered post is deemed to have been received in the ordinary course of the post, whether the recipient sees it or not but the presumption of due service is rebuttable. See *Italica Holdings SA v Bayadea* [1985] 1 EGLR 70; *Lex Service plc v Johns* [1990] 1 EGLR 92, CA.

13   *Smith v Draper* [1990] 2 EGLR 69, CA. An exception to the rule that a valid s 25 notice cannot be withdrawn is provided by Sch 6, para 6 to the 1954 Act, which applies where a competent landlord has served a s 25 notice on the tenant and within two months thereof, a new landlord becomes the competent landlord.

14   Landlord and Tenant Act 1954 Part II (Notices) Regulations 1983, SI 1983/133, notably Form 1.

15   As in *JT Developments Ltd v Quinn* [1991] 2 EGLR 257, CA.

16   See e g *Lewington v Trustees of the Society for the Protection of Ancient Buildings* (1983) 45 P & CR 336; *Mehmet v Dawson* [1984] 1 EGLR 74, CA.

17   Cf *Snook v Schofield* [1975] 1 EGLR 69 (outdated form which did not materially depart from Act valid).

18   *Tegerdine v Brooks* (1977) 36 P & CR 261, CA; also *Sun Alliance and London Assurance Co Ltd v Hayman* [1975] 1 All ER 248, CA; *Morris v Patel* [1987] 1 EGLR 75, CA.

in which the space for the date and signature was left blank, was valid.[19] The tenant will suffer no loss from such trifling deviations, provided the notice conveys the substance of what is required.[20] Should a notice fail in a serious respect to comply with the regulations, it will be invalid, as where a notice failed to state the correct name and address of the competent landlord (a vital piece of information for any tenant).[1] Likewise invalid was a notice which failed to state the names of all the joint landlords.[2] This information is necessary for the correct service of the tenant's notices, but no reasonable tenant could be expected to know the names of all the competent landlords.

3   The notice must specify the date on which the current tenancy is to come to an end – the date of termination (s 25(1)). The date so specified must not be earlier than the date on which, in the case of a fixed-term tenancy, it would have expired by effluxion of time (s 25(4)).[3] In the case of a periodic tenancy, the specified date must be no earlier than the earliest date on which the tenancy could have been brought to an end by a notice to quit served by the landlord on the giving of the s 25 notice (s 25(3)(a)). However, it is not necessary for the date of termination to fall on the correct expiry date at common law,[4] no doubt because, as seen, the statutory method of termination is the sole permissible means of ending a business tenancy.

4   The landlord (which expression includes one of two or more joint landlords)[5] may give a s 25 notice not less than six nor more than twelve months before the specified termination date (s 25(2)).[6] Where the tenancy requires a period of notice above six months, the time-limit is altered from twelve months to the period equal to the period required under the tenancy plus six months (s 25(3)(b)).

5   The s 25 notice must state whether or not the landlord would oppose an application to the court for a new tenancy and, if so, on what grounds he will rely (s 25(6)). The landlord will, in proceedings, be limited to the grounds stated in his s 25 notice,[7] which cannot later be changed.[8] The paragraphs of s 30(1) (which are the grounds of opposition to a new tenancy, discussed in chapter 25) need not be set out in full.[9] If, after service of a s 25 notice, the reversion is assigned, the successor in title may rely on, but will be bound by, the grounds specified in the notice.

---

19 *Falcon Pipes Ltd v Stanhope Gate Property Co Ltd* (1967) 117 NLJ 1345; also *British Railways Board v AJA Smith Transport Ltd* [1981] 2 EGLR 69.
20 See eg *Barclays Bank v Ascott* [1961] 1 WLR 717; also *Sabella Ltd v Montgomery* [1997] EGCS 15, where the cumulative effect of individual minor omissions was to invalidate a s 25 notice, even though any one of these alone might not have done so.
1   *Morrow v Nadeem* [1987] 1 All ER 237, [1986] 1 WLR 1381, CA.
2   *Pearson v Alyo* [1990] 1 EGLR 114, CA; also *Yamaha-Kemble Music (UK) Ltd v ARC Properties Ltd* [1990] 1 EGLR 261.
3   See *Re Crowhurst Park, Sims-Hilditch v Simmons* [1974] 1 All ER 991, [1974] 1 WLR 583.
4   *Hogg Bullimore & Co v Co-operative Insurance Society Ltd* (1984) 50 P & CR 105.
5   *Leckhampton Dairies v Artus Whitfield Ltd* (1986) 130 Sol Jo 225.
6   See *Hogg Bullimore & Co v Co-operative Insurance Society Ltd*, supra.
7   *XL Fisheries v Leeds Corpn* [1955] 2 QB 636, CA.
8   See *Betty's Cafés Ltd v Phillips Furnishing Stores Ltd* [1957] Ch 67, [1957] 1 All ER 1, CA; *Hutchinson v Lamberth* [1984] 1 EGLR 75, CA.
9   *Biles v Caesar* [1957] 1 All ER 151; also *Philipson-Stow v Trevor Square Ltd* [1981] 1 EGLR 56.

A s 25 notice must generally relate to the whole demised premises, and this may be of importance where the tenant occupies premises which are not physically contiguous, as with an office-floor and ground-floor storage facilities.[10] A s 25 notice will be invalid unless it relates to the whole of the holding, and not just to part of it.[11] Therefore, if the reversion has been severed since the grant of the tenancy, it may be impossible for any valid s 25 notice to be served, since neither landlord may serve a notice to terminate which applies to the whole holding.[12] Where there were held to be two leases in one document, a s 25 notice served in respect of the whole premises demised by one of the leases was upheld.[13]

Competent landlord

A s 25 notice must be served by a 'landlord' within s 44(1), and this person may not necessarily be the tenant's immediate landlord. Section 44(1) imposes three requirements on the nature of the landlord's interest before the landlord is a competent landlord within Part II.[14]

1   The landlord's interest must be in reversion expectant (whether immediately or not) on the termination of the tenancy.
2   The interest must be either the fee simple or a tenancy which will not come to an end within fourteen months by effluxion of time. If the interest is a qualifying tenancy, the mesne landlord must have given no notice by which his interest will come to an end within fourteen months or any further time it may be continued under s 36(2) or s 64.
3   The landlord's interest must not itself be an interest on a reversion expectant (immediately or not) on an interest which fulfils those conditions.

These provisions are apparently aimed at disentitling a mesne landlord with no substantial interest in the premises from taking any direct part in the proceedings, where there is a business sub-tenant in occupation of the holding in question. They are not free from difficulty. Where the interest of an intermediate landlord is continuing under Part II, he remains a 'competent landlord' for the purpose of service of s 25 and s 26 notices.[15] This applies whether or not the mesne landlord has granted a reversionary lease to the sub-tenant of part of the premises.[16] Once the head landlord has served a s 25 notice on the intermediate landlord, who applies for a new tenancy, the latter ceases to be a 'competent landlord' and so, if his own tenant (of part of the whole premises) desires to request a new tenancy, he should serve any relevant notice on the head landlord. If he serves notices on the mesne landlord, he risks losing the right to apply for a new tenancy as time begins

10   See *Herongrove Ltd v Wates City of London Properties plc* [1988] 1 EGLR 82.
11   *Southport Old Links Ltd v Naylor* [1985] 1 EGLR 66, CA; also *M&P Enterprises (London) Ltd v Norfolk Square Hotels Ltd* [1994] 1 EGLR 129.
12   As in *Dodson Bull Carpet Co Ltd v City of London Corpn* [1975] 2 All ER 497, [1975] 1 WLR 781 (tenancy of two properties not determinable by s 25 notice from landlord of severed part of reversion).
13   *Moss v Mobil Oil Co Ltd* [1988] 1 EGLR 71, CA.
14   What is said here applies with equal force to notices served on the landlord by the tenant.
15   *Cornish v Brook Green Laundry* [1959] 1 QB 394, [1959] 1 All ER 373, CA.
16   *Bowes-Lyon v Green* [1963] AC 420, [1961] 3 All ER 843, HL.

to run against him under s 29(3). In one case, where the mesne landlord had served a s 25 notice on his tenant (of part of the premises) and had subsequently requested a new tenancy from the head landlord, so ceasing to qualify as a 'competent landlord', the mesne landlord was under a duty to his tenant to correct the misrepresentation involved in his earlier s 25 notice that he was the 'competent landlord' and, since he had not, the (sub) tenants were entitled to apply for a new tenancy.[17]

4 A head landlord may terminate both the tenancy and any sub-tenancies derived out of it where the tenant is protected by Part II.[18]

III TENANT'S REQUEST FOR A NEW TENANCY

The request

A tenant holding under a tenancy granted for a term of years certain exceeding one year, whether or not continued under s 24(1), or for a term of years certain and thereafter from year to year, is entitled to apply for a new tenancy under s 26 (s 26(1)).[19] The s 26 procedure cannot be used by a tenant who has already been given a s 25 notice by his landlord; nor where the tenant has given a notice to terminate under s 27 and a landlord cannot serve a s 25 notice if the tenant has already made a request for a new tenancy under s 26 (s 26(4)). In other words, the procedures under sections 25 and 26 are mutually exclusive. A tenant for a fixed term which does not exceed one year and periodic tenants have no right to request a new tenancy under s 26, although they may apply for a new tenancy if the landlord serves on them a s 25 notice of termination. The tenant's request must comply with a number of requirements.

1 It must be in the prescribed form.[20] It must be served on the 'competent landlord' within s 44(1) – see the discussion earlier in this chapter.

2 The notice must specify the date on which the proposed tenancy is to begin, which must be not more than twelve nor less than six months after the date specified in the request (s 26(2)). This date must not be any earlier than the date on which the current tenancy would otherwise have expired by effluxion of time or could have been brought to an end by notice to quit given by the tenant (s 26(2), proviso). The reference to effluxion of time relates to fixed term tenancies exceeding one year; that to notice to quit to periodic tenancies, according to the High Court. It ruled that a tenant holding a twenty-year fixed term business tenancy granted in June 1985 would not have been able to break the tenancy in June 1995, a right preserved by s 24(2), and at the same time serve a s 26 request for a new tenancy.[1] The

---

17 *Shelley v United Artists Corpn* [1990] 1 EGLR 103, CA.

18 1954 Act, Sch 6, paras 6 and 7; *Lewis v MTC (Cars) Ltd* [1975] 1 All ER 874, [1975] 1 WLR 457, CA (competent landlord may determine business sub-tenancy before mesne tenancy expired).

19 See *Watkins v Emslie* [1982] 1 EGLR 81, CA.

20 Landlord and Tenant Act 1954 Part II (Notices) Regulations 1983, SI 1983/133, Form No 8.

1 *Garston* v *Scottish Widows Fund* [1996] 1 WLR 834. In fact, the tenant's break clause notice was invalid. A petition to appeal to the House of Lords was refused [1996] 1 WLR 102.

court did not wish to confer on a tenant who validly broke his tenancy the right to obtain a new tenancy on more favourable terms in times of recession.

3   The tenant must, in his request, set out his proposals as to the property to be comprised in the new tenancy and as to the rent payable thereunder and as to the other terms of the new tenancy, otherwise his request is of no effect (s 26(3)). The property to be comprised in the new tenancy need not necessarily be the whole premises held under the current lease. Indeed, where a tenant has sub-let part of the premises, it seems that he cannot properly claim renewal for that part, as it no longer forms part of the 'holding' within s 23(3). If he has sub-let the whole, retaining only common parts, he seemingly cannot claim renewal at all.[2] The tenant should specify the length of the proposed new tenancy, as this is one of the 'terms' required by s 26(3), and where a tenant failed to specify a term, but held under a seven-year term, it was held that he had impliedly requested a seven-year new tenancy by requesting that the other terms of the new tenancy should be the same as those of the current tenancy.[3]

Once the tenant has applied for a new tenancy, the current tenancy terminates immediately before the date specified in the request for the beginning of the new tenancy (s 25(5)) subject to interim continuation (s 64). Where, therefore, a tenant requested a new tenancy with a date specified in June 1971, but did nothing further until early 1973, at which time the landlord obtained an order for possession, his existing tenancy was held to have terminated immediately before the date specified in 1971 and his application failed as he was no longer a tenant.[4] In principle, the time-limits laid down in s 26 are strict. The tenant, moreover, must apply to the court, following a request, within the four months specified by s 29(3), which run from the date of his request. If he fails to comply with this limit, he cannot make a second request under s 26, having purportedly withdrawn the first, since s 25(5) terminates his current tenancy, and it makes no difference to this that he may have followed up his second request with an application to the court which is on time.[5]

Landlord's counter notice

The prescribed form of a tenant's request for a new tenancy makes it clear that the landlord has the right to oppose the request. This he may do by serving a counter-notice on the tenant within two months of the making of the request for a new tenancy (s 26(6)). The landlord's notice must state on which of the grounds given by s 30 of the 1954 Act Part II the landlord will oppose the application. No prescribed form of notice is required for this particular notice.

---

2   *Graysim Holdings Ltd v P & O Property Holdings Ltd* [1996] AC 329, [1995] 4 All ER 831, HL.
3   *Sidney Bolsom Investment Trust Ltd v E Karmios & Co (London) Ltd* [1956] 1 QB 529, [1956] 1 All ER 536, CA.
4   *Meah v Sector Properties Ltd* [1974] 1 All ER 1074, [1974] 1 WLR 547, CA.
5   *Polyviou v Seeley* [1979] 3 All ER 853, CA; also *Stile Hall Properties Ltd v Gooch* [1979] 3 All ER 848, CA.

Time-limits

Section 26 imposes various time-limits on the tenant as a condition precedent of his making a valid request, but these are imposed for the sole benefit of the landlord, who may, if he so wishes, waive them by accepting an otherwise procedurally invalid notice.[6] In addition, the landlord may be estopped by conduct from insisting on a strict compliance with the statutory time-limits, as where a tenant served a s 26 request which did not comply with these time-limits, but the landlord, neither party realising the error, initially indicated that it would not oppose a new tenancy and gave no counter-notice under s 26(6), but subsequently, having applied for an interim rent (on the basis of the tenancy continuing) took the invalidity point.[7] The two grounds for upholding the tenant's request were, first, that the landlord accepted the notice; second, that he had in any case affirmed the tenancy by asking for an interim rent. By contrast, where, following a s 26 request, the tenant applied too soon to the court, and the parties conducted abortive negotiations, the landlord had not impliedly represented to the tenant that he would not oppose a new tenancy, and the tenant lost his right to apply under s 26.[8]

IV INTERIM RENT

The landlord may apply to the court, if he has given a s 25 notice or following a s 26 tenant's request for a new tenancy, for the determination of a 'rent which it would be reasonable for the tenant to pay' during continuation under s 24 and the court has a discretion to fix what is known as an 'interim rent' (s 24A(1)). The purpose of s 24A is seemingly to prevent a tenant, in times of inflation, spinning out the steps required by the 1954 Act, Part II, so as unfairly to prolong the continuation of the old rent. The interim rent is deemed to be payable either from the date on which the proceedings were commenced,[9] or the date specified in the landlord's notice or the tenant's request, whichever is the later (s 24A(2)). In determining a rent under s 24A, the court is bound to have regard to the rent payable under the terms of the tenancy, but otherwise s 34(1) and (2) of the 1954 Act apply to the determination as if a new tenancy from year to year of the whole of the property comprised in the tenancy were granted to the tenant by order of the court (s 24A(3)). Therefore an interim rent is an open market rent, taking into account the disregards required by s 34, for a hypothetical new yearly tenancy on the same terms as the existing tenancy, so far as compatible with a yearly tenancy.[10] The effect of the requirement that the court must have

---

6 *Kammins Ballrooms Co Ltd v Zenith Investments (Torquay) Ltd* [1971] AC 850, [1970] 2 All ER 871, HL.
7 *Bristol Cars Ltd v RKH (Hotels) Ltd* (1979) 38 P & CR 411, CA.
8 *Stevens and Cutting Ltd v Anderson* [1990] 1 EGLR 95, CA.
9 See *R v Gravesend County Court, ex p Patchett* [1993] 2 EGLR 125 (L applied in February and T discontinued proceedings in July, unaware of L's application; court could not later backdate L's application for the purposes of securing an interim rent).
10 As notably in *Woodbridge v Westminster Press Ltd* [1987] 2 EGLR 97.

regard to the existing rent is that the court may at its discretion determine an interim rent which is less than the full market rent.[11] The courts may, at their discretion, permit a discount from the interim rent so as to shield the tenant from too steep a jump in the rent from its old level, but the question of whether any allowance may be made, and, if so, as to its amount, is at the discretion of the court, and the Court of Appeal will only interfere with the exercise of a county court judge's discretion if it is obviously wrong.[12] However, in one case a county court decision was held to be erroneous in law because the judge had paid insufficient attention to the fact that at the contractual termination date, a major company was leaving the precinct concerned, so adversely affecting the value of the tenant's unit; and so a 3.275% reduction in the interim rent for the tenancy from year to year by way of a cushion was insufficient, and it was increased to 10%.[13] Subject to issues as to errors of law, the amount of any reduction is a question of fact. A 50% reduction has been allowed, exceptionally.[14] More modest reductions of the order of 6% to 10% have properly been made.[15] It is, subject to these points, implicit in s 24A(3) that the interim rent is to be a market rent throughout the whole period for which it is payable: thus, where proceedings were delayed for some three years and the interim rent was fixed at 300% above the old rent, the decision was upset on appeal, since for the earlier part of the three-year period, the rent was above the market level.[16] But where a tenant had enjoyed the benefit of a low rent in times of inflation, his advantage was not perpetuated, so as to cause injustice to the landlord, and no discount was conferred.[17]

Regard must be had to the state of the premises, at the time when the relevant period starts: if they are then out of repair, in breach of a landlord's covenant, the court may determine a differential interim rent, so that the landlord only recovers the full amount if and when he remedies his breaches.[18] Once the application for an interim rent has been made, the fact that the tenant later withdraws his application does not affect the jurisdiction to order an interim rent.[19] The fact that the reversion is assigned once an application for interim rent is made also makes no difference and the new landlord obtains the benefit of it.[20]

11   *English Exporters (London) Ltd v Eldonwall Ltd* [1973] Ch 415, [1973] 1 All ER 726; also *Ratners (Jewellers) Ltd v Lemnoll* [1980] 2 EGLR 65; *UDS Tailoring Ltd v BL Holdings Ltd* [1982] 1 EGLR 61.
12   *Halberstam v Tandalco Corpn NV* [1985] 1 EGLR 90, CA; *Khalique v Law Land plc* [1989] 1 EGLR 105, CA.
13   *French v Commercial Union Life Assurance Co Ltd* [1993] 1 EGLR 113, CA.
14   *Charles Follett Ltd v Cabtell Investment Co Ltd* (1987) 55 P & CR 36, CA.
15   As in *Janes (Gowns) Ltd v Harlow Development Corpn* [1980] 1 EGLR 52.
16   *Conway v Arthur* [1988] 2 EGLR 113, CA.
17   *Department of the Environment v Allied Freehold Property Trust Ltd* [1992] 2 EGLR 100 (Cty ct).
18   *Fawke v Viscount Chelsea* [1980] QB 441, [1979] 3 All ER 568, CA.
19   *Michael Kramer & Co v Airways Pension Fund Trustees Ltd* [1978] 1 EGLR 49; *Artoc Bank and Trust Ltd v Prudential Assurance Co plc* [1984] 3 All ER 538, [1984] 1 WLR 1181; *Benedictus v Jalaram Ltd* [1989] 1 EGLR 251, CA.
20   *Bloomfield v Ashwright Ltd* (1983) 47 P & CR 78, CA.

V TENANT'S RIGHT TO APPLY TO THE COURT FOR A NEW TENANCY

If the tenant considers that the landlord has uncontestable grounds of opposition, he may decide to quit and not to apply to the court for a new tenancy under s 24(1). In that event, the current tenancy will come to an end on the date specified in the landlord's s 25 notice or the tenant's s 26 request for a new tenancy. If the tenant decides to quit after receiving a landlord's counter-notice relying on grounds (e) to (g) of s 30(1), having applied for a new tenancy, and seeks leave to withdraw his application, leave will generally be given unconditionally in the absence of intervening prejudice to the landlord; if the landlord withdraws his opposition, he cannot in these circumstances avoid paying compensation to the tenant.[1]

The parties may negotiate, after the service of the various statutory notices and counter-notices, for the grant of a new tenancy by agreement out of court: but the tenant should beware of allowing the time-limit laid down by s 29(3) of not less than two[2] nor more than four months after the original notice was served to pass: if he does so, and fails to apply to court within the prescribed time-limit, he will be unable to apply unless the parties have agreed to extend the time-limits.[3] If the parties agree on all the terms of a new tenancy, the current tenancy is continued until the new tenancy commences (s 28).

If the tenant applies to the court under s 24(1) for a new tenancy, but before the hearing the parties agree on the grant of a new tenancy, the tenant may withdraw his application or the parties may ask the court to order a new tenancy on the terms agreed. The court has a discretion to allow a tenant to amend an application, provided it is made on time, so that a tenant was allowed to amend an application so as to apply to the whole holding, in view of the substantial detriment she would otherwise suffer.[4]

---

1 *Lloyds Bank Ltd v City of London Corpn* [1983] Ch 192, [1983] 1 All ER 92; also *Fribourg & Treyer Ltd v Northdale Investments Ltd* (1982) 44 P & CR 284.
2 Two months means just that: the period ends on the corresponding date in the relevant month: *EJ Riley Investments v Eurostile Holdings Ltd* [1985] 3 All ER 181, [1985] 1 WLR 1139, CA.
3 As in *Saloman v Akiens* [1993] 1 EGLR 101, CA, where correspondence in negotiations for a new tenancy following a s 25 notice was 'subject to contract'.
4 *Nurit Bar v Pathwood Investments Ltd* (1987) 54 P & CR 178, CA.

Chapter 26

Grounds of opposition

A landlord who cannot terminate a business tenancy by one of the permitted common law or other methods is entitled to terminate a continuing tenancy or defeat a tenant's application for a new tenancy and to regain possession of the premises if he is able to establish one of a number of statutory grounds of opposition. He must inform the tenant in his s 25 notice or s 26(6) counter-notice of which, if any, ground he intends to rely on, and then prove the ground at the hearing. The court must dismiss the application if it is satisfied that the landlord has established any ground stated in his notice (s 31(1)). 'Landlord' includes any successor in title, so that the latter may rely on his predecessor's notice, if he is landlord at the date of the hearing.[1] The statutory grounds, with the exception of that relating to alternative accommodation, fall into two classes: those which relate to breaches of tenants' obligations, which, if proved, enable the landlord to evict the tenant without having to pay him 'disturbance' compensation, and those which entitle the tenant to such compensation, if established, as the price for the landlord to obtain possession.[2] The largest number of reported cases centres, as might be imagined, around the grounds entitling the landlord to re-possession in order to redevelop the premises or to occupy them for his own business. These two grounds emphasise the overriding rights of the landlord and the qualified nature of the statutory renewal rights, as being subordinate to the landlord's rights in both these important aspects of property control and management.

Para (a): breach of repairing obligations:

> where under the current tenancy the tenant has any obligations as respects the repair and maintenance of the holding, that the tenant ought not to be granted a new tenancy in view of the state of repair of the holding, being a state resulting from the tenant's failure to comply with the said obligations.

The breach must exist at the date of service of the notice. It is not enough for the landlord to prove that the tenant is in substantial breach of a repairing obligation: he must satisfy the court that the breach is so serious that the tenant 'ought not', in the court's discretion, to be granted a new tenancy because the

---

1 *Betty's Cafés Ltd v Phillips Furnishing Stores Ltd* [1957] Ch 67, CA; *Marks v British Waterways Board* [1963] 3 All ER 28, [1963] 1 WLR 1008, CA.
2 However, if alternative accommodation is availiable, below, the tenant does not need such compensation and so is not given it.

court may grant a new tenancy despite the breach.[3] An undertaking by the tenant to remedy the breach would be taken into account by the court in the exercise of its discretion.[4] The question is whether it would be unfair to the landlord, having regard to the tenant's part conduct, to grant the latter a new tenancy: where the past breaches, which will be taken into account, were serious and the tenant had neglected his covenant to repair, a new tenancy was refused.[5]

Para (b): persistent delay in paying rent:

> the tenant ought not to be granted a new tenancy in view of his persistent delay in paying rent due under the current tenancy.

'Persistent delay' means a course of conduct over a period of time, and so the court will have regard to the frequency and extent of the delays,[6] and the steps the landlord was obliged to take to secure repayment and the question of how the landlord may be secured in any new tenancy against future breaches of this covenant.[7] Once persistent delay has been proved by the landlord, the tenant may persuade the court to grant him a new tenancy if, for example, he has a good explanation for the delay and can demonstrate that it was exceptional.[8] Thus, where a county court judge was satisfied with a tenant's explanation for persistent delays in paying rent over two and a half years, payments having thereafter been prompt, the Court of Appeal declined to interfere with his decision, on such a question of fact, to order a new tenancy.[9]

Para (c): other substantial breaches:

> the tenant ought not to be granted a new tenancy in view of other substantial breaches by him of his obligations under the current tenancy, or for any other reason connected with the tenant's use or management of the holding.

The seriousness of any alleged breach will thus be considered,[10] and the question of whether the breach is or is not continuing in nature is relevant. In the case of a remediable breach, the court will take into account whether it has been remedied and whether the breach has in any case been waived. Paragraph (c) is based on fault generally, going beyond any breaches of obligation. The landlord may thus rely on the fact that the tenant's continued user of the holding would constitute a breach of a planning enforcement order.[11] In its discretion (para (c) being a discretionary ground in view of the words 'ought not') the court has regard to all relevant circumstances, and the general conduct of the

3 *Nihad v Chain* (1956) 167 Estates Gazette 139.
4 *Lyons v Central Commercial Properties Ltd* [1958] 2 All ER 767, 775, CA.
5 *Lyons v Central Commercial Properties Ltd, supra.*
6 *Hopcutt v Carver* (1969) 209 Estates Gazette 1069, CA.
7 *Rawashdeh v Lane* [1988] 2 EGLR 109, CA.
8 *Betty's Cafes Ltd v Phillips Furnishing Stores, supra.*
9 *Hurstfell Ltd v Leicester Square Property Co Ltd* [1988] 2 EGLR 105, CA.
10 See eg *Norton v Charles Deane Productions Ltd* (1969) 214 Estates Gazette 559.
11 *Turner and Bell v Searles (Stanford-le-Hope) Ltd* (1977) 33 P & CR 208, CA.

tenant,[12] but the landlord's interest must be shown to be prejudiced and where a county court judge did not indicate which matters he took into account, apart from the tenant illegally keeping his van on a grass verge, the case was remitted.[13] However, only if the county court's decision is vitiated by an error of law will the Court of Appeal interfere, as where there was no evidence to support a finding that rooms in a basement flat had been converted into a laundry.[14]

Para (d): suitable alternative accommodation:

> the landlord has offered and is willing to provide or secure the provision of alternative accommodation for the tenant. The terms on which the alternative accommodation is available are reasonable having regard to the terms of the current tenancy and to all other relevant circumstances. The accommodation and the time at which it will become available must be suitable for the tenant's requirements (including the requirement to preserve goodwill), having regard to the nature and class of his business and to the situation and extent of, and facilities afforded by, the holding.

The landlord must have made an offer in good faith, which he is still able and willing to honour. Despite the use of the present tense in para (e), the offer need only be made before the issue is joined in pleadings, and need not be made before the service of a s 25 notice.[15] If the offer is of part only of the accommodation, he must prove that the part in question is sufficient for the tenant's business purposes as at the date of the hearing. Paragraph (d) is not discretionary so that if the landlord establishes it, the application must be dismissed.[16] Thereafter the tenant must accept the landlord's offer or run the risk of having to quit the premises with no compensation for disturbance.

Para (e):   possession required for letting or disposing of the property as a whole:

> the tenant ought not to be granted a new tenancy where the current tenancy was created by the sub-letting of part only of the property comprised in a superior tenancy and the landlord is the owner of a superior interest in reversion expectant on the termination of that superior tenancy; the aggregate of the rents reasonably obtainable on separate lettings must be substantially less than the rent reasonably obtainable on a letting of the property as a whole; and on the termination of the current tenancy the landlord requires possession of the holding for the purpose of letting or otherwise disposing of the property as a whole.

Where paragraph (e) applies, a superior landlord has, under s 44(1), become the competent landlord as against a sub-lessee of part of the premises. If, at the date of the hearing, the landlord is merely the immediate landlord of the tenant, para (e) cannot therefore be invoked by him. The landlord's requirement of

12   *Eichner v Midland Bank Executor and Trustee Co Ltd* [1970] 2 All ER 597, [1970] 1 WLR 1120; *Hutchinson v Lamberth* [1984] 1 EGLR 75.
13   *Beard v Williams* [1986] 1 EGLR 148, CA.
14   *Jones v Jenkins* [1986] 1 EGLR 113, CA.
15   *M Chaplin Ltd v Regent Capital Holdings Ltd* [1994] 1 EGLR 249 (Cty ct).
16   *Betty's Cafés Ltd v Phillips Furnishing Stores Ltd* [1957] Ch 67 at 84, [1957] 1 All ER 1 at 8.

possession must arise on the termination of the current tenancy (that held by the tenant requesting a new tenancy) so that the landlord has to prove that the intermediate tenancy will come to an end by the termination date of the current sub-tenancy. It is, however, sufficient if the landlord proves that the intermediate tenancy will come to an end within the period specified as sufficient to entitle him to a s 31 declaration. Paragraph (e) is discretionary: the court would presumably take into account the fact that the landlord had consented to the sub-letting. Because of the requirement that the landlord must show that the total rents for the whole premises would be substantially higher if let as a whole then if it were re-let in parts, it was not sufficient for a landlord to prove only that the aggregate rents of parts of the premises were less, but not substantially less, than the total rent of the whole.[17]

Para (f): landlord intends to demolish or reconstruct:

> on the termination of the current tenancy the landlord intends to demolish or reconstruct the whole or a substantial part of the premises, or to carry out substantial work of construction on the holding or part, and he cannot reasonably do so without obtaining possession of the holding.

Landlord's intention The landlord[18] must have a clear intention. Often this intention is proved by the existence of a works programme. Should the execution of this involve a technical illegality (as where the works might as planned contravene a conservation order) this will not prevent reliance on para (f) provided that the incidental illegality can be avoided, as by a different method of carrying out the works.[19] The intention must be proved at the time of the hearing.[20] The court may direct that the issue of intention is to be tried as a preliminary issue,[1] and it appears that such directions are not uncommon,[2] as a way of saving costs to both parties.

In the case of a company, its resolutions may afford evidence of the requisite intention,[3] and in the case of a local authority, the requisite intention may be gathered from committee minutes or from its officers.[4] If the landlord gains possession and subsequently changes his mind, the tenant has no recourse against him.[5] The 'intention', whose existence is ultimately one of fact and degree,[6] must have moved out of the zone of contemplation into the valley of

17 *Greaves Organisation Ltd v Stanhope Gate Property Co Ltd* (1973) 228 Estates Gazette 725.
18 Or, in the case of joint landlords, the survivor, if one of them dies before the hearing: *Biles v Caesar* [1957] 1 All ER 151, [1957] 1 WLR 156, CA.
19 *Palisade Investments Ltd v Collin Estates Ltd* [1992] 2 EGLR 94, CA (but the result in this case would have been different if the works could only have been carried out illegally).
20 *Betty's Cafés Ltd v Phillips Furnishing Stores Ltd* [1957] Ch 67, [1957] 1 All ER 1, CA.
1 *Dutch Oven Ltd v Egham Estate and Investment Co Ltd* [1968] 1 WLR 1483.
2 Such a direction was made in eg *Barth v Pritchard* [1990] 1 EGLR 109, CA.
3 *Betty's Cafes Ltd v Phillips Furnishing Stores Ltd*, supra.
4 *Poppetts (Caterers) Ltd v Maidenhead Corpn* [1971] 1 WLR 69, CA.
5 See *Reohorn v Barry Corpn* [1956] 2 All ER 742, CA (where the requisite intention not proved).
6 *Fleet Electrics Ltd v Jacey Investments Ltd* [1956] 3 All ER 99, CA; *DAF Motoring Centre (Gosport) Ltd v Hatfield & Wheeler Ltd* [1982] 2 EGLR 59, CA.

decision.[7] The landlord must show that his project is viable and has a reasonable prospect of being carried out, and the court does not expect to examine all the details of the scheme provided such a prospect is shown,[8] once planning permission has been obtained, and finance and other general arrangements, such as with a building contractor, duly made, even if not all the details of the latter two points have been settled.[9] It is not necessary to show that binding contracts have been entered into in connection with the work.[10] On the other hand, there must not be too many obstacles left for the landlord to clear, as where a planning permission for site clearance imposed onerous conditions, which the landlord was not able to comply with at the date of the hearing; he had also not selected a developer, without whose participation his development project would fail, and so the landlord failed under para (f).[11]

The landlord is entitled to choose his own method of work, even if a different scheme would not involve the tenant quitting the whole holding.[12] If the landlord intends, on regaining possession, as opposed to at some future date,[13] to sell his interest, he cannot satisfy para (f); but since he does not necessarily have to carry out the work personally, para (f) may be satisfied if the landlord definitely intends to grant a building lease to a developer.[14] The precise length of any building lease is not, in itself, a significant matter: in one case, para (f) was satisfied by a local authority landlord which intended to grant a developer a four-year lease, once it had cleared and re-planted the site.[15]

An intention to carry out work within para (f) need not be the primary purpose, and hence, neither the fact that the landlord intended, after demolition works, to incorporate the premises in an agricultural holding,[16] nor that he intended, after demolition, to rebuild the premises and occupy them himself,[17] precluded him from invoking para (f).

Although the intention must be to carry out work at the termination of the tenancy, this refers to the time the landlord actually obtains possession, which may be a few weeks after the hearing.[18] Under s 31(2), if the landlord fails under para (f) but would have succeeded at such later date (within one year of the date specified in the s 25 notice or s 26 request) as the court determines, the court may make a declaration to that effect, and is not to order a new tenancy.[19] The

---

7   *Cunliffe v Goodman* [1950] 2 KB 237 at 254, CA.
8   *A Levy & Son Ltd v Martin Brent Developments Ltd* [1987] 2 EGLR 93; also *Peter Goddard & Sons Ltd v Hounslow London Borough Council* [1992] 1 EGLR 281, CA; also *Aberdeen Steak Houses plc v Crown Estates Comrs* [1997] EGCS 14.
9   *Capocci v Goble* [1987] 2 EGLR 102, CA.
10 Ibid.
11 *Edwards v Thompson* [1990] 2 EGLR 71. However, owing to the prospect of a successful scheme being worked out, the tenant obtained a one-year tenancy.
12 *Decca Navigator Co Ltd v Greater London Council* [1974] 1 All ER 1178, [1974] 1 WLR 748, CA.
13 *Turner v Wandsworth London Borough Council*, infra.
14 *PE Ahern & Sons Ltd v Hunt* [1988] 1 EGLR 74 (125-year term); *Spook Erection Ltd v British Railways Board* [1988] 1 EGLR 76, CA (99-year term).
15 *Turner v Wandsworth London Borough Council* [1994] 1 EGLR 134, CA.
16 *Craddock v Hampshire County Council* [1958] 1 WLR 202, CA.
17 *Fisher v Taylors Furnishing Stores Ltd* [1956] 2 QB 78, [1956] 2 All ER 78, CA.
18 See also *Livestock Underwriting Agency v Corbett and Newson* (1955) 165 Estates Gazette 469.
19 The tenant has 14 days from the making of the declaration to have the termination date of the tenancy put off by up to one year to the date indicated by the court (s 31(2)).

landlord did not have to rely on para (f) where, the tenant having left the premises voluntarily for new temporary accommodation, thus giving the landlord possession, his premises had ceased to exist as a separate entity due to works of reconstruction.[20]

Since the court is supposed to make a finding as to which part of para (f) particular work comes,[1] it is necessary to examine the various terms used therein, although the court is not to adopt an item by item approach and if, taken as a whole, the work is, for example, structural or building work, it will satisfy para (f) even if it may contain individual items of work which, in isolation would not,[2] since the position as a whole is looked at.

Demolition in para (f) presents no difficulty, but *substantial work of construction* in the second limb of para (f) is less simple and whether work falls within this category is a question of degree and impression.[3] To take two extreme contrasts, it includes the amalgamation of two shops by the substantial removal of a party wall and other major structural alterations,[4] but does not include the removal of material, infilling and landscaping.[5] The nature and extent of the proposed work must be taken into account in order to decide if it involves 'substantial' work of construction. A plan to build an extension over a period of nearly four months, at a cost of upwards of £8,000, so considerably improving the premises, qualified.[6] The requirement that the work is 'substantial' limits the landlord, since, if the work, taken as a whole, is not building work, affecting the structure of a building, it will not qualify. Thus, work involving the re-siting of a staircase, re-wiring, the installation of central heating, re-roofing and redecoration, was not 'substantial work of construction'.[7] Similarly, the word 'reconstruct' in the first part of para (f) requires there to be a substantial interference with the structure of the premises and then a measure of re-building, before work may qualify.[8]

Section 31A defences

To prevent the landlord from gaining possession of the whole premises where he only intends to carry out work on part of the premises, or where the duration of the work to the whole premises will be very short, the tenant has a defence under s 31A. The tenant must establish a defence under s 31A but since it is related to para (f), the court must consider this ground in the light of s 31A. The tenant may put forward conditional arguments so that if para (f) were to be satisfied, the tenant would then accept a tenancy of part of the holding.[9] Section

---

20 *Aireps Ltd v City of Bradford Metropolitan Corpn* [1985] 2 EGLR 143, CA.
 1 *Romulus Trading Co Ltd v Henry Smith's Charity Trustees* [1990] 2 EGLR 75, CA.
 2 *Joel v Swaddle* [1957] 3 All ER 325, [1957] 1 WLR 1094, CA; *Romulus Trading Co Ltd v Henry Smith's Charity Trustees*, supra.
 3 *Cook v Mott* (1961) 178 Estates Gazette 637, CA.
 4 *Bewlay (Tobacconists) Ltd v British Bata Shoe Co Ltd* [1958] 3 All ER 652, [1959] 1 WLR 45, CA.
 5 *Botterill v Bedfordshire County Council* [1985] 1 EGLR 82, CA.
 6 *Morar v Chauhan* [1985] 3 All ER 493, [1985] 1 WLR 1263, CA.
 7 *Barth v Pritchard* [1990] 1 EGLR 109, CA; also *Joel v Swaddle*, supra.
 8 *Percy E Cadle & Co Ltd v Jacmarch Properties Ltd* [1957] 1 QB 323, [1957] 1 All ER 148, CA.
 9 *Romulus Trading Co Ltd v Henry Smith's Charity Trustees (No 2)* [1991] 1 EGLR 95, CA.

31A provides that the court cannot hold that the landlord could not reasonably carry out the demolition or other work without obtaining possession if:

(a) the tenant agrees to the inclusion in the terms of the new tenancy of terms giving the landlord access and other facilities for the carrying out of the work intended and, given that access and facilities, the landlord could reasonably carry out the work without obtaining possession of the holding and interfering to a substantial extent or for a substantial time with the use of the holding for the purpose of a business carried on by the tenant; or
(b) the tenant is willing to accept a tenancy of an economically separable part of the holding[10] and either para (a) of s 31A is satisfied with respect to that part or possession of the remainder of the holding would be reasonably sufficient to enable the landlord to carry out the intended work.

The expression 'work intended' in s 31A(1)(a) refers to work which could not be done by the landlord without obtaining possession (and not, therefore, work which he is entitled to enter and carry out pursuant to an express term in the lease).[11] If the landlord's right of access is wide enough to enable him to complete the work, as where it refers to improvement, alteration and addition, and this is what the landlord intends to do, s 31A(1)(a) will preclude him relying on para (f).[12] Should the work go outside the contemplation of an entry clause, as with total rebuilding, it is otherwise.[13] If the right of entry is wide enough to allow the landlord to do part of the work, but not the whole, the court must decide which part falls within and which without the clause, and then, in relation to the work outside the clause, the effect of that work on the tenant's business and whether s 31A(1)(a) applies.[14]

The court looks at the physical effects of the work, as opposed to their results from a business point of view.[15] Whether the proposed work will, within para (a), interfere with the use of the holding 'to a substantial extent and for a substantial time' is a question of fact, and the duration, extent and nature of the work are all relevant factors, as is the nature of the tenant's business.[16] If the tenant's business will be closed or severely disrupted for more than a very few weeks, he cannot invoke s 31A(1)(a). Where the works would last for two weeks, closing and vacating the premises, there was an insufficient interference with the tenant's business.[17] By contrast, where, owing to the works, the tenant's cafe would be closed for at least 12 weeks, the interference was very

10 See s 31A(2): the aggregate of rents reasonably obtainable on separate lettings of that part, after completion of the work, in addition to those from the rest of the premises, must not, for para (b) to apply, be substantially less than the rent reasonably obtainable from letting the whole premises.
11 *Heath v Drown* [1973] AC 498, [1972] 2 All ER 561, HL; see Wilkinson (1985) 135 NLJ 145.
12 *Price v Esso Petroleum Ltd* [1980] 2 EGLR 58, CA.
13 *Leathwoods Ltd v Total Oil (Great Britain) Ltd* (1985) 51 P & CR 20, CA.
14 *Cerex Jewels Ltd v Peachey Property Corpn plc* (1986) 52 P & CR 127, CA.
15 *Redfern v Reeves* (1978) 37 P & CR 364, CA. As with para (f), the landlord is entitled to choose his method of work: if this requires possession of the whole, the tenant cannot invoke s 31A by showing that an alternative scheme would involve possession of part only of the holding.
16 *Mularczyk v Azralnove Investments Ltd* [1985] 2 EGLR 141, CA.
17 *Cerex Jewels Ltd v Peachey Property Corpn plc* [1986] 2 EGLR 65, CA.

substantial, having regard to the type of business, and the tenant failed to make out a s 31A(1)(a) defence.[18]

Para (g): landlord's intention to occupy the premises:

> on the termination of the current tenancy the landlord intends to occupy the premises for the purposes or partly for the purposes of a business to be carried on there by him, or as his residence.

Intention   The test for the sufficiency of the landlord's intention is similar to that applicable to paragraph (f): it is objective, and requires proof by the landlord of his settled and firm intention to occupy[19], to be carried out in the reasonable future, which may be within a reasonable time of the termination of the lease if the landlord first intends to carry out work,[20] which is ultimately a question of fact for the county court.[1] In the case of a company landlord, evidence of its intention may be proved by a manager with authority delegated to him by the board of directors,[2] or it may be established by a resolution of the board of directors. Where relevant, a reasonable prospect of his obtaining any necessary planning permission must be shown by the landlord, as opposed to a fanciful prospect or one which could sensibly be ignored by a reasonable landlord.[3] The relevant date is thus the date of the hearing[4] and it is not necessary to adduce evidence that the relevant intention existed before then.[5] However, a landlord who intends to occupy even only for a short time prior to selling the premises will generally come within paragraph (g).[6] A company (or other) landlord with the requisite intention does not have to show what particular part of the business it intends to transfer to the subject premises.[7] In any event, once a sufficient intention is shown by the landlord, he does not have to show that he intends to make physical use of the entire holding.[8]

Legislation imposes a solution in two cases where the person who is likely to occupy is not the person who gave the s 25 or s 26(6) notice.

---

18 *Blackburn v Hussain* [1988] 1 EGLR 77, CA.
19 *Europark (Midlands) Ltd v Town Centre Securities plc* [1985] 1 EGLR 88; *Mirza v Nicola* [1990] 2 EGLR 73, CA.
20 As in *London Hilton Jewellers Ltd v Hilton International Hotels Ltd* [1990] 1 EGLR 112, CA.
1   See *Cox v Binfield* [1989] 1 EGLR 97, CA.
2   *Manchester Garages Ltd v Petrofina (UK) Ltd* [1975] EGD 69, CA.
3   *Gregson v Cyril Lord Ltd* [1962] 3 All ER 907, [1963] 1 WLR 41, CA, approved in *Westminster City Council v British Waterways Board* [1985] AC 676, [1984] 3 All ER 737, HL; *Cadogan v McCarthy & Stone Developments Ltd* [1996] EGCS 94, CA.
4   It is assumed, as with para (f), that, if the landlord proves a sufficient intention, this will be the same at the date of the hearing and the expiry of interim continuation: *Expresso Coffee Machine Co Ltd v Guardian Assurance Co* [1958] 2 All ER 692, [1958] 1 WLR 900; affd [1959] 1 All ER 458, [1959] 1 WLR 250, CA; *Chez Gerard Ltd v Greene Ltd* [1983] 2 EGLR 79, CA.
5   *JW Thornton Ltd v Blacks Leisure Group plc* (1986) 53 P & CR 223, CA. Thus a resolution of a company board was accepted as evidence of the required intention during the hearing: *London Hilton Jewellers Ltd v Hilton International Hotels Ltd* [1990] 1 EGLR 112, CA.
6   *Willis v Association of Universities of the British Commonwealth* [1965] 1 QB 140, CA.
7   *Mash & Austin Ltd v Odhams Press Ltd* (1957) 169 Estates Gazette 655; *Pelosi v Bourne* (1957) 169 Estates Gazette 656.
8   *Method Development Ltd v Jones* [1971] 1 All ER 1027, [1971] 1 WLR 168, CA.

(a) *Trusts* By s 41(2), if the landlord's interest is held on trust[9] then, because references to the 'landlord' include the beneficiaries, or any of them, para (g) may be invoked if either the landlord or any beneficiary intends to carry on a business on the premises.[10] However, any beneficiary claiming thus to invoke para (g) must be entitled to occupy solely under his trust interest and not otherwise, as under a lease granted by the beneficairies to some, but not all of their number.[11]

(b) *Groups of Companies* By s 42(3)(a), where the landlord's interest is held by a member of a group of companies, an intended occupation by any member of the group includes intended occupation by any member of the group for the purposes of a business to be carried on by that member.[12]

There is a further special rule for companies in which the landlord has a controlling interest:[13] any business carried on by the company is to be treated, within para (g), as a business to be carried on by him (s 30(3)); otherwise, however, the business will be treated as carried on by the company and not the landlord, owing to the general principle that a company is a separate entity from the landlord.[14]

Occupation   While the landlord must intend to occupy the whole premises, personally or through an agent,[15] or manager, at least where the landlord retains practically complete control over the running of the business,[16] he need not necessarily intend to use the whole for business purposes. Where the landlord intended, having obtained possession, to re-let the whole premises, para (g) was inapplicable, even though during the planned works of conversion, the landlord would be in temporary occupation.[17] It seems that para (g) is not available where the landlord intends to demolish existing buildings and to put new ones on the site.[18] This may be because it is not possible to occupy the holding with buildings which one is intent on demolishing. By contrast, where a site was vacant and the landlord intended to erect a building on part of it, the landlord could invoke para (g), as the intention of the ground is to hand back the landlord his land if he wishes to carry on his own business on it.[19]

The five-year rule   Paragraph (g) is subject to a qualification under s 30(2). This precludes the landlord from invoking the ground:

9   See *Maurar v Chauhan* [1985] 3 All ER 493, [1985] 1 WLR 1263, CA.
10 See *Sevenarts Ltd v Busvine* [1969] 1 All ER 392, [1968] 1 WLR 1929, CA.
11 *Meyer v Riddick* [1990] 1 EGLR 107, CA.
12 Two bodies corporate are taken as members of a group if and only if one is a subsidiary to the other or both are subsidiaries of a third body corporate (s 42(1)).
13 As defined by s 30(3) and applies if (a) the landlord is a member of the company and able, without the consent of any other person, to appoint or remove the holders of at least a majority of the directorships; or (b) he holds more than half of the company's share capital, disregarding any shares held by him in a fiduciary capacity or as nominee for another person.
14 See *Tunstall v Steigmann* [1962] 2 QB 593, [1962] 2 All ER 417, CA.
15 See *Skeet v Powell-Sheddon* [1988] 2 EGLR 112, CA.
16 As in *Teesside Indoor Bowls Ltd v Stockton-on-Tees Borough Council* [1990] 2 EGLR 87, CA.
17 *Jones v Jenkins* [1986] 1 EGLR 113, CA.
18 *Nursey v P Currie (Dartford) Ltd* [1959] 1 All ER 497, [1959] 1 WLR 273, CA.
19 *Cam Gears Ltd v Cunningham* [1981] 2 All ER 560, [1981] 1 WLR 1011, CA.

(a) if his interest or an interest which has merged in that interest and but for the merger would be the landlord's interest was purchased or created[20] within the five years preceding the date specified in the original s 25 notice or s 26 request; and

(b) if throughout that period there has been a tenancy or succession of tenancies of the holding within Part II of the 1954 Act.

A landlord who has 'purchased', that is bought for money,[1] the freehold or a tenancy (by grant or assignment),[2] within the five year period, he cannot rely on ground (g), unless there was a time during that period when there was no business tenancy of the holding in being.[3] Where the landlord's interest is leasehold, a succession of tenancies is treated as a single continuing tenancy for the purpose of determining when the landlord acquired his interest.[4]

---

20 The interest is created on the date of execution of the lease and not the commencement date of the term, or that of taking possession if different: *Northcote Laundry Ltd v Frederick Donnelly Ltd* [1968] 2 All ER 50, [1968] 1 WLR 562, CA.

1 *HL Bolton (Engineering) Co Ltd v T J Graham & Sons Ltd* [1957] 1 QB 159, [1956] 3 All ER 624, CA.

2 But not by surrender without consideration: cf *Frederick Lawrence Ltd v Freeman, Hardy and Willis* [1959] Ch 731, [1959] 3 All ER 77, CA.

3 For successful avoidance of s 30(2) by the grant of a reversionary lease by the freeholders to sub-lessees see *Wates Estate Agency Services v Bartleys Ltd* [1989] 2 EGLR 87, CA.

4 See *Artemiou v Procopiou* [1966] 1 QB 878, [1965] 3 All ER 539, CA.

Chapter 27

Dismissal of tenant's application

I TERMINATION OF THE CURRENT TENANCY

The court is precluded by s 31(1) from ordering a new tenancy to be granted if the landlord establishes any one or more of the grounds of opposition under s 30(1) to its satisfaction. Otherwise, the court will order a new tenancy. Where a notice to terminate or a tenant's request for a new tenancy has been given, followed by an application to the court, the effect of the notice is to terminate the tenancy at the expiration of three months as from the date on which the application[1] is finally disposed of (s 64(1)).[2] In one case, a tenant's application for a new tenancy was dismissed but some ten days before the date the right to occupation ended, the landlords' computer sent out a routine rent demand. The tenants paid the sum demanded but the landlords were not estopped by conduct from treating the lease as duly terminated.[3]

If the landlord fails to establish any of the grounds specified in s 30(1)(d), (e) or (f) to the satisfaction of the court, but the court would have been satisfied as to any of those grounds if the date of termination specified in the landlord's notice or the date specified in the tenant's request for a new tenancy had been such later date as the court may determine, but which is no later than one year from the specified date:

(a) the court must make a declaration to that effect, stating which of the above grounds would have been satisfied and specifying the date so determined: it cannot order a new tenancy;
(b) if, within 14 days from the making of the declaration, the tenant requires this, the court is to make an order substituting the date specified in the declaration for that specified in the landlord's notice to terminate or the tenant's request for a new tenancy (s 31(2)).

1 This provision applies even to a tenant's application which contravenes the time-limits laid down in s 29(3): *Zenith Investments (Torquay) Ltd v Kammins Ballrooms Co Ltd (No 2)* [1971] 2 All ER 901, [1971] 1 WLR 1032, with the result that in that case the tenancy ended when the tenants surrendered possession.
2 This latter expression is to be construed in accordance with s 64(2).
3 *Legal & General Assurance Society v General Metal Agencies Ltd* (1969) 212 Estates Gazette 159. This result is seemingly unaffected by the strict development of the common law of waiver (see eg *Central Estates (Belgravia) Ltd v Woolgar (No 2)* [1972] 3 All ER 610, CA) since a similar result arises in the case of Rent Act statutory tenancies (see *Trustees of Henry Smith's Charity v Willson* [1983] QB 316, [1983] 1 All ER 73, CA).

Where the court refuses an order for a new tenancy, and it is subsequently proved that the court was induced to refuse the grant, by misrepresentation or concealment of material facts, the court may order the landlord to pay the tenant such sum as appears sufficient compensation for damage or loss sustained by the tenant as a result of the refusal (s 55(1)). It seems that if the landlord, in good faith, establishes a ground of opposition, and subsequently changes his mind, s 55(1) will not avail the tenant.

II DISTURBANCE COMPENSATION

A tenant who fails to obtain an order for a new tenancy may qualify for compensation under s 37, if the landlord has established any of the grounds specified in s 30(1)(e), (f) or (g), and no other ground within s 30(1) had been made out by the landlord (s 37(1)). He is also entitled to such compensation where no other ground was specified in his s 25 notice or s 26(6) reply, except for grounds (e), (f) or (g), and no application was made for a new tenancy, or, if it was, it was withdrawn (s 37(1)).[4]

The amount of compensation is the product of the appropriate multiplier[5] and either (a) the rateable value of the holding or (b) twice the rateable value of the holding (s 37(2)).[6] The rateable value of the holding is that as it appears in the valuation list in force at the time when the original notice or request was made: it makes no difference that, subsequently, the list may have been amended so as to reflect an increased rateable value as such amendment cannot be retrospectively applied.[7]

The higher rate of compensation is only available if, by s 37(3):

(a) during the whole of the 14 years immediately preceding the termination of the current tenancy, premises being or comprised in the holding have been occupied for the purpose of a business carried on by the occupier or for those and other purposes;

(b) if, during those 14 years there was a change in the occupier of the premises, the person who was the occupier immediately after the change was the successor to the business carried on by the person who was the occupier immediately before the change.

The words 'the premises comprised in the holding' in s 37(3) refer to the particular premises which had been occupied by the tenant (or where relevant,

---

4 The court has power to require the tenant, as a condition of obtaining leave to withdraw, that he should not seek compensation under s 37: see *Young, Austen & Young Ltd v British Medical Association* [1977] 2 All ER 884, [1977] 1 WLR 881; *Fribourg and Treyer v Northdale Investments Ltd* (1982) 44 P & CR 284.

5 The multiplier is fixed at three levels, notably at three where the relevant date for determining the rateable value of the holding is before 1 April 1990 and at one where the relevant date is on or after 1 April 1990: Landlord and Tenant Act 1954 (Appropriate Multiplier) Order 1990, SI 1990/363.

6 As calculated under s 37(5) and (5A) to (5D) – the latter being applicable where any part of the holding is domestic property as defined by Local Government and Housing Act 1989, s 66.

7 *Plessy Co plc v Eagle Pension Funds Ltd* [1990] 2 EGLR 209.

any sub-tenant) for the purposes of his business. Provided that at least part thereof, such as one floor of a demised building, was occupied by the tenant for the purposes of his business for the continuous period of 14 years prior to the termination of the tenancy, he qualifies for the higher rate compensation, because the premises in question need only be 'comprised' in the holding.[8] But the tenant will not qualify for the higher rate of compensation unless the requisite occupation is for the full period of 14 years from taking possession; any period short of that, by no matter how short a margin even if it is as little as one day, qualifies for the lower rate only.[9] As to the words 'the termination of the current tenancy' within s 37(3), from which the period of occupation is to be calculated, this expression refers to the date of termination specified in the landlord's s 25 notice or the tenant's s 26 request for a new tenancy (s 37(7)). Therefore, the effect of any interim continuation under s 64 is left out of account for this purpose; but as a rule, the relevant date for assessing compensation is the date when the tenant quits the holding.[10] In any event, no compensation under s 37 may be claimed unless the tenant has first served a s 29(2) notice of unwillingness to give up possession on the landlord.[11] On the other hand, once a landlord has served a counter-notice to a tenant's application which invokes grounds (e), (f) or (g), he cannot both recover possession and avoid the payment of compensation, because by serving a counter-notice he has presented the tenant with the choice of the doubtful possibility of a new tenancy and the certainty of s 37 compensation.[12]

8 *Edicron Ltd v William Whiteley Ltd* [1984] 1 All ER 219, [1984] 1 WLR 59, CA.
9 *Department of the Environment v Royal Insurance plc* (1986) 54 P & CR 26.
10 *International Military Services Ltd v Capital and Counties plc* [1982] 1 WLR 575; *Cardshops Ltd v John Lewis Properties Ltd* [1983] QB 161, [1982] 3 All ER 746, CA; *Sperry Ltd v Hambro Life Assurance Ltd* [1983] 1 EGLR 70.
11 *Re 14 Grafton Street, London W1* [1971] Ch 935.
12 *Lloyds Bank Ltd v City of London Corpn* [1983] Ch 192, [1983] 1 All ER 92.

Chapter 28

Court order of a new tenancy

I POWERS OF THE COURT AS TO TERMS

Where the tenant has applied to the court for a new tenancy, the court is bound, by s 29(1), to make an order for the grant of a new tenancy comprising such property, at such a rent and on such other terms as are provided in ss 32-35. The court cannot do this where:

(a) the landlord successfully establishes one or more grounds of opposition under s 30; or
(b) the court is precluded by s 31(2) from ordering a new tenancy.

If the parties reach an enforceable agreement on any of the matters specified in these provisions, the court's power to determine terms is limited to those not agreed.

Property to be comprised in the holding

The parties may agree on what is to constitute the holding; if not, s 32(1) requires the court to designate the holding with regard to the circumstances existing at the date of the order. The tenant's application must relate only to the premises or part, occupied by him for business purposes. As mentioned earlier (chapter 23), where the whole or part of the premises, is, at the relevant date, occupied by a sub-tenant, the latter is entitled to renewal and not the tenant, in respect of the parts he occupies. If the tenant's originating application is defective, for example, it fails to cover the whole holding, the court has a discretion to allow subsequent corrections.[1] The landlord may insist under s 32(2), that all property comprised in the current tenancy be included in the new tenancy.[2] In addition, the court has the power, under s 32(1A), to order a new tenancy in respect of the part of the premises of which the tenant has indicated[3] that he was willing to accept a tenancy; but the tenant cannot be forced to accept the landlord's offer of a tenancy of part only of the business premises where he cannot obtain the grant of a new tenancy of the whole and he will be given leave to withdraw his application.[4]

1 *Nurit Bar v Pathwood Investments Ltd* (1987) 54 P & CR 178, CA.
2 Even if he cannot offer vacant possession of the property over and above the holding: *Re No 1, Albemarle Street W1* [1959] Ch 531, [1959] 1 All ER 250.
3 See s 31A(1)(b) and ch 26; this would follow a s 30(1)(f) application by the landlord.
4 *Fribourg and Treyer Ltd v Northdale Investments Ltd* (1982) 44 P & CR 284.

Section 32 distinguishes between property to be comprised in the new tenancy and 'rights enjoyed in connection with the holding', such as purely contractual rights (eg to erect advertising signs),[5] fixtures, easements and quasi-easements such as would pass under s 62 of the Law of Property Act 1925, unless expressly excluded. Such rights as were enjoyed by the tenant under the current tenancy will be included in the new tenancy except as otherwise agreed between the parties, or in default of agreement, as determined by the court.[6]

Duration (s 33)

The court may order a new tenancy for any duration it thinks reasonable in all the circumstances: if it is a tenancy for a term of years certain, its duration cannot exceed 14 years (s 35). The new tenancy begins on the coming to an end of the current tenancy. The parties, by contrast, may agree on a tenancy of any duration they like: if so, the court has power to order a tenancy for that agreed term,[7] where other terms are in dispute. Thus, relative hardship may be a relevant factor, or that the landlord would in a matter of months be able to establish the ground specified in s 30(1)(g) or (f).[8] The length of the current tenancy, the nature of the business, the age and the state of the property and its prospects of redevelopment are all material circumstances.[9]

Therefore, if the landlord is able to show a bona fide intention to redevelop, which is not capable of immediate realisation, the court may order a tenancy for a given period with a break clause on suitable terms to enable him to terminate the lease and redevelop if and when able to do so.[10] Similarly, a landlord was given the right to break a new tenancy on six months' notice where there was a real possibility that he might redevelop the site, during the ten years proposed by the tenant.[11] There is no inevitability that a break clause will be inserted to suit the convenience or requirements of the landlord, so that where the tenant intended to retire at a given date, the landlord was refused a break clause exercisable for redevelopment at any time on six months' notice, having regard to the hardship caused to the tenant in possible relocation so close to his retirement date.[12] Equally, where the tenant requested a one-year term and the landlord sought a 14-year term, a one-year term was granted, giving the landlord time in which to find new tenants.[13] Essentially, the length of the term is at discretion: in one case a tenant was given a longer lease than he would have liked.[14] Since the policy of the Act is not to give the tenant security if the landlord

---

5   *Re No 1 Albemarle Street W1* [1959] Ch 531 [1959] 1 All ER 250; *G Orlik (Meat Products) Ltd v Hastings and Thanet Building Society* (1974) 29 P & CR 126, CA.
6   Evidence is admissible to show the true extent of the intended demise if the parcels clause is incorrect: *I S Mills (Yardley) Ltd v Curdworth Investments Ltd* (1975) 119 Sol Jo 302, CA.
7   *Janes (Gowns) Ltd v Harlow Development Corpn* [1980] 1 EGLR 52.
8   See *Upsons Ltd v E Robins Ltd* [1956] 1 QB 131, [1955] 3 All ER 348, CA.
9   See eg *London and Provincial Millinery Stores Ltd v Barclays Bank Ltd* [1962] 1 WLR 510, CA.
10 *McCombie v Grand Junction Co Ltd* [1962] 2 All ER 65n, [1962] 1 WLR 581, CA; *Adams v Green* [1978] 2 EGLR 46, CA; *Amika Motor Ltd v Colebrook Holdings Ltd* [1981] 2 EGLR 62, CA.
11 *National Car Parks Ltd v Paternoster Consortium Ltd* [1990] 1 EGLR 99.
12 *Becker v Hill Street Properties Ltd* [1990] 2 EGLR 78, CA.
13 *CBS United Kingdom Ltd v London Scottish Properties Ltd* [1985] 2 EGLR 125.
14 *Re Sunlight House, Quay St, Manchester* (1959) 173 Estates Gazette 311.

proves that he intends to occupy the premises himself in the near future, but could not at the date of the hearing, where the five-year rule precluded this, the effect of this was taken into account in determining the duration of a new tenancy.[15]

To prevent long appeals prolonging a term, the court may well direct that the term should start from the final disposal of the application and end on a specified date.[16]

The discretion of the county court regarding the term is wide and generally the Court of Appeal will not interfere in the absence of error of law.[17] Special rules exist to order the grant of any necessary reversionary leases, where required, because the new tenancy extends beyond the immediate landlord's interest.[18]

Rent

In the event of non-agreement as to the rent payable under the new tenancy, s 34(1) provides that the court shall determine it as that at which, having regard to the terms of the current tenancy (other than those relating to rent), the holding might reasonably be expected to be let in the open market by a willing lessor. By s 34(4),[19] the matters taken into account by the court in determining the rent include any effect (on the new tenancy) of the operation of the provisions of the Landlord and Tenant (Covenants) Act 1995. That Act, among other things, abrogates the liability of a tenant holding a tenancy granted as from 1 January 1996 to observe leasehold covenants after an assignment of the tenancy, and enables the landlord in certain circumstances to pre-specify in a commercial tenancy that it is a condition of any assignment that the assigning tenant guarantees the immediate assignee's performance of his covenants.

Both ss 34 and 35 direct the court to have regard to the terms of the current tenancy; the court must first consider other terms before deciding on the new rent: if any new term is added or if any existing term is altered or excluded in the new tenancy, this may well have an effect on the new rent.[20] If a party seeks a departure from the terms of the current tenancy, the onus of justifying the departure is on him; hence the court refused both to relax a user clause where the effect would be to raise the rent[1] and to narrow a user clause where the effect would be to depress it.[2] Where the county court altered a covenant against assignment or underletting so as to incorporate a surrender-back clause after fixing the new rent, the case was remitted to enable reconsideration of the rent.[3]

---

15 *Wig Creations v Colour Film Services* (1969) 20 P & CR 870, CA (tenants obtained a three-year term, not the 12-year lease they asked for).
16 *Chipperfield v Shell UK Ltd* (1980) 42 P & CR 136, CA.
17 *Upsons Ltd v E Robins Ltd* [1956] 1 QB 131, [1955] 3 All ER 348, CA.
18 Landlord and Tenant Act 1954, s 44 and Sch 6, para 2, which applies both where the parties agree on duration and where it is fixed by the court.
19 Added by the Landlord and Tenant Act 1995, Sch 1, para 3; a similar rule applies to s 35 of the 1954 Act (para 4).
20 *O'May v City of London Real Property Co Ltd* [1983] 2 AC 726, 740, HL.
 1 *Charles Clements (London) Ltd v Rank City Wall Ltd* [1978] 1 EGLR 47.
 2 *Aldwych Club Ltd v Copthall Property Co Ltd* (1962) 185 Estates Gazette 219.
 3 *Cardshops Ltd v Davies* [1971] 2 All ER 721, [1971] 1 WLR 591, CA.

Section 34(1) postulates an open market rent. This expression has been said to require the inclusion of a sufficient number of (notional) lessors and lessees to create the opportunity of comparing rents, enabling the forces of supply and demand to operate. There must be a willing lessor and a willing lessee (as might happen in a rent review matter) and a reasonable period in which to negotiate the new tenancy at arm's length. Any rent payable by a lessee with a special interest must, in accordance with general valuation principles, be disregarded. The landlord will no doubt seek to obtain the best rent for the premises on the terms offered and the tenant to persuade the landlord to accept the lowest rent possible.[4]

The new rent may be decided having due regard to expert evidence from a surveyor, perhaps one for each side, experienced in current values for comparable neighbourhood property,[5] taking into account the terms of the new tenancy[6] and, on occasion, a firm offer of a rent to be paid in respect of the same premises with vacant possession.[7] The court will not admit new evidence of rents for leases of allegedly comparable premises, where it has, on the basis of evidence already available to it, already exercised its discretion as to the amount of the new rent.[8] The rent of neighbouring property is relevant, however, only to compare the relative trading position of the premises.[9] If there are no comparables, general rent increases in the area may be applied.[10] The matter is, at the end of the day, at the general discretion of the judge.[11] There is no general rule that the tenant is bound to disclose the trading accounts of his business[12] but they may be admissible with special types of premises whose profitability fluctuates, such as hotels, restaurants and so on, as a relevant indication of earnings capacity.[13] The tenant cannot set up his own breaches of covenant to repair in reduction of the rent under s 34(1).[14] In contrast, the court has power, under s 34(1), to order that the rent is not to commence, or is to commence at a lower rate, until repairs are carried out, where it is the landlord who is in breach of a covenant to repair under the contractual term.[15] Since an assessment of the rent is objective, s 34 does not allow a rent below the market level to be fixed simply because the tenant cannot afford the new rent.[16] On the other hand,

---

4 *Baptist v Masters of the Bench and Trustees of the Honourable Society of Gray's Inn* [1993] 2 EGLR 136 (where an open market at Gray's Inn could operate despite the fact that the occupiers were all in the same profession).
5 The court is the ultimate arbiter of the weight of such evidence and in one case a re-hearing was ordered on appeal where excessive reliance had been placed on the evidence of one expert, the tenant not having his own expert: *Miah v Bromley Park Garden Estates Ltd* [1992] 1 EGLR 98, CA.
6 Cf *English Exporters (London) Ltd v Eldonwall Ltd* [1973] Ch 415, [1973] 1 All ER 726.
7 *Re 52–56 Osnaburgh Street* (1957) 169 Estates Gazette 656.
8 *Khalique v Law Land plc* [1989] 1 EGLR 105, CA.
9 *Rogers v Rosedimond Investments (Blakes Market) Ltd* [1978] 2 EGLR 48, CA.
10 *National Car Parks v Colebrook Estates Ltd* [1983] 1 EGLR 78.
11 *Turone v Howard de Walden Estates Ltd* [1982] 1 EGLR 92, CA; *Oriani v Dorita Properties Ltd* [1987] 1 EGLR 88, CA; *Khalique v Law Land plc*, supra.
12 *WJ Barton Ltd v Long Acre Securities Ltd* [1982] 1 All ER 465, [1982] 1 WLR 398, CA.
13 See *Harewood Hotels Ltd v Harris* [1958] 1 All ER 104, [1958] 1 WLR 108, CA.
14 *Family Management v Gray* [1980] 1 EGLR 46, CA.
15 *Fawke v Viscount Chelsea* [1980] QB 441, [1979] 3 All ER 568, CA.
16 *Giannoukakis Ltd v Saltfleet Ltd* [1988] 1 EGLR 73, CA.

other factors relevant to the premises which might reduce the rent, such as the fact that, in times of recession, retailers may not be ready and willing to take leases of inferior sites without some substantial incentive, may be taken into account.[17]

It is provided (s 34(1)) that four matters must be disregarded in assessing the rent for a new tenancy:

(a) Any effect on rent attributable to occupation by the tenant (or a predecessor in title) of the holding. Therefore, the tenant is not protected against the open market rent by the fact that he is a sitting tenant.[18]
(b) Any goodwill attaching to the premises by reason of the business carried on by the tenant or any predecessor in title of his in the same business.
(c) Any increase in value attributable to certain improvements carried out by the person who was current tenant other than in pursuance of an obligation to his immediate landlord.[19] The following conditions apply to this, by s 34(2):
   (i) that the improvement was completed either during the current tenancy or not more than 21 years before the application for a new tenancy;
   (ii) that the holding or the part improved was at all times since completion of the improvement, subject to tenancies to which Part II applies; and
   (iii) that on the termination of any tenancy the tenant did not quit. As with rent review, it is not possible to treat the premises as though no improvement had ever been made, as a matter of valuation.[20]
(d) In the case of licensed premises, the increase in value attributable to the licence, if its benefit is to be regarded as the tenant's.

The court has power, under s 34(3), to include a rent review clause in the new tenancy on such terms as it thinks fit. This provision was passed (as an amendment to the 1954 Act, Part II) to confirm a High Court ruling.[1] It has been decided that the court in the exercise of its discretion may, if the parties agree on the insertion of a rent review clause for the first time in the new tenancy, but not as to its terms, render the clause both upwards and downwards.[2] Thus, the court ordered that a new nine-year tenancy of shop premises should have such a clause every three years, where the original lease had been for a 21-year term, without any rent review, on the ground that an upwards-only clause would be unfair to the tenant, due to a continuing local recession.[3]

17 *French v Commercial Union Life Assurance Co plc* [1993] 1 EGLR 113, CA.
18 *O'May v City of London Real Property Co Ltd* [1983] 2 AC 726, 740, HL.
19 If the improvement is carried out under a licence prior to the lease, the disregard will not apply: *Euston Centre Properties Ltd v H & J Wilson Ltd* [1982] 1 EGLR 57. If under a licence to improve, disregard is a question of construction: *Godbold v Martin the Newsagents Ltd* [1983] 2 EGLR 128.
20 Cf *Estates Projects Ltd v Greenwich London Borough* [1979] 2 EGLR 85.
 1 *Stylo Shoes Ltd v Manchester Royal Exchange Ltd* (1967) 204 Estates Gazette 803.
 2 *Janes (Gowns) Ltd v Harlow Development Corpn* [1980] 1 EGLR 52 (where owing to a neighbouring development, a fall in rental values was quite possible); also *Boots the Chemists Ltd v Pinkland Ltd* [1992] 2 EGLR 98 (Cty Ct).
 3 *Forbouys plc v Newport County Council* [1994] 1 EGLR 138 (Cty ct) (the possibility of an upwards review discounted any unfairness to the landlord); also *Amarjee v Barrowfen Properties Ltd* [1993] 2 EGLR 133.

Where the contractual tenancy already contains an upwards-only rent review clause, the position is more open. In one case, the judge refused, in his discretion, to alter the terms of an upwards-only clause which he regarded as suitable for reproduction in the new tenancy.[4] There is no reason why the court should not alter the terms of an existing upwards-only rent review clause as they apply to the new tenancy, so as to allow for a downwards review, if it has a general unfettered discretion. If, however, the issue is governed by s 35 of the 1954 Act, Part II, the court would have to incorporate the clause in an unaltered form in the new tenancy, unless persuaded by the tenant of the fairness and justice of altering its terms, with some compensation to the landlord. By reason of s 35, there is power in the court to include a term dealing on a fixed or variable basis, with service charges.[5]

As to the date from which the new rent is payable: if the parties agree on the commencement date for the new tenancy, they may provide that rent is payable from the date of commencement, even if this precedes execution of the lease.[6] If there is no agreement as to a commencement date, the relevant date is that of the hearing.[7]

Other terms

The court is enabled by s 35, in the absence of agreement between the parties, to determine any other terms under the new tenancy, having regard to the terms of the current tenancy and to all relevant circumstances.

As was seen above, the courts will be reluctant to impose, without good reason, new terms and the party seeking to do this must justify a change as fair, reasonable, and adequately compensated for. Hence, where under the current tenancy the landlords were responsible for all maintenance, repairs and services, without recourse to the tenants, and sought to impose a term in a new tenancy on the tenants providing for service charges in respect of these items, in return for a small cut in the overall basis of calculation of the rent payable, the House of Lords refused to force this proposal on the tenants as it was a significant, unjustified and inadequately compensated for change.[8] A change in the terms of the current tenancy will be allowed if essentially fair with adequate compensation to the party adversely affected by the change.[9] Accordingly, the county court ordered that a shop tenant must in future contribute to a service charge referable to the whole of the parade concerned, having regard to the common features of the particular development.[10] But the court refused to insert a tenants' option to purchase the freehold in a new tenancy where the option in the current tenancy had expired.[11] Nor is the court able to enlarge the

---

4   *Charles Follett Ltd v Cabtell Investments Ltd* [1986] 2 EGLR 76. This aspect was not considered on appeal. Also *Blythewood Plant Hire Ltd v Spiers Ltd* [1992] 2 EGLR 103 (Cty Ct).
5   *Hyams v Titan Properties Ltd* (1972) 24 P & CR 359, CA.
6   *Bradshaw v Pawley* [1979] 3 All ER 273, [1980] 1 WLR 10.
7   *Lovely and Orchard Services Ltd v Daejan Investments (Grove Hall) Ltd* (1977) 121 Sol Jo 711.
8   *O'May v City of London Real Property Co Ltd* [1983] 2 AC 726, [1982] 1 All ER 660, HL.
9   *Gold v Brighton Corpn* [1956] 3 All ER 442, [1956] 1 WLR 1291, CA.
10   *Amarjee v Barrowfen Properties Ltd* [1993] 2 EGLR 133.
11   *Kirkwood v Johnson* (1979) 38 P & CR 392, CA.

current holding by incorporating against the landlord's will, easements or rights over his own land not hitherto enjoyed by the tenant.[12] As to user clauses, see the text dealing with s 34. Where the residue of a business lease was assigned subject to a newly imposed term on assignment that the tenant would obtain guarantors of his obligations under the lease, it was held that the court could, on a ten-year new tenancy order, impose the like guarantee requirement, even though it would last for ten years rather than, under the contractual term, one year.[13] However, the court should not impose a term on the tenant requiring him to pay the landlord's costs of preparing the new tenancy.[14] Where the original leases of business premises contained break-clauses exercisable in the event of the landlord's wishing to redevelop, new leases were granted for fixed terms with break-clauses in each after five years.[15] The result of the above considerations may be that there is relatively little scope for 'modernising' leases under s 35.[16]

II EFFECT OF THE ORDER

Carrying out of the court's order

Even though the court makes an order for the grant of a new tenancy, on the application of the tenant, the tenant is not bound to take the tenancy and the parties may agree not to act on its terms. First, the tenant is entitled under s 36(2) to apply to the court within 14 days for the revocation of the order, and the court is bound to revoke it.[17] In that event, the parties may agree, or the court may determine, that the current tenancy shall continue beyond what would otherwise have been its date of termination (ie the date specified in the original notice or a later date by virtue of s 64) for such period as is 'necessary to afford to the landlord a reasonable opportunity for reletting or otherwise disposing of the premises which would have been comprised in the new tenancy'. This provision is necessary for the protection of a tenant who cannot afford the rent, for example, or accept the terms, as finally determined by the court, for where these were matters in dispute, he was not necessarily sure of their outcome when he made the application; nevertheless, the court has a discretion to order costs, or vary an order for costs, in the original application, as well as to order costs in the revocation (s 36(3)), which will tend to discourage abuses on the part of tenants. Second, the parties are free, by a written agreement (s 69(2)), to modify or exclude any of the terms determined by the court which may suit neither of them.

---

12 *G Orlik (Meat Products) Ltd v Hastings and Thanet Building Society* (1974) 29 P & CR 126, CA.
13 *Cairnplace Ltd v CBI (Property Investment) Co Ltd* [1984] 1 All ER 315, [1984] 1 WLR 696, CA.
14 Ibid. Otherwise the tenant would lose the protection of the Costs of Leases Act 1958, s 1.
15 *JH Edwards & Sons Ltd v Central London Commercial Estates Ltd* [1984] 2 EGLR 103. The landlords did not have any firm proposals: hence the measure of security given to the tenants. Cf *Leslie & Godwin Investments Ltd v Prudential Assurance Co Ltd* [1987] 2 EGLR 95.
16 See further Law Com No 162 (1987), paras 4.54-4.56 and their 1992 Report (ch 22).
17 There is no discretion in the court not to revoke: *Broadmead Ltd v Corben-Brown* (1966) 201 Estates Gazette 111.

Those two cases apart, the landlord is bound to execute and the tenant bound to accept, a lease or agreement for a tenancy of the holding embodying the terms as agreed between them or determined by the court; and the tenant may be required by the landlord to execute a counterpart of the instrument. Default in execution is not only a contempt of court; compliance may be enforced by specific performance.[18] Until then, equity treats the parties as landlord and tenant.[19]

Termination of the current tenancy

The current tenancy will continue until the new lease or binding agreement for a new lease takes effect. Where the court determines the duration of the new tenancy under s 33, that will commence on the date specified in the original notice, or a later date by virtue of s 64. Where the parties have themselves agreed upon the duration of the new tenancy, however, there appears to be nothing in s 33 to prevent them from agreeing to some other date, except possibly that if the agreed date were earlier, it is arguable that this would be a surrender of the current tenancy, which in turn would have to be authorised under s 38(4)(b). Once there is a binding agreement for a new tenancy, the tenant loses all his rights under Part II in relation to the current tenancy.

---

18 *Pulleng v Curran* (1980) 44 P & CR 58, CA.
19 *Greaves Organisation Ltd v Stanhope Gate Property Co Ltd* (1973) 228 Estates Gazette 725.

Chapter 29

Compensation for improvements

I APPLICATION OF PART I OF THE 1927 ACT

Holdings within the Act

A tenant's right to compensation for improvements is governed by Part I of the Landlord and Tenant Act 1927, and Part III of the 1954 Act. The 1927 Act applies to holdings other than an agricultural holding or a farm business tenancy under a lease (defined by s 25 as including any under-lease) other than a mining lease, used wholly or partly for carrying on thereat any trade or business, whether created before or after the commencement of the Act (s 17(1)). Service tenancies created after 25 March 1928 are excluded as long as the tenant's employment or appointment continues if the contract is in writing and expresses the purpose for which the tenancy is created (s 17(2)). Trade or business is defined as including any profession regularly carried on upon the premises, but not the business of sub-letting premises as residential flats (s 17(3)); but beyond that, there is no definition of trade, business or profession, which are open to the same meanings as under the 1954 Act. Where premises are used partly for other purposes, the right to compensation is limited to improvements in relation to trade or business (s 17(4)). Tenancies of on-licensed premises are not excluded, and therefore a tenant is entitled to compensation for improvements under the 1927 Act.

Improvements within the Act

Under s 1, a tenant is entitled to claim compensation for improvements (including the erection of any building but not trade or other fixtures which he is entitled to remove) on his holding made by him or his predecessors in title, which add to the letting value of the holding. 'Tenant' is defined by s 25(1) as 'any person entitled in possession to the holding under any contract of tenancy'; hence, 'predecessor in title' receives a wide construction and includes an improving sub-lessee assigning to an assignee.[1] Improvements made before 25 March 1928 do not qualify for compensation, nor improvements made pursuant to any contract for valuable consideration including a building lease (s 2(1)), whenever made, and whether the agreement was made between the tenant and his landlord or a sub-tenant.[2] Improvements made after the passing

1 *Pelosi v Newcastle Arms Brewery (Nottingham) Ltd* (1981) 43 P & CR 18, CA.
2 *Owen Owen Estate v Livett* [1956] Ch 1, [1955] 2 All ER 513.

of the 1954 Act pursuant to any statutory requirements qualify for compensation and an improvement made less than three years before the termination of the tenancy and begun on or after 1 October 1954, qualifies for compensation.[3] There is no general definition of 'improvement': it may include the erection, demolition and rebuilding of buildings, whether for the same or a different business;[4] but does not include any trade or other fixtures which the tenant is entitled to remove.

II   QUALIFYING CONDITIONS

In order to qualify for the right to claim compensation on quitting on the termination of the tenancy, the tenant must observe certain conditions laid down in s 3. Before making the improvement,[5] the tenant must under s 3(1) first serve on his landlord a notice of his intention to make it, together with a specification[6] and plan showing the proposed improvement and any part of the premises affected thereby, and if the landlord raises no objections, within three months of the service of the notice, the tenant may proceed with the work. However, the landlord is, within three months, entitled to serve on the tenant a notice of objection, and if he does, the tenant must apply to the court to certify that the proposed improvement is a 'proper improvement'. On such an application, any superior landlords are to be notified and are entitled to be heard, and the court must give a certificate if it is satisfied that the improvement:

(a) is of such a nature as to be calculated to add to the letting value of the holding at the termination of the tenancy; and
(b) is reasonable and suitable to the character thereof; and
(c) will not diminish the value of any other property belonging to the same landlord or any superior landlord from whom the immediate landlord or tenant directly or indirectly holds.

In certifying the improvement, the court may make such modifications to the plans and specifications proposed by the tenant as it thinks fit. The court may also impose such other conditions as it thinks reasonable. No certificate will be given, however, if the landlord can prove that he has offered to make the proposed improvement himself in consideration of a reasonable increase in rent, or of an increase to be determined by the court, unless he has failed to carry out such an undertaking. As regards the reasonableness and suitability of the proposed improvement to the character of the holding, the court is directed by s 3(2) to have regard to any evidence adduced by the landlord or superior landlord (but no one else) to show that the improvement is calculated to injure the amenity or convenience of the neighbourhood. Where the landlord serves

---

3   Landlord and Tenant Act 1954, s 48.
4   *National Electric Theatres Ltd v Hudgell* [1939] Ch 553, [1939] 1 All ER 567.
5   The following does not apply to statutory improvements, where the tenant may proceed as soon as he gives notice of intention to the landlord.
6   See *Deerfield Travel Services Ltd v Wardens etc of the Leathersellers of the City of London* (1982) 46 P & CR 132, CA.

no notice of objection, or the improvement is certified as proper, the tenant may execute the improvement in accordance with the plans and specifications (s 3(4)), and on completion within the time agreed with the landlord, or determined by the court, is entitled to require of the landlord a certificate of completion, to be issued at the tenant's expense; and if the landlord fails to give one within one month, the tenant may apply for one to the court (s 3(6)). Once the tenant has carried out an improvement, he cannot subsequently apply to the court for a certificate under s 3, if he has not previously done so, even though the provision does not in terms impose a requirement that a certificate may only be granted before any work is carried out.[7]

III THE TENANT'S CLAIM FOR COMPENSATION

The claim

A tenant's claim for compensation for improvements in respect of which the qualifying conditions are satisfied must, under s 1(1) of the Act, be made in the prescribed manner[8] in writing, and signed by the tenant or his agent. It must specify the holding and the business and state the nature of the claim, the cost and other particulars of the improvement, the date when it was completed, and the amount claimed.[9] The claim must be served on the landlord in accordance with s 23 of the Act[10] within the strict time limits imposed by s 47 of the 1954 Act:

1 within three months of the giving of a notice to quit or a notice to terminate (or if the tenancy is terminated under s 26 of the 1954 Act, within three months of the landlord's counter-notice);
2 not more than six but not less than three months before the termination of a tenancy which will expire by effluxion of time;
3 within three months of the effective date of an order for possession in forfeiture proceedings, or within three months of re-entry without an order for possession.

Service of the claim must be made within the requisite time-limits and these limits cannot be extended.[11]

The importance of Part I of the 1927 Act has been greatly reduced since 1954, in relation to claims for compensation, since under s 1(1) of the 1927 Act the right to compensation arises only if the tenant quits the holding on the termination of the tenancy. However, it is nevertheless important that a tenant should satisfy the qualifying conditions in respect of improvements which he

---

7 *Hogarth Health Club Ltd v Westbourne Investments Ltd* [1990] 1 EGLR 89, CA.
8 County Court Rules 1981, Ord 43, r 3, or RSC, Ord 97, r 4.
9 It is vital to state the amount claimed: *British and Colonial Furniture Co Ltd v William McIlroy Ltd* [1952] 1 KB 107, [1952] 1 All ER 12.
10 *Sector Properties Ltd v Meah* (1973) 229 Estates Gazette 1097, CA (service at place of business a proper method).
11 *Donegal Tweed Co v Stephenson* (1929) 98 LJKB 657.

proposes to make, in order not only to get compensation should the landlord establish a ground for possession in due course, but also to have their added value disregarded in fixing the rent under s 34 in respect of any new tenancy granted under Part II within the next 21 years.

The amount of compensation

In the absence of agreement between the parties, all questions as to the right to compensation are determined by the court (s 1(3)); and under s 1(1) the amount shall not exceed:

(a) the net addition to the value of the holding as a whole which may be determined to be the direct result of the improvement; or
(b) the reasonable cost of carrying out the improvement at the termination of the tenancy, subject to a deduction of an amount equal to the cost (if any) of putting the works constituting the improvement into a reasonable state of repair, except so far as such cost is covered by the liability of the tenant under any covenant or agreement as to the repair of the premises.

In determining the amount under (a), regard must be had to the purposes for which it is intended to use the premises after the termination of the tenancy, and if it is shown that it is intended to demolish or to make structural alterations in the premises or any part of them or to use the premises for a different purpose, regard must be had to the effect of such demolition, alteration or change of user on the additional value attributable to the improvement, and to the length of time likely to elapse between the termination of the tenancy and the proposed changes (s 1(2)). If the claim for compensation is on that account reduced by the court, the tenant may later make a further application to the court to vary the amount originally determined, if he can show that the landlord has not carried out his intentions within the time specified. Further, the amount is to be reduced by any benefit received by the tenant or his predecessor in title from the landlord 'in consideration expressly or impliedly of the improvement' (s 2(3)). On the question as to what constitute 'benefits', there is little authority, and it is arguable that any reductions in rent under successive tenancies by virtue of s 34(2) of the 1954 Act might be set off against the tenant's claim.

IV   REFORM

A major defect of the present rules, applicable to commercial tenants, is that because compensation is not payable for an improvement which he is contractually bound to carry out, the landlord can avoid liability by taking a covenant obliging the tenant to carry out a proposed improvement to which the landlord agrees. In any event, an obligation to re-instate demised premises at the end of the term removes any benefit to the landlord from an improvement carried out during the lease and so avoids any liability to pay compensation. Besides, many lessees only make improvements of a short-term nature, designed not to benefit anyone but themselves or their successors in title to the lease. The

Law Commission, which re-examined the topic, found that the statutory compensation procedure was little used.[12] The claims procedure only laid a foundation for a successful claim later, if it was justified. Thus, a claim could be defeated because the improvement had no residual value or because the landlord decided to build or alter the use of the property.[13] The Law Commission said that the statutory procedures were complex and pointed out that statutory continuation under Part II of the Landlord and Tenant Act 1954 means that no compensation for improvements under the 1927 Act may be claimed by a tenant whose tenancy is continued or who claims a new lease.

The Law Commission concluded that the scheme for compensation for improvements in its present form should be abolished; this would not affect the right of the parties to negotiate compensation.[14] There would be transitional rules to preserve potential compensation claims for which notice was served before any legislation took effect, and no claim would be allowed after 25 years from the commencement of the legislation.[15] The Law Commission also recommended the retention of the authorisation procedures of s 3(4), with the application of the definition of trade, business or profession which applies under Part II of the Landlord and Tenant Act 1954.[16] So far, however, this useful report has not been implemented.

---

12 Compensation for Tenants' Improvements (Law Com No 178) (1989), para 3.3.
13 Ibid, para 3.9.
14 Ibid, paras 3.20-3.21.
15 Ibid, paras 3.26-3.28. The legislation would not come into effect until a six-month period from its enactment had elapsed, so as to give due warning: para 3.29.
16 Ibid, paras 4.8-4.9.

PART F
AGRICULTURAL HOLDINGS

Chapter 30

Statutory protection of old-style agricultural tenancies

I INTRODUCTION AND POLICY

The common law, and customary rights, governed the relationship of the parties to an agricultural tenancy until the latter part of the nineteenth century, but from then on statute intervened, at first so as to provide compensation for agricultural tenants who carried out improvements to the land or buildings concerned and then quit the holding. With the passing of the Agricultural Holdings Act 1948, and subsequent legislation consolidated into the Agricultural Holdings Act 1986, security of tenure was conferred on an agricultural tenant whose tenancy, from year to year, had been terminated by notice to quit: generally the landlord cannot regain possession except where there is default in the performance of his obligations by the tenant or he is able to prove some other specified statutory ground such as an intention to put the land to non-agricultural use. The 1986 Act also provides for a statutory succession scheme to an agricultural tenancy after the death of the tenant: the scheme was introduced in 1976 and had been curtailed in 1984. However, the security of tenure provisions, coupled with the possibility of successions on death, were both blamed by the government and some in the farming industry itself for a reduction in the availability of farming land for letting. In addition, it was said that it was unsatisfactory that farming tenants should be at risk of losing statutory protection because they might have diversified away from farming into business ventures such as the use of their land for leisure or tourism. Therefore, as from 1 September 1995, the Agricultural Tenancies Act 1995 replaces the 1986 Act, subject to transitional provisions for certain tenancies of agricultural land granted as from that date. Knowledge of the previous rules continues to be necessary, since the new rules are not retrospective.

II APPLICATION OF THE ACT

The Agricultural Holdings Act 1986 applies to a contract of tenancy of an agricultural holding, entered into before the commencement of the Agricultural Tenancies Act 1995. An agricultural holding is defined as: 'the aggregate of land (whether agricultural or not) comprised in a contract of tenancy which is a contract for an agricultural tenancy' (s 1(1)). The land concerned must not be 'let to the tenant during his continuance in any office, appointment or employment held under the landlord' (s 1(1)). 'Agricultural land' is defined by s 1(4) as being, in particular: 'land used for agriculture which is so used for the purpose of a trade or business'. The expression 'agriculture' has a wide meaning (s 96(1)) and so includes 'horticulture, fruit growing, seed growing, dairy farming and livestock[1] breeding and keeping the use of the land as grazing land, meadow land, osier land, market gardens and nursery gardens, and the use of the land for woodlands where that use is ancillary to the farming of the land or for other agricultural purposes'. Since land used for agriculture includes land forming part of an agricultural unit (s 96(5)), the protection of the 1986 Act may extend to any dwelling-house occupied by the tenant for the purpose of farming the land, such as a cottage and its garden let with a farm. Thus, as long as the tenant continues to use the land for agricultural purposes in the statutory sense, he retains security of any residence let with the land.

The extended statutory definition of 'agriculture' meant that it was possible to hold that a tenancy of a field used for grazing horses from a riding school came within statutory protection,[2] but not, by contrast, such activities as merely keeping a horse or pony for pleasure, and the keeping of pigeons, as no business activity was involved as required by the Act.[3]

Land used for agriculture

Section 1(2) deals with the question of deciding whether a contract of tenancy is within s 1. A contract of tenancy relating to any land is a contract for an agricultural tenancy if, having regard to three factors, the whole of the land is let for use as agricultural land – subject to such exceptions only as do not substantially affect the character of the tenancy. The three factors are:

(a) the terms of the tenancy;
(b) the actual or contemplated use of the land at the time of the conclusion of the contract and subsequently; and
(c) any other relevant circumstances.

The use of the land at the commencement of the tenancy and at all times during the tenancy must, therefore, be at least partly as agricultural land in connection with a trade or business (as required by s 1(4)), for agricultural purposes, otherwise the protection of the 1986 Act cannot apply. In one case, the High Court found on the facts that the main use of the land was as a retail shop for selling horticultural products: the raising, caring and culture of such products on part of the land was merely ancillary to the main purpose, and the tenancy was not of an agricultural holding within the legislation.[4] By contrast, where a

---

1 'Livestock' is widely defined by s 96(1) as including any creature kept for the production of food, wool, skins or fur or for the purpose of its use in the farming of land or the carrying on in relation to land of any agricultural activity.
2 *Rutherford v Maurer* [1962] 1 QB 16, [1961] 2 All ER 775, CA.
3 See *Hickson & Welch Ltd v Cann* (1977) 40 P & CR 218n, CA.
4 *Monson v Bound* [1954] 1 WLR 1321.

tenant held an inn and garden, with 12 acres of land comprising an orchard and pasture, and made substantial profits from the land by selling fruit, as well as from the inn, it was held that the tenancy taken as a whole was within the legislation, which contemplated, in contrast to earlier legislation, that a tenancy could fall within the 1948 (now 1986) Act where the land was an aggregate of agricultural and non-agricultural land.[5]

However, if a tenancy is originally within the 1986 Act, but agricultural activity in the statutory sense is wholly or substantially abandoned during the tenancy, without the consent of the landlord, the 1986 Act ceases to apply to the tenant. Strong evidence is required to support a claim by the landlord of unilateral abandonment, and in one case, where it was said that the tenant, who had originally used the land to graze horses and cattle, now used it only for jumping horses, the landlord failed as the county court had made no findings relevant to the issue of abandonment.[6] If the tenant unilaterally wholly alters the user of the tenancy, without the landlord's consent, the 1986 Act ceases to apply to the tenancy, as where a tenancy contemplated that the tenant would use the premises as an orchard, but she instead changed the user to accommodate animals and for recreational purposes. The tenant could not claim the protection of the Rent Act 1977, merely because she resided on the premises.[7] It is open to a landlord to prove that the tenant has, during the tenancy, partly altered the user of the land so that a substantial part of it is put to non-agricultural purposes. This type of contention raises difficult questions of fact and degree. Where, for example, a tenant held a letting of land for use as a garden centre, and was required by the tenancy agreement to manage the property in accordance with the rules of good husbandry and to preserve the fertility of the soil, and so originally for agricultural purposes, but later, as well as growing roses, the tenant had diversified into such things as selling bought-in produce from his shop, the fact that most of his turnover came from the latter source did not render a finding that the tenancy was still within the 1986 Act wrong in law.[8]

The 1986 Act envisages that a tenant may, by commencing agricultural and related activities on his land, bring the tenancy within the Act even though the tenancy was not subject to the Act when it commenced (s 1(3)), but for this to occur, the landlord must give his permission, or have consented to the change of use, or have acquiesced in it.

It has already been observed that the 1986 Act requires the use of agricultural land for the purposes of a trade or business, rather than personal or pleasure uses, but the words 'trade or business' are not limited to a specified type of trade or business, as it was held that a field used under licence for grazing horses used in connection with a riding school was used for agriculture and for the riding school business, and so the licence was protected by the Act.[9]

5 *Dunn v Fidoe* [1950] 2 All ER 685, CA.
6 *Wetherall v Smith* [1980] 2 All ER 530, [1980] 1 WLR 1290, CA.
7 *Russell v Booker* [1982] 2 EGLR 86, CA.
8 *Short v Greeves* [1988] 1 EGLR 1, CA; and see Rogers [1988] Conv 431.
9 *Rutherford v Maurer* [1962] 1 QB 16, [1961] 2 All ER 775, CA.

According to the High Court, if the land is let for agricultural business purposes, it may at the same time be used for other purposes, such as keeping a mare for pleasure, provided that the main business user does not become so minor that it is no longer the purpose of the letting.[10]

Contract of tenancy – further

The 1986 Act applies only to certain types of contract of tenancy,[11] viz, those defined as being a letting of land,[12] or an agreement for the letting of land, for a term of years or from year to year (s 1(5)).[13] Exclusive possession must be conferred on the tenant by the letting and the onus of proving this is on the tenant.[14] The 1986 Act reflects an old principle that agricultural tenancies were often tenancies from year to year.

Special provision is made by s 3(1) of the 1986 Act for a tenancy granted for a term of two years or more. Instead of terminating at the expiry date of the tenancy, it continues as a tenancy from year to year on the terms of the original tenancy so far as applicable. If either party, not more than two years and not less than one year before the termination date of the initial fixed term gives written notice to terminate, this statutory conversion will not take place (s 3(2)). However, by s 4, should the tenant, or, where a joint tenancy had been granted, the surviving tenant, die within the last year of the initial fixed term, with no notice having been given, the only continuation under s 3 is for 12 months from the original termination date of the tenancy.[15]

Despite the terms of s1(5) and of s 2, considered below, it is relatively easy by means of a simple device for landlords to avoid the 1986 Act rules. This is because it has been held that a fixed-term tenancy granted for a term of more than one year but for less than two years is not protected by any provision of the Act. Section 2(1) does not apply as the tenancy is not for an interest of less than from year to year. Section 3 is excluded, as it applies only to tenancies from two to five years.[16] Thus, a fixed-term tenancy for 23 months certain fell outside these provisions of the 1986 Act, yet, because it was a tenancy of agricultural land within the 1986 Act, it could not be protected by Part II of the Landlord and Tenant Act 1954, owing to s 43(1)(c) of the latter Act.[17]

---

10 *Brown v Teirnan* [1993] 1 EGLR 11.
11 Ie a single contract of tenancy: *Blackmore v Butler* [1954] 2 QB 171, [1954] 2 All ER 403.
12 There are no lower acreage limits to the application of the Act: *Stevens v Sedgeman* [1951] 2 KB 434, [1951] 2 All ER 33, CA.
13 Special provision is made for a lease for life or lives to which Law of Property Act 1925, s 149(6) applies: this is deemed for the purposes of the 1986 Act to be a tenancy for years and so caught by the latter Act.
14 *Evans v Tompkins* [1993] 2 EGLR 6, CA.
15 The parties to an agricultural tenancy granted before 1 September 1995 may contract out of s 4 with Ministerial approval under s 5 as to which a generous construction applies. See *Pahl v Trevor* [1992] 1 EGLR 22, CA (requiring a clear consent in such approval but not a specified date) and *Ashdale Land & Property Co Ltd v Manners* [1992] 2 EGLR 5 (approval may be for a period during which any agreement may be granted).
16 *Gladstone v Bower* [1960] 2 QB 384, [1960] 3 All ER 353, CA.
17 *EWP Ltd v Moore* [1992] 2 EGLR 4, CA.

Extensions to protection

Were it not for special provisions, it would be easy to avoid the protection of the 1986 Act simply by granting a tenancy for less than a year, or a licence to occupy. Section 2(1) and (2) of the 1986 Act therefore provide that any letting of land for use as agricultural land for an interest less than a tenancy from year to year, or any licence to occupy such land shall take effect, with the necessary modifications, as if it were an agreement for the letting of land for a tenancy from year to year. There are two specific exclusions from this extension of protection.

(a) The agreement was made in contemplation (express or implied) of the use of the land only[18] for grazing or mowing (or both) during some specified period of the year.
(b) The lessor's (or licensor's) interest is itself an interest in land less than from year to year, and has not by virtue of s 2 taken effect as such a tenancy.

In deciding whether s 2 applies to a tenancy, the court examines the tenant's interest in the land as actually granted by the agreement: and if a tenant when taking possession is then entitled to such an interest, s 2 applies; moreover, since the provision is mandatory, even if the tenant knows that the landlord did not intend the 1986 Act to apply, he may properly invoke s 2 if it applies.[19] This mandatory rule cannot be overridden by any estoppel.[20]

We turn now to the principal exceptions, set out above, to the extended protection of s 2 of the 1986 Act: grazing or mowing agreements and licences.

Grazing or mowing As with any document, an agreement granting grazing or mowing rights will be construed objectively and, if it is express, whether in writing or not, it may only be gone behind if it is a sham.[1] However, a requirement that the tenant cultivate the land, in the agreement, prevents the exception in s 2 from applying, being outside its contemplation, and the tenant enjoys full security under the Act.[2] The fact that the tenancy includes the use of outbuildings is not sufficient to exclude s 2,[3] provided the agreement is genuinely intended to fall within the exception. While s 2(2)(a) requires that the period of the year for grazing or mowing be specified in the agreement, if the latter contemplates use of the land only for the season when grazing or mowing is possible, it may, on a beneficial construction, fall within the exception.[4] Indeed, an agreement for seasonal grazing which does not refer to specific dates falls within the present exception: the onus of proving that it does is on the

---

18 See *Brown v Teirnan* [1993] 1 EGLR 11 (if the contemplated use is *more* than grazing or mowing or for grazing or mowing only for one year or more, the tenancy or licence may be protected nonetheless).
19 So that disputes with respect to the application of the provision must be settled by arbitration under the Act (s 2(4)).
20 *Keen v Holland* [1984] 1 All ER 75, [1984] 1 WLR 251, CA.
 1 *Chaloner v Bower* [1984] 1 EGLR 4, CA.
 2 *Lory v London Borough of Brent* [1971] 1 All ER 1042, [1971] 1 WLR 823.
 3 Cf *Avon County Council v Clothier* (1977) 75 LGR 344, CA.
 4 *Stone v Whitcombe* (1980) 40 P & CR 296, CA.

landlord: in this, the court is entitled to have regard to what was in fact done on the land and to the conduct of the parties subsequent to the agreement.[5]

Licences   By s 2(2)(b), the 1986 Act confers security on a person granted a licence to occupy land for use as agricultural land 'if the circumstances are such that if his interest were a tenancy from year to year he would in respect of that land be the tenant of an agricultural holding'. This provision, which appeared in the 1948 Act, was enacted well before the House of Lords re-interpreted the way licence agreements should be interpreted at common law (see chapter 3). A licence agreement, whether express or implied, will now only fall within this specific provision (which might be said to have been made unnecessary by subsequent developments) if it grants the occupier, for consideration, exclusive possession of the land, or at any rate the right to make exclusive use of the land for agricultural purposes, as against the owner or any person authorised by him.[6] Thus, for example, where a person entered and cleared land at his expense, on the understanding that he was to have an interest in the land, he was held, to make sense of the agreement, to be in occupation as an exclusive licensee for consideration in anticipation of the grant of a tenancy, and s 2 conferred on him the protection of the 1986 Act.[7]

If the owner genuinely retains and exercises a right to make co-extensive or contemporaneous use of the land, or exercises overriding control over it, the occupation agreement will be a licence outside s 2(2)(b).[8] This principle supplies a means of avoiding the extension of statutory security to licences by making sure that the grant of exclusive possession is in substance and in form withheld from the occupier. For example, an agreement under which the owner made available land and buildings to another person, who was to milk his cows and share the profits, but the owner had the express right to alter the land, from time to time available, was a genuine licence.[9]

However, it will be appreciated that to reserve a limited right of access to the land is not inconsistent with the grant of exclusive possession to the occupier.[10] Moreover, where an occupier under a long-standing agreement with the owner farmed the land and marketed its produce and paid the owner annual sums, he held a protected licence caught by s 2(2)(b).[11] Similarly, where an occupier was let into exclusive possession in order to erect an agricultural building at his expense, he held an implied protected licence.[12]

5   *Watts v Yeend* [1987] 1 All ER 744, [1987] 1 WLR 323, CA.
6   *University of Reading v Johnson-Houghton* [1985] 2 EGLR 113, where the occupier made exclusive use of gallops and had exclusive possession over adjacent scrubland; also *Harrison v Wing* [1988] 2 EGLR 4; *Sparkes v Smart* [1990] 2 EGLR 245, CA.
7   *Mitton v Farrow* [1980] 2 EGLR 1; also *Gold v Jacques Amand Ltd* [1992] 2 EGLR 1.
8   *Bahamas International Trust Co Ltd v Threadgold* [1974] 3 All ER 881, [1974] 1 WLR 1514, HL; also eg *Collier v Hollinshead* [1984] 2 EGLR 14.
9   *McCarthy v Bence* [1990] 1 EGLR 1, CA.
10   *Lampard v Barker* [1984] 2 EGLR 11, CA. The reservation of concurrent rights of grazing (for example) would presumably be a different matter.
11   *Padbury v York* [1990] 2 EGLR 3.
12   *Gold v Jacques Amand Ltd* [1992] 2 EGLR 1; also *Ashdale Land & Property Co Ltd v Manners* [1992] 2 EGLR 5 (where a 'licence' granted following an approval by the Minister under s 5 was held to be within s 2(2)(b) and so protected by s 3 since it conferred exclusive possession).

III SECURING A WRITTEN AGREEMENT

Right to secure a written agreement

Where there is no written agreement between the landlord and tenant of an agricultural holding, or such agreement as there is fails to contain any of the basic statutory terms mentioned below, by s 6(1) of the 1986 Act, either party has the right to refer the terms of the tenancy to arbitration,[13] provided he has first requested the other party to enter into a written agreement embodying the basic terms but no agreement could be arrived at. With the commencement of the new regime of farm business tenancies, in relation to any tenancy of an agricultural holding entered into on or after 1 September 1995, these provisions do not apply (1995 Act s 4(1)): indeed, they are not replaced by any corresponding rules enabling a farm business tenant to secure a written agreement, still less to enable him to require specified terms to be included in the tenancy. While the policy of the 1986 Act rules is to secure minimum terms for tenants, that of the 1995 Act is seemingly to allow the parties freedom as to the terms they wish to include in the tenancy, in keeping with the promotion of policies of general deregulation.[14]

On a reference, the arbitrator must, in his award, specify the existing terms of the tenancy, subject to any variations agreed between the parties, and make provision for all the matters specified in Schedule 1 to the 1986 Act, in such a manner as is agreed between the parties or, in default of agreement, as appears to the arbitrator to be reasonable and just between them (s 6(2)). No provision inconsistent with the Act may be included.

The award may include (s 6(2)) any further provisions, apart from those in Schedule 1 and those relating to repairs, as may be agreed between the parties. The award of an arbitrator under s 6 has effect as from the making of the award or any later date therein specified and has the same effect as if contained in a written agreement varying the tenancy between the parties (s 6(4)). If, by reason of any provision which the arbitrator is required to include in the tenancy, it appears to him equitable that the rent of the holding should be varied, he has a statutory discretion to vary such rent (s 6(3)).

With a view to protecting the landlord against an assignment, sub-letting or parting with possession of the land during the period of a landlord's request for arbitration, or agreement, and ending with an award or agreement, in a case where no provision is made in the tenancy, s 6(5) precludes the tenant from assigning, sub-letting or parting with the possession of the holding or any part of it without the landlord's written consent while an agreement or arbitration is pending, and a transaction contravening this provision is void.

Terms of written agreement

The matters for which, in accordance with Schedule 1, provision is to be made in a written tenancy agreement are these.

13 As to the procedure see 1986 Act, s 84 and Sch 11.
14 The RICS has issued Guidance notes as to the matters which ideally ought to be included in farm business tenancy agreements, but there is no compulsion to include these.

1   The names of the parties.
2   Particulars of the holding with sufficient description, by reference to a map or plan, of the fields and other parcels of land comprised therein, to identify the extent of the holding.
3   The term or terms for which the holding, or different parts thereof, is or are agreed to be let.
4   The rent reserved and the dates on which it is payable.
5   The incidence of liability for rates (including drainage rates).
6   A covenant by the tenant in the event of destruction by fire of harvested crops grown on the holding for consumption thereon, to return to the holding the full equivalent manurial value of the crops destroyed, in so far as that is required in accordance with the rules of good husbandry.
7   Except where the tenant is a government department, or the tenant has made alternative provision with the approval of the Minister, a covenant by the tenant to insure all dead stock on the holding, and all such harvested crops as aforesaid, against damage by fire.
8   A power for the landlord to re-enter on the holding in the event of the tenant not performing his obligations under the agreement.
9   A covenant by the tenant not to assign, sub-let or part with the possession of the holding or of any part thereof without the landlord's consent in writing.

IV   LIABILITY FOR MAINTENANCE, REPAIR AND INSURANCE OF FIXED EQUIPMENT

The provisions of what are known as the 'model clauses'[15] are incorporated by s 7(3) into every contract of tenancy of an agricultural holding entered into, in principle, before 1 September 1995, except in so far as they would impose on one of the parties to an agreement in writing a liability which under the agreement is imposed on the other party.[16] Unless and until a party avails himself of his statutory right to refer a term which effects substantial modifications to the model clauses to arbitration, the express term will continue to prevail.[17] If there is a reference to arbitration, the arbitrator must consider whether the modifications of the tenancy to the model clauses are justifiable in all the circumstances. If he is satisfied that they are not justifiable, he has a discretion to vary the terms to the extent that appears to him to be reasonable and just between the parties (s 8(3)) and he may in consequence, vary the rent up or down (s 8(4)). Such a variation may transfer liability to repair from the tenant to the landlord. The landlord then has three months from the effective date of

---

15   Ie Agriculture (Maintenance, Repair and Insurance of Fixed Equipment) Regulations 1973, SI 1973/1473, as amended from 24 March 1988 by SI 1988/281.
16   The Agricultural Tenancies Act 1995 makes no provision as to model clauses, in keeping with its *laissez-faire* principles; see however ch 33.
17   *Burden v Hannaford* [1956] 1 QB 142, [1955] 3 All ER 401, CA. This does not apply to oral tenancies.

the transfer[18] to serve a notice under s 9(1) of the 1986 Act requiring the tenant to pay any compensation for which the tenant would otherwise have been liable to pay to the landlord for deterioration of the holding under s 71, on the supposition for this purpose that the tenancy had terminated at the date of transfer of liability.[19]

The terms of the model clauses in their current form, may be summarised as follows.

Part I: Rights and liabilities of landlord

The landlord is liable to repair the structure and exterior of the farmhouse, cottages and farm buildings, including the roofs, chimney stacks and pots, eaves-guttering and downpipes, main walls and exterior walls, including walls and fences of open and covered yards and garden walls, plus any interior repairs made necessary as a result of structural defects. He must also repair floors, floor joists, ceiling joists and timbers, exterior and interior staircases, fixed ladders, doors, windows and skylights. In the case of repairs, eg to floorboards, interior staircases, doors and windows, eaves-guttering and downpipes, the landlord may recover half the reasonable cost from the tenant (para 1(1)).

The landlord must also replace anything which it was, under para 5, the tenant's responsibility to repair but which has become worn out or otherwise incapable of further repair, unless by virtue of para 6(2), the tenant is liable to replace it because it has worn out or otherwise become incapable of repair if its condition has been brought about by or is substantially due to the tenant's failure to replace it.

The landlord is liable also for external decoration when required to prevent deterioration and in any case at intervals of not more than five years (para 3) but he may recover half the reasonable cost of certain items from the tenant.

By para 4 the landlord is not liable:

(a) to execute repairs etc to buildings which are the tenant's property; nor
(b) to execute repairs etc rendered necessary by the wilful act or negligence of the tenant or any members of his household or his employees.

The landlord must keep the farmhouse, cottages and farm buildings insured to their full value against loss or damage by fire (para 2(1).

As to things other than buildings, the landlord must by para 1(2) execute all repairs and replacements to the underground water supply pipes, wells, bore-holes and reservoirs and all underground installations connected therewith and to the sewage disposal systems, including septic tanks, filtering media and cesspools.

If the landlord fails to execute repairs, other than repairs to an underground water pipe,[20] within three months of receipt of a written notice from the tenant specifying the repairs, the tenant may then carry out the repairs and recover the

18 Thanks to the Agriculture (Time-Limit) Regulations 1988, SI 1988/282.
19 1986 Act, s 9(3) makes a similar provision where the transfer of liability is from landlord to tenant.
20 In the case of these latter repairs, the period concerned is one week (para 12(2)).

reasonable cost from the landlord forthwith. A similar right applies to replacements, except that there is an upper limit of £2,000 or the annual rent of the holding, whichever is the less (para 12(1), (3) and (4)). In this connection it has been held that the tenant is entitled to recover to the relevant limit in respect of every year from the execution of the replacements until he recoups his total outlay.[1]

If the landlord wishes to contest his liability for any repairs or replacements specified in the tenant's notice, he must serve a written counter-notice on the tenant, within one month of the service of the tenant's notice, specifying the items of which he denies liability and requesting arbitration. Once a counter-notice is served, the tenant's right to recover the cost of the work arises only if the question of liability is decided in his favour by the arbitrator (para 12(5)). Once the one month period for service of a landlord's counter-notice expires, liability is presumed against the landlord; once the three-month period in which he may execute repairs runs out, he cannot any longer do them as of right, so that the tenant may either himself do the work or claim specific performance or damages.[2]

Part II: Rights and liabilities of the tenant

The tenant is liable, so far as the buildings, farmhouse and cottages are concerned, to repair and keep and leave clean and in good tenantable repair, order and condition, those parts which do not fall to the landlord. The duty extends to all fixtures and fittings. The duty is to carry out interior repairs on the farmhouse, cottages and farm buildings: plus the full maintenance of drains, sewers, gulleys, grease-traps, manholes and inspection chambers, electrical and water supply systems and fittings so far as above ground, and hydraulic rams (above or below ground). The tenant is responsible for the maintenance of the following on the land: fences, hedges, field walls, stiles, gates and posts, cattlegrids, bridges, culverts, ponds, watercourses, sluices, ditches, roads and yards in and on the holding (para 5). The tenant must also keep clean and in good working order all roof valleys, eaves-guttering and downpipes, wells, septic tanks, cesspools and sewage disposal systems.

The tenant is bound to redecorate as often as may be necessary and in any case at intervals of not more than seven years the inside of the farmhouse, cottages and farm buildings (para 7) and he must renew all broken or cracked tiles or slates and replace all slipped tiles or slates from time to time as the damage occurs, up to an annual limit of, from 24 March 1988, £100 (para 8(1)).

The tenant must cut, trim or lay a proper proportion of the hedges in each year of the tenancy so as to maintain them in good and sound condition (para 9) and is bound also to dig out, scour and cleanse all ponds, water-courses, ditches and grips as may be necessary to keep them at sufficient depth and keep clear and free from obstruction all field drains and their outlets (para 10).

---

1 *Grayless v Watkinson* [1990] 1 EGLR 6, CA.
2 *Hammond v Allen* [1993] 1 EGLR 1.

If the tenant fails to comply with his obligations the landlord may serve a written notice on him, and if he does not start work on repairs or replacements for which he is liable within two months or fails within three months of such notice to complete the work, the landlord has a right to enter and execute the repairs or replacements and to recover the reasonable cost of these from the tenant forthwith (para 4(2)). The tenant may within one month of this notice contest liability by means of a counter-notice, which refers the disputed items to arbitration: this suspends the landlord's notice until the termination of the arbitration (para 4(3)).

Part III: General provisions

By para 13(1), if at any time either the landlord or the tenant is of opinion that any item of fixed equipment is redundant, either may serve a two months' notice on the other requiring arbitration (if no agreement can be reached). If the arbitrator decides that the item is indeed redundant to the farming of the holding, he must so award, and then neither party is under any obligation to maintain, replace or repair that item. With regard to redundant and obsolete buildings, para 13 applies but para 14(2) adds a category to redundancy following an award (as for fixed equipment) viz that there is no liability to execute work which is impossible except at prohibitive or unreasonable expense by reason of subsidence of the land or the blocking of outfalls not under either party's control.

V RENT PROVISIONS

Arbitration

If the parties to a tenancy which falls within the rules of the Agricultural Holdings Act 1986 cannot agree on the rent payable then by s 12(1), the landlord or tenant may by notice in writing served on the other demand that the rent payable as from the next termination date[3] is referred to arbitration.[4] The earliest date for the new rent to take effect is 12 months after the demand for arbitration. There is a limit to the frequency of arbitrations under s 12, which applies mainly to periodic tenancies, so that the parties to a fixed-term tenancy will only be able to obtain a rent review if such is provided for by the lease itself.

The general rule[5] is that no demand for arbitration is valid if the next termination date after the date of the demand is earlier than the end of three years from any of the following dates:

(a) the commencement of the tenancy; or
(b) the date from which a previous increase or reduction in rent took effect under s 12 or otherwise (as by agreement); or

---

3 This means the next day, following the date of the demand, on which the tenancy could have been determined by notice to quit on the date of the demand (s 12(4)).
4 For a comparison between these rules and those applicable to farm business tenancies see ch 33.
5 1986 Act, Sch 2, para 4(1).

(c) the date from which a previous arbitrator's direction that the rent should continue unchanged took effect under s 12.[6]

In calculating the dates under exception (b) above, there are three disregards to be made.[7]

(a) the date of an increase or reduction in rent under s 6(3) or 8(4) of the Act;
(b) the date of an increase in rent under s 13(1) or (3);[8]
(c) the date of a reduction in rent under s 33.

An arbitration notice lapses on the next termination date after the date of the demand (s 12(3)) unless before then either an arbitrator has been appointed by agreement or an application has been made under s 84 to appoint an arbitrator. If, after a landlord's arbitration notice, the tenant duly applies for the appointment of an arbitrator, the landlord is precluded from unilaterally withdrawing his notice.[9] It should be noted that the s 12 procedure merely operates to revise the rent and does not determine the tenancy.[10]

Determination of the rent

The general rule (s 12(2)) is that the arbitrator must determine a rent properly payable for the holding at the date of the reference and must then increase or reduce the previous rent or direct that it continues unchanged.[11] The new rent takes effect, generally, 12 months from the date of the demand.

The rent is to be that at which the holding might reasonably be expected to be let by a prudent and willing landlord to a prudent and willing tenant,[12] taking into account all relevant factors and including:

(i) the terms of the tenancy including those relating to rent;
(ii) the character, situation and locality of the holding; and
(iii) its productive capacity and its related earnings capacity.[13]

6 A special rule applies where a new tenancy commences between the same tenant and a landlord entitled to a severed part of the reversion and the rent is a proportion of the old. Sch 2, para 5 relates back references to the commencement of the tenancy or to rent to the start of the tenancy of the original holding or the last agreement, arbitration, etc, as to rent, as the case may be.
7 1986 Act, Sch 2, para 4(2).
8 Also by Sch 2, para 4(2)(b) there is disregarded any reduction in rent agreed between the parties in consequence of any change in the fixed equipment provided on the holding by the landlord; and see *Mann v Gardner* [1991] 1 EGLR 9 (surrender of part of holding not within this disregard, as being a change in holding itself).
9 *Buckinghamshire County Council v Gordon* [1986] 2 EGLR 8.
10 1986 Act, Sch 2, para 6. An agreement adjusting the boundaries of the holding or varying any term apart from the rent does not, unless the agreement otherwise provides, determine the tenancy nor cause the three-year time bar to start running afresh. If solely due to these things, the rent is adjusted, the same result follows.
11 Guidance to arbitrators is given in the RICS Guidance Notes for Valuers applicable to agricultural holdings valuations.
12 1986 Act, Sch 2, para 1(1); presumably, the term 'willing' bears a similar meaning to that applicable to rent reviews; cf eg *FR Evans v English Electric Ltd* (1977) 36 P & CR 185.
13 Defined on the assumption that the holding is occupied by a competent tenant practising a suitable system of farming taking fixed equipment and any other facilities on the holding into account (productive capacity), or the extent to which, in the light of this, a competent tenant

In this, it is by no means clear whether the existing rent is to be taken into account, as strictly it does not relate to rent,[14] but it is the better view that it must be left out of account.

The arbitrator must also, by Sch 1, para 1(3), take into account the current level of rent for comparable lettings. This means any available evidence of rents currently paid or likely to become payable for other tenancies of agricultural holdings on similar terms other than terms fixing the rent. From this figure there are three disregards:

(a) any appreciable scarcity element in the rents for comparable holdings available for letting on similar terms to the subject holding;[15]
(b) any element in the rent due to the fact that the tenant or a person tendering for a comparable holding occupies land in its vicinity conveniently capable of occupation together with the holding (as opposed to the 'marriage value' resulting from the holding itself);[16] and
(c) any effect on rents of comparable holdings due to allowances or reductions due to the charging of premiums.

The arbitrator must also disregard (Sch 1, para 2) any increases or decreases in the rental value due to:

(a) tenants' improvements or fixed equipment[17] other than those executed or provided under tenants' obligations in the tenancy;
(b) landlords' grant-aided improvements;
(c) the effect of the tenant's occupation;
(d) the effect of dilapidation or deterioration of or damage to buildings or land caused or permitted by the tenant;
(e) any increase in rental value caused by registered quota.[18]

On the general approach to be taken, any enhancement of rental values to a scarcity of farms for letting must be discounted; but if there is sufficient evidence of a balanced market, the full 'open market value' prevails.[19] The term 'open market value' or 'open market rent' is only a shorthand for the detailed

could reasonably be expected to profit from farming the holding (related earning capacity): Sch 2, para 1(2). See *Enfield London Borough Council v Pott* [1990] 2 EGLR 7 (clear and separate assessment of both factors is required of arbitrator).
14 Cf *British Gas Corporation v Universities Superannuation Scheme Ltd* [1986] 1 All ER 978, where in a contractual rent review the existing level of rent was not taken into account in relation to the hypothetical lease after review. However, s 8(1) of the 1948 Act, the predecessor to the 1986 Act, refers to disregarding terms 'other than those relating to rent'.
15 *Enfield London Borough Council v Pott,* supra (rent previously payable of holding not to be taken into account as a comparable); as to scarcity generally, see the discussion of regulated rents in ch 17 and below.
16 See further Muir Watt, pp 52-53.
17 Tenants' fixed equipment means (para 2(3)) fixed equipment (itself as defined s 96(1)) provided by the tenant during the current or a previous tenancy. On 'improvements' cf *Tummon v Barclays Bank Trust Co Ltd* (1979) 39 P & CR 300 (no necessity that these be agricultural).
18 Agriculture Act 1986, s 15(1). Such quota is to be registered under regulations, details of which lie outside the scope of this book. See Rodgers, ch 13.
19 *Aberdeen Endowments Trust v Will* 1985 SLT 23.

statutory requirements, whose detailed effect must be taken into account in each given case. A wide range of factors may be relevant, as where the existence of both a designation of the premises as a site of special scientific interest and of a management agreement with the tenant (which latter might limit the uses he could put the land to but the former might give him offsetting compensation) were relevant matters for an arbitrator to take into account and then evaluate in calculating the new rent.[20]

Tenants' improvements within the above disregards mean, in effect, improvements executed on the holding wholly or partly at his expense (grant-aided or not) but without any allowance or benefit in return from the landlord in consideration thereof. If the tenant held a previous tenancy of the holding, then this disregard extends to those improvements[1] executed under that tenancy and the same extended disregard applies to tenants' fixed equipment (1986 Act, Sch 2, para 2). Excluded from the extended disregard are tenants' improvements or fixed equipment for which the tenant received any compensation on termination of that or any other tenancy.

Increase in rent for landlords' improvements

The landlord is entitled by s 13(1) of the 1986 Act to an increase in rent on account of any improvement carried out by him on the holding, whether or not compensation would be payable under the Act, provided he serves on the tenant a six month written notice after completion of the works. Only those improvements carried out at the request of or in agreement with the tenant or pursuant to a s 67(5) notice[2] will qualify. An increase under s 13 does not operate the three-year bar on rent arbitrations (1986 Act, Sch 2, para 4(2))(b)). The amount of the increase is the increase in rental value attributable to the improvement (any dispute being referable to arbitration (s 13(7)): if the latter is grant-aided then the scale of the increase is reduced proportionately (s 13(4)). By s 13(3), there will be no increase in rent if before the six month period of any notice expires, the parties agree on an increase in rent or other benefit to the landlord, in respect of the improvement.

VI   OUTLINE OF THE ROLE ALLOTTED TO ARBITRATION UNDER THE 1986 ACT

It is convenient at this point to examine the role of arbitrators appointed under the 1986 Act.

---

20 *JW Childers Trustees v Anker* [1996] 1 EGLR 1, CA.
 1 If the tenant continuously adopted a system of farming or 'high farming' more beneficial than that required or customary, this counts as an improvement for the present purposes (Sch 2, para 2(4)).
 2 Ie where the landlord elected to carry out an improvement which the tenant had applied to the Agricultural Land Tribunal for consent to execute.

Claims on termination of the tenancy

Section 83(1) of the Act provides for any claim, of whatever nature, arising between the parties to a tenancy of an agricultural holding to be compulsorily determined by arbitration, if the claim arises:

(a) under the Act or any custom or agreement; and
(b) on or out of the termination of the tenancy of the holding or part of the holding.

In order to preserve such a claim, the claimant must serve a notice in writing on the other party within two months after the termination of the tenancy, of his intention to make the claim (s 82(3)). The notice must specify the nature of the claim, if only by reference to the statutory provision, custom, or term of an agreement under which it is made (s 83(3)).

The parties are given eight months after the termination of the tenancy within which to reach agreement in writing upon the matters of the claim (s 83(4)).[3] If the claim has not been settled when the time-limit expires it is to be determined by arbitration under the 1986 Act (s 83(5)).

Claims during the tenancy

The settlement of a number of claims arising during the currency of a tenancy are also made referable to arbitration, e g rent (s 12), increases of rent for certain improvements carried out by the landlord (s 13(7)), variation of terms as to permanent pasture (s 14), assessment of the tenant's farming methods in proceedings for an injunction (s 15(6)), disputes as to any amount of fair value payable by the landlord to the tenant in relation to fixtures of buildings (s 10(6)), compensation for damage by wild animals or birds (s 20(4)). There is nothing to prevent the parties from agreeing to refer other matters to arbitration, which would otherwise be the subject of litigation, but it is doubtful whether the parties may agree to invoke the special arbitration procedures under the Agricultural Holdings Act 1986 in such cases; consequently, they would be subject to the Arbitration Act 1996.

Outline of procedure

Section 84(1) provides that any matter which by virtue of the Act or regulations made under the 1986 Act is required to be determined by arbitration under the Act, must be determined by a single arbitrator in accordance with Sch 11, and not in accordance with the Arbitration Act 1996. The arbitrator is either appointed by agreement between the parties or in default of agreement, by a person appointed by the Minister on the application of one of the parties, from a panel (Sch 11, para 1). Appointment by the Minister must be made by him as soon as possible after receiving the application.

The detailed procedure to be followed by an arbitrator is laid down in Sch 11 and regulations deal with ancillary aspects.[4] In particular, there is a statutory

---

3 See *Hallinan v Jones* [1984] 2 EGLR 20.
4 Agricultural Holdings Rules 1948, SI 1948/1943 as amended by SI 1985/1829.

requirement that reasons for the award be given whether the arbitrator is appointed by agreement or not (para 21). Also that the county court may remove an arbitrator for misconduct (para 27) and it may remit the award or any part to the arbitrator for reconsideration; and in the case of error of law on the face of the award, the county court may, as an alternative to remission, vary the award itself (para 28). An example of an error of law of the latter kind was where an arbitrator misconstrued a tenant's covenant to pay rent as conditional on the landlord's compliance with his covenant to repair certain items.[5] The parties must deliver a statement to the arbitrator of their respective cases, with all necessary particulars within 35 days of his appointment (para 7), and no amendments, except with his consent, are allowed. Leave to amend should be given to the arbitrator, despite this time-limit, which is not mandatory and inflexible, if no undue prejudice will result to the other side.[6]

VII   SPECIAL RULES AS TO PERMANENT PASTURE

Where the terms of a tenancy of an agricultural holding granted prior to the commencement of the Agricultural Tenancies Act 1995 provide for the maintenance of specified land, or a specified proportion of the holding, as permanent pasture, either party may, by notice in writing served on the other, demand a reference to arbitration under s 14 of the question whether it is expedient in order to ensure the full and efficient farming of the holding that the amount of land required to be maintained as permanent pasture should be reduced (s 14(2)). But for this provision, the ploughing up of such pasture land might constitute waste. On a reference, the arbitrator may by his award:

(a) modify the terms of the tenancy as to the land which is to be maintained as permanent pasture or is to be treated as arable land, and as to cropping, and
(b) if he gives a direction reducing the area of the land to be maintained as permanent pasture, order the terms of the tenancy to be modified so as to require the tenant, on quitting the holding on termination of the tenancy to leave a specified amount of land as permanent pasture or as temporary pasture sown with seeds mixture of a specified kind.

The Agricultural Tenancies Act 1995, in accordance with its refusal to regulate detailed aspects of the relationship of the parties to a farm business tenancy, has no provisions corresponding to s 22 of the 1986 Act.

VIII   OTHER SPECIAL PROVISIONS IN THE 1986 ACT

In contrast to farm business tenancies, tenancies of agricultural holdings granted before 1 September 1995 enjoy the benefit of specific regulatory

---

5   *Burton v Timmis* [1987] 1 EGLR 1, CA.
6   *ED & AD Cooke Bourne (Farms) Ltd v Mellows* [1983] QB 104, [1982] 2 All ER 208, CA.

provisions. A party who wishes any of the matters covered by these provisions to apply to a farm business tenancy would need to make express provision for the matter in question in the tenancy agreement.

Compensation for damage by wild animals

Section 20 of the 1986 Act provides for payment by the landlord of compensation where the tenant has sustained damage to his crops from any wild animals or birds, the right to kill and take which is vested in the landlord or anyone claiming under the landlord (other than the tenant), which are not wild animals or birds which the tenant has permission in writing to kill. Such compensation is payable only if (s 20(2)):

(a) the tenant gave notice of the damage to the landlord, in writing, within one month of first becoming aware of it (or of the time that he ought reasonably to have become aware of it) and gave the landlord a reasonable opportunity to inspect the damage, ie before harvesting or removing the crops; and

(b) the tenant gave a notice in writing of the claim, with particulars, to the landlord within one month of the expiration of the year (as to which see s 20(3)(b)) in respect of which the claim is made.

The amount of compensation is settled by agreement after the damage has been caused, or, in default of agreement, by arbitration under the Act (s 20(4)). Where the rights in respect of the wild animals or birds that did the damage are vested in someone other than the landlord, he is entitled to be indemnified by that person against all claims for compensation under s 20 (s 20(5)).

Restriction on landlord's remedies for breach of contract of tenancy

The amount of extra rent or liquidated damages recoverable by the landlord against the tenant for breach of obligation (by distress or otherwise) is restricted by s 24 of the 1986 Act to the extent of the damage actually suffered by the landlord in consequence of the breach. This precludes, for example, the recovery of a penal rent by distress and also limits the right of the landlord to recover an increased rent, if the tenant breaks any covenant in the tenancy, to his actual loss. This provision cannot be contracted out of.

Record of the condition of the holding

By s 22(1) either party is entitled at any time during the tenancy to require the making of a record of the condition of the fixed equipment on the holding and of the general condition of the holding (including any parts not under cultivation). The tenant may, at any time during the tenancy, make a similar request with respect to:

(a) existing improvements executed by him or in respect of which, with the landlord's consent, he paid compensation to an outgoing tenant; and

(b) any fixtures or buildings which, under s 10 of the 1986 Act, he is entitled to remove.

Such a record, the cost of making which is borne in equal shares unless the parties otherwise agree (s 22(3)) is essential to any tenant's claim for compensation under s 70 (special systems of farming) and useful in connection with assessing the liability of the parties for repairs. Any record is to be made, in default of agreement between the parties, by a person appointed by the President of the Royal Institution of Chartered Surveyors and this person may enter the holding at all reasonable times for the purpose of making the record (s 22(2)).

Landlord's powers of entry

The landlord or any person authorised by him has under s 23 of the 1986 Act the right to enter the holding at all reasonable times for the purpose of:

(a) viewing the state of the holding;
(b) fulfilling the landlord's responsibilities to manage the holding in accordance with the rules of good estate management; or
(c) providing or improving fixed equipment for the holding otherwise than in fulfilment of those responsibilities.

Distress for rent

If the amount of any compensation due to the landlord has been ascertained (whether by agreement, custom or under the Act) before any distress, then the compensation is to be set off against the rent and distress may only be levied for the balance if any (s 17 of the 1986 Act).

Chapter 31

The security of tenure regime of the 1986 Act

I GENERAL RULES

Tenants of an agricultural holding granted before the commencement of the Agricultural Tenancies Act 1995 benefit from strict statutory rules whose result is to confer substantial security of tenure on them, despite the landlord having served a notice to quit.

In the first place, the common law rule that a yearly tenancy is determinable by a valid six months' notice, which puts an end to the tenancy, is overridden by s 25(1) of the Agricultural Holdings Act 1986. This provides that a notice to quit an agricultural holding or part of it is invalid if it purports to terminate the tenancy before the expiration of 12 months from the end of the current year of tenancy. Although s 25(1) cannot be contracted out of, it does not prevent the tenant from agreeing, if it suits him, say owing to financial difficulties, to accept a shorter notice, waiving his right to a longer notice.[1] There are exceptions to the 12-month minimum notice rule,[2] including the following:

(a) where the tenant is insolvent;
(b) where notice to quit is given under a provision in the tenancy authorising the resumption of possession of the whole or part of the holding for a specified and non-agricultural purpose;[3]
(c) where the tenant gives a sub-tenant notice to quit;
(d) where an arbitrator has specified a date for the termination of the tenancy on the failure of the tenant to do work after a notice to remedy or where the time under such a notice has been extended;
(e) where on a reference under s 12 of the 1986 Act the arbitrator determines an increase in rent (s 25(3)) – this rule overrides any term in the tenancy (s 25(5)). In this case, a six months' notice may validly be given by the tenant,

---

1 *Elsden v Pick* [1980] 3 All ER 235, [1980] 1 WLR 898, CA.
2 1986 Act, s 25(2) and Agricultural Holdings (Arbitration on Notices) Order 1987, SI 1987/710.
3 See *Paddock Investments Ltd v Lory* [1975] 2 EGLR 5, CA; where this provision is invoked, then additional compensation may be payable to the tenant under 1986 Act, s 62.

though it terminates the tenancy immediately before the increase in rent is effective.

II   TENANT'S COUNTER-NOTICE

General rules

Section 26(1) of the 1986 Act is the second aspect of the strict security of tenure conferred on the tenant of an agricultural holding granted before the commencement of the Agricultural Tenancies Act 1995. If, within one month of the giving of the landlord's notice to quit,[4] whether it relates to the whole or any part of the holding, the tenant serves on the landlord a counter-notice in writing that s 26(1) is to apply, the notice to quit takes effect only if the Agricultural Land Tribunal for the area consents to its operation. Conversely, if no counter-notice is served on time, there is no requirement of any such consent and the landlord is under no implied duty to the tenant to set out his right to serve a counter-notice.[5] The 1986 Act does not expressly prohibit contracting out of the right to serve a counter-notice, but s 26(1) has been held to be mandatory and to override any contrary stipulation in the tenancy.[6] Since this rule is of public policy, it was also held that where, with a view to evading the 1986 Act, a landlord let a farm to his wife who sub-let it to the tenant, there was an agricultural tenancy, stripped of security; this grant contravened the 1986 Act and could only be terminated subject to the fetters of that statute and not freely, as at common law.[7] If, therefore, A grants a tenancy to B and C and they as tenants agree with A as landlord that they will not without A's consent serve a counter-notice, this stipulation is void.[8] A counter-notice served by one of two individual joint tenants is of no effect: all must consent to preserve the tenancy.[9] If one of the joint tenants is also the landlord, a notice served by all the tenants except for the landlord-tenant is valid.[10] Where the tenancy is a trust asset, the landlord, if a partner, may be compelled to join in the service of the notice, where requisite to preserve the tenancy.[11]

Where the landlord serves a notice to quit which does not specify any of the grounds for possession and a tenant's counter-notice follows, the landlord has one month from the service of the latter to apply in the prescribed form for the consent of the Agricultural Land Tribunal to the operation of the notice.[12] If the

---

4   Which must be validly given at common law: *Crawford v Elliott* [1991] 1 EGLR 13, CA; *Divall v Harrison* [1992] 2 EGLR 64, CA (notice not identifying correct landlord invalid).
5   *Crawford v Elliott,* supra.
6   *Johnson v Moreton* [1980] AC 37, [1978] 3 All ER 37, HL.
7   *Gisborne v Burton* [1988] 3 All ER 760, CA; J Martin (1988) 138 NLJ 792; Rodgers [1989] Conv 196.
8   *Featherstone v Staples* [1986] 2 All ER 461, [1986] 1 WLR 861, CA.
9   *Newman v Keedwell* (1977) 35 P & CR 393, CA.
10   *Featherstone v Staples,* supra.
11   *Sykes v Land* [1984] 2 EGLR 8, CA.
12   1986 Act, s 27(1) and Agricultural Land Tribunals (Rules) Order 1978, SI 1978/259. The one-month period is inflexible: *Parrish v Kinsey* [1983] 2 EGLR 13, CA.

landlord's notice specifies a statutory ground then no tenant's counter-notice is possible, but the onus is on the landlord to prove the ground on which he relies and he cannot obtain possession if no statutory ground applies.

Consent to unspecified notice to quit

The landlord must establish one of five matters to obtain the consent of the Tribunal but, under a provision which emphasises the security offered to the tenant under the pre-1995 Act régime, it may in any case withhold its consent if a fair and reasonable landlord would not insist on possession (s 27(2)). The matters are:

(a) *Good husbandry* (s 27(3)(a)): that the carrying out of the purpose for which the landlord proposes to terminate the tenancy is desirable in the interests of good husbandry as respects the land to which the notice relates, treated as a separate unit. This means that, under the landlord's proposals, the land would be farmed better, comparing the merits of each party.[13]

(b) *Sound estate management* (s 27(3)(b)): that the carrying out of the above purpose is desirable in the interests of sound management of the estate of which the land in question forms part or which that land constitutes. In this case, the question may be considered in relation to the land to which the notice relates and any other relevant land (say with which it may be amalgamated).[14] A scheme to sell off parts of the holding and to apply the sale proceeds to improving the fixed equipment on what remained might suffice within s 27(3)(b).[15]

(c) *Agricultural research* (s 27(3)(c) and (d)): that the carrying out of the above purpose is desirable for the purposes of agricultural research, education, experiment or demonstration, or for the purposes of enactments relating to smallholdings or allotments.

(d) *Greater hardship* (s 27(3)(e)): that greater hardship (including hardship to third parties) would be caused by withholding than by giving consent to the operation of the notice. This matter is up to the discretion of the Tribunal.[16] The financial result to the parties from a decision is always important.[17] The tenant's poor performance, if any, as a farmer, is relevant.[18] Where the landlord wished to manage a farm, assisted by his son, the Tribunal accepted that he had proved greater hardship from the refusal of consent compared with the hardship to the tenant by granting it and yet the landlord was refused consent under the Tribunal's discretion because the tenant was found to be more experienced than the landlord and so the productivity of the holding would suffer.[19]

---

13 *Davies v Price* [1958] 1 All ER 671, [1958] 1 WLR 434, CA. Merely to show that the land would be farmed better if amalgamated with another unit does not suffice.
14 *Evans v Roper* [1960] 2 All ER 507, [1960] 1 WLR 814.
15 *Lewis v Moss* (1961) 181 Estates Gazette 685.
16 *Wickington v Bonney* (1982) 47 P & CR 655.
17 *Purser v Bailey* [1967] 2 QB 500, [1967] 2 All ER 189, CA.
18 *R v Agricultural Land Tribunal for the South Eastern Area, ex p Parslow* [1979] 2 EGLR 1.
19 *Jones v Burgoyne* (1963) 188 Estates Gazette 497.

(e) *Non-agricultural use* (s 27(3)(f)): that the landlord proposes to terminate the tenancy for the purpose of the land being used for a use, other than agriculture, which falls outside Case B. This is a non-agricultural use such as private forestry for which planning permission is not required.

III   EXCLUSION OF TENANT'S RIGHT TO SERVE A COUNTER-NOTICE

The landlord may preclude the tenant of a pre-1995 Act agricultural tenancy from serving a counter-notice if he serves a notice to quit which specifies one or more of a series of statutory grounds or Cases. So as to avoid losing security, the tenant has the right to refer a notice which relies on Cases A, B, D or E to arbitration.

It is a general ground of invalidity of a notice to quit that the landlord has made a false statement (as opposed to a careless one) in relation to his chosen statutory ground. Where a landlord served a notice to quit specifying Case E, but the tenant failed to refer the notice to arbitration, he was entitled to prove that the notice was invalid because it contained fraudulent statements, i e assertions which the landlord knew to be false or as to the truth or falsity of which he was recklessly careless.[20] In that case, the landlord acted as he did because his main objective was to remove the tenant from the premises. It is immaterial that a false statement does not in fact deceive the recipient, since the test of validity is whether the landlord honestly believed in the truth of the statement.[1] It is a further general defence to a notice to quit relying on a statutory Case that the landlord is estopped by conduct from relying on his notice, as where he has previously promised not to serve a notice to quit relying on the ground concerned and the tenant relies on that promise. But, allegations of estoppel are difficult to prove. However, a landlord who explored with his tenant the possibility of converting existing buildings and putting up a new bungalow for the tenant, whose plans were frustrated by a refusal of planning permission, was estopped from serving a Case B notice, as the tenant had altered his position in reliance on the landlord's conduct.[2] It was said to have been unconscionable of the landlord to have gone back on the common assumption of the parties, that the tenant would remain in occupation of the farm concerned, unless and until he had been given new buildings, had the planning application succeeded.

The statutory grounds or 'cases' are as follows.

Case A: Smallholdings

This is where the holding was let as a smallholding by a smallholdings authority or by the Minister on or after 12 September 1984 and:

---

20 *Rous v Mitchell* [1991] 1 All ER 676, CA; Rodgers [1991] Conv 144.
 1 *Omnivale Ltd v Boldan* [1994] EGCS 63.
 2 *John v George* [1996] 1 EGLR 7, CA.

(a) the tenant has attained 65, and
(b) if the notice would deprive him of living accommodation occupied under the tenancy, suitable alternative accommodation is available or will be available to him, when the notice takes effect, and
(c) the tenancy acknowledges that Case A applies.

The notice to quit must state that it is given under Case A and is referable to arbitration within one month.

Case B: *Planning consent*

The notice to quit states that it is given under Case B and is given on the ground that the land is required for a use, other than agriculture:

(a) for which permission has been granted on an application made under the enactments relating to town and country planning;
(b) for which permission has been granted under a General Development Order for a non-agricultural use;
(c) for which any statutory permission other than the Planning Acts deems permission under those enactments to have been granted;
(d) which any statute other than the Planning Acts deems not to constitute development for the purpose of those enactments;
(e) for which permission is not required under the Planning Acts by reason only of Crown immunity.

The landlord must give a 12 month notice of his intention to rely on Case B but the tenant may contest this by counter-notice, served within one month of the notice to quit, requiring arbitration.[3]

Case C: *Certificate of bad husbandry*

Not more than six months before the notice to quit was given, the Tribunal granted a certificate (under Sch 3, para 9) that the tenant was not fulfilling his responsibilities to farm in accordance with the rules of good husbandry, and this fact is stated in the notice.[4]

The landlord may apply to the Tribunal for a certificate of bad husbandry but its power to grant a certificate is limited (Sch 2, para 9) because it must disregard any practice adopted by the tenant under any provision of the tenancy or otherwise agreed with the landlord, indicating its object to further any of the following three things:

(a) the conservation of flora or fauna or geological etc features of special interest;

---

3 Agricultural Holdings (Arbitration on Notices) Order 1987, SI 1987/710, art 9; see *Cawley v Pratt* [1988] 2 EGLR 6, CA.
4 For procedure, see Agricultural Land Tribunals (Rules) Order 1978, SI 1978/259. By s 25(4), the Tribunal may specify in the certificate a minimum period of at least two months' notice instead of the usual 12 months: if a notice to quit states this fact and is for at least that period it will be valid.

(b) the protection of buildings etc of archaeological, architectural or historic interest;
(c) the conservation or enhancement of the natural beauty or amenity of the countryside, or promoting public access.

Case D: Non-compliance with notice to pay rent or to remedy breaches

This important Case states that at the date of the notice to quit, the tenant has failed to comply with a landlord's written notice in the prescribed form requiring him:

(a) within two months of the service of the notice, to pay any rent due; or
(b) within a reasonable period specified in the notice, to remedy any breach capable of being remedied by him of the terms and conditions of the tenancy.[5]

Rent   Once the tenant fails to pay all the rent due (and in the correct manner) within two months of the landlord's notice to pay, the notice to quit becomes indefeasible.[6] The sole and exclusive means for the tenant to contest a notice to pay is to require arbitration (Sch 4) and if none is sought, no relief is possible and the notice takes effect to deprive the tenant of his tenancy. This procedure is not equivalent to forfeiture and equity cannot intervene.[7]

There are certain formalities in relation to a notice to pay with which a landlord must strictly comply: he must correctly state his name,[8] the rent due,[9] and give the correct name and address of all joint tenants.[10] However, not all the owners of the reversion need necessarily be parties to a Case D notice: one owner alone may validly serve a Case D notice.[11]

The strict requirement that all rent due must be paid by the stated date is capable of waiver by agreement, express or implied, as where the landlord indicates preparedness to accept a cheque posted by the due date.[12] This rule does not apply where the cheque is not one which the paying bank is bound to honour, as where it was sent with only one of the necessary signatures.[13] Where a tenant presented two cheques which were not accepted by the landlord and which became outdated by the date of service of a Case D notice, the tenant had not discharged his obligation to pay.[14]

Section 48 of the Landlord and Tenant Act 1987 applies to an agricultural tenant whose premises include a dwelling, owing to the wide statutory definition of the latter expression in s 46(1), so that where the landlord of such a tenant failed to serve the requisite s 48 notice before serving a Case D notice, no rent was due within the latter Case until a separate 1987 Act notice had been served.

---

5 For forms of notice see Agricultural Holdings etc Regulations 1987, SI 1987/711, Sch.
6 *Stoneman v Brown* [1973] 2 All ER 225, [1973] 1 WLR 459, CA.
7 *Parrish v Kinsey* [1983] 2 EGLR 13, CA.
8 *Pickard v Bishop* (1975) 31 P & CR 108, CA.
9 *Dickinson v Boucher* [1984] 1 EGLR 12, CA.
10 *Jones v Lewis* (1973) 25 P & CR 375, CA.
11 *Parsons v Parsons* (1983) 47 P & CR 494.
12 *Beevers v Mason* (1978) 37 P & CR 452, CA.
13 *Luttenberger v North Thoresby Farms Ltd* [1993] 1 EGLR 3.
14 *Official Solicitor v Thomas* [1986] 2 EGLR 1, CA.

However, as from service of such a notice some eight weeks later, all the rent stated as owing in the notice remained due: s 48(1) did not provide that a failure to service a 1987 Act notice destroyed the landlord's right to claim the rent due prior to such service.[15] It is questionable what benefit s 48(1) of the 1987 Act adds to the existing security of the tenant: it seems merely to have added an unnecessary additional formality.

Other breaches Owing to its importance, a notice to remedy other breaches must be in the prescribed form and must specify a period for remedy of the breach.[16] If the notice requires any work of repair, maintenance or replacement, it must be in Form 2 of the regulations: if not, in Form 3. If the tenant wishes to contest a reason stated, he must, within one month of service of the landlord's notice to do work, serve a written notice specifying the items in respect of which he denies liability and requiring arbitration.[17] The landlord's notice must describe the items of repair, maintenance or replacement required and must allow at least six months in which the tenant is to do the work specified. The arbitrator, in the interests of the tenant, has wide powers to modify or alter a notice to do work, including a power to extend the time allowed by the landlord.

The original or modified notice to do work must be complied with in full: substantial compliance is insufficient as a defence to a later notice to quit.[18] If the failure to comply is due to non-supply of materials to be provided by the landlord, this was excusable, although the time specified in the notice for remedy was not thereby rendered unreasonable from the start.[19] If more than one breach is to be remedied, a reasonable time must be allowed for all breaches to be remedied or the notice will be bad.[20]

Despite non-compliance with a notice to do work, the tenant has an additional safeguard: he may, under s 28, by written counter-notice within one month of the landlord's notice or an arbitration award, require the consent of the Tribunal to the Case D notice. By s 28(5), the Tribunal must consent to the operation of the notice unless it appears to them that a fair and reasonable landlord would not insist on possession, having regard to:

(a) the extent of the tenant's failure to comply with the notice to do work;
(b) the consequences of his failure to comply in any respect; and
(c) the circumstances surrounding the failure.

Case E: Irremediable breaches

This ground is that at the date of giving the notice to quit, the landlord's interest has been materially prejudiced by the tenant committing an irremediable

15 *Dallhold Estates (UK) Pty Ltd v Lindsey Trading Properties Inc* [1994] 1 EGLR 93, CA.
16 Agricultural Holdings (Forms of Notice etc) Regulations 1987, SI 1987/711.
17 Agricultural Holdings (Arbitration on Notices) Order 1987, SI 1987/710, art 3; but the tenant remains liable to carry out any items which he does not contest: *Ladds Radio and Television Ltd v Docker* (1973) 226 Estates Gazette 1565; and note that both or all joint tenants must serve an arbitration notice: see *Combey v Gumbrill* [1990] 2 EGLR 7.
18 *Price v Romilly* [1960] 3 All ER 429, [1960] 1 WLR 1360.
19 *Shepherd v Lomas* [1963] 2 All ER 902, [1963] 1 WLR 962, CA.
20 *Wykes v Davis* [1975] QB 843, [1975] 1 All ER 399, CA.

breach of a term or condition of his tenancy, if it is a term not inconsistent with his responsibilities to farm in accordance with the rules of good husbandry. Where a tenant granted an unlawful sub-tenancy to a company, and the landlord served a Case E notice, there was no 'material prejudice' merely owing to the risk that the tenant might serve a notice to quit on the landlord, leaving him saddled with the sub-tenant, since the effect at common law of such an upwards notice would be to terminate the sub-tenancy by operation of law.[1]

The notice must clearly specify this ground if relied upon (especially as it has to be clear, where relevant, whether Case D or E is being invoked). Although great care must be taken in the preparation of a Case E notice, it was held that where a notice omitted to state that the reversion had, after the grant of the tenancy, been severed, the notice was upheld, having regard to the knowledge of both parties, as the court leant in favour of validity.[2] The tenant may require an arbitration within one month of the service of the notice.[3]

The tenant cannot validly contract out of his right to serve an arbitration notice (under this or any other case): to enforce a covenant not to require arbitration is contrary to public policy.[4] Where the parties in negotiations and dealings both assumed that, contrary to the fact, a tenancy did not restrict assignments, and went to arbitration on their false assumption, the landlords were estopped by convention from invoking Case E.[5]

Case F: Insolvency

It is a ground for possession, which must be stated as a reason in the notice, that at the date of giving the notice to quit, the tenant has become insolvent (defined s 96(1)).

Case G: Death of tenant

Under this it is provided that the notice to quit is given:

(a) following the death of a person who immediately before his death was the sole (or sole surviving) tenant under the contract of tenancy; and
(b) not later than three months beginning with the date of any relevant notice[6]

and it is stated in the notice to quit that it is given by reason of that person's death.

The date of any relevant notice in (b) above means either (1) the date of service of a written notice on the landlord by or on behalf of an executor or administrator of the tenant's estate informing the landlord of the tenant's death;[7] or (2) the date on which the landlord is given notice by virtue of s 40(5)

---

1 *Pennell v Payne* [1995] QB 192, [1995] 2 All ER 592, CA.
2 *Land v Sykes* [1992] 1 EGLR 1, CA.
3 Agricultural Holdings (Arbitration on Notices) Order1987, supra, art 9.
4 *Johnson v Moreton* [1980] AC 37, [1978] 3 All ER 37, HL.
5 *Troop v Gibson* [1986] 1 EGLR 1, CA.
6 See *BSC Pension Fund Trustees v Downing* [1990] 1 EGLR 4.
7 See *Lees v Tatchell* [1990] 1 EGLR 10 (return of rent demand with cheque by executors insufficient as notice).

of an application for a succession to the tenancy. If both of the above events occur, the three month period above runs from the first to take place.

There is no provision for arbitration on a Case G notice. Even though it may state the death as the reason for the notice, where it is possible to apply for a succession and such is applied for, the notice takes effect only if, after an application, no person is determined by the Tribunal to be suitable to succeed, or the Tribunal consents to the operation of the notice in relation to the whole or part of the holding (s 43). The importance of the succession provisions will be progressively curtailed, since where the tenant holding under most, but not all, tenancies granted on or after 12 July 1984 dies, no succession to the tenancy may be applied for (s 34).

Case H: Ministerial certificates

This Case states that the Minister has certified that the notice to quit is given by him to enable him to use or dispose of the land to effect an amalgamation under s 26(1) of the Agriculture Act 1967 or the re-shaping of any agricultural unit, and the tenancy itself contains an acknowledgment signed by the tenant that Case H is to apply.

IV NOTICE TO QUIT PART OF THE HOLDING

A tenancy of an agricultural holding granted prior to 1 September 1995 may expressly enable the landlord to serve a notice to quit part of the holding. If it does not, a notice to quit part only is void. By s 31(1) of the 1986 Act, a notice to quit part of the holding is, however, valid if given for the purpose of adjusting the boundaries between agricultural units or amalgamating agricultural units or parts; or if it is given for a list of purposes in s 31 for which it is intended to use the land. Examples of this include the erection of cottages or other houses for farm labourers, and the provision of gardens for cottages. By s 32 the tenant may within 28 days of a notice to quit part of the holding accept it as notice to quit the whole and notify the landlord. By s 33, where notice to quit part is given, the tenant is entitled to a reduction in rent proportionate to the part lost and to any depreciation in value to the rest and if the amount of any reduction cannot be agreed, it will be settled by arbitration.

V SUCCESSION SCHEME OF THE 1986 ACT

Introduction

There is a succession scheme under which, in the case of an agricultural tenancy granted before 12 July 1984, there may be succession to the tenancy of an agricultural holding on the death or retirement of the tenant (s 34 of the 1986 Act). This scheme, introduced only in 1976, has been removed in relation to a tenancy within the 1986 Act granted on or after 12 July 1984. There are four exceptional cases where it survived, but there is no possibility of any statutory succession to a farm business tenancy governed by the Agricultural Tenancies Act 1995. Indeed, the 1976 succession scheme was blamed in some quarters for a reduction in the availability of farm land to let. The four exceptional cases where a tenancy within the 1986 Act regime may be succeeded to are these:

(a) where the tenancy was obtained under a Tribunal direction under s 39 or s 53;
(b) where the landlord granted the tenancy under s 45(6) to a person or persons entitled, after a Tribunal direction, to a tenancy;
(c) where the tenancy is written and the parties agree that the succession scheme is to apply;
(d) the tenancy was granted to a person who, immediately before 12 July 1984, was the tenant of the whole or a substantial part of the land comprised in the holding.

Outline of succession on death rules

The succession scheme following the death of the tenant does not apply where, at the date of the death, the tenancy is subject to a valid notice to quit under s 26 or to a Case B or Case F notice (s 38). Moreover, it cannot apply where two successions have already taken place (s 37). The scheme is excluded where the landlord and the current tenant agree on the grant of a new tenancy of the holding, which need not be the whole holding (s 37(2) and (4)) or a related holding to a close relative of the tenant, and an assignment of an existing tenancy to an eligible person operates the succession rules (s 37(2) and (4)).

1. *Application by eligible person*: A person eligible to succeed, namely any surviving close relative (widely defined in s 35(2) so as to include spouses, brothers, sisters or children) of the deceased, may apply under s 36(1) for a direction under s 39 from the Tribunal within three months of the death of the tenant. The Tribunal must be satisfied that the applicant has not ceased to be eligible since the date of the death (s 39(2)).
2. *What eligible person must prove*: An eligible person must show that he is not the occupier of a commercial unit of agricultural land (s 36(3)(b)). He must also prove that in the seven years ending with the death, his only or principal source of income for a continuous period of five years or for two or more discontinuous periods amounting to five years, was derived from his agricultural work on the holding or on a unit of which it forms part (s 36(3)(a)). A purposive approach is adopted: so, where a person had no sufficient source of income other than his drawings on a partnership account, and made these because of his full-time work on an agricultural holding, he 'derived' his livelihood from that work.[8]
3. *Occupation rule*: A claimant must also comply with an occupation rule. There are special deeming rules with respect to occupation so that, for example, joint occupation by a close relative of the deceased and others is treated as occupation by the former person of the whole holding, with a right

8 *Welby v Casswell* [1995] 2 EGLR 1, CA.

of apportionment of income if his share of income falls below that attributable to a commercial unit.[9]

4. *Suitability to succeed*: Assuming the above conditions are complied with, the Tribunal must then determine whether the applicant or each of a number of joint applicants, is suitable to succeed, using a large number of criteria such as the training and practical experience of the applicant, his age, health and financial standing. Indeed all relevant matters must be taken into account as must the landlord's views, if any (s 39(8)).

5. *Direction*: If the Tribunal decides that the applicant is entitled to succeed, they must give a direction entitling him to a tenancy of the holding within three months from the day after the date of death (s 39(1)) but the landlord may consent to accept a joint tenancy, where relevant, of up to four applicants (s 39(9)). After a direction, the landlord is deemed to grant the applicant a new tenancy (s 45). The terms of the new tenancy are generally the same as those of the old tenancy unless varied by arbitration (ss 47-48) and the tenancy is generally granted so as to run as from 12 months immediately after the end of the year in which the deceased tenant dies (s 46(1)). Before giving a direction, the Tribunal must allow the landlord to apply for its consent to the operation of any Case G notice (s 44), and they may consent to the operation of such notice in relation to the whole or any part of the holding. If no application is made, or the application fails, a Case G notice is consented to, it is provided that it takes effect in relation to the whole holding (s 43(1)).

9 Sch 6, para 7. As to occupation under a list of short interests, eg licences etc, which does not count, see ibid, para 6; as to the position where the close relative already occupies a holding under a direction, para 8; and for occupation by a close relative's spouse or company controlled by a close relative, see para 9.

Chapter 32

Rights on termination, compensation and miscellaneous matters

I LANDLORD'S CLAIMS ON TERMINATION

The landlord of the tenant of an agricultural holding who is governed by the Agricultural Holdings Act 1986 may have claims for damage or dilapidation from the tenant after quitting, and these fall under three heads.[1] The following rules do not apply to farm business tenancies, which are governed by the express provisions of the tenancy and the common law rules discussed elsewhere.

Claim under contract of tenancy

By s 71(3) of the 1986 Act, the landlord may claim damages for dilapidation, deterioration or damage due to the tenant's failure to farm in accordance with the rules of good husbandry, under the written contract of tenancy.[2] In no case, by s 71(5), is the amount of compensation to exceed the amount, if any, by which the value of the landlord's reversion is diminished by the breach in question.[3] The expression 'dilapidation' bears a wide meaning and includes not only the disrepair of buildings but also such things as the neglect of fences and hedges, or damage to gates and hedges.[4]

Claim under statute

The landlord may, alternatively, claim under s 71(1) for breaches of the implied obligation of the tenant to farm in accordance with the rules of good husbandry. This right applies only on the tenant's quitting the holding. The amount of compensation in this case is (s 71(2)) the cost, as at the date of quitting, of making good the dilapidation, deterioration or damage. This is subject to the ceiling on claims imposed by s 71(5).

---

1 For further details see eg West, ch 13.
2 This head of claim may also be made during the currency of the contract of tenancy: *Kent v Conniff* [1953] 1 QB 361, [1953] 1 All ER 155, CA.
3 Similar considerations presumably apply to s 71(4) as apply to Landlord and Tenant Act 1954, s 18(1); see ch 9 above.
4 *Evans v Jones* [1955] 2 QB 58, [1955] 2 All ER 118, CA.

General deterioration

There is an additional right in the landlord under s 72 to claim for general deterioration. The amount recoverable is that by which the value of the holding has been reduced, having regard to the character and situation of the holding and the average requirements of tenants reasonably skilled in husbandry. A claim of the present kind might be made where the landlord proves additional general damage to the farm as a whole, beyond any specific heads of claim, as where owing to neglect of ditches, he has to re-let to a different tenant at a reduced rent.

No claim can be made under s 71 or s 72 unless an arbitration notice is given under s 84 within two months of the termination of the tenancy s 83(1). On arbitration, the terms of the tenancy are always relevant,[5] as are, where applicable, those of the model clauses. In the case of s 72 claims, additionally, there must be a preliminary notice of intention to claim compensation served by the landlord not later than one month prior to termination.

It appears that the landlord may claim damages at common law, during the tenancy, for dilapidations to particular buildings, fixed equipment or parts of the holding despite the statutory provisions, which do not in terms derogate from the landlord's common law rights.[6] Such claims would be subject to the ceiling of s 18(1) of the Landlord and Tenant Act 1927.

II COMPENSATION FOR TENANTS' IMPROVEMENTS[7]

Rights to compensation

At common law, an agricultural tenant had no right to compensation for any improvements which he had acquired or carried out at his own expense. In time, such rights came to be established by custom of the country, and local customary rights were often incorporated expressly in the terms of the tenancy.

The 1986 Act supersedes customary rights, except that in the case of 'old improvements', a claim may be made, in the alternative, under custom or agreement. 'Old improvements' mean those begun before 1 March 1948 (s 64(4) and Sch 9, Part I) and are not further considered in this book. 'New improvements' refer to those begun on or after 1 March 1948. The statutory rights to compensation are available to any tenant of agricultural land (including land belonging to the Crown (s 95)). The following rules do not apply to farm business tenancies within the Agricultural Tenancies Act 1995, in relation to which revised compensation rules, which pose general principles rather than reliance on lists of matters eligible for compensation.

The rights of the tenant of an agricultural holding within the 1986 Act to compensation arise on his quitting the holding on the termination of his

---

5   *Barrow Green Estate Co v Walker's Executors* [1954] 1 All ER 204, [1954] 1 WLR 231, CA.
6   *Kent v Coniff* supra.
7   As to the right of a tenant of an agricultural holding within the 1986 act to remove fixtures, see ch 15; his right to security of tenure in place of emblements is governed by s 21 of the 1986 Act, where such right arises.

tenancy, and therefore a tenant who is granted a new tenancy is not entitled to compensation on the termination of the earlier tenancy, but such rights as he would have had will be preserved until ultimately he quits (s 69(1)). A tenant who on entry, and with the written consent of the landlord, paid any compensation to the outgoing tenant for improvements, may, on quitting the holding, claim the same compensation as the outgoing tenant would have been entitled to claim, if he had remained in occupation and was now quitting (s 69(2)).

Compensation for 'new improvements'

'New improvements' are defined by s 64(1) as improvements specified in Sch 7 and Part I of Sch 8 to the 1986 Act, which were begun on or after 1 March 1948. Rights to compensation in respect of them are governed by ss 64-69 of the Act.

Improvements within Part I of Sch 7 may only be carried out by the tenant with the landlord's written consent (s 67(1)). Improvements within Part II of Sch 7 require the consent of the landlord,[8] or, if it is refused, the consent of the Agricultural Land Tribunal (s 67(3)). The Tribunal may approve the carrying out of the improvement, unconditionally or on terms, or it may withhold approval (s 67(4)).[9] The landlord may in writing notify the Tribunal and the tenant, if approval is given, that he proposes himself to carry out the improvement (s 67(5)), so avoiding the need to pay compensation.[10] An approval where no subsequent landlords' notice is served, has effect as if it were the consent of the landlord (s 67(6)). The work which qualifies for compensation is set out in Sch 7 to the 1986 Act as follows.

'New improvements' for which the consent of the landlord is required

1   Making or planting of osier beds.
2   Making of water meadows.
3   Making of watercress beds.
4   Planting of hops.
5   Planting of orchards or fruit bushes.
6   Warping or weiring of land.
7   Making of gardens.
8   Provision of underground tanks.

'New improvements' for which the consent of the landlord or approval of the Tribunal is required

9   Erection, alteration or enlargement of buildings, and making or improvement of permanent yards.

---

8   The requirement of landlords' prior consent is also a condition precedent to carrying out work or making any claim for compensation by a farm business tenant within the Agricultural Tenancies Act 1995.
9   For forms of application, see Agricultural Land Tribunals (Rules) Order 1978, SI 1978/259, Form 6.
10 The relevant period is one month from receipt of the Tribunal's decision: 1978 Order, supra, r 7(2).

10 Carrying out works in compliance with an improvement notice served, or an undertaking accepted, under Part VII of the Housing Act 1985 or Part VIII of the Housing Act 1974.

11 The creation or construction of loading platforms, ramps, hard standings for vehicles or other similar facilities.

12 Construction of silos.

13 Claying of land.

14 Marling of land.

15 Making or improvement of roads or bridges.

16 Making or improvement of water courses, culverts, ponds, wells or reservoirs, or of works for the application of water power for agricultural or domestic purposes or of works for the supply, distribution or use of water for such purposes (including the erection or installation of any structures or equipment which form part of or are to be used in connection with operating any such works).

17 Making or removal of permanent fences.

18 Reclaiming of waste land.

19 Making or improvement of embankments or sluices.

20 Erection of wirework for hop gardens.

21 Provision of permanent sheep-dipping accommodation.

22 Removal of bracken, gorse, tree roots, boulders or other like obstructions to cultivation.

23 Land drainage (other than mole drainage and works carried out to secure the efficient functioning thereof).

24 Provision or laying-on of electric light or power.

25 Provision of facilities for the storage or disposal of sewage or farm waste.

26 Repairs to fixed equipment, being equipment reasonably required for the proper farming of the holding, other than repairs which the tenant is under an obligation to carry out.

27 The grubbing up of orchards or fruit bushes.

28 Planting trees otherwise than as an orchard and bushes other than fruit bushes.

The measure of compensation for improvements under Sch 7 is not the cost of the improvements, but an amount equal to the increase attributable to the improvement in the value of the holding as a holding, having regard to the character and situation of the holding and the average requirements of tenants reasonably skilled in husbandry (s 66(1)).

The following short-term 'new improvements' (listed in Sch 8, Part I) may be made by the tenant of an agricultural holding who is subject to the 1986 Act without the consent of the landlord, though he must follow a merely formal notification procedure in the case of item 1 – one month's advance notice being required in this instance (s 68(1)).

'New improvements' which do not require the consent of the landlord

1 Mole drainage and works carried out to secure the efficient functioning thereof.

2 Protection of fruit trees against animals.

3 Clay burning.
4 Liming (including chalking) of land.
5 Application to land of purchased manure and fertiliser, whether organic or inorganic.
6 Consumption on the holding of corn (whether produced on the holding or not) or of cake or other feeding stuff not produced on the holding by horses, cattle, sheep, pigs or poultry.

The measure of compensation for improvements set out in the Eighth Schedule is their value to an incoming tenant, calculated in accordance with regulations (s 66(2)).[11] The landlord is entitled to make certain deductions in respect of benefits allowed to the tenant and improvement grants or local government grants paid to the tenant (s 66(5)). Otherwise the tenant would gain more than sufficient compensation.

III TENANT-RIGHT MATTERS

Certain 'tenant-right matters' appear in Sch 8, Part II, in respect of which the tenant is entitled to compensation by virtue of the 1986 Act. The measure of compensation for these improvements is the same as for those under Part I, unless the parties have agreed in the contract of tenancy that it should be calculated in some other way (s 66(4)). The matters are listed as follows:

a   Growing crops and severed or haxrvested crops and produce, being in either case crops or produce grown on the holding in the last year of the tenancy, but not including crops or produce which the tenant has a right to sell or remove from the holding.
b   Seeds sown and cultivations, fallows and acts of husbandry performed on the holding at the expense of the tenant (including the growing of herbage crops for commercial seed production).
c   Pasture laid down with clover, grass, lucerne, sainfoin or other seeds, being either:
(a) pasture laid down at the expense of the tenant otherwise than in compliance with an obligation imposed on him by an agreement in writing to lay it down to replace temporary pasture comprised in the holding when the tenant entered thereon which was not paid for by him; or
(b) pasture paid for by the tenant on entering on the holding.
d   Acclimatisation, hefting or settlement of hill sheep on hill land.
e   In areas of the country where arable crops can be grown in an unbroken series of not less than six years and it is reasonable to grow them on the holding or part, the residual fertility value of the sod of the excess qualifying leys on the holding, if any.

---

11 Agriculture (Calculation of Value for Compensation) Regulations 1978, SI 1978/809, as amended.

IV SPECIAL SYSTEMS OF FARMING

The tenant may claim compensation under s 70, whereby he is entitled to an amount equivalent to any increase in the value of the holding as a result of his continued adoption of a special system of farming (sometimes called 'high farming') during his tenancy. In order to establish such a claim, the tenant must show that the system adopted was more beneficial than the system of farming required by the terms of the tenancy, or if none was specified, then the system of farming normally practised on comparable agricultural holdings (s 70(1)). Section 70(2) further requires that:

(i) the tenant has, not later than one month before the termination of the tenancy, given the landlord notice in writing of his intention to claim compensation under this head, and
(ii) a record has been made under s 22 of the Act of the condition of the fixed equipment on the holding and of the general condition of the holding.

Compensation under s 70 is not payable in respect of matters arising before that record was made (or the first of them), nor of improvements for which compensation has, or should have been, claimed separately under any other head (s 70(3)). As this compensation is additional compensation, due allowance must be made, in assessing the value of the holding, for compensation for improvements (s 64) or in respect of tenant-right matters, if these have caused or contributed to the benefit (s 70(4)) and the tenant is not entitled to s 70 compensation in respect of improvements or other matters (such as under s 64 or in respect of market gardens) recoverable elsewhere in the Act (s 70(5)).

V DISTURBANCE COMPENSATION

Where the tenancy of an agricultural holding to which the 1986 Act applies terminates in two circumstances, and the tenant quits, he is entitled to disturbance compensation (s 60(1)).[12] These are:

(a) where a notice to quit is given by the landlord; or
(b) where the tenant gives a counter-notice under s 32, having been given notice to quit part of the holding.

Compensation is restricted by s 63(3) of the 1986 Act where the tenant serves a counter-notice after a notice to quit[13] part of the holding, which enlarges the notice to cover the whole holding which the tenant then quits. If the notice

---

12 Since there is no security of tenure apparatus equivalent to that of the 1986 Act in the Agricultural Tenancies Act 1995, farm business tenants are not entitled to disturbance compensation; but one aim of the revised compensation for improvement rules is seemingly to assist the latter tenants with their relocation expenses.
13 Ie a notice given by the original landlord or any other person entitled to a severed part of the reversion: s 63(4).

related to less than one quarter of the holding and the rest was reasonably capable of being farmed as a separate unit, then compensation for disturbance is for that relating to the original part to which the notice related (s 63(3)). On the other hand, a tenant who becomes liable to pay compensation for disturbance to a sub-tenant, in consequence of being served with a notice to quit by his own landlord, is not debarred from claiming compensation under this head against his landlord by reason only that he cannot strictly be said to 'quit' the holding on the termination of his tenancy, owing to the fact that he was not in occupation of the holding (s 63(2)). Section 63(1) gives a sub-tenant the right to claim compensation for disturbance on quitting after termination of his sub-tenancy consequent on termination by operation of law of the head tenancy after notice or counter-notice.

Compensation for disturbance is payable notwithstanding any agreement to the contrary (s 78(1)). No compensation is payable where the landlord is entitled to regain possession under Cases C to G inclusive of Sch 3 to the 1986 Act (s 61(1)). Nor is additional compensation payable where the Agricultural Land Tribunal consented to a landlord's notice to quit for reasons of good husbandry, agricultural research or greater hardship, and the notice stated that it was given on one of these grounds (s 60(3)). It is seemingly not the intention of Parliament to allow a tenant who, through his own fault or for some other reason justifying the loss of security of tenure, is removed involuntarily from the holding to claim compensation.

Where the landlord resumes possession following a landlord's notice to quit part of the holding under s 31 or s 43(2), the compensation provisions apply to the part concerned as if it were a separate holding which the tenant had quitted under a notice to quit (s 74(2)(a)). The same result follows where a landlord entitled to a severed part of the reversion resumes possession following notice to quit served with respect to the relevant part of the holding (s 74(3)).[14]

'Basic' compensation

There are two types of compensation: 'basic' and 'additional' compensation. Basic compensation is the amount of the loss or expense directly attributable to the tenant's quitting the holding, which is unavoidably incurred by him on sale or removal of household goods, implements of husbandry, fixtures, farm produce or farm stock on or used in connection with the holding; and it includes expenses reasonably incurred by him in the preparation of his claim for 'basic' compensation, but not costs incurred as a result of a reference to arbitration (s 60(5)). The minimum 'basic' compensation is one year's rent of the holding at the rate at which rent was payable immediately before the termination of the tenancy (s 60(3)(a)). If the tenant considers that his losses or expenses exceed that figure, he may claim his actual losses or the maximum of two years' rent, provided that a least one month before the termination of the tenancy he has given the landlord notice in writing of his intention to make a claim under this head, and before selling any of the goods, etc, he has given the landlord a reasonable opportunity of making a valuation thereof (s 60(6)).

14   Such notice being given by the landlord under Law of Property Act 1925, s 139.

'Additional' compensation

The tenant is entitled to claim 'additional' compensation (s 60(2)(b)), to assist in the reorganisation of his affairs following the loss of his tenancy. The amount concerned is that equal to four years' rent of the holding at the rate at which the rent was payable immediately before the termination of the tenancy of the holding (s 60(4)). This compensation is not payable where the landlord is entitled to regain possession despite the security of tenure of the tenant, which he gives up on quitting, under Case A or H of Sch 3 (s 61(2)).

Certain tenants are also entitled to compensation on quitting in respect of milk quota allocated to the tenant,[15] inasmuch as the value of the land will have been increased by the allocation of such quota, and so the tenant is entitled to claim additional sums if the amount of quota allotted to him exceeds the standard quota.

VI ADDITIONAL COMPENSATION RIGHTS FOR MARKET GARDEN TENANTS

Where under a tenancy granted prior to the commencement of the Agricultural Tenancies Act 1995, an agricultural holding is let or treated as a market garden,[16] additional rights with respect to compensation for improvements apply, notably:

(a) Before the termination of the tenancy, the tenant may remove all fruit trees and fruit bushes planted by him (but not permanently set out) although if he leaves them, he will not be entitled to compensation in respect of them (s 79(4)).
(b) An incoming tenant may claim compensation for improvements which he purchased, although the landlord did not consent in writing to the purchase (s 79(5)).
(c) Those improvements listed in Sch 10 begun on or after 1 March 1948 are to be treated as if they were improvements not requiring the consent of the landlord as a condition precedent to claiming compensation (s 79(2)).

The relevant improvements are as follows:
1 Planting of standard or other fruit trees permanently set out.
2 Planting of fruit bushes permanently set out.
3 Planting of strawberry plants.
4 Planting of asparagus, rhubarb and other vegetable crops which continue productive for two or more years.
5 Erection, alteration or enlargement of buildings for the purposes of the trade or business of a market gardener.

---

15 Agriculture Act 1986, s 13 and Sch 1.
16 Where the land is part of an agricultural holding, the special rules apply as if the market garden portion were a separate holding (s 79(1)).

The tenant of a market garden has the specific right, under s 10 of the 1986 Act, to remove any building erected on the holding by him for the purposes of his trade or business as a market gardener (s 79(3)(a)).

The tenant may wish to have the holding or any part of it treated as a market garden, so as to obtain these special rights, and if the landlord refuses, or fails within a reasonable time to agree to this, the tenant may apply to the Agricultural Land Tribunal for a direction (s 80(1)). If the Tribunal is satisfied that the holding or part is suitable for market gardening, they must direct that s 79(2) to (5) is to apply to all or some of the improvements specified in Sch 10, provided the improvements are executed after the date of the direction (s 80(2)).

Where any such direction is given and the tenancy is determined by notice to quit given by the tenant or by reason of the tenant's insolvency, he loses any rights to compensation, unless within one month of the insolvency he produces to the landlord an offer in writing (which must remain open for three months) from a substantial and otherwise suitable person to accept a tenancy of the holding as from the termination of the tenancy, and to pay the tenant the amount of compensation due to him, and the landlord fails to accept that offer within the three months (s 80(4)). If the landlord accepts the offer, the incoming tenant must pay on demand all sums due to the landlord from the outgoing tenant, which sums the incoming tenant is entitled to deduct from any compensation he is liable to pay to the outgoing tenant (s 80(5)). These provisions as to compensation, known as the 'Evesham custom', may be substituted for the provisions as to compensation which would otherwise be applicable to a tenancy of land agreed to be let or treated as a market garden (s 81(2)). Nevertheless, the parties are free to contract out of the provisions of the Act relating to compensation for improvements, provided that the compensation agreed is fair and reasonable having regard to the circumstances existing when the agreement was made (s 81(1)).

VII   SPECIFIC RULES FOR SMALLHOLDINGS, ALLOTMENTS AND ALLOTMENT GARDENS

Smallholdings

Part III of the Agriculture Act 1970 constitutes county councils as 'smallholdings authorities' (s 38). The authorities are required by s 39, having regard to the general interests of agriculture and of good estate management, to make it their general aim to provide opportunities for persons to be farmers on their own account by letting holdings to them. There was an upper limit of 50 acres under the earlier Acts, but by s 39(2), a holding is to be treated as within the upper limit, if in the opinion of the Minister, it is capable of providing full-time employment for not more than two men (including the person to whom it is let) with or without additional part-time employment of another man. Smallholdings may be let only to a person who is to farm the holding, and either:

(a) is regarded by the authority as being qualified by reason of his agricultural experience to farm the holding on his own account, or

(b) is a person in respect of whom the authority is satisfied that within a reasonably short time he will become eligible to be so regarded (s 44(2)).

More than one smallholding may be let to several similarly qualified persons proposing to farm the land together on a co-operative system (s 44(3)). In determining the rent at which a smallholding should be let, the authority is required by s 45(1) to have regard to the rent which, in its opinion, might reasonably be expected to be determined by arbitration under the 1986 Act in respect of a tenancy of that land if it were let as an agricultural holding on the same terms as under the proposed letting.

Section 46 of the 1970 Act gives the authorities the necessary powers to equip smallholdings. If a tenancy of a smallholding falls within s 1 of the Agricultural Holdings Act 1986, then Case A of Sch 3 of that Act is available to the authority and also, no person claiming to succeed to a tenancy of a smallholding granted before or after Part III of the 1970 Act was passed may claim a succession to it under the succession scheme (s 38(4) of the 1986 Act).

Allotments

The tenant of an allotment, which is defined by s 1 of the Allotments Act 1922, as any parcel of land, whether attached to a cottage or not, of not more than two acres in extent let as a farm or a garden, or partly as a garden and partly as a farm, is entitled by s 3(2) of that Act (which cannot be contracted out of), on the termination of his tenancy,[17] to specific compensation for:

(a) crops, including fruit, growing upon the land in the ordinary course of cultivation and for labour expended upon and manure applied to the land; and

(b) fruit trees or bushes provided and planted by the tenant with the landlord's prior consent in writing, and for drains, outbuildings, pigsties, fowl-houses, or other structural improvements made or erected by and at the expense of the tenant on the land with such consent.

The measure of compensation is the value to an incoming tenant (s 22(3)), and the amount is subject to deductions in respect of any arrears of rent, breach of the terms of the contract of tenancy and of any wilful or negligent damage caused or permitted by the tenant (s 3(3)).

Allotment gardens

By s 22(1) of the Allotments Act 1922, the expression 'allotment garden' means an allotment not exceeding 40 poles in extent, which is wholly or mainly cultivated for the production of vegetables or fruit for consumption by the tenant or his family. On quitting the land on the termination of his tenancy by the landlord, the tenant is entitled, by s 2(3), notwithstanding any agreement to the contrary, to compensation for crops growing upon the land in the

---

17 But not where the tenancy was granted on or after 1 September 1995 and is a farm business tenancy within the Agricultural Tenancies Act 1995 (1995 Act, Sch, paras 3 and 4).

ordinary course of the cultivation of the land as an allotment garden and for manure applied to the land.

He may remove his fruit trees and bushes, and any erection or improvement made by him, before the end of his tenancy; and in addition, he may be entitled to claim compensation for disturbance (amounting to one year's rent), provided that his tenancy is terminated:

(a) by re-entry under the Allotments Act 1922;
(b) where the landlord is himself a tenant by the termination of *his* tenancy; or
(c) where the landlord is a local authority which has let the land under s 10 of the 1922 Act, by the termination of the authority's right of occupation.

Termination by the landlord must generally be by a 12 months' notice to quit expiring on or before the sixth day of April or on or after the twenty-ninth day of September (s 1(1)). Re-entry may be made on three months' notice, however, where the land is required for certain statutory purposes (s 1(1)). On re-entry for non-payment of rent, bankruptcy or other breach of obligation, there are no rights to compensation. It is thought that, as the user of the land is outside the purposes contemplated by s 1 of the Agricultural Holdings Act 1986, a tenancy of an allotment garden cannot fall within that Act, nor within the Agricultural Tenancies Act 1995.

Chapter 33

Farm business tenancies

I INTRODUCTION AND POLICY

General background

The common law rules governing tenancies of farm land and associated buildings have long been subjected to statutory controls. Yet, during most of this century, the proportion of agricultural land which is farmed by tenants as opposed to landowners under various different arrangements has been in steady and seemingly irreversible decline.

With the avowed intention of deregulating the law, and of encouraging new lettings of farm land for agricultural and other more diversified uses, such as the provision of leisure facilities, Parliament has enacted the Agricultural Tenancies Act 1995.[1] The machinery of the Act is a break with most aspects of the previous statutory regime. It confers no security on an agricultural tenant and shifts the balance of advantage firmly into the landlord's favour in that respect. The new legislation is supposed to mark a change away from the making of detailed statutory provisions as to most aspects of the contractual relationship, once established within the 1995 Act, between the parties to a tenancy of farming land. Parliament now favours freedom of contract. However, it has been said that the rules in relation to the establishment of a farm business tenancy, a prerequisite to taking advantage of the new rules, may put off new entrants to tenanted farming, owing to their complexity.[2]

A deregulated approach

That the 1995 Act follows a deregulation policy is illustrated by its approach to the contractual obligations of the parties to a farm business tenancy (other than as to rent review and compensation). These are left for the parties to insert into the tenancy. Thus, the 1995 Act does not enable the tenant to refer the terms of a non-written agreement to arbitration, as does the 1986 Act.

The freedom of contract approach is further shown by the fact that the 1995 Act has no specific statutory rules dealing with damages on account of tenants'

---

1 For commentaries on the 1995 Act see Sydenham and Mainwaring, *Farm Business Tenancies*; Evans, *Agricultural Tenancies Act 1995*; see also Bright [1995] Conv 445.
2 See Gibbard and Ravenscroft, *Reform of Agricultural Holdings*, 1996, CELTS (University of Reading No 96/3), para 6.8.

dilapidations. The issue is left to the common law as adjusted by s 18(1) of the Landlord and Tenant Act 1927. Model clauses as to repairs and maintenance in the form of delegated legislation, a feature of the old rules, are not part of the 1995 scheme of things.

The most dramatic illustration, however, of the deregulation promoted by the 1995 Act is that it confers no security of tenure on a farm business tenant. He has no automatic right to renewal of his tenancy. One reason for the lack of security has been said to be that 'the farming industry today does not need protection but rather deregulation and competition'.[3]

There is thus a sharp contrast between the new rules and the right of the tenant of an agricultural holding within the old system to prevent, by service of a counter-notice, his landlord from terminating the tenancy by a general notice to quit. It is unlikely that any farm business tenant will enjoy a tenancy of the land for his life, or perhaps for any long period. The effects of the 1995 Act in relation to the length of tenancies and on farming practices remain to be seen, but it is possible that in relation to tenancies of 'bare land' these may lead to short terms and the adoption of farming practices to enable market rents to be paid, at the possible expense of the long-term interest of the land itself.[4]

The 1995 Act is not retrospective, and having regard to the exceptional cases in which a post 1 September 1995 tenancy of farm land may still be subject to the 1986 Act, the old rules may take some considerable time to die out.[5] There is nothing, however, to prevent the landlord of a sitting tenant within the 1986 Act to offer his tenant a new farm business tenancy, in return for the surrender of his previous tenancy: special deterrents against this type of replacement such as exist in the private residential sector were not deemed necessary, so emphasising the need for old-style tenants to be wary of offers of new land to be incorporated into their tenancy.

Two planks of the Act

The full-blown security of tenure provisions of the Agricultural Holdings Act 1986, combined with its succession provisions, were blamed by the government for a fall in the amount of tenanted agricultural land in England and Wales, so that by 1994, one of the Ministers sponsoring the then Bill thought that only about one-third of such land was at that time rented, and much of that under short-term, non-secure, tenancies.[6] Moreover, it was supposed that a farm tenant who diversified his initial farming business into other activities, during the tenancy, such as the provision of leisure facilities, might take the tenancy out of the protection of the new rules into that of Part II of the 1954 Act, and specific provision is made to cover this contingency, so as not to frustrate one of the

---

3   Sydenham and Mainwaring, p 5.

4   For these and other considerations see Bishop [1996] Conv 243; cf Gibbard and Ravenscroft, supra, para 6.4.

5   Moreover, to judge by their resistance during the passage of the legislation eg to the absence of security of tenure of a farm tenant's home, the Labour Party, if elected after the next general election, might wish to modify some aspects of the new rules.

6   Earl Howe, *Hansard*, 28 November 1994, Col 486, in second reading debate of the Agricultural Tenancies Bill.

main planks of the new Act. The Agricultural Tenancies Act 1995, passed with the agreement of the landlords' and tenants' representative organisations, creates a 'farm business tenancy'. The Act is not retrospective.[7] By s 2(1), a tenancy which begins before the commencement of the Act, on 1 September 1995, cannot be a farm business tenancy.

Main objectives and principles of Act

It appears convenient to provide a summary of the main objectives and principles of the Agricultural Tenancies Act 1995, as derived from its terms, before examining its terms in a little more detail.[8]

1　A principal aim is to get rid of the *security of tenure* apparatus applicable to lettings of agricultural holdings. Although the 1995 Act requires a farm business tenancy to be determined by a notice to quit by either party, the Act imposes merely formal requirements as to the form and duration of a notice to quit, which, if valid, takes effect in the same way as would any common law notice, to determine the tenancy. There is no automatic right to renewal of a farm business tenancy, once such a tenancy is validly ended by the landlord.

2　The 1995 Act precludes any *succession scheme* applying to a farm business tenancy. The attainment of this objective was simple enough, by precluding the 1986 Act rules from applying to most tenancies granted on or after 1 September 1995. The statutory double succession scheme had already been curtailed by the Agricultural Holdings Act 1986.

3　The *constitution of farm business tenancies* is provided for in specific rules. Following an exchange of notices at the beginning of the tenancy, the parties may enter into a tenancy which initially envisages the undertaking of farming activities for the purposes of a trade or business, but which also allows the tenant who continues to run parts of the land concerned as a farm, to also enter into major diversification away from agriculture, while ensuring that the tenancy does not cease to be a farm business tenancy for that reason alone.[9] The government believed that, without this safeguard for landlords, the tenant, by diversification, might risk bringing a tenancy which was originally a farm business tenancy within the 1995 Act into the (more stringent) protection of Part II of the 1954 Act, without the landlord's consent.[10]

4　The farm business tenancies legislation introduces a fresh statutory framework for *compensation to farm business tenants for improvements* carried out during the tenancy. This scheme was not thought of as being a 'rigid straitjacket', owing to the ability of a farm business tenant to diversify away from farming activities.[11] The new provisions seemingly provide for rapid compensation

---

7　It applies to land in which the Crown holds or has held an interest (s 37).
8　The new statutory right to remove tenants' fixtures is however discussed in ch 15.
9　As stated by the government spokesman in the House of Lords at the Committee Stage of the Agricultural Tenancies Bill, *Hansard*, 12 December 1994, col 1091.
10　If the parties do not exchange notices, a risk of the tenancy being subject to the 1954 Act, Part II was envisaged: *Hansard*, 12 December 1994, col 1090.
11　In the words of Earl Howe, *Hansard*, 13 December 1994, Col 1208.

to the tenant so that he is able to have the funds to start a new farming business after having to quit his former premises, seeing that he has no security of tenure under the Act. A novel feature of the rules is that the tenant may claim compensation in respect of his having obtained a planning permission which was not implemented during his tenancy (s 16). The basis of compensation is generally the increase attributable to the improvement in the value of the holding at the termination of the tenancy (s 20(1)), which in itself does not represent a break with the previous rules.

What is new is that instead of providing lists of matters for which the tenant may claim compensation, with or without the landlord's consent,[12] the 1995 Act imposes a general requirement that no compensation may be claimed unless the landlord has given his written consent to the making of an improvement. The government resisted an amendment which would have required the consent of the landlord not to be unreasonably withheld, because, it was said, a landlord of an agricultural tenant had a close personal interest in the land, its management and development.[13] The tenant is protected, however, by a new enabling provision which allows him to refer a refusal of consent or condition attached to a consent to arbitration.

5   The Act introduces altered statutory rules as to the *revision of rent payable under a farm business tenancy*, which rules may yield to the contrary intention of the parties, as where they provide in the tenancy for a fixed rent during the term. Subject to that, the rent may be reviewed in accordance with a formula, such as the retail Prices Index, or, if the parties so agree, at specified intervals. Either party has the right to refer a rent to arbitration under the general law – in contrast to the position under the 1986 Act, where arbitrations are within the umbrella of that Act.

II DEFINITION AND SCOPE OF 1995 ACT

Application of new rules

Part I of the Agricultural Tenancies Act 1995 establishes a farm business tenancy – a new form of tenancy where land is to be used for the purposes of agriculture.[14] The Agricultural Holdings Act 1986 does not apply to any tenancy beginning on or after 1 September 1995. Equally, the 1995 Act is not applicable to tenancies which began before 1 September 1995 (s 2(1)), which, if of an agricultural holding, may be governed by the Agricultural Holdings Act 1986. A tenancy at will and a genuine licence to occupy fall outside the 1995 Act.[15] There are a

---

12 Which method dates back at least to the Agricultural Holdings Act 1883, and was repeated in the Agricultural Holdings Acts 1923, 1948 and 1986.
13 Earl Howe, HL Committee, *Hansard*, 13 December 1994, col 1233; yet there seems, at first sight, a lack of complete consistency between this reason and the much-stressed ability of farm business tenants to diversify away from farming activities.
14 'Agriculture' is defined by s 38(1) of the 1995 Act, and is the same as that of s 96(1) of the 1986 Act.
15 Tenancies at will are excluded by s 38(1). There is no anti-avoidance provision corresponding to s 2(2)(b) of the 1986 Act but similar principles would presumably apply to the 1995 Act.

number of cases, specified where the 1986 Act applies to a tenancy of an agricultural holding created on or after 1 September 1995 (1995 Act, s 4). The principal exceptions are as follows.[16]

1. *Pre-Act contracts* The 1995 Act does not apply where a tenancy was granted by a written contract of tenancy entered into before 1 September 1995 which indicates that the 1986 Act is to apply to the tenancy (1995 Act s 4(1)(a)).[17] This exception might apply where, for some reason, the parties have contracted say in August 1994 for a tenancy under which possession is to be taken, and rent paid, only on or after 1 September 1995.

2. *Preservation of established successions* A number of related matters are here covered. Thus, where a tenancy was obtained by succession under the curtailed succession scheme by virtue of a direction of an Agricultural Land Tribunal under ss 39 or 53 of the 1986 Act (s 4(1)(b)), the 1995 Act does not apply to it.[18] This exemption applies, therefore, where a direction is made for a succession either in favour of a person eligible to succeed to a tenancy of an agricultural holding within the 1986 Act, or the person nominated by the tenant of such a holding applies for a Tribunal direction. It is also possible for the parties, in a written contract of tenancy entered into after the 1995 Act commences, to contract into the 1986 Act statutory succession rules, where the parties agree on the name of the successor (s 4(2)(d)).[19]

3. *Variation of 1986 Act tenancy* The aim of non-retrospectivity for farm business tenancies would have been at risk, where a tenancy of an agricultural holding to which the 1986 Act applied is varied after the commencement of the 1995 Act, owing to the common law principle that should an existing tenancy be varied by, notably, adding land to the holding, in consideration of an increased rent, the effect of this transaction is seemingly to surrender the existing tenancy and to re-grant a new tenancy.[20] Although s 4(1)(f) of the 1995 Act affirms this principle, it provides that the new tenancy is to be subject to the 1986 Act, provided that the tenant had been the tenant of the holding 'or of any agricultural holding which comprised the whole or a substantial part of the land comprised in the holding' under a tenancy to which the 1986 Act applied.[1]

---

16 See further Evans, loc cit, notes to s 4. It is said that the policy of s 4 is that 1986 Act tenancies should disappear as soon as possible.

17 Where an incoming tenant accepts a post-1 September 1995 tenancy of an agricultural holding as a result of the 'Evesham custom' (see ch 32) that tenancy is subject to the 1986 Act (s 4(1)(e)).

18 There is a related exception (s 4(1)(c)) where a direction is made to one of a number of joint tenants under s 39 of the 1986 Act.

19 This principle is subject to the limitations of s 4(2) so as to avoid overlapping with the remainder of the succession exceptions in s 4(1).

20 *Jenkin R Lewis v Kerman* [1971] Ch 477, as explained by Woodfall, 17.026.

1 However, the new tenancy will only be subject to the 1986 Act if the sole reason for an (implied) surrender and re-grant is the variation in the old tenancy; therefore there is nothing in s 4(1)(f) to preclude the parties to a tenancy of an agricultural holding from agreeing in express terms on the grant, after the commencement of the 1995 Act, of a farm business tenancy.

Definition of farm business tenancy

There are two types of farm business tenancy (s 1(1)). The 1995 Act leaves it to the parties to decide about the length of the tenancy – there is no upper or lower limit on duration. Both types of farm business tenancy are however subject to the 'business conditions'. However, if these conditions are satisfied, the tenancy[2] must either comply with the agriculture condition or the notice conditions. For reasons advanced, if the tenant wishes to diversify outside farming activities during the tenancy and the landlord wishes to protect himself, at the outset of the tenancy, against it ceasing to be subject to the 1995 Act and falling within, say, Part II of the Landlord and Tenant Act 1954, the notice conditions should be complied with.

Business conditions

The business conditions are as follows (s 1(2)):

(a) all or part of the land comprised in the tenancy must be farmed for the purposes of a trade or business, and
(b) since the beginning of the tenancy,[3] all or part of the land so comprised has been so farmed.

Although it appears from s 38(1) that references to the farming of land include references to the carrying on in relation to land of any agricultural activity, so referring back to the wide definition of 'agriculture' in s 38(1), the expression 'trade or business' is not defined in the 1995 Act. It is therefore thought that, at least at the beginning of the tenancy, the whole or part of the land must be farmed as a business. It may well be that to satisfy the business condition, it is not necessary for the same part of the holding always to have been farmed for the purposes of a trade or business: the overriding requirement is that some part of the holding is at all times used for commercial farming.[4]

The business conditions must be satisfied throughout the tenancy, so that, since the tenant is required to farm at least part of the land throughout for the purposes of a trade or business, he would cease to have a farm business tenancy if such farming discontinued completely.[5] It remains to be seen, where the 'notice condition' applies, how much diversification away from farming would be allowed – presumably the question would be one of fact and degree. If all farming activity ceased, the tenancy would fall within Part II of the Landlord and Tenant Act 1954.

---

2 Which expression includes a sub-tenancy and an agreement for a tenancy or sub-tenancy but not a tenancy at will (s 38(1)).
3 Ie since the day on which, under the terms of the tenancy, the tenant is entitled to possession under the tenancy (s 38(4)) and not, therefore, the date of the contract, if possession is postponed.
4 See Sydenham and Mainwaring, p 18.
5 Subject to s 1(7): if at the date of proceedings, for example, all or part of the land is farmed for the purposes of a trade or business, it is presumed that it had been so farmed since the beginning of the tenancy.

Agriculture condition

The agriculture condition is that the character of the tenancy must be 'primarily or wholly agricultural' having regard to:

(a) the terms of the tenancy;
(b) the use of the land comprised in the tenancy;
(c) the nature of any commercial activities carried on on the land; and
(d) any other relevant circumstances (s 1(3)).

Nevertheless, should the tenant of a farm business tenancy where the notices envisaged immediately below were not exchanged discontinue wholly or substantially all agricultural activities then, even if this is without the landlord's consent, the 1995 Act would cease to apply to the tenancy. However, the tenant is precluded by s 1(8) from claiming in breach of the terms of his tenancy, that he carries on only non-agricultural commercial activities on the land so as, for example, to bring the tenancy within the protection of Part II of the Landlord and Tenant Act 1954.

Notice conditions

If the notice conditions are complied with at the beginning of the tenancy[6] or the day on which the parties enter into any instrument creating the tenancy,[7] diversification from primary farming activities may safely take place, and the tenancy remains firmly within the 1995 Act. It has been said that parties ought ideally to comply with the notice conditions so as to avoid uncertainty about the nature of the tenancy.[8]

The landlord and tenant must give each other a written notice, which must be a separate notice: it is not sufficient if the terms of the tenancy incorporate it (s 1(6)).[9] The notices must be served in accordance with the 1995 Act (s 36) as by delivery to the party concerned,[10] though in the case of service on the landlord, service on any managing agent of his is sufficient (s 36(5)(a)).

The *contents* of the notice are as follows. The land to be comprised in the tenancy must be identified. The notice must state that the person giving the notice intends the tenancy to be and to remain a farm business tenancy (s 1(4)(a)). Moreover, at the beginning of the tenancy, having regard to the terms of the tenancy and to any other relevant circumstances, the tenancy must have a character which is primarily or wholly agricultural (s 1(4)(b)).

The tenant of a farm business tenancy where initial notices have been exchanged may diversify into non-farming business activities during the duration of his tenancy in principle, without a risk that the 1995 Act rules will

6　See s 38(1) above.
7　Other than an agreement to enter into a tenancy at a future date (s 1(5)(a)), so ruling out the creation of reversionary tenancies from the notice conditions but not the agriculture condition.
8　See Sydenham and Mainwaring, p 20.
9　In contrast to the position with, eg, an owner-occupier notice under an assured tenancy.
10　It is specifically provided that transmission by fax or other electronic means is not sufficient service of a notice (s 36(3)).

not apply, provided that the tenancy was initially wholly or mainly agricultural, and that he continues to farm part of the land for the purposes of his trade or business (s 1(2)(a)). However, such diversification must not be into activities in breach of the terms of the tenancy: if it is, then the tenancy ceases to be a farm business tenancy, on account of failure to comply with the 'business condition', unless the landlord or his predecessor consented to the breach or the landlord acquiesced in it (s 1(8)). Thus, if the tenant wishes to open a leisure park and this is prohibited by the terms of the tenancy, in principle the 1995 Act would cease to apply to him and the landlord could regain possession untrammelled by the Act, by common law means. It may also be presumed that where a tenant runs a business on the land in breach of a planning enforcement order, this could be relied on by the landlord as a breach of s 1(8), so entitling him to possession.

Where a fixed-term (but not a periodic) farm business tenancy is granted subject to the protection of the notice conditions, the landlord and tenant may subsequently vary the amount of land comprised in the tenancy, provided that any additions or subtractions are 'small in relation to the size of the holding and do not affect the character of the holding' without any need to serve fresh notices on each other (s 3(2)). Were it not for this provision, it might have been held that the previous tenancy had been surrendered and a new tenancy re-granted which would have entailed the service of fresh notices so as to preserve the advantages of allowing diversification out of farming activities.[11]

III TERMINATION PROVISIONS OF THE 1995 ACT

With the avowed aim of encouraging landlords to let more agricultural land, the 1995 Act does not confer any security of tenure on the tenant, save on an interim basis, after the expiry or termination of a farm business tenancy. However, the legislation does not allow either party to a farm business tenancy to bring it to an end merely by serving a notice to quit valid at common law on the other party. Instead, it continues fixed-term farm business tenancies for a term of more than two years as tenancies from year to year. The only way the landlord or tenant may prevent such continuation is by serving a notice of intention to terminate on the other party. In the case of a farm business tenancy from year to year, whether a periodic yearly tenancy or a continuing fixed-term tenancy for more than two years, the Act requires either party to give the other a notice to quit of at least twelve months before its stated termination date. These limited restrictions may be intended to allow the parties sufficient time either to negotiate a new tenancy or the tenant to find alternative accommodation and premises for his farm business and his family, if he lives on the premises.

Tenancies for more than two years

A farm business tenancy for a term of more than two years, but not for any shorter term, is subject to statutory continuation by s 5(1) of the 1995 Act.

11 According to the government at the Committee Stage of the Bill in the House of Lords: *Hansard*, 12 December 1994, col 1144.

Instead of terminating on its term date,[12] the tenancy continues from that date as a tenancy from year to year 'but otherwise on the terms of the original tenancy so far as applicable'. Either party has the right, under s 5(1), to prevent statutory continuation by a written notice to the other party of his intention to terminate the tenancy. A notice of intention must be given at least twelve but less than 24 months before the term date. The effect of a valid notice under s 5(1) is to terminate the farm business tenancy for a term of more than two years on the term date originally agreed, and to entitle the landlord to possession as from then, unless a new tenancy is agreed between the parties. Since, after a valid notice under s 5(1) has been given, there is no continuing tenancy from year to year, no separate notice to quit is seemingly required from the party serving the s 5(1) notice under s 6(1).

The statutory method of termination has effect notwithstanding 'any agreement to the contrary' (s 5(4)). This seemingly precludes the parties from agreeing, by either a term in the tenancy itself or a subsequent variation to it, to surrender a fixed-term farm business tenancy for two years or more by, say, a two months' notice. If either the landlord or tenant fails to serve a notice of intention to terminate within the prescribed time-limits before the term date, the tenancy will continue under s 6 of the 1995 Act.

The special position of a farm business tenancy for more than two years is re-enforced by s 7. By s 7(1) 'any notice to quit the holding or part ... given in pursuance of any provision of the tenancy ... shall be invalid unless it is in writing and is given at least twelve months but less than twenty-four months before the date on which it is to take effect'. This particular requirement overrides 'any provision to the contrary in the tenancy'.[13] This wording contrasts with the words 'any agreement to the contrary' in s 5(1) and might invite a narrow construction of them, so that the parties could, by a separate agreement to the tenancy provide for, say, a different length of notice to that laid down in s 7(1).[14]

Section 7(1) is presumably directed at landlords' or tenants' options to break the tenancy following a unilateral notice. Should such a notice be required by the terms of the tenancy to be served six months in advance, the terms of the tenancy would be disregarded. It may be that nothing in s 7(1) would prevent a landlord, in such a case, from serving a notice to determine under his break clause which gave the tenant the minimum twelve-month period of notice, if the only effect of the provision is to substitute a statutory period and form of notice for that agreed between the parties.

The relationship between sections 5(1) and 7(1) is not free from difficulty where the tenancy is for a fixed term of over two years. It is thought that, if, for example, the landlord serves a valid notice to break a fixed term tenancy for 10 years, expiring in December 2005, to expire in December 2000, the 'term date' of the tenancy is, for the purposes of s 5(1), December 2000, since the purpose

---

12 Ie the date fixed for the expiry of the term in the case of a fixed-term tenancy (s 5(2)).

13 Section 7(1) of the 1995 Act does not apply to a tenant's counter-notice under Law of Property Act 1925, s 149(2) (s 7(2) – and see below) nor to a tenancy caught by Law of Property Act 1925, s 149(6) (s 7(3)).

14 Cf also the wider language of s 38(1) of the Landlord and Tenant Act 1954, referring to contrary agreements the instrument creating the tenancy or not.

of s 7(1) is presumably to give the tenant a minimum period of notice which is of at least 12 months. The continuation provisions of the 1995 Act would seemingly, following the first part of s 5(1), apply, as would those of s 6(1). The landlord would seemingly need to serve a separate notice to quit on the tenant, complying with s 6(1), and expiring in December 2001, as his break clause notice ('to quit') could not be saved by s 6(2), discussed below, not being a notice of intention 'which complies with' s 5(1).

Length of notice to quit

A notice to quit by the landlord or the tenant of a farm business tenancy from year to year is subject to the limited protection conferred by s 6 of the 1995 Act. This imposes a minimum 12 month requirement on landlords' and tenants' notices to quit. These requirements apply 'notwithstanding any provision to the contrary in the tenancy'. A notice to quit the whole or part of the holding concerned will be invalid unless:

(a) it is in writing;
(b) it is to take effect at 'the end of a year of the tenancy'; and
(c) it is given at least twelve months but less than twenty-four months before the date on which it is to take effect.

Section 6(1) applies to periodic tenancies from year to year and to continuing fixed-term tenancies of over two years, as well as to fixed-term tenancies of up to two years. However, it is provided that where a landlord or tenant gives a valid notice of intention to terminate under s 5(1), in relation to a tenancy for a term of two years or more, provided it takes effect on the first anniversary of the term date, a notice to quit under s 6(1) is not invalid merely because it is given before the term date (s 6(2)). Thus, if L granted T a farm business tenancy on 1 January 1996 with a term date of 31 December 1999, he may decide to give T a notice of intention to terminate the tenancy in November 1998 (13 months before the term date, and so valid). L could at the same time, in November 1998, serve on T a notice to quit, complying with s 6(1), which takes effect on 31 December 1999, that date being the end of a year of the tenancy. The notice to quit would not be invalid because it was served during the term certain.

Where a tenant of a farm business tenancy receives a notice to quit part of the land, because the reversion has been severed as between two or more landlords, he has the specific right under Law of Property Act 1925, s 140(2) to give a one month notice to quit to the reversioner in relation to the rest of the land. Although the landlord's notice must comply with the minimum twelve-month requirement of s 6(1), a tenant's counter-notice under s 140(2) of the 1925 Act is saved by s 6(3) from having to do so.

IV RENT REVIEW PROVISIONS

Part II of the Agricultural Tenancies Act 1995 provides for the review of the rent of a farm business tenancy. However, the parties are free to fix the initial rent for the tenancy at any level they like.

The statutory provisions may be contracted out of by the parties, but only in three cases. First, where the terms of the tenancy expressly state that there is to be no review of rent during the tenancy (s 9(a)) but the rent is otherwise to remain fixed, as where it is reserved throughout. The second case where the statutory provisions do not apply is where, although the rent is, apart from any review, to remain fixed, the tenancy allows for the variation of rent at a specified time or times during the tenancy by or to a specified amount (s 9(b)(i)). The third case is where, again subject to the rent otherwise remaining fixed, there is to be a rent review in accordance with a specified formula which is not upwards only ('does not preclude a reduction') and which does not require or permit the 'exercise by any person of any judgment or discretion in relation to the determination of the rent of the holding' (s 9(b)(ii)). Thus a rent review formula, requiring the parties to agree on an open market rent, to a level which may be above or below the current level of rent, but which does not envisage any arbitration or determination by an expert, would seemingly operate to the exclusion of the statutory rules. By contrast, a formula which required the agreement of the parties to an increase only in the rent would not be excepted, and this provision of the 1995 Act is the first known manifestation of some legislative hostility to upwards-only rent review clauses.

Arbitration notices

The statutory machinery operates by entitling the landlord or the tenant to refer the rent to arbitration at regular intervals. Accordingly, both the landlord and tenant of a farm business tenancy may give a notice in writing to the other (called a 'statutory review notice') which requires that the rent payable for the holding is referred to arbitration under the 1995 Act (s 10(1)). This provision overrides any agreement to the contrary (s 9). The new rent is to be paid as from the 'review date', but specific provisions are made as to this date, so governing the minimum life of a rent review.

The review date must, in any case, be at least 12 months but less than 24 months from the date of giving of the 'statutory review notice' (s 10(3)). The terms of the tenancy itself, if they provide for shorter periods, are overridden. Moreover, so giving primacy to the agreement of the parties, if they have agreed in writing (seemingly in the tenancy or by separate agreement) that the rent is to be varied as from a specified date or dates, or at specified intervals, the review date must be a date as from which the rent could be varied under the agreement (s 10(4)).[15] Subject to this, the date as from which the new rent is payable, the review date, must:

(a) must be an anniversary of the beginning of the tenancy,[16] or some other day of the year as agreed between the landlord and tenant, and

15 Likewise, if the parties have agreed in writing that the statutory review date is to be a specified date or dates, the review date must be one of those dates (s 10(5)).
16 Where the tenant takes a new tenancy of part of the holding from a landlord of a split reversion, the expression 'beginning of the tenancy' refers to the original tenancy until the first occasion following the beginning of the new tenancy that an arbitration etc under s 10 takes effect (s 11). Thus, if L1 grants T a tenancy for 10 years in 1996 and T is granted a new tenancy of a smaller holding by L2, who holds part of the freehold, in 1998, T cannot seemingly avoid a rent reference in 1999.

(b) must be not before the end of three years beginning with the latest of four dates, notably, the beginning of the tenancy, or any date as from which a previous direction of an arbitrator as to the amount of the rent took effect (s 10(6)).[17]

Where, therefore, the parties to a farm business tenancy of substantial length have agreed that the rent is to be reviewed at five-yearly intervals, this agreement prevails and no reference to arbitration under the Act may be made by either party at shorter intervals. Although the interval between reviews which applies in the absence of agreement for statutory purposes is three years, there is nothing in the Act to prevent the parties from agreeing on shorter intervals, even annually.

Arbitrations – further

Once a statutory review notice has been given under the 1995 Act, the parties may agree on the new rent or, failing agreement, may appoint an arbitrator, but, if within six months ending with the review date, they cannot agree even on a name, either party has the right under s 12 to apply to the President of the RICS for the appointment of an arbitrator. Where the parties have agreed that the new rent is to be decided on some other basis, as by an expert, but that person has not been appointed within the six months already mentioned, the same default provision applies, and either party may apply for the appointment of an arbitrator to the President of the RICS.

The amount of the rent referred to an arbitration is to be determined in accordance with s 13. The government's stated policy was to avoid the prescriptive approach of the 1986 Act.[18] The policy of these provisions of the Act is seemingly to allow the rent for a farm business tenancy to reflect the law of supply and demand.[19] The new rent is payable as at the review date, and the arbitrator must determine what rent is properly payable in respect of the holding. He may increase or reduce the rent previously payable or direct that it is to continue unchanged (s 13(1)).

The arbitrator must ascertain the rent 'at which the holding might reasonably be expected to be let on the open market by a willing landlord to a willing tenant' taking into account all relevant factors, including in every case the terms of the tenancy (s 13(2)). While the arbitrator is entitled to have regard to the intervals agreed between reviews, he is to disregard the criteria for the determination of any new rent. Any effect of the fact of the occupation of the tenant who is a party to the arbitration on the rent is to be disregarded (s 13(4)(a)). Thus, any effect of the occupation of his predecessor in title under the current or even a previous tenancy might be taken into account.

17 By s 10(6) of the 1995 Act, the other dates are (i) the date as from which a previous determination of rent took effect, where made by a person appointed under an agreement of the parties who was not an arbitrator, but was, eg, an expert and (ii) the date of a previous written agreement between the parties, since the beginning of the tenancy, as to the amount of the rent.
18 *Hansard*, HL Committee on the Agricultural Tenancies Bill, 12 December 1994, col 1188.
19 Sydenham and Mainwaring, p 45 (as opposed, it appears, to any profits made by the tenant from the land).

So as not to give the tenant the benefit of his own wrongdoing, the rent is not to be fixed at a lower amount by dilapidation or deterioration of, or damage to, buildings or land caused or permitted by the tenant (s 13(4)(b)). The words 'caused or permitted' not only seem to apply to deliberate breaches of repairing covenant, but to neglect amounting to waste. There again being no reference to the tenant's predecessor in title under the current or a previous tenancy, it could be argued that any effect on rent of dilapidations due to such predecessor's fault could be taken into account – unless the tenant is subject not only to an obligation to repair but to put or to keep in repair.

Disregard of tenant's improvements

So as to protect the tenant against having to pay a new rent inflated by his own improvements which have a lasting value, any increase in the rental value of the holding which is due to tenants' improvements[20] is to be disregarded (s 13(3)). However, the following increases owing to such improvements are not to be disregarded, because the tenant is presumed to have been adequately compensated already for these.

(a) Any tenant's improvement provided under an obligation imposed on the tenant by the terms of his present or any previous tenancy, and which arose on or before the beginning of the tenancy in question;
(b) Any tenant's improvement to the extent that any allowance or benefit has been made or given by the landlord in consideration of its being provided; and
(c) Any tenant's improvement to the extent that the tenant has received any compensation from the landlord for the improvement.

Increases in value resulting from improvements of a predecessor in title fall outside s 13(3) and 15, and so may, if their effect is not spent, presumably be taken into account, unless the parties otherwise agree.

Comparison with previous rules

The rules for rent review under the 1995 Act are largely a break with the previous system. Those applying to farm business tenancies envisage an arbitration under the general law as the principal dispute resolution. The fact that the 1995 Act allows the parties' agreement as to the intervals of rent review to prevail over the statutory three-year intervals, which are provided in default, is new: the previous principle was that there should be three-year reviews. A further novelty of the 1995 Act is that it enables the parties, by agreement, to have their dispute as to a reviewed rent referred to an expert, rather than to an arbitrator. However, one party cannot refuse to agree to such a reference without risking the other from invoking the statutory default provision for reference to an arbitrator. Although the parties are thus free to agree as to the machinery of a rent review, neither of them can avoid a rent review itself taking place if the other requires it to do so. The fact that the new formula does not require in terms that the character,

---

20 The definition of 'tenant's improvement' in s 15, below, applies (s 13(5)).

situation and locality of the holding, nor its produce or related earnings capacity – in contrast to the requirements of the 1986 Act – be taken into account is a result of the flexible approach of the Act, so as to make the tenant pay a market rent no matter what his profits or lack of them may amount to.

V   COMPENSATION FOR TENANTS' IMPROVEMENTS

Introduction

Part III of the 1995 Act provides for a fresh set of rules governing compensation payable by the landlord to the tenant of an oral or written farm business tenancy, on the tenant quitting the holding. The general policy of these provisions is seemingly two-fold. The aim of Part III was said to be to compensate tenants quickly for any useful improvements to incoming new tenants, thus putting them in funds with which to establish a new business, and to provide for the rapid resolution of any disputes. The tenant has, accordingly, only four months from the date of his request for the landlord's consent within which to seek arbitration (s 19(3)). The landlord's position is protected to some extent by the fact that compensation is only payable for relevant improvements for which the landlord's written consent[1] has been given (s 17).[2]

The second strand of policy is that, since the Act was said by the government to allow for diversification away from traditional farming, it was essential not to attempt to prescribe a legal straitjacket of permitted improvements, requiring further amendment in time.[3] This, and the argument that one could not predict in advance which improvements a diversifying tenant might make,[4] may explain why lists of permitted improvements (which have appeared since at least 1883) are not present in the 1995 Act. Moreover, which is new, the obtaining of an unimplemented planning permission by a farm business tenant counts as a tenants' improvement qualifying for compensation within Part III. If, however, the tenant has implemented a planning permission, this form of compensation is not available, seemingly because the tenant would be able to claim, where relevant, compensation for any improvements made to the holding as a result.[5]

Definition of tenant's improvement and amount of compensation

The tenant of a farm business tenancy is entitled to claim compensation under Part III of the 1995 Act in respect of any tenant's improvement. Claims

---

1   Written consent was said by the government spokesman in the HL Committee to be required to ensure that there was evidence at the time of assessment of compensation that the tenant was entitled to claim it (*Hansard*, 13 December 1994, col 1219) – a point of obvious importance where the reversion has changed hands since the giving of consent.
2   The government resisted an attempt to make such consent subject to a test of reasonableness on the ground of the special character of agricultural tenancies: *Hansard*, HL Committee, 13 December 1994, col 1223.
3   HL Committee, supra, col 1208.
4   See Sydenham and Mainwairing, p 67.
5   HL Committee, *Hansard*, 13 December 1994, col 1232.

for compensation are to be settled by arbitration (s 22(1)) although the parties may avert this by settling the claim by agreement in writing.[6] A tenant's right arises on the termination of his tenancy, when he quits the holding, and the landlord[7] pays the compensation (s 16(1)). However, there are certain absolute bars to compensation, notably, where the tenant removes any physical improvement, notably a fixture, under s 8 of the Act (as to which, see chapter 15). No compensation is payable for improvements which do not have the landlord's prior consent, and the tenant has only a two month period from the termination of the tenancy in which to claim compensation, failing which, his right is lost (s 22(2)).

Section 15 of the 1995 Act gives a wide definition of 'tenant's improvement'. Two types of improvement qualify for compensation:[8]

(a) Any physical improvement made on the holding by the tenant by his own effort or wholly or partly[9] at his own expense, or
(b) any 'intangible advantage' obtained for the holding by the tenant by his own effort or wholly or partly at his own expense, which becomes attached to the holding.

The first limb of this provision would cover permanent improvements to the holding, such as the erection of a new building or the installation of equipment which the tenant does not or cannot remove on expiry of the tenancy. Paragraph (b) is designed to cover planning permissions obtained by the tenant but not implemented by him, which will benefit his successor in title or the landlord, as well as compensation for loss of EU milk or other production quotas.

So as to prevent the landlord from having to pay a large amount of compensation for an improvement which, say because it was specially suited for the particular outgoing tenant's needs, might be of little value to an incoming tenant, the amount of compensation for a tenant's improvement, other than one consisting of planning permission, is the amount equal to the 'increase in value attributable to the improvement in the value of the holding at the termination of the tenancy' (s 20(1)). However, if the tenant has, by written agreement with the landlord, received a benefit in consideration of the improvement, such as a premium, there is to be a proportionate reduction in any compensation payable (s 20(2)). In the case of an improvement consisting of planning permission, the amount of compensation is the amount equal to the increase 'attributable to the fact that the relevant development is authorised by the planning permission in the value of the holding at the termination of the tenancy' (s 21(1)).

6 Which must not provide for compensation in a manner not in accordance with Part III (s 26(1)).
7 The policy of preserving full compensation is shown by the fact that where the reversionary estate is vested in more than one landlord, the tenant is entitled to compensation as if the estate were not severed (s 25(1)) but the amount of any compensation payable may be apportioned by the arbitrator as between the different landlords (s 25(2)).
8 Compensation for 'routine improvements' (tenant-right matters such as growing crops, acts of husbandry and so on) is provided for in s 19(10). The tenant may apply for compensation in this case even without the landlord's prior consent (s 19(9)).
9 So as not to overcompensate a tenant, where he has received a grant out of public money for an improvement, the amount of any compensation is proportionately reduced (s 20(3)).

In view of the stated importance of the right to compensation at the termination of a farm business tenancy to a tenant, specific provisions preserve the tenant's right to claim compensation. So, the fact that the tenant may have remained in the holding during two (or more) farm business tenancies does not deprive him of his right to compensation in relation to an improvement he carried out during an earlier tenancy (s 23(1)). The parties may, however agree on the payment of compensation on the termination of the relevant earlier tenancy (s 23(2)).[10] Equally, where, following a severance of the reversion and the resumption of possession of part of the holding by the landlord of part, the tenant's right to claim compensation in relation to the part he quits is triggered as at that time (s 24). The affected part of the holding is treated as if it were a separate holding.

Requirement of landlord's consent

The tenant is only able to claim compensation for an improvement (of any kind) where the landlord[11] has given his consent in writing to the provision of the improvement (s 17(1)). The tenant must not have commenced the improvement before he seeks consent – or he loses any right to compensation – unless the improvement is a 'routine improvement'. Consent may be given unconditionally or on condition that the tenant agrees to a specified variation in the terms of the tenancy (s 17(3)). The consent may be given in the instrument creating the tenancy – as where the tenant undertakes to make certain improvement – or elsewhere, as in a landlord's letter (s 17(2)).

However, where the improvement consists of a planning permission, a specific rule applies. The landlord must have given his consent in writing to the making of the application (s 18(1)). If that consent is refused, the tenant obtains no right to compensation (s 19(1)). Otherwise, the tenant might presumably make an application for a change of use which might be inconsistent with the landlord's interests.

There is no requirement that the landlord is not to refuse his consent unreasonably, for reasons mentioned earlier. However, as a counterpart to this, if, except in the case of planning permission applications, the tenant is aggrieved by a refusal of consent, he may give a written notice to the landlord which demands that the question is referred to an arbitration (s 19(1)). He may also serve such a notice where the landlord fails to give consent within two months of a written request by the tenant for consent, or where he objects to a variation in the terms of the tenancy – such as a rent increase – required by the landlord as a condition of consent.

So as to promote speed of dispute resolution, the tenant must give notice referring a landlord's refusal of consent or disputed variation within two months beginning with the day the landlord gives him notice (s 19(3)). In the case of a failure of the landlord to give consent following a tenant's request, the

10 Such agreement does not, in terms, have to be in writing but s 23(3) precludes the tenant in such a case from claiming any further compensation at the termination of his last tenancy.
11 'Landlord' for this and any purpose under the 1995 Act includes a person holding a leasehold estate or a limited owner, such as a tenant for life (s 32).

tenant must give his arbitration notice within four months beginning with the day he gave his request to the landlord (s 19(3)).[12]

Arbitrations as to compensation

Arbitrations over compensation fall into two classes, those which relate to disputes about landlords' consents, and those relating to the amount of compensation itself. Regarding the first of these categories, the arbitrator has a general power to consider whether, having regard to the terms of the tenancy and any other relevant factors, it is reasonable for the tenant to provide the improvement (s 19(5), but his powers are balanced against the policy of giving weight to the landlord's wishes while not allowing the tenant's compensation to be diminished. Thus, in particular, although an arbitrator has the power unconditionally to approve the provision of an improvement, he cannot make his approval subject to any condition, otherwise the amount of compensation could be reduced[13] and he has no power to vary any condition required by the landlord (s 19(6)).

As far as arbitrations over the amount of compensation are concerned, where the parties cannot settle the claim by a written agreement, and the tenant has claimed compensation before the end of two months as from the date of termination of the tenancy (s 22(2)) either party has the right, within four months from the termination date of the tenancy, to apply to the President of the RICS to appoint an arbitrator (s 22(3)). No doubt the arbitrator, in assessing the amount of compensation, is mainly concerned to find the amount of the increase in the value of the holding attributable to the improvement at the termination of the tenancy, as required by s 20(1)).

VI MISCELLANEOUS PROVISIONS

There is a role assigned by the 1995 Act to arbitrations and the provision made for an alternative means of dispute resolution. There is an important, but not exclusive, role to arbitrations.[14] Any arbitrations are to be under the general law and not, as is the case under the 1986 Act, pursuant to a specific set of rules applicable to agricultural holdings alone.

In disputes not concerned with statutory rent reviews, consents to improvements or compensation claims, all of which have specific rules, s 28(1) of the 1995 Act provides that any dispute other than in these three matters

---

12 It is envisaged that, to prevent the landlord frustrating the compensation provisions, following a tenant's arbitration notice, the parties may reach an agreement, but if not, the tenant may apply to the President of the RICS for the appointment of an arbitrator (s 19(4)).

13 This result, if permitted, would, in the government view, run against the key provision in the Act of full compensation: HL Committee, *Hansard*, 13 December 1994, col 1235.

14 This is because provision is made in s 29 for joint references to a third party who is not an arbitrator, where the tenancy agreement expressly provides for this method of dispute resolution. However, as a safeguard, if only one party makes a reference the other has a four-week period in which to refer the dispute to arbitration.

which concerns the rights and obligations of the parties under the Act is to be determined by arbitration.[15] Where a dispute of this kind has arisen, the landlord or tenant may give a written notice to the other specifying the dispute and stating that unless the parties have appointed an arbitrator by agreement, he proposes to apply to the President of the RICS to appoint an arbitrator (s 28(2)). Although s 28(2) requires that two months must elapse from the date of giving the notice before any such application is made, no time-limit is imposed by s 28(3) for the making of the application to the President of the RICS. The application must be in writing (s 30(2)).

15 The provisions of s 30 apply.

Appendix

[Precedents 1 and 2 below are reproduced with the kind permission of the Law Society, who hold the copyright in the documents. The latest versions of both leases were published in 1996.]

Precedent No 1

Law Society Business Lease (Whole of Building)

Date

Landlord

of

Lets to

Tenant

of

The property known as

Property

Residential Accommodation

[Which includes   ]

For the period starting on

Lease Period

And Ending on

For use (except any residential accommodation) as

Use Allowed

Or any other use to which the Landlord consents (and the Landlord is not entitled to withhold that consent unreasonably) The Tenant paying the Landlord rent at the rate of

Rent

  Pounds

                    (£   )

                    A year by these instalments:

                    (A) on the date of this lease, a proportionate sum for
                    the period starting on

                                                                        to

                                                            and then

                    (B) equal monthly instalments in advance on the Rent
                    days

                                                    Day of each month

Rent Review dates

                    the rent may be increased (under clause 8) with effect
                    from every Anniversary of the start of the lease period

Tenant's Obligations

1.   Payments

1. The tenant is to pay the Landlord:

1.1   The rent

1.2   the amount of every premium which the Landlord pays to insure the
      property under this lease, to be paid within 14 days after the Landlord
      gives written notice of payment (and this amount is to be paid as rent)

and the following sums on demand:

1.3   a fair proportion (decided by a surveyor the Landlord nominates) of the
      cost of repairing maintaining and cleaning:

      party walls, party structures, yards, gardens, roads, paths, gutters, drains,
      sewers, pipes, conduits, wires, cables and things used or shared with other
      property

1.4   the cost (including professional fees) of any works to the property which
      the Landlord does after the Tenant defaults

1.5   the cost and expenses (including professional fees) which the Landlord
      incurs in:
      (a)   dealing with any application by the Tenant for consent or approval,
            whether or not it is given

(b) preparing and serving a notice of a breach of the Tenant's obligations, under section 146 of the Law of Property Act 1925, even if forfeiture of this lease is avoided without a court order

(c) preparing and serving schedules of dilapidations either during the lease period or recording failure to give up the property in the appropriate state or repair when this lease ends

1.6 interest at the Law Society's interest rate on any of the above payments when more than fourteen days overdue, to be calculated from its due date

and in making payment under this clause:

(a) nothing is to be deducted or set off

(b) any value added tax payable is to be added.

2. The tenant is also to make the following payments, with value added tax where payable:

2.1 all periodic rates, taxes and outgoings relating to the property, including any imposed after the date of this lease (even if of a novel nature), to be paid promptly to the authorities to whom they are due

2.2 the cost of the grant, renewal or continuation of any licence or registration for using the property for the use allowed, to be paid promptly to the appropriate authority when due

2.3 a registration fee of £20 for each document which this lease required the Tenant to register, to be paid to the Landlord's solicitors when presenting the document for registration

3. **Use**

3. The Tenant is to comply with the following requirements as to the use of the property and any part of it and is not to authorise or allow anyone else to contravene them:

3.1 to use the property, except any residential accommodation, only for the used allowed

3.2 to use any residential accommodation only as a home for one family

3.3 not to do anything which might invalidate any insurance policy covering the property or which might increase the premium

3.4 not to hold an auction sale in the property

3.5 not to use the property for any activities which are dangerous, offensive, noxious, illegal or immoral, or which are or may become a nuisance or annoyance to the Landlord or to the owner or occupier of any neighbouring property

3.6   not to display any advertisement on the outside of the property or which are visible from the outside unless the Landlord consents (and the Landlord is not entitled to withhold that consent unreasonably)

3.7   not to overload the floors or walls of the property

3.8   to comply with the terms of every Act of Parliament, order, regulation, bye-law, rule, licence and registration authorising or regulating how the property is used, and to obtain, renew and continue any licence or registration which is required.

4. Access

4.   The Tenant is to give the Landlord, or anyone authorised by him in writing, access to the property:

4.1   for these purposes:
   (a)   inspecting the condition of the property, or how it is being used
   (b)   doing works which the Landlord is permitted to do under clause 5.8(c)
   (c)   complying with any statutory obligation
   (d)   viewing the property as a prospective buyer or mortgagee or, during the last six months of the lease period, as a prospective tenant
   (e)   valuing the property
   (f)   inspecting, cleaning or repairing neighbouring property, or any sewers, drains, pipes, wires, cables serving neighbouring property

4.2   and only on seven days' written notice except in an emergency

4.3   and during normal business hours except in an emergency

4.4   and the Landlord is promptly to make good all damage caused to the property and any goods there in exercising these rights.

5. Condition and Work

5.   The Tenant is to comply with the following duties in relation to the property:

5.1   to maintain the state and condition of the property but the Tenant need not alter or improve it except if required under clause 5.7

5.2   to decorate the inside and outside of the property:
   (a)   in every fifth year of the lease period
   (b)   in the last three months of the lease period (however it ends) except to the extent that it has been decorated in the previous year
and on each occasion the Tenant is to use the colours and the types of finish used previously

5.3 but the Tenant need only make good damage caused by an insured risk to the extent that the insurance money has not been paid because of any act or default of the Tenant

5.4 not to make any structural alterations, external alterations or additions to the property

5.5 not to make any other alterations unless with the Landlord's consent in writing (and the Landlord is not entitled to withhold that consent unreasonably)

5.6 to keep any plate glass in the property insured for its full replacement cost with reputable insurers, to give the Landlord details of that insurance on request, and to replace any plate glass which becomes damaged

5.7 to do the work to the property which any authority acting under an Act of Parliament requires, even if it alters or improves the property. Before the Tenant does so, the Landlord is to:
   (a) give his consent in writing to the work
   (b) contribute a fair proportion of the cost of the work taking into account any value to him of the work

5.8 if the Tenant fails to do any work which this lease requires him to do and the Landlord gives him written notice to do it, the Tenant is to:
   (a) start the work within two months, or immediately in case of emergency, and
   (b) proceed diligently with the work
   (c) in default, permit the Landlord to do the work

5.9 any dispute arising under clause 5.7(b) is to be decided by arbitration under clause 14.5

6 Transfer etc.

6. The Tenant is to comply with the following:

6.1 the Tenant is not to share occupation of the property and no part of it is to be transferred, sublet or occupied separately from the remainder

6.2 the Tenant is not to transfer or sublet the whole of the property unless the Landlord gives his written consent in advance, and the Landlord is not entitled to withhold that consent unreasonably

6.3 any sublease is to be in terms which are consistent with this lease, but is not to permit the sub-tenant to underlet

6.4 within four weeks after the property is transferred mortgaged or sublet, the Landlord's solicitors are to be notified and a copy of the transfer mortgage or sublease sent to them for registration with the fee payable under clause 2.3

6.5 if the Landlord requires, a tenant who transfers the whole of the property is to give the Landlord a written guarantee, in the terms set out in the Guarantee Box, that the Transferee will perform his obligations as Tenant

7 Other matters

7. The Tenant:

7.1 is to give the Landlord a copy of any notice concerning the property or any neighbouring property as soon as he receives it

7.2 is to allow the Landlord, during the last six months of the lease period, to fix a notice in a reasonable position on the outside of the property announcing that it is for sale or to let

7.3 is not to apply for planning permission relating to the use or alteration of the property unless the Landlord gives written consent in advance

8. Rent Review

8.1 On each rent review date, the rent is to increase to the market rent if that is higher than the rent applying before that date

8.2 The market rent is the rent which a willing tenant would pay for the property on the open market, if let to him on the rent review date by a willing landlord on a lease on the same terms as this lease without any premium and for a period equal to the remainder of the lease period, assuming that at the date:
  (a) the willing tenant takes account of any likelihood that he would be entitled to a new lease of the property when the lease ends, but does not take account of any goodwill belonging to anyone who had occupied the property
  (b) the property is vacant and had not been occupied by the Tenant or any sub-tenant
  (c) the property can immediately be used
  (d) the property is in the condition required by this lease and any damage caused by any of risks insured under clause 11 has been made good
  (e) during the lease period no tenant nor sub-tenant has done anything to the property to increase or decrease its rental value and "anything" includes work done by the Tenant to comply with clause 5.7, but nothing else which the Tenant was obliged to do under this lease

8.3 If the Landlord and the Tenant agree the amount of the new rent, a statement of that new rent, signed by them, is to be attached to this lease

8.4 If the landlord and the Tenant have not agreed the amount of the new rent two months before the rent review date, either of them may require the new rent to be decided by arbitration under clause 14.5

8.5 (a) The Tenant is to continue to pay rent at the rate applying before the rent review date until the next rent day after the new rent is agreed or decided

    (b) Starting on that rent day, the Tenant is to pay the new rent

    (c) On that rent day, the Tenant is also to pay any amount by which the new rent since the rent review date exceeds the rent paid, with interest on that amount at 2% below the Law Society's interest rate.

9. Damage

9. If the property is damaged by any of the risks to be insured under clause 11 and as a result of that damage the property, or any part of it, cannot be used for the use allowed:

9.1 the rent, or a fair proportion of it, is to be suspended for three years or until the property is fully restored, if sooner

9.2 if at any time it is unlikely that the property will be fully restored within three years from the date of the damage, the Landlord (so long as he has not delayed the restoration) or the Tenant can end this lease by giving one month's notice to the other during the three year period, in which case

    (a) the insurance money belongs to the Landlord and

    (b) the Landlord's obligation to make good damage under clause 11 ceases

9.3 a notice given outside the time limits in clause 9.2 is not effective

9.4 the Tenant cannot claim the benefit of this clause to the extent that the insurers refuse to pay the insurance money because of his act or default

9.5 any dispute arising under any part of this clause is to be decided by arbitration under clause 14.5

Landlord' Obligations and Forfeiture Rights

Quiet Enjoyment

10. While the Tenant complies with the terms of this lease, the Landlord is to allow the Tenant to possess and use the property without lawful interference from the Landlord or any trustee for the Landlord

Insurance

11. The Landlord agrees with the Tenant:

11.1 the Landlord is to keep the property (except the plate glass) insured with reputable insurers to cover:
   (a)   full rebuilding, site clearance, professional fees, value added tax and three years' loss of rent
   (b)   against fire, lighting, explosion, earthquake, landslip, subsidence, heave, riot, civil commotion, aircraft, aerial devices, storm, flood, water, theft, impact by vehicles, damage by malicious persons and vandals and third party liability and any other risks reasonably required by the Landlord so far as cover is available at the normal insurance rates for the locality and subject to reasonable excesses and exclusions

11.2 and to take all necessary steps to make good as soon as possible damage to the property caused by insured risks except to the extent that the insurance money is not paid because of the act or default of the tenant

11.3 and to give the Tenant at his request once a year particulars of the policy and evidence from the insurer that it is in force

11.4 and that the Tenant is not responsible for any damage for which the Landlord is compensated under the insurance policy

Forfeiture

12   This lease comes to an end if the Landlord forfeits it by entering any part of the property, which the Landlord is entitled to do whenever:
   (a)   payment of any rent is fourteen days overdue, even if it was not formally demanded
   (b)   the Tenant has not complied with any of the terms in this lease
   (c)   the Tenant if any individual (and if more than one, any of them) is adjudicated bankrupt or an interim receiver of his property is appointed
   (d)   the Tenant if a company (and if more than one, any of them) goes into liquidation (unless solely for the purpose of amalgamation or reconstruction when solvent), or has an administrative receiver appointed or has an administration order made in respect of it

The forfeiture of this lease does not cancel any outstanding obligation of the Tenant or a Guarantor

End of Lease

13   When this lease ends the Tenant is to:

13.1 return the property to the Landlord leaving it in the state and condition in which this lease required the Tenant to keep it

13.2 (if the Landlord so requires) remove anything the Tenant fixed to the property and make good any damage which that causes.

General

14 Parties' Responsibility

14.1 Whenever more than one person or company is the Landlord, the Tenant or the Guarantor, their obligations can be enforced against all or both of them jointly and against each individually

Landlord

14.2 (a) The obligations in this lease continue to apply to the Landlord until he is released by the Tenant or by a declaration of the court

(b) The current owner of the Landlord's interest in the property must comply with the Landlord's obligations in this lease

Tenant

14.3 (a) A transfer of this lease releases the Tenant from any future obligations under it. This does not apply in the case of a transfer made without the Landlord's consent or as a result of the Tenant's death or bankruptcy

(b) After a transfer, the Tenant's successor must comply with the Tenant's obligations in this lease

Service of Notices

14.4 The rules about serving notices in Section 196 of the Law of Property Act 1925 (as since amended) apply to any notice given under this lease

Arbitration

14.5 Any matter which this lease requires to be decided by arbitration is to be referred to a single arbitrator under the Arbitration Acts. The Landlord and the Tenant may agree the appointment of the arbitrator, or either of them may apply to the President of the Royal Institution of Chartered Surveyors to make the appointment.

Headings

14.6 The headings do not form part of this lease

Stamp Duty

15. This lease has not been granted to implement an agreement for a lease

Signed as a deed by/on behalf of the Landlord and delivered in the presence of:

....

Witness

....
Witness's occupation and address

Signed as a deed by/on behalf of the Tenant and delivered in the presence of:

....
Witness

....
Witness's occupation and address

GUARANTEE BOX

The terms in this box only take effect if a guarantor is named and then only until the Tenant transfers this lease with the Landlord's written consent. The Guarantor must sign this lease.

'Guarantor':

of

agrees to compensate the Landlord for any loss incurred as a result of the Tenant failing to comply with an obligation in this lease during the lease period or any statutory extension of it. If the Tenant is insolvent and this lease ends because it is disclaimed, the Guarantor agrees to accept a new lease, if the Landlord so requires, in the same form but at the rent then payable. Even if the Landlord gives the Tenant extra time to comply with an obligation, or does not insist on strict compliance with terms of this lease, the Guarantor's obligation remains fully effective.

THIS DOCUMENT CREATES LEGAL RIGHTS AND LEGAL OBLIGATIONS. DO NOT SIGN IT UNTIL YOU HAVE CONSULTED A SOLICITOR. THERE IS A CODE OF PRACTICE CONCERNING COMMERCIAL LEASES IN ENGLAND AND WALES PUBLISHED UNDER THE AUSPICES OF THE DEPARTMENT OF THE ENVIRONMENT.

....
Landlord

....
Tenant

....
Guarantor

<u>Notes</u> - At the end of the above lease, there is a reference to the Code of Practice concerning commercial leases in England and Wales. This Code was published at the end of 1995. The government, in a Department of the Environment Press Release of 14 December 1995, have stated that one aim of the Code is to encourage flexibility in lease negotiations and greater transparancy. The "promulgation" of this Code is but one aspect of what has been called an "age of encouragement" (JE Adams [1996] Conv 241) such as the Property Managers' Association's Guide on Service Charges in Commercial Properties of 1994. The difficulty is of course that, rather like Revenue Extra Statutory Concessions, the present Code is not legally binding and the sanctions for its disregard seem solely moral.

The Code explains the basic terms of commercial leases such as those relating to repairs and service charges. It says that the parties should be told about the existence of the Code at the beginning of negotiations. It also examines some of the risks of certain clauses, such as upwards-only rent review clauses as well as the risks undertaken by guarantors. In addition, it encourages what it regards as being good practice. There are statements about the role of the legal advisor. The terms and conditions of a lease ought to be explained to clients before they sign. If there are disputes, the parties are encouraged to settle these by agreement. If a client has special requirements, then the wording of the lease ought to correspond as closely as possible to these; and if not, the client should be given an explanation of the consequences. The Code is to be reviewed, once it has been in operation for three years. If it is thought to fail - and there may be no certain or reliable way of knowing this- the question might arise whether legislation would be considered to remedy any perceived ills not cured as a result of the Code - such as upwards-only rent review clauses. However, the existence of the Code has been invoked by the government in a Consultation Paper published in mid-1996 by the Department of the Environment as affording a justification for recommending legislation to implement certain reforms recommended by the Law Commission to Part II of the Landlord and Tenant Act 1954, notably to make it much easier for the parties to a business tenancy to contract out of Part II of the Landlord and Tenant Act 1954.

For a further discussion and evaluation of the Code, see Gower (1995) 92/44 LS Gazette 28, 30; JE Adams Commercial Leases (1996) Vol 10 Issue 1, p 1f and also [1996] Conv 9; also the comments of PH Kenny [1996] Conv 83.

Precedent No 2
<u>Law Society Business Lease (Part of Building)</u>

<u>Note</u> - The following are extracts from the Law Society Business Lease (Part of a Building).

3 SERVICE CHARGES

3.   The Landlord and the Tenant agree that:

3.1   the service charge is the Tenant's fair proportion of each item of the service costs

3.2   the service costs:
   (a)   are the costs which the Landlord fairly and reasonably incurs in complying with his obligations under clauses 12 and 13
   (b)   include the reasonable charges of any agent contractor consultant or employee whom the Landlord engages to provide the services under clauses 12 and 13
   (c)   include interest at no more than the Law Society's interest rate on sums the Landlord borrows to discharge his obligations under clauses 12 and 13

3.3   the Tenant is to pay the Landlord interim payments on account of the service charge within 21 days of receiving a written demand setting out how it is calculated

3.4   an interim payment is to be the Tenant's fair proportion of what the service costs are reasonably likely to be in the three months following the demand

3.5   the Landlord is not entitled to demand interim payments more than once in every three months

3.6   the Landlord is to keep full records of the service costs and at least once a year is to send the Tenant an account setting out, for the period since the beginning of the lease period or the last account as the case may be:
   (a)   the amount of the service costs
   (b)   the service charge the Tenant is to pay
   (c)   the total of any interim payments the Tenant has paid
   (d)   the difference between the total interim payments and the service charge

3.7   within 21 days after the Tenant receives the account, the amount mentioned in clause 3.6(d) is to be settled by payment between the parties except that the Landlord is entitled to retain any overpayment towards any interim payments he has demanded for a later accounting period

3.8 the Landlord is either:
  (a) to have the account certified by an independent chartered accountant, or
  (b) to allow the Tenant to inspect the books records invoices and receipts relating to the service costs

3.8 disagreements about the amounts of the service charge or the service costs are to be decided by arbitration under clause 17.5

13 SERVICES

13 The Landlord is to comply with the following duties in relation to the building:

13.1 to maintain the state and condition (including the decorations) of:
  (a) the structure, outside, roof, foundations, joists, floor slabs, load bearing walls, beams and columns of the building
  (b) those parts of the building which tenants of more than one part can use ("the common parts")

13.2 to decorate the common parts and the outside of the building very five years, using colours and types of finish reasonably decided by the Landlord

13.3 to pay promptly all periodic rates, taxes and outgoings relating to the common parts, including any imposed after the date of this lease (even if of a novel nature)

13.4 to pay or contribute to the cost of repairing, maintaining and cleaning party walls, party structures, yards, gardens, roads, paths, gutters, drains, sewers, pipes, conduits, wires, cables and other things used or shared with the other property

13.5 to provide the services listed on page 5, but the Landlord is not to be liable for failure or delay caused by industrial disputes, shortage of supplies, adverse weather conditions or other causes beyond the control of the Landlord.

PROPERTY RIGHTS

BOUNDARIES

16.1 This lease does not let to the Tenant the external surfaces of the outside walls of the property and anything above the ceilings and below the floors

FACILITIES

16.2 The Tenant is to have the use, whether or not exclusive, of any of the following facilities:

the right for the Tenant and visitors to come and go to and from the property over the parts of the building designed or designated to afford access to the property, the rights previously enjoyed by the property for shelter and support and for service wires, pipes and drains to pass through them, and the right to park vehicles in any designated parking area subject to any reasonable rules made by the Landlord

16.3 The Landlord is to have the rights previously enjoyed over the property by other parts of the building for shelter and support and for service wires, pipes and drains to pass through it, and the right for the Landlord and his tenants and their visitors to come and go to and from the other parts of the building over the parts of the property designated for that purpose.

Precedent No 3

Short Form of Tenancy Agreement for a Letting for
One Year and Thereafter of a Furnished House or Bungalow

[Permission to reproduce this precedent, which appears in Precedents for the Conveyancer, No 5-5, is gratefully acknowledged of Messrs Sweet & Maxwell and of the author of the precedent.]

AN AGREEMENT made this .... day of ....19 ...BETWEEN AB of etc. and CD of etc. (hereinafter called "the Landlords") of the one part and EF of etc. (hereinafter called "the Tenant") of the other part.

Tenancy for One Year and Thereafter from Year to Year

1. The Landlords agree to let and the Tenant agrees to take the [dwelling house] [bungalow] garage and premises situate and being etc. (hereinafter called "the premises") furnished as stated in the inventory contained in the Schedule hereto for a term of one year certain commencing on the ... day of ... 19 ... and thereafter from year to year until the tenancy shall be determined at the end of the second or any subsequent year calculated from the date of commencement aforesaid by either of the parties giving to the other or others at least six calendar months' previous notice in writing in that behalf AT THE HALF-YEARLY rent of £... payable in advance on the ... day of .... and the .... day of .... in each year the first payment to be made on the ... day of ... 19 .

Tenant's Obligations

2. The Tenant agrees with the Landlords and each of them as follows:

(1)　To pay the said rent on the days and in the manner aforesaid.

(2)　To pay all rates taxes assessments and outgoings whatever (whether imposed by statute or otherwise and whether of a national or local character) now or at any time during the tenancy payable in respect of the premises or any part thereof or by the owner or occupier thereof.

(3)　To keep the interior of the premises including the fixtures and fittings thereof in good tenantable repair and condition both as respects fabric and decoration and in such repair and condition to deliver up the same together with all fixtures and fittings at the expiration of the tenancy Provided that the Tenant shall not without the consent in writing of the Landlords first had and received redecorate replace or repair the whole or any part of the woodwork of the premises which at the date of commencement of the tenancy is grained or consists of natural wood finish.

(4)　To replace and make good all breakages deficiencies and damage to the furniture fixtures fittings and effects in the premises which may happen during the period of the tenancy (save when caused by reasonable use) and at the expiration of the tenancy to deliver up the same according to the said inventory and in the same rooms in which the same now are in as sound perfect and clean a condition as at the commencement of the tenancy (save as aforesaid).

(5)   To maintain the gardens and pleasure-grounds of the premises in good order and properly cultivated and planted.

(6)   To permit the Landlords or their agents to enter at all reasonable times for the purpose of viewing the condition of the premises and at the Tenant's expense to make good all deficiencies of repair for which the Tenant is liable hereunder within one calendar month after notice thereof shall have been given or left upon the premises.

(7)   Not to use the premises or any part thereof or suffer the same to be used for any purpose other than a single private dwelling-house.

(8)   Not to assign his interest under this agreement or underlet or part with [or share] possession of the premises or any part thereof.

Landlords' Obligation

3. The Landlords hereby jointly and severally agree with the Tenant as follows:

(1)   That the Tenant duly pay the rent and observing and performing the agreements on his part hereinbefore contained may peaceably hold and enjoy the premises during the tenancy without any disturbance by the Landlords or any person claiming under them.

(2)   To maintain and keep the roof or roofs external main walls and timbers of the premises in good repair and condition with power to enter on the premises for the purposes of this clause.

Proviso for Re-entry

4. IN CASE of non-payment of rent (whether formally or legally demanded or not) or any other breach of this agreement by the Tenant the Landlords shall be at liberty to re-enter and take possession of the premises whereupon this agreement shall thencefore cease to have effect but without prejudice to the Landlords' right to recover all rent then due and any damages for any prior breach of this agreement.

AS WITNESS, etc.

SCHEDULE OF FURNITURE

Index